Tricks of the Game-Programming Gurus

André LaMothe
John Ratcliff
Mark Seminatore
Denise Tyler

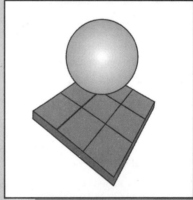

SAMS
PUBLISHING

A Division of Macmillan Computer Publishing,
A Prentice Hall Macmillan Company
201 West 103rd Street, Indianapolis, IN 46290

I dedicate this book to my mother and father for letting me chase my dreams. —AL

To my fiancée Erin—thanks for the support. I couldn't have done it without you. —MS

To Ed, for his endless support and understanding that creativity knows no timeclock. —DT

Overview

Contents

Acknowledgments

I would like to first thank Chris Denny for giving me the opportunity to be one of the authors on this project. Now that it's all over, I guess staying up 20 hours a day isn't too bad! Also, I want to thank the development editor Scott Parker for being the easiest editor I've ever worked with, Anne Barret for making sure not to hurt my feelings too much with her edits, and finally for that free dinner from Robert Bogue who did an excellent job with the technical editing.

As far as my crew here at the lab, I want to thank Ash Patel from the bottom of my heart for helping me write this book. He was instrumental in editing for technical content as well as keeping me motivated, not to mention that he is the only person on Earth who can watch *Real Genius* over and over and not get bored of it! I want to thank Jaime Mayol for helping me get that darn modem game working that night we stayed up till 2 a.m., and for letting me borrow his laptop computer and completely dissect his 486 for experiments. My dear friend Mark Bell deserves thanks for his creative input, and for always arguing with me (even though I'm always right!). And I want to thank Dione Phillips for letting me borrow his camcorder.

Finally, I want to thank all the people at SAMS who I didn't get to meet. The poor souls who had to decipher my cryptic figures, the software development editor, and last but not least, Carol Ackerman who sent me my checks!

—André LaMothe

Introduction

Ever have an idea for a computer game and wonder how to turn your idea into reality? Did you play your favorite computer game and determine that it would be perfect if only you could have a slightly different creature running out of the dark at you? Did you ever ask yourself, "How did they do that?" when playing computer games? This book opens the door to creating your own computer games.

Computer Games

If you haven't visited your local video arcade and blown a roll of quarters lately, you're working too hard! Try walking into a video arcade or your local computer store; the computer game craze will slap you in the face. The days of Hunt the Wampus and Lunar Lander are gone forever and are being replaced by sleeker, slinkier, more sophisticated games.

Today's personal computer games contain miles of tunnels, roads, and grotesque creatures. They are booming with dazzling graphics and sound. DOOM, included on the CD-ROM with this book, is one of the most popular of these games. It includes corridors of treasures to find and creatures to hunt and kill before they kill you. If you have ever played DOOM, you couldn't miss the acid baths, guns, multiple creatures, sliding doors, elevators, hidden passages, explosions...the list goes on and on. These features were created with combinations of graphics and sound.

The graphics in DOOM give you the impression of distance and space—as if you're actually standing in the middle of the scenery. DOOM employs 3-D graphics for this effect. PC game-programming professionals are using 3-D graphics to add realism to every type of game. Go to the computer store and check out 7th Guest, MYST. X-wing, Outpost, and Indy Car Racing. This technology is also surfacing in the video arcade with games such as Virtual Racing and Virtual Boxing.

When you add a great storyline and hi-fi sound to these games, the journey into the PC game world is complete. You feel that you're in the midst of the action—fighting, racing, and sleuthing your way through the game in a struggle to stay alive.

This Book!

Tricks of the Game-Programming Gurus takes graphics and sound to the extreme. Most game books focus on how to *play* the game. This book is different. It teaches you how to *program* your own game using techniques developed by the professionals. You learn from the professional PC game developers how to create games that use graphics and sound. If you're a beginner to game programming, this book is an excellent introductory text. It will teach you how to scroll, score tables, program 3-D graphics, create textures, and more. If you're a game developer and need to learn newer techniques, this book will be good source for your endeavors.

What You Need to Know

To use this book, you should know C fairly well. Most game books focus on assembly language. Although this book talks a little about assembly, it primarily focuses on writing games in C. It does contain a small assembly language primer for the assembly you'll need to know.

How This Book is Organized

This book is about techniques to develop PC games. It is not written in a progressive manner, but you will see a pattern in the organization of some chapters.

In Chapter 1, "A Video-Game Primer," you learn who writes games, where ideas come from, and the phases of PC game design.

Chapter 2, "Assembly Language Basics," gives you a short assembly language tutorial. You learn the basic terminology and the methods used to create games in this book.

Chapter 3, "Input Device Basics," introduces you to programming the interface between the games and input devices such as joysticks, mice, and keyboards.

Chapter 4, "The Mechanics of Two-Dimensional Graphics," shows you the workings of 2-D graphics used in games like Commander Keen. You learn programming techniques for scrolling, scaling, translating, rotating, and clipping in 2-D games.

Chapter 5, "The Mysteries of the VGA Card," reveals the workings of VGA Graphics. You learn about the power of 256 colors, color look-up tables, bit blitting, vertical ray tracing, and so on.

In Chapter 6, "The Third Dimension," you enter the world of the third dimension. Here you learn how to create DOOM worlds using 3D graphic techniques.

Chapter 7, "Advanced Bit-Mapped Graphics and Special FX," introduces you to creating collisions, fast bit blitting, lighting, special game effects, and so on. Sharpen your sword; the action begins here!

Chapter 8, "High-Speed 3-D Sprites," takes you to the ultra dimension of creating high-speed 3-D sprites. This chapter shows you how to take a real-world model of a space craft and incorporate it into your games.

In Chapter 9, "Sound FX and Music," you learn the fundamentals of PC sound in your game. You can create excitement and terror using your Sound Blaster card. In games, the music can make your heart surge with the on-screen action.

In Chapter 10, "Implementing Computer Game Music," you learn about DIGPAK and MIDPAK, real packages that enable you to create and enhance the music and sound in your games. With these packages, you can add orchestrated music and sounds to your creations and give them that professional edge. Several popular games already use this package: The 7th Guest, Terminator 2029 and Mechwarrior II.

Chapter 11, "Video Game Algorithms, Data Structures, and Methodologies," introduces you to the internal building constructs of professional games. You learn modeling of real-world data structures for game universes and saving game positions.

Chapter 12, "Surreal Time, Interrupts, and Multitasking," explains how to add the dimension of time to your games. You learn programming techniques to multitask different game operations, how to create the game loop, and how to call interrupts to access input/output devices.

Chapter 13, "Synthetic Intelligence," reveals how to give your game characters a little intelligence. You don't want your characters to roll over and play dead time after time. Teach them to think and react based on your movements and input so that you have a "realer" feeling game.

Chapter 14, "Linking Up," shows you how to give your game another dimension. You can use your modem to dial up a friend, and then play that friend head-to-head from across the country. Multiplayer games are becoming very popular and surprisingly inexpensive to implement.

Chapter 15, "The Toolchest," gives you a complete set of tools to build your games. Build textures, characters, sound files, maps, and backgrounds with these tools. A complete set can be found on the CD-ROM.

Chapter 16, "Creating Art for Your Game," introduces an artist's point of view to your game. Using the skills learned in this chapter, you can make your game art snappier and more professional.

Chapter 17, "Parallax Scrolling Techniques," introduces a perspective of viewing objects close up faster than objects in the distance. Parallax scrolling technique makes this perspective come to life in your games.

Chapter 18, "Optimization Techniques," provides techniques and tricks to optimize your game for performance. Your game should be faster and more fluid if you follow the tricks set forth in this chapter.

Chapter 19, "Warlock," introduces you to the computer game creation of author André LaMothe.

Conventions Used in This Book

This book uses the following conventions:

- Text that you type in is presented in a special monospace font.

- Placeholders in the text—text that represents other words or characters you are to type in—appear in a *monospace italicized* font.

- New terms are *italicized* in the text.

- Notes, tips, warnings, and cautions are used throughout the book to give you additional, relevent information about the subject at hand.

1

A Video-Game Primer

Where to begin? So much to tell, so few pages in which to do it. The journey we are about to embark on is going to be, as Bill and Ted would say, "an excellent adventure." When we're through, there will be another person—you—who will be able to give the world an experience that it never would have had. You'll be able to let someone else see into your "mind's eye." I think that's probably the most important reason for writing a video game. (Making millions of dollars does come in a close second!)

Creating a video game is like creating a work of art or a poem. The creator gets to share with the world something that was once completely imaginary. A great sculptor once said, "The statue was always there; I merely released it from the rock" (or something along those lines). A video game has the same air about it. The computer has a bunch of little bits in it, and you're simply turning them on or off. Turn the right ones on (and the right ones off), and you'll have created a work of art.

by André LaMothe

I want to put you into a creative frame of mind. We need to be on the same wavelength, or at least in the same band! In this first chapter I describe how to go about designing a video game. (Be warned: this chapter might get weird! It's the only one where I get to express myself without having the necessity of structure clouding up my "creative space." The other chapters have to be a bit more serious.) We cover the following topics in this chapter:

- Who writes video games
- Where ideas come from
- The phases of video-game design
- What you'll learn from this book

The pages after this chapter describe how to *write* a video game.

Who Writes Video Games?

Video games are written by a plethora of different people. The factor that connects all of us in a special way is the fulfillment we get out of creating little worlds and watching others enjoy our creations. A painting is nice, but it can't make you laugh, cheer, or jump 10 feet out of your chair—well, maybe *some* paintings can! But if you like to make others happy, a video game is definitely one of the most rewarding types of applications you can write. (Frankly, I don't think anyone really likes writing compilers or word processors, do you?)

Video games are a way of expressing something that can't be expressed. Some people need a channel for their incredible imagination. I think that's why our world has movies and the theater. We thirst for fantasy and an escape from reality. Video games are a way for ordinary people to become little gods of their own universes. They can then let someone loose and watch them explore.

Where Do the Ideas Come From?

The ideas for video games come from your imagination, that's where! Within your mind is an endless universe filled with unicorns, robotic worlds, and cities of elves. A video game can be anything you want it to be. If you're having a creative block, however, the best place to start is a video-game arcade. Pay an arcade a visit. Take a friend and throw away 20 bucks. But be careful: while you *are* seeing other people's creations when you go to a video game arcade, they've had a lot of input from that dreaded dragon, the Marketing Department. The games in the arcades are designed to do one thing: make money! You shouldn't design your games based on possible financial rewards, though. Base them on what you think will make people smile—or scream!

What you can extract from such a quest is *inspiration*. (But, please—I don't think I could take another Street Fighter, OK?) Also, remember that it's easy to just copy a game and then change it around. If you're going to use someone else's game idea as your foundation, you'd better give them credit. (Otherwise, you may find legal action taken against you!)

If the arcades don't get the creative juices flowing, I suggest you go to the nearest video store and rent a half-dozen science fiction and fantasy movies. Also, get a couple animated films. Movies are almost as good as video games. You can't control the characters, but they can create moments of suspension of disbelief, and a conviction that the universe on the screen is real.

Finally, your dreams are an incredible source of ideas for video games. I've gotten at least a dozen amazing video-game ideas from my dreams. Where else do you think a game like Pac Man came from? Little ghosts chasing a round yellow ball with a chomping mouth? That had to come from a dream—or long periods of oxygen deprivation!

Remember: we want to create a little universe where players can immerse themselves in another reality, one where each player is the focus and the main character.

When you finally come up with an idea, take your time and think about it over a week or two before you do anything. Develop a story in your mind. When you have a complete plot, you can extract a video game from *that*. One of the worst things you can do is make up a video game as you go. (Don't get me wrong. It's OK to add things, or to change things as you're writing. However, your game must have a solid, cohesive plot—from beginning to end—before you begin.)

Oh, and please don't try to make up games with a bunch of digitized CD-ROM animation and sound. Players don't want to watch movies allowing limited interaction. They want to be in a computer world that's surrealistic. Using recorded video of live actors doesn't fit into the imaginary world of the computer.

The Phases of Video-Game Design

A video game, like any piece of software, can be constructed using a standard design methodology. However, we aren't making cheese sandwiches here; we can deviate from the standard sometimes. Here are the phases a design methodology must include, and a suggested order in which they might be accomplished:

- First, you need the idea. We've talked about that.

- Once you have a clear idea of what the game is going to be, I suggest writing a storyboard of sorts. If the game is going to have multiple levels, describe and sketch each level.

- You then need to populate the levels with interesting creatures and goals. You must make each level challenging and rewarding; the player needs a reason to play, and keep on playing. There has to be a goal of some sort for each section or level of the game.

- Once you have an idea of what each level will look like and the goals of each level, you should start thinking about *game play*. How are game objects going to move and act/react? What abilities will the player have? Will the player be able to get extra power, lives, strength, and so on? Will there be digitized sound effect, music, or both? Get a rough idea of these kinds of things down on paper.

At this point you have sufficient information and enough ideas to start writing down a more exact plan. You have the general concepts and flow of the game. Now try to get specific in areas that you're sure about. For instance:

- Select which video mode you're going to use for the game. You might use high-resolution and give up color, for example.

- Think out how complex the graphics are going to be. Is the game going to be 2-D, 3-D, or a mixture?

You learn more about the kinds of choices you have as you go through the book.

Once you have these factors nailed down, it's time to start seeing what kind of resources you'll need. Start designing, in detail, the easiest level first. Make an inventory of the kinds of animations, algorithms, and tools you'll need to make that single level. Once you come up with an inventory, try to generalize it to the other levels. A small subset of a typical inventory might look like this:

- A paint program to create the bit maps

- An animation program to animate the bit maps so you can see them before using them

- C code to do bit blitting (that is, binary block image transferring), bit scaling, and line drawing

- Algorithms for the artificial intelligence of the creatures in the game

- A tool to digitize and manipulate sounds

- C code for all input devices, such as the keyboard, mouse, and joystick

- A tool to draw the levels and to save them on disk

- A collection of musical instrument digital interface (MIDI) tracks for each level

All right, I think you get the idea: you need to figure out everything you don't have lying around the hard drive. Complete the list to the best of your abilities, then start creating or acquiring the things in the list.

Then it's time to put your money where your mouth is and dive into the software design. But be careful: don't bury yourself. For instance, if you're going to write a multiplayer or networked game, you must keep this in mind from beginning to end when writing the software. We go into the reasons for this in the chapters on networked and multiplayer games.

When writing the software, try to break it down into small sections that perform specific tasks. A video game can roughly be broken up into the following sections:

- The game world and its data structures

- The renderer engine, which draws the image on the video screen

- The input/output system

- The artificial intelligence system

- The main game loop

- The user interface

- The sound system

Of course, each one of these can be further broken down. However, this is a reasonable start at it.

When writing a video game, don't try to blow the doors out on the first try. Don't bite off more than you can chew. Just make something and build on it the next time around. Otherwise, I guarantee you won't finish. If you go through the steps I've described, you'll have implemented a better design phase than 90 percent of the software engineers I know! Most of them type now—and pay later.

That's about all there is to it. The rest has to come from you. Take your time, make things simple, and don't shoot for the stars your first time out. If you follow those guidelines, you should have a success on your first try.

What Will You Learn from This Book?

This book is designed to give you the necessary framework, software, tools, and algorithms to create a textured, 3-D video game of the DOOM and Wolfenstein 3-D genre. This is not a textbook on 2-D and 3-D graphics. Video games are full of tricks and techniques. Even though there are chapters on 2-D and 3-D, they concentrate on the types of operations and functionality you need to create the aforementioned games.

We do, however, need to cover a great deal of ground. To put it plainly, a video-game programmer has to know everything about everything. That's all there is to it. In going through this book you will do and see things that you've always wondered about, but never had the chance or time to figure out. You see, there are a lot of little details to making a video game. You must address each and every one of them before you can write one line of code.

When you've finished this book you'll have what you need to make a serious video-game application. To make sure of this, we're going to write a video game at the end of the book. When I started writing this book I hadn't decided exactly what that would be; I considered something like Wolfenstein 3-D, or maybe something completely different with ghosts and goblins. In the event, it evolved interactively with the book. When you start that section, you'll see what developed.

Summary

In this chapter we learned about some of the background we need to write video games. We learned that there are many aspects to creating a video game other than the obvious technical ones (which are a great task to conquer in themselves). These nontechnical aspects are:

- Creating storyboards
- Creating scripts

- Exercising your creativity in general
- Planning your game design
- Having some idea of your target market

Well, we've had enough fun talking about video games; now let's learn exactly what's needed to write one! Without further ado, get comfortable and turn the page...

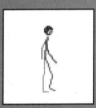

Assembly Language Basics

D r. Rudy Rucker, a friend and former professor of mine, once said "Assembly language is really cool; it's like programming with DNA." I think that statement is appropriate for this chapter. Assembly language is the native tongue of the computer and, if mastered, allows you to wield unimaginable powers. In this chapter we take a review course in assembly language. We learn to interface assembly with our programs and to use Microsoft's C in-line assembler. Also, we get a bit ahead of ourselves and write a couple of graphics routines. This chapter covers the following topics:

- Why we need assembly language in video games

- An overview of the 80x86 family

- The CPU registers

- The form of an assembly language function

by André LaMothe

- Passing parameters
- Local variables
- Making external references
- Talking back to the caller
- Some useful control structures
- Setting the video mode
- Clearing the screen at the speed of light
- Using the in-line assembler

Why Do We Need Assembly Language in Video Games?

Even for the compiler gods at Microsoft and Borland, assembly language today is still faster than C code. However, the gap is closing. I remember a day (a long time ago in a galaxy far, far away) where all video games were written in pure assembly language! Can you imagine that? Be glad we have hundreds of computer scientists and software engineers creating compilers. These compilers are almost as good as the best assembly language programmers. The fact is, compilers can do only about 95 percent of our work. That last 5 percent we still have to do ourselves. We still must use assembly language to do things such as plot pixels, draw lines, draw polygons, bit blits, and so on. We must use it wherever we need lightning speed—usually, anytime we're doing graphics.

There are a couple of ways we can use assembly language in our programs:

- We can make assembly language functions and call them from C. We'll do this in places that are time restrictive (such as the aforementioned pixel plotting, line and polygon drawing, bit blits, and so on).

- We also can use a fairly new tool called the *in-line assembler*. The in-line assembler allows you to place assembly language instructions within your C code itself. This is an incredible asset to a video-game programmer, because it allows you to use assembly language without using a separate assembler and associated tools. This can save a lot of time.

Before we move on, I want to caution you to *not* get crazy and use assembly language for everything. Use it sparingly, and only where you really need it. Otherwise, your code will become complex and not portable. (Did you know that DOOM has only a couple of assembly modules? The rest is efficient C code.) If you need more than a thousand to two thousand lines of assembly, you need to rethink your approach, optimize your code, or maybe just take a sledge hammer and start over again!

The 80x86 Family Overview

The 80x86 family of processors is truly diversified. Intel has made more processors than any of us can shake a stick at. The games and programming we do in this book support only the 80386, 80486, and 80586/Pentium processor. For our purposes, we'll be talking about the real mode of each of these processors: the 8086 emulation mode used by DOS, with the 640K barrier.

You see, the first real processor Intel made was the 8088. It was in the first PC. It was replaced by the 8086—and the rest is history. However, the world got hooked on DOS, which was an 8086-based operating system. When Intel produced the 286, 386, 486, 586, and—believe it or not—the soon-to-be-released 686 (I have friends in low places), they had to keep the processors downwardly compatible with the original 8086. What that means for us is that we must program our 586/60MHz PC with the same instructions and 640K barrier constraints that the original 8086s had!

It's a real shame, because the 386 and so on are 32-bit processors with flat memory-model (no segments) addressing, advanced instructions, and more. Using the new instructions alone would give us an edge in our games. Alas, we must bite the bullet and use our processors as if they were 8086s running at 250MHz. Moreover, the flat memory model eliminates segment registers, the 640K barrier, and all the headaches they bring. We can tell the compiler to use 286 instructions with the _62 compiler option, but these are still 16 bit instructions and don't help us utilize the 32-bit capabilites of the 386, 486, and 586.

So let's get started reviewing what we have to work with. For the rest of this chapter I refer synonymously to the 386, 486, and 586 as "the CPU."

The function of the CPU is to move data from place to place and do simple operations on that data. These operations include mathematics, testing, and logical operations (such as OR, NOT, and AND). For any CPU to be programmed efficiently, it must have a sufficient number of registers to hold results and accomplish the task at hand. The registers of the PC's CPU are described in the following section.

CPU Registers

General-Purpose Registers

> These registers are used in the general program execution and are, in many cases, interchangeable. However, each register has a special talent:
> AX—16-bit, used both for general purposes and math results
> BX—16-bit, used both for general purposes and indexing
> CX—16-bit, used both for general purposes and counting
> DX—16-bit, used for general purposes
> BP—16-bit, used for general purposes, holding offsets, and indexing
> SI—16-bit, used both for general purposes and as the source in data-movement operations
> DI—16-bit, used both for general purposes and as the destination in data-movement operations

Segment Registers

> These registers are used to point to segments. A *segment* is a 64K block of memory that represents an area that has a specific function (such as code space or data space):
> DS—The data segment, used to point to the active area from which data references are made
> CS—The code segment, used to point to the current place from which the CPU is executing code
> ES—The extra segment, used to alias another segment or to point to another 64K block of interest; *aliasing* is to provide an additional name for an object so that it can be accessed by either name
> SS—The stack segment, used to point to the current portion of memory to be used as stack memory
> IP—This register points to the current instruction being executed

Flag Register

> The flag register holds the CPU status, such as the Z (zero) flag, C (carry) flag, and so on. This register can't be directly accessed, but its status can be obtained through the use of instructions.

The Form of an Assembly Language Function

Assembly language functions are much like C functions. They have a beginning, an end, and code in the middle. (Kinda like a corndog.) This book references Microsoft's macro assembler MASM 5.1 through 6.1, because these newer versions of MASM support new directives that make interfacing to C an easier task.

 NOTE

MASM 5.0 will suffice for our first discussions. However, you'll need MASM 5.1 or higher to get the full benefit of the book.

In a while we'll get to passing parameters and all that fun stuff, but for now let's see what we need as a minimum in an external assembly language program that will be called by C and linked in by the linker (the program that builds the final executable from the objects). Listing 2.1 shows a prototype procedure for MASM 5.0 and later.

Listing 2.1. A prototype procedure for MASM 5.0 and later.

```
; A Prototype Procedure for MASM 5.0 or Later Version.

.MODEL MEDIUM           ; This is the memory model. It also
                        ; could be SMALL or LARGE.
.CODE                   ; This is the beginning of the code.

PUBLIC _function_name   ; This lets the linker have access to
                        ; the function name so the function
                        ; can be exported.

_function_name PROC FAR ; This is the name and type (NEAR or
                        ; FAR) of the function. NEAR can use
                        ; the SMALL or COMPACT memory models
                        ; FAR can use the MEDIUM, LARGE, and
                        ; HUGE memory models.

push BP                 ; This sets up the stack-frame prolog
                        ; code.
mov BP,SP               ; This rests the stack frame.

; do work in here


pop BP                  ; This cleans up the stack-frame epilog
                        ; code.

_function_name ENDP     ; This is the end of the procedure.

END                     ; This is the end of the code.
```

Let's analyze the skeleton program shown in Listing 2.1:

■ The first directive we see is .MODEL. As with the C compiler, MASM must know what memory model the program is going to use. The MEDIUM keyword signifies that we want to use MEDIUM memory model. To refresh your memory, here are the properties of the memory models:

The SMALL memory model has one 64K segment for code and another for data.
The COMPACT memory model has one 64K code segment, but allows multiple data segments.
The MEDIUM memory model has one 64K segment for data, but multiple segments for code.
The LARGE memory model has multiple 64K segments for both code and data.
The HUGE memory model allows data items to be larger than 64K, but is almost identical to the LARGE memory model.
Most of the time we'll be using the MEDIUM or LARGE memory models.

■ Continuing with our analysis, we see that the next directive is PUBLIC. This tells MASM that the next name should be exported and visible to other modules.

■ Now, we come to the beginning of the function. A function in assembly language is started with the PROC directive, which immediately follows the name of the function.

One little caveat: if you're using a version of MASM that doesn't allow the C attribute to be used in the model directive, you must place an underscore in all assembly language names if you want them to be properly referenced by the linker when it links it to your C code.

■ At this point we enter into the executable portion of the code. The first two instructions you see set up the stack frame so that the assembly language procedure can access parameters on the stack. We get into this later.

■ At the end of the procedure we clean up the stack frame we created so that the procedure can return to the caller.

■ Finally, there's the directive ENDP. This tells the assembler that this is the end of the procedure.

■ We could have more procedures if we wished, but at the very end of the source code we must place an END directive. This indicates to the assembler the end of the entire program.

The next logical topic of discussion is passing parameters. Our assembly language functions won't be very exciting unless we can exchange information with them.

Passing Parameters

Assembly language and C are like distant cousins: they adhere to a lot of the same constraints and premises. However, assembly is more primal. When we pass parameters to an assembly function, we must go through a couple of extra steps to obtain the parameters that the code expects. First, you must set up a stack frame (as we did in Listing 2.1). Next, you must extract the parameters off the stack.

To do this extraction you must understand how the parameters are passed on to the stack. Say you want to write an assembly language procedure that adds two numbers and returns the result to the AX register. The procedure would look like this:

```
int Add_Int(int number_1, int number_2);
```

If you were to execute this procedure, C would create a stack frame and push the parameters on the stack. In this case, number_1 and number_2 would be pushed on the stack.

You might think that number_1 would be pushed, then number_2 would be pushed. However, C does things a little different. The C compiler pushes all parameters in reverse order, unless it is specifically ordered not to. This reverse ordering makes it easier to access variables. By reversing the order of pushing variables on the stack, parameters are always accessed as positive offsets from BP, which makes life easier. This allows functions such as printf to pass a changeable number of parameters. With that in mind, if we made the call to the Add_Int procedure, the stack frame would look like either Figure 2.1 or Figure 2.2. The difference is in the memory model used.

The reason the memory model makes a difference is that the return address of the instruction immediately following the function call is placed on the stack. If the memory model is SMALL (meaning that all data and code is in the same segment), only an offset is necessary to continue execution. This offset takes up two bytes. However, if the memory model is MEDIUM or LARGE, both an offset and a segment are necessary to continue execution. The combined segment and offset take up a full four bytes.

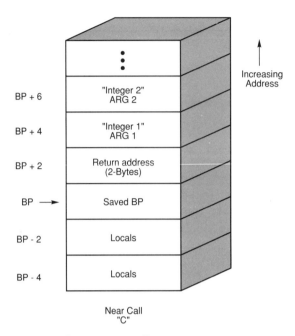

Figure 2.1. *Diagram of a C NEAR call.*

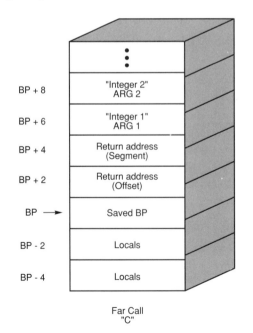

Figure 2.2. *Diagram of a C FAR call.*

As you can see from Figures 2.1 and 2.2, the parameters are pushed in an order such that, when the stack frame is set up, you can access the parameters as positive offsets from the BP register. Therefore, if you want to access number_1, you could use the syntax [BP+4] or [BP+6] (depending on the memory model of the call).

As an example, let's write this addition procedure. This procedure will take two integers as parameters and add them. The result will be sent to the AX register, which is the convention for a standard C function when returning 16-bit values. Listing 2.2 shows this simple addition procedure, which is an implementation of the prototype procedure in Listing 2.1.

Listing 2.2. A simple addition procedure.

```
; equates section

integer_1 EQU [BP+6]     ; This is an alias for integer one.
integer_2 EQU [BP+8]     ; This is an alias for integer two.

.MODEL MEDIUM            ; This tells the procedure to use the
                         ; MEDIUM memory model.

.CODE                    ; This is the beginning of the code.

PUBLIC _Add_Int          ; This lets the linker have access to
                         ; the function name so the function
                         ; can be exported.

_Add_Int PROC FAR        ; This is the name of the function
                         ; (Add_Int) and its type (FAR).

push BP                  ; These two instructions set up the
                         ; stack frame prolog code.
mov BP,SP

mov AX,integer_1         ; This moves the first operand into the
                         ; accumulator.
add AX,integer_2         ; This adds the second operand into the
                         ; accumulator.

pop BP                   ; This cleans up the stack-frame epilog
                         ; code.

_Add_Int ENDP            ; This is the end of the procedure.

END                      ; This is the end of the code.
```

The only changes we have made to the prototype in Listing 2.1 is that we actually made it do something, and we added a couple of lines to set up aliases. As before, let's analyze the procedure:

■ As in Listing 2.1, I use assembler directives to set up the memory model and the start and end of the function.

■ The EQU directive is simply a string-replacement facility to alias one string to another. I didn't want to use the syntax [BP+6] and [BP+8] to access the variables on the stack. I would much rather use aliases that represent [BP+6] and [BP+8]. The lines that accomplish these substitutions read:

```
integer_1 EQU [BP+6]
integer_2 EQU [BP+8]
```

Aliasing variable names and values can, in general, make assembly language programs much easier to read. Otherwise, complex expressions or register-based expressions would have to be used to reference variables.

The USES Directive

I've hinted that MASM 5.1 and later have some new directives to make parameter passing and function-frame creation easier. You can use one of the new directives, called USES, in conjunction with the PROC directive to inform the assembler about the registers that will be used in the function. The USES directive takes care of all the chores of setting up the stack frame and aliasing the variable names for you. Moreover, it generates prolog and epilog code to save the registers that tell you it will be used in the function, so that these registers are not corrupted when the function returns back to C.

Remember, C must use the same registers your assembly language programs use. If you use a register in your assembly program, you must save it on the stack and restore it when your function is complete. Otherwise, your C program will probably crash when execution flow continues from where it left off before the assembly call.

The PROC directive, and its added qualifier USES, have the following generalized syntax:

```
label PROC [[attributes]] [[USES register_list]] [[,]]
[[parameter_list[[:type]]...]]
```

■ The label field is the name of the procedure.

■ The attributes field tells the assembler the properties of your procedure that you would like enforced. It can have a conglomeration of the parameters, such as the distance of the procedure (NEAR or FAR); the visibility of the procedure (PUBLIC or PRIVATE); and, finally, the language type (C, PASCAL, and so on). Being able to enforce properties in a procedure allows our assembly program to be more like a high-level language procedure. It ties our hands a little, but it forces more structure.

■ The *register_list* field indicates which register(s) will be used by the function with the USES directive. This tells the assembler to generate code that will save these registers on the stack during entry of the procedure from the caller, and to restore them on exit from the procedure.

■ The *parameter_list* field closely resembles a normal C parameter list.

■ The name of each variable and its type is listed for all the variables that will be passed to the procedure. The type field denotes the size of the variable passed (such as BYTE or WORD).

For example, if you were to write a procedure to which three integers were passed, and which was to use the SI, DI, and CX registers, you could include the following statement:

```
foo PROC USES SI DI CX, integer_1:WORD, integer_2:WORD, integer_3:WORD
```

Using the PROC and USES directives, let's now reimplement the procedure from Listing 2.2 as shown in Listing 2.3.

Listing 2.3. A modified version of Add_Int.

```
.MODEL MEDIUM, C        ; This tells the procedure to use the
                        ; MEDIUM memory model with C parameter
                        ; passing.

.CODE                   ; This is the beginning of the code.

PUBLIC _Add_Int         ; This lets the linker have access to
                        ; the function name so the function can
                        ; be exported.

_Add_Int PROC USES integer_1:WORD, integer_2:WORD

mov AX,integer_1        ; This moves the first operand into the
                        ; accumulator.
add AX,integer_2        ; This adds the second operand into the
                        ; accumulator.

_Add_Int ENDP           ; This is the end of the procedure.

END                     ; This is the end of the code.
```

As you can see from Listing 2.3, the burden of saving the BP register and creating and destroying the stack frame is now left up to the assembler. Moreover, the parameters integer_1 and integer_2 can be accessed without aliases or stack references.

Passing Pointers

We must address the issue of pointers before we move on. We know how to pass value parameters, such as bytes and words, but how are pointers passed?

Pointers are passed as double words, or DWORDs. To access pointers on the stack, we could use the old technique of aliasing two WORD locations to the names segment and offset, and use these aliases in our assembly program.

For example, if we called the assembly language function in the MEDIUM memory model (say, in a FAR call) with the following line:

```
pfoo(&x)
```

we could access the address of the variable x with the following aliases:

```
offset      EQU [BP+6]
segment     EQU [BP+8]
```

If we wanted to change the value of x, we could do the following:

```
mov DI, offset      ; This moves the offset in the DI register.
mov AX, segment     ; We can't move data directly into a segment
mov ES,AX           ; register, so use AX as a temp.
mov ES,AX           ; Now "x" is pointed to by ES:DI.
mov ES:[DI], CX     ; This moves whatever is in CX into "x".
```

This program has two distinct steps:

■ The first step creates a pointer to x via the ES and DI registers.

■ The second step actually changes the variable x.

That about wraps it up for parameter passing. The new extensions to the PROC and USES directives are great, and you should use them if you feel comfortable doing so. However, if you prefer doing things MASM 5.0 style, by all means do so. There's no difference at all as far as speed of execution.

Local Variables

You now know how to pass variables to your procedures, but what about temporary and local variables that have scope only in the procedure itself?

When we write C programs, we use local variables to help with computations, save results, and so on. As in C, we can implement local variables in our assembly functions by way of the stack. Although it's possible to create local variables in the automatic data area (that is, in the *data segment*), we won't. Why? The stack was created to hold data and local variables, so let's use it for what it was made for.

Here's how to do it. When we create a stack frame by pushing the BP register, we access the parameters (if any) by adding positive offsets to the BP register, such as [BP+6] and so on. However, the stack really is a region of contiguous memory, which we can use if we wish. To do so, we need only use a negative offset from the BP register to get a free memory location.

Therefore, if we want two local variables named *local_1* and *local_2*, we would use the following aliases:

```
local_1 EQU [bp-2]
local_2 EQU [bp-4]
```

This gives us two integers to play with. While we have no idea what's in these locations, we can rest assured that it's valid memory that can be used. However, we must remember that we just used the stack for data storage, so we have to change the SP register to reflect this. Otherwise, the next push instruction will push something right into our variable and clobber it!

To remedy this inconvenience, we must adjust the SP register by an amount equal to the amount of storage you've allocated manually. In this case we used four bytes, so we would have to include the code fragment shown in Listing 2.4 to make sure things operate smoothly:

Listing 2.4. Adjusting the SP register.

```
push BP                 ; This sets up the stack frame, as
                        ; usual.
mov BP,SP
sub SP,4                ; This adjusts the stack pointer so
                        ; our local variables don't get stepped
                        ; on.

; Do work here.



add SP, 4               ; The stack pointer must be readjusted
                        ; before stack frame cleanup.
pop BP                  ; This cleans up the stack frame (that
                        ; is, it restores the BP register).
```

The LOCAL Directive

Note that in Listing 2.4 we not only adjusted the SP register at the beginning of the procedure, but also at the end (just before we restored the BP register). This is technique generally used to allocate variables in an assembly language procedure called from any high-level language. Listing 2.4 does this manually. However, MASM 5.1 and later have a directive that takes care of all the hassle and generates the code for us. The new directive is called, appropriately, LOCAL. The LOCAL directive has the following syntax:

```
LOCAL variable_name:type, variable_name:type,...
```

(MASM is getting more like C every day.)

Using the LOCAL directive, let's write a program called Timer that takes one parameter, time, and places it into a local variable, asm_time. The C call would look like this:

```
Timer(25);
```

Listing 2.5 shows the implementation of Timer in assembly language using all the directives discussed in this chapter so far.

Listing 2.5. A timer assembly implementation using local variables.

```
.MODEL MEDIUM           ; This tells the procedure to use the
                        ; MEDIUM memory model.

.CODE                   ; This is the beginning of the code.


_Timer PROC FAR USES AX, time:WORD   ; AX will be destroyed
      LOCAL asm_time:WORD

mov AX, time
mov asm_time, AX

_Timer ENDP             ; This is the end of the procedure.

END                     ; This is the end of the code.
```

This program would take quite a bit more code to implement without the new MASM directives, so they're worth getting a grasp on. If you have only MASM 5.0, however, you can get by without them.

TIP I suggest you create a general template that supports parameters and locals. Modify your template to take into consideration memory models and extra directives for each procedure.

Making External References

When you write a C module that uses variables or functions from other modules, you can use the EXTERN keyword to let the compiler know that the variables or function will be resolved later (at link time). MASM 5.0 and later also supports this functionality.

In our assembly language functions we may want to reference global variables back in the main C program. We could just pass the variable to the assembly function every time and not worry about external variables. However, this is time consuming and, frankly, a bit prehistoric. In video games especially, we must use more globals than we would in any other type of program. The reason for this is speed: we don't want the overhead of parameters being pushed and popped during function calls slowing things up.

Use the EXTRN directive to reference a global or external variable defined in another module. It has the following syntax:

```
EXTRN symbol:type, symbol:type,...
```

where *symbol* is the variable name and *type* is the size of the variable (for example, BYTE, WORD, DWORD).

The EXTRN directive enables you to allocate a variable in your C code and access it in your assembly language parameters. There is a drawback: the variable defined as EXTRN assumes that it resides in the current data segment pointed to by DS. If you're in the SMALL or MEDIUM memory models, that won't be a problem. However, if you're in the LARGE memory model there's no guarantee that the global variable in your C program will be accessed properly using the current value of the DS register when an assembly language function is entered. To remedy this, use the SMALL or MEDIUM memory models all the time. For this reason, I suggest you use the MEDIUM memory model for all your programming.

As an example, let's write a procedure that adds two integers together and places the result in a third integer. The twist is that all these integers will be global and external from the assembly language procedure's point of view. Listing 2.6 shows the code for this procedure, while Listing 2.7 shows the MASM portion of an external example.

Listing 2.6. The C portion of an external example.

```
#include <stdio.h>

int first=1, second=2, third=0;  // These are the integers with
                                 // which we want to work.

void main(void)
{

printf("\nBefore adding third =%d",third);
Add_Ext();                       // This calls the assembly
                                 // program that will add
                                 // externals.
printf("\nAfter adding third = %d",third);

} // end main
```

Listing 2.7. The MASM portion of an external example.

```
.MODEL MEDIUM           ; This tells the procedure to use the
                        ; MEDIUM memory model.

EXTRN first:WORD, second:WORD, third:WORD

.CODE                   ; This is the beginning of the code.

_Add_Ext PROC FAR       ; The procedure is type FAR.
mov AX, first           ; This moves the first number into the
                        ; accumulator.
add AX, second          ; This adds the second number to the
                        ; accumulator.
mov third, AX           ; This stores the result back into
                        ; third.

_Add_Ext ENDP           ; The procedure ends here.

END                     ; This is the end of the code segment.
```

Listings 2.6 and 2.7 are examples of using external variables. Three variables are defined: first, second, and third. Both programs call Add-Ext, which adds first to second and stores the result into third.

This brings us to passing data and results back to the C program that called the assembly procedure, covered in the next section.

Talking Back to the Caller

When C was originally designed, one of its specifications was that it was to be a "functional" language. By functional I don't mean that it doesn't crash a lot, but that functions themselves can return results and be used in complex expressions. For example, the following C expression would be perfectly valid:

```
coeff = Factorial(n) * cos(r) * Scale(z);
```

This expression evaluates three functions and performs the operations required by the math operators binding them. The result is then stored in the variable coeff. This functionality makes C a "functional" language.

Of course, this is only one of C's many assets. Therefore, if we want our assembly functions to emulate C functions, we must have a way to return results to the calling functions, as do C functions themselves.

If you were to compile a few C functions that returned values and look at the assembly listings, you soon would figure out that the functions always return results in a specific set of registers. In fact, if you follow the conventions I'm about to describe, your assembly functions will work exactly like C functions (as far as returning results).

Parameters returned from assembly to C should be placed into the following registers depending on their size:

- BYTEs should be returned in the AL register.

- WORDs should be returned in the AX register.

- DWORDs should be returned in the DX and AX register, where AX holds the low word.

- Pointers that are NEAR should be returned in the AX register.

- Pointers that are FAR should be returned in DX:AX, where the DX register holds the segment and the AX register the offset.

For an example of returning results back to C, review Listing 2.2. In Listing 2.2 we added two integers and accumulated the results in the AX register. Luckily for us, this is the register in which an integer would properly be placed to be sent back to C. If we had a slightly different situation (such as the result in the CX register), we would have moved CX into AX before exiting to ensure that the results were returned properly.

We've belabored MASM and its directives and techniques long enough. (I'm starting to see little 1s and 0s everywhere!) Let's move on to some "real world" examples of what we would use assembly language for.

Setting the Video Mode

A video game has many tasks, such as sound, artificial intelligence, and so on. Before we can do anything about these, however, we must set the video display! Now, we could dive right in and start fiddling with the VGA cards, registers, and setting, but this is dangerous: what works on one card may not work on another. Therefore, to avoid the possibility of embarrassment, we'll use the basic input/output system (BIOS) to set the video mode.

The general graphics functionality of the PC is contained in INT 10h. Using this interrupt is easy: we need only set up the proper registers with the function we wish executed, along with any other values that the specific function needs. We will use mode 13h for the games we'll be writing. (This is the graphics mode with 320 bytes per line, 200 lines per screen, and 256 colors.) Therefore, we need a way to place the system into this mode. With that in mind, let's write an assembly program to set the video mode, along with a C program to test it. Listing 2.8 does the job, while Listing 2.9 shows a C test function (setmodec.c) to test the video mode.

Listing 2.8. An assembly procedure to set the video mode (setmodea.asm).

```
.MODEL MEDIUM, C        ; This tells the procedure to use the
                        ; MEDIUM memory model with C parameter
                        ; passing.

.CODE                   ; This is the beginning of the code.

PUBLIC Set_Mode         ; This lets the linker have access to
                        ; the function name so the function
                        ; can be exported.

Set_Mode PROC FAR C vmode:WORD
                        ; The function takes one parameter.

mov AH,0                ; Video function 0:set video mode
mov AL, BYTE PTR vmode  ; This sets the mode to which you
                        ; want to change.
int 10h                 ; Use BIOS to set the mode.

ret                     ; This causes the procedure to return
                        ; to the caller.

Set_Mode ENDP           ; This is the end of the procedure.

END                     ; This is the end of the code.
```

Listing 2.9. A C function to test the video mode (setmodec.c).

```c
#include <stdio.h>

#define VGA256 0x13
#define TEXT_MODE 0x03

extern Set_Mode(int mode);


void main(void)
{

// This sets the video mode to 320x200 256 color mode.

Set_Mode(VGA256);

// Wait for keyboard to be hit.

while(!kbhit()){}

// Put the computer back into text mode.

Set_Mode(TEXT_MODE);

} // end main
```

If you type in and execute Listings 2.8 and 2.9, you'll probably see a blank screen. In this instance, a blank screen doesn't mean that your computer crashed, but that the program has changed your VGA card to mode 13h. When you press a key, the default (80x25) text mode will be reset. If we wished, we could have used Microsoft's graphics library function _setvideomode() to accomplish the same task. (However, we want to build up a library of our own—hopefully about a hundred times faster!)

Now that we've set the video mode to the one desired, it's probably a good idea to clear it out. Guess what's next?

Clearing the Screen at Light Speed

The video screen in mode 13h is really just a continuous block of memory. This region of memory starts at A000:0000 and continues on until A000:fBFF. In mode 13h, each pixel is represented by exactly one byte. Take a look at Figure 2.3 to visualize this.

With this configuration, each pixel can have one of 256 values. These values are not (as you might think) the colors of each pixel. Instead, they are the *look-up values*.

Here's how it works. The pixel value (that is, the byte that is stored in every memory location of the screen buffer) is used as an index to a giant color look-up table. A value of 26, then, doesn't mean "color 26." Instead, it means "Index into the 26th element of the color look-up table, and use that value as the color."

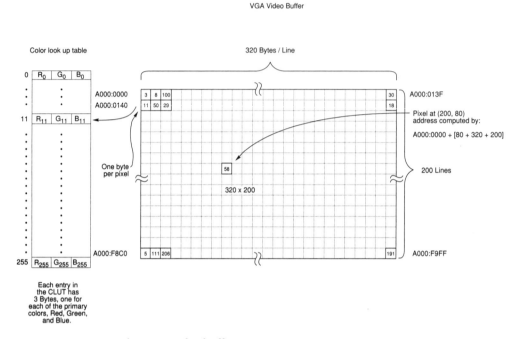

Figure 2.3. *The VGA video buffer.*

The color value contains one byte for each of the three primary colors. However, only the first six bits in each byte are used for each. This means that each element in the color look-up table has three elements: R (red), G (green), and B (blue). We therefore can have a total of 2^{18}, or 262,144, colors. However, because of limits on the color look-up table, only 256 of them can be displayed on the screen at once.

If you're a little confused at this point, don't worry! It will all become much more confusing later.

In video games such as the ones in which we're interested, the screen will be drawn frame-by-frame 15 to 30 times a second. However, before we can draw the screen, we must erase the old one! To do this, we need a way of filling the screen buffer with a value, usually the background color. This value will represent the data that the buffer is filled with and, ultimately, the color of the screen.

The fastest way to accomplish this is to use the assembly instruction stosw. You may well ask, "Why use stosw when each pixel is represented by a BYTE, not a WORD?" The answer is twofold:

- First, as we're storing the same value in every location, we might as well store as many bytes as possible per video write as possible.

- Second, we want to minimize the accesses to the video because it's about ten times slower than normal memory (unless you have a local bus, high-performance VGA card. Whenever you can, therefore, it's better to write a WORD rather than a BYTE.

Listing 2.10 shows an assembly function to set the video mode (filla.asm), while Listing 2.11 shows a C program to test it (fillc.c).

Listing 2.10. A fill-screen assembly procedure (filla.asm).

```
screen_ram EQU 0A000h      ; This starts video ram at A000:0000.

.MODEL MEDIUM, C           ; This tells the procedure to use the
                           ; MEDIUM memory model with C parameter
                           ; passing.

.CODE                      ; This is the beginning of the code.

PUBLIC Fill_Screen         ; This let's the linker have access
                           ; to the function name so the function
                           ; can be exported.

Fill_Screen PROC FAR C color:WORD
                           ; The function takes one parameter.

mov AX, screen_ram         ; This sets ES:DI to screen ram.
mov ES, AX
xor di,di                  ; This zeros DI out.

mov CX,320*200/2           ; This is the number of words we want
                           ; filled.
mov AL, BYTE PTR color     ; This moves the color into AL.
mov AH,AL                  ; This moves the color into AH.
rep stosw                  ; This blasts the video RAM with the
                           ; color at the fastest possible rate.

ret                        ; This causes the procedure to return
                           ; to the caller.

Fill_Screen ENDP           ; This is the end of the procedure.

END                        ; This is the end of the code.
```

Listing 2.11. Fill screen C main test program (fillc.c).

```c
#include <stdio.h>

#define VGA256 0x13
#define TEXT_MODE 0x03

extern Set_Mode(int mode);
extern Fill_Screen(int color);


void main(void)
{
int t;

// This sets the video mode to 320x200 256 color mode.

Set_Mode(VGA256);

// Fill the screen with 1s, which in the default palette will
// be blue.

for (t=0; t<1000; t++)
Fill_Screen(1);

// Wait for keyboard to be hit.

while(!kbhit()){}

// Put the computer back into text mode.

Set_Mode(TEXT_MODE);

} // end main
```

These programs will clear the screen just about as fast as it's going to be cleared.

A note on a subtlety of the VGA card: I clocked my computer, and the fastest I could possibly clear the screen was at 22 frames/sec. This seems ultra slow, but the frame rate is bottlenecked by the VGA card. I computed that my CPU could, theoretically, have a screen-refresh rate of 250 frames/sec, but the video card's memory is just too slow—the CPU is sitting and waiting most of the time while the screen is being updated. We use this little quirk later to our advantage. For now, just make note of it.

On the companion CD that accompanies this book you'll find a program called gauge.exe. You can use it to compute the maximum refresh rate of your video system.

Our refresher course in assembly went very well. I learned a lot, and I hope you did, too. We must cover one more topic: the in-line assembler.

Using the In-Line Assembler

The current trend in the computer industry is toward doing everything in one language. The in-line assembler is a response to this.

The in-line assembler is a platform-dependent extension of the standard C language. It allows programmers to include assembly language instructions directly in their programs, rather than having to create a separate assembly language procedure and link it in. This has two advantages:

- First, the C programmer doesn't need to know as much as before.

- Second, in-line assembly is the ultimate convenience in mixed language programming.

The in-line assembler is invoked by the following syntax:

```
_asm
    {
    ; assembly instructions go here
    }
```

That's all there is to it: no directives, no prolog, no epilog. Just one _asm and a couple of braces, and we're in business.

Now, about a million questions should come to mind about using the in-line assembler. I'll try to address at least half—just kidding! However, here are a couple of the most important points:

- You don't have to save the registers that could be corrupted on the stack. This is is done for you.

- Parameter passing is greatly simplified. If the variable you wish to access is within the scope of the procedure the in-line assembly code is in, you can use the variable name as you normally would with any inner block.

For example, if we wanted to swap two values using the in-line assembler, the following C code would do it:

```
void Swap(int num_1, int num_2)
{

_asm
    {
    mov AX, num_1
```

```
    mov BX, num_2
    mov num_2, AX
    mov num_1, BX
    } // End the in-line assembler.

} // end Swap
```

This procedure would do the swap and the working registers wouldn't be corrupted at all. The compiler would take care of saving them for you.

As long as you don't get carried away with things, you can use the in-line assembler as you would MASM. Of course, the in-line assembler doesn't have nearly the functionality of MASM. It does have a generous subset of the functionality of MASM, which will suffice for most tasks. I have found it to be more than ample for almost everything.

A game-programming guru should always be asking, "How fast is it?" Well, the in-line assembler is just about as fast as using pure assembly. There's almost no overhead, so what you see is what you get. The only overhead that might occur happens during entrance and exit from the in-line assembly section, as there may be extraneous prolog and epilog code.

Nevertheless, I suggest you use the in-line assembler all the time, if you can. For instance, I wrote an entire sound system using the in-line assembler, and it only took a few hours. If I'd had to use external assembly language procedures, it would have taken twice the time because of all the debugging, assembling, and linking I would have had to do. The only drawback is compatibility with non-PC systems—but then, that's not really an issue because we're PC programmers!

Oh, and there's one more tiny little fact. I said before that we'll be using the CPU as if it's a fast 8086. However, if you wish, it's OK to use 286 instructions with the in-line assembler. Use the -G2 option on the C compiler. Of course, you can make external assembly modules using 386, 486, or even 586 specific code if you wish, but be careful! If you use code that only works on a 586, you shrink your target market considerably.

Summary

This chapter probably took the wind out of you! Indeed, we covered a lot of material in a short time:

■ We learned about the architecture of the 80xxx family of processors, and how this architecture can be a bit of an inconvenience to video-game programmers as far as the memory models are concerned.

- We learned how to use the new directives the macro assembler provides to help ease our assembly language programming.

- We learned how to interface our C programs to assembly language, and why we need to use assembly language at all.

- We also covered the in-line assembler. This probably will be the tool of choice used throughout the book to accomplish small tasks that need to be in assembly language.

- Finally, we wrote some programs that placed the PC into mode 13h, and saw how to call these from C.

You now should have a much firmer grip on MASM and assembly language on the PC. We've discussed all the important topics that concern us in programming video games, such as interfacing between assembly and C, and the in-line assembler.

By no means is it my intent to teach assembly language. (As my friend said, it's like programming in DNA—definitely a correct statement.) You must have a good grasp on assembly to use it wisely. There are a number of times in the following chapters where we resort to assembly language, and you must know what I'm talking about. Otherwise, you'll be lost in a sea of 1s and 0s. If you must, therefore, pick up your favorite book on assembly and read it cover to cover. Come back when you're ready.

3

Input Device Basics

At this point in time computers can't read our minds—yet—and we can't read what passes for the mind of a computer. Taking that into consideration, we must communicate with the computer through mechanical *interfaces*. These interfaces include the keyboard, joystick, and mouse. We use standard tactics—such as BIOS, interrupts, and assembly language—to communicate with the computer through these devices. This chapter covers the following topics:

- ■ Interfacing to video games

- ■ The joystick

- ■ The keyboard

- ■ The mouse

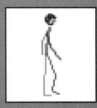

by André LaMothe

Interfacing to Video Games

Playing a video game wouldn't be very exciting if we couldn't interact with it. The whole idea of video games is to be able to interact with a virtual world in real time. When the first games started popping up in arcades and, later, in homes, they had very crude interfaces. Some games had a few buttons that the player could press that would represent the choices and will of the player. As time marched on, more input devices became available. Atari and others started producing games with joysticks and more elaborate control systems, such as flight sticks.

Today, the PC has a wealth of input devices: the products of years of theoretical and applied research. As video-game programmers, we must pay close attention to the use of input devices so the players of our games have smooth and responsive interfaces with which to experience our worlds. If our input system is sluggish and primitive, it won't matter if we can output color holographs with surround sound: players won't play a game they can't control the way they want to.

Now is really a great time to be in the video-game business. Unlike a couple years ago, we can today count on a few common denominators that we couldn't before. For example:

- Most people have a 386 or better.

- Most people have at least VGA graphics, with a large percentage of game players owning sound cards.

- Finally, with Bill Gates at the helm of Microsoft, we can almost bank on most people having a mouse—because almost everyone owns a copy of Windows.

The thing we still have to question is whether our prospective game player has a joystick. Some do, some don't. Many people still prefer the keyboard.

No matter the device used, we must make our use of input intuitive to the player, not clumsy or unnatural. We have to make the mouse glide, the joystick rock, and the keyboard pound—or, through the magic of software, make it seem that way.

So the upshot is: it isn't up to us to decide which input devices to support. We must support all of them. We must be slaves to our game players in this area. Our philosophies may be, and probably are, very different from those of our players as far as selecting the ultimate input device. Hence, we must learn to work with *all* input devices with equal skill and cunning.

Without further ado, let's begin with the joystick.

The Joystick

The joystick has a rather unfortunate name; only the PC gods know what the inventor was thinking. The joystick interface on the PC was really an afterthought. The hardware utilized is—although some would tend to disagree with me on this—crude and unfriendly. Reading the joystick(s) and joystick buttons isn't a terribly complex task; it's just a bit unorthodox and inconsistent compared to the joystick hardware of other computers.

You see, joysticks are *analog devices*: they have a continuous output throughout their travel. This continuum is an "analog" value; see Figure 3.1.

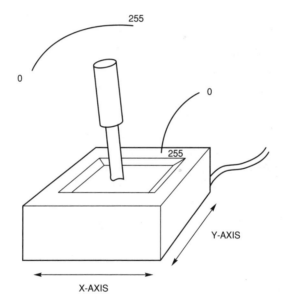

Figure 3.1. *The analog movement of a joystick.*

Our task is to somehow convert this analog value into more palatable data; that is, a digital word. We've all heard of analog-to-digital (A/D) converters, and if the PC were designed today that's what would be in every joystick card.

However, back in the late 70s and early 80s, when the PC was designed and finally marketed, A/D converters were expensive. Hardware engineers had to "hack" together crude A/D converters just for the joystick cards. What they came up with was mildly ingenious at the time, but has since then been a thorn in the side of every video-game programmer.

How Joysticks Work

This is how joysticks work:

■ Each axis on the joystick has a potentiometer connected to it. When the joystick is deflected along the x- or y-axis, the resistance of this potentiometer changes.

■ This potentiometer is used, along with a capacitor, to create a charging circuit.

■ We know from elementary electronics that if you apply voltage to a simple circuit with a resistor and capacitor in series, the capacitor will charge faster (or slower) depending on the resistance and applied voltage.

■ The voltage from the charging capacitor is compared to a pre-established value. When the voltage hits a threshold, the system sets a flag.

■ The time this entire process takes is proportional to the resistance—which, itself, is proportional to the joystick position. Thus, we have a way of figuring out the position of the joystick, scaled by a factor based on the CPU speed.

There's a problem with this wonderful plan: we can time the charging of the system, but "timing" really means "counting." The faster the PC, the faster the counting. (Gotcha!) Therefore, a fast PC will give a different count than a slow PC, even though the capacitors on each system take the same time to charge. That's why we have the joy of *calibrating the joystick* before playing most video games. The video game has to register the range of your particular joystick on your particular computer. (Don't worry: when we're done with this discussion there won't be a joystick in town that you won't be able to conquer.)

Joystick Buttons

The buttons on the joystick are simple switches. (This should make you happy! They could have been some kind of charge-coupled, field-actuated ion pumps.) To read simple switches, we just scan a certain port.

There are some joysticks with multiple buttons, such as the Thrustmaster. Nevertheless, their basic operation is the same, and the extra buttons are read through another I/O port. This I/O port and the further functionality of these advanced types of joysticks can be obtained from the manufacturer's development documentation.

The I/O port 201h is the window into the joystick. As shown in Figure 3.2, this port controls both joystick A and joystick B.

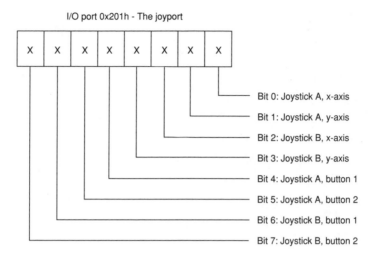

I/O port 0x201h - The joyport

Bit 0: Joystick A, x-axis
Bit 1: Joystick A, y-axis
Bit 2: Joystick B, x-axis
Bit 3: Joystick B, y-axis
Bit 4: Joystick A, button 1
Bit 5: Joystick A, button 2
Bit 6: Joystick B, button 1
Bit 7: Joystick B, button 2

Figure 3.2. *Joystick-port bit definitions.*

We go into the explanation of bits 0-3 in a moment, in the section "Reading the Joystick Position." Bits 4-7 are the switch states of the joystick buttons. When one of the buttons on joystick 1 or 2 is pressed, the appropriate bit is set in port 201h. There's *one* little detail: the buttons are inverted. For example, if you were to press button one on joystick 1, bit 0 would toggle from 1 to 0. This isn't a big deal, however: we just invert the bits.

Listing 3.1 contains code to read the buttons.

Listing 3.1. Reading the joystick buttons.

```
// D E F I N E S ///////////////////////////////////////////////

#define JOYPORT      0x201  // The joyport is at 201 hex.

#define BUTTON_1_A   0x10   // Joystick 1, button A
#define BUTTON_1_B   0x20   // Joystick 1, button B
#define BUTTON_2_A   0x40   // Joystick 2, button A
#define BUTTON_2_B   0x80   // Joystick 2, button B

#define JOYSTICK_1_X 0x01   // Joystick 1, x-axis
#define JOYSTICK_1_Y 0x02   // Joystick 1, y-axis
#define JOYSTICK_2_X 0x04   // Joystick 2, x-axis
#define JOYSTICK_2_Y 0x08   // Joystick 2, y-axis

#define JOY_1_CAL    1      // This command calibrates
                            // joystick #1.
```

continues

Listing 3.1. continued

```
#define JOY_2_CAL        2    // This command calibrates
                              // joystick #2.


/////////////////////////////////////////////////////////////

unsigned char Buttons(unsigned char button)
{
// Read the joystick buttons by 'peeking' at the port to which
// the switches are attached.

outp(JOYPORT,0); // Clear the latch and request a sample.

// Invert buttons, then mask with request.

return( ~inp(JOYPORT) & button);

} // end Buttons


/////////////////////////////////////////////////////////////

unsigned char Buttons_Bios(unsigned char button)
{
// BIOS version of buttons read.

union _REGS inregs, outregs;

inregs.h.ah = 0x84; // This is joystick function 84h.
inregs.x.dx = 0x00; // This is read-buttons subfunction 0h.

// Call DOS.

_int86(0x15,&inregs, &outregs);

// Invert buttons, then mask with request.

return( (~outregs.h.al) & button);

} // end Buttons_Bios
```

Let's look at Listing 3.1 in detail:

- The functions `Buttons()` and `Buttons_Bios()` get the same result. `Buttons()` first sends a 0 to the joystick port, then reads the data back. The 0 has to be sent because it tells the joystick port to take a sample.

- Once the data has been retrieved, we mask off the lower four bits and invert the upper four bits.

- This listing includes definitions (`#defines`) so that numerical constants don't have to be used, making the interface more convenient.

■ Buttons_Bios() uses the system BIOS to read the joystick. When this call is made, the result is placed in register AL. Personally, for something as simple as the buttons I'd probably use the port directly. As a rule, the BIOS is slow. When it comes to joysticks, however, it's not bad. If you want to use the BIOS, do so.

Reading the Joystick Position

Reading the joystick position is a bit tedious, but nothing we can't handle. All we need to do is send the sample joystick command by writing 0 to joystick port 201h. Then we wait for the appropriate bit (0-3) to be set in the joystick port. While we wait, we must be counting. When the bit of interest gets set, the sum we have been accumulating is the position of the joystick. Listing 3.2 contains code that does all this for us.

Listing 3.2. Reading the joystick position.

```
unsigned int Joystick(unsigned char stick)
{
// This reads the joystick values manually by counting how long
// the capacitors take to charge/discharge.
// (Let's use the in-line assembler. It's cool!)

__asm
    {
    cli                     ; Disable interrupts.

    mov ah, byte ptr stick  ; Get a mask into AH to select the
                            ; joystick to read.
    xor al,al               ; Zero out AL, XOR is a trick.
    xor cx,cx               ; Do the same with CX, which we'll
                            ; use as a counter.
    mov dx,JOYPORT          ; DX is used by inp and outp.
    out dx,al               ; Write 0s to the port.
discharge:
    in al,dx                ; Read the data back from the port.
    test al,ah              ; Has the bit in question changed?
    loopne discharge        ; If the stick isn't ready, decrement
                            ; cx and loop.

    sti                     ; Reenable interrupts.
    xor ax,ax               ; Zero out AX.
    sub ax,cx               ; AX now holds the position of the
                            ; axis switch.

    } // end asm

// As AX has the result, the function will return it properly.

} // end Joystick
```

(I'm starting to like the in-line assembler.) This program is quite simple:

■ On entry, the program zeros out the AX and CX registers.

■ The program then polls the joystick port, which instructs the joystick hard-ware to take a sample.

■ The program then sits in the discharge loop and counts while waiting for the appropriate bit—the joystick axis potentiometer we wanted to read—to be set.

■ Counting is accomplished by using the CX register and the loopxx instruction. In this case, the program uses loopne, which makes a decision based on the zero flag that was previously set (or reset, depending on the result of the test instruction).

■ The test instruction is what keeps testing to see if the joystick is done with its discharging.

■ When the proper bit is set, the program exits out of the loop. The result is then passed back to the caller by way of the AX register.

That's all there is to it. Later in the book I provide a demo program that uses all of the joystick functions. That program has a BIOS version of Joystick() called Joystick_Bios(). The BIOS version is reliable and almost self-calibrating. I suggest you use it instead of reading the joystick(s) manually.

(Throughout the book I try to show you there are at least two ways to skin a cat, and usually more if you're clever.)

Joystick Calibration

Now let's address the matter of calibration. As I said earlier, the result we get from reading the joystick by way of a timing loop will vary on different computers. On some computers the x-axis may range from 0-255; on others, it may range from 0-10,000. Therefore, we must *normalize* this data, or map its domain to the same range. The standard tactic is to have the player go through a calibration phase during game setup. During this phase, the player operates the joystick and the software records and saves the calibration data somewhere on the disk for later retrieval.

To calibrate a joystick, our program must:

■ Find the minimum and maximum deflection values for both the x- and y-axes.

■ Save this information.

■ Use this information to compute how much the player is moving the joystick.

For example, say the joystick was calibrated and we found that the x-axis ranged from 0-255. We then would know that if we read the joystick x-axis and retrieved a 128, the joystick was probably in the middle. (Actually, during calibration the neutral position is also recorded. This is because many joysticks don't fall to neutral in the exact middle of the potentiometer travel.)

There's one final detail we should cover about using joysticks: detecting them. The common technique to detect whether a joystick is present is to start the joystick-charging circuit and wait for it to time out. This can be accomplished by reading the joystick(s) with the BIOS call and testing whether each axis is 0. If this is true, no joystick is plugged in.

I think we've said enough about joysticks, so here's some code that uses the functions in Listings 3.1 and 3.2. Listing 3.3 starts up and then asks the player to:

■ Swirl the joystick

■ Release the joystick

■ Press a button

The program then saves this calibration information in global variables for future use.

Listing 3.3. A joystick program (joy.c).

```
// I N C L U D E S ////////////////////////////////////////////////

#include <dos.h>
#include <bios.h>
#include <stdio.h>    // Include the basics.
#include <math.h>     // Include math stuff.
#include <conio.h>
#include <graph.h>    // Include Microsoft's Graphics Header.


// D E F I N E S ////////////////////////////////////////////////


#define JOYPORT       0x201  // The joyport is at 201 hex.

#define BUTTON_1_A    0x10   // Joystick 1, button A
#define BUTTON_1_B    0x20   // Joystick 1, button B
#define BUTTON_2_A    0x40   // Joystick 2, button A
#define BUTTON_2_B    0x80   // Joystick 2, button B

#define JOYSTICK_1_X  0x01   // Joystick 1, x-axis
#define JOYSTICK_1_Y  0x02   // Joystick 1, y-axis
#define JOYSTICK_2_X  0x04   // Joystick 2, x-axis
#define JOYSTICK_2_Y  0x08   // Joystick 2, y-axis
```

continues

Listing 3.3 continued

```c
#define JOY_1_CAL       1   // This command calibrates
                            // joystick #1.
#define JOY_2_CAL       2   // This command calibrates
                            // joystick #2.


// G L O B A L S ////////////////////////////////////////////////

unsigned int joy_1_max_x,   // These are the global joystick
                            // calibration variables.
             joy_1_max_y,
             joy_1_min_x,
             joy_1_min_y,
             joy_1_cx,
             joy_1_cy,
             joy_2_max_x,
             joy_2_max_y,
             joy_2_min_x,
             joy_2_min_y,
             joy_2_cx,
             joy_2_cy;


// F U N C T I O N S ////////////////////////////////////////////////

unsigned char Buttons(unsigned char button)
{
// Read the joystick buttons by 'peeking' at the port to which
// the switches are attached.

outp(JOYPORT,0); // Clear the latch and request a sample.

// Invert buttons, then mask with request.

return( ~inp(JOYPORT) & button);

} // end Buttons

////////////////////////////////////////////////////////////////////

unsigned int Joystick(unsigned char stick)
{
// This reads the joystick values manually by counting how long
// the capacitors take to charge/discharge.
// Let's use the in-line assembler. It's cool!

__asm
    {
    cli                     ; Disable interrupts.

    mov ah, byte ptr stick  ; Get a mask into AH to select the
                            ; joystick to read.
    xor al,al               ; Zero out AL, XOR is a trick.
    xor cx,cx               ; Same with CX, which we'll use as a
                            ; counter.
```

```
        mov dx,JOYPORT          ; DX is used by inp and outp.
        out dx,al               ; Write 0s to the port.
discharge:
        in al,dx                ; Read the data back from the port.
        test al,ah              ; Has the bit in question changed?
        loopne discharge        ; If the stick isn't ready, decrement
                                ; cx and loop.

        sti                     ; Reenable interrupts.
        xor ax,ax               ; Zero out AX.
        sub ax,cx               ; AX now holds the position of the
                                ; axis switch.

    } // end asm

// As AX has the result, the function will return it properly.

} // end Joystick

/////////////////////////////////////////////////////////////////

unsigned int Joystick_Bios(unsigned char stick)
{
// BIOS version of joystick read
union _REGS inregs, outregs;

inregs.h.ah = 0x84; // This is joystick function 84h.
inregs.x.dx = 0x01; // This is read-joystick subfunction 1h.
// Call DOS.

_int86(0x15,&inregs, &outregs);

// This returns the proper value, depending on the sent command.

switch(stick)
    {
    case JOYSTICK_1_X:
        {
        return(outregs.x.ax);
        } break;

    case JOYSTICK_1_Y:
        {
        return(outregs.x.bx);
        } break;

    case JOYSTICK_2_X:
        {
        return(outregs.x.cx);
        } break;

    case JOYSTICK_2_Y:
        {
        return(outregs.x.dx);
        } break;

    default:break;
```

continues

Listing 3.3. continued

```
       } // end switch stick

} // end Joystick_Bios


/////////////////////////////////////////////////////////////

unsigned char Buttons_Bios(unsigned char button)
{
// BIOS version of buttons read

union _REGS inregs, outregs;

inregs.h.ah = 0x84; // This is joystick function 84h.
inregs.x.dx = 0x00; // This is read-buttons subfunction 0h.

// Call DOS.

_int86(0x15,&inregs, &outregs);

// Invert buttons, then mask with request

return( (~outregs.h.al) & button);

} // end Buttons_Bios

/////////////////////////////////////////////////////////////

void Joystick_Calibrate(int stick)
{
// This calibrates the joystick by finding the min and max
// deflections in both the x- and y-axes, then stores it in a
// global data structure for future use.

unsigned int x_new,y_new; // Temporary joystick positions

// This sets variables so we can find their actual values.

if (stick==JOY_1_CAL)
    {

    printf("\nCalibrating Joystick #1: Swirl stick, then release
it and press FIRE");

    // This sets calibrations to impossible values.

    joy_1_max_x=0;
    joy_1_max_y=0;
    joy_1_min_x=10000;
    joy_1_min_y=10000;

    // Now the player should swirl the joystick, let the stick
    // fall neutral, and then press any button.

    while(!Buttons(BUTTON_1_A | BUTTON_1_B))
        {
```

```
            // This gets the new values and tries to update
            // calibration.
            x_new = Joystick_Bios(JOYSTICK_1_X);
            y_new = Joystick_Bios(JOYSTICK_1_Y);

            // Process the x-axis:

            if (x_new >= joy_1_max_x)
                joy_1_max_x = x_new;

            if (x_new <= joy_1_min_x)
                joy_1_min_x = x_new;

            // Process the y-axis:

            if (y_new >= joy_1_max_y)
                joy_1_max_y = y_new;

            if (y_new <= joy_1_min_y)
                joy_1_min_y = y_new;

            } // end while

            // The player has let the stick go to neutral, so that
            // must be the center.

            joy_1_cx = x_new;
            joy_1_cy = y_new;

    } // end calibrate joystick #1
else
if (stick==JOY_2_CAL)
    {
    printf("\nCalibrating Joystick #2: Swirl stick, then release
it and press FIRE");

    // This sets the calibrations to impossible values.

    joy_2_max_x=0;
    joy_2_max_y=0;
    joy_2_min_x=10000;
    joy_2_min_y=10000;

    // Now the player should swirl the joystick, let the stick
    // fall neutral, and then press any button.

    while(!Buttons(BUTTON_2_A | BUTTON_2_B))
        {
        // This gets the new values and tries to update
        // calibration.
        x_new = Joystick(JOYSTICK_2_X);
        y_new = Joystick(JOYSTICK_2_Y);

        // Process the x-axis:

        if (x_new >= joy_2_max_x)
            joy_2_max_x = x_new;
        else
```

continues

Listing 3.3. continued

```
        if (x_new <= joy_2_min_x)
            joy_2_min_x = x_new;

        // Process the y-axis:

        if (y_new >= joy_2_max_y)
            joy_2_max_y = y_new;
        else
        if (y_new <= joy_2_min_y)
            joy_2_min_y = y_new;

        } // end while

        // The player has let the stick fall neutral, so that
        // must be the center.

        joy_2_cx = x_new;
        joy_2_cy = y_new;


    } // end calibrate joystick #2

printf("\nCalibration Complete... hit any key to continue.");

getch();

} // end Joystick_Calibrate

/////////////////////////////////////////////////////////////////////

void main(void) // Test the joystick interface.
{

// This calibrates the joystick.

Joystick_Calibrate(JOY_1_CAL);

_clearscreen(_GCLEARSCREEN);

// Let the player fiddle with the joystick.

while(!kbhit())
    {

    _settextposition(2,0);

    printf("Joystick 1 = [%u,%u]
",Joystick_Bios(JOYSTICK_1_X),Joystick_Bios(JOYSTICK_1_Y));

    if (Buttons_Bios(BUTTON_1_A))
        printf("\nButton 1 pressed   ");
    else
    if (Buttons_Bios(BUTTON_1_B))
        printf("\nButton 2 pressed   ");
    else
        printf("\nNo Button Pressed   ");
    } // end while
```

```
// Let the player know what the calibrations turned out to be.

printf("\nmax x=%u, max y=%u,min x=%u,min y=%u,cx=%u,cy=%u",joy_1_max_x,
                                                            joy_1_max_y,
                                                            joy_1_min_x,
                                                            joy_1_min_y,
                                                            joy_1_cx,
                                                            joy_1_cy);

// Later!

} // end main
```

If you type in and execute Listing 3.3, you can press a key and watch joystick 1 change its values in real time as you move the stick around and press the buttons.

The Keyboard

The keyboard is the most complex input device the PC has to offer. It has its own small controller chip—and a mind of its own, so to speak. I've spent many late nights digging into IBM's technical-reference BIOS listings trying to unravel the mysteries of the PC keyboard.

There are some things that are uncertain in life, like the value of the dollar, the thermal-expansion coefficient of rubidium, and so on. One thing that *is* for sure is that the keyboard will live forever. I think Scotty said it best in *Star Trek IV:* "Ah. A keyboard. How quaint."

For our purposes as video-game programmers, we must get input from the keyboard in a clean manner that works all the time. With that in mind, we're not going to mess with interrupts and nebulous internal registers and ports. We're going to use the functions provided by C and the BIOS to query the keyboard. I don't mean functions such as getch() and scanf(), but the _bios_keyboard() functions that C provides.

Let's stop here for a reality check. As a rule, you should never use the BIOS... right? Well, in some cases—such as file I/O and memory allocation—it's OK. Basically, you can use BIOS calls for functions that aren't time-dependent. Using the BIOS for reading the keyboard or the joystick is not going to kill us. (Using it for drawing lines or pixels will bury us!) As I said before, PCs are fast enough that we don't have to optimize everything and hand assemble our programs anymore. Just don't get careless.

The BIOS supports a few functions that we'll be using, as shown in Table 3.1.

Table 3.1. Keyboard BIOS Functions

Bios INT 16h

Function: 00h—Read character from keyboard

Entry: AH:00h

Exit: AH: Keyboard Scan Code

        AL: ASCII Character

Function: 01h—Read Keyboard Status

Entry: AH:01h

Exit: AH: Keyboard Scan Code

        AL: ASCII Character

        Zero Flag: If 0 then character waiting, if 1 then no character.

Function: 02h—Return Keyboard Flags

Entry: AH:02h

Exit: AL: Keyboard Flag Byte

        Bit 0:Right Shift Key Down

        Bit 1:Left Shift Key Down

        Bit 2:Control Key Down

        Bit 3:Alt Key Down

        Bit 4:Scroll Lock On

        Bit 5:Num Lock On

        Bit 6:Caps Lock On

        Bit 7:Insert On

The bits returned from each function are self explanatory.

Scan Codes

Let's examine a nuance of the keyboard called *scan codes*. You see, we're used to thinking when the A key is pressed on the keyboard, an ASCII 'a' is sent to the keyboard handler. Not true! What's sent is a scan code. Moreover, a scan code is sent when a key press is made *and* when a release is made.

In video games we're not so interested in ASCII codes as we are in making keys like A, S, and the space bar represent right, left, and FIRE. Therefore, we really only need to get the scan codes.

This is exactly what we do. Table 3.2 shows these scan codes.

Table 3.2. Scan codes.

Key	Scan Code
ESC	1
1	2
2	3
3	4
4	5
5	6
6	7
7	8
8	9
9	10
0	11
MINUS	12
EQUALS	13
BKSP	14
TAB	15
Q	16
W	17

continues

Table 3.2. continued

Key	Scan Code
E	18
R	19
T	20
Y	21
U	22
I	23
O	24
P	25
LFT_BRACKET	26
RGT_BRACKET	27
ENTER	28
CTRL	29
A	30
S	31
D	32
F	33
G	34
H	35
J	36
K	37
L	38
SEMI	39
APOS	40
LEFT_SHIFT	42
BACK_SLASH	43
Z	44

Key	Scan Code
X	45
C	46
V	47
B	48
N	49
M	50
COMMA	51
PERIOD	52
FOWARD_SLASH	53
RIGHT_SHIFT	54
PRT_SCRN	55
ALT	56
SPACE	57
CAPS_LOCK	58
F1	59
F2	60
F3	61
F4	62
F5	63
F6	64
F7	65
F8	66
F9	67
F10	68
F11	133
F12	134
NUM_LOCK	69

continues

Table 3.2. continued

Key	Scan Code
SCROLL_LOCK	70
HOME	71
UP	72
PGUP	73
NUM_MINUS	74
LEFT	75
CENTER	76
RIGHT	77
NUM_PLUS	78
END	79
DOWN	80
PGDWN	81
INS	82
DEL	83

As you review this information, notice that keys that have two symbols on them have only one scan code. This is because the single scan code is further qualified by the shift state, discussed in the next section. And, *viola!* We can compute the ASCII code by using a look-up table.

Shift States

We want to be able to:

■ Detect whether a key has been pressed.

■ Get that key.

■ Read the key's shift state.

The *shift state* is just a bit vector that relays information about the Shift, Alt, Ctrl, and other keys. The shift state can be found in memory locations 417h and 418h. However, we aren't going to read shift states directly. We'll use the BIOS and C instead.

Listing 3.4 contains the code to get the shift state.

Listing 3.4. Retrieving the shift state from the keyboard.

```
// bitmasks for control keys/shift status

#define SHIFT_R                 0x0001
#define SHIFT_L                 0x0002
#define CTRL                    0x0004
#define ALT                     0x0008
#define SCROLL_LOCK_ON          0x0010
#define NUM_LOCK_ON             0x0020
#define CAPS_LOCK_ON            0x0040
#define INSERT_MODE             0x0080
#define CTRL_L                  0x0100
#define ALT_L                   0x0200
#define CTRL_R                  0x0400
#define ALT_R                   0x0800
#define SCROLL_LOCK_DWN         0x1000
#define NUM_LOCK_DWN            0x2000
#define CAPS_LOCK_DWN           0x4000
#define SYS_REQ_DWN             0x8000

/////////////////////////////////////////////////////////////////

unsigned int Get_Control_Keys(unsigned int mask)
{
// This returns the status of all requested control keys.

return(mask & _bios_keybrd(_KEYBRD_SHIFTSTATUS));

} // end Get_Control_Keys
```

In Listing 3.4, the Get_Control_Key() function uses a C BIOS call to query the shift state. I've included a convenient set of definitions so you can call the Get_Control_Key() function with one of the commands in the #defines lines. The sent command request is logically combined with the shift state using an AND. This capability enables you to call the function and query a specific state in a single function call.

Obtaining Scan Codes from Keyboard Input

The code in Listing 3.5 reads the scan code directly and reports it back. If there is no key ready, the function returns a 0.

Listing 3.5. Retrieving scan codes from the keyboard.

```
/////////////////////////////////////////////////////////////////

unsigned char Get_Scan_Code()
{
// This gets the scan code of a key press.
// Let's use the in-line assembler.

// Is a key ready?

__asm
    {
    mov ah,01h          ; Function 1: is a key ready?
    int 16h             ; Call the interrupt.
    jz empty            ; There was no key, so exit.
    mov ah,00h          ; Function 0: get the scan code, please.
    int 16h             ; Call the interrupt.
    mov al,ah           ; The result was in AH, so put it
                        ; into AL.
    xor ah,ah           ; Zero out AH.
    jmp done            ; The data's in AX... let's blaze!

empty:
    xor ax,ax           ; Clear out AX. 0 means no key.
done:

    } // end asm

// As the data is in AX, it will be returned properly.

} // end Get_Scan_Code

/////////////////////////////////////////////////////////////////
```

Again, we're using the in-line assembler. We could have made the BIOS call with the C function _int86(), but doing it in line is just cooler!

Obtaining ASCII Characters from Keyboard Input

Now let's take a look at how we would retrieve an ASCII character from the keyboard. This could be useful when the player is typing in, say, a name and we want the actual ASCII codes. We could use the scan codes and translate—but why, when we can also read the ASCII code?

Listing 3.6 shows the last function we'll be using regarding the keyboard. This program queries the keyboard for a waiting character. If there is one, the program retrieves it and sends back the ASCII code. If there was no waiting character, the function returns 0.

Listing 3.6. Retrieving an ASCII character from the keyboard.

```
///////////////////////////////////////////////////////////

unsigned char Get_Ascii_Key()

{

// If there is a normal ASCII key waiting, return it. Otherwise,
// return 0.

if (_bios_keybrd(_KEYBRD_READY))
 return(_bios_keybrd(_KEYBRD_READ));
else return(0);

} // end Get_Ascii_Key

///////////////////////////////////////////////////////////
```

To use the function in Listing 3.6, you would do something like this:

```
if ((c=Get_Ascii_Key()) > 0)
    {
    process character
    }
else
    {
    no character ready, take appropriate action
    }
```

All Together Now: a Keyboard Demo Program

That about wraps it up for the keyboard. Listing 3.7 is a demo program that makes calls to the functions in the previous listings, and also defines scan codes for ease of processing. This program displays the scan code of the key you're pressing and tracks the Ctrl and Alt keys. When you press the Q key, the program quits. Note how the scan code is printed out and is not the same as the ASCII code of the depressed key.

Listing 3.7. A keyboarder program (key.c).

```
// I N C L U D E S //////////////////////////////////////////

#include <dos.h>
#include <bios.h>
#include <stdio.h>    // Include the basics.
#include <math.h>     // Include math stuff.
#include <conio.h>
#include <graph.h>    // Include Microsoft's Graphics Header.
```

continues

Listing 3.7. continued

```
// D E F I N E S ///////////////////////////////////////////////

// Bitmasks for control keys/shift status:

#define SHIFT_R            0x0001
#define SHIFT_L            0x0002
#define CTRL               0x0004
#define ALT                0x0008
#define SCROLL_LOCK_ON     0x0010
#define NUM_LOCK_ON        0x0020
#define CAPS_LOCK_ON       0x0040
#define INSERT_MODE        0x0080
#define CTRL_L             0x0100
#define ALT_L              0x0200
#define CTRL_R             0x0400
#define ALT_R              0x0800
#define SCROLL_LOCK_DWN    0x1000
#define NUM_LOCK_DWN       0x2000
#define CAPS_LOCK_DWN      0x4000
#define SYS_REQ_DWN        0x8000

// Scan code values. Note: keys showing two symbols yield the
// same value for either symbol, so I will consistently use the
// lower symbol. For example, the 1 key also has a ! above it,
// but we just call it the SCAN_1 key.

#define SCAN_ESC           1
#define SCAN_1             2
#define SCAN_2             3
#define SCAN_3             4
#define SCAN_4             5
#define SCAN_5             6
#define SCAN_6             7
#define SCAN_7             8
#define SCAN_8             9
#define SCAN_9             10
#define SCAN_0             11
#define SCAN_MINUS         12
#define SCAN_EQUALS        13
#define SCAN_BKSP          14
#define SCAN_TAB           15
#define SCAN_Q             16
#define SCAN_W             17
#define SCAN_E             18
#define SCAN_R             19
#define SCAN_T             20
#define SCAN_Y             21
#define SCAN_U             22
#define SCAN_I             23
#define SCAN_O             24
#define SCAN_P             25
#define SCAN_LFT_BRACKET   26
#define SCAN_RGT_BRACKET   27
#define SCAN_ENTER         28
#define SCAN_CTRL          29
#define SCAN_A             30
```

```
#define SCAN_S              31
#define SCAN_D              32
#define SCAN_F              33
#define SCAN_G              34
#define SCAN_H              35
#define SCAN_J              36
#define SCAN_K              37
#define SCAN_L              38
#define SCAN_SEMI           39
#define SCAN_APOS           40
#define SCAN_TILDE          41
#define SCAN_LEFT_SHIFT     42
#define SCAN_BACK_SLASH     43
#define SCAN_Z              44
#define SCAN_X              45
#define SCAN_C              46
#define SCAN_V              47
#define SCAN_B              48
#define SCAN_N              49
#define SCAN_M              50
#define SCAN_COMMA          51
#define SCAN_PERIOD         52
#define SCAN_FOWARD_SLASH   53
#define SCAN_RIGHT_SHIFT    54
#define SCAN_PRT_SCRN       55
#define SCAN_ALT            56
#define SCAN_SPACE          57
#define SCAN_CAPS_LOCK      58
#define SCAN_F1             59
#define SCAN_F2             60
#define SCAN_F3             61
#define SCAN_F4             62
#define SCAN_F5             63
#define SCAN_F6             64
#define SCAN_F7             65
#define SCAN_F8             66
#define SCAN_F9             67
#define SCAN_F10            68
#define SCAN_F11            133
#define SCAN_F12            134
#define SCAN_NUM_LOCK       69
#define SCAN_SCROLL_LOCK    70
#define SCAN_HOME           71
#define SCAN_UP             72
#define SCAN_PGUP           73
#define SCAN_NUM_MINUS      74
#define SCAN_LEFT           75
#define SCAN_CENTER         76
#define SCANE_RIGHT         77
#define SCAN_NUM_PLUS       78
#define SCAN_END            79
#define SCAN_DOWN           80
#define SCAN_PGDWN          81
#define SCAN_INS            82
#define SCAN_DEL            83
```

continues

Listing 3.7. continued

```c
// F U N C T I O N S /////////////////////////////////////////////

unsigned char Get_Ascii_Key(void)

{

// If there's a normal ASCII key waiting, return it. Otherwise,
// return 0.

if (_bios_keybrd(_KEYBRD_READY))
 return(_bios_keybrd(_KEYBRD_READ));
else return(0);

} // end Get_Ascii_Key

/////////////////////////////////////////////////////////////////

unsigned int Get_Control_Keys(unsigned int mask)
{
// This returns the status of all requested control keys.

return(mask & _bios_keybrd(_KEYBRD_SHIFTSTATUS));

} // end Get_Control_Keys

/////////////////////////////////////////////////////////////////

unsigned char Get_Scan_Code(void)
{
// This gets the scan code of a key press.
// Let's use the in-line assembler.


// Is a key ready?

__asm
   {
   mov ah,01h          ; Function 1: is a key ready?
   int 16h             ; Call the interrupt.
   jz empty            ; There was no key, so exit.
   mov ah,00h          ; Function 0: get the scan code, please.
   int 16h             ; Call the interrupt.
   mov al,ah           ; The result was in AH, so put it
                       ; into AL.
   xor ah,ah           ; Zero out AH.
   jmp done            ; The data's in AX... let's blaze!

empty:
    xor ax,ax          ; Clear out AX. 0 means no key.
done:

   } // end asm

// As the data is in AX, it will be returned properly.

} // end Get_Scan_Code
```

```
///////////////////////////////////////////////////////////
void main(void) // Keyboard demo
{
int done=0;
unsigned int control;

_clearscreen(_GCLEARSCREEN);

while(!done)
    {

    _settextposition(2,0);

    if ( (key = Get_Scan_Code()) )
       printf("%c %d   ",key,key);

    // This tests for the Ctrl and Alt keys.

    if (Get_Control_Keys(CTRL))
       printf("\ncontrol key pressed");

    if (Get_Control_Keys(ALT))
       printf("\nalt key pressed     ");

    if (key==16) done=1; // 16 is the scan code for 'q'

    } // end main

} // end main
```

The Mouse

The mouse really was a milestone in the evolution of input devices. Originally, it was part of research done at the Xerox PARC center in California. It has now become the input device of choice for millions of users. The mouse enables a user to directly navigate on the video screen and simply "point to" and "click" the icon of interest.

The word *icon*, although used for centuries to mean "an image or likeness" (and having sacred connotations in some religions), was imported into the computer lexicon by a video game programmer back in the days of the Apple I.

The mouse usually connects to a serial port on the computer or, on some modified serial ports and laptops, in a DIN connector. There are *bus mice* that have dedicated cards that interface to the PC, but they haven't been too successful. (Most users don't feel like cracking open their PC to install a simple mouse.)

The mice of today work either optically or mechanically. (Actually, I soon expect them to use mind control.) In any case, the motion is encoded as a series of pulses and converted into a packet that indicates the motion of the mouse and the status of the buttons. This packet is sent over the serial communications port to which the mouse is connected, and then interpreted by the application.

Writing a mouse driver isn't too bad, but—luckily for us—Microsoft and other companies have already written about a million or so mouse drivers. Unlike the keyboard and the joystick, we interface with the mouse solely through driver functionality. We don't, for example, try to decode the position packets.

A copy of the latest version of the Microsoft mouse driver is included on the companion CD at the back of the book. The driver itself has about 50 or 60 functions. We'll be using only the bare minimum needed to get the position of the mouse and the state of the buttons. Table 3.3 lists these driver functions.

A *mickey* is the smallest unit of distance the mouse can discern. It's about 1/200th of an inch.

Table 3.3. Mouse Driver Functions.

Bios INT 33h

Function: 00h—Reset Mouse Driver

Entry: AH: 0000h

Exit: AX: FFFFh is success, 0000h failed

        BX: Number of Mouse Buttons

Function: 01h—Show Mouse Pointer

Entry: AX: 0001h

Exit: None

Function: 02h—Hide Mouse Pointer

Entry: AX:0002h

Exit: None

Function: 03h—Get Pointer Position and Button Status

Entry: AX: 0003h

Exit: BX: Button Status

       Bit 0: Left Mouse Button, 1 if pressed, 0 otherwise

       Bit 1: Right Mouse Button, 1 if pressed, 0 otherwise

       Bit 2: Center Mouse Button, 1 if pressed, 0 otherwise

       CX: X Coordinate

       DX: Y Coordinate

Function: 0Bh—Get Relative Mouse Position

Entry: AX: 000bh

Exit: CX: Relative Horizontal Motion in Mickeys

       DX: Relative Vertical Motion in Mickeys

Function: 1Ah—Set Sensitivity

Entry: AX: 001Ah

Exit: BX: X Axis Sensitivity 0 - 100

       CX: Y Axis Sensitivity 0 - 100

       DX: Double Speed Value 0 - 100

As you can see, the driver functions are called using BIOS interrupt 0x33h. We usually send parameters in the AX register and receive output from the calls by way of the AX, BX, CX, and DX registers.

I've designed an easy-to-use interface for you to use with the mouse, including a master function called Squeeze_Mouse(). The Squeeze_Mouse() function is multipurpose; its action depends on the parameter sent as its command. The prototype looks like this:

```
int Squeeze_Mouse(int command, int *x, int *y, int *buttons);
```

I created a set of definitions to direct Squeeze_Mouse() to do our bidding. They are:

```
// Mouse subfunction calls:

#define MOUSE_INT              0x33 // Mouse interrupt number.
#define MOUSE_RESET            0x00 // Reset the mouse.
#define MOUSE_SHOW             0x01 // Show the mouse.
#define MOUSE_HIDE             0x02 // Hide the mouse.
#define MOUSE_BUTT_POS         0x03 // Get buttons and mouse
                                    // position.
#define MOUSE_SET_SENSITIVITY  0x1A // Set the sensitivity of
                                    // the mouse to 0-100.
#define MOUSE_MOTION_REL       0x0B // Query motion counters to
                                    // compute relative motion.
```

Therefore, if we want to query the x,y position of the mouse, we could do the following:

```
Squeeze_Mouse(MOUSE_BUTT_POS, &mouse_x, &mouse_y,&mouse_buttons);
```

where mouse_x, mouse_y, and mouse_buttons are local variables in which we want the results stored.

Let's consider the two different ways the mouse driver sends back the mouse position:

■ The mouse driver can send back absolute coordinates. In absolute mode, accomplished by calling Squeeze_Mouse() with MOUSE_BUTT_POS, the returned values in x and y are the screen coordinates of the mouse.

For example, if the mouse is in the upper-left corner of the screen, the function returns (0,0).

■ The mouse driver can send back relative coordinates. In relative mode, the *delta*, or difference since the last call, is sent back.

For example if the mouse has moved 20 mickeys along the x-axis 10 mickeys along the y-axis from its last position, that's what will be sent back. To read relative motion, use the command MOUSE_MOTION_REL.

One final tidbit about the mouse: you can change its sensitivity to motion using the command MOUSE_SET_SENSITIVITY. Send a value from 1-100 in the x and y variables and then call Squeeze_Mouse(). After the call the sensitivity will be changed; in other words, the ratio of physical motion to logical motion will be adjusted.

Listing 3.8 shows a demo program that uses the mouse. This program enables you to draw on the screen by pressing the left mouse button, and to change color with the right mouse button.

I'm outta here; meet you in the next chapter!

Listing 3.8. Mickie Mouse (mouse.c).

```c
// I N C L U D E S ////////////////////////////////////////////////

#include <dos.h>
#include <bios.h>
#include <stdio.h>    // Include the basics.
#include <math.h>     // Include math stuff.
#include <conio.h>
#include <graph.h>    // Include Microsoft's Graphics Header.


// D E F I N E S ////////////////////////////////////////////////

// Mouse subfunction calls:

#define MOUSE_INT              0x33 // Mouse interrupt number.
#define MOUSE_RESET            0x00 // Reset the mouse.
#define MOUSE_SHOW             0x01 // Show the mouse.
#define MOUSE_HIDE             0x02 // Hide the mouse.
#define MOUSE_BUTT_POS         0x03 // Get buttons and mouse
                                    // position.
#define MOUSE_SET_SENSITIVITY  0x1A // Set the sensitivity of
                                    // the mouse to 0-100.
#define MOUSE_MOTION_REL       0x0B // Query motion counters to
                                    // compute relative motion.

// Definitions to make reading buttons easier:

#define MOUSE_LEFT_BUTTON      0x01 // Left button mask.
#define MOUSE_RIGHT_BUTTON     0x02 // Right button mask.
#define MOUSE_CENTER_BUTTON    0x04 // Center button mask.


// G L O B A L S ////////////////////////////////////////////////


// F U N C T I O N S ////////////////////////////////////////////////


int Squeeze_Mouse(int command, int *x, int *y,int *buttons)
{
// Mouse interface. We'll use _int86 instead of in-line asm.
// (Why? No real reason.)
// What function is the caller requesting?
```

continues

Listing 3.8. continued

```c
union _REGS inregs, outregs;

switch(command)
      {

    case MOUSE_RESET:
         {

         inregs.x.ax = 0x00; // Subfunction 0: reset.
         _int86(MOUSE_INT, &inregs, &outregs);
         *buttons = outregs.x.bx; // Return the number of
                                  // buttons.
         return(outregs.x.ax);    // Return overall success
                                  // or failure.

         } break;

    case MOUSE_SHOW:
         {
         // This function increments the internal show-mouse
         // counter.
         // When it is equal to 0, the mouse is displayed.

         inregs.x.ax = 0x01; // Subfunction 1: increment show
                             // flag
         _int86(MOUSE_INT, &inregs, &outregs);

         return(1);

         } break;

    case MOUSE_HIDE:
         {
         // This function decrements the internal show-mouse
         // counter.
         // When it is equal to -1, the mouse is hidden.

         inregs.x.ax = 0x02; // Subfunction 2: decrement show
                             // flag
         _int86(MOUSE_INT, &inregs, &outregs);

         return(1);

         } break;

    case MOUSE_BUTT_POS:
         {
         // This function gets the buttons and returns the
         // absolute mouse positions in the vars x,y, and
         // buttons, respectively.

         inregs.x.ax = 0x03; // Subfunction 3: get position
                             // and buttons.
         _int86(MOUSE_INT, &inregs, &outregs);

         // Extract the info and send it back to the caller
```

```
                // via pointers.
                *x      = outregs.x.cx;
                *y      = outregs.x.dx;
                *buttons = outregs.x.bx;

                return(1);

                } break;

        case MOUSE_MOTION_REL:
                {

                // This functions gets the relative mouse motions
                // from the last call and puts them in the variables
                // x and y, respectively.

                inregs.x.ax = 0x03; // Subfunction 11: get relative
                                    // motion.
                _int86(MOUSE_INT, &inregs, &outregs);

                // Extract the info and send it back to the caller
                // via pointers.
                *x      = outregs.x.cx;
                *y      = outregs.x.dx;

                return(1);

                } break;

        case MOUSE_SET_SENSITIVITY:
                {
                // This function sets the overall "sensitivity" of
                // the mouse. Each axis can have a sensitivity from
                // 1-100, so the caller should put 1-100 in both x
                // and y before calling. Also "buttons" is used to
                // send in the doublespeed value, which also ranges
                // from 1-100.
                inregs.x.bx = *x;
                inregs.x.cx = *y;
                inregs.x.dx = *buttons;

                inregs.x.ax = 0x1A; // Subfunction 26: set
                                    // sensitivity.
                _int86(MOUSE_INT, &inregs, &outregs);

                return(1);

                } break;

        default:break;

        } // end switch

} // end Squeeze_Mouse

//////////////////////////////////////////////////////////////////

void main(void)
```

continues

Listing 3.8. continued

```
{

int x,y,buttons,num_buttons;
int color=1;

// Put the computer into graphics mode.

_setvideomode(_VRES16COLOR); //  640x480 in 16 colors

// Initialize the mouse.

Squeeze_Mouse(MOUSE_RESET,NULL,NULL,&num_buttons);

// Show the mouse.

Squeeze_Mouse(MOUSE_SHOW,NULL,NULL,NULL);

while(!kbhit())
    {

    _settextposition(2,0);

    Squeeze_Mouse(MOUSE_BUTT_POS,&x,&y,&buttons);

    printf("mouse x=%d y=%d buttons=%d    ",x,y,buttons);

    // Video easel

    if (buttons==1)
        {
        _setcolor(color);
        _setpixel(x-1,y-2);
        _setpixel(x,y-2);
        _setpixel(x-1,y-1);
        _setpixel(x,y-1);
        } // end if draw on

    if (buttons==2)
        {
        if (++color>15) color=0;

        // Wait for mouse release.

        while(buttons==2)
            {
            Squeeze_Mouse(MOUSE_BUTT_POS,&x,&y,&buttons);
            } // end while

        } // end if draw on

    } // end while

// Put the computer back into text mode.

_setvideomode(_DEFAULTMODE);

} // end main
```

Summary

In this chapter we learned about the different input devices that the video-game player will use to communicate with our games: the keyboard, mouse, and joystick. Furthermore, we created simple, clean functions to interface with these devices. We also learned that BIOS is probably not the way to go when communicating with input devices, especially when trying to read the keyboard.

The Mechanics of Two-Dimensional Graphics

Y ou can think of the computerscreen as a blank piece of paper that can tranform and morph before your very eyes. To achieve this, we must know the proper language to use. The language is mathematics.

In this chapter we take a journey into the abyss known as the *two-dimensional plane*. We cover the following topics:

- The Cartesian, or two-dimensional, plane

- Points, lines, and polygons

- Translation

- Scaling

- Rotation

- Clipping

- Using matrices

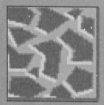

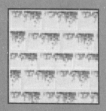

by André LaMothe

The Two-Dimensional Plane

The two-dimensional (2-D) plane, sometimes called the *Cartesian plane*, is like a piece of writing paper. More precisely, it's like a piece of graph paper that extends infinitely in both directions. Figure 4.1 is a representation of this.

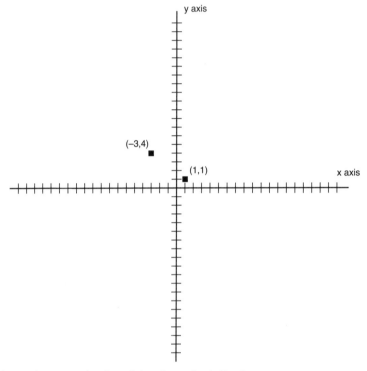

Figure 4.1. *The points (1,1) and (-3,4) on the 2-D plane.*

Each point on the 2-D plane can be located by specifying two coordinates. Usually, these coordinates are (x,y), where the x coordinate specifies a point on the horizontal axis and the y coordinate specifies a point on the vertical axis. For example, if we wanted to plot the points (1,1) and (-3,4) on the 2-D plane, we would plot them as you see in Figure 4.1.

The 2-D plane is important because it gives us a place to begin that isn't too complicated. (Video games are complicated enough without piling on a ton of abstract math up front.) We begin by exploring the 2-D plane and its properties, so that when we move into the third dimension we won't shock anyone! Moreover, there are a lot of video games that are still 2-D, especially on home-video game systems such as Sega, Genesis, and Nintendo. It's therefore worthwhile to understand 2-D graphics and graphic manipulations.

Points, Lines, and Polygons

We've all seen games such as Asteroids, Spectre, and Major Havoc. These were some of the first video games ever made, and they have something in common: they're all made out of lines—lots of them—in the 2-D plane (which I refer to affectionately from now on as just "the plane"). We can't do much in the plane except draw little dots and collections of little dots (that is, lines).

Points

We've already defined a point: it's simply a position on the plane that we can specify with two coordinates (x,y). Let's write a little C program that plots points on the screen. Listing 4.1 shows the Pointy program pointy.c.

Listing 4.1. Pointy: a program to plot points (pointy.c).

```
#include <stdio.h> // This includes the basics.
#include <graph.h> // This includes Microsoft's Graphics Header.

void main(void)
{

int x,y,color,index;

// Put the computer into graphics mode.

_setvideomode(_VRES16COLOR); // This sets the mode to 640x480
                             // in 16 colors.

// Let's draw 10,000 points randomly on the screen.

for (index = 0; index<10000; index++)
    {
    // Get a random position and color and plot a point there.

    x = rand()%640;
    y = rand()%480;
    color = rand()%16;
    _setcolor(color); // Set the color of the pixel to be drawn.
    _setpixel(x,y);   // Draw the pixel.
```

continues

Listing 4.1. continued

```
    } // end for index

// Wait for the user to hit a key.

while(!kbhit()){}

// Put the computer back into text mode.

_setvideomode(_DEFAULTMODE);

} // end main
```

Let's understand what the program in Listing 4.1 does:

- The computer is placed into a VGA graphics mode by way of the call to _setvideomode(_VRES16COLOR). This is a Microsoft graphics library call.

- The program then falls into the main loop: a for structure that, each time through the loop, obtains three random numbers: one for color and two for the (x,y) position of the point we want to plot.

- We then use the library function _setpixel(x,y) to plot the point in the color we previously set with _setcolor(color). The program does this 10,000 times and then stops.

- The program then waits for you to hit a key, upon which it exits and returns you to DOS.

If you run the program over and over you may notice that the points are always in the same place. How could this be? Well, we use the function rand(). This is not a true random-number generator, but a pseudo-random number generator. It uses a math technique to generate numbers that have an even distribution for all integers. It's random in that sense, but each time it gives the same numbers.

To get around this you can *seed* the random number generator with a different number every time you run the program. Use the srand(int) function to seed the random number generator.

Lines

A line is the shortest path between two points. A line between the point at (1,1) and the point at (5,5) in the plane would look like Figure 4.2.

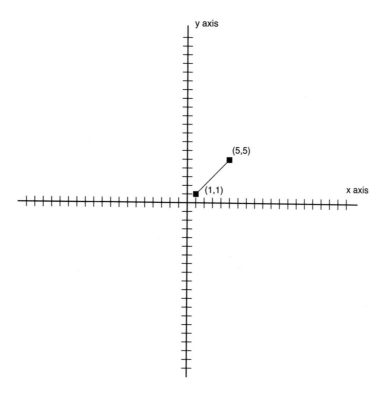

Figure 4.2. *A line in a plane.*

Let's improve the program in Listing 4.1 to draw lines instead of points. To do this, we add a couple things. Instead of having only two random numbers for x and y, Listing 4.2 has two points, represented by (x1,y1) and (x2,y2). The program then draws a line between them using a library call. The code looks like this:

Listing 4.2. Liner: a program to draw a line (liner.c).

```
#include <stdio.h> // This includes the basics.
#include <graph.h> // This include Microsoft's Graphics Header.

void main(void)
{

int x1,y1,x2,y2,color,index;

// Put the computer into graphics mode.

_setvideomode(_VRES16COLOR); // This sets the mode to 640x480
                             // in 16 colors.
```

continues

Listing 4.2. continued

```
// Let's draw 1,000 lines randomly on the screen.

for (index = 0; index<1000; index++)
    {
    // Get a random position and color and draw a line there.

    x1 = rand()%640;   // This is the x-axis location of the
                       // starting point.
    y1 = rand()%480;   // This is the y-axis location of the
                       // starting point.
    x2 = rand()%640;   // This is the x-axis location of the
                       // ending point.
    y2 = rand()%480;   // This is the y-axis location of the
                       // ending point.
    color = rand()%16;
    _setcolor(color);  // Set the color of the pixel to be drawn.
    _moveto(x1,y1);    // Move to the start of the line.
    _lineto(x2,y2);    // Draw the line.

    } // end for index

// Wait for the user to hit a key.

while(!kbhit()){}

// Put the computer back into text mode.

_setvideomode(_DEFAULTMODE);

} // end main
```

Polygons

Lines are cool, and with some luck you might be able to make a screen saver out of Program 4.2. But video games have more interesting graphics on the screen than lines—except, maybe, Quix!—so let's meet the polygon.

A polygon is a collection of points connected by lines. The points of a polygon are called *vertices*. Figure 4.3 shows a triangle composed of three vertices: vertex 1, vertex 2, and vertex 3.

All polygons are closed. (I don't even have a name for an open polygon; a nonagon?) Polygons can be concave or convex. Convex polygons are shapes such as squares, triangles, and rectangles. Concave polygons are polygons that have an irregular shape with some "dents." Figure 4.4 shows both a convex and a concave polygon.

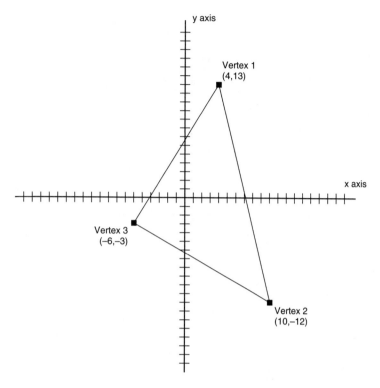

Figure 4.3. *A simple polygon: the triangle.*

There's a mathematical way to compute whether a polygon is concave or convex, but for now we know enough to write a program that draws a polygon. The Polydraw program is shown in Listing 4.3.

Listing 4.3. Polydraw: a program to draw a polygon (polydraw.c).

```
#include <stdio.h> // This includes the basics.
#include <graph.h> // This includes Microsoft's Graphics Header.

main()
{

// Put the computer into graphics mode.
_setvideomode(_VRES16COLOR); // This sets the mode to 640x480
                             // in 16 colors.

// Draw a simple polygon:
_setcolor(1);        // Make it blue.
_moveto(100,100);    // This defines vertex 1.
_lineto(120,120);    // This defines vertex 2.
```

continues

Listing 4.3. continued

```
_lineto(150,200);    // This defines vertex 3.
_lineto(80,190);     // This defines vertex 4.
_lineto(80,60);      // This defines vertex 5.
_lineto(100,100);    // Draw the line back to vertex 1 to close
                     // up the polygon

// Wait for the user to hit a key.
while(!kbhit()){}

// Put the computer back into text mode.

_setvideomode(_DEFAULTMODE);

} // end main
```

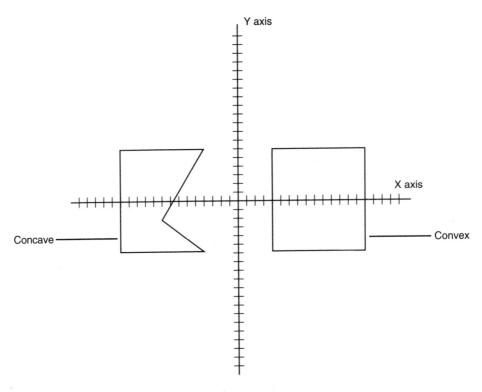

Figure 4.4. *A concave and a convex polygon.*

Objects

It's time to start picking up the pace—we need to start turning and burning, so hold on tight!

I want now to define a general object with a data structure. If we want to use lines to draw ships and creatures, we need a data structure to hold the attributes of the object. For now, let's keep it simple. Each of our objects will have up to sixteen vertices, a color, and a position. We will calculate the position in a minute, but the code for defining the vertices of a data structure should look like the fragment in Listing 4.4.

Listing 4.4. Data structures used for defining vertices and objects.

```
// Defining the structure of a vertex.

typedef struct vertex_typ
        {
        float x,y; // This is a single point in the 2-D
                   // plane.
        } vertex, *vertex_ptr;

// Define the structure for an object.

typedef struct object_typ
        {
        int num_vertices;    // This is the number of
                             // vertices in this object.
        int color;           // This is the color of this
                             // object.
        float xo,yo;         // This is the position of this
                             // object.
        vertex vertices[16]; // This defines 16 vertices.
        } object, *object_ptr;
```

This stucture is all we need to define an object that's constructed of a single polygon with a specific color at a certain position.

Positioning an Object

We must talk about the line defining the position of the object in the object structure in Listing 4.4. The coordinates xo,yo specify the starting position of the object in the 2-D plane. The polygon or object is drawn relative to the starting position.

This brings us to the notion of a *local coordinate system*. The Cartesian plane is called a *world coordinate system*, meaning it's really big. The screen itself has its own coordinate system called the *screen coordinate system*, and all objects on the screen have their own local coordinate systems. Figure 4.5 sheds some light on this.

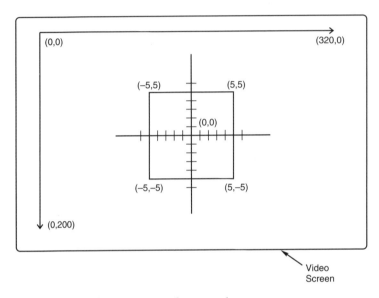

Figure 4.5. *Local coordinate system relative to the screen.*

What we must do is define our object in its own local coordinate system, translate it to its position in world coordinates, and then draw it on the screen in screen coordinates. That seems like a long haul to draw a polygon, but it's not as complex as it sounds. For now, let's assume that world coordinates and screen coordinates are the same, so:

- ▪ (0,0) is the upper-left corner of the screen.

- ▪ As you move to the right, the x coordinate increases.

- ▪ As you move down, the y coordinate increases.

This gives us a screen that's similar to quadrant 1 (positive x and y values) of a Cartesian coordinate system, but with the y-axis inverted relative to the computer screen. Having the y-axis inverted is alright but, because it tends to confuse the issues a bit, let's invert it from now on. Therefore, the origin (0,0) is now in the lower-left corner of the screen, and the screen is an exact replica of quadrant 1; see Figure 4.6.

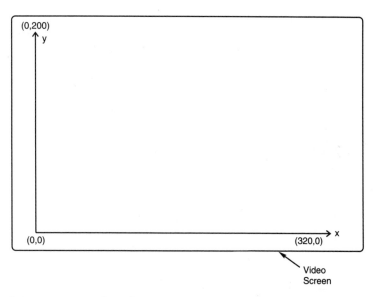

Figure 4.6. *Remapping the video screen to match quadrant 1 of the Cartesian plane.*

We have all the tools we need to represent a set of objects in the computer. The next sections discuss how to move them about the screen, rotate them, and make them bigger or smaller (that is, scale them).

Translating an Object

To *translate* an object is to move it to another position without changing its rotation or size. Let's use our data structures to define an object that we can use for the following discussion. An asteroid is a good subject. Figure 4.7 shows a graph-paper representation of our asteroid.

Listing 4.5 holds the code fragment defining our asteroid.

Listing 4.5. Defining an asteroid.

```
// Define an asteroid.

object asteroid;

// Fill in the fields.

asteroid.num_vertices = 6;  // Six vertices should be enough.
asteroid.color = 1;         // Color the asteroid blue.
```

continues

Listing 4.5. continued

```
asteroid.xo  = 320;              // Initially, locate the asteroid
                                 // in the center of the screen (in
                                 // 640x480 mode).
asteroid.yo  = 240;

// Now let's define the vertices of the asteroid. Remember: the
// local origin is (0,0).

asteroid.vertices[0].x = 4.0
asteroid.vertices[0].y = 3.5
asteroid.vertices[1].x = 8.5
asteroid.vertices[1].y = -3.0
asteroid.vertices[2].x = 6
asteroid.vertices[2].y = -5
asteroid.vertices[3].x = 2
asteroid.vertices[3].y = -3
asteroid.vertices[4].x = -4
asteroid.vertices[4].y = -6
asteroid.vertices[5].x = -3.5
asteroid.vertices[5].y = 5.5
```

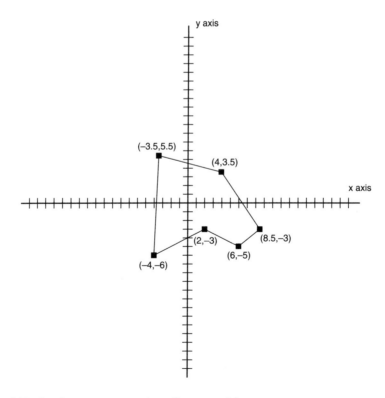

Figure 4.7. *A polygon representation of an asteroid.*

That wasn't so bad—although, in a real video game, you wouldn't want to define objects in this way because it's too complex a structure. Instead, you might load the vertices using a file, or have them generated algorithmically. (For instance, AutoCad uses a file format called DXF, which holds lists of vertices along with various other properties. After a DXF file is loaded, the vertices are parsed from the file and inserted into the appropriate data structure.) For our present purposes, however, manually defining a single asteroid this way is OK.

All right, let's start building up some ideas. We'll draw the object's vertices relative to its position on the screen. This position is defined by (xo,yo). If we want to translate the object, we simply do the following:

```
xo = xo + dx
yo = yo + dy
```

where dx and dy are the number of pixels we want to move in the x- and y-axis, respectively. (We can think of dx and dy as the velocity along the x- and y-axes.)

That's all there is to translation. Now let's move to scaling.

Scaling an Object

Scaling means to change the size of an object. Take a look at Figure 4.8 for an example of scaling. The asteroid in Figure 4.8 is twice as big as the one in Figure 4.7.

This is a big clue on how scaling works. All we need to do to scale an object is multiply each vertex that comprises the object by the scaling factor. The code fragment shown in Listing 4.6 does the job for an object structure.

Listing 4.6. Scaling an object structure.

```
void Scale_Object(object_ptr object,float scale)
{
int index;

// For all vertices, scale the x and y component.

for (index = 0; index<object->num_vertices; index++)
    {
    object->vertices[index].x *= scale;
    object->vertices[index].y *= scale;
    } // end for index

} // end Scale_Object
```

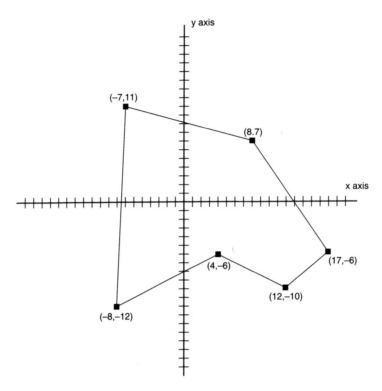

Figure 4.8. *A bigger asteroid.*

The function in Listing 4.6 works by scaling each component of each individual vertex. If we want to scale our "asteroid" object and make it twice as big, we would use the following code:

```
Scale_Object((object_ptr)&asteroid, 2.0);
```

That's all there is to it. Now, were ready to do some rotation.

Rotating an Object

To rotate an object, we must spin it around some axis. In 2-D space this axis is the *z-axis*. Even though we're working in 2-D, the third dimension still exists—we just aren't paying much attention to it.

If the screen is the x,y plane, the z-axis is sticking out at you, perpendicular to both the x- and y-axes. Therefore, if we define our objects as we have in the 2-D plane, we must rotate them about the z-axis. The following math rotates an arbitrary point (x,y) about the z-axis:

```
new_x  = x * cos(angle)  -  y * sin(angle)
new_y  = y * cos(angle) + x * sin(angle)
```

where `angle` is the angle you want to rotate the point. You should note a couple of things:

■ Positive angles have the effect of clockwise rotation.

■ Negative angles have the effect of counterclockwise rotation.

C uses radians, *not* degrees. Alas, any calls you make to the trigonometric functions must have radians as their parameters. To convert radians to degrees, we can write simple macros that allow conversion to and from each angular system:

```
Deg_To_Rad(deg) {pi*deg/180;}
Rad_To_Deg(rad) {180*rad/pi;}
```

In other words, there are 360 degrees, or 2*[pi] radians, in a circle.

We have the rotation formulas down—how they work nobody knows, but let's write some code with them. We need a function to rotate an object. The function in Listing 4.7 does precisely that.

Listing 4.7. Rotating an object.

```
void Rotate_Object(object_ptr object, float angle)
{
int index;
float x_new, y_new,cs,sn;

// Precompute the sine and cosine.
cs = cos(angle);
sn = sin(angle);

// For each vertex, rotate it by angle.
for (index=0; index<object->num_vertices; index++)
    {
     // Rotate the vertex.
     x_new  = object->vertices[index].x * cs -  object->vertices[index].y * sn;
     y_new  = object->vertices[index].y * cs + object->vertices[index].x * sn;

     // Store the rotated vertex back into structure.
     object->vertices[index].x = x_new;
     object->vertices[index].y = y_new;

     } // end for index

} // end Rotate_Object
```

This function may need a bit of explaining. I precomputed the sine and cosine of the angle. Why, you ask? Because of speed. Even with a floating-point processor, doing trigonometric functions takes up precious compute time that could be used more productively. (Actually, later in the book we learn how to use look-up tables that have the sin and cos precomputed for all angles from 0 through 360, so no trig functions need to be computed during run time. Moreover, we learn not to use floating-point numbers at all—but, again, we get to that later (in Chapter 18, "Optimization Techniques").

It's time now, I think, to write some code. It seems fitting that we should somehow do something more extravagant with the asteroid example we've been using thus far. I think we should make an asteroid field! That sounds like fun. Let's do a little design work first, just as we would in a video game.

I want to have an asteroid field of a dozen or so asteroids with lots of different sizes. I want them to move around on the screen and, when they get to an edge, I want them to bounce off it. Therefore, our program should have the following structure:

Step 1—Initialize the asteroid field.
Step 2—Erase the asteroid field.
Step 3—Transform the asteroid field.
Step 4—Draw the asteroid field.
Step 5—Go to Step 2 until the user hits a key.

To make this easier, I'm going to add three fields to our structures: one for the scale factor and two for the *velocities* (that is, the translation factors). The entire program is given in Listing 4.8.

Listing 4.8. A program that draws an asteroid field.

```
// I N C L U D E S ///////////////////////////////////////////

#include <stdio.h> // Include the basics.
#include <graph.h> // Include Microsoft's Graphics Header.
#include <math.h>  // Include math stuff.

// D E F I N E S  ///////////////////////////////////////////

#define NUM_ASTEROIDS 10
#define ERASE 0
#define DRAW  1

// T Y P E D E F S ///////////////////////////////////////////

// Define the structure for a vertex.

typedef struct vertex_typ
        {
        float x,y; // This is a single point in the
```

```
                              // 2-D plane.
                     } vertex, *vertex_ptr;


// Define the structure for an object.

typedef struct object_typ
            {
            int num_vertices;      // The number of vertices in
                                   // this object.
            int color;             // The color of this object.
            float xo,yo;           // The position of this object.
            float x_velocity;      // The x velocity of this
                                   // object.
            float y_velocity;      // The y-velocity of this
                                   // object.
            float scale;           // The scale factor to be used.
            float angle;           // The rotation rate to be used.
            vertex vertices[16];   // This defines 16 vertices.
            } object, *object_ptr;


// G L O B A L S //////////////////////////////////////////////


object asteroids[NUM_ASTEROIDS];


// F U N C T I O N S //////////////////////////////////////////

void Delay(int t)
{

// Take up some compute cycles.

float x = 1;

while(t—>0)
     x=cos(x);


} // end Delay

//////////////////////////////////////////////////////////////////

void Scale_Object(object_ptr object,float scale)
{
int index;

// For all vertices, scale the x and y components.

for (index = 0; index<object->num_vertices; index++)
     {
     object->vertices[index].x *= scale;
     object->vertices[index].y *= scale;
     } // end for index

} // end Scale_Object
```

continues

Listing 4.8. continued

```
////////////////////////////////////////////////////////////////

void Rotate_Object(object_ptr object, float angle)
{
int index;
float x_new, y_new,cs,sn;

// Precompute the sine and cosine.
cs = cos(angle);
sn = sin(angle);

// For each vertex. rotate it by angle.
for (index=0; index<object->num_vertices; index++)
    {
     // Rotate the vertex.
     x_new  = object->vertices[index].x * cs - object->vertices[index].y * sn;
     y_new  = object->vertices[index].y * cs + object->vertices[index].x * sn;

     // Store the rotated vertex back into structure.
     object->vertices[index].x = x_new;
     object->vertices[index].y = y_new;

     } // end for index

} // end Rotate_Object

////////////////////////////////////////////////////////////////

void Create_Field(void)
{

int index;

for (index=0; index<NUM_ASTEROIDS; index++)
    {

    // Fill in the fields.

    asteroids[index].num_vertices = 6;
    asteroids[index].color = 1 + rand() % 14; // This is always
                                              // visable.
    asteroids[index].xo    = 41 + rand() % 599;
    asteroids[index].yo    = 41 + rand() % 439;

    asteroids[index].x_velocity = -10 + rand() % 20;
    asteroids[index].y_velocity = -10 + rand() % 20;
    asteroids[index].scale      = (float)(rand() % 30) / 10;
    asteroids[index].angle      = (float)(- 50 + (float)
                                     (rand() % 100)) / 100;

    asteroids[index].vertices[0].x = 4.0;
    asteroids[index].vertices[0].y = 3.5;
    asteroids[index].vertices[1].x = 8.5;
    asteroids[index].vertices[1].y = -3.0;
    asteroids[index].vertices[2].x = 6;
    asteroids[index].vertices[2].y = -5;
    asteroids[index].vertices[3].x = 2;
```

```
    asteroids[index].vertices[3].y = -3;
    asteroids[index].vertices[4].x = -4;
    asteroids[index].vertices[4].y = -6;
    asteroids[index].vertices[5].x = -3.5;
    asteroids[index].vertices[5].y = 5.5;

    // Now scale the asteroid to the proper size.

    Scale_Object((object_ptr)&asteroids[index], asteroids[index].scale);

    } // end for index

} // end Create_Field

////////////////////////////////////////////////////////////////

void Draw_Asteroids(int erase)
{

int index,vertex;
float xo,yo;

for (index=0; index<NUM_ASTEROIDS; index++)
    {

    // Draw the asteroid.

    if (erase==ERASE)
      _setcolor(0);
    else
      _setcolor(asteroids[index].color);

    // Get position of the object.
    xo = asteroids[index].xo;
    yo = asteroids[index].yo;


    // Move to the first vertex.

  _moveto((int)(xo+asteroids[index].vertices[0].x),(int)(yo+asteroids[index].vertices[0].y));

    for (vertex=1; vertex<asteroids[index].num_vertices; vertex++)
        {
  _lineto((int)(xo+asteroids[index].vertices[vertex].x),(int)(yo+asteroids[index].vertices[vertex].y));

        } // end for vertex

    // close object

  _lineto((int)(xo+asteroids[index].vertices[0].x),(int)(yo+asteroids[index].vertices[0].y));

    } // end for index

} // end Draw_Asteroids

////////////////////////////////////////////////////////////////
```

continues

Listing 4.8. continued

```c
void Translate_Asteroids(void)
{

int index;

for (index=0; index<NUM_ASTEROIDS; index++)
    {
    // Translate the current asteroid.

    asteroids[index].xo += asteroids[index].x_velocity;
    asteroids[index].yo += asteroids[index].y_velocity;

    // Collision detection (that is, bounds check).

    if (asteroids[index].xo > 600 ¦¦ asteroids[index].xo < 40)
        {
        asteroids[index].x_velocity = -asteroids[index].x_velocity;
        asteroids[index].xo += asteroids[index].x_velocity;
        }

    if (asteroids[index].yo > 440 ¦¦ asteroids[index].yo < 40)
        {
        asteroids[index].y_velocity = -asteroids[index].y_velocity;
        asteroids[index].yo += asteroids[index].y_velocity;
        }

    } // end for index

} // end Translate_Asteroids

///////////////////////////////////////////////////////////////

void Rotate_Asteroids(void)
{

int index;

for (index=0; index<NUM_ASTEROIDS; index++)
    {
    // Rotate the current asteroid.
    Rotate_Object((object_ptr)&asteroids[index], asteroids[index].angle);

    } // end for index

} // end Rotate_Asteroids


///////////////////////////////////////////////////////////////

void main(void)
{

// Put the computer into graphics mode.

_setvideomode(_VRES16COLOR); // This sets the mode to 640x480
                             // in 16 colors.
```

```
// Initialize asteroid field
Create_Field();

while(!kbhit())
      {
      // Erase the field.

      Draw_Asteroids(ERASE);

      // Transform the field.

      Rotate_Asteroids();

      Translate_Asteroids();

      // Draw the field.

      Draw_Asteroids(DRAW);

      // Wait a bit...

      Delay(500);

      } // end while
// Put the computer back into text mode.

_setvideomode(_DEFAULTMODE);

} // end main
```

If you type in and execute the code in Listing 4.8, you should see an asteroid field on your screen with a collection of multicolored rocks bouncing off the screen edges. (Collision detection is discussed more fully in this chapter under "Basic Collision Detection," and in Chapter 11, "Video Game Algorithms, Data Structures, and Methodologies.")

There are some issues to discuss at this point:

■ The first thing you should notice is that the images flicker quite a bit. This is because we are rendering the lines at the same time the video display is being drawn.

The screen is a collection of pixels. These pixels are being drawn from left to right and from top to bottom by the hardware in your video card and monitor. The problem is, we must not alter the video screen while it's being drawn. In Chapter 5, "The Mysteries of the VGA Card," we discuss drawing the entire screen in a separate buffer and then moving it to the video buffer in one blast. For now, rest assured that flicker can be dealt with.

■ Another problem causing flicker is the fact that we're using Microsoft's Graphics Library, which is, to put it bluntly, about as fast as your tax refunds. You see, Microsoft hasn't optimized its drawing functions for high performance. These drawing functions are meant to be used in slower applications that don't need the response or speed of a video-game display.

■ The program uses floating-point numbers, which we eradicate later by using fixed-point numbers instead.

■ Finally, the whole program is terribly inefficient as video games go. It does things in "standard, textbook" ways. Video-game programmer rule number one: there's always a clever way to do something that seems impossible. If there weren't, half the PC video games you see wouldn't exist—because the PC doesn't have the performance. We must trick it into doing the magic we make it do.

(Believe me, DOOM is a perfect example of this. If I hadn't seen it for myself, I wouldn't believe it was possible—but, as we know, DOOM is quite real, and probably the best example of using clever methods and incredible creativity to make an impossibly complex world come to life on the computer screen.)

Remember, most video-game programmers are still too young to buy a drink! They don't know yet what they're not supposed to be able to do; they just think things up and use the tools they have at their disposal to make them happen. These tools are addition, subraction, and maybe a trig function or two. Try to unlearn all you've learned about what's possible and impossible!

Clipping

Although we aren't going to delve deeply into this topic, I want to cover it for completeness. We're more interested in the special cases of clipping that we discuss in chapters to follow than we are in the general theory of clipping. For now, however, let's learn about the concept and how to implement it in its most basic form.

Clipping means drawing only the portions of a video image that are within some predefined boundary. Consider, for example, the case in which you see an object in a game move off the screen. As it's occluded by the edge of the screen, the visible portion of it remains geometrically intact. The object is being clipped as it moves off the screen. You take this for granted, but the programmer knows exactly how much of the image to display—and not to display. This computation can be complex or simple, depending on the situation.

Clipping can be done at two levels:

■ Image space

■ Object space

Image-space clipping is based on testing every single point that has the possibility of being drawn on the screen against the clipping region. For example, if we have a rectangular clipping region that coincides with the boundaries of the video screen in mode 13h (320x200), we don't draw any pixels that are outside this range. Pixels that are within the region bounded by 0-319 on the x-axis and 0-199 on the y-axis are drawn. The others are not.

Because all objects that can be drawn on a computer screen are ultimately made up of pixels, this method is the simplest to implement. Which geometrical entities are being drawn is irrelevant. It doesn't matter if they're lines, squares, bit maps, or whatever: in the end, everything calls the pixel-plotting function, which has the final word. If the pixel-plotting function determines that the pixel is out of bounds, it isn't drawn.

The problem with image-space alorithms and implementations is speed. Take drawing a line, for example. It's fairly easy to test whether a line is within a clipping region. You can test the line's endpoints with the region, or perform an intersection test—so why test every single pixel against the clipping region? Some preprocessing can be done to decide where the line should be clipped. This is the basis of object-space clipping algorithms.

Object-space clipping takes into consideration the geometry of the object being clipped, and processes it into an object that doesn't require clipping. This new object is then passed to the rendering engine and drawn without regard for the parts that are out of the clipping region, as we know the object has already been processed.

The problem with object-space algorithms is that their implementation can be rather complex, depending on the types of objects being drawn. Clipping simple lines in object space isn't too difficult, but it can be much more difficult to find efficient algorithms for complex, solid, polygon-based objects.

Luckily for us, the most complex things we'll ever have to clip are bit maps, which we learn to do in Chapter 7, "Advanced Bit-Mapped Graphics and Special FX." For now, realize that we must try to somehow use object-space algorithms whenever possible because speed is our biggest concern. We can't add any overhead to our pixel-plotting functions that isn't absolutely necessary.

To be complete, we must next touch upon a topic that many people don't like to hear about. The next section discusses matrices.

Matrices

Matrices are used here and there within these pages. They really aren't very hard to understand or use. Moreover, we need them because they can help us write faster transformations, and are useful tools to represent mathematical operations in a very compact form.

A matrix is, as you might suspect, a collection of numbers. These numbers are oriented in a set of rows and columns. The number of rows and columns make up the dimensions of the matrix. Here are two matrices, Matrix A and Matrix B:

```
        ¦ 1   0   2 ¦                  ¦ 3   5  -1 ¦
A   =   ¦ 3  -1   4 ¦           B  =   ¦ 2   7   0 ¦
                                       ¦ 4   3   3 ¦

Dimension is 2x3                  Dimension is 3x3
```

Matrix A is 2x3 (that is, it has two rows and three columns), while Matrix B is 3x3. We can access an element of Matrix A, for example, by using the notation A[m,n], where m is the row and n is the column. The element in the upper-left corner of the Matrix A would be A[0,0], which is equal to 1.

Doing Operations on Matrices

You can do most operations to matrices that you can to normal, scalar numbers. However, operations effect the entire matrix. For instance, you can add and subtract matrices. To do so, you add or subract each individual component, respectively.

As an example, note the following two 2x3 matrices, Matrix A and Matrix C:

```
        ¦ 1   0   2 ¦          ¦ 3   5  -1 ¦
A   =   ¦ 3  -1   4 ¦   C  =   ¦ 2   7   0 ¦
```

To add Matrix A and Matrix C, for each element m,n of each matrix, you add each component. The outcome goes into the respective position in the results matrix:

```
          ¦ 1   0   2 ¦     ¦ 3   5  -1 ¦     ¦ 4   5   1 ¦
A + C =   ¦ 3  -1   4 ¦  +  ¦ 2   7   0 ¦  =  ¦ 5   6   4 ¦
```

We also can multiply a matrix by a scalar k. For example, to multiply Matrix A by 3, we would multiply each component of matrix by 3. The outcome goes into the respective position in the results matrix:

```
3A = 3 *  ¦ 1   0   2 ¦         ¦ 3   0   6  ¦
          ¦ 3  -1   4 ¦    =    ¦ 9  -3   12 ¦
```

Now let's talk about matrix multiplication. This is much different than the scalar multiplication we did previously, and can be a bit confusing. There are some rules, however, that you can memorize:

■ The number of columns in the first matrix (*n*) must be equal to the number of rows in the second (also *n*). This means that if one matrix is *m*x*n*, the other must be *n*x*r*. The other two dimensions, *m* and *r*, can be anything.

■ Matrix multiplication is *not* commutative: AB is not equal to BA.

Multiplying an *m*x*n* matrix by an *n*x*r* matrix can be defined algorithmically as follows:

1. For each row in the first matrix:

   Multiply that row by each column in the second matrix, element-by-element. Sum up the result.

2. Place the result into postion *i,j* of the results matrix, where *i* is the row of the first matrix being processed and *j* is the column of the second matrix being processed.

   Take a look at Figure 4.9 to see this more clearly.

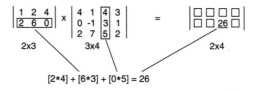

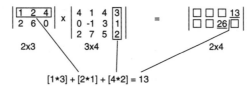

Figure 4.9. *The results of matrix multiplication.*

We can do the operation easily with C code. Let's define a general 3x3 matrix and make a function to multiply matrices. Listing 4.9 shows the C code to do this.

Listing 4.9. Defining and multiplying two matrices.

```
// A general matrix structure

typedef struct matrix_typ
        {
        float elem[3][3];  // This is storage for a 3x3
                           // matrix.
        } matrix, *matrix_ptr;
```

continues

Listing 4.9. continued

```
void Mat_Mult3X3(matrix_ptr matrix_1, matrix_ptr matrix_2,
                 matrix_ptr result)
{
index i,j,k;
for (i=0; i<3; i++)
    {
    for (j=0; j<3; j++)
        {
        result[i][j] = 0; // Initialize the element.
        for (k=0; k<3; k++)
            {
            result->elem[i][j] += matrix_1->elem[i][k]
                   * matrix_2->elem[k][j];
            } end for k
        } // end for j
    } // end for i


} // end Mat_Mult3X3
```

Upon exit from this function, the result of the matrix multiplication is stored in
result.

The Identity Matrix

One more thing before we get to the point of this whole conversation about matrices:
the *identity matrix*. To be technical, every closed algebraic space has to have a few
things that mathematicians have stated to be a bare minimum to be considered viable.
Without diverging into a Ph.D. dissertation, we need something by which we can
multiply a matrix and get the same matrix! In other words, we need the multiplicative
identity. (That sounds like an ailment, huh?)

In simpler terms, we need a general matrix $m \times n$, which we can call Matrix I. When we
multiply any matrix by Matrix I, the result always leaves the original matrix unscathed.
If you think about it for a while you'll realize that the matrix we desire has its main
diagonal filled with 1s, with 0s everywhere else. Here's a 3x3 identity matrix:

$$
I = \begin{vmatrix} 1 & 0 & 0 \\ 0 & 1 & 0 \\ 0 & 0 & 1 \end{vmatrix}
$$

If we were to multiply Matrix A by Matrix I:

$$
A = \begin{vmatrix} 1 & 0 & 2 \\ 3 & -1 & 4 \\ 6 & -2 & 0 \end{vmatrix} \quad I = \begin{vmatrix} 1 & 0 & 0 \\ 0 & 1 & 0 \\ 0 & 0 & 1 \end{vmatrix}
$$

the result would be the original Matrix A:

```
      | 1   0   2 |       | 1   0   0 |        | 1    0   2 |
      | 3  -1   4 |       | 0   1   0 |        | 3   -1   4 |
A  =  | 6  -2   0 |   I = | 0   0   1 |  AI = A| 6   -2   0 |
```

Using Matrices in Games

Enough said about how matrices work. Let's get to the reason we want to use them.

In Listing 4.8 we made an asteroid field that had asteroids translating, scaling, and rotating. If we represent our objects as collections of matrices, we can use matrix multiplication to transform them. The beauty of matrices is that you can concatenate matrix operations into a single matrix and multiply the objects' vertices by a single matrix that represents translation, rotation, and scaling in one matrix-multiplication operation!

Remember: when writing video games we must continually search for faster, more efficient ways to do things. The bigger our bag of tricks, the better. Now, let's look at the matrices for translation, scaling, and rotation.

A General Translation Matrix

Here's a general translation matrix, where x_translation and y_translation are the amounts by which you want to scale the object in the x- and y-axis, respectively:

```
| 1                0               0 |
| 0                1               0 |
| x_translation    y_translation   1 |
```

A General Scaling Matrix

Here's a general scaling matrix, where scale_x and scale_y are the amounts by which you want to scale the object in the x- and y-axis, respectively:

```
| scale_x          0               0 |
| 0                scale_y          0 |
| 0                0               1 |
```

Note that we're allowing for non-uniform scaling; that is, we can make the object scale in one axis differently than in the other. However, if we wanted to scale uniformly, we would make scale_x = scale_y.

A General Rotation Matrix

Here's a general rotation matrix, where `angle` is the angle by which you wish to rotate the object or vertex:

```
┆ cos(angle)      -sin(angle)     0 ┆
┆ sin(angle)       cos(angle)     0 ┆
┆ 0                0              1 ┆
```

A General Scaling, Rotation, and Translation Matrix

Here comes the cool part: we can now take the translation, scaling, and rotation matrices and multiply them (or, as it's called, *concatenate* them) to get a single matrix that will do all three functions in one multiplication. The final matrix looks like this:

```
┆ scale_x*cos(angle)      scale_x* -sin(angle)     0 ┆
┆ scale_y*sin(angle)      scale_y* cos(angle)      0 ┆
┆ x_translation           y_translation            1 ┆
```

If you multiply the vertices of your object by this matrix, the result is an object that is scaled, rotated, and translated. Neat, huh!?

The Vertex Normalizing Component

Well, I've been putting off a little detail that I hope you've caught on to by now. How do we multiply each vertex by a 3x3 transformation matrix? Good question; I'm glad you asked.

What we must do is change the representation of our vertex structure slightly to accomodate a *normalizing component.* This normalizing component is just a 1 tacked onto the end of each vertex. We can therefore modify the code fragment in Listing 4.4, which defines the vertices of a data structure, to that shown in Listing 4.10.

Listing 4.10. A new and improved vertex for data structures.

```
// A new and improved vertex

#define X_COMP 0
#define Y_COMP 1
#define N_COMP 2

typedef struct vertex_typ
        {
        float p[3];  // A single point in the 2-D plane
                     // with a normalizing factor.
        } vertex, *vertex_ptr;
```

As you can see, we've made Matrix P, which is really a vertex, into an array. (If you recall, we can multiply two matrices as long as their inner dimensions are the same: $m \times n$ times $n \times r$, for example.) Our final transformation matrix is 3x3, so we needed a 1x3 matrix to multiply with. Matrix P now satisfies this condition.

An Asteroid Program with Matrices

I think we've had enough talk; let's see some action! We're going to rewrite our asteroid program from Listing 4.8 with matrices. (This still isn't our final program; the asteroid concept doesn't lend itself well to being done completely with matrices. Alas, I don't want to force a structure on the program that will make it so complex that we lose the essence of what we're trying to do.) Listing 4.11 shows the Asteroids Deluxe program.

Listing 4.11. Asteroids Deluxe (field_dlx.c).

```c
// I N C L U D E S ///////////////////////////////////////////////

#include <stdio.h> // include the basics
#include <graph.h> // include Microsoft's Graphics Header
#include <math.h>  // include math stuff

// D E F I N E S ///////////////////////////////////////////////

#define NUM_ASTEROIDS 10
#define ERASE 0
#define DRAW  1

#define X_COMP 0
#define Y_COMP 1
#define N_COMP 2


// T Y P E D E F S ///////////////////////////////////////////////

// A new and improved vertex

typedef struct vertex_typ
        {
        float p[3]; // A single point in the 2-D plane with
                    // a normalizing factor.
        } vertex, *vertex_ptr;

// Define a general matrix structure.

typedef struct matrix_typ
        {
        float elem[3][3]; // This is storage for a 3x3
                          // matrix.
        } matrix, *matrix_ptr;
```

continues

Listing 4.11. continued

```
// Define the structure for an object.

typedef struct object_typ
        {
        int num_vertices;    // This is the number of
                             // vertices in this object.
        int color;           // This is the color of this
                             // object.
        float xo,yo;         // This is the position of this
                             // object.
        float x_velocity;    // This is the x velocity of
                             // this object.
        float y_velocity;    // This is the y velocity of
                             // this object.
        matrix scale;        // This is the object scaling
                             // matrix.
        matrix rotation;     // This is the object's rotation
                             // and translation matrix.

        vertex vertices[16]; // This defines 16 vertices.
        } object, *object_ptr;


// G L O B A L S ///////////////////////////////////////////


object asteroids[NUM_ASTEROIDS];


// F U N C T I O N S ///////////////////////////////////////

void Delay(int t)
{

// Take up some compute cycles.
float x = 1;

while(t-->0)
    x=cos(x);


} // end Delay

//////////////////////////////////////////////////////////////

void Make_Identity(matrix_ptr i)
{

// Make the sent matrix an identity matrix.

i->elem[0][0] = i->elem[1][1] = i->elem[2][2] = 1;
i->elem[0][1] = i->elem[1][0] = i->elem[1][2] = 0;
i->elem[2][0] = i->elem[0][2] = i->elem[2][1] = 0;


} // end Make_Identity
```

```
/////////////////////////////////////////////////////////////////

void Clear_Matrix(matrix_ptr m)
{

// Zero out the sent matrix.

m->elem[0][0] = m->elem[1][1] = m->elem[2][2] = 0;
m->elem[0][1] = m->elem[1][0] = m->elem[1][2] = 0;
m->elem[2][0] = m->elem[0][2] = m->elem[2][1] = 0;


} // end Clear_Matrix

/////////////////////////////////////////////////////////////////

Mat_Mul(vertex_ptr v,matrix_ptr m)
{

// Do a multiplication of a 1x3 * 3x3. The result is again 1x3.
// For speed, do the multiplication manually by specifying each
// multiplication and addition (an apprentice's trick).

float x_new, y_new;

x_new = v->p[0]*m->elem[0][0] + v->p[1]*m->elem[1][0]
                  + m->elem[2][0];
y_new = v->p[0]*m->elem[0][1] + v->p[1]*m->elem[1][1]
                  + m->elem[2][1];

v->p[X_COMP] = x_new;
v->p[Y_COMP] = y_new;

// Note: we need not change N_COMP because it's always 1.

} // end Mat_Mul

/////////////////////////////////////////////////////////////////

void Scale_Object_Mat(object_ptr obj)
{

int index;

// Scale the object: multiply each point in the object by its
// scaling matrix.

for (index=0; index<obj->num_vertices; index++)
    {

    Mat_Mul((vertex_ptr)&obj->vertices[index],(matrix_ptr)&obj->scale);

    } // end for index

} // end Scale_Oject_Mat
```

continues

Listing 4.11. continued

```
/////////////////////////////////////////////////////////////

void Rotate_Object_Mat(object_ptr obj)
{

int index;

// Rotate the object: multiply each point in the object by its
// rotation matrix.

for (index=0; index<obj->num_vertices; index++)
    {

    Mat_Mul((vertex_ptr)&obj->vertices[index],(matrix_ptr)&obj->rotation);

    } // end for index

} // end Rotate_Oject_Mat


/////////////////////////////////////////////////////////////

void Create_Field(void)
{

int index;
float angle,c,s;

// This function creates the asteroid field.

for (index=0; index<NUM_ASTEROIDS; index++)
    {

    // Fill in the fields.

    asteroids[index].num_vertices = 6;
    asteroids[index].color = 1  + (rand() % 14); // This is always
                                                 // visable.
    asteroids[index].xo    = 41 + (rand() % 599);
    asteroids[index].yo    = 41 + (rand() % 439);
    asteroids[index].x_velocity = -10 + (rand() % 20);
    asteroids[index].y_velocity = -10 + (rand() % 20);

    // Clear out the matrix.

    Make_Identity((matrix_ptr)&asteroids[index].rotation);

    // Now set up up rotation matrix.

    angle = (float)(- 50 + (float)(rand() % 100)) / 100;

    c=cos(angle);
    s=sin(angle);

    asteroids[index].rotation.elem[0][0] = c;
    asteroids[index].rotation.elem[0][1] = -s;
    asteroids[index].rotation.elem[1][0] = s;
```

```
            asteroids[index].rotation.elem[1][1] = c;

            // Set up a scaling matrix.

            // Clear out the matrix and set scale in one blow.

            Make_Identity((matrix_ptr)&asteroids[index].scale);

            asteroids[index].scale.elem[0][0] = (float)(rand() % 30) / 10;
            asteroids[index].scale.elem[1][1] = asteroids[index].scale.elem[0][0];


            asteroids[index].vertices[0].p[X_COMP] = 4.0;
            asteroids[index].vertices[0].p[Y_COMP] = 3.5;
            asteroids[index].vertices[0].p[N_COMP] = 1;

            asteroids[index].vertices[1].p[X_COMP] = 8.5;
            asteroids[index].vertices[1].p[Y_COMP] = -3.0;
            asteroids[index].vertices[1].p[N_COMP] = 1;

            asteroids[index].vertices[2].p[X_COMP] = 6;
            asteroids[index].vertices[2].p[Y_COMP] = -5;
            asteroids[index].vertices[2].p[N_COMP] = 1;

            asteroids[index].vertices[3].p[X_COMP] = 2;
            asteroids[index].vertices[3].p[Y_COMP] = -3;
            asteroids[index].vertices[3].p[N_COMP] = 1;

            asteroids[index].vertices[4].p[X_COMP] = -4;
            asteroids[index].vertices[4].p[Y_COMP] = -6;
            asteroids[index].vertices[4].p[N_COMP] = 1;

            asteroids[index].vertices[5].p[X_COMP] = -3.5;
            asteroids[index].vertices[5].p[Y_COMP] = 5.5;
            asteroids[index].vertices[5].p[N_COMP] = 1;

            // Now scale the asteroid to the proper size.

            Scale_Object_Mat((object_ptr)&asteroids[index]);

            } // end for index

} // end Create_Field

//////////////////////////////////////////////////////////////////

void Draw_Asteroids(int erase)
{

int index,vertex;
float xo,yo;

// This function draws the asteroids, or erases them, depending
// on the sent flag.
for (index=0; index<NUM_ASTEROIDS; index++)
    {

    // Draw the asteroid.
```

continues

Listing 4.11. continued

```
if (erase==ERASE)
   _setcolor(0);
else
   _setcolor(asteroids[index].color);

// Get the position of object.
xo = asteroids[index].xo;
yo = asteroids[index].yo;


// Move to the first vertex.

_moveto((int)(xo+asteroids[index].vertices[0].p[X_COMP]),
        (int)(yo+asteroids[index].vertices[0].p[Y_COMP]));

for (vertex=1; vertex<asteroids[index].num_vertices; vertex++)
    {
    _lineto((int)(xo+asteroids[index].vertices[vertex].p[X_COMP]),
            (int)(yo+asteroids[index].vertices[vertex].p[Y_COMP]));

    } // end for vertex

// Close object

_lineto((int)(xo+asteroids[index].vertices[0].p[X_COMP]),
        (int)(yo+asteroids[index].vertices[0].p[Y_COMP]));


} // end for index

} // end Draw_Asteroids

////////////////////////////////////////////////////////////////

void Translate_Asteroids(void)
{

int index;

// This function moves the asteroids.

for (index=0; index<NUM_ASTEROIDS; index++)
    {
    // Translate the current asteroid.

    asteroids[index].xo += asteroids[index].x_velocity;
    asteroids[index].yo += asteroids[index].y_velocity;

    // Collision detection (that is, bounds check).

    if (asteroids[index].xo > 600 || asteroids[index].xo < 40)
        {
        asteroids[index].x_velocity = -asteroids[index].x_velocity;
        asteroids[index].xo += asteroids[index].x_velocity;
        }

    if (asteroids[index].yo > 440 || asteroids[index].yo < 40)
```

```
        {
        asteroids[index].y_velocity = -asteroids[index].y_velocity;
        asteroids[index].yo += asteroids[index].y_velocity;
        }

    } // end for index

} // end Translate_Asteroids

//////////////////////////////////////////////////////////////////

void Rotate_Asteroids(void)
{

int index;

for (index=0; index<NUM_ASTEROIDS; index++)
    {
    // Rotate the current asteroid.
    Rotate_Object_Mat((object_ptr)&asteroids[index]);

    } // end for index

} // end Rotate_Asteroids


//////////////////////////////////////////////////////////////////

void main(void)
{

// Put the computer into graphics mode.
_setvideomode(_VRES16COLOR); // This sets the mode to 640x480
                             // in 16 colors.

// Initialize asteroid field
Create_Field();

while(!kbhit())
    {
    // Erase the field.

    Draw_Asteroids(ERASE);

    // Transform the field.

    Rotate_Asteroids();

    Translate_Asteroids();

    // Draw the field.

    Draw_Asteroids(DRAW);

    // Wait a bit...

    Delay(500);
```

continues

Listing 4.11. continued

```
    } // end while

// Put the computer back into text mode.

_setvideomode(_DEFAULTMODE);

} // end main
```

You should spend some time and study each of these programs. Pay special attention to the way the asteroids are being rotated and scaled. If you compare the execution speed of Listings 4.8 and 4.11, you shouldn't notice any difference in speed, because Listing 4.8 does the same thing as Listing 4.11. However, if we took some time and re-thought Listing 4.11, we could put all the transformations (rotation, scaling, and translation) in a single matrix. Listing 4.11 would then be considerably faster.

This is where matrix multiplying really shines: when you're performing multiple transformations using a single, precomputed transformation matrix that is the concatenation of all the transformation operations we want to perform on the object in question.

In Case You Were Wondering...

Keep in mind why we're doing all this: to learn how to write video games—preferably, 3-D video games. However, we have to build slowly. If I were to just show you how to go about making something like Wolfenstein 3-D or DOOM, we'd lose a lot of the philosophy and tactics of writing video games. These issues are the same whether you're writing Pong or Afterburner.

If you're a true video-game sorcerer, at this very moment you should be thinking about taking what I've given you and turning it into a small version of the classic Asteroids. Don't worry: I'm not going to say "As an exercise, convert Listing 4.8 into an Asteroids game." We'll write a game together, and soon, but for now let's just talk about how we would do the conversion. With that in the back of your mind, you'll make important connections later on.

If, however, you happened to ask *me* to convert Listing 4.8 into a simple version of Asteroids, this is what I'd do:

1. Take inventory on what I was missing. I need a ship, a score-keeping system, some missiles, and a graceful entrance and exit to the game. (I need some collision detection, too. Collision detection is discussed more fully in the next section, "Basic Collision Detection.")

2. Get a ship working. To do this I would define an object that resembles the insignia from *Star Trek*. This would be my ship.

   Write a few routines. You have everything you need to do this. From Chapter 3, "Input Device Basics," we know how to read the keyboard and detect key presses.

3. I'd write a routine to draw or erase the ship's object (just like the `Draw_Asteroids()` function in Program 4.11).

4. I'd write one that would allow the player to move the ship.

5. I'd write a routine that, depending on the status of the keyboard, would rotate the ship clockwise or counter clockwise. I'd do this by changing the `angle` member of the object structure.

6. I'd then need some way to move the ship foward in the direction it's pointing, so I would need to update the object members' `x_velocity` and `y_velocity`, depending on the direction the ship was pointing. Here's a hint:

   x_velocity = cos(angle) * speed
   y_velocity = sin(angle) * speed

   where speed would increase or decrease by the player's pressing or releasing a thrust key.

7. To get the ship in the game, I would place a call to the erase function in the same place the asteroids are erased, then place a call to the movement routine that queries the keyboard in the middle (between the erase section and the draw section).

8. Finally, I'd put a call to the draw ship function at the end of the code.

That would do it.

Basic Collision Detection

Let's hold off on weapons for now and try and see if we can get hit by an asteroid. (I hear they pack a punch!) We'll have to do some *collision detection* for this.

What that means is we need to see if the asteroids have hit the ship. A rough cut at this would be to do the following:

1. Forget about the actual shape of the asteroids and the ship and create a virtual *bounding box* around each object, for test purposes only. Don't actually draw a bounding box, but put one into the software. Figure 4.10 shows what I mean.

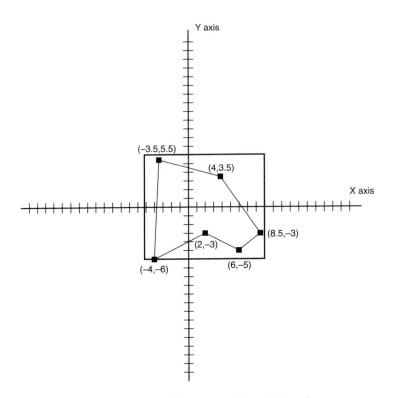

Figure 4.10. *A bounding box around the asteroid for collision detection.*

2. If we can figure out that the bounding box of the ship has entered the bounding box of the asteroids, we can tell whether the ship has been obliterated! This is easy to do: just test each vertex of one of the boxes and see if it's within the other bounding box. If you find a winner, you're done—and there's been a collision.

3. Now, when I detect a collision, I probably would do something spectacular, as a 500-ton ship with antimatter drive was just hit by an asteroid. However, a bunch of random pixels in the vicinity would probably do for now.

4. Scoring is easy: just create a variable named score and print the score out on the screen every time through the main loop. You can use the _outtext() function to print using Microsoft's Library—which, by the way, we would never actually use in a video game because it's so slow, but which suffices now to get the point across.

Finally, we need to be able to score points, so we need some weapons. The ship in Asteroids uses photon torpedoes—actually, little dots. What I would do is:

1. Let a certain key, such as the space bar, be the firing button.

2. When I detected that the player pressed the key and wanted to fire, I'd set up some variables that reflected the direction the ship was pointing in, such as `miss_xv` and `miss_yv`. (These variables are computed using sin and cos, as is the ship's velocity.)

3. I then would store the position of the missile, which is the center of the ship, in two more variables named `miss_x` and `miss_y`.

4. I would set a `life` variable to some value such as 100.

5. I'd move the missile the same way we've moved everything else, but every time I moved it I'd do a bounding box test to see if it had hit an asteroid. If so, I would increase the score and remove the asteroid completely.

6. If the `life` variable went to zero, I would kill the missile and allow the player to fire another.

Summary

This chapter could have been about a hundred times bigger. We really had to take a crash course in 2-D graphics and polygon-based rendering. We learned a lot of new concepts and terminology, and we learned how to perform simple transformations with points and objects in the plane. We also learned quite a bit about matrices (probably more than you wanted to know) and how they can be used in computer graphics and video games to simplify geometrical transformations into a more compact form. Finally, we got to see some asteroid fields animated on the screen. Things are definitely getting more exciting!

I'm sure you have many questions; probably, many more than when you began. However, I keep giving you pieces of the puzzle as we go. Remember, there are no hard-and-fast rules to making video games. They're not like bubble-sort programs. They have many forms and flavors. What we want as video-game programmers is a set of techniques and technologies to implement our ideas, so let's keep building.

5

The Mysteries of the VGA Card

I n the PC games we write, we use the computer to synthesize worlds and little creatures on the video screen. We use the video-graphics array (VGA) card to draw these images. The VGA card is our only communication between our programs and the video display. How we program it ultimately impacts the realism and excitement our games create. In this glorious chapter, therefore, we talk about the following subjects:

- An overview of the VGA card

- The 256-color mode

- The configuration of video memory

- The color look-up table

- Remapping the color palette

- Color rotation

- Plotting pixels

- Drawing lines

by André LaMothe

- PCX files

- Bit blitting

- Sprites

- Text blitting

- Double buffering

- Vertical retrace syncing

- Tombstone

An Overview of the VGA Card

The VGA card is the hardware that generates the video signal that is fed into the video display. This video signal is a series of pulses that define the color and intensity of each pixel on the screen. We aren't concerned with how this video signal is created or how the VGA card creates all the complex timings it takes to control the video display. We have one, single concern: how do we place a pixel on the screen in any color we wish? Once we've answered that question, we can do just about anything.

Plotting a single pixel on the video screen can be quite a challenge, and we must know a great many details to do it—but once we've done it and understand the VGA card, we can call the function and never have to worry about it again.

As you may know, the VGA card supports many different graphics modes, and can actually be programmed to display resolutions that most people aren't even aware it can support. (I've created a 320x400-pixel mode with 256 colors by directly reprogramming the VGA timing registers!) This functionality comes from the architecture of the VGA card, which is a good step up from that of the color-graphics adapter (CGA) and enhanced-graphics adapter (EGA) cards of the past. The VGA card has many registers that can be programmed to accomplish different goals. In any case, programming the registers is a topic for a book on the VGA card, and not a primary concern of ours. If you're curious, don't worry: there isn't a shortage of such publications. In my small home library, I have over thirty books on the VGA card. If you want to know more about its secrets, you'll have no problems finding information.

The way we're going to approach the VGA card is to think of it as a video system that supports a single mode; for example, the mode that we'll use for our games. (That mode is the 320x200, 256-color mode, mode 13h—the details of which we explore later in this chapter.) What we gain by using the VGA card to support only one mode is a bit of machine dependence. Our games will work only on VGA or higher cards. We won't be supporting EGA, monochrome, and so on. The reason? Video-game programmers have had just about enough of writing twenty different display drivers to support every possible video mode and monitor in existence. If we concentrate on a single mode, we can exploit it to its fullest and write very specific code.

Normally, when you write a program, you try to make it quite general. Not so in a video game for the PC. If we know that objects will always be moving to the right, we can take advantage of this. PC games are so graphically and computationally intensive that we must practically rewrite all our code for each game. That's right: no more reusing libraries or cutting, pasting, and otherwise hacking at old software. We aren't making word processors—we're making new worlds, and they must be perfect!

We'll be using the VGA card in mode 13h. But how does this mode work? Good question. Read on and find out.

The 256-Color Mode

Mode 13h (or mode 19, in decimal) is the 320x200, 256-color graphics mode supported by the VGA card. The video screen is 320 pixels horizontally by 200 pixels vertically, and it can support 256 different colors on the screen at once.

Now, here comes the real beauty of mode 13h. In the other VGA modes all kinds of bit shifting and twiddling had to be done because the EGA's video buffer was a multiplane mess that drove many a programmer to drink. However, the VGA's mode 13h is a frightfully easy one in which to program. You see, all graphics modes (such as CGA, EGA, VGA, SVGA, XGA, and whatever new acronyms come along) use a portion of memory to represent the bit map to be displayed on the screen. This portion of memory is called the *video buffer*. For mode 13h and the VGA card, the video buffer starts at A000:0000 and ends at A000:F9FF. If you're good at hexadecimal math, you'll realize that the video buffer is exactly 64000 bytes long. If we multiply 320 by 200, the result is 64000! That means that each pixel in mode 13h is represented by exactly one byte. That's almost exciting enough for me to actually like the VGA card.

Figure 5.1 shows a representation of the VGA video buffer.

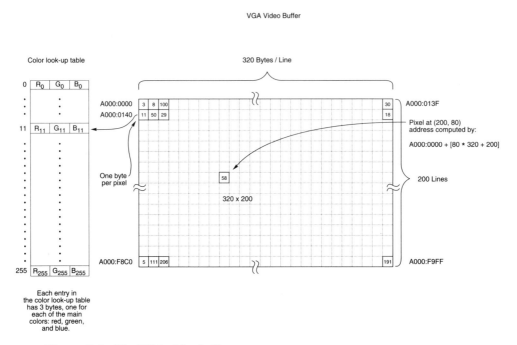

Figure 5.1. *The VGA video buffer.*

Later in this chapter we get to how to address the video buffer and blast pixels into it. At the moment, however, I want to address a topic that might be causing some concern about now: won't the 320x200 mode be too blocky and jagged? The answer is: yes and no. A resolution of 320x200 is definitely substandard today, but with 256 colors on the screen, and clever rendering, it won't be as apparent. Moreover, we'll be making video games that have a lot of animation, color, and motion. These factors tend to blur the resolution. The player won't even notice that the game is in low resolution (unless, of course, Data from *Star Trek* is playing).

The Configuration of Video Memory

Let's talk about writing into the video buffer. As you can see in Figure 5.1, the video buffer begins at A000:0000 and ends at A000:FF9F. Because each pixel is represented by exactly one byte, addressing the video buffer is easy. All we need to do is create a pointer to the video buffer, and then write into the video buffer using the pointer. That's it!

Well, that's almost it. The video buffer is one big, contiguous block of memory, or an array of bytes. We see that there are 320 bytes per line, and 200 lines. Therefore, to plot a pixel at any x,y location, we would:

■ Multiply the y coordinate by 320.

■ Add the x coordinate to the result of the multiplication.

■ Use the final result as an offset from the base pointer to the video buffer.

■ Write a value from 0-255 into this final address.

Whammo: a pixel miraculously appears on the screen. If we draw a series of pixels we have a line, and so on.

The Color Look-Up Table

I just said that we could put a number from 0-255 into the final address we compute. However, what does this number mean? Answer: it's the color we want the pixel to be.

The VGA card is capable of displaying 256 colors at a time on the screen; therefore, the color we wish to be displayed can be represented by a number in the range of 0-255. Great—but what's the relationship between the numbers and the actual color? The number is used as an index into a *color look-up table* that holds the real value of the color to be displayed on the screen.

The VGA card is actually capable of producing 262,144 colors! However, if we needed to place a value that represented that number in every pixel location, we'd need roughly three bytes to represent a number that large—and the video buffer would get really big. Therefore, what designers decided to do was to design a graphics adapter with some indirection. *Indirection* means that a value is not taken literally, but is used to locate another value (just as a pointer can be dereferenced in C).

Instead of allowing all 262,144 colors to be displayed simultaneously, designers allowed a subset of 256 of them to be displayed simultaneously. (The number 256 comes from the different number of values a single byte can have; that is, 0-255, or a total of 256.) Therefore, the VGA card has a color look-up table that hold 256 values. Each value is composed of three components, each one byte long. These components hold the red, green, and blue components of the desired color. (Remember: red, green and blue are sufficient to create any color.)

The color look-up table contains a total of 768 bytes (3x256). Alas, when the video hardware reads a 72 in the video buffer, it looks in location 72 of the color look-up table. Location 72 starts at 72x3 from the base address of the table itself, because there are three bytes per entry. The red, green, and blue components then are extracted from the entry and used as the signals for the final color to be displayed. Take a look at Figure 5.2 to see a detailed example of this.

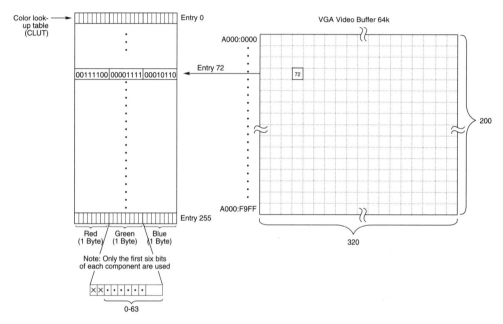

Figure 5.2. *Looking up a color in the color look-up table.*

It would have been really nice if we had access to the color look-up table directly—say, at some block of memory. Unfortunately, the color registers are accessible only through the use of I/O ports on the VGA card. This isn't too bad, but it makes things ugly!

Next, we learn how to change the values in the color look-up table.

Remapping the Color Palette

The color look-up table is implemented as a register file on the VGA card. (I use the word *register* to mean an entry in the color look-up table. Each palette register is 24 bits.) To access any entry in the register file we must do things a certain way. We can't just say "Change the red component of entry 123." We must change *all three* components of any entry we wish to alter, and we must do it in a certain order.

Even though each entry consists of three bytes (one for each primary component), only the first six bits of each byte are used for the color. There are 64 shades of each color, or a total of 2^{18} different colors (which is where we get the total number of colors: 262,144). If you place a value larger than six bits, or 63, in a color register, it won't hurt anything—but it won't change the color.

We need only the following three I/O ports to accomplish the task of changing the entries in the color look-up table:

```
#define PALETTE_MASK          0x3C6
#define PALETTE_REGISTER_RD   0x3C7
#define PALETTE_REGISTER_WR   0x3C8
#define PALETTE_DATA          0x3C9
```

Here's how this breaks down:

■ Port number 0x3C6, called the *palette mask*, is used to mask the bits of the requested palette register. For example, if you place a mask of 0x00 in this port you get register 0, no matter what register you requested. Alternatively, if you place a 0xFF in the mask register, you're able to access any register you wish by way of palette index registers 0x3C8 and 0x3C7. (One is used for writing and the other for reading.)

■ Port 0x3C7, called the *palette read register*, is used to select the entry in the color look-up table from which you want to read.

■ Port 0x3C8, called the *palette write register*, is used to select the entry in the color look-up table to which you want to write.

■ Finally, data from the red, green, and blue components is written to or read from by way of the single port 0x3C9, called the *palette data port.*

You should be asking: "How can we get three different bytes from one port?" Well, you get them in sequence. After you select the appropriate register (the entry in the color look-up table you want to access), the first byte you write to the palette register goes into the red byte of the entry. The second byte you write goes into the green byte of the entry. Finally, the third byte you write goes into the blue byte of the entry. When reading, the same is true—but instead of writing three bytes, each time you read the palette data port you get the next component of the selected register. To write to palette register, we must:

■ Change the mask to 0xFF every time you read or write a color register, so you're sure of its state.

■ Select the register you want to change.

■ Do three port writes to the data register.

Listing 5.1 contains the code to do these steps.

Listing 5.1. Writing to a palette register.

```
///////////////////////////////////////////////////////////////////

void Set_Palette_Register(int index, RGB_color_ptr color)
{

// This function sets a single color look-up table value indexed
// by index with the value in the color structure.

// Tell the VGA card we are going to update a palette register.

_outp(PALETTE_MASK,0xff);

// Tell the VGA card which register we will be updating.

_outp(PALETTE_REGISTER_WR, index);

// Now update the RGB triple. Note that the same port is used
// each time.

_outp(PALETTE_DATA,color->red);
_outp(PALETTE_DATA,color->green);
_outp(PALETTE_DATA,color->blue);

} // end Set_Palette_Color

///////////////////////////////////////////////////////////////////
```

Notice that I use a data structure called RGB_color. It's a structure with three fields, one for each primary color. It looks like this:

```
typedef struct RGB_color_typ
        {
        unsigned char red;      // This is the red component of
                                // color 0-63.
        unsigned char green;    // This is the green component of
                                // color 0-63.
        unsigned char blue;     // This is the blue component of
                                // color 0-63.

        } RGB_color, *RGB_color_ptr;
```

It seems as though reading a palette register would be the next thing to do, so let's do it. We do the same thing as in the Set_Palette_Register, except we read the values from the palette data port and place them into the sent RBG_color structure. Listing 5.2 contains the code to do that.

Listing 5.2. Reading a palette register.

```
////////////////////////////////////////////////////////////////

void Get_Palette_Register(int index, RGB_color_ptr color)
{

// This function gets the data out of a color register
// and places it into color.

// Set the palette mask register in case it was changed
// by another process.

_outp(PALETTE_MASK,0xff);

// Tell the VGA card which register we will be reading.

_outp(PALETTE_REGISTER_RD, index);

// Now extract the data.

color->red   = _inp(PALETTE_DATA);
color->green = _inp(PALETTE_DATA);
color->blue  = _inp(PALETTE_DATA);

} // end Get_Palette_Color

////////////////////////////////////////////////////////////////
```

Now that we know how to read from and write to a palette register, why don't we create a function that makes a neat color palette?! Sounds good to me! To create this nifty palette, we create a function that builds a palette that has 64 shades each of gray, red, green, and blue. Listing 5.3 contains the code to do this.

Listing 5.3. Creating a nifty color palette.

```
////////////////////////////////////////////////////////////////

void Create_Cool_Palette(void)
{

// This function creates a nifty palette: 64 shades of gray, 64
// of red, 64 of green, and 64 of blue.
```

continues

Listing 5.3. continued

```
RGB_color color;

int index;

// swipe through the color registers and create four banks
// of 64 colors each.
for (index=0; index < 64; index++)
    {
    // These are the grays:

    color.red   = index;
    color.green = index;
    color.blue  = index;

    Set_Palette_Register(index, (RGB_color_ptr)&color);

    // These are the reds:

    color.red   = index;
    color.green = 0;
    color.blue  = 0;

    Set_Palette_Register(index+64, (RGB_color_ptr)&color);

    // These are the greens:

    color.red   = 0;
    color.green = index;
    color.blue  = 0;

    Set_Palette_Register(index+128, (RGB_color_ptr)&color);

    // These are the blues:

    color.red   = 0;
    color.green = 0;
    color.blue  = index;

    Set_Palette_Register(index+192, (RGB_color_ptr)&color);

    } // end index

} // end Create_Cool_Palette

/////////////////////////////////////////////////////////////////
```

Being able to remap the color palette enables us to create all kinds of interesting lighting and animation effects in our games. (For instance, that's how the lighting effects are done in DOOM. A portion of the color palette is remapped "on the fly" during game play.) This is how effects such as local lighting and gunfire are accomplished. It's especially good for turning the lights completely off!

You'll just have to take it on faith that we've created a nifty color palette in Listing 5.3, because there's no way to see it yet. We must create a few functions to plot pixels and draw lines first. We'll get to that in a moment, but first I want to talk about a technique we just might find some use for in the near future.

Color Rotation

When I purchased my first computer back in 1978 (well, actually, Dad bought it for me), I was utterly fascinated by computer graphics and video games. The computer we bought was an Atari 800. It was well ahead of its time for what it could do. One of the interesting effects that could be accomplished was called color rotation. *Color rotation* can be implemented only on computers that have color look-up tables. Basically, an image is drawn on the screen; for instance, a waterfall. The waterfall is comprised of, say, 16 shades of blue, which are indexed in the color look-up table with consecutive integers—in other words, the entries are all next to each other. So, what we have on the screen is a waterfall comprised of the 16 shades of blue that are located in, for instance, color registers 100-115.

What if we take each one of those values and shift it into the next register? That is, what if we take 100 and place it into 101, take 101 and place it into 102, and so on until, finally, we take 115 and place it back into 100? What would happen is the colors would rotate and give the illusion of motion. Back in the 70s you had to do things like this because a 1.79MHz 6502 wasn't going to redraw half the screen at 30 frames per second; that much was certain!

We may use this technique later. There are all kinds of cool things that can be done with color rotation, and with the PC having 256 color registers you can do a lot. So, keep it in mind as a good trick! Now, on to plotting little dots.................

Plotting Pixels

I once said, "Give me the address of the video buffer and I'll take over the world!" This remains a true statement (although I'm still working on Eastern Europe). In any memory-mapped video-display system such as the PC's, rendering graphics can be a pleasurable experience as long as the video buffer has some kind of logic to its organization. And, as we've seen, it does. It's one big array. We couldn't ask for more. As we discovered earlier in this chapter, we need only compute the offset from the base of the video buffer at A000:0000 and store a byte there representing the color of the pixel we wish to see. There's not much more to it. Listing 5.4 contains a code fragment that enables you to plot a pixel of a specific color at any x,y position.

Listing 5.4. Plotting a pixel at any x,y position.

```
//////////////////////////////////////////////////////////////

void Plot_Pixel(int x,int y,unsigned char color)
{
// This function plots the pixel in the desired color. Each row
// contains 320 bytes; therefore, multiply y times the row and
// add x.

video_buffer[y*320+x] = color;

} // end Plot_Pixel

//////////////////////////////////////////////////////////////
```

Plotting a pixel is *so simple*. I almost wish it were harder so I had more to write about, but the fact is that in mode 13h IBM has really hit a home run. The Plot_Pixel function is simple. In fact, it's a single line. However I would like to make a suggestion: let's optimize it.

This book has an entire chapter on optimization techniques (Chapter 18), but for now that single multiplication in the code is driving me crazy! Let's get rid of it. As a rule, multiplication of integers should be avoided, and floating-point calculations should be illegal! So how do we get rid of the calculation y*320? We use base-2 math. All numbers in a computer are ultimately represented in binary, and we can use this to our advantage. If you take a binary number and shift it to the left or right, it's like multiplying or dividing by 2. Figure 5.3 shows this in more detail.

Because shifting is anywhere from two to 10 times faster than multiplication, we can have a much faster plot function. The only catch is that 320 is not a multiple of two—so how can we achieve y*320? Here's the trick: that 320 we want is 256+64. If we multiply y by 256 and then add it to y multiplied by 64, we have y*320. Listing 5.5 contains the the code to do fast pixel plotting.

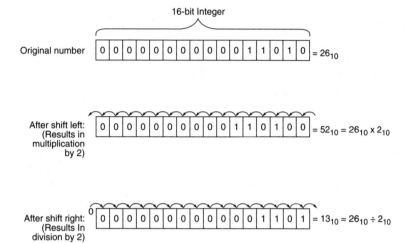

Figure 5.3. *Shifting bits to perform multiplication and division.*

Listing 5.5. A program to do some fast pixel plotting.

```
///////////////////////////////////////////////////////////////

void Plot_Pixel_Fast(int x,int y,unsigned char color)
{
// This function plots the pixel in the desired color a little
// quicker using binary shifting to accomplish the
// multiplications.

// Use the fact that 320*y = 256*y + 64*y = y<<8 + y<<6

video_buffer[((y<<8) + (y<<6)) + x] = color;

} // end Plot_Pixel_Fast


///////////////////////////////////////////////////////////////
```

This function works about twice as fast—definitely worth a few moments of optimizing. Later we learn to optimize functions so well the folks at Microsoft will be saying, "How did they do that?"

Now that we have a pixel plotter, let's expand our graphics library by making functions to draw lines.

Drawing Lines

We're not interested in doing general line drawing, also known as Breshenham's Algorithm. In the PC games that we'll be writing, we need not draw lines *from* any point *to* any point. Instead, we'll be drawing a lot of vertical lines, and maybe a few horizontal lines. Furthermore, most games are totally bit-mapped—we may not draw *any* lines!

Also, we'll be the only ones calling our own functions, so we can always leave the coordinates in some order and count on them staying in that order. (Otherwise, the functions would have to order them. That takes time—something we don't have an infinite amount of!) If we were writing these functions for a general graphics library, we couldn't assume the coordinates were in any particular order.

We're going to create two functions. One of them draws horizontal lines from left to right, and the other draws vertical lines top to bottom. Figure 5.4 shows the geometry of these lines.

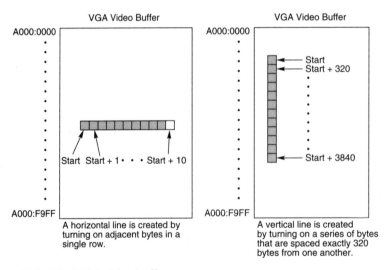

Figure 5.4. *The VGA video buffer.*

Drawing horizontal lines is the easiest, so let's begin there. As you can see in Figure 5.4, you can create a horizontal line by turning on a row of pixels in the 320x200-pixel matrix. To accomplish this, we must find the starting address of the row and then blast the pixels from the starting position of the line to the ending position of the line. We do this using the memset function. This is one of the fastest ways to do this. Listing 5.6 contains code that draws a horizontal line.

Listing 5.6. Drawing a horizontal line.

```
////////////////////////////////////////////////////////////////

void H_Line(int x1,int x2,int y,unsigned int color)
{
// This function draws a horizontal line using the memset
// function. Note: x2 > x1.

_fmemset((char far *)(video_buffer + ((y<<8) + (y<<6)) + x1),color,x2-x1+1);

} // end H_Line

////////////////////////////////////////////////////////////////
```

Notice some things about the code in Listing 5.6:

■ We use the `_fmemset` function because `_fmemset` is the model-independent version of `memset`, and works properly with far pointers.

■ We compute the starting address of the line and the function blasts a number of bytes of a certain value (the color).

■ The number of bytes is the length of the line, which is the right endpoint minus the left endpoint. The 1 is added because if we don't add it we'll be off by one. This is a typical software bug called the "off-by-one error."

Other than that, the function is straightforward.

We can't use one of the functions from the `memset` family to draw vertical lines because they operate only on contiguous blocks of memory. In the case of a vertical line, every pixel is 320 bytes away from the previous address (because there are 320 bytes per line). If you're at a specific position in the video buffer and you want to move to exactly below the current position, you add 320. If you want to move to exactly above your current position, you subtract 320 from your current address. Therefore, we must make a loop that increments the address by 320 bytes every cycle and draws the vertical line a pixel at a time, from top to bottom. Listing 5.7 contains the code to do this.

Listing 5.7. Drawing a vertical line.

```
////////////////////////////////////////////////////////////////

void V_Line(int y1,int y2,int x,unsigned int color)
{
// This function draws a vertical line. Note: y2 > y1.

unsigned int line_offset,
                    index;
```

continues

Listing 5.7. continued

```
// Compute the starting position.

line_offset = ((y1<<8) + (y1<<6)) + x;

for (index=0; index<=y2-y1; index++)
    {
    video_buffer[line_offset] = color;

    line_offset+=320; // Move to the next line.

    } // end for index

} // end V_Line

///////////////////////////////////////////////////////////////////
```

The function V_Line is a bit longer than H_Line because it must do all the address calculations itself. The function is fairly efficient; notice the use of shifting to accomplish multiplication. (If you still don't understand binary shifting, don't worry about it. We get into a complete treatment in Chapter 18, "Optimization Techniques.")

Before we move on to the next topic, I want to give you a cool program that uses the palette and vertical-line drawing functions to create a neat palette and display it. This program uses the Set_Mode() function from Chapter 2, "Assembly Language Basics." I haven't included the source here because you already have it from that chapter. The Set_Mode() function is declared as EXTERNAL, so you must compile and link it with the program. Listing 5.8 shows the Palette Demo program.

NOTE

I found a little problem with the VGA card in reading a palette register. It seems that the register you request is not the one you get all the time. This bug is hardware-specific and manifests itself only on some VGA cards. For now, my solution is to read each color register twice. That seems to fix it. In your code, you may want to try to detect this and use different palette-register functions if this bug exists. However, the time gained by making this observation during runtime is hardly worth it.

Listing 5.8. Creating and displaying a color palette (paldemo.c).

```c
// I N C L U D E S ///////////////////////////////////////////
#include <io.h>
#include <conio.h>
#include <stdio.h>
#include <stdlib.h>
#include <dos.h>
#include <bios.h>
#include <fcntl.h>
#include <memory.h>
#include <math.h>
#include <string.h>

// D E F I N E S ///////////////////////////////////////////
#define VGA256          0x13
#define TEXT_MODE       0x03

#define PALETTE_MASK      0x3c6
#define PALETTE_REGISTER  0x3c8
#define PALETTE_DATA      0x3c9

#define SCREEN_WIDTH    (unsigned int)320
#define SCREEN_HEIGHT   (unsigned int)200

// S T R U C T U R E S ///////////////////////////////////////////

// This structure holds an RGB triple in three bytes.

typedef struct RGB_color_typ
        {

        unsigned char red;    // This is the red component of
                              // color 0-63.
        unsigned char green;  // This is the green component of
                              // color 0-63.
        unsigned char blue;   // This is the blue component of
                              // color 0-63.

        } RGB_color, *RGB_color_ptr;

// E X T E R N A L S ///////////////////////////////////////////


extern Set_Mode(int mode);


// P R O T O T Y P E S ///////////////////////////////////////////

void Set_Palette_Register(int index, RGB_color_ptr color);
void Get_Palette_Register(int index, RGB_color_ptr color);
void Create_Cool_Palette(void);
void V_Line(int y1,int y2,int x,unsigned int color);

// G L O B A L S ///////////////////////////////////////////
```

continues

Listing 5.8. continued

```c
unsigned char far *video_buffer = (char far *)0xA0000000L;
// vram byte ptr
unsigned int far *video_buffer_w= (int far *)0xA0000000L;
// vram word ptr

// F U N C T I O N S ////////////////////////////////////////////

void Set_Palette_Register(int index, RGB_color_ptr color)
{

// This function sets a single color look-up table value indexed
// by index with the value in the color structure.

// Tell the VGA card that we are going to update a pallete
// register.

_outp(PALETTE_MASK,0xff);

// Tell the VGA card which register we will be updating.

_outp(PALETTE_REGISTER, index);

// Now update the RGB triple> Note: the same port is used
// each time.

_outp(PALETTE_DATA,color->red);
_outp(PALETTE_DATA,color->green);
_outp(PALETTE_DATA,color->blue);

} // end Set_Palette_Color

//////////////////////////////////////////////////////////////////

void Get_Palette_Register(int index, RGB_color_ptr color)
{

// This function gets the data out of a color register
// and places it into color.

// Set the palette mask register.

_outp(PALETTE_MASK,0xff);

// Tell the VGA card which register we will be reading.

_outp(PALETTE_REGISTER, index);

// Now extract the data.

color->red   = _inp(PALETTE_DATA);
color->green = _inp(PALETTE_DATA);
color->blue  = _inp(PALETTE_DATA);

} // end Get_Palette_Color
```

```
/////////////////////////////////////////////////////////////

void Create_Cool_Palette(void)
{

// This function creates a cool palette: 64 shades of gray, 64 of red,
// 64 of green, and 64 of blue.

RGB_color color;

int index;

// swipe through the color registers and create four banks
// of 64 colors each.

for (index=0; index < 64; index++)
    {

    // These are the grays:

    color.red   = index;
    color.green = index;
    color.blue  = index;

    Set_Palette_Register(index, (RGB_color_ptr)&color);

    // These are the reds:

    color.red   = index;
    color.green = 0;
    color.blue  = 0;

    Set_Palette_Register(index+64, (RGB_color_ptr)&color);

    // These are the greens:

    color.red   = 0;
    color.green = index;
    color.blue  = 0;

    Set_Palette_Register(index+128, (RGB_color_ptr)&color);

    // These are the blues:

    color.red   = 0;
    color.green = 0;
    color.blue  = index;

    Set_Palette_Register(index+192, (RGB_color_ptr)&color);

    } // end index

} // end Create_Cool_Palette

/////////////////////////////////////////////////////////////

void V_Line(int y1,int y2,int x,unsigned int color)
```

continues

Listing 5.8. continued

```
{
// Draw a vertical line. Note: y2 > y1.

unsigned int line_offset,
                      index;

// Compute the starting position.

line_offset = ((y1<<8) + (y1<<6)) + x;

for (index=0; index<=y2-y1; index++)
    {
    video_buffer[line_offset] = color;

     line_offset+=320; // Move to the next line.

    } // end for index

} // end V_Line

//M A I N /////////////////////////////////////////////////////////

void main(void)
{
int index;
RGB_color color,color_1;

// Set the video mode to the 320x200, 256 color mode.

Set_Mode(VGA256);

// Create the color palette.

Create_Cool_Palette();
// Draw a bunch of vertical lines, one for each color.

for (index=0; index<320; index++)
    V_Line(0,199,index,index);
// Wait for the player to press a key.

while(!kbhit())
    {
    Get_Palette_Register(0,(RGB_color_ptr)&color_1);
    Get_Palette_Register(0,(RGB_color_ptr)&color_1);

    for (index=0; index<=254; index++)
        {
        Get_Palette_Register(index+1,(RGB_color_ptr)&color);
        Get_Palette_Register(index+1,(RGB_color_ptr)&color);
        Set_Palette_Register(index,(RGB_color_ptr)&color);

        } // end for

    Set_Palette_Register(255,(RGB_color_ptr)&color_1);
```

```
        } // end while

// Put the computer back into text mode.

Set_Mode(TEXT_MODE);

} // end main
```

The program in Listing 5.8 creates a new palette that has 64 shades of all the primary colors, plus gray. It then draws a vertical line in each one of these colors, and then rotates the colors.

Enough with little dots and lines! We have to be able to read whole image files. Enter, stage left: .PCX files.

PCX Files

In the computer-graphics industry there are so many standards the word *standard* doesn't even mean what it's supposed to! Today's popular graphics formats are .GIF, .TIF, .RGB, .TGA, and .PCX—to name a few. We're interested in .PCX files because they're the PC's most popular format.

A .PCX file is a representation of an image that has been encoded. The encoding is necessary because we wouldn't want to save every pixel in a 320x200x256 image: a single image would take almost 64K of memory! However, drawn images have a great deal of *color coherence*; that is, there are a lot of the same colors in the same picture. We can use this to our advantage to compress the image into a smaller space.

> Photographs, on the other hand, don't have a lot of color coherence. They consist of many colors distributed all over the place, so they're harder to compress. As we'll be doing most of our artwork by hand, though, we needn't concern ourselves with digitized images and the problems that go along with them.

Take a look at Figure 5.5, which is a screen from Warlock. As you can see, there aren't that many colors—as a matter of fact, there are many large areas that have the exact same color.

Figure 5.5. *A screen from Warlock, which demonstrates that a limited number of colors are available to you.*

Why can't we just count the number of pixels with the same color and store the image as a group of counts, along with position and the color to replicate? We can. However, that technique is even more advanced than what we'll use, which is the .PCX format. The .PCX format uses *run-length encoding* (RLE). RLE operates on a line-by-line basis; that is, it's unaware of the vertical aspect of the image, and looks only at the horizontal aspect of each line of the image.

Take a look at Figure 5.6. The .PCX format processes each line of the image separately and compresses the line if it can. It does this by finding large runs of the same pixel. When a run is found, the number of pixels and the actual pixel value is recorded. This is done over and over for each line until the image is compressed.

This technique works great on many images, but it can backfire when an image has very few pixel runs. In those cases, RLE can actually expand the file. This happens when there are many adjacent pixels with different values. These pixels are recorded as runs with a length of one, therefore taking up two bytes instead of one.

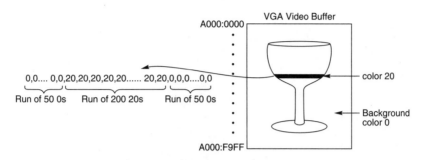

Each run can be encoded in the following manner:

(number of pixels that are the same), (pixel value)

In this case,

50, 0, 200, 20, 50, 0

Figure 5.6. *A run-length encoding (RLE) scheme.*

The .PCX file has three components:

- The first section of the .PCX file is 128 bytes long and contains a header with various kinds of information.

- The next section is the actual RLE image data, which can be any length.

- The last 768 bytes are the color palette, if there is one. In our case there's always a palette because we're using the 256-color mode 13h. The 768 bytes are the RGB bytes, in order, from color register 0 to 255.

Summing up, the .PCX file looks like Figure 5.7.

Reading the header section is straightforward: just read the first 128 bytes and format them as in the structure contained in Listing 5.9.

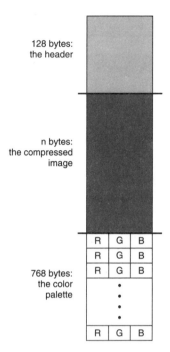

128 bytes: the header

n bytes: the compressed image

768 bytes: the color palette

Figure 5.7. *The .PCX file format.*

Listing 5.9. Reading and formatting the RLE header.

```
typedef struct pcx_header_typ
        {
        char manufacturer;        // This is always 10.
        char version;             // 0-Ver 2.5 Paintbrush,
                                  // 2-Ver 2.8 with palette.
                                  // 3-Ver 2.8 use default
                                  // palette, 5-Ver 3.0 or
                                  // better of Paintbrush.
        char encoding;            // This is always 1, meaning
                                  // RLE encoding.
        char bits_per_pixel;      // This is the bits per pixel;
                                  // in our case, 8.
        int x,y;                  // This is the upper-left corner
                                  // of the image.
        int width,height;         // This is the size of the image.
        int horz_res;             // This is the number of pixels
                                  // in the x direction.
        int vert_res;             // This is the number of pixels
                                  // in the y direction.
        char ega_palette[48];     // This is the EGA palette; we
                                  // can ignore it.
        char reserved;            // Nothing.
        char num_color_planes;    // This is the number of planes
                                  // in the image.
```

```
int bytes_per_line;      // This is the number of bytes
                         // per single horizontal line.
int palette_type;        // Don't worry about it.
char padding[58];        // Fat at end of file

} pcx_header, *pcx_header_ptr;
```

The last portion of the .PCX file, which is the palette, also can be obtained easily:

■ Move the file pointer to the end of the file.

■ Back up 768 bytes.

■ Read the palette in.

Now, I've purposely left out some details of the exact encoding of the .PCX file, just to let you think for a moment that it made sense. The problem is the stuff in the middle, which is the compressed data for the .PCX image.

After the first 128 bytes, the next byte and every byte thereafter is the .PCX data. As we're only concerned with mode 13h .PCX files, we must make sure that, after we have decompressed the .PCX file, all 64,000 pixels have been accounted for. Here comes the hard part, though. The compression is encoded in the following manner:

■ If the byte read is in the range of 192-255, we subtract 192 from it and use the result as the number of times to replicate the next byte.

■ If the byte read is from 0-191, we use that as the next value; therefore, we place it in the bit map unchanged.

If you're sharp (and I know you are), you'll see a little problem here. What about pixels that have the values from 192-255? Are they interpreted as RLE runs? In fact, yes. The brilliant solution to this—I'm being sarcastic—is to encode the values of 192-255 as runs of length one. For example, if I actually wanted a 200 in the image, I'd first place a 193 in the data stream and *then* a 200. Take a look at Figure 5.8 to see an example of decompression.

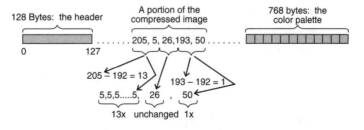

Decompressed data: 5,5,5,5,5,5,5,5,5,5,5,5,5,26,50

Figure 5.8. *Decompressing the .PCX file.*

Implementing a .PCX reader isn't as bad as it looks. Listing 5.10 does just that.

Listing 5.10. A .PCX reader.

```c
// Screen dimensions:
#define SCREEN_WIDTH 320
#define SCREEN_HEIGHT 200

// This structure is used to hold an entire .PCX entity.

typedef struct pcx_picture_typ
        {
        pcx_header header;         // This is the 128 byte header.
        RGB_color palette[256];    // This is storage for the
                                   // palette.
        char far *buffer;          // This is an area in which to
                                   // place the decompressed image.

        } pcx_picture, *pcx_picture_ptr;

//////////////////////////////////////////////////////////////////

void PCX_Load(char *filename, pcx_picture_ptr image,int enable_palette)
{
// This function loads a .PCX file into a picture structure. The
// actual image data for the .PCX file is decompressed and
// expanded into a secondary buffer within the picture structure.
// The separate images can be grabbed from this buffer later.
// The header and palette also are loaded.

FILE *fp;
int num_bytes,index;
long count;
unsigned char data;
char far *temp_buffer;

// Open the file.

fp = fopen(filename,"rb");

// Load the header.

temp_buffer = (char far *)image;

for (index=0; index<128; index++)
    {
    temp_buffer[index] = getc(fp);
    } // end for index

// Load the data and decompress it into the buffer.

count=0;

while(count<=SCREEN_WIDTH * SCREEN_HEIGHT)
    {
    // Get the first piece of data.
```

```
    data = getc(fp);

    // Is this an RLE?

    if (data>=192 && data<=255)
        {
        // How many bytes are in the run?

        num_bytes = data-192;

        // Get the actual data for the run.

        data  = getc(fp);

        // Replicate the data in the buffer num_bytes times.

        while(num_bytes—>0)
            {
            image->buffer[count++] = data;

            } // end while

        } // end if rle
    else
        {
        // Copy the actual data into the buffer at the next
        // location.

        image->buffer[count++] = data;

        } // end else not rle

    } // end while

// Move to the end of file, then back up 768 bytes (that is, to
// the beginning of the palette.

fseek(fp,-768L,SEEK_END);

// Load the palette into the VGA registers.

for (index=0; index<256; index++)
    {
    // Get the red component.

    image->palette[index].red   = (getc(fp) >> 2);

    // Get the green component.

    image->palette[index].green = (getc(fp) >> 2);

    // Get the blue component.

    image->palette[index].blue  = (getc(fp) >> 2);

    } // end for index
```

continues

Listing 5.10. continued

```
fclose(fp);

// Change the palette to the newly loaded palette if commanded
// to do so.

if (enable_palette)
   {

   for (index=0; index<256; index++)
       {

       Set_Palette_Register(index,(RGB_color_ptr)&image->palette[index]);

       } // end for index

   } // end if change palette

} // end PCX_Load

/////////////////////////////////////////////////////////////////
```

The PCX_Load() function is the workhorse of the .PCX file loader. This function loads a .PCX file, decompresses it into a buffer, and loads the palette (if you specify that it do so). I made the PCX_Load() function take a flag that denoted whether you wished the palette to be updated. Every .PCX file has its own palette attached at the end, and I thought you should have the option of loading a new palette into the color look-up table.

The function does exactly what you'd think it does. There's no magic:

■ The .PCX file is opened.

■ The header is read in.

■ The .PCX file is loaded and decompressed until we have decoded 64000 pixels.

■ Finally, the color palette is loaded.

Simple enough. Great, thrilling—but what are we supposed to do with a picture that takes up the whole screen? The answer is: we extract little pieces of the picture. These little pieces are 24x24 pixel bit maps. Moreover, they are regularly spaced in the 320x200-pixel matrix that represents the screen.

I've created a template for you called charplate.pcx, which you'll find on the companion CD. If you examine it, you'll see that it has a bunch of little white squares on it. You can use this template by drawing your game characters in the little white squares. We then extract the bit maps from the larger .PCX image and use them for the characters in our examples.

How are you going to draw and modify .PCX files in the 320x200x256 mode 13h format? I've included a couple of shareware programs, called VGA-Paint and Pro-Paint, on the companion CD-ROM. However, I suggest that you bite the bullet and purchase a copy of Electronic Arts' Deluxe Paint & Animation program. It's one of the most widely used PC paint programs, and works perfectly in 320x200x256 mode 13h. Also, it has all kinds of morphing and animation functions to help create your images.

Bit Blitting

Bit blitting is short for *binary block image transfer*. It's a term used by video-game players and programmers to describe the process of moving a group of bits (an image) from one place to another. In PC games, we're interested in moving images of our characters from their off-screen data storage areas to the video buffer. Take a look at Figure 5.9 to see a bit blit in action.

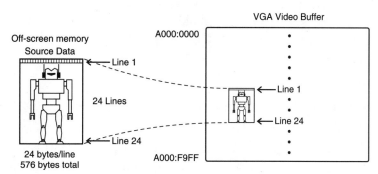

Figure 5.9. *Bit blitting in action.*

As you can see, a matrix of pixels is copied one-by-one from a source memory region to a destination memory region; usually, the screen buffer, although there are times when we would scan a portion of the video buffer and store it somewhere for further processing.

To get the concept of blitting down, we could write some functions that take a bit map that has been scanned from a .PCX and place it on the screen. That would get the point across, but I thought we might take a little "artistic freedom" here and dip into sprites and their animation.

Sprites

What is a sprite, you ask? (A lemon drink. Just kidding!) Sprites are little moveable objects on the video game field. The term was coined in the 70s by Apple and Atari people. So, let's talk about sprites and animation. Although we cover the topic of sprites and animation in Chapter 7, "Advanced Bit-Mapped Graphics and Special FX," it's good to at least preview what's to come. With that in mind, I've created a "sprite" class, which is what we'll use to represent our sprites.

A sprite is a little "player" in a PC game. This little player can move around the screen, animate, and change size and color—and do all this without much complication. Sounds like a video-game programmer's dream, huh? But guess what: IBM PCs don't have sprites! Sprites normally are implemented with hardware. PCs such as the Amiga, Atari, Commodore and newer Apples have hardware sprite engines, but the IBM PC does not. We have to emulate them ourselves, with software.

No problem. This will give us something to do.

Making a sprite engine takes a lot of time and effort, and we don't want to waste either just for demonstration purposes. All we want to do here is get a basic idea of how to place images on the screen with the ability to animate them and move them. Because a sprite is a high-level object, we first must take care of its low-level implementation. This is a good time to do another design phase, as we did with the asteroids game.

Here's what we need:

■ We must be able to grab a matrix of pixels from the loaded .PCX image and store it in a buffer associated with the sprite.

■ Moreover, we'd like to scan multiple images from the .PCX file and load them into an array that's associated with a single sprite. This would allow us to animate the sprite.

Figure 5.10 shows a sequence of frames that make an animated cowboy, which we use later.

After we load the data from the .PCX file for the sprite imagery, we want to be able to display the sprite at any location on the video screen. To do this, we must be careful. If we blast pixels onto the video display, we destroy whatever was there. Therefore, we must be able to scan what's under the place on which we'll be placing our sprite, so that we can replace it later.

Figure 5.10. *A walking cowboy.*

Let's take a tangent here for a moment and talk about animation structures. In a PC game there are two ways of building up a display:

■ We can redraw the entire screen frame by frame, as Wolfenstein-3D does.

■ We can redraw only portions of the screen.

Which track we take depends on the type of PC game we're making, and what kind of performance we need. If we redraw the entire screen, we'd best do it quickly because 64,000 pixels is a lot of little dots to be drawing. If we only draw portions of the screen, we'd better be careful not to destroy any of the background behind the images. As I've said before, each PC game is different, and you must use the best technique for the specific application.

Let's look at the method we use in this chapter, which is redrawing only portions of the screen. Take a look at Figure 5.11 to see the sequence of events that must occur to move a sprite properly.

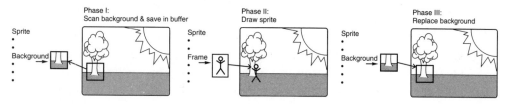

Figure 5.11. *The phases of animation.*

Now that we know what must be done, let's get to it. First let's create a sprite structure. Listing 5.11 contains code to take a first stab at it.

Listing 5.11. A sprite structure with fields for animation.

```
typedef struct sprite_typ
        {
        int x,y;              // This is the position of
                              // the sprite.
        int x_old,y_old;      // This is the old position of
                              // the sprite.
        int width,height;     // These are the dimensions of
                              // the sprite, in pixels.
        int anim_clock;       // This is the animation clock.
        int anim_speed;       // This is the animation speed.
        int motion_speed;     // This is the motion speed.
        int motion_clock;     // This is the motion clock.

        char far *frames[MAX_SPRITE_FRAMES];
                              // This is an array of pointers
                              // to the images.
        int curr_frame;       // This is the current frame being
                              // displayed.
        int num_frames;       // This is the total number of
                              // frames.
        int state;            // This is the state of the sprite
                              // (alive, dead...)
        char far *background; // This is what's underneath the
                              // sprite.

        } sprite, *sprite_ptr;
```

The sprite has fields for its positions, dimensions, imagery and a few other elements that might not make too much sense right now. We get to them later, but for now we're almost ready to write our first function.

Before we can do anything we must extract a bit map from the .PCX file and place it into the array that holds the images for the sprite. If you remember, I created a .PCX template in which you can draw the characters and their animations (charplate.pcx). The function that extracts the bit map from the .PCX image assumes you have drawn your images with this template. The code in Listing 5.12 enables you to send the sprite you want updated, along with the coordinate of the template "cell" you want scanned into the sprite, to the function.

Listing 5.12. A function to extract a rectangle from a loaded .PCX file.

```
////////////////////////////////////////////////////////////

void PCX_Grap_Bitmap(pcx_picture_ptr image,
                     sprite_ptr sprite,
                     int sprite_frame,
                     int grab_x, int grab_y)

{
// This function grabs a bit map from the .PCX frame buffer. It
```

```
// uses the convention that the 320x200-pixel matrix is sub-
// divided into a smaller matrix of 12x8 adjacent squares, each
// being a 24x24-pixel bit maps. The caller sends the .PCX
// picture along with the sprite to save the image into along
// with the frame of the sprite. Finally, the position of the
// bit map to be grabbed is sent.

int x_off,y_off, x,y, index;
char far *sprite_data;

// First, allocate the memory for the sprite in the sprite
// structure.

sprite->frames[sprite_frame] = (char far *)malloc(SPRITE_WIDTH * SPRITE_HEIGHT);

// Create an alias to the sprite frame for ease of access.

sprite_data = sprite->frames[sprite_frame];

// Now load the sprite data into the sprite-frame array from the
// .PCX picture

// We must find which bit map to scan. Remember: the .PCX
// picture is really a 12x8 matrix of bit maps, where each bit
// map is 24x24 pixels. Note: 0,0 is the upper-left bit map and
// 11,7 is the lower-right bit map.

x_off = 25 * grab_x + 1;
y_off = 25 * grab_y + 1;

// Compute the starting y address.

y_off = y_off * 320;

for (y=0; y<SPRITE_HEIGHT; y++)
    {

    for (x=0; x<SPRITE_WIDTH; x++)
        {

        // Get the next byte of the current row and place it
        // into the next position in the sprite-frame data
        // buffer.

        sprite_data[y*24 + x] = image->buffer[y_off + x_off + x];

        } // end for x

        // Move to the next line of the picture buffer.

        y_off+=320;

    } // end for y

// Increment the number of frames.

sprite->num_frames++;

// Done! Let's bail!
```

continues

Listing 5.12. continued

```
} // end PCX_Grap_Bitmap

//////////////////////////////////////////////////////////////////
```

The function in Listing 5.12 takes a sprite pointer and a cell location and scans it out of a loaded .PCX image for you. Moreover, it allocates the memory for image storage and initiates the data structure. (I've decided to make the sprites 24x24. There's no compelling reason to do this other than that 24x24 makes a good sprite.)

Now that we have the images for a sprite, the next step is to place sprites on the video screen. To place a sprite, we must:

- Compute its starting position, based on its x,y coordinates.
- Convert these coordinates into an address in the video buffer.
- Move the bytes of the image into the screen buffer.

To draw a sprite, we must perform the above operations with the current frame of animation. The code in Listing 5.13 does this.

Listing 5.13. Drawing a sprite.

```
//////////////////////////////////////////////////////////////////

void Draw_Sprite(sprite_ptr sprite)
{

// This function draws a sprite on the screen, row by row, very
// quickly. Note the use of shifting to implement multplication.

char far *work_sprite;
int work_offset=0,offset,x,y;
unsigned char data;

// Alias a pointer to the sprite for ease of access.

work_sprite = sprite->frames[sprite->curr_frame];

// Compute the offset of the sprite in the video buffer.

offset = (sprite->y << 8) + (sprite->y << 6) + sprite->x;

for (y=0; y<SPRITE_HEIGHT; y++)
    {

    for (x=0; x<SPRITE_WIDTH; x++)
        {

        // Test for a transparent pixel; that is, 0. If the
        // pixel isn't transparent, proceed with the drawing.
```

```
        if ((data=work_sprite[work_offset+x]))
            video_buffer[offset+x] = data;

    } // end for x

// Move to the next line in the video buffer and in the
// sprite bit-map buffer.

offset      += SCREEN_WIDTH;
work_offset += SPRITE_WIDTH;

    } // end for y

} // end Draw_Sprite
```

The function in Listing 5.13 works in much the same manner as does the pixel plotter in Listing 5.5. The start address of the sprite's destination is computed, and then the bytes of the sprite are blasted into the video buffer line by line.

Note that we could have made an optimization. Why not use the memcpy function to copy each line, as it's really a series of 24 bytes? The reason why is that we need to take into consideration *transparent pixels*. You see, the sprite usually is drawn with a background color, such as black. Moreover, we usually use color 0 to denote background (or "transparent"). Whenever we see a 0 in the data stream of the sprite, therefore, we want the background to show through. Take a look at Figure 5.12 to see an example of transparency.

Figure 5.12. *Transparency.*

This is why we must have an `if` clause in the draw loop. There are ways around this. Assembly language is one way to speed it up, but for now this is fast enough.

The next function we want to implement is something that scans the background just before we place a sprite. Remember: once we draw something into the video buffer, the image or data that was there is obliterated. Therefore, we must scan the background under a sprite *before* placement so we can restore the background later, when the sprite is moved. The code in Listing 5.14 does this.

Listing 5.14. Scanning the background behind the sprite.

```
/////////////////////////////////////////////////////////////////

void Behind_Sprite(sprite_ptr sprite)
{

// This function scans the background behind a sprite so that
// the background isn't obliterated when the sprite is drawn.

char far *work_back;
int work_offset=0,offset,y;

// Alias a pointer to the sprite background for ease of access.

work_back = sprite->background;

// Compute the offset of the background in the video buffer.

offset = (sprite->y << 8) + (sprite->y << 6) + sprite->x;

for (y=0; y<SPRITE_HEIGHT; y++)
    {
    // Copy the next row of the screen buffer into the sprite
    // background buffer.

    _fmemcpy((char far *)&work_back[work_offset],
            (char far *)&video_buffer[offset],
            SPRITE_WIDTH);

    // Move to the next line in the video buffer and in the
    // sprite background buffer.

    offset      += SCREEN_WIDTH;
    work_offset += SPRITE_WIDTH;

    } // end for y

} // end Behind_Sprite

/////////////////////////////////////////////////////////////////
```

The Behind_Sprite() function scans the 24x24-pixel matrix where the sprite is about to be placed. The data from this scan is stored in the *background field* of the sprite. The background field is a pointer to a block of memory where the actual data bytes are stored.

That's all the functionality we need to draw little creatures on the screen and move them around. As far as animation goes, we must change the curr_frame field in the sprite structure before drawing the sprite. We discuss animation later in this chapter, but I think you get the idea. We just erase the sprite, move the sprite and draw the sprite—and do that over and over—and that's all there is to it.

Text Blitting

One last topic that's important in PC games is printing text! Many people leave this topic untouched and don't even point you in the right direction. Being able to print out text in a PC game is absolutely necessary, and this section spends some time on it.

Because our PC game will be running in a graphics mode and not in a text mode, the only way we're going to be able to "print" text is to blit it on the screen pixel by pixel. However, where are we going to get the data for the bit maps? We could draw all 128 characters and load them using a .PCX file, but this would be overkill for our purposes. I'd much rather find the PC's bit maps for the internal character set, hidden away in the darkest regions of its memory. If we could find these, we could use the data to blit characters and strings on the screen in any color or size we wanted. Guess what? I know exactly where the ROM character sets are and how to address them. (Should I tell? I guess so.)

The data for the 8x8 ROM Character Set can be found at the starting address F000:FA6E. The characters are in order of the ASCII sequence; therefore, the character 'A' would be the 65th in the sequence. Each character is composed of eight bytes, where each byte is a single line of the bit map for the respective character. Hence, we must multiply the 65 from our previous example by eight to find the offset of the first byte of data in the character set. This offset is then added to the base address of F000:FA6E, and the eight bytes found there are each line of the character. Take a look at Figure 5.13 to get a byte on this.

We have just one little problem in mode 13h: we need a byte for each pixel—not a bit, as we have in this case. This is because each line of any character in the ROM character set has one byte per line. Well, no matter. What we do is to send the color we want the character to be, then replicate this color into a line of pixels depending on the value of each bit in the current line of the character (which itself is a single byte).

The algorithm works like this:

- Get the next line of the character data (that is, the next byte).

- Draw eight horizontal pixels, where pixels 0-7 are turned on or off depending on whether bits 0-7 in the data byte are on or off.

- Do this for each line.

Listing 5.15 contains the code to blit a character on the screen at any location and color.

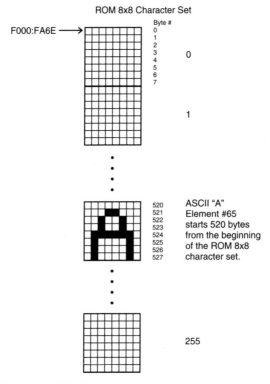

Figure 5.13. *The 8x8 ROM Character Set.*

Listing 5.15. Character-blitting code.

```
//////////////////////////////////////////////////////////////

void Blit_Char(int xc,int yc,char c,int color)
{
// This function uses the ROM 8x8 Character Set to blit a
// character on the video screen. Notice the trick used to
// extract bits from each character byte that comprises a line.
```

```c
int offset,x,y;
unsigned char data;
char far *work_char;
unsigned char bit_mask = 0x80;

// Compute the starting offset in the ROM character
// look-up table.

work_char = rom_char_set + c * CHAR_HEIGHT;

// Compute the offset of the character in the video buffer.

offset = (yc << 8) + (yc << 6) + xc;

for (y=0; y<CHAR_HEIGHT; y++)
    {
    // Reset the bit mask.

    bit_mask = 0x80;

    for (x=0; x<CHAR_WIDTH; x++)
        {
        // Test for a transparent pixel; that is, 0. If the
        // pixel isn't transparent, proceed with the drawing.

        if ((*work_char & bit_mask))
            video_buffer[offset+x] = color;

        // Shift the bit mask.

        bit_mask = (bit_mask>>1);

        } // end for x

    // Move to the next line in the video buffer and in the ROM
    // character data area.

    offset    += SCREEN_WIDTH;
    work_char++;

    } // end for y

} // end Blit_Char

/////////////////////////////////////////////////////////////////////
```

Printing out a whole string is easy now. We need only space the characters out by their width, which is eight, and print them one by one until a NULL is encountered in the string. The demo program at the end of this chapter uses a function like this.

We've covered a ton of ground in this chapter, and your brain is probably frying right about now. Let's slow down the pace and talk about a couple of details of animation and rendering that we must consider in video-game programming.

Double Buffering

No, double buffering is *not* adding a base to an acid to neutralize it. It's a method used in displaying graphics to get rid of the flicker that can occur when objects are drawn and moved. When the functions we have written draw sprites on the screen, they do it without regard for the VGA card's state; that is, they draw and erase without synchronizing with the video display. There are two ways to minimize the flickering that can occur:

■ Method one is *double buffering*. The entire screen is draw on an off-screen buffer, then the entire screen is blasted to the video buffer at once. This minimizes messing with all the small sections of the video buffer, and does its job in one big movement of data. Take a look at Figure 5.14 for a graphical example.

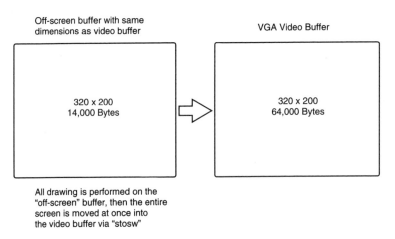

Off-screen buffer with same
dimensions as video buffer

VGA Video Buffer

320 x 200
14,000 Bytes

320 x 200
64,000 Bytes

All drawing is performed on the
"off-screen" buffer, then the entire
screen is moved at once into
the video buffer via "stosw"

Figure 5.14. *Double buffering.*

■ *Page flipping* is a twist on double buffering. Using this method, two video pages are in existence. When one is being displayed, the other is being re-drawn. The fresh page is then displayed by way of moving a hardware pointer to the new page—and, instantly, the new view is displayed. See Figure 5.15 for a graphical representation of page flipping.

Both these methods have their drawbacks—twice as much drawing has to be done—but there is virtually no flicker, and the animation will look as smooth as polished silica.

We see these concepts in action in Chapter 7, "Advanced Bit-Mapped Graphics and Special FX." For now, just know they exist and that we can get rid of the flicker.

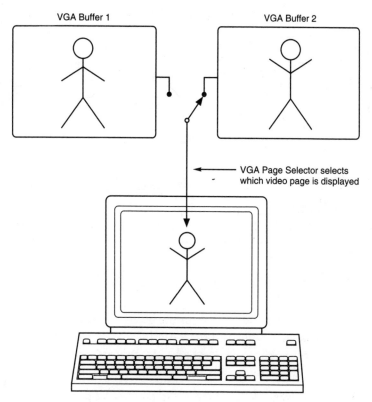

Figure 5.15. *Page flipping.*

Vertical Retrace Syncing

The image drawn on the screen by the CRT and controlled by the VGA card is done in an exact manner:

- A beam of electrons swipes across the screen, left to right, top to bottom, drawing the picture.

- When it reaches the bottom it moves back up to the top and starts again. Figure 5.16 shows a representation of this.

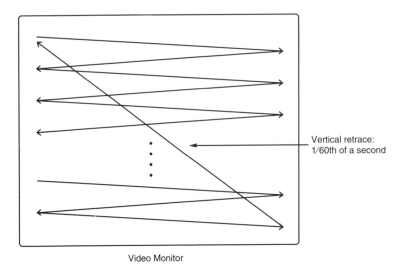

Video Monitor

Figure 5.16. *The vertical retrace.*

■ The 1/60th of a second it takes for the beam to move back to the top (the *retrace period*, as it's called) is the ideal time to change the video buffer. The video buffer is not accessed by the VGA hardware during the retrace period. The 1/60th of a second is a hardware-dependent timing parameter.

In Chapter 7, "Advanced Bit-Mapped Graphics and Special FX," we learn how to "synchronize" our game to this signal and create flicker-free screen updates.

Timing is Everything

I tried to think up a cool demo of the sprite software here. I figured you could make a little town with a cowboy who walked across a street. So far, so good. Then I thought you could shoot him and watch his guts get splattered all over the place. Then I decided that, for now, that's a bit much. We don't want to cloud the use of the graphics functions with a lot of game logic yet.

To perform realistic animation, we must pay attention to *timing*. If a character has ten frames of animation, and we arbitrarily change frames or move the character, it will look like the character is moonwalking! We must have timers that count clicks so our characters do things when the proper number of clicks has occurred. In our case, we use four variables to keep track of the motion and animation timing:

■ `anim_clock`

■ `anim_speed`

■ `motion_clock`

■ `motion_speed`

The speed variables are set, constant values; the clock variables are updated every time they go through the main loop. When the clock variables become larger than the speed variables, we perform an action such as moving the sprite or changing frames. The clocks are then reset. This enables us to make the animation and motion independent of each other and (to an extent) independent of the speed of the machine.

We talk at length about animation, timing, and so on in Chapter 7, "Advanced Bit-Mapped Graphics and Special FX."

Tombstone

We've gone from knowing nothing about the VGA card to actually knowing a great deal. I would bet that you could write a decent 2-D game at this point. To help you along, I've created a demo called Tombstone.

In Tombstone, a little cowboy walks across an Old Western town at different speeds. You have all the tools you need to add a gun and some shooting. Also, within the .PCX file the cowboy is in, there are "pain" or "death" frames I drew for the cowboy if he were to meet with the barrel of a Colt .45. See if you can add a gun, shooting, and a death sequence. The entire program is given in Listing 5.16, with the exception of the `Set_Mode()` function. Link `Set_Mode()` in when you create the executable file.

Press any key to exit the demo, and you'll see the coolest single line of code at work! Have fun—that's what games are about.

Listing 5.16. TOMBSTONE (Tomb.c).

```
// I N C L U D E S /////////////////////////////////////////////////

#include <io.h>
#include <conio.h>
#include <stdio.h>
#include <stdlib.h>
#include <dos.h>
#include <bios.h>
#include <fcntl.h>
#include <memory.h>
```

continues

Listing 5.16. continued

```c
#include <math.h>
#include <string.h>

// D E F I N E S //////////////////////////////////////////////

#define ROM_CHAR_SET_SEG 0xF000     // This is a segment of the
                                    // ROM 8x8 Character Set.
#define ROM_CHAR_SET_OFF 0xFA6E     // This is the beginning
                                    // offset of the ROM 8x8
                                    // Character Set.

#define VGA256          0x13
#define TEXT_MODE       0x03

#define PALETTE_MASK        0x3c6
#define PALETTE_REGISTER    0x3c8
#define PALETTE_DATA        0x3c9

#define SCREEN_WIDTH        (unsigned int)320
#define SCREEN_HEIGHT       (unsigned int)200

#define CHAR_WIDTH      8
#define CHAR_HEIGHT     8

#define SPRITE_WIDTH        24
#define SPRITE_HEIGHT       24
#define MAX_SPRITE_FRAMES 16
#define SPRITE_DEAD         0
#define SPRITE_ALIVE        1
#define SPRITE_DYING        2

// S T R U C T U R E S /////////////////////////////////////////

// This structure holds an RGB triple in three bytes.

typedef struct RGB_color_typ
        {

        unsigned char red;      // This is the red component of
                                // color 0-63.
        unsigned char green;    // This is the green component of
                                // color 0-63.
        unsigned char blue;     // This is the blue component of
                                // color 0-63.

        } RGB_color, *RGB_color_ptr;

typedef struct pcx_header_typ
        {
        char manufacturer;
        char version;
        char encoding;
        char bits_per_pixel;
        int x,y;
        int width,height;
        int horz_res;
        int vert_res;
```

```
          char ega_palette[48];
          char reserved;
          char num_color_planes;
          int bytes_per_line;
          int palette_type;
          char padding[58];

          } pcx_header, *pcx_header_ptr;


typedef struct pcx_picture_typ
          {
          pcx_header header;
          RGB_color palette[256];
          char far *buffer;

          } pcx_picture, *pcx_picture_ptr;


typedef struct sprite_typ
          {
          int x,y;              // This is the position of
                                // the sprite.
          int x_old,y_old;      // This is the old position of
                                // the sprite.
          int width,height;     // These are the dimensions of
                                // the sprite, in pixels.
          int anim_clock;       // This is the animation clock.
          int anim_speed;       // This is the animation speed.
          int motion_speed;     // This is the motion speed.
          int motion_clock;     // This is the motion clock.

          char far *frames[MAX_SPRITE_FRAMES];
                                // This is an array of pointers
                                // to the images.
          int curr_frame;       // This is the current frame being
                                // displayed.
          int num_frames;       // This is the total number of
                                // frames.
          int state;            // This is the state of the sprite
                                // (alive, dead...)
          char far *background; // This is what's underneath the
                                // sprite.

          } sprite, *sprite_ptr;


// E X T E R N A L S ///////////////////////////////////////////


extern Set_Mode(int mode);


// P R O T O T Y P E S /////////////////////////////////////////

void Set_Palette_Register(int index, RGB_color_ptr color);

void Plot_Pixel_Fast(int x,int y,unsigned char color);
```

continues

Listing 5.16. continued

```c
void PCX_Init(pcx_picture *image);

void PCX_Delete(pcx_picture *image);

void PCX_Load(char *filename, pcx_picture_ptr image,int enable_palette);

void PCX_Show_Buffer(pcx_picture_ptr image);

// G L O B A L S ////////////////////////////////////////////////

unsigned char far *video_buffer = (char far *)0xA0000000L;
    // vram byte ptr
unsigned int far *video_buffer_w= (int far *)0xA0000000L;
    // vram word ptr
unsigned char far *rom_char_set = (char far *)0xF000FA6EL;
    // ROM characters 8x8


// F U N C T I O N S ////////////////////////////////////////////

//////////////////////////////////////////////////////////////////

void Blit_Char(int xc,int yc,char c,int color)
{
// This function uses the ROM 8x8 Character Set to blit a
// character on the video screen. Notice the trick used to
// extract bits from each character byte that comprises a line.
int offset,x,y;
unsigned char data;
char far *work_char;
unsigned char bit_mask = 0x80;

// Compute the starting offset in the ROM character
// look-up table.

work_char = rom_char_set + c * CHAR_HEIGHT;

// Compute the offset of the character in the video buffer.

offset = (yc << 8) + (yc << 6) + xc;

for (y=0; y<CHAR_HEIGHT; y++)
    {
    // Reset the bit mask.

    bit_mask = 0x80;

    for (x=0; x<CHAR_WIDTH; x++)
        {
        // Test for a transparent pixel; that is, 0. If the
        // pixel isn't transparent, proceed with the drawing.

        if ((*work_char & bit_mask))
            video_buffer[offset+x] = color;

        // Shift the bit mask.

        bit_mask = (bit_mask>>1);
```

```
        } // end for x

    // Move to the next line in the video buffer and in the ROM
    // character data area.

    offset      += SCREEN_WIDTH;
    work_char++;

    } // end for y

} // end Blit_Char

//////////////////////////////////////////////////////////////////

void Blit_String(int x,int y,int color, char *string)
{
// This function blits an entire string on the screen with fixed
// spacing between each character, and calls the blit_char
// function.

int index;

for (index=0; string[index]!=0; index++)
    {

    Blit_Char(x+(index<<3),y,string[index],color);

    } /* end while */

} /* end Blit_String */

//////////////////////////////////////////////////////////////////

void Delay(int t)
{

float x = 1;

while(t—>0)
    x=cos(x);

} // end Delay

//////////////////////////////////////////////////////////////////

void Set_Palette_Register(int index, RGB_color_ptr color)
{

// This function sets a single color look-up table value indexed by index
// with the value in the color structure.

// Tell the VGA card we are going to update a palette register.

_outp(PALETTE_MASK,0xff);

// Tell the VGA card which register we will be updating.

_outp(PALETTE_REGISTER, index);
```

continues

Listing 5.16. continued

```c
// Now update the RGB triple. Note: the same port is used
// each time.

_outp(PALETTE_DATA,color->red);
_outp(PALETTE_DATA,color->green);
_outp(PALETTE_DATA,color->blue);

} // end Set_Palette_Color

///////////////////////////////////////////////////////////////

void PCX_Init(pcx_picture_ptr image)
{
// This function allocates the buffer region needed to load a
// .PCX file.

if (!(image->buffer = (char far *)malloc(SCREEN_WIDTH * SCREEN_HEIGHT + 1)))

   printf("\ncouldn't allocate screen buffer");

} // end PCX_Init

///////////////////////////////////////////////////////////////

void Plot_Pixel_Fast(int x,int y,unsigned char color)
{

// This function plots the pixel in the desired color a little
// quicker by using binary shifting to accomplish the
// multiplications.

// Use the fact that 320*y = 256*y + 64*y = y<<8 + y<<6.

video_buffer[((y<<8) + (y<<6)) + x] = color;

} // end Plot_Pixel_Fast

///////////////////////////////////////////////////////////////

void PCX_Delete(pcx_picture_ptr image)
{
// This function deallocates the buffer region used for the
// .PCX file loaded.

_ffree(image->buffer);

} // end PCX_Delete

///////////////////////////////////////////////////////////////

void PCX_Load(char *filename, pcx_picture_ptr image,int enable_palette)
{
// This function loads a .PCX file into a picture structure. The
// actual image data for the .PCX file is decompressed and
// expanded into a secondary buffer within the picture structure.
// The separate images can be grabbed from this buffer later.
```

```
// The header and palette also are loaded.

FILE *fp, *fopen();
int num_bytes,index;
long count;
unsigned char data;
char far *temp_buffer;

// Open the file.

fp = fopen(filename,"rb");

// Load the header.

temp_buffer = (char far *)image;

for (index=0; index<128; index++)
    {
    temp_buffer[index] = getc(fp);
    } // end for index

// Load the data and decompress it into the buffer.

count=0;

while(count<=SCREEN_WIDTH * SCREEN_HEIGHT)
    {
    // Get the first piece of data.

    data = getc(fp);

    // Is this an REL?

    if (data>=192 && data<=255)
        {
        // How many bytes are in the run?

        num_bytes = data-192;

        // Get the actual data for the run.

        data  = getc(fp);

        // Replicate the data in the buffer num_bytes times.

        while(num_bytes—>0)
            {
            image->buffer[count++] = data;

            } // end while

        } // end if rle
    else
        {
        // Copy the actual data into the buffer at the next
        // location.

        image->buffer[count++] = data;
```

continues

Listing 5.16. continued

```
            } // end else not rle

        } // end while

    // Move to the end of file, then back up 768 bytes (that is, to
    // the beginning of the palette.

    fseek(fp,-768L,SEEK_END);

    // Load the palette into the VGA hardware.

    for (index=0; index<256; index++)
        {
        // Get the red component.

        image->palette[index].red   = (getc(fp) >> 2);

        // Get the green component.

        image->palette[index].green = (getc(fp) >> 2);

        // Get the blue component.

        image->palette[index].blue  = (getc(fp) >> 2);

        } // end for index

    fclose(fp);

    // Change the palette to the newly loaded palette if commanded
    // to do so.

    if (enable_palette)
        {

        for (index=0; index<256; index++)
            {

            Set_Palette_Register(index,(RGB_color_ptr)&image->palette[index]);

            } // end for index

        } // end if change palette

} // end PCX_Load

///////////////////////////////////////////////////////////////////

void PCX_Show_Buffer(pcx_picture_ptr image)
{
// Copy the .PCX buffer into the video buffer.

_fmemcpy((char far *)video_buffer,
         (char far *)image->buffer,SCREEN_WIDTH*SCREEN_HEIGHT);

} // end PCX_Show_Picture
```

```
//////////////////////////////////////////////////////////////////

Sprite_Init(sprite_ptr sprite,int x,int y,int ac,int as,int mc,int ms)
{
// This function initializes a sprite with the sent data.

int index;

sprite->x            = x;
sprite->y            = y;
sprite->x_old        = x;
sprite->y_old        = y;
sprite->width        = SPRITE_WIDTH;
sprite->height       = SPRITE_HEIGHT;
sprite->anim_clock   = ac;
sprite->anim_speed   = as;
sprite->motion_clock = mc;
sprite->motion_speed = ms;
sprite->curr_frame   = 0;
sprite->state        = SPRITE_DEAD;
sprite->num_frames   = 0;
sprite->background   = (char far *)fmalloc(SPRITE_WIDTH * SPRITE_HEIGHT+1);

// Set all bit-map pointers to null.

for (index=0; index<MAX_SPRITE_FRAMES; index++)
    sprite->frames[index] = NULL;

} // end Sprite_Init

//////////////////////////////////////////////////////////////////

void Sprite_Delete(sprite_ptr sprite)
{
// This function deletes all the memory associated with
// a sprite.

int index;

_ffree(sprite->background);

// Now deallocate all the animation frames.

for (index=0; index<MAX_SPRITE_FRAMES; index++)
    _ffree(sprite->frames[index]);

} // end Sprite_Delete

//////////////////////////////////////////////////////////////////

void PCX_Grap_Bitmap(pcx_picture_ptr image,
                sprite_ptr sprite,
                int sprite_frame,
                int grab_x, int grab_y)

{
```

continues

Listing 5.16. continued

```
// This function grabs a bit map from the .PCX frame buffer. It
// uses the convention that the 320x200-pixel matrix is sub-
// divided into a smaller matrix of 12x8 adjacent squares, each
// being a 24x24-pixel bit maps. The caller sends the .PCX
// picture along with the sprite to save the image into along
// with the frame of the sprite. Finally, the position of the
// bit map to be grabbed is sent.

int x_off,y_off, x,y, index;
char far *sprite_data;

// First, allocate the memory for the sprite in the
// sprite structure.

sprite->frames[sprite_frame] = (char far *)fmalloc(SPRITE_WIDTH * SPRITE_HEIGHT);

// Create an alias to the sprite frame for ease of access.

sprite_data = sprite->frames[sprite_frame];

// Now load the sprite data into the sprite-frame array from the
// .PCX picture.

// We must find which bit map to scan. Remember: the .PCX
// picture is really a 12x8 matrix of bit maps, where each bit
// map is 24x24-pixels. Note: 0,0 is the upper-left bit map and
// 11,7 is the lower-right bit map.

x_off = 25 * grab_x + 1;
y_off = 25 * grab_y + 1;

// Compute the starting y address.

y_off = y_off * 320;

for (y=0; y<SPRITE_HEIGHT; y++)
    {

    for (x=0; x<SPRITE_WIDTH; x++)
        {

        // Get the next byte of the current row and place it
        // into the next position in sprite-frame data buffer.

        sprite_data[y*24 + x] = image->buffer[y_off + x_off + x];

        } // end for x

        // Move to the next line of the picture buffer.

        y_off+=320;

    } // end for y

// Increment the number of frames.

sprite->num_frames++;
```

```
// Done! Let's bail!

} // end PCX_Grap_Bitmap

////////////////////////////////////////////////////////////////

void Behind_Sprite(sprite_ptr sprite)
{

// This function scans the background behind a sprite so that
// the background isn't obliterated when the sprite is drawn.

char far *work_back;
int work_offset=0,offset,y;

// Alias a pointer to the sprite background for ease of access.

work_back = sprite->background;

// Compute the offset of the background in the video buffer.

offset = (sprite->y << 8) + (sprite->y << 6) + sprite->x;

for (y=0; y<SPRITE_HEIGHT; y++)
    {
    // Copy the next row of the screen buffer into the sprite
    // background buffer.

    _fmemcpy((char far *)&work_back[work_offset],
            (char far *)&video_buffer[offset],
            SPRITE_WIDTH);

    // Move to the next line in the video buffer and in the
    // sprite background buffer.

    offset      += SCREEN_WIDTH;
    work_offset += SPRITE_WIDTH;

    } // end for y

} // end Behind_Sprite

////////////////////////////////////////////////////////////////

void Erase_Sprite(sprite_ptr sprite)
{
// Replace the background that was behind the sprite.

// This function replaces the background that was saved from
// where a sprite was going to be placed.

char far *work_back;
int work_offset=0,offset,y;

// Alias a pointer to sprite background for ease of access.

work_back = sprite->background;
```

continues

Listing 5.16. continued

```c
// Compute the offset of the background in the video buffer.

offset = (sprite->y_old << 8) + (sprite->y_old << 6) + sprite->x_old;

for (y=0; y<SPRITE_HEIGHT; y++)
    {
    // Copy the next row of the screen buffer into the sprite
    // background buffer.

    _fmemcpy((char far *)&video_buffer[offset],
             (char far *)&work_back[work_offset],
             SPRITE_WIDTH);

    // Move to the next line in the video buffer and in the
    // sprite background buffer.

    offset      += SCREEN_WIDTH;
    work_offset += SPRITE_WIDTH;

    } // end for y


} // end Erase_Sprite

/////////////////////////////////////////////////////////////////

void Draw_Sprite(sprite_ptr sprite)
{

// This function draws a sprite on the screen, row by row, very
// quickly. Note the use of shifting to implement
// multiplication.

char far *work_sprite;
int work_offset=0,offset,x,y;
unsigned char data;

// Alias a pointer to the sprite for ease of access.

work_sprite = sprite->frames[sprite->curr_frame];

// Compute the offset of the sprite in the video buffer.

offset = (sprite->y << 8) + (sprite->y << 6) + sprite->x;

for (y=0; y<SPRITE_HEIGHT; y++)
    {
    // Copy the next row into the screen buffer using memcpy
    // for speed.

    for (x=0; x<SPRITE_WIDTH; x++)
        {

        // Test for a transparent pixel; that is, 0. If the
        // pixel isn't transparent, proceed with the drawing.
```

```
        if ((data=work_sprite[work_offset+x]))
            video_buffer[offset+x] = data;

        } // end for x

    // Move to the next line in the video buffer and in the
    // sprite bit-map buffer.

    offset       += SCREEN_WIDTH;
    work_offset += SPRITE_WIDTH;

    } // end for y

} // end Draw_Sprite


// M A I N ///////////////////////////////////////////////////


void main(void)
{

long index,redraw;
RGB_color color;
int frame_dir = 1;

pcx_picture town, cowboys;

sprite cowboy;

// Set the video mode to the 320x200, 256 color mode.

Set_Mode(VGA256);

// Set up the global pointers to screen RAM.

// Load the background.

PCX_Init((pcx_picture_ptr)&town);
PCX_Load("town.pcx", (pcx_picture_ptr)&town,1);
PCX_Show_Buffer((pcx_picture_ptr)&town);

PCX_Delete((pcx_picture_ptr)&town);

// Print the header.

Blit_String(128, 24,50, "TOMBSTONE");

// Load in the cowboy imagery.

PCX_Init((pcx_picture_ptr)&cowboys);
PCX_Load("cowboys.pcx", (pcx_picture_ptr)&cowboys,0);

// Grab all the images from the cowboy's .PCX picture.

Sprite_Init((sprite_ptr)&cowboy,SPRITE_WIDTH,100,0,7,0,3);

PCX_Grap_Bitmap((pcx_picture_ptr)&cowboys,(sprite_ptr)&cowboy,0,0,0);
```

continues

Listing 5.16. continued

```
PCX_Grap_Bitmap((pcx_picture_ptr)&cowboys,(sprite_ptr)&cowboy,1,1,0);
PCX_Grap_Bitmap((pcx_picture_ptr)&cowboys,(sprite_ptr)&cowboy,2,2,0);
PCX_Grap_Bitmap((pcx_picture_ptr)&cowboys,(sprite_ptr)&cowboy,3,1,0);

// Kill the .PCX memory and buffers now that we're done.

PCX_Delete((pcx_picture_ptr)&cowboys);

Behind_Sprite((sprite_ptr)&cowboy);
Draw_Sprite((sprite_ptr)&cowboy);

// main loop

cowboy.state = SPRITE_ALIVE;

while(!kbhit())
     {

     redraw = 0; // used to flag if we need a redraw

     if (cowboy.state==SPRITE_ALIVE)
        {
        // Test to determine if it's time to change frames.

        if (++cowboy.anim_clock > cowboy.anim_speed)
           {
           // Reset the animation clock.

           cowboy.anim_clock = 0;

           if (++cowboy.curr_frame >= cowboy.num_frames)
              {
              cowboy.curr_frame = 0;

              } // End if reached last frame

           redraw=1;

           } // end if time to change frames

        // Now test to determine if it's time to move
        // the cowboy.

        if (++cowboy.motion_clock > cowboy.motion_speed)
           {
           // Reset the motion clock.

           cowboy.motion_clock = 0;

           // Save the old position.

           cowboy.x_old = cowboy.x;

           redraw = 1;

           // Move the cowboy.
```

```
            if (++cowboy.x >= SCREEN_WIDTH-2*SPRITE_WIDTH)
               {

               Erase_Sprite((sprite_ptr)&cowboy);
               cowboy.state = SPRITE_DEAD;
               redraw          = 0;

               } // end if reached last frame

            } // end if time to change frames

         } // end if cowboy alive
      else
         {
         // Try to start up another cowboy.

         if (rand()%100 == 0 )
            {
            cowboy.state       = SPRITE_ALIVE;
            cowboy.x           = SPRITE_WIDTH;
            cowboy.curr_frame = 0;
            cowboy.anim_speed   = 3 + rand()%6;
            cowboy.motion_speed = 1 + rand()%3;
            cowboy.anim_clock   = 0;
            cowboy.motion_clock = 0;

            Behind_Sprite((sprite_ptr)&cowboy);
            }

         } // end else dead, try to bring back to life

      // Now the sprite has had its state updated.

      if (redraw)
         {
         // Erase the sprite at the old position.

         Erase_Sprite((sprite_ptr)&cowboy);

         // Scan the background at the new postition.

         Behind_Sprite((sprite_ptr)&cowboy);

         // Draw the sprite at the new position.

         Draw_Sprite((sprite_ptr)&cowboy);

         // Update the old position.

         cowboy.x_old = cowboy.x;
         cowboy.y_old = cowboy.y;

         } // end if sprites needed to be redrawn

   Delay(1000);

   } // end while
```

continues

Listing 5.16. continued

```
// Make a cool clear screen and dissolve the screen (in one
// line, eye might add!).

for (index=0; index<=300000; index++,Plot_Pixel_Fast(rand()%320, rand()%200, 0));

// Put the computer back into text mode.

Set_Mode(TEXT_MODE);

} // end main
```

Summary

This is probably the most important chapter of the entire book. Even though most of the information within doesn't directly relate to video games, the information and concepts are absolutely necessary if we are to write games. So if there's anything you didn't understand, stop right here and read the chapter again. (Don't worry; I'll wait.)

If you've read and mastered the information within this chapter, you know that:

- We covered the VGA card and briefly discussed its architecture.

- Then we focused on the video mode that we're most interested in: mode 13h. This mode offers the best resolution and color of all standard VGA modes, and is the easiest to program.

- We covered myriad topics relating to programming the VGA in mode 13h, such as programming color registers, plotting pixels, loading .PCX files, and bit blitting.

- We also began our first discussions of sprites, and we even implemented a simple sprite engine.

- We touched upon some advanced topics that are further explored in later chapters. Among these were concepts such as double buffering and vertical syncing.

- Finally, we put everything together and made a demo program that displays a little cowboy walking across the street (although he looks a bit stiff at this point!)

I'll meet you in the next chapter. Grab a slide rule—you may need one!

The Third Dimension

R ecent advances in both hardware and software have brought the fantasy of three-dimensional video games into tangible reality on the PC. Video-game programmers today can create 3-D games on inexpensive PCs, allowing players to have experiences that a couple years ago would have been impossible.

Granted, there have been flight simulators and a few 3-D games on the market in the past. However, they were always too slow or impractical to market to the general public: to run at a reasonable rate they needed at least a 386, with a 486 being desirable. These limitations forced video-game programmers to find ways of creating 3-D rendering techniques that are quite different from the traditional methods used in polygon-based 3-D graphics. These new techniques are incredibly clever and can make a PC perform in ways that simply wouldn't have been believed a few years ago.

In this chapter we discuss traditional methods by which 3-D graphics are rendered on the PC, and then dive into ray casting. Ray casting is a

by André LaMothe

technique that renders 3-D views with lightning speed. It also lends itself naturally to texture mapping and shading.

In this chapter we cover:

- Three-dimensional space
- Points, lines, polygons, and objects in 3-D
- Translation, scaling, and rotation in 3-D
- Projections
- Solid modeling
- Hidden-surface removal
- The "Painter's Algorithm"
- The "Z-Buffer Algorithm"
- Texturing
- Ray tracing
- Ray casting
- Implementing a ray caster
- Improving that ray caster
- Implementing doors and transparency
- Lighting, shading, and our color palette

We begin our lesson with some general 3-D concepts to refresh your memory and understanding. Then we jump right in and figure out how to create games like Wolfenstein, DOOM, and Terminator Rampage!

Three-Dimensional Space

Three-dimensional space... it sounds like something out of a science fiction book, doesn't it? Three-dimensional (3-D) space is really an extension of the 2-D plane. Rendering 3-D graphics is *not* easy. Somehow, the complexity of rendering graphics seems to increase in an exponential way to accommodate the paltry addition of one more dimension. The reason for this, in my opinion, is that the image complexity increases proportionally to the square of the dimension; therefore, whatever the complexity of rendering and manipulating a 2-D scene, it becomes easily many times more complex when we add that third dimension.

Learning how to deal with that added dimension is our goal. This should all be review for you by this time. However, one more time can't hurt, so here we go.

Mathematically speaking, a point in 3-D space is uniquely described by three coordinates: x, y, and z. As discussed in Chapter 4, "The Mechanics of Two-Dimensional Graphics," if the screen is the x,y plane, then the z-axis is sticking out at you, perpendicular to both the x- and y-axes.

Unlike the two-dimensional plane, which simply has the x-axis running horizontally and the y-axis running vertically, the 3-D coordinate system comes in two flavors:

■ The right-handed system

■ The left-handed system

The names of these systems are derived from the fact that, if you take your right or left hand and roll your fingertips from the positive x-axis into the y-axis, your thumb points in the direction of the positive z-axis. Figure 6.1 shows a representation of these two ways to visualize and define a 3-D system.

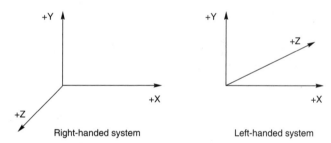

Figure 6.1. *The 3-D coordinate system.*

We use the right-handed system for all of our discussions and code examples. There are two reasons for this:

■ The right-handed system is easier to work with simply because visualization is a bit easier with it.

■ The right-handed system is widely accepted as the standard.

Of course, you realize that the computer screen is a 2-D plane and we surely cannot render 3-D images on a 2-D plane. True... However, we can project them onto the 2-D plane. In essence, we can see their "shadows," at least in the sense that they have been de-dimensionalized. (Yes, I did make that word up.) This projection does work fairly well, and a completely believable model can be rendered on a 2-D screen so that viewers can extrapolate the "feel" of a full three dimensions in their minds.

Games such as Wolfenstein and DOOM are 3-D—in a sense. However, they are special cases of 3-D space, with certain attributes that allow them to be rendered quickly and efficiently. Much of this is due to their regular geometry (that is, the geometry of the rectangular hallways and solids that make up much of the scenery).

At any rate, we get to that later in this chapter. For now let's begin our review of 3-D graphics with simple geometrical entities.

Points, Lines, Polygons, and Objects

As we previously have seen, a point in 3-D has a triple set of coordinates (x,y,z). This is the only information needed to uniquely specify a single point in 3-D space.

Logically, the next object we would want to be able to represent would be the line. A line is created simply by connecting two points in 3-D space.

We might use code such as that in Listing 6.1 to define points and lines in 3-D.

Listing 6.1. Defining points and lines in 3-D.

```
// A structure for a point in 3-space:

typedef struct point_typ
{
  float x,y,z;      // These are the coordinates of a point
                    // in 3-space.
} point, *point_ptr;

// A structure for a line in 3-space:

typedef struct line_typ
{
  point start,end;      // These are the two points of our line.
} line, *line_ptr;
```

Using the structures in Listing 6.1, let's define a line that extends from the origin (0,0,0) to (100,200,300):

```
// Allocate a line structure.

line line1;

// Define the starting point at the origin.

line1.start.x = 0;
line1.start.y = 0;
line1.start.z = 0;
```

```
// Define the endpoint at (100,200,300).

line1.end.x = 100;
line2.end.y = 200;
line3.end.z = 300;
```

At this point we have a representation of a line from the origin to the point (100,200,300). If we wished, we could build up 3-D models and worlds with lines; however, this would be a bit crude.

What we would like is a higher level of abstraction with which to model objects. This higher level comes from the use of polygons. As we learned in Chapter 4, "The Mechanics of Two-Dimensional Graphics," a polygon is a collection of vertices. These vertices define the endpoints of the polygon and are connected with lines. Polygons in 3-D are exactly like polygons in 2-D—except that, of course, they have one more coordinate, or dimension. If we defined a 3-D triangle, it might look like the one in Figure 6.2.

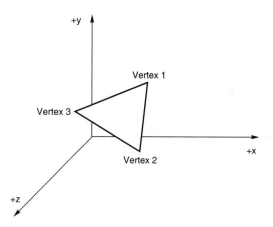

Figure 6.2. *A 3-D triangle.*

As you can see, representing 3-D objects on a 2-D piece of paper is rather awkward. We have to use a kind of "diagonal view." We deal with this shortcoming later in this chapter, but you get the general idea.

Representing polygons is quite easy: we use the definition of a polygon plus a few attributes to create a reasonable structure. Listing 6.2 contains a possible polygon definition.

Listing 6.2. Defining polygons in 3-D.

```
// A structure for a polygon

typedef struct polygon_typ
{
  int num_vertices;        // This is the number of vertices
                           // in this polygon.
  vertices[MAX_VERTICES];  // This is the vertices that make
                           // up the polygon.
  int color;               // This is the color of the
                           // polygon.
} polygon, *polygon_ptr;
```

The code in Listing 6.2 contains the vertices of the polygon, along with the color, which should be enough information to draw it reasonably.

Now that we have a polygon structure, the next logical step is to make an object based on polygons. Figure 6.3 is a representation of such an object.

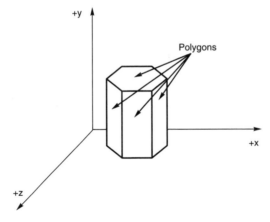

Figure 6.3. *A 3-D object based on polygons.*

Again, we can add one more level to our definition. An object is a collection of polygons, so let's make a structure that encapsulates that concept. Listing 6.3 does just that.

Listing 6.3. Defining 3-D objects based on polygons.

```
// An object structure:

typedef struct object_typ
{
```

```
int num_faces;                  // How many faces are in
                                // the object?
polygon faces[MAX_FACES];       // These are the faces (that is,
                                // the polygons) of the object.
float xo,yo,zo;                 // This is the position of the
                                // object in the world.
int visible;                    // This is the object in the
                                // world right now.
} object, *object_ptr;
```

The structure in Listing 6.3 defines an object that's composed of a collection of polygons, or *faces*. Using these structures and definitions, we could create a couple 3-D objects, such as a starship and a planet, and place them somewhere in 3-D space.

To place objects in 3-D space we need to know *where they are* in that space. That is, we need to know where each component's xo,yo,zo come into play. As with the 2-D objects discussed in Chapter 8, we define 3-D objects so that they have a local coordinate system based at (0,0,0). Then, when we want to move the object somewhere in 3-D space, we translate the object to its final position in the world. In the case of our structures, this final position would be at (xo,yo,zo). Accomplishing this task is simply a matter of translating each point of the object, just as we've seen in our discussions of 2-D objects.

We should examine our representations of 3-D objects to see if they are reasonable. As an example, let's take a look at an imaginary cube that's centered at the origin, with dimensions 2x2x2. Figure 6.4 helps you visualize this.

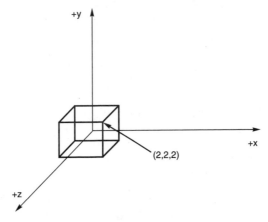

Figure 6.4. *A cube centered at the origin.*

When we inspect the cube, we see that it's composed of eight points and six faces. Using our definitions and data structures, we could define the cube as an object with six faces—and we'd be done. The problem with this is that it's not the most efficient way to represent the object. Each face has four points, and each of these points is common to two other faces. That means that we're wasting memory.

Maybe a better data structure would be one that contains a general vertex list, along with a polygon list that uses pointers or indices to build a polygon out of the vertices. This way, there'd be no waste of memory. However, the data structure would become more complex and difficult to handle because:

- We would have to have pointers, indices, or both to refer to the vertices required to build up the geometry of the object. Either one of these increases the dereferencing time of the object's data.

- Our structures would use preallocated arrays to hold vertices and polygons. This is inefficient memory use. These arrays will always be the same size: whether we use one element in the array or the full size of the array, the maximum number of elements will always be allocated.

These are factors to consider when you create 3-D data structures. However, for our purposes the structures in Listings 6.2 and 6.3 are the simplest to work with. If you were to make a set of real 3-D structures, you would probably use other tactics.

In general, the way 2-D or 3-D objects is represented is very much affected by the game you are writing, how much memory you can use, and so on. (Our mission of the moment is to understand the mechanics of 3-D graphics and rendering, not to determine the most efficient way to represent them in the computer. This changes depending on the algorithms and data structures used.)

To summarize:

- 3-D objects are composed of vertices.

- These vertices connect faces, or polygons, that make up the surfaces of the object itself.

- Objects are defined relative to the origin, and are later transformed to specific positions and orientations in the world.

- There are many ways to represent 3-D objects, and you must pick one that suits your specific needs for speed and memory.

Translation, Scaling, and Rotation in 3-D Space

Whether the objects in your video game are points, lines, or solid objects, we must always break each of the higher-level entities down to their primal part: the point. Once we do this, we can transform all the points—the vertices—that make up an object separately, and the object itself is transformed when the procedure is complete. For example, if we want to rotate or translate a 3-D cube, we would have our algorithm break the object down into polygons, and then into points, before doing the transformations.

With that in mind, we should concentrate on learning to transform single points.

Translating a 3-D Object

To translate a point (x,y,z) by an amount (dx,dy,dz), we would do the following operation:

```
x = x + dx;
y = y + dy;
z = z + dz;
```

If we wished to use a matrix, we would have to represent our point as a "four-tupple," such as (x,y,z,1). This matrix multiplication then would do the job:

$$[x' \; y' \; z' \; 1] = [x \; y \; z \; 1] \begin{vmatrix} 1 & 0 & 0 & 0 \\ 0 & 1 & 0 & 0 \\ 0 & 0 & 1 & 0 \\ dx & dy & dz & 1 \end{vmatrix}$$

where dx, dy, and dz are the translation factors respectively, and x', y', and z' are the new points after the transformation. (The tacked-on 1 you see is just to make the transformations work out properly; without it, translation couldn't be achieved with matrix multiplication. See Chapter 4, "The Mechanics of Two-Dimensional Graphics," for more information on this.)

Scaling a 3-D Object

The next transformation we would wish to implement is scaling. Scaling a 3-D object is the same as scaling a 2-D object, with one more multiplication for the last (z) component. Here's the math to scale the point (x,y,z) by a factor of s:

```
x = x * s;
y = y * s;
z = z * s;
```

That's so easy, it's a wonder 3-D graphics are so hard!

To implement the transformation with a matrix, we must again represent the point with a "four-tupple" (x,y,z,1). Here is the scaling matrix:

```
                             ┆ S   0   0   0 ┆
[x' y' z' 1'] = [x y z 1]    ┆ 0   S   0   0 ┆
                             ┆ 0   0   S   0 ┆
                             ┆ 0   0   0   1 ┆
```

Of course, if you wished to scale each component of the object by a different factor (for example, only along the x-axis), you could use separate scaling factors for each dimension, as in:

```
                             ┆ Sx  0   0   0 ┆
[x' y' z' 1'] = [x y z 1]    ┆ 0   Sy  0   0 ┆
                             ┆ 0   0   Sz  0 ┆
                             ┆ 0   0   0   1 ┆
```

Using this matrix allows the object to be non-uniformly scaled; for example, if the scale factors sx, sy, and sz are not equal.

Rotating a 3-D Object

The final transformation that can be done on an object is rotation. Rotating a 3-D object is the same as rotating a 2-D object—we just need one more dimension. The following sections give transformation matrices to rotate a point (x,y,z) by an arbitrary angle about each of the axes.

Rotation Parallel to the X-Axis

The following transformation matrix rotates a point (x,y,z) parallel to the x-axis:

```
                            ┆ 1    0       0      0 ┆
[x' y' z' 1] = [x y z 1]    ┆ 0    cos r   sin r  0 ┆
                            ┆ 0   -sin r   cos r  0 ┆
                            ┆ 0    0       0      1 ┆
```

where r is the angle, in radians.

Rotation Parallel to the Y-axis

The following transformation matrix rotates a point (x,y,z) parallel to the y-axis:

```
                            ┆ cos r   0   -sin r   0 ┆
[x' y' z' 1] = [x y z 1]    ┆ 0       1    0       0 ┆
                            ┆ sin r   0    cos r   0 ┆
                            ┆ 0       0    0       1 ┆
```

where r is the angle, in radians.

Rotation Parallel to the Z-Axis

The following transformation matrix rotates a point (x,y,z) parallel to the z-axis:

$$[x'\ y'\ z'\ 1] = [x\ y\ z\ 1] \begin{vmatrix} \cos r & \sin r & 0 & 0 \\ -\sin r & \cos r & 0 & 0 \\ 0 & 0 & 0 & 0 \\ 0 & 0 & 0 & 1 \end{vmatrix}$$

where r is the angle, in radians.

The Last Word on 3-D Transformations

That about sums it up for transformations that can be done to an object in 3-D space. Realize, of course that these transformations by no means comprise a complete list. This is only a subset of the major transformations you can do. There are many variations on these, and there are completely new transformations (such as deformation transformations, shearing transformations, and other weird matrices) that can be applied to points in 3-D space. However, we know enough to continue on to... *projections*.

Projections

At this point we know how to represent a 3-D object in space and how to perform operations such as translation, scaling, and rotation on this object. The burning question now should be, "How do we draw 3-D objects on a 2-D screen?" The answer is simple: we "project" them onto the surface.

Projecting a 3-D object on a 2-D plane is easy, and gives fairly good results. Unfortunately, the results never look real. Your eyes have a single viewpoint; therefore, the image will look 3-D, but never really "feel" 3-D.

There actually exist head-mounted displays with stereovision systems: a little CRT for each eye, each with a different viewpoint to simulate a real, 3-D view. These HMDs are used in virtual reality systems. The problem with them is that the *parallax*, or focal point, of each person is different and the HMD must be adjusted. If the adjustment isn't adequate, the wearer gets a headache.

Nevertheless, we'll stick to using the plain old video monitor, along with some math, to project the 3-D image on the screen. I want to discuss two kinds of projection that can be used for this purpose: *parallel* (or *orthogonal*) *projection* and *perspective projection*. Figure 6.5 shows a diagram of each type of projection.

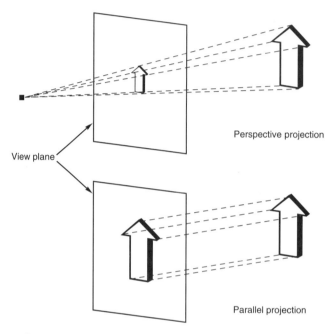

Figure 6.5. *The two standard kinds of 3-D projections.*

Parallel projections are the easiest to implement, but the images don't look 3-D. They look like 2-D images drawn to look 3-D. To implement a parallel projection, we simply throw away the z component of each point in the 3-D object and then draw the object as if it were 2-D.

On the other hand, perspective projections take a more complex approach, and actually do look 3-D. They have the quality of looking down a long road. The farther you look down the road, the smaller the road gets. Figure 6.6 shows an example of this.

The perspective projection takes the z component into consideration and appropriately modifies the x and y components. The elements that achieve perspective turn out to be:

- Simple division and multiplication by the z component
- A viewing distance

Figure 6.6. *A road to nowhere.*

In a moment we get to the details of projections, but first let's talk about the video screen and its relationship to the coordinates in the virtual 3-D world.

Coping with the 2-D Video Screen

Implementing a true, 3-D graphics system is *complicated*. Entire books (rather large ones, I might add) have been written on the subject. At the very least, we need:

- Some 3-D models
- A viewing volume
- A projection onto the view plane

The part about the 3-D objects we have under control: we define polygons as collections of vertices, and build up an object composed of polygons. The parts about the viewing volume and the view plane, however, need some explaining.

When we view our 3-D world, we must be positioned at some location in the 3-D world; moreover, we must be looking in some direction. Figure 6.7 shows both these concepts.

Using this information and the objects in the world, we can compute what objects are visible from that viewpoint and in that view direction—and then render them appropriately on the screen, which is our view plane. This kind of thing is, in general, extremely complex; many transformations must be done to solve the general case. (By *general case* I mean arbitrary geometry, multiple light sources, and completely realistic environments.) Alas, being video-game programmers, we are not interested in the general case; we are instead interested in making a game look 3-D! Therefore, we can apply some constraints to the problem at hand and find ways to come up with a 3-D view need not be created with general 3-D environments in mind.

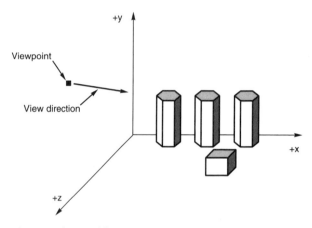

Figure 6.7. *Looking at the world.*

■ First, we pretend that the center of the video screen is the origin of a right-handed system. The illustration in Figure 6.8 shows how a right-handed system is mapped onto the video screen.

■ Second, we add the convention that the player will be looking down the z-axis in the negative direction, into the screen.

We could therefore project a single pixel at (0,0,0) on the screen using parallel projection and see a dot in the center of the screen.

Figure 6.9 shows the difference between a parallel projection and a perspective projection.

As you can see in Figure 6.9, the center of projection is really the perpendicular distance from the player to the view plane (that is, the surface of the video screen).

The math to project 3-D objects on the screen is fairly simple, and we get to it in a minute. First we need to talk about scale.

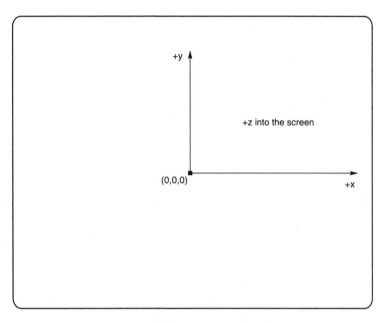

Figure 6.8. *Mapping the right-handed system onto the video screen.*

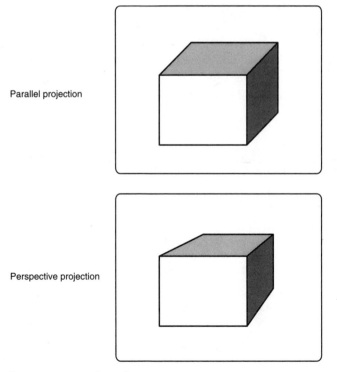

Figure 6.9. *Projecting onto the video screen.*

Video-Screen Scale

The video screen in mode 13h is 320x200, so how can we see a universe that is 1000x1000? There are many ways to approach this problem. One way is to use perspective projection so that, as we back away from an object, it gets smaller. At some point a 1000x1000-pixel universe would be scaled small enough to fit on the video screen.

If we use parallel projection, of course, this would never occur. To remedy this, we must scale the screen and pretend it's another size, such as MxN. To accomplish this we must normalize the screen, then compute the position of any coordinate based on this normalization and the virtual screen size we have simulated. For instance, to make the screen 1000x1000, we would do the following.

To plot a point (x,y) on the screen, where each component can range from 0-1000, we could use the following transformation:

```
x_screen = 320 * x / 1000;
y_screen = 200 * y / 1000;
```

where x_screen and y_screen would be the actual, final coordinates of the pixel plotted on the 320x200 screen.

That's how you can change the size of the screen. Of course, there is a penalty for this: if your real screen is 320x200, transforming the screen to 1000x1000 isn't going to give you more resolution. In actuality, some points will be plotted at the same position. For instance, both 999 and 1000 on the y-axis would be plotted at 199, so you couldn't tell the difference between them. This doesn't really matter, though, when viewing a 3-D world based on polygons rather than a bit-map based world (such as that in a 2-D game).

Parallel-Projection Math

The math needed to do a parallel projection is simple: you just throw away the z-coordinate and plot the x- and y-coordinates of each point in the object. Here's the transformation: given the point (x,y,z),

```
x_parallel = x;
y_parallel = y;

plot x,y
```

Perspective-Projection Math

Doing a perspective transformation is a little different. We use the z component to scale the x and y components to make the object look more realistic as it gets closer to and farther from the view plane (the surface of the screen). Here's the transformation: given the point (x,y,z) and a viewing distance of *D* from the screen,

```
x_perspective = D * x/z;
y_perspective = D * y/z;
```

That's all there is to it. We multiply each component by the distance and divide the result by the z-coordinate—and, magically, the image will look like it's 3-D.

The Viewing Volume

We've talked about the objects in 3-D space and projections, but what about the viewing volume? The *viewing volume* is analogous to the clipping region in 2-D space (discussed in Chapter 4, "The Mechanics of Two-Dimensional Graphics"). Similarly to when we clip the objects from the sides of the screen in a 2-D game, we must clip 3-D objects to a volume. This volume is composed of six sides and looks like a 3-D trapezoid. It's sometimes referred to as the *viewing frustum*. Figure 6.10 shows a viewing volume.

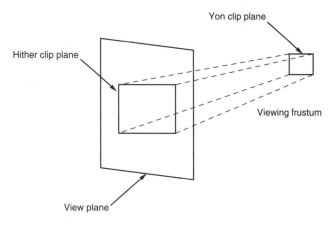

Objects within the view volume are visible;
objects outside it are clipped.

Figure 6.10. *The viewing volume.*

In essence, we want to clip each object, or portion of an object, that extends beyond any of the clipping planes. This is done because they probably won't be visible with perspective projection anyway, and therefore there's no need to even render them.

The hither and yon clipping planes (see Figure 6.10) are probably the most important. When an object gets too close to the screen, it should disappear (as if it has gone behind you). Furthermore, when an object get too far away to be of any concern, we should clip it away because it will only look like a single pixel if we were to render it. (I'm sure you've seen driving games or 3-D texture-mapped games where objects seem to "pop up" from nowhere. This is an effect of having the hither clip plane too close to the screen and, ultimately, the player.)

I'm not going to get any further into 3-D clipping: we don't need it to create DOOM- and Wolfenstein-type games. It's more appropriate for flight simulators and driving games, or any polygon-based 3-D simulation in general. However, you can use the same tactics employed for 2-D clipping to achieve 3-D clipping.

There's just one more element to deal with: modeling solid objects.

Solid Modeling

Solid modeling is the ultimate in realism that a computer can offer. Objects rendered by the computer in solid modeling look solid. Taking this step into the domain of solid objects has taken a long time for both hardware and software engineers, due to the sheer number of computations that must be done to render a solid object. Take a look at Figure 6.11 to see a comparison of a solid model and a wire frame model, and to make sure you and I are on the same wavelength.

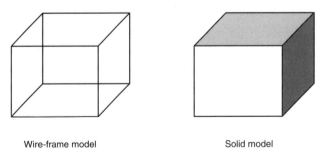

Wire-frame model   Solid model

Figure 6.11. *Wire-frame and solid models.*

As you can see, the solid model is much more believable. The wire-frame model has its uses; however, today we expect objects in a computer game to be solid—no ifs, ands, or buts!

Creating solid models is not much different than making wire frame models. We can use all the same data structures, transformations and projections. The problem arises when we try to draw solid 3-D objects. You see, there are hidden surfaces. Hidden surfaces are the surfaces that shouldn't be visible to the player (for example, the surfaces that are behind the object from the direction the player is viewing the object). This turns out to be a really big problem. The computer doesn't know the difference between visible surfaces and hidden surfaces, so it goes along and draws *all* of them and the object turns out looking like a transporter malfunction on *Star Trek!* To remedy this, we must figure out ways to remove these hidden surfaces. This is the topic of our next discussion.

Hidden-Surface Removal

Hidden-surface removal, or HSR, has been a thorn in the side of graphics engineers and video-game programmers alike. It's a mathematically intensive and time-consuming problem to solve. There are algorithms to accomplish it, but they aren't easy to implement and seldom run at the speeds we need for a PC video game.

There are two phases to HSR. Phase 1 is removing totally invisible surfaces, called *backfaces.* Backfaces are the surfaces that couldn't possible be visibly from the viewpoint of the viewer. To remove these surfaces we can use the dot product of the view vector and the surface normal of each surface. We compute this value. If the angle is less than 90 degrees, the surface is visible; if it's more than 90 degrees, it's not visible and we can throw it away.

We can compute the surface normal of each surface using the cross product between two co-planer edges on the same surface. The view vector is generated from the viewpoint to any point on the surface; preferably, the point from which the normal was computed.

If I just lost you, take a look at Figure 6.12 to see the whole process drawn out.

In Phase 2, after backfaces have been removed, the visible faces must be drawn. However, you must take care during this phase to draw the faces in order such that the objects look right.

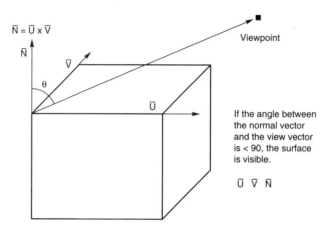

Figure 6.12. *Testing whether a surface is visible.*

There's a popular algorithm, the Painter's Algorithm, that does this ordering. It works by performing five tests on each pair of visible polygons (surfaces), and then creating an order in which to draw them, from back to front, much as a painter would paint them.

Another technique to do this ordering is called the Z-Buffer Algorithm. It operates in *image space*, at the pixel level. It's easy to implement, but is slow and consumes much memory.

Video-game programmers don't have the luxury of being able to use either algorithm in a general way. We must cheat the system, coming up with special cases and hybrids to do our bidding. (Otherwise, games such as DOOM just wouldn't exist.) In any case, let's review each algorithm briefly.

The Painter's Algorithm

Be forewarned: the Painter's Algorithm is one of those algorithms that can be a pain to implement in reality. The basic idea of the Painter's Algorithm is to sort the surfaces in some way so that when they're rendered it's in a manner that looks correct. The simplest version of the Painter's Algorithm can be implemented when each surface is parallel to the view plane (that is, flat to the screen). In this case, we can just sort each surface in order of decreasing z value. We then draw the farthest surfaces first and continue drawing nearer and nearer surfaces. This is a specific case, but it does have its uses. (For instance, in a Space Harrier-type game there are many 2-D bit maps flying around. They're all parallel to the view plane—the screen—so they can be drawn in proper order using this technique.)

Problems start occurring when the surfaces are not parallel to the view plane. Then everything falls to pieces, and we're stuck with doing a bunch of tests. This means that we could, at worst, be doing a lot of computations.

Figure 6.13 shows a top-down view of two polygons in one of the worst cases you might end up testing.

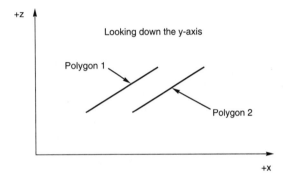

Figure 6.13. *The worst-case ordering of two polygons.*

No matter how we sort these polygons based on their minimum, maximum, or average z values, we always come up with the wrong ordering. To remedy this, we must perform the following five tests on each pair of polygons.

The tests must be done if (and only if) the z-extents of the two polygons in question overlap. Otherwise, they can be drawn in any order: it won't make a difference.

Painter's Algorithm Test 1

Do the x-extents of polygon 1 and polygon 2 overlap, as shown in Figure 6.14?

- If they *do not*, you're done with that pair of polygons. Their order doesn't matter as they can't possible occlude each other.

- If they *do* overlap, proceed to Test 2.

Painter's Algorithm Test 2

Do the y-extents of polygon 1 and polygon 2 overlap, as shown in Figure 6.15?

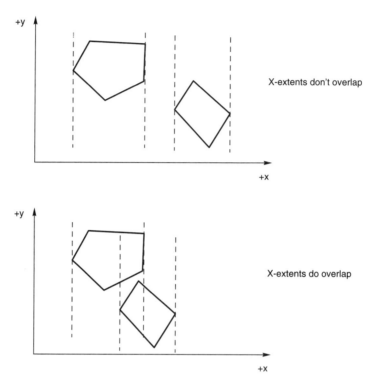

Figure 6.14. *Testing the x-extents.*

- If they *do not*, we can throw them out again.
- If they *do* overlap, proceed to Test 3.

Painter's Algorithm Tests 3 and 4

Tests 3 and 4 are similar because they both have to do with cutting planes. To understand the test, imagine extending the extents of a polygon to infinity in both directions, creating a plane. This is a *cutting plane*.

Take a look at Figure 6.16.

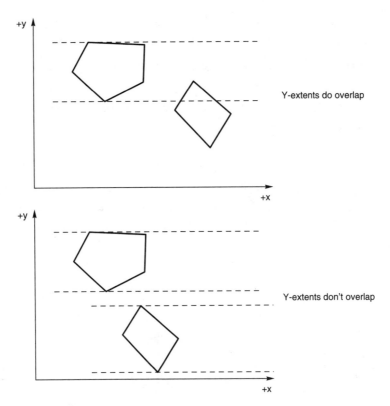

Figure 6.15. *Testing the y-extents.*

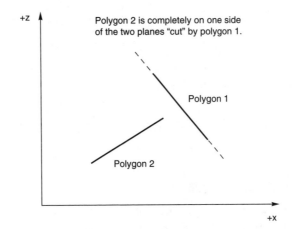

Figure 6.16. *Cutting planes.*

To do the test, create a cutting plane with polygon 1 and test polygon 2 against it. Then create a cutting plane with polygon 2 and test polygon 1 against it.

- ■ If either polygon can be contained within the cutting plane of the other, the polygons are correctly ordered.

- ■ If neither polygon can be contained within the cutting plane of the other, proceed to Test 5.

Painter's Algorithm Test 5

At this point we can be almost certain that the polygons are in the incorrect order, save one case. The case occurs when the polygons are concave—that is, have dents in them—and their extents overlap while their actual edges do not. Figure 6.17 shows an example of this case.

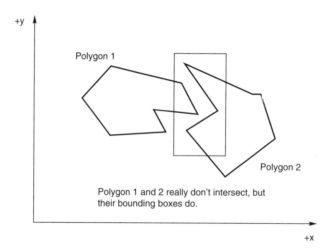

Figure 6.17. *Testing invalid intersection.*

Figuring this situation out is so complex, your best bet is to just swap the polygons and be done.

Painter's Algorithm at Runtime

The Painter's algorithm works fine, but it has bad runtime behavior. In worst case, it can take it $O(n^2)$, where n is the number of polygons. For those of you who are not familiar with asymptotic analysis, the notation translates to a number of swaps equal to the square of the number of polygons.

The Z-Buffering Algorithm

Due to the speed and increased memory capabilities of PCs today, another algorithm is taking precedence over the Painter's Algorithm: the Z-Buffer Algorithm. This algorithm is much easier to comprehend than the Painter's Algorithm. (Besides, most high-performance graphics systems and dedicated graphics boards now have hardware z-buffering built in, so you don't have to solve the hidden-surface removal problem yourself.)

Implementing a z-buffer is easy. All we need is the z-buffer itself, which is just a screen buffer the same size as the video screen. In our case, that would be a 320x200 matrix of integers (or floats, depending on how you wanted to do the math). We then fill this array with the z values of the polygons, along with the color of each pixel at any particular position, using the following procedure:

1. Given a collection of 3-D surfaces (that is, polygons), we first compute their projections onto the view plane. Again, in our case this view plane is the screen.

    To draw a 3-D polygon on a 2-D screen, we must project it onto the view plane using one of the two kinds of projection discussed earlier in this chapter, such as perspective projection. After projection, the polygon has a set of vertices that are really 2-D points. We then fill in the polygon using these 2-D points to create the edges.

2. As we scan convert the polygon (that is, draw it as a collection of horizontal or vertical strips), we generate the x and y components for each point. (Remember: there could be hundreds of points with the same x and y value, but with differing z values.)

3. We then use the *plane equation*, described in a moment, for a plane that lies coplanar with the polygon, solving it for the z component at each x and y position. We obtain the z value for every point within the polygon's boundary.

4. We record each point's z value and color and store these values in the z-buffer.

5. We then see which points would be plotted at each pixel of the video screen. To do that, we find the point with the z value nearest to the view plane. We compare that z value to the one currently in the z-buffer for that x and y. If the new z value is nearer to the view plane than the old one, it overwrites the old one. We do this continually until we've done each pixel on the display screen.

6. We then plot the pixel with that point's color.

The Plane Equation

I said that we can use the plane equation for the polygon to get the z component for each interior pixel of the scan-converted polygon. That equation is as follows.

Given the point (x,y) and the normal vector to the polygon <Nx,Ny,Nz>

```
            Nz
z = ------------------
      1 - Nx * x - Ny * y
```

Using the Plane Equation on Polygon Vertices

So how do we get the plane equation from the polygon vertices? Easy: we know that all the vertices of the polygon are coplanar—they'd better be! Therefore, we can take two adjacent edges and create a normal vector based on this.

We do this by taking the cross-product of the two adjacent, coplanar vectors. Figure 6.18 illustrates how to compute a normal vector. This normal vector can be used in the plane equation, along with the x and y components of the current pixel, to compute the z component.

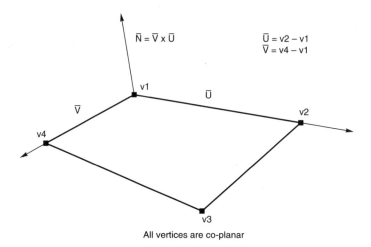

Figure 6.18. *Computing the normal vector.*

Given the normal vector of the polygon, the plane equation solves for the z component at any given (x,y) pixel location. Given the point (x,y) and the normal vector to the polygon <Nx,Ny,Nz>,

```
            Nz
z = ------------------
      1 - Nx * x - Ny * y
```

Image Space vs. Object Space

The Z-Buffer Algorithm works flawlessly and can be implemented with ease. The only problem is that it works at the pixel level; therefore, it's an *image space* algorithm. Its weak point is that it does not take into account the geometrical properties (that is, *object space* elements) of the object. That single weakness has made necessary the existence of hybrid algorithms that can be used for special cases. These hybrids try to take into consideration some of the geometry of the object before removing hidden surfaces.

Next, let's learn how to make the surfaces of our 3-D objects a bit more realistic.

Texturing

Texturing is an extremely mathematical area, and for that reason I'm going to leave it to other sources for a complete discussion. For our purposes we need only look at it from a video-game programmer's point of view.

Texturing simply means mapping some bit-mapped image onto a flat or curved surface. Doing this can greatly increase the realism of a scene—but, as I mentioned, it's mathematically intensive and hardly a task that can be accomplished on a PC in the general case. We can, however, perform texturing in some specific cases.

For instance, in Chapter 7, "Advanced Bit-Mapped Graphics and Special FX," you discover how to scale a bit map. You could think of this as mapping a texture onto a square polygon. The mapping of the texture is easy, as the texture is mapped directly onto a flat surface. If the surface was bent, curved, or at an angle not parallel to the view plane, this mapping would have instantly become hard to do. Therefore, when we texture something we want to make sure that the destination of the texture (which is a bit map) is always parallel to the view plane (the screen).

After playing games like DOOM and Wolfenstein, you would quickly come to the conclusion that textures are mapped in ways that put them at angles to the view plane. This is not entirely true. The screen is actually made up of vertical strips that are each separately textured. You could think of them as 1-D vertical lines that have a 1-D texture mapped onto them. This is the "trick" that makes these kinds of games able to attain the frame rates they do. Instead of building up the screen out of polygons and trying to map textures on these polygons at angles, with perspective and other transformations, the screen is built out of 320 vertical strips that are each parallel to the view plane. We cover this technique in depth in a moment, but before we do I want to talk about ray tracing and ray casting.

Ray Tracing

Ray tracing is a method used to generate photo-realistic images on a computer using complete models of the objects in the 3-D world. Ray tracing can support several different attributes and solves many problems that in the past had to be handled with brute-force methods. In one, single algorithm ray tracing can accomplish these effects:

- Hidden surface removal
- Transparency
- Reflections
- Refraction
- Ambient lighting
- Point source lighting
- Shadows

The original ray-tracing algorithm was invented to solve the hidden-surface removal problem. However, the inventor quickly realized that it could do much more. Ray tracing creates an image by simply building it according to the physical model by which we see real objects. This, of course, consists of rays of light hitting objects and being absorbed, refracted, reflected, and so on until they finally find their way into our eyes. Figure 6.19 shows a general scene that could be ray traced. As you see, we have some objects, a light source, a viewer, and a view plane.

To ray trace the scene as nature would, we would have to emit trillions of light rays from the light source and then let them intersect with the objects in the scene, hoping that some of them would pierce the view plane and create an image for the viewer. This is how nature does it—but it's not the way we do it. Why trace every possible ray? We're only concerned with the rays that can possibly intersect the view plane.

With that in mind, why not do the ray tracing backwards? We draw rays from the viewpoint through the view plane for each pixel position in the screen, and then allow the ray to intersect objects in the scene. When we detect an intersection, we can stop there and color the pixel with the color of the object that particular ray hit. This is called *primary ray tracing*.

This technique renders a 3-D image; however, effects such as shadows, refraction, reflections, and so on are not seen. To make these effects happen we must emit more rays, called *secondary rays*, from the intersection point. This is done recursively up to some level of detail. Then all the results of all the rays are summed up, and the original pixel from which the first primary ray was drawn is colored appropriately, based on this information.

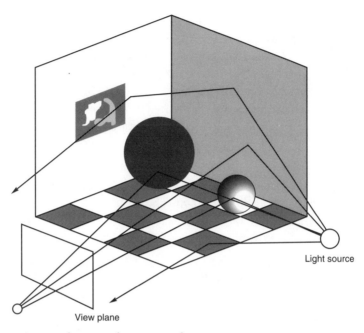

Figure 6.19. *A general scene to be ray traced.*

Ray tracing is one of the most computationally intensive methods of rendering 3-D images, and the results are startling. The only problem is that even a supercomputer can't do it in real time, which is how we'd need it done for a PC video game. We must instead extract the fundamentals and some of the mechanics of ray tracing to create another method with which to obtain real-time performance in a 3-D game world on a PC. This new method could be used only in limited cases; optimally, those of walls that are perpendicular to the floor and ceiling, with a view direction looking straight into the screen. In these cases, we can do simple ray tracing using primary rays to generate the scene, or what's called ray casting.

With further optimizations and insights, it's possible to get real-time performance out of a PC with this method even with a fully textured world. If you're interested in how to do this, read on!

Ray Casting

Ray casting is a technique used in video games to create a realistic 3-D view. However, there are a few conditions that have to be met and a few rules we must abide by. These rules are derived from the fact that ray casting is really a derivative of ray tracing; hence, it inherits many of the same computational difficulties of ray tracing.

The key to using ray casting in a video game is to keep it simple and to make the geometry of the world being rendered extremely primitive. In general, ray casting wouldn't work for an arbitrary 3-D application, such as a flight simulator or 3-D modeling system. Nonetheless, for a PC video game that takes place in a building with perpendicular walls and ceilings, ray casting works miracles. A world such as the one you see in DOOM uses far more advanced techniques than ray casting. However, even those advanced techniques evolved from ideas based on ray casting.

We're going to try something a little less ambitious—at least for now—than creating a technique to render something like DOOM. We want to shoot for a Wolfenstein 3-D level of technology; moreover, I want to make sure you have a firm grasp on ray casting and the idea behind it. If you absorb and comprehend ray casting and all its subtleties, creating new techniques to accomplish such ground-breaking rendering as that seen in DOOM will be within your grasp.

With that in mind, I've written a crude ray-casting engine built around a demo program that allows you to walk around in a 3-D world that consists of cubes used as building blocks. This world is read into a 2-D matrix as an ASCII file, and then the ray-casting engine renders the world in full 3-D perspective.

I decided to use Microsoft's graphics libraries for this program because speed isn't the issue during these discussions. (I want you to understand, and have solid footing in, this topic. If you learn nothing during this chapter save one concept, make it ray casting!) The second reason I used Microsoft's graphics libraries is because I want you to see the 2-D world and the 3-D world simultaneously while the ray casting is being done, so I had to use a high-resolution mode and Microsoft's libraries, accordingly. This gives you a better feel for the mechanics of the process and the final results.

The next pages are going to be quite technical and detailed. Ray casting is theoretically simple; however, implementing it in practice is not easy because of the many little details that must be taken into consideration. These details are the very ones that I'm the most interested in uncovering. I could have written a fully textured, real-time ray caster with shading for this chapter, but I'd rather that you see a simple version of one that is not cluttered with all kinds of bells and whistles that obscure the underlying functions of the ray caster.

Finally, the ray-casting engine is quite slow due to the way I wrote it. I used floating-point mathematics (rather than the fixed-point mathematics you learn in Chapter 18, "Optimization Techniques"), and I did no optimization other than using precomputed look-up tables for the trigonometric functions.

At this point I want you to execute the program ray.exe from the companion CD, and experiment with the ray caster for a few moments to see what it does and how it does it. When you execute the program you see three displays, shown in Figure 6.20.

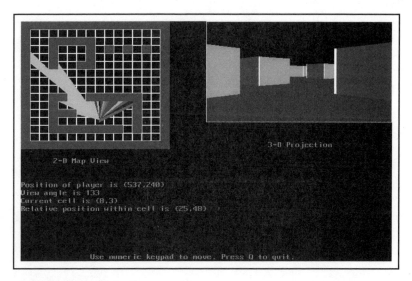

Figure 6.20. *A screen shot of ray.exe.*

The display on the left side of the screen is a 2-D overview, or *map view*, of the world being rendered. The world is a matrix composed of *cells* or *blocks*, each being 64x64x64 virtual units.

From this 2-D database, a full 3-D model is created through the use of ray casting. This 3-D view is seen through a viewport on the right side of the screen. The world is not textured. However, I have placed white vertical lines on the image to delineate cell boundaries. To move the viewpoint and view angle of the player around, use the numeric keypad (press the NumLock key first).

When you've seen enough of the program, press Q. The program exits.

Hopefully, you've now played with the ray caster and developed a feel for what it does. You should have noticed how the 3-D image is built up: vertical strip by vertical strip. These strips are generated by a *sweeping ray* that emanates from the player's viewpoint and sweeps out a specific number of degrees (that is, an arc length). As each ray is cast out from the viewpoint, it intersects a cell either on a horizontal or vertical boundary. This intersection is calculated along with the distance from the player to the point of intersection. This is used to resolve the height of the current vertical strip.

You could think of ray casting in the following way. Imagine you're looking forward in a room. You see the wall in front of you and, with your peripheral vision, you also see some of the walls on either side of you. The view you see is created by light rays reflecting off the wall into your eyes and, ultimately, creating an image on your retina.

Ray casting works in reverse. Instead of light reflecting off walls into your eye, as in reality, ray casting "casts" rays to generate an image. Figure 6.21 shows a scene being generated by ray casting.

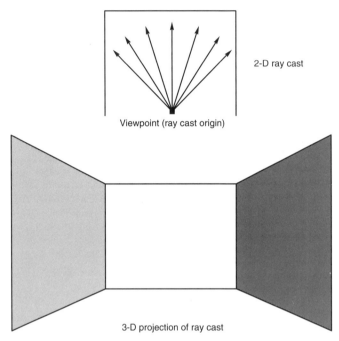

2-D ray cast

Viewpoint (ray cast origin)

3-D projection of ray cast

Figure 6.21. *Generating a scene by ray casting.*

Like a laser scanning system, we scan the area around us and then build up an image based on the results of the scan. The image that we generate has to be based on a *field of view*, or FOV. This field of view is the amount of information we can see at once as a function of the angle from dead ahead. If we can see 45 degrees in each direction relative to the view direction, as shown in Figure 6.22, we would have an FOV of 90 degrees.

FOV is important in ray casting: we must decide what FOV we want so that we can generate the proper tables and so on. Most humans have a large FOV: 90 degrees or more. However, for our discussions, I have picked 60 degrees just because I like the way it looks on the screen. You can have any FOV you wish, but try to stay between 60-90 degrees, or your 3-D view will look truly bizarre!

At this point we know that we need to cast out a collection of rays that span a certain FOV. We then must calculate the intersections of these rays with the walls, and use the information about each intersection to generate a 3-D view. As an example, take a look at Figure 6.23.

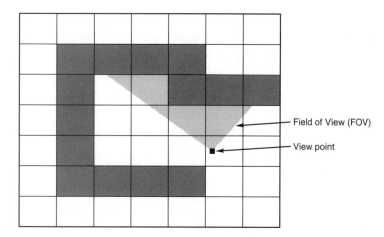

Rays will only be cast out within the FOV.

Figure 6.22. *The field of view.*

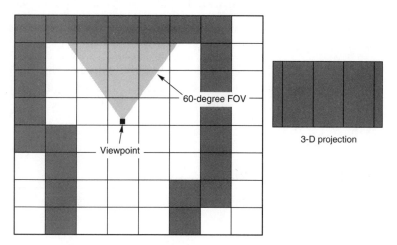

Figure 6.23. *A sample ray cast out with a 60-degree field of view.*

In Figure 6.23, the player is in an 8x8 world. We've set the player's viewpoint looking straight up; that is, 90 degrees. If we wanted to have a 60-degree field of view, we would start casting out rays from the view direction less 30 degrees to the view direction plus 30 degrees, or from 30 to 120 degrees. As you can see, I've shown the casting of a few rays and the final result of the cast in Figure 6.23.

The first question is: "How many rays do we need to cast?" The answer is simple: we cast a number of rays equal to the horizontal resolution of the screen on which we will be projecting the image. In our case this is 320 rays, as we're using mode 13h. Your intuition should tell you that we need to break up 60 degrees into 320 subangles, and cast a ray out for each angle.

Because the world in which we're casting rays is really 2-D, the problem of computing intersections becomes quite simple. Moreover, the world has a regular architecture; that is, it's a regular grid with blocks either solid or not. Both the ray-casting math and the number of rays that are cast are greatly decreased in comparison to ray casting in a general world with arbitrary geometry. That means to us that we can use a lot of little tricks to make the ray caster work at incredible speeds. (We get to that later in this chapter. For now, let's keep delving into the way it's done.)

We have a collection of rays that are cast out from the view direction of the player, minus 30 degrees to plus 30 degrees from the view direction. This gives us a total FOV of 60 degrees. To generate this FOV:

1. We cast out 320 rays (one for each vertical column of the screen) and compute the intersection of each ray with the blocks that make up the 2-D map world.

2. Using this information, we compute the distance from the player to the point of intersection.

3. We then use this distance to scale the vertical strip, rendering the vertical strip with the proper scale on the screen at our specific horizontal position. The horizontal position is the current ray being cast, 0-319.

Algorithm 6.1 is an algorithmic definition for ray casting a scene.

Algorithm 6.1. A ray-casting algorithm.

```
// Let the player be at position (xp,yp) with a view direction
// of view_angle.

// Initialize all variables.

// Start the cast -30 degrees from the player's view direction.

start_angle = view_angle - 30;

// We must cast 320 rays, one for each screen column.

for (ray = 0; ray < 320; ray++)
{
  compute the slope of the current ray

  while(the ray is not done casting)
  {
    // Test for vertical intersection.
```

```
    if (not intersected yet withj vertical wall)
        if (the ray has hit a block on a vertical boundary)
        {
            compute distance from xp,yp to point of intersection
            save distance
        } // end if vertical intersection

        if (not intersected yet with horizontal wall)
            if (the ray has hit a block on a horizontal boundary)
            {
                compute distance from xp,yp to point of intersection
            } // end if horizontal

    } // end while

    // At this point the ray has made both a horizontal and a
    // vertical intersection.

    if (the horizontal intersection is closer than the vertical intersec-
tion)
    {
        compute scale based on horizontal distance
        and render a sliver of the image
    } // end if horizontal intersection is closer
    else
    {
        compute the scale based on the vertical distance
        and render a sliver of the image
    } // end else vertical intersection is closer

} // end ray
```

Of course, there are about a million details left out of Algorithm 6.1—in particular, *slivers* are discussed in much more detail in this chapter under "Drawing the Sliver." However, you get the basic idea!

One question that should be bothering you is: "Why does this work at all?" The reason it works is that we're modeling how photons of light create an image. Granted, we're doing it backward—but this model does just about everything. It removes hidden surfaces, creates perspective, and has all the information needed to do shading, lighting, and texturing. This is why ray casting is such an incredibly powerful tool for the video-game programmer. We can make games and environments that would be literally impossible using standard polygon techniques.

You may say that a world that's made out of a bunch of regularly spaced blocks is boring. Yes, that would be the case—without texture and shading. Once you add textures and shading to the walls, however, you can create frighteningly real-looking game environments to play in. Furthermore, you can always decrease the size of the basic building block of the world to create more complex shapes. You could even add other geometric shapes (such as halfblocks that have 45-degree faces, and so on). It's up to you. The only thing that will stop you is speed, so you have to figure out ways to do everything quickly. After all, DOOM has surely proven that anything is possible on a PC!

Now that we've covered the basics behind ray casting, let's get into the exact details of how it's done, and all the math needed to do it. This is one of the most important parts of this chapter. I've read many books that contain algorithms on how to do something, but then don't provide the exact methods and specific cases in which to use them, which are always discovered with much agony and frustration on the part of the programmer. Therefore, I'll try to give you as many details, and answer as many questions, as I can.

Remember one thing: I wrote this ray caster to be readable and understandable. It is by no means as fast as it could be; furthermore, it's not complete (with doors, transparency, and so on). However, these additions shouldn't be hard for you to implement once you understand the technology behind the ray caster.

The Math Behind Ray Casting

Theoretically, ray casting is simple. A number of rays are cast out, and intersections with either a horizontal line or vertical line must be computed. That seems easy enough. The problem is doing it wickedly fast without complex code.

In this section we concentrate on the intersection problem, because it's the area where most of the time is consumed during the ray cast. There are seven main areas that we must analyze and understand:

- Generating lines
- Computing the first intersection
- Computing the remaining intersections
- Calculating distance
- Computing the scale
- Rectifying view distortion
- Drawing slivers

These are covered next.

Generating Lines

The rays we cast out are basically lines. These lines originate from the player's viewpoint, which is really a position in the 2-D game grid map. We have chosen to have a field of view of 60 degrees; therefore, we need a look-up table of all the possible rays that could be cast out from any view angle. This table must hold the slopes of all the possible rays. From these slopes we can create lines from the player's viewpoint for the ray cast.

Formula 6.1.

Calculating the number of elements in the slope look-up table.

The questions before us are: how many elements should be in this slope look-up table, and how do we create all the slopes? The table needs a sufficient number of entries so that, when the player is viewing the ray-cast world, the 320 rays equal a *total span*, or arc, of 60 degrees (which is our field of view). Therefore, we must have a table with 1920 elements, or *slopes*. This is calculated using the following formula:

```
table size = (screen width) * 360/FOV
```

In our case, the screen width is 320 and the FOV is 60 degrees, so the result would be:

```
320 * 360/60 = 1920
```

for 1920 elements in the slope look-up table.

Defining a Slope

Now we need to know what the elements in the slope look-up table should be. They're the actual slopes of all the possible lines that will be cast out from the player's viewpoint. Because we have broken up the circle into 1920 arcs, each arc is exactly 360/1920 degrees, or 0.1875 degrees. We therefore must figure out some method of computing the slope of all the lines—from 0-360 degrees—with angular increments of 0.1875 degrees. Well, this seems as though it should be difficult to do! However, the transcendental function tangent does the trick.

If you recall, the definition of a tangent is sin/cos, which is based on a right triangle. This results in the opposite side divided by the adjacent side—or, more rigorously:

```
                  sin 0           opposite side
    tan 0  =    -----------  =   ----------------
                  cos 0           adjacent side
```

So the tangent of any angle is equal to the opposite over the adjacent. It turns out that opposite over adjacent is M, or the slope of the hypotenuse relative to the horizon. Therefore, we can write:

```
M = tan q
```

If we create a slope look-up table of 1920 elements, each being the tangent of the angle, we'll in essence have created a table of slopes for all the possible lines. We'll use these slopes to generate the rays. However, there's a catch: the tangent function has a few problems.

- First, quadrant I is the only place where the signs of the tangent will be correct. In the other quadrants, the tangent can be positive or negative—but you don't know what the sign of the slope *really* was because the tangent is a quotient. Therefore, when we generate the tables we must put in conditional code so that the signs of the slopes are generated correctly for the other three quadrants (II, III and IV).

- Secondly, the tangent function goes to infinity at the vertical asymptotes (that is, 90 and 270 degrees), so care must be taken to avoid a floating-point or general mathematics error at the asymptotes.

Calculating the Lines to be Generated

Once we've taken care of all the details of creating the slope look-up tables, we're ready to use them to calculate the lines to be generated:

1. We find the position of the player for the current ray cast, or rendering.

2. We then compute the first intersection of each ray that's cast with the perimeter of the cell the player currently is in.

Remember, the player runs around in a 2-D map world that's used to generate a 3-D view. In our case, the world is 16x16 cells, with each cell being 64x64; therefore, the world has 1024x1024 virtual dimension units. (These units are totally relative; that's why I call them virtual.) Anyway, the player—irrelevant of position—will always be within some cell of the game world. This position is computed by simply dividing the player's global position, which can range from 0-1023 for both the x and y, by the number 64; or, more precisely:

```
cell_x = x_world/64;
cell_y = y_world/64;
```

where x_world and y_world both range from 0-1023.

Once the current game cell has been computed, we can find the first intersection of the current ray. Let's see the math for that.

Computing the First Intersection

A line has many equations, from parametric to the point-slope form. For our purposes, we can use the point-slope form of a line to figure out a fast way to compute intersections with the line and horizontal or vertical asymptotes (that is, cell boundaries).

Formula 6.2.

Computing the first y-intersection.

Here's the point-slope from of a line:

```
(yi - yp)
----------- = M
(xi - xp)
```

where (xi,yi) is the point of intersection of the line and (xp,yp) is the position of the player. After some algebraic manipulations, we see that

```
yi = M(xi - xp) + yp
```

Formula 6.3.

Computing the next x-intersection.

```
xi = M⁻¹ (yi - yp) + xp
```

To find the first intersection of the current ray being cast and the exterior perimeter of the block containing the player, we need only do two multiplications and four additions. That's not bad. We could probably optimize this, but it will do for our discussions here.

The variables M and M-1 are the slope and the inverse of the slope, respectively, which we have precomputed in the slope look-up table. The only thing about these equations that should bother you is that they're *circular*—in other words, each equation needs the result of the other. This is a bit misleading. You see, the term xi in the first equation really means "the first bounding vertical line," and the term yi in the second equation really means "the first bounding horizontal line." This is the beauty of ray casting in a regular-square matrix. We know that a ray has to intersect with each cell on a specific vertical or horizontal boundary. Figure 6.24 clarifies this.

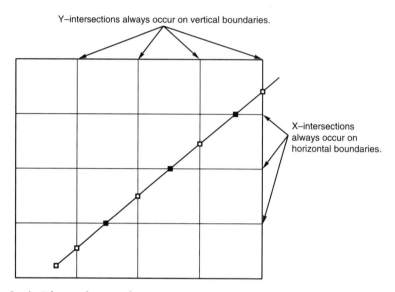

Figure 6.24. *The mechanics of an intersecting line.*

Once we've computed the first intersection we can continue finding the intersections with the ray and the rest of its trajectory.

Before we continue on to finding other intersections, I want to make clear that each ray can make both intersections with each horizontal asymptote and each vertical asymptote. We must compute both the horizontal and vertical intersections as the ray is being cast. Some programmers prefer to cast the same ray twice: once for the possible horizontal intersections and once for the possible vertical intersections. Figure 6.25 illustrates this.

This is fine, but I prefer to do both simultaneously. Their runtime is roughly equivalent, so when you write a ray caster it's up to you if you want to separate each intersection test.

There's one final detail relating to intersections: at each intersection (including the first), we test to see if there's a solid object there. We must look either up, down, right, or left of the intersection to see if there's a solid block there. The direction we look depends on the quadrant we're in. For instance, if we're casting a ray at 45 degrees, we know that all x intersections must occur as the ray moves upward. Therefore, we should find the first intersection and then look to the block above the intersection to see if it's solid.

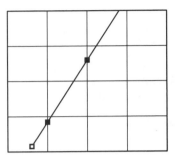

First ray cast tests for vertical
intersections.

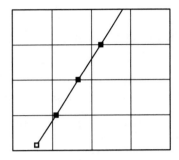

Second ray cast tests for horizontal
intersections.

Figure 6.25. *Casting the same ray twice.*

If there's a solid block, we stop and record the distance to the intersection (along with a couple other pieces of information that we get to later). However, if there is no solid block, we must continue casting the ray until it hits something or goes out of the world boundaries. We use the same technique for the rest of the quadrants.

Computing the Remaining Intersections

Once we've found the first intersections for both the horizontal and vertical walls, we can find the next possible intersection point by simply adding a constant to the current point of intersection. For example, if an intersection has just been found at a y_i of 100, some factor times the slope (or inverse of the slope) plus the 100 would be the next y_i. The factor is just the size of the cell in the world. In our case, each cell is 64x64, so to find the next intersection we use the following formulas.

> **Formula 6.4.**
>
> Computing the next possible x-intersection.

```
Next xi = xi + M⁻¹ (cell width)
```

> **Formula 6.5.**
>
> Computing the next possible y-intersection.

```
Next yi = yi + M (cell height)
```

where cell width and cell height are each 64.

That's not bad for a start: finding the next possible intersection takes just two multiplications and two additions. Remember, ray casting has to be done quickly, or else we won't get the frame rates necessary to simulate reality.

After we compute the next possible intersection points, we test to see if there's a block there. If so, we compute the distance from the player to the intersection. This is used later to render the perspective 3-D image. If there is no intersection, we continue casting.

Calculating Distance

So, how do we calculate distance once we do find an intersection that has a solid block next to it? Once we've computed the intersection point, we're in a position to compute the distance from the player to the point. This distance is used for two things:

- As a comparison to qualify which intersection (vertical or horizontal) was closer

- To compute the scale of the wall

Formula 6.6.

The Pythagorean Theorem.

We might think to use the Pythagorean Theorem, which states that the hypotenuse equals the square root of the sum of the squares of the sides of a right triangle; or, more precisely:

$$H = (x^2 + y^2)^{1/2}$$

This is great if you have about a billion machine cycles to waste! Unfortunately, we're not so lucky. We must use some other, much less complex technique to compute distance. The squares aren't so bad—they're just multiplications—but the square root is out of the question. We could use some super-fast square root look-up table, but there's a simpler way to compute distance if you know the length of the sides and have the ability to compute sin and cos. Normally, we would laugh at the use of trigonometric functions: they're so slow, what would be the use in deference to the square root? The catch is, we can precompute them and save them in a table. With that in mind, take a look at Figure 6.26.

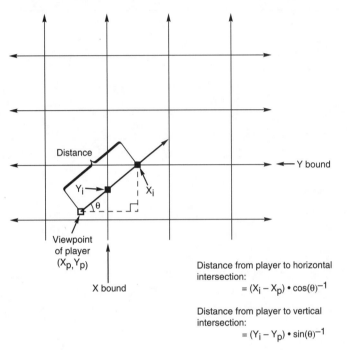

Distance from player to horizontal intersection:
$$= (X_i - X_p) \cdot \cos(\theta)^{-1}$$

Distance from player to vertical intersection:
$$= (Y_i - Y_p) \cdot \sin(\theta)^{-1}$$

Figure 6.26. *Computing the distance from the player to the point of intersection.*

Once we've computed both the vertical and horizontal intersections, we can use the fact that the sin and cos are in terms of:

■ The angle of the ray (which we have)

■ The length of the hypotenuse (which we're trying to find)

■ The length of the sides of the triangle (which we have)

Using Figure 6.26 as a frame of reference for variable names, the following formulas compute the lengths of the hypotenuse (or, in other words, the distance from the player to the point of intersection).

> ### Formula 6.7.
>
> Calculating the distance to the x-intersection.

```
distance = (xi - xp) * cos⁻¹ angle
```

> ### Formula 6.8.
>
> Calculating the distance to the y-intersection.

```
distance = (yi - yp) * sin⁻¹ angle
```

where *angle* is the current angle of the ray being traced, which would in implementation just be an index number from 0-1920 into a look-up table of precomputed sin-1 and cos-1 functions.

This seems like a long process but, if written properly and optimized, the entire ray cast can be done in only a few milliseconds. Once the distances have been computed, a decision is made on which one is closer, and a sliver of the screen is rendered.

Computing the Scale

Now let's talk about scale. *Scale* means how big something is—or seems to be. In the virtual world of the computer, scale is absolutely meaningless unless there are objects to compare, giving *relative scale*. Therefore, the only way we can even comprehend or talk about scale is relative to something else.

To compute scale, we make a comparison between the x-and y-intersections. The scale, or height, of the sliver of the screen that is to be drawn is computed based on the nearer interesection. The sliver is drawn with some height, symmetrically positioned about the center of the screen on the vertical axis. Using the 320x200 mode as an example, and a final height of 100 pixels, we would draw the sliver of screen from 50-150 on the vertical axis. We get more specific about that in a moment.

When computing the scale of the bit map we could use the distance itself, as in:

```
scale = distance to intersection
```

This doesn't exactly work: objects should get bigger as they get closer, not bigger as they get farther away. So we must invert this expression to obtain:

```
scale = 1/distance to intersection
```

Formula 6.9.

The scale of a strip.

This does work. However, the images will have an artificial look to them. We must multiply by another factor, which we can think of as the view distance and aspect ratio combined. The final expression is:

```
scale = K / distance to intersection
```

where K is whatever gives the most pleasing image. (Personally, I choose K such that the block on the screen looks square, but that's up to you.)

Rectifying View Distortion

The final problem we must talk about is what's called *projection distortion*. You see, we broke a rule to implement ray casting: we used polar coordinates and rectangular coordinates together. This has the effect of modulating the scale by a sinusoidal disturbance that makes the image look as if you're looking at it through a spherical lens (or, in deference to you, Kent) a fishbowl. (That's an inside joke for those of you who have seen *Real Genius*).

This spherical viewing distortion is caused by the radial method with which we are casting the ray. We cast each ray from the same source point (that is, the player's viewpoint). Spherical distortion occurs because the objects with which we're testing intersections are defined in a rectangular space, and the rays we're casting are in a spherical, or polar, space. Figure 6.27 shows a polar ray-casting space.

Now, take a look at Figure 6.28. Here we see what the player sees looking directly at a flat wall.

The view the player should see is a rectangle. However, due to the difference in distance to intersections as a function of deviance from the central ray, the view is distorted. In essence, a sin wave has been superimposed on the distance function.

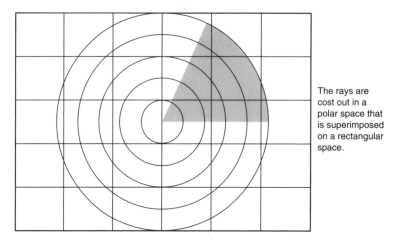

The rays are cost out in a polar space that is superimposed on a rectangular space.

Figure 6.27. *The polar ray-casting space.*

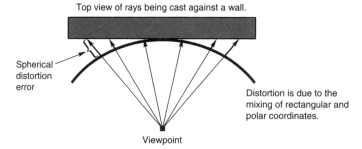

Top view of rays being cast against a wall.

Spherical distortion error

Distortion is due to the mixing of rectangular and polar coordinates.

Viewpoint

Figure 6.28. *Viewing distortion.*

Figure 6.29 shows two actual views of the ray caster. The first view is without distortion compensation; the second is with compensation.

This is all very interesting and intriguing, but how do we get rid of it? The answer is: a simple multiplication by an inverse function. The sinusoidal distortion can be nullified by multiplying the scale by the $\cos^{-1}$ of the current ray angle relative to the 60-degree field of view. By *relative*, I mean that a 60-degree field of view is swept out from -30 degrees from the player's view direction to +30 degrees from the player's view direction. We must multiply each ray's scale, from -30 to +30, by the $\cos^{-1}$ of the same angle, -30 to +30. This cancels out the distortion.

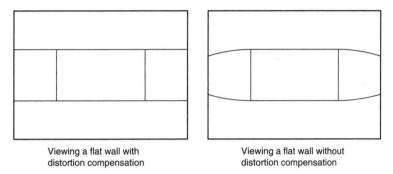

Viewing a flat wall with
distortion compensation

Viewing a flat wall without
distortion compensation

Figure 6.29. *Viewing distortion caused by polar ray-casting space.*

Drawing the Sliver

We're finally ready to draw the sliver of bit map that is one of the vertical strips composing the final, rendered screen. As I said before, we draw the sliver such that its extents are centered about the midline that divides the screen into two horizontal planes. Therefore, once we compute the final scale, we can find the top and bottom of the sliver using the following pseudocode:

```
top = 100 - scale/2
bottom = top+scale;
```

where `scale` is the final height of the sliver we wish rendered.

Implementing a Ray Caster

I've written a fully operational ray caster for you so that you can understand how it's done. This ray caster is commented extensively to enable you to follow the logic. This ray caster is embedded in a demo program on the companion CD at the back of this book. The ray-casting demo program and engine code can be found in the file ray.c, and the executable file is ray.exe.

The demo program loads a 2-D world that is an ASCII file. Take a look at Figure 6.30 to see a sample world that we will ray cast. It was generated with an ASCII text editor.

```
1 1 1 1 1 1 1 1 1 1 1 1 1 1 1 1
1                             1
1   1 1 1 1 1                 1
1   1       1  1  1  1        1
1   1       1                 1
1   1     1 1                 1
1                             1
1                             1
1                             1
1   1 1     1 1 1 1 1 1       1
1   1               1         1
1   1 1 1           1         1
1   1               1         1
1   1 1 1 1 1 1 1   1         1
1                             1
1 1 1 1 1 1 1 1 1 1 1 1 1 1 1 1
```

16 x16

Figure 6.30. *ASCII file representation of the game grid.*

The entire program is too long to list here, and we're only really interested in the ray-casting engine anyway. Let's take a look at the ray-casting engine in detail, and see what each section of the code does and why.

Listing 6.4. The ray-casting engine (raylist.c).

```c
void Ray_Caster(long x,long y,long view_angle)
{
  // This function casts out 320 rays from the viewer and builds
  // up the video display based on the intersections with the
  // walls. The 320 rays are cast in such a way that they all
  // fit into a 60-degree field of view.
  //
  // After a ray is cast, the distance to the first horizontal
  // and vertical edge that has a cell in it is recorded. The
  // intersection that has the closer distance to the player is
  // the one used to draw the bit map. The distance is used to
  // compute the height of the "sliver" of texture or line that
  // is drawn on the screen.
  //
  // Note: this function uses floating point (slow), no
  // optimizations (slower), and, finally, makes calls to
  // Microsoft's Graphics libraries (slowest!). However, writing
  // it in this manner makes it many-orders-of-magnitude easier
  // to understand.

  int rcolor;

  long xray=0,       // This tracks the progress of a ray looking
                     // for y interesctions.
       yray=0,       // This tracks the progress of a ray looking
                     // for x intersections.
       next_y_cell,  // This is used to figure out the quadrant
                     // of the ray.
```

```
        next_x_cell,
        cell_x,      // This is the cell the ray currently is in.
        cell_y,
        x_bound,     // This is the next vertical and horizontal
                     // intersection point.
        y_bound,
        xb_save,     // This is storage in which to record
                     // intersection cell boundaries.
        yb_save,
        x_delta,     // This is amount by which to move to get to
                     // the next cell position.
        y_delta,
        ray,         // This is the current ray being cast, from
                     // 0-320.
        casting=2,   // This tracks the progress of the x- and y-
                     // components of the ray.
        x_hit_type,  // This records the block that was
                     // intersected, and is used to figure out
        y_hit_type,  // which texture to use.

        top,         // This is used to compute the top and
                     // bottom of the sliver that is drawn
        bottom;      // symmetrically around the bisecting plane
                     // of the screen's vertical extents.


    float xi,        // This is used to track the x- and y-
                     // intersections.
          yi,
          xi_save,   // This is used to save exact x- and y-
                     // intersection points.
          yi_save,
          dist_x,    // This is the distance of the x- and y-
                     // intersections from the viewpoint.
          dist_y,
          scale;     // This is the final scale in which to draw
                     // the "sliver."

// S E C T I O N  1 ////////////////////////////////////////////

// Initialization

// Compute the starting angle from the player. The field of view
// is 60 degrees, so subtract half of that for the current view
// angle.

if ( (view_angle-=ANGLE_30) < 0)
{
   // Wrap the angle around.
   view_angle=ANGLE_360 + view_angle;
} // end if

//Select a color for the cast.
rcolor=1 + rand()%14;

// Loop through all 320 rays.
```

continues

Listing 6.4. continued

```
// section 2

  for (ray=0; ray<320; ray++)
  {

// S E C T I O N  2 ///////////////////////////////////////////////

      // Compute the first x-intersection.

      // We need to know which halfplane we are casting from
      // (relative to the y-axis).

      if (view_angle >= ANGLE_0 && view_angle < ANGLE_180)
      {

        // Compute the first horizontal line that could be
        // intersected with the ray. Note: it will be above
        // the player.

        y_bound = CELL_Y_SIZE + CELL_Y_SIZE * (y / CELL_Y_SIZE);

        // Compute the delta to get to the next horizontal
        // line.

        y_delta = CELL_Y_SIZE;

        // Based on the first possible horizontal intersection
        // line, compute the x-intercept so that casting can
        // begin.

        xi = inv_tan_table[view_angle] * (y_bound - y) + x;

        // Set the cell delta.

        next_y_cell = 0;

      }  // end if upper half plane
      else
      {

        // Compute the first horizontal line that could be
        // intersected with the ray. Note: it will be below
        // the player.

        y_bound = CELL_Y_SIZE * (y / CELL_Y_SIZE);

        // Compute the delta to get to the next horizontal
        // line.

        y_delta = -CELL_Y_SIZE;

        // Based on the first possible horizontal intersection
        // line, compute the x-intercept so that casting can
        // begin.

        xi = inv_tan_table[view_angle] * (y_bound - y) + x;
```

```
    // Set the cell delta.

    next_y_cell = -1;

} // end else lower half plane


// S E C T I O N  3 ///////////////////////////////////////////

    // Compute the first y intersection.

    // We need to know which halfplane we are casting from
    // relative to the x-axis.

    if (view_angle < ANGLE_90 || view_angle >= ANGLE_270)
    {
        // Compute the first vertical line that could be
        // intersected with the ray. Note: it will be to the
        // right of the player.

        x_bound = CELL_X_SIZE + CELL_X_SIZE * (x / CELL_X_SIZE);

        // Compute the delta to get to the next vertical line.

        x_delta = CELL_X_SIZE;

        // Based on the first possible vertical intersection
        // line, compute the y intercept so that casting can
        // begin.

        yi = tan_table[view_angle] * (x_bound - x) + y;

        // Set the cell delta.

        next_x_cell = 0;

    } // end if right half plane
    else
    {
        // Compute the first vertical line that could be
        // intersected with the ray. Note: it will be to the
        // left of the player.

        x_bound = CELL_X_SIZE * (x / CELL_X_SIZE);

        // Compute the delta to get to the next vertical line.

        x_delta = -CELL_X_SIZE;

        // Based on the first possible vertical intersection
        // line, compute the y intercept so that casting can
        // begin.

        yi = tan_table[view_angle] * (x_bound - x) + y;
```

continues

Listing 6.4. continued

```
            // Set the cell delta.

            next_x_cell = -1;

        } // end else right half plane

        // begin cast

        casting   = 2;              // These are two rays to
                                    // cast simultaneously.
        xray=yray = 0;              // Reset the intersection
                                    // flags.


// S E C T I O N  4 /////////////////////////////////////////////

        while(casting)
        {

            // Continue casting each ray in parallel.

            if (xray!=INTERSECTION_FOUND)
            {

                // Test for an asymtotic ray.

                if (fabs(y_step[view_angle])==0)
                {
                    xray = INTERSECTION_FOUND;
                    casting--;
                    dist_x = 1e+8;

                } // end if asymtotic ray

                // Compute the current map position to inspect.

                cell_x = ( (x_bound+next_x_cell) / CELL_X_SIZE);
                cell_y = (long)(yi / CELL_Y_SIZE);

                // Test whether there is a block where the current
                // x ray is intersecting.

                if ((x_hit_type = world[(WORLD_ROWS-1) - cell_y][cell_x])!=0)
                {
                    // Compute the distance.

                    dist_x  = (yi - y) * inv_sin_table[view_angle];
                    yi_save = yi;
                    xb_save = x_bound;

                    // Terminate x casting.

                    xray = INTERSECTION_FOUND;
                    casting-;

                } // end if a hit
```

```
        else
        {
            // Compute the next y intercept.

            yi += y_step[view_angle];

        } // end else

    } // end if x-ray has intersected

// S E C T I O N  5 /////////////////////////////////////////////

        if (yray!=INTERSECTION_FOUND)
        {

            // Test for an asymtotic ray.

            if (fabs(x_step[view_angle])==0)
            {
                yray = INTERSECTION_FOUND;
                casting--;
                dist_y=1e+8;

            } // end if asymtotic ray

            // Compute the current map position to inspect.

            cell_x = (long)(xi / CELL_X_SIZE);
            cell_y = ( (y_bound + next_y_cell) / CELL_Y_SIZE);

            // Test whether there is a block where the current
            // y ray is intersecting.

            if ((y_hit_type = world[(WORLD_ROWS-1) - cell_y][cell_x])!=0)
            {
                // Compute the distance.

                dist_y  = (xi - x) * inv_cos_table[view_angle];
                xi_save = xi;
                yb_save = y_bound;

                // Terminate y casting.

                yray = INTERSECTION_FOUND;
                casting--;

            }  // end if a hit
            else
            {
                // Compute the next x intercept.

                xi += x_step[view_angle];

            } // end else

        } // end if y ray has intersected
```

continues

Listing 6.4. continued

```
        // Move to the next possible intersection points.


        x_bound += x_delta;
        y_bound += y_delta;


        // _settextposition(38,40);
        // printf("x_bound = %ld, y_bound = %ld    ",x_bound,y_bound);

    } // end while not done

// S E C T I O N  6 ////////////////////////////////////////////////

    // At this point, we know that the ray has succesfully
    // hit both a vertical wall and a horizontal wall, so we
    // must see which one was closer and then render it.
    //
    // Note: We later replace the crude monochrome line with a
    // sliver of texture, but this is good enough for now.

    if (dist_x < dist_y)
    {

        sline(x,y,(long)xb_save,(long)yi_save,rcolor);

        // There was a vertical wall closer than the
        // horizontal wall.

        // Compute the actual scale and multiply the result
        // by the view filter so that spherical distortion is
        // cancelled.

        scale = cos_table[ray]*15000/(1e-10 + dist_x);

        // Compute the top and bottom and do a very crude clip.

        if ((top    = 100 - scale/2) < 1)
            top = 1;

        if ((bottom = top+scale) > 200)
            bottom=200;

        // Draw the wall sliver and put some dividers up.

        if (((long)yi_save) % CELL_Y_SIZE <= 1 )
            _setcolor(15);
        else
            _setcolor(10);

        _moveto((int)(638-ray),(int)top);
        _lineto((int)(638-ray),(int)bottom);

    }
    else // Must have hit a horizontal wall first.
    {
```

```
        sline(x,y,(long)xi_save,(long)yb_save,rcolor);

        // Compute the actual scale and multiply the result by
        // the view filter so that spherical distortion is
        // cancelled.

        scale = cos_table[ray]*15000/(1e-10 + dist_y);

        // Compute the top and bottom and do a very crude clip.

        if ( (top     = 100 - scale/2) < 1)
           top = 1;

        if ( (bottom = top+scale) > 200)
           bottom=200;

        // Draw the wall sliver and put some dividers up.

        if ( ((long)xi_save) % CELL_X_SIZE <= 1 )
           _setcolor(15);
        else
           _setcolor(2);

        _moveto((int)(638-ray),(int)top);
        _lineto((int)(638-ray),(int)bottom);

        } // end else

// S E C T I O N  7 ///////////////////////////////////////////////

     // Cast the next ray.

     if (++view_angle>=ANGLE_360)
     {
        // Reset the angle back to zero.

        view_angle=0;

     } // end if

   } // end for ray

} // end Ray_Caster
```

The ray-casting engine has been separated into seven main sections so that we can discuss it in a reasonable manner. Let's begin with section one.

■ The first section of the code does a bit of initialization. It takes the player's current view direction and subtracts 30 degrees from it to arrive at the starting angle with which to begin the ray cast. This section also sets a random number that's used to color the current ray-cast in the 2-D map.

■ The second and third sections of the code compute the first x- and y-intersection of the current ray with the perimeter of the cell the player is currently in. Once the first intersection is found for both the x-axis and y-axis, a couple of variables are set to record which way the cast should continue along both the x-axis and y-axis. This helps the fourth and fifth sections of code.

General direction is determined by testing the halfplane from which the ray is being cast. In the case of a ray that is traveling to the right, we know that all possible y-axis intersections will occur to the right of the player's current position, and so on. This logic is applied to both x- and y-intersections to come up with a set of general *traversal variables*.

■ The fourth and fifth sections of the code continue testing for x- and y-intersections. As each intersection is found along the x-axis (which is really a vertical wall) and the y-axis (which is really a horizontal wall), the cell adjacent to the intersection is tested to see if it contains a solid block. If so, the distance from the player to the intersection is recorded for later use, along with the position of the intersection relative to the cell's local origin.

This position can be used for texturing. Although this particular ray caster doesn't do texturing, it does have enough information to accomplish it. For instance, if the ray intersected the middle of the cell wall, we would know to extract the 32nd vertical strip of some texture and map it on the screen. We learn about this later in the book, when we write the Warlock game.

■ The sixth section is where the action finally happens. At this point in the program flow we have computed both the horizontal and vertical intersections, along with their respective distances. Hence, we're ready to display a vertical strip, or sliver, on the screen. To do this, we test each distance to see which one is nearer, and take the closer intersection as the one to be rendered. The current x-position is just the number of the ray, which varies from 0-319. The height of the strip is calculated from the distance with a couple constants to give a pleasing look, along with a square aspect.

■ The seventh section bumps up the current ray angle and loops back to the beginning for another ray cast until all 320 rays have been cast.

The engine we've created is a good place to start; although it doesn't have texturing or lighting, these things aren't that difficult to implement. The reason I opted to keep them out is that they tend to cloud the purity of the ray caster and its operation. It's better that you understand exactly how to do a simple ray cast rather than have a slippery grasp on a fully textured, shaded ray caster.

Now that we have a functioning ray caster, let's see what improvements we can make to it.

Improving Our Ray Caster

The ray caster is hardly complete at this point. It doesn't have textured walls or shading. This much we know, but—ignoring those deficiencies for a moment—how can we speed it up?

- The first and foremost way to speed the ray caster up is to use fixed-point math instead of floating-point. This optimization alone will speed the engine up at least two to four times.

- Secondly, there are a lot of little optimizations that can be made in the C code. Implementing them will extract another 20-50 percent more in performance.

- Next, we might decide to split the x-cast and y-cast into two separate programs. This may allow an optimization that's hiding in the forced parallelism I've given the ray caster.

- Finally, a real ray caster would never use Microsoft's graphics library or the high-resolution mode of 640x480. Once the ray caster uses our library functions and the 320x200 mode 13h, I expect it to run at least 10 times faster, or a minimum of 30 frames/second, which is more than enough for a game. Even if it ran at only 15 frames/second, I'd be happy.

Implementing Doors and Transparency

I'm sure you've seen the doors in Wolfenstein and DOOM open. As they open, you can see into the next room. This turns out to be a fairly complex problem, and implementing it in the ray caster is a bit of a hack. The door must be rendered, but what's behind it also has to be drawn. What has to be done to solve this problem is that the ray has to be cast until it hits the door, and then goes beyond the door.

Let's try to understand this by discussing *transparency*, or seeing through portions of a wall. Say, for example, we draw a wall texture that has holes in it, which we want to see through to the other side. If there was a monster, we could see it through the wall by way of the hole.

This functionality is implemented in the following way:

1. The ray is cast and hits the solid wall.

2. If the wall has holes in it, the ray's intersection and distance from the player are recorded. The ray is cast further through the wall until it hits another wall.

3. At this point that intersection is recorded.

This process could go on forever, but let's say it stopped after the second wall was hit. We now have two intersections, shown in Figure 6.31.

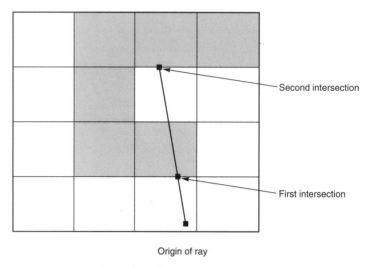

Origin of ray

Figure 6.31. *Casting a ray beyond its first intersection.*

The first intersection would amount to a vertical strip being drawn on the screen. However, there's a hole in the strip where we should see the wall behind it. Therefore, the ray caster buffers both intersections, drawing the farther one first and the nearer one second. This is a form of the Painter's Algorithm, but with a single vertical strip of the screen instead of a polygon. Two strips would be drawn, with the first being partially occluded by the second—but this is exactly what we want. The final image would look as if you were seeing through a hole in the wall.

Implementing a door works in much the same way. As the door opens to the left or right, part of its bit map disappears into the recess in the door channel. This means that you should be able to see through the portion of the door that physically isn't there anymore. This is done by casting the ray until it hits the door, and then continuing on with it until the next intersection. However, unlike the wall with holes in it, the door isn't semi-transparent. We don't need to buffer both intersections; just the last one. This is the one we render, because it's the intersection beyond the door.

In general, effects such as holes, doors, push walls, and so on are done in some manner similar to these two examples, using multiple ray casts along with a simple z-buffering system to record the depth of the ray intersections for a multiple-intersection cast.

Lighting, Shading, and the Color Palette

I want to explain how all those incredible lighting effects are done in DOOM, and how 3-D texture-mapped worlds can be shaded and lit up. You'll find more on the topic when you get to Chapter 7, "Advanced Bit-Mapped Graphics and Special FX."

Realize that there are many clever tricks and techniques used in a game such as DOOM. Moreover, the map editor for DOOM allows a great deal of control of the rooms, colors, and so on. In general, however, all the lighting effects you see in DOOM are done using the color palette in some manner or form.

Basically, the environment in DOOM was created in such a way that it seems almost miraculous. Close, but let's take a crack at it! As an example, I'm going to show a possible method of creating a shaded environment with local lighting and global ambient lighting.

Let's pause for a moment and talk about local and ambient lighting so that we can be sure we're on the same page, if you know what I mean.

Ambient Lighting

Ambient lighting is the average light in a room coming from all directions. For instance if you have an adjustable ceiling lamp, you can increase or decrease the level of ambient light in a room. Figure 6.32 shows a room with two different levels of ambient light.

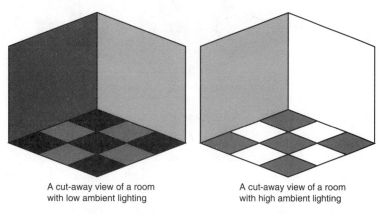

A cut-away view of a room with low ambient lighting

A cut-away view of a room with high ambient lighting

Figure 6.32. *Two rooms with different ambient lighting.*

Of course, the more lights you have, the more even you make ambient light throughout the space. The best example of ambient light is the outdoors. The Sun is so far away that all the light rays impinging on Earth are, for all intents and purposes, parallel. This creates an average, or ambient, light level outside that changes as a function of the angle of the sun.

Local Lighting

Local lighting is a concentration of light intensity in a specific location to highlight something. For example, if you were in your bedroom and had the lights on, you would have an average, or ambient, light level in your room. Now imagine shining a flashlight on the wall. You'd see an increase of reflected light from the wall area at which the flashlight was pointed, as shown in Figure 6.33.

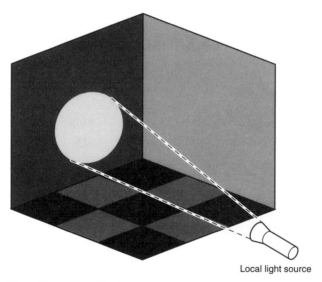

Local light source

Figure 6.33. *The effects of local lighting.*

This is a *local light source*. Even if you turned the ambient lights brighter or dimmer, the local area that you illuminated with the flashlight would stay at roughly the same intensity. (Of course, you could drown out the local light by turning the ambient lights up so bright that their intensity was equal to that of the flashlight.)

Lambert's Law

Now let's talk about reflection and light intensity. If a light source is directed at a surface at some angle and the viewer views the surface parallel to its normal position, the intensity of the light changes according to Lambert's Law, which states:

$$I_d = I_i \; k_d \; \cos \theta \qquad 0 \le \theta \; \pi/2$$

where:

- I_d is the resulting light intensity.

- I_i is the intensity of the light source.

- k_d is the diffuse reflectivity of the surface material.

- θ is the angle between the surface normal and the light source.

What this means in English is that the intensity of reflected light increases as the direction of the light source becomes co-linear with the surface normal—in other words, when the light source is pointing right at the surface and is not at an angle.

The Inverse Square Law

There's another law that is in effect when lighting is concerned: the *inverse square law*. This law states that the intensity of light decreases as the inverse of the square of the distance. Put another way, the farther you get from an illuminated object, the dimmer it gets. (This seems reasonable, doesn't it?)

Let There Be a Light Model

We now have all the physics we need to create a light model that looks good. We know that:

- The farther away a light source gets, the darker it gets.

- As the angle of a surface moves away from the light source, the surface gets dimmer.

- As the ambient light level increases or decreases, so does the brightness of all objects in a room.

We take all three factors into consideration to create a realistic light model.

We could take the angle of the viewer, the ambient light, and the distance to each wall into account for shading. The question is: do we need to? Maybe, maybe not. It depends on what you're willing to call *realistic*. Our whole goal here is to shade the walls in some way that looks real—but at the same time they have to be textured.

How can we accomplish this? There are two ways to do it.

We could compute the exact intensity "on the fly" for each pixel, and render the pixel in that color. The only problem here is that we would quickly run out of color registers. As we only have 256 color registers, we can only have 256 different colors on the screen at once. This amounts to us having to be clever with the use of the colors that we have.

However, here's a method that works and can look quite good. Whether or not "good" means "realistic" is up to you; however, it will look good enough for a PC video game. We know that we need to change the intensity of the walls depending on their angle relative to the view and their distance. We also know, of course, that the intensity of the walls will uniformly increase or decrease relative to the ambient light level. For now, let's concentrate on the effects that distance and angle have on light intensity.

At some point when doing the ray cast, we render a strip of texture on the screen. This texture is rendered with some set of colors that are, in essence, the result of a collection of RGB values that are placed in the color look-up table. (See Chapter 5, "The Mysteries of the VGA Card," for more about the color look-up table.) To do any kind of shading, we need to have the angle the view makes with the walls and the distance between the view and the walls. Luckily, we already have both. We know the angle at which the ray is being cast, and we compute the distance to each intersection as the ray casting is being done. The only thing left to do is to figure out how to use this information to shade the walls.

If we wished, we could use both the distance from the player to the wall and the angle between the player and the wall for the shading algorithm. In practice, we don't need a model that's that complete. We can actually use either the angle or the distance and obtain an effect that looks like the walls are being shaded. The problem is, where are we going to get all the shades from when we only have 256 colors?

To solve this problem, we can create a color palette that has the following attributes:

■ The first 16 colors are the standard EGA colors.

■ We then put additional colors in the next 56 locations. These colors are the only colors that will ever be shaded, and the only colors that will exist in the game. These colors must be chosen such that there are enough base colors to draw all the objects in the game. Furthermore, these 56 colors will be the brightest versions of the colors in the game, so you would create them with that in mind.

■ Now, here's the tricky part. The remaining 184 colors are broken up into three more banks of 56 colors, and a single bank of 16 colors at the end of the color look-up table:

The three banks of 56 colors will be generated algorithmically in software and used by the shading engine.

The bank of 16 colors will be used as extra colors for rotation effects, glowing images, and palette animation.

Let's take a look at what we have. The color palette would look like this:

Table 6.1. The Color Palette for Shading.

Color Register #	Function
0-15 :	The basic EGA colors
16-71:	The primary colors
72-127:	The second shade of the primaries
128-183:	The third shade of the primaries
184-239:	The fourth shade of the primaries
240-255:	Extra colors used for color rotation effects, and so on

The shading engine works as follows: as the sliver of texture is being drawn, the shading engine adds a constant to each pixel value. This constant indexes into the next shade bank of 56 colors, and so forth. For example, if a texture was drawn with solid texture, all color register 16, the other shades would be 16+56, 16+2*56, 6+3*56 (or 72, 128, and 184, respectively). Basically, the shading engine uses the texture data as a basis, and then shades the texture by using other color registers that are accessed by adding a constant. If an object is drawn in the first 16 colors, the shading engine does not add a constant to the values based on the calculated intensity. The color will be plotted unscathed.

We now have four shades of each color in the primary palette of 56 colors. When a hallway is drawn, the ray-casting engine can use four different shades to shade the walls. This is just enough to make it look as though there's shading going on. The remaining three shades are generated by software, by taking the primaries and decreasing their intensities some amount. Therefore, there are a total of four banks of the same colors with decreasing intensities.

The questions now are: how do we use the table, and how should we draw our bit maps? When drawing your bit maps, draw anything that you'll ever want to appear shaded with the bank of the first 56 colors. If you don't want objects to be shaded, use the first 16 colors—and they'll never be touched by the shading engine.

This is how we can obtain local lighting. We draw objects that are lights, or are illuminated by a constant light, with the first 16 colors. Alas, they may never change shade.

Our final problem is: how do we select which shade to use? As I mentioned earlier, we can use either the angle or the distance to obtain the effect of shade. I suggest you try both and see which one you like. To implement either, break the range of possible values for angle or distance into *zones*. If the current value is within zone one, use shade one; if the current value is in zone three, use shade three; and so on. For example, you could say "If the ray angle is within 20 degrees of the view direction, use shade one or the primary colors; if the ray angle is between 20-30 degrees from the view direction, use the second shade of colors," and so on.

The same logic can be used for distance. The only thing to remember is that the intensity should fall off non-linearly; therefore, you should generate your other shades in a non-linear manner. Your zones should be non-linear also (that is, each zone shouldn't have the same amount of range). For example, Table 6.2 shows a possible delineation of distance with which to select shades:

Table 6.2. Selecting a shade based on distance.

Virtual-Distance Units	Shade Bank
0-20	Bank 0 (colors 16-71)
20-50	Bank 1 (colors 72-127)
50-100	Bank 2 (colors 128-183)
100-infinity	Bank 3 (colors 184-239)

A similar table could be made for view angles. At this point in the book, we aren't ready to write an advanced program that would demonstrate the shading engine because of the optimizations that would be needed to get reasonable performance. Hopefully, however, you get the idea.

To reiterate, we break the color palette into six regions:

- The first and last region contain colors that aren't used by the shading engine.
- The middle four regions are four banks of 56 colors each, where each bank is a different shade of the same 56 hues.

When the screen image is rendered, each pixel is drawn with the brightest colors (bank 0), with a constant added to the pixel value that accesses another shade. This constant is a function of the light model, which can be based on either distance or angle.

That's about all there is to it.

Summary

In this chapter we covered standard 3-D polygon-based graphics.

We learned about the mathematics behind 3-D transformations, and methods used to render 3-D images (such as hidden surface removal, doors, and transparency).

We also learned the most important things of all to the PC video-game programmer (as far as DOOM-type games are concerned): ray tracing and ray casting. Moreover, we learned how to implement a ray caster and how to shade and texture the world.

Finally, we learned that ray casting is a complex process (relative to other video game-related topics) and that it must be done quickly—or at least fast enough to obtain a reasonable frame rate of 15 frames/second or more.

Later, when we write Warlock, we take what we've learned here and implement a fully functioning ray caster with texture and shading. Until then, have fun with the next chapter!

Advanced Bit-Mapped Graphics and Special FX

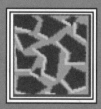

T he line between a good video game and an *incredible* one is usually narrow. The algorithms, themes, and sounds are roughly the same from game to game. What separates one game from another—and, consequently, what makes one person rich and another not so rich—is that little extra: clever screen transitions, smooth scrolling, proper video synchronization, and so on. Like a warrior with a sword, therefore, we must sharpen our blade to a razor-fine edge.

This chapter has some really interesting (yet simple) programs that deliver effects comparable to the most complex and state-of-the-art effects seen in video games today. Within these pages we also learn some advanced bit-map techniques, such as scaling, that we use later. This chapter covers:

by André LaMothe

- Faster bit blitting
- Logical bit operations
- Transparency encoding
- Bit clipping
- Sprite collision
- More on double buffering
- Locking on target with the vertical sync
- Color-register animation
- More on lighting
- Context-sensitive animation
- "Animotion"
- Scrolling
- Special FX
- Background animation
- Screen transitions
- Textures
- Bit-mapped image scaling
- Bit-mapped image rotation

Without further verbage, let's get busy!

Faster Bit Blitting

Taking into consideration the types of video games we want to create in this part of the book, we should concentrate our programming efforts on the areas that we know are going to "bottleneck" game performance. One area will be the primary culprit: the graphics.

Within a 3-D, texture-mapped, Wolfenstein- or DOOM-type game, most of the computer's computational time is spent either on rendering the walls (that is, the 3-D view) or drawing the 2-D sprite images that represent game objects, such as monsters. We discuss the 3-D rendering part in depth in Chapter 6, "The Third

Dimension." However, I want to say a few things about sprite optimization because it's so important to the type of game in which we're interested.

We've seen in previous chapters how to blit bits (in Chapter 5, "The Mysteries of the VGA Card") and transfer bit-mapped images from one region of memory to another. I'd bet that 90 percent of the time spent developing a game is spent figuring out the fastest possible way to do this. In Chapter 18, "Optimization Techniques," we cover general optimization theory and see some examples of applying the techniques to our code. However, those techniques are to be used on the last pass of the code (meaning that, after the code is already fast, we make it wickedly fast using optimization techniques).

What you should realize is that you must rewrite your bit-blitting algorithms and code almost every time you create a new game; moreover, you may have two to five different blitters in a single game. Each blitter is designed specifically for a special case. For instance, you may find that some kind of optimization could be made to your general blitter for objects that are always stationary. If so, go ahead and make two blitters: one for moving objects and one for stationary objects. The code for each blitter takes around 1K to 2K bytes, if even that much.

Here's another example of a possible optimization: your blitters may read data in a way that replicates the most obvious way it can be stored. However, consider whether blitting would be faster if the data were in another form. For instance, is storing data pixel by pixel (based on a 2-D matrix) less efficient than storing it column by column (based on 16 bits)? If you find such an improvement, maybe the form could be synthesized with the original data, and the data preprocessed for use by the modified blitter.

In any case, think about ways to make your blitting as fast as possible, because a video game will have anywhere from 2 to 20 moving objects on the screen that are, on average, 32x32 pixels. That's quite a bit of data to be moving around in real time!

> As you know, I've supplied blitters and some tools with this book. *Please do not use these in a video game!* They're too slow. They're for demonstration purposes only. You must alter them for your specific needs.

There's one more aspect of blitting objects that you can use to your advantage: if you always know that the objects will be 16x16 or 32x32, or whatever, you can write a blitter for each different size, optimized specifically for the dimensions in question.

Remember: there are no hard-and-fast rules for making video games. There are no exact algorithms and no shrinkwrapped libraries. You must be mega-creative and mega-clever. There is, however, something that should make you feel better: every game in history that has been a hit didn't use more than high school algebra and trigonometry. What this means to you is that there may be an obvious way to do something using higher mathematics and complex algorithms, but most of the time a 12-year-old will find another way that's 100 times faster and more efficient—just because a 12-year-old doesn't know better!

Logical Bit Operations

When an object is blitted to the video screen, or even to an off-screen work area, we can do a logical operation with the source and destination pixels. If you review our Draw_Sprite() function given in Listing 5.13 (in Chapter 5, "The Mysteries of the VGA Card"), you'll see that it basically does a blind replacement of data, depending on the source data:

- If the data is nontransparent (that is, not black), the source data replaces the current pixel on the screen.

- If the source data is transparent, the data on the screen is left untouched.

We do this so that we can see through the object if it has holes. To implement this transparency we must put an IF statement similar to the following in the inner loop of the blitter:

```
if ((data=work_sprite[work_offset+x]))
            video_screen[offset+x] = data;
```

This IF statement is executed many times; to be exact, it's executed sprite_width times sprite_height. For a 64x64 image, therefore, there are 4096 IFs. That's 4,095 too many!

However, there's another possible optimization that can be made in certain cases. If we take the IF out, the sprite image creates a black rectangular region with the sprite in the middle. If the sprite we're drawing is rectangular and takes up the whole 64x64, there's no need to have the IF statement: we know that the source pixels will always be drawn on the destination (that is, there are no transparent portions of the source bit map). Alas, this is seldom the case! Although we can surely make versions of the blitter for when this does occur (such as for wall textures), we should try to see if there's a "happy medium" between the two extremes.

One possibility is to use logical bitwise operations—such as OR, XOR, AND, and NOT—to place our data on the screen. This way we don't use an IF statement; we use a logical operator, which is performed quickly by the CPU. The only questions are: which operator should we use, and what will that operator do?

Recall how data is represented in mode 13H: each pixel is represented by a single byte. That byte is used as a color index into the color look-up table. If we start using logical operators on the source and destination, we'll be mixing colors and changing the color index—which we don't want to do!

Let's see some examples. Say that we're blitting a single pixel with value 10 (red) onto the screen at position (100,100). At this position there's another pixel with the value of 56 (magenta). We'd like to see a red pixel on the screen after plotting (100,100) with value 10. However, using the logical operations that we have at our disposal, the values in Table 7.1 will occur instead:

Table 7.1. The results of logical operations on source and destination data.

Given that 56 = 00111000b and 10 = 00001010b:

Source (bit image)	Operation	Destination Data (screen data)	Result
00111000	OR	00001010	00111010 = 58
00111000	AND	00001010	00001000 = 8
00111000	XOR	00001010	00110010 = 50

As you can see, doing a logical operation on the data transforms the color index to that of another color. This might even be what we want; in certain cases discussed in a moment, in fact, it's exactly what we want. However, we still haven't got what we originally wanted, which is to replace the screen pixel with our data pixel only in the case when it is nonzero.

Now, no one said we couldn't do more than one logical operation on the source and destination data. We can do so if we wish, but we would start to lose what gains we have made. An IF statement is basically a comparison and a jump—so, if we start using multiple logical operations, at some point the logical operations will take more time than the IF statement. To illustrate this, let's see the code generated both by doing an IF statement (in Listing 7.1) and by doing a logical operation (in Listing 7.2), and see just how much slack we really have.

Listing 7.1. The disassembly of an IF statement.

```
; File if.c
;
; #include <stdio.h>
;
;
; char far *source, *dest;  // These are the source and
                            // destination data regions.
;
; main()
; {
; Line 8
                        _main:
 *** 000000 c8 00 00 00 enter OFFSET L00181,OFFSET 0
     *** 000004    56              push si
     *** 000005    57              push di
; index = fffc
; data = fffa
;
; int index;
; Line 10
; unsigned data;
; Line 11
;
; // if version
;
; if (data=source[index])
; Line 15
     *** 000006    8b 46 fc    mov  ax,WORD PTR -4[bp]
     *** 000009    8b 1e 00 00     mov  bx,WORD PTR _source
     *** 00000d    8b 0e 02 00     mov  cx,WORD PTR _source+2
     *** 000011    03 d8           add  bx,ax
     *** 000013    8e c1           mov  es,cx
     *** 000015    26 8a 07     mov  al,BYTE PTR es:[bx]


     *** 000018    98              cbw
     *** 000019    89 46 fa        mov  WORD PTR -6[bp],ax
     *** 00001c    3d 00 00        cmp  ax,OFFSET 0
     *** 00001f    75 03 e9 00 00      je   L00180
;     dest[index]=data;


; Line 16
     *** 000024    8b 46 fa     mov  ax,WORD PTR -6[bp]
     *** 000027    8b 4e fc     mov  cx,WORD PTR -4[bp]
     *** 00002a    8b 1e 00 00  mov  bx,WORD PTR _dest
     *** 00002e    03 d9        add  bx,cx
     *** 000030    88 07        mov  BYTE PTR [bx],al
;
; } // end main
; Line 18
                    L00180:
; Line 18
                    L00177:
     *** 000032    5f              pop  di
     *** 000033    5e              pop  si
```

```
    *** 000034    c9              leave
    *** 000035    cb              ret   OFFSET 0
Local Size: 6
; Line 0
```

Listing 7.2. The disassembly of a logical OR operation.

```
; File or.c
;
; #include <stdio.h>
;
;
; char far *source, *dest;   // These are the source and
                             // destination data regions.
;
; main()
; {
; Line 8
                        _main:
 *** 000000 c8 00 00 00 enter OFFSET L00180,OFFSET 0
     *** 000004    56              push  si
     *** 000005    57              push  di
; index = fffc
; data = fffa
;
; int index;
; Line 10
; unsigned data;
; Line 11
;
; // logical operator version (OR)
;
; dest[index]=dest[index]=data ¦ source[index];
; Line 15
     *** 000006    8b 46 fc    mov   ax,WORD PTR -4[bp]
     *** 000009    8b 1e 00 00     mov   bx,WORD PTR _source
     *** 00000d    8b 0e 02 00     mov   cx,WORD PTR _source+2
     *** 000011    03 d8           add   bx,ax
     *** 000013    8e c1           mov   es,cx
     *** 000015    26 8a 07        mov   al,BYTE PTR es:[bx]


     *** 000018    98          cbw
     *** 000019    0b 46 fa    or    ax,WORD PTR -6[bp]


     *** 00001c    8b 4e fc        mov   cx,WORD PTR -4[bp]
     *** 00001f    8b 1e 00 00     mov   bx,WORD PTR _dest
     *** 000023    03 d9           add   bx,cx
     *** 000025    88 07           mov   BYTE PTR [bx],al
     *** 000027    8b 4e fc        mov   cx,WORD PTR -4[bp]
     *** 00002a    8b 1e 00 00     mov   bx,WORD PTR _dest
     *** 00002e    03 d9           add   bx,cx
     *** 000030    88 07         ⁙ mov   BYTE PTR [bx],al
```

continues

Listing 7.2. continued

```
;
; } // end main
; Line 17
; Line 17
                           L00177:
    *** 000032      5f               pop   di
    *** 000033      5e               pop   si
    *** 000034      c9               leave
    *** 000035      cb               ret   OFFSET 0
Local Size: 6
; Line 0
```

If you take a close look at Listings 7.1 and 7.2, you'll see that I've highlighted the areas that are generated specifically by the intrinsic differences between the two programs. We see that the code that uses the logical OR operation is about half as big as the code that uses the IF statement. However, we must count cycles to be precise. This is difficult, because we can't be sure if the code is running on a 386, 486, or 586. Nevertheless, we can roughly guess that the code that uses the logical operation is almost 100 percent faster than the IF statement version. This translates to our being able to use only one logical operation, maybe two, before the performance is matched by the original IF statement. We must, therefore, figure out a way to use a single logical operation to obtain the results we desire.

One way is to take advantage of the many special effects and clever operations which can be done with logical manipulations that change the pixel value in a predictable manner. For example, one way we can use a logical operation is to create the color look-up table in such a way that the results of certain logical operations (such as OR, AND, or XOR) result in a new color index. This index obtains a color value that has the same RGB values as the original source data but has the numerical value of the source data and the destination data logically combined.

Let's create a color model for purposes of illustration. The background in our world has only 16 colors, with the indices of 0, 16, 32, 48, 64, 80, 96, 112, 128, 144, 160, 176, 192, 208, and 224. The foreground, or sprite, images also have 16 colors; however, their indices are 0-15. Therefore, when a source pixel and destination pixel are used in a logical OR operation, the resulting lower four bits are always the foreground color, while the resulting upper four bits are always the background color.

Now say that we replicate the first 16 colors over and over in the color look-up table and create multiple banks of 16 colors with the same RGB values, as shown in Figure 7.1.

Figure 7.1. *Creating multiple color banks with the same RGB values.*

Bank 0 would range from 0-15, bank 1 would range from 16-31, and so on. Each bank would have the same RGB values, so when the background data was zero, the foreground color (0-16) would stay intact. Put more precisely:

```
0 OR (0-16) = (0-16)
```

Things get interesting when a nonzero value is used for the source data. Assume that the source data is a 5 (or color 6, from the source image's point of view), and the background data is 32 (or color 2). When these values are used in a logical OR operation, the result is 37, which is the fifth color in the third bank of 16 colors. Color 37 has the same RGB values as color 6 or index 5, because we replicated the colors in banks of 16.

Once all the smoke clears, you can see that we have indeed accomplished our goal: with a single logical operation, we have implemented transparency! The only drawback is that we now have only 16 colors. (Having only 16 colors in a game isn't going to cut it, but for the moment it's worth it to have discovered a clever use of the color look-up table to speed up our blitter.)

Admittedly, we probably won't use this exact color model. However, it gives us a new tool—and some ideas that we might use elsewhere.

Transparency Encoding

As I alluded to in the previous section, it may be possible to speed up the blitter if another data structure is used. Our major problem in blitting rectangular sprites is in implementing transparency: whenever the transparent pixel (usually 0, or black) is in the source image, the background image pixel is left intact (that is, not replaced). The problem, as we just saw, is the execution of the IF statement.

Another possible solution to our pixelated dilemma, however, is to create a sort of *run-length encoded* (RLE) version of our sprite data that encodes "runs" of transparency, as shown in Figure 7.2.

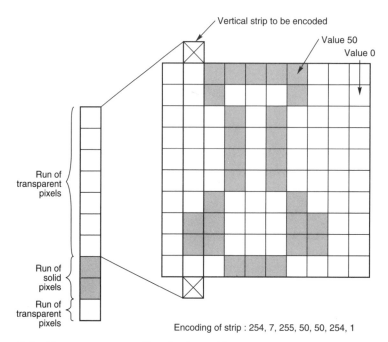

Figure 7.2. *Transparency encoding for faster blitting.*

If the object to be blitted were broken down into horizontal or vertical strips, we could scan for runs of transparency and encode them in some way. Then we could turn transparency on and off, much like using a toggle switch a few dozen times rather than doing thousands of IF operations. The choice is up to you; however, as a starting point, I suggest something like the following:

- Make sure the sprite has data in the following format:
  Vertical Strip 1, Vertical Strip 2,...Vertical Strip N
  where each vertical strip is composed of runs of solid and transparent pixels.

- In addition, set a flag up to denote each type of run, such as 255 and 254.

- The next data item after the flag should be the length of the run, in bytes.

- The last elements are the actual data bytes themselves.

Our single strip of data would look like this:

```
Let,

255: solid
254: transparent

(255 ¦254), number of data bytes,data,
```

This pattern would repeat over and over. For example, the first strip of Figure 7.2 would encode as:

```
254,3,0,0,0,255,13,5,5,5,5,5,5,5,4,4,4,26,31,28
```

The algorithm we could write would skip over the transparent pixels and only draw the solid pixels for each vertical strip.

We can make one further optimization: when there's a transparent run, we know that the data will be zero (or whatever color index represents "transparent"), so why waste space and place streams of redundant zeroes in the sprite data? We can just take them out. Therefore, our new data type can contain the solid data, some flags, and the run-length indicator bytes. There is one little problem with this scheme: we can't use 255 or 254 as color indexes anymore, because they're used as control flags. (However, I don't think two colors out of 256 is going to kill us, do you?)

Again, this is just an idea that can speed up your blitting. You may not use this exact encoding. You may decide to do things horizontally instead, but his would make your rendering harder when you were tyring to mix a ray-cast world with a sprite world. (You saw why in Chapter 6, "The Third Dimension.") However, it's one more trick up your sleeve. Of course, you'd need to write extra functions to convert your standard bit images so the Draw_Sprite() function would work on them.

We've covered a few ideas on ways to improve bit blitting and the rendering of sprites in this section. I want to emphasize, though, that these are just ideas. I want you to come up with new twists and ways of looking at the problem. You now know a few ways to attack bit blitting, but the blitters in your code will continually change and evolve as you learn and become more experienced. (I know ways to bit blit 20 times faster than anything we've talked about or seen; however, these blitters work only in a specific case, and are so optimized that I have a hard time understanding them—and I wrote them!) The point is, there's more than one way to do something. You must be clever in your programming if you are ever going to attain the performance levels of Wolfenstein or DOOM.

Bit Clipping

Bit clipping means clipping a bit map to the edges of the screen or some other arbitrary shape. We're not interested in general clipping here. We're only interested in rectangular or window-type clipping. Even in a Wolfenstein- or DOOM-type game, the only clipping that's done with a sprite is against some rectangular region, such as the edges of the screen or some other, smaller rectangle within the boundaries of the screen. Figure 7.3 shows a bit-mapped image clipped against the screen.

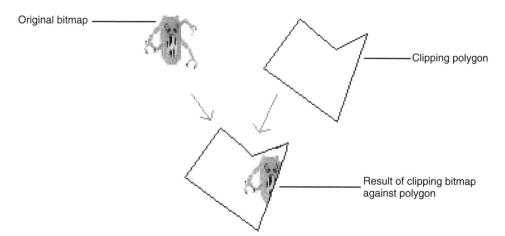

Original bitmap

Clipping polygon

Result of clipping bitmap against polygon

Figure 7.3. *Clipping a bitmap against a polygon.*

So how do we clip an image against a rectangular region? First, do we need to even *do* clipping? The answer is yes, and maybe no. If your game objects and creatures are transformed in ways that never make them extend past the bounding region, clipping is unnecessary; the case of the object extending off its domain will never occur. To ensure that an object would never move off the screen, its control logic would keep the object in its bounding region during motion or transformations.

However, this isn't always achievable. For example, in the 3-D view in DOOM, there are many times when a monster is barely on the screen. Maybe only the right half of its body is visible. That means the left half is being clipped, so clipping is a must.

We must clip a bit-mapped image any time it's possible the image may extend past any edge of the screen (or past the bounding domain we've set up for it). For instance, in Wolfenstein 3-D the player can change the size of the view window. No matter what happens, you never see any of the images go beyond this view window because they're clipped against it.

Now, there are two ways to attain a clipped bit-mapped image:

- We can test every single pixel to see if it's within the bounding region. Clipping in this fashion is called *image-space clipping*. In other words, we process the image all the way down to the pixel level, and then make decisions.

  This technique doesn't take into consideration the geometry of the object. This is slow (and, I suspect, is the method Microsoft uses for graphics— because no one can write blitters that run as slow as the ones in Microsoft's Graphics Library!). Anyway, we don't want to do that.

■ We can consider the geometrical properties of the object during the clipping operation: its size, shape, and position relative to the bounding (clipping) region. Clipping in this fashion is called *object-space clipping*.

What we really want to do is object-space clipping. Clipping is simple—at least, the kind of clipping we're going to need is simple. However, we always want to be insightful and resourceful. Clipping the bit image is going to slow the blitting down a bit, and we want to minimize this slowdown.

The first insight we can make is the following preprocessing test: *Is the object even within the bounding region?* For example, say we have a 16x16 bit map and it's at position (1000,1000). The screen is the bounding region. Because the screen is 320x200, obviously the bit map isn't even visible, and neither clipping nor rendering is necessary. For every object in the game world, then, we should test whether it's partially visible. Algorithm 7.1 does this.

Algorithm 7.1. Testing whole object visibility.

```
// Let the object be at (x,y) with a size of WidthXHeight.
// Let the screen be size Screen_Width x Screen_Height.
// For each object in world:

// Process the current object.

if (X >0 and X<Screen_Width and Y>0 and Y<Screen_Height)
   then partially visible goto clip
else
   not in view goto next object
```

Algorithm 7.1 is not the most efficient. However, it shows the point clearly: if the object is wholly or even partially on the screen, it should be clipped and displayed. Otherwise, process the next object.

Once we've made the decision to clip the object, we simply have to figure out the new top, bottom, left, and right edges of the bit map to be drawn after the other parts are clipped off by the bounding region. If you think about this, you'll see that, in most instances, only two edges get clipped at any time: one vertical edge and one horizontal edge. This works for all bit maps that are smaller than the screen.

If the bit maps are bigger than the screen in either dimension, that idea goes out the window. This can actually happen when we start scaling sprites to make them look as though they're getting closer. For now, though, we'll assume that the sprites will always be smaller than the bounding region—at least for the rest of the discussion.

If you've studied the Draw_Sprite() function in Chapter 5, or any of its derivatives, you'll see that it does a double FOR loop on the bit-mapped data and draws the object row by row, where each row starts at the x position of the sprite and progresses downward using the sprites starting at y. What we must do, therefore, is change the mechanics of the two FOR loops to take into consideration a new starting and ending (x,y), and we must change the starting position of the sprite if either the x component or y component is off the screen. Remember: just because the x, y, or both are off the screen doesn't mean the whole sprite is. Figure 7.4 shows an example of this.

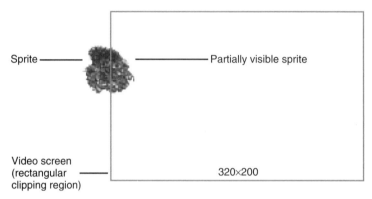

Figure 7.4. *A partially visible sprite.*

Let's modify the Draw_Sprite() function to clip a sprite to the video screen. This new version is about 5 percent slower; however, it will always draw the sprite correctly. Listing 7.3 contains the code.

Listing 7.3. The Draw_Sprite()**function, with clipping.**

```
void Draw_Sprite_Clip(sprite_ptr sprite)
{

// This function draws a sprite on the screen and clips it to
// the screen boundaries. The function is drawn out to show each
// step clearly.

char far *work_sprite;
int work_offset=0,offset,x_off,x,y,xs,ys,xe,ye,
    clip_width,clip_height;
unsigned char data;

// Extract the sprite position.

xs = sprite->x;
ys = sprite->y;

// Compute the end of the bounding box in screen coordinates.
```

```
xe = xs + sprite_width  - 1;
ye = ys + sprite_height - 1;

// Test whether the sprite is totally invisible (i.e., is beyond
// the screen boundaries).

if ( (xs >= SCREEN_WIDTH) ¦¦ (ys >= SCREEN_HEIGHT) ¦¦
     (xs <= (-sprite_width)) ¦¦ (ys <= (-sprite_height)) )
    {
    return;
    } // End if the sprite is invisible.

// The sprite must be partially visible; therefore, compute the
// region to be drawn.

// Clip in the x direction.

if (xs < 0)
   xs=0;

else
if (xe >= SCREEN_WIDTH)
    xe=SCREEN_WIDTH-1;

// Clip in the y direction.

if (ys < 0)
   ys=0;

else
if (ye >= SCREEN_HEIGHT)
    ye=SCREEN_HEIGHT-1;

// Compute the new width and height.

clip_width  = xe - xs + 1;
clip_height = ye - ys + 1;

// Compute working offsets based on the new starting y.

work_offset = (sprite->y - ys) * sprite_width;

x_off = (xs-sprite->x);

// Now render the clipped sprite.

// Alias a pointer to the sprite for ease of access.

work_sprite = sprite->frames[sprite->curr_frame];

// Compute the offset of the sprite in the video buffer.

offset = (ys << 8) + (ys << 6) + sprite->xs;

for (y=0; y<clip_height; y++)
    {
    // Copy the next row into the screen buffer, using memcpy
    // for speed.
```

continues

Listing 7.3. continued

```
    for (x=0; x<clip_width; x++)
        {

        // Test for a transparent pixel (that is, 0); if not
        // transparent, draw.

        if ((data=work_sprite[work_offset+x + x_off]))
            double_buffer[offset+x+x_off] = data;

        } // end for x

    // Move to the next line in the video buffer and in the
    // sprite bit-map buffer.

    offset      += SCREEN_WIDTH;
    work_offset += sprite_width;

    } // end for y

} // end Draw_Sprite_Clip
```

As with the first two listings in this chapter, take the program in Listing 7.3 with a grain of salt. It does what it's supposed to do; however, it has no context. Context is everything! For example, you may make a game where all images stay in the middle. In that case you wouldn't need bit clipping. Maybe your game objects always move horizontally; in that case, you wouldn't have to worry about clipping the object vertically, and you could optimize the preprocessing portion. Always try to write your graphics functions for the particular game and problems at hand. In these discussions the most important thing is that you understand the problem. Once you understand the problem, finding a solution is just a matter of time and hard work.

Sprite Collision

Many times in a game we want to test whether two or more sprites have crashed into each other. Testing for sprite collision is no different than testing for the asteroid/ship collision discussed in Chapter 4, "The Mechanics of Two-Dimensional Graphics." To test whether two sprites have collided or intersected, we simply test to see whether any of the four bounding vertices of one sprite are contained within the bounding region of the other sprite. This test looks something like Algorithm 7.2.

Algorithm 7.2. Sprite collision testing.

```
// Let each sprite have size (width x height) and assume that
// the sprites are located at (x1,y1) and (x2,y2), respectively.
if (x1 > x2  and  x1 < x2+width  and  y1 > y2  and  y1 < y2+height)
   {
   do collision
   }
else
   {
   no collision
   }
```

The interesting aspect of Algorithm 7.2 is that it tests for a collision by testing for intersection. We could try an optimization by testing for the converse; that is, test whether the objects *don't* intersect. (Many times it's easier to test whether something didn't occur than to test whether it did...just an idea to generate other points of view!)

Double Buffering

We had a brief introduction to double buffering in Chapter 5, "The Mysteries of the VGA Card." Now I want to really nail down the concept and its *raison d'être*.

Double buffering is used to minimize the flicker induced by blasting pixels to the video screen. A double buffer is an off-screen region of memory used to build up the display. Then, when the display is built up and the image is ready for viewing, a high-speed chunk of code copies the double buffer to the video buffer. Usually, this copy is done using a stosw instruction, which moves WORDS at a time. This is the most efficient way to access the video buffer.

We should be asking whether drawing to the double buffer is going to slow things down compared to directly writing to the video buffer. Here are the things to consider:

- First, the video RAM is quite slow, and doing read or write operations is anywhere from two to 10 times slower than normal memory.

- Second, once the screen is built up in the double buffer, we can blast all 64,000 bytes of it into the video buffer in one single shot using the stosw instruction.

- Finally, if we were to do all our drawing and image rendering in the video buffer itself, we would see all kinds of flickering and shearing effects.

Taking all that into consideration, using a double buffer is usually faster than direct video access, and the animation and graphics will be an order of magnitude smoother. The single drawback to using a double buffer is that it needs 64,000 bytes of memory; however, it's worth it.

Also, the whole screen need not be double-buffered. For instance, if the viewport to the game world is only 100 pixels high, the double buffer need only be big enough to hold 100 rows of 320 pixels, or 32,000 bytes. In Chapter 14, "Linking Up," we make a game called Net-Tank to show you how to do serial communications and multiplayer games. In Net-Tank we only double buffer the first 176 lines of the display. The rest of the display is made up of instruments that can be drawn once and are static images.

Now that we know what a double buffer is and what it's used for, let's see some examples of how to create a double buffer and render in it. The original 2-D bit-mapped graphics code that we saw in Chapter 5, "The Mysteries of the VGA Card," has been modified and extended in Listing 7.4 to use a double buffer instead of the video buffer. Making this change boils down to changing one line of code in each function: we simply change the word `video_buffer` to `double_buffer` in all the sprite functions. This program, circles.c:

- Allocates a double buffer
- Draws 1,000 circles in it
- Blasts the buffer to the video screen in a single bound

Listing 7.4. Circles in the double buffer (circles.c).

```c
// I N C L U D E S /////////////////////////////////////////////

#include <stdio.h>
#include <math.h>
#include <graph.h>
#include <malloc.h>
#include <memory.h>
#include <string.h>

// D E F I N E S /////////////////////////////////////////////

#define SCREEN_WIDTH      (unsigned int)320
#define SCREEN_HEIGHT     (unsigned int)200

// G L O B A L S  /////////////////////////////////////////////

unsigned char far *video_buffer = (char far *)0xA0000000L;
    // vram byte ptr
unsigned char far *double_buffer = NULL;

// F U N C T I O N S /////////////////////////////////////////////

void Init_Double_Buffer(void)
```

```
{

double_buffer =
 (char far *)_fmalloc(SCREEN_WIDTH * SCREEN_HEIGHT);

_fmemset(double_buffer, 0, SCREEN_WIDTH * SCREEN_HEIGHT);

} // end Init_Double_Buffer

////////////////////////////////////////////////////////////////

void Show_Double_Buffer(char far *buffer)
{
// Copy the double buffer into the video buffer.

_asm
   {
   push ds                   // Save the data segment.
   les di, video_buffer      // Set the destination (that is, the
                             // video buffer).
   lds si, buffer            // Set the source (that is, the
                             // double buffer).
   mov cx,320*200/2          // We want to move 320*200 bytes, or
                             // half that number of words.
   rep movsw                 // Do the movement.
   pop ds                    // Restore the data segment.
   }

} // end Show_Double_Buffer

////////////////////////////////////////////////////////////////

void Plot_Pixel_Fast_D(int x,int y,unsigned char color)
{

// Plot pixels into the double buffer.
// Use the fact that 320*y = 256*y + 64*y = y<<8 + y<<6.

double_buffer[((y<<8) + (y<<6)) + x] = color;

} // end Plot_Pixel_Fast_D

////////////////////////////////////////////////////////////////

void Circles(void)
{
// This function draws 1,000 circles into the double buffer. (In
// a game we would never use a crude algorithm like this to draw
// circles. Instead, we would use look-up tables or other means.
// However, we just want something to be drawn in the double
// buffer.)

int index,xo,yo,radius,x,y,color,ang;

// Draw 100 circles at random positions, with random colors and
// sizes.
```

continues

Listing 7.4. continued

```
for (index=0; index<1000; index++)
    {

    // Get the parameters for the next circle.

    xo     = 20 + rand()%300;
    yo     = 20 + rand()%180;
    radius = 1 + rand()%20;
    color  = rand()%256;

    for (ang=0; ang<360; ang++)
        {

        x = xo + cos(ang*3.14/180) * radius;
        y = yo + sin(ang*3.14/180) * radius;

        Plot_Pixel_Fast_D(x,y,(unsigned char)color);

        } // end ang

    } // end index

} // end Circles


// M A I N ////////////////////////////////////////////////////////

void main(void)
{
// Set the video mode to the 320x200, 256 color mode.

_setvideomode(_MRES256COLOR);

// Create a double buffer and clear it.

Init_Double_Buffer();

_settextposition(0,0);
printf("Drawing 1000 circles to double buffer.
printf("\nPlease wait...");

// Draw the circles to the double buffer.

Circles();

printf("Done, press any key.");

// Wait for the player to hit a key, then blast the double
// buffer to the video screen.

getch();

Show_Double_Buffer(double_buffer);

_settextposition(0,0);
```

```
printf("That was quick. Hit any key to exit.");

getch();

// Restore the video mode.

_setvideomode(_DEFAULTMODE);

} // end main
```

Admittedly, the program in Listing 7.4 isn't the most exciting thing in the world, but it gets the point across. Notice how the plot pixel function writes to the double buffer instead of the video buffer.

Using a double buffer makes the video display almost flicker-free; however, we still can't ensure that the video buffer isn't being written to at the moment it's being accessed by the video hardware to drive the monitor. This can cause screen sheer. Screen sheer, and how to avoid it, is discussed in the next section.

Locking on Target with the Vertical Sync

As you know, the video image is created by an electron gun that paints the screen pixel by pixel until it reaches the bottom. At that point, it retraces along a diagonal line back to its starting position and the process is repeated. During this *vertical retrace period*, the screen memory is not begin accessed by the video hardware—and, if we make changes to the video RAM, we don't see them until the next frame.

This is exactly what we want. The most opportune time to update the video buffer is when it isn't being accessed: during the vertical retrace period. The beginning of the retrace is initiated by the vertical syncrhonization pulse (*vertical sync*) sent by the VGA card. This pulse and the period immediately after it are what we're interested in detecting and using to lock our animation to the 70Hz CRT timing.

To accomplish this, we must figure out a way to detect the start of the vertical retrace, and then use this knowledge to help us synchronize our graphics updates to times when the video buffer is not being accessed by the rendering hardware.

It just so happens that this VGA card has a register that monitors the vertical retrace. The register, called the *VGA input status word*, can be found at port number 0x3DA. Of the eight bits that comprise the register, we're interested in the fourth bit, bit number d3:

■ When the bit is 1, there's a retrace in progress.

■ When the bit is 0, there's no retrace in progress.

Now, if we merely tested the bit and detected a retrace in progress, we wouldn't know if it was at the beginning, middle, or end of its cycle. If a retrace is in progress, therefore, we must wait for it to end. By doing this, we can know that the next action marks the beginning of a retrace. Hence, we can write a routine that polls the status bit and waits for the beginning of a retrace. Our routine can then return and let the caller know that, for the next 1/70th of a second (for VGA modes, or 1/60th of a second for EGA modes), the video buffer can be accessed without contingency.

I've written a demo program, vsync.c, that does this synchronization and counts the number of vertical retraces as a function of time. Because there are 70 retraces per second, if you let the program run for 60 seconds the count should be 4,200. Listing 7.5 contains the code.

Listing 7.5. Counting retraces (vsync.c).

```
// I N C L U D E S ////////////////////////////////////////////////

#include <dos.h>
#include <bios.h>
#include <stdio.h>
#include <math.h>
#include <conio.h>
#include <graph.h>

// D E F I N E S ////////////////////////////////////////////////

#define VGA_INPUT_STATUS_1    0x3DA // VGA status reg 1, bit 3 is
                                    // the vsync:
                                    // 1 = retrace in progress
                                    // 0 = no retrace

#define VGA_VSYNC_MASK 0x08         // Masks off unwanted bits of
                                    // status reg.


// G L O B A L S ////////////////////////////////////////////////

unsigned char far *video_buffer = (char far *)0xA0000000L;
    // vram byte ptr


// F U N C T I O N S ////////////////////////////////////////////////

void Wait_For_Vsync(void)
{
// This function waits for the start of a vertical retrace. If a
// vertical retrace is in progress, it waits until the next one.

while(_inp(VGA_INPUT_STATUS_1) & VGA_VSYNC_MASK)
    {
    // Do nothing; VGA is in retrace.
    } // end while
```

```
// Now wait for vysnc and exit.

while(!(_inp(VGA_INPUT_STATUS_1) & VGA_VSYNC_MASK))
     {
     // Do nothing; wait for the start of the retrace.
     } // end while

// At this point a vertical retrace is occuring, so return to
// the caller.

} // Wait_For_Vsync

// M A I N ////////////////////////////////////////////////////

void main(void)
{

long number_vsyncs=0;  // Tracks the number of retrace cycles.

while(!kbhit())
     {

     // Wait for a vsync.

     Wait_For_Vsync();

     // Do graphics or whatever now that we know electron gun is
     // retracing. We have only 1/70th of a second, though!
     // Usually, we would copy the double buffer to the video
     // RAM.

     // ....

     // tally vsyncs

     number_vsyncs++;

     // Print to the screen.

     _settextposition(0,0);
     printf("Number of vsync's = %ld    ",number_vsyncs);


     } // end while
} // end main
```

There are a multitude of things that the vertical sync can be used for:

- We can use it as a time base for some process or event.

- We can use it to lock a game to a 70Hz running frequency on any machine.

- Finally, we can use it to synchronize our graphics updates with the retrace period.

I have to tell you something that I wish I didn't have to: it's possible to have a vertical-retrace interrupt. The PC does have hardware support to vector to an interrupt when a vertical retrace occurs. However, this interrupt support is not truly IBM compatible, and won't always work. Furthermore, it uses INT2, which is used for fatal hardware faults and is marked by IBM as reserved. Therefore, I'm not going to cover it: it's hardware-dependent, and most programmers don't even use it.

Let's move on to the next interesting and exciting topic: color-register animation.

Color-Register Animation

Many things in life are not as they seem to be. Analogously, many effects and animations are not done as you would think. Color-register animation is one of those techniques that can make something that would be extremely difficult or computationally expensive quite simple to implement.

Color-register animation is based on the fact that an image is a collection of colors. These colors are, in turn, defined by RGB values in a color look-up table. For example, let's say we have two identical objects—say, two trees, each comprised of eight shades of green. We create two set of colors, each with the same eight shades. Then we draw the two trees next to each other. We draw one tree using the first set of colors and the other tree using the second set of colors, as shown in Figure 7.5.

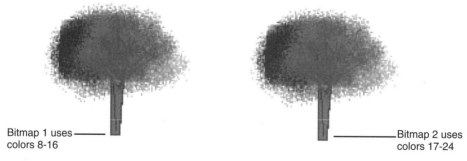

Bitmap 1 uses colors 8-16

Bitmap 2 uses colors 17-24

Figure 7.5. *Using two sets of identical colors with different color-register values.*

If we were to blit both trees on the screen, we'd see two otherwise identical trees that were, in fact, drawn with different color registers. Here comes the interesting part: what if we zeroed out the first set of color registers? The first tree would disappear.

That's the basis of color-register animation. In short:

- We make all the images of interest out of different sets of color registers containing the same RGB values.

- Then we turn each object invisible by zeroing out the color registers for that specific image.

- Then we sequentially turn back on each of the color registers that make up each separate object, while keeping the other banks of the color registers zeroed.

This makes the object seem to move from one position to another, although there was no movement or pixel blasting. We simply changed a few color registers.

This technique can be used to make objects metamorphosize (*morph*) into other shapes, move across the screen, and disappear. To show you how this can work I've created a demo called birdani.c, which makes a little bird fly around in a circle without actually moving. I drew the bird in 13 shades of gray in a paint program, then loaded the image in with the PCX software we wrote in Chapter 5, "The Mysteries of the VGA Card," then zeroed out all the color registers that made up the 13 shades of gray. At this point I placed a green in the first color register, then zeroed it out and placed the same green in the next color register, and so on. This makes the bird look like it's flapping its wings and flying in a circle. Listing 7.6 contains birdani.c.

From now on in the book I use precompiled libraries of functions so that we don't have to see the same old functions in all the listings. I've taken most of the functions we've looked at so far in the book and placed them into a single C file named graph0.c. Along with this is a header file named graph0.h. We can link this object in with our other C source to make all the functions in the C file accessible. Just compile the file graph0.c—be sure to use the MEDIUM memory model—and, during your link phase, add it to the main program you're working with. If you want access to the functions in the graphics library, be sure to include the header file graph0.h.

You could also create a library with the graphics functions using Microsoft's Library Manager, LIB. We have only one source file, so that might be overkill. It's up to you. As long as all the code in graph0.c, graph0.h, and the set mode function is included somehow with the rest of the programs in this chapter, everything will be just fine.

As with all the programs discussed in ths book, though, I've included an .EXE file on the companion CD. You can simply execute it if you don't feel like compiling and linking the program.

Listing 7.6. Color-register animation (birdani.c).

```c
// I N C L U D E S //////////////////////////////////////////////

#include <io.h>
#include <conio.h>
#include <stdio.h>
#include <stdlib.h>
#include <dos.h>
#include <bios.h>
#include <fcntl.h>
#include <memory.h>
#include <malloc.h>
#include <math.h>
#include <string.h>
#include <graph.h>
#include "graph0.h" // Include our graphics library.

// D E F I N E S //////////////////////////////////////////////

#define BIRD_START_COLOR_REG 16
#define BIRD_END_COLOR_REG   28

// G L O B A L S //////////////////////////////////////////////

unsigned int far *clock = (unsigned int far *)0x0000046C;
     // Pointer to internal
     // 18.2 clicks/sec

pcx_picture birds;

////////////////////////////////////////////////////////////////

void Timer(int clicks)
{
// This function uses the internal timekeeper (the one that runs
// at 18.2 clicks/sec to time a delay). You can find the 32-bit
// value of this timer at 0000:046Ch.

unsigned int now;

// Get the current time.

now = *clock;
```

```
// Wait until the time has gone past the current time plus the
// amount we wanted to wait. Note that each tick is
// approximately 55 milliseconds.

while(abs(*clock - now) < clicks){}

} // end Timer

////////////////////////////////////////////////////////////////

void Animate_Birds(void)
{
// This function animates a bird drawn with 13 different colors
// by turning on a single color and turning off all the others
// in a sequence.

RGB_color color_1, color_2;
int index;

// Clear out each of the color registers used by birds.

color_1.red   = 0;
color_1.green = 0;
color_1.blue  = 0;

color_2.red   = 0;
color_2.green = 63;
color_2.blue  = 0;

// Clear out all the colors.

for (index=BIRD_START_COLOR_REG;
     index<=BIRD_END_COLOR_REG; index++)
    {

    Set_Palette_Register(index, (RGB_color_ptr)&color_1);

    } // end for index

// Make the first bird green, then rotate the colors.

Set_Palette_Register(BIRD_START_COLOR_REG,
                (RGB_color_ptr)&color_2);

// Animate the colors.

while(!kbhit())
    {
    // Rotate the colors.

    Get_Palette_Register(BIRD_END_COLOR_REG,
                    (RGB_color_ptr)&color_1);

    for (index=BIRD_END_COLOR_REG-1;
        index>=BIRD_START_COLOR_REG; index—)
        {
```

continues

Listing 7.6. continued

```
            Get_Palette_Register(index,(RGB_color_ptr)&color_2);
            Set_Palette_Register(index+1,(RGB_color_ptr)&color_2);

            } // end for

            Set_Palette_Register(BIRD_START_COLOR_REG,
                                (RGB_color_ptr)&color_1);

        // Wait a while...

        Timer(3);

        } // end while

} // end Animate_Birds

// M A I N //////////////////////////////////////////////////////

void main(void)
{
int index,
    done=0;

// Set the video mode to the 320x200, 256 color mode.

Set_Mode(VGA256);

// Initialize the .PCX file that holds all the birds.

PCX_Init((pcx_picture_ptr)&birds);

// Load the .PCX file that holds the cells.

PCX_Load("birds.pcx", (pcx_picture_ptr)&birds,1);

PCX_Show_Buffer((pcx_picture_ptr)&birds);

PCX_Delete((pcx_picture_ptr)&birds);

_settextposition(0,0);
printf("Hit any key to see animation.");

getch();

_settextposition(0,0);
printf("Hit any key to Exit.          ");

Animate_Birds();

// Restore the video mode.

Set_Mode(TEXT_MODE);

} // end main
```

The birdani.c program in Listing 7.6 is rudimentary. However, incredible effects can be mastered with the use of this technique, including the ones discussed in the next section.

Illuminating Your Games

Lighting, shading, and similar effects are traditionally done with complex mathematics based on physical models that take into consideration such factors as the angle of incidence, light source distance, light source type, specular and refractive properties of the reflecting material, transmission properties of the space around the object, and so on. (Chapter 6, "The Third Dimension," has more to say about this.) No wonder it takes a Cray XMP hours or days to ray trace a photorealistic image! The equations that would need to be solved, and the number of operations that would need to be done to obtain those solutions, are a bit too much to ask of a little PC. Therefore, we're going to have to use a bit of creativity and some light models that are "good enough" for our needs as video-game programmers. The incredible lighting effects you see in DOOM are impressive but, none the less, not impossible to implement. As usual, let's learn to fly before we try transporting!

As an example, say we've drawn a room using color registers 1-32. These color registers are full of shades of gray (along with some reds—there have been some altercations recorded on the walls.) Anyway, what if we slowly increased the RGB values in each of the color registers, 1-32? Well, you would see the room get *brighter*. And if we decreased each RGB value in each color register, the room would get darker.

Of course, you must make sure to keep the percentage of each component the same. Otherwise, the color will start changing hue along with intensity. In other words, you must increase or decrease the components of each color register proportionally to its original value. Therefore, to decrease the intensity of a specific color register—say, 26—you would first see what percent of the color was red, green, and blue. Then you would compute a factor to be added or subtracted to each component so that the original color balance stays intact.

As an example, let's decrease each RGB value by 5 percent on each iteration. To do this we must recompute 5 percent of each RGB value and subtract it from each RGB component. Table 7.2 shows the results of doing this a few times on an arbitrary RGB color.

Table 7.2. Decreasing a color's intensity while keeping the color balance the same.

Color Components	R	G	B	(Color balance using red as reference)
Iteration 1	60	40	20	1: .66 : .30
Iteration 2	57	38	19	1: .66 : .33
Iteration 3	54	36	18	1: .66 : .33

As you can see, if we iteratively decrease each component by 5 percent, a constant color balance stays in flux. Of course, computing 5 percent of each value on each iteration is computationally expensive. To avoid this, we might try simply decrementing a constant value from each color register component, disregarding the color balance. This works. However, as the intensity of the color goes up or down, you may notice that the hue of the color starts to shift.

A compromise between the two extremes would be to compute three constants based on the original color balance, and use those constants as the incremental or decremental amounts. This would decrease the error as the components were altered. In our case, we might use a 5 for the red component, .66*5 for the green, and .3*5 for the blue. This actually produces reasonable results. Using this technique, we would get the following RGB values after one iteration.

R	G	B	(Color balance using red as reference)
55	37	19	1: .67 : .34

The error based on the true color balance is negligible—and, as we would only increment or decrement the RGB components a few times, the color shift would hardly be noticeable.

Context-Sensitive Animation

This is a fairly unexplored topic in video-game technology. *Context* means "relating to the environment or basis." For our purposes, the context will be whatever is currently happening in the game world. Is the player dying, jumping, being shot at, or what? Whatever it is, that's part of the context—and having animation and effects that are sensitive to the context adds another dimension of reality to the game play.

Let me clarify what the heck I'm talking about with an example. Say we have a game where the player's character can walk, jump, run, and shoot. Whether the character is jumping over a spider or jumping over a lake, he or she always does this same animation during the jump. What if we were to make a separate set of animation cells for each different case, or context, in which players could find themselves? For example, when the character jumps over a pool of water, he or she doesn't do much except jump. However, if the test of jumping skill is leaping over a spider, the player's character might look at you, utter a shriek of terror, and exhibit markedly enhanced jumping abilities. (Landing on that big, juicy spider probably wouldn't be a very nice experience for the little character trapped in the virtual computer world.)

Summing up: context-sensitive animation systems try to take into account the environment or set of circumstances at that particular point in the game to help in selecting a set of animation cells that add a little more variety to the visualization of the game.

"Animotion"

Animotion is a word I made up and hereby put forth into the dictionary of video-game terminology. (As you'll continue to find out, I make up words when there isn't a good one already.) Animotion describes the proper merging of animation and motion.

In the Tombstone demo in Chapter 4, "The Mechanics of Two-Dimensional Graphics," a little cowboy walked across the street. Actually, it looked more like he was hobbling and moonwalking all in one. The problem was that his motion, or translation, wasn't in sync with his animation cells. Many objects in a video game can have constant velocities. Game objects such as missiles and other flying objects are good examples. However, objects that must somehow look real and be in contact with a surface, such as the ground, are another story.

Animotion is absolutely necessary if motions such as walking, running, jumping, and so on are to look real. Otherwise, when objects are animated, they'll look artificial. We can't just run through the animation cells and move the object some number of pixels at every cycle. We must take a look at each cell and compute just how much motion should *really* occur. Then, we create a motion look-up table that uses the current frame as an index into the table. The motion look-up table contains the translation values used during animation.

Figure 7.6 shows the cells for a stick figure, whom we'll call Stickman.

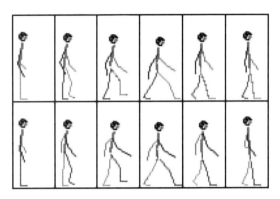

Figure 7.6. *Animation cells for Stickman.*

(Stickman has a serious vision problem: he has only one eye.) There are 12 animation cells for Stickman walking. For each cell, I sat and estimated how much the object should translate to make the image look like it's really walking. After a little tweaking, I obtained the values shown in Table 7.3 for each cell of animation:

Table 7.3. Translation values for a smooth walk.

Cell 1 - 17

Cell 2 - 0

Cell 3 - 6

Cell 4 - 2

Cell 5 - 3

Cell 6 - 0

Cell 7 - 17

Cell 8 - 0

Cell 9 - 6

Cell 10 - 2

Cell 11 - 3

Cell 12 - 0

To show you an example of animotion versus constant motion, I've created a program that allows the player to alternate between these methods by hitting the Spacebar. Our guinea pig will be poor, defenseless Stickman. We're going to place him in a really bad part of town with nothing but his two arms, two legs, and two eyes. (—oops! I mean one eye.) Anyway, watch him walk across the screen. Then hit the Spacebar to toggle his motion mode from constant velocity to animotion. You'll see a big difference. This program, shown in Listing 7.7, also uses the code in graph0.c, so remember to link it in to make a final, executable program. (If you can't wait, don't worry: there's a precompiled .EXE file, called stick.exe, on the companion CD.)

Listing 7.7. A demonstration of animotion.

```c
// I N C L U D E S //////////////////////////////////////////////////

#include <io.h>
#include <conio.h>
#include <stdio.h>
#include <stdlib.h>
#include <dos.h>
#include <bios.h>
#include <fcntl.h>
#include <memory.h>
#include <malloc.h>
#include <math.h>
#include <string.h>

#include "graph0.h" // Include our graphics library.

// D E F I N E S //////////////////////////////////////////////////

#define VEL_CONST -1
    // Flags that motion should use constant velocity.

// G L O B A L S //////////////////////////////////////////////////

unsigned int far *clock = (unsigned int far *)0x0000046C;
    // Pointer to internal
    // 18.2 clicks/sec.

sprite object;
pcx_picture stick_cells,
            street_cells;


// The motion look-up table has a separate entry for each frame
// of animation so a more realistic movement can be made based
// on the current frame.

int object_vel[] = {17,0,6,2,3,0,17,0,6,2,3,0};

// F U N C T I O N S //////////////////////////////////////////////////
```

continues

Listing 7.7. continued

```c
voidTimer(int clicks)
{
// This function uses the internal timekeeper (the one that runs
// at 18.2 clicks/sec to time a delay). You can find the 32-bit
// value of this timer at 0000:046Ch.

unsigned int now;

// Get the current time.

now = *clock;

// Wait until the time has gone past the current time plus the
// amount we wanted to wait. Note that each tick is
// approximately 55 milliseconds.

while(abs(*clock - now) < clicks){}

} // end Timer


// M A I N ////////////////////////////////////////////////////

void main(void)
{
int index,
    done=0,
    vel_state=VEL_CONST;

// Set the video mode to the 320x200, 256 color mode.

Set_Mode(VGA256);

// Set the sprite system size so functions use the correct
// sprite size.

sprite_width = 32;
sprite_height = 64;

// Initialize the .PCX file that holds the street.

PCX_Init((pcx_picture_ptr)&street_cells);

// Load the .PCX file that holds the cells.

PCX_Load("street.pcx", (pcx_picture_ptr)&street_cells,1);

PCX_Show_Buffer((pcx_picture_ptr)&street_cells);

// Use the .PCX buffer for the double buffer.

double_buffer = street_cells.buffer;

Sprite_Init((sprite_ptr)&object,0,0,0,0,0,0);

// Initialize the .PCX file that holds the stickman.
```

```
PCX_Init((pcx_picture_ptr)&stick_cells);

// Load the .PCX file that holds the cells.

PCX_Load("stickman.pcx", (pcx_picture_ptr)&stick_cells,1);

// Grab six walking frames.

PCX_Grap_Bitmap((pcx_picture_ptr)&stick_cells,
               (sprite_ptr)&object,0,0,0);
PCX_Grap_Bitmap((pcx_picture_ptr)&stick_cells,
               (sprite_ptr)&object,1,1,0);
PCX_Grap_Bitmap((pcx_picture_ptr)&stick_cells,
               (sprite_ptr)&object,2,2,0);
PCX_Grap_Bitmap((pcx_picture_ptr)&stick_cells,
               (sprite_ptr)&object,3,3,0);
PCX_Grap_Bitmap((pcx_picture_ptr)&stick_cells,
               (sprite_ptr)&object,4,4,0);
PCX_Grap_Bitmap((pcx_picture_ptr)&stick_cells,
               (sprite_ptr)&object,5,5,0);

PCX_Grap_Bitmap((pcx_picture_ptr)&stick_cells,
               (sprite_ptr)&object,6, 0,1);
PCX_Grap_Bitmap((pcx_picture_ptr)&stick_cells,
               (sprite_ptr)&object,7, 1,1);
PCX_Grap_Bitmap((pcx_picture_ptr)&stick_cells,
               (sprite_ptr)&object,8, 2,1);
PCX_Grap_Bitmap((pcx_picture_ptr)&stick_cells,
               (sprite_ptr)&object,9, 3,1);
PCX_Grap_Bitmap((pcx_picture_ptr)&stick_cells,
               (sprite_ptr)&object,10,4,1);
PCX_Grap_Bitmap((pcx_picture_ptr)&stick_cells,
               (sprite_ptr)&object,11,5,1);

// Don't need the stickman .PCX file anymore.

PCX_Delete((pcx_picture_ptr)&stick_cells);

// Set up the stickman.

object.x          = 10;
object.y          = 120;
object.curr_frame = 0;

// Scan the background.

Behind_Sprite((sprite_ptr)&object);

// main loop

while(!done)
    {

    // Erase the sprite.

    Erase_Sprite((sprite_ptr)&object);
```

continues

Listing 7.7. continued

```
// Increment the current frame of the stickman.

if  (++object.curr_frame > 11)
    object.curr_frame = 0;

// Move the sprite using either a constant velocity or a
// look-up table.

if (vel_state==VEL_CONST)
   {
   object.x+=4;
   } // end if constant velocity mode
else
   {
   // Use the current frame to index into the table.

   object.x += object_vel[object.curr_frame];

   } // End, or use the look-up table to create
     // a more realistic motion.

// Test whether the stickman is off the screen.

if (object.x > 280)
    object.x=10;

// Scan the background.

Behind_Sprite((sprite_ptr)&object);

// Draw the sprite.

Draw_Sprite((sprite_ptr)&object);

// Copy the double buffer to the screen.

Show_Double_Buffer(double_buffer);

// Wait a bit...

Timer(2);

// Test whether the player is hitting the keyboard.

if (kbhit())
   {
   switch(getch())
       {
       case ' ': // Toggle motion mode
            {
            vel_state = -vel_state;
            } break;

       case 'q': // exit system
            {
            done=1;
```

```
                   } break;
              } // end switch

        } // end if kbhit
    } // end while

// Delete the .PCX file.

PCX_Delete((pcx_picture_ptr)&street_cells);

// Restore the video mode.
Set_Mode(TEXT_MODE);
} // end main
```

After running the program, I'll bet your glad not to be Stickman. That thing in the tunnel looks pretty mean!

Now let's move to scrolling.

Scrolling

Many video games have really huge game worlds. In fact, these worlds are so large that displaying the entire world at once is impossible. Therefore, a technique called *scrolling* (or *panning*) is used to display a window into the game universe. This window may be the same size as the video display, or smaller. Figure 7.7 shows an example game world that has six screens' worth of image data.

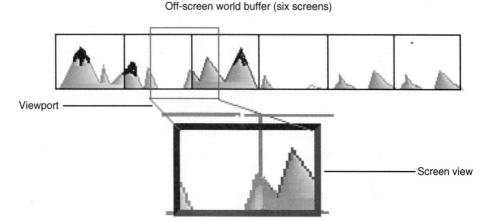

Figure 7.7. *Scrolling around.*

As you can see in Figure 7.7, the viewport has some position within the game world, and everything within the viewport is then mapped to the screen. The scrolling effect occurs when the viewport is continually moved in some direction, and the data within it is continually mapped to the view screen. (A perfect example of scrolling can be seen in the Mario Brothers games. Most of the appeal of these games is due to their large game universes.)

Although scrolling has traditionally been an effect used in 2-D games, there are many uses for it in 3-D games. For instance, in DOOM you may notice that you can see mountains and terrain outside the windows and in the exterior world that scrolls as you rotate. This scenery is really a 2-D image that's scrolled in the background. The image has been tweaked a bit to make it look 3-D; however, it's basically a scrolling, 2-D image.

The PC does have special hardware to facilitate scrolling. Also, because the VGA card can have up to a megabyte of video RAM, it's possible to draw your game world in the VGA video buffer and let the hardware do the scrolling for you. There are two problems with this, however:

■ First, if we use the hardware we become hardware-dependent, and some VGA cards may not have enough memory.

■ Second, scrolling in mode 13h is more problematic than in other EGA-based modes because the video memory is no longer organized in a multiplane fashion, as it is in the other EGA modes. This feature (or, I should say, lack of one) means we can't use the hardware to scroll for us as we can in EGA modes that are planar.

The bottom line is that we will not be using the PC's hardware to do scrolling. We will do it manually, using block copies of off-screen memory to the video buffer. We are completely hardware-independent using this technique, and our software will be more portable in the long run.

Scrolling the whole screen, or a portion of the screen, can be done two ways:

■ We can draw the entire game world in a large memory buffer. However, six predrawn screens would take 6*64,000 bytes, or 384,000 bytes. This is quite a waste of memory. In any case, as we said a moment ago, we would then make an imaginary window move over the world and map that region to the screen.

■ The second method is a bit slower, but consumes much less memory. It's based on generating the image on the fly. By *on the fly* I mean that the world is represented by some other data structure—perhaps a 2-D cell matrix, where each cell is 8x8 pixels and represents a bit map we want placed in the world. A cell world that was six screens would only take 6,000 bytes. Then, as the window would be moved around the cell world, the cells would be interpreted and the appropriate bit maps for each cell rendered.

The problem with this method is speed. Because each cell must be translated to a bit map and blitted to the double buffer or screen, a lot of time is needed to draw the screen. You may have seen some video games that look pretty bad when they scroll. You can actually see the screen being drawn. This is the problem you're seeing.

We either sacrifice speed or memory; the choice is yours.

To show you an example of scrolling, I've made a program that creates a world that is 640x100. I then move a view window over the game world and map it to a window in the middle of the video screen. The game world has some stars and a mountainscape drawn in it. (It looks a little like the game Defender.) Use the keyboard to move the view window to the right and left and scroll the scene. Listing 7.8 contains the code for this program, called defend.c.

Listing 7.8. An example of scrolling (defend.c).

```
// I N C L U D E S //////////////////////////////////////////////

#include <stdio.h>
#include <math.h>
#include <graph.h>
#include <malloc.h>
#include <memory.h>
#include <string.h>

// D E F I N E S //////////////////////////////////////////////

#define SCREEN_WIDTH      (unsigned int)320
#define SCREEN_HEIGHT     (unsigned int)200

// G L O B A L S  //////////////////////////////////////////////

unsigned char far *video_buffer = (char far *)0xA0000000L;
     // vram byte ptr
unsigned char far *double_buffer = NULL;

// F U N C T I O N S //////////////////////////////////////////////

void Show_View_Port(char far *buffer,int pos)
{
// Copy a portion of the double buffer to the video screen.

unsigned int y,double_off, screen_off;
```

continues

Listing 7.8. continued

```
// There are 100 rows that must be moved; move the data row
// by row.

for (y=0; y<100; y++)
    {

    // Compute the starting offset into the double buffer.
    // y * 640 + pos

    double_off = ((y<<9) + (y<<7) + pos );

    // Compute the starting offset in the video RAM.
    // y * 320 + 80

    screen_off = (((y+50)<<8) + ((y+50)<<6) + 80 );

    // Move the data.

    _fmemmove((char far *)&video_buffer[screen_off],
            (char far *)&double_buffer[double_off],160);

    } // end for y

} // end Show_View_Port

//////////////////////////////////////////////////////////////////

void Plot_Pixel_Fast_D2(int x,int y,unsigned char color)
{

// Plot pixels into the double buffer with our new virtual
// screen size of 640x100.

// Use the fact that 640*y = 512*y + 128*y = y<<9 + y<<7.

double_buffer[((y<<9) + (y<<7)) + x] = color;

} // end Plot_Pixel_Fast_D2

//////////////////////////////////////////////////////////////////

void Draw_Terrain(void)
{

// This function draws the terrain into the double buffer, which
// in this case can be thought of as being 640x100 pixels.

int x,y=70,index;

// Clear out memory first.

_fmemset(double_buffer,0,(unsigned int)640*(unsigned int)100);

// Draw a few stars.
```

```
for (index=0; index<200; index++)
    {
    Plot_Pixel_Fast_D2(rand()%640,rand()%70,15);
    } // end for index

// Draw some mountains.

for (x=0; x<640; x++)
    {

    // Compute the offset.

    y+=-1 + rand()%3;

    // Make sure the terrain stays within a reasonable boundary.

    if (y>90) y=90;
    else
    if (y<40) y=40;

    // Plot the dot in the double buffer.

    Plot_Pixel_Fast_D2(x,y,10);

    } // end for x

} // end Draw_Terrain

// M A I N ///////////////////////////////////////////////////////

void main(void)
{

int done=0,sx=0;

// Set the video mode to the 320x200, 256 color mode.

_setvideomode(_MRES256COLOR);

_settextposition(0,0);

printf("Use < > to move. Press Q to quit.");

// Draw a little window.

_setcolor(1);

_rectangle(_GBORDER, 80-1,50-1,240+1,150+1);

// Allocate memory for the double buffer.

double_buffer = (char far *)
                _fmalloc(SCREEN_WIDTH * SCREEN_HEIGHT+1);

Draw_Terrain();

Show_View_Port(double_buffer,sx);
```

continues

Listing 7.8. continued

```
// main loop

while(!done)
     {

    // Has the player hit a key?

    if (kbhit())
       {

      switch(getch())
           {
           case ',': // Move the window to the left, but
                     // don't go too far.
                {
                sx-=2;

                if (sx<0)
                    sx=0;

                } break;

           case '.': // Move the window to the right, but
                     // don't go too far.
                {
                sx+=2;

                if (sx > 640-160)
                   sx=640-160;

                } break;

           case 'q': // Is the player trying to bail?
                {
                done=1;

                } break;

           } // end switch

      // Copy the viewport to the screen.

      Show_View_Port(double_buffer,sx);

      _settextposition(24,0);

      printf("Viewport position = %d  ",sx);

      } // end if

    } // end while

// Restore the video mode.
```

```
_setvideomode(_DEFAULTMODE);

} // end main
```

If you're like me, you probably want to make a little Defender game now. If that's the case, put the book down and go for it. Don't worry; I'll wait. At least try to put in a ship with joystick control.

Back already? No video game would be complete without some cool visual effects, so let's cover some topics in that area.

Special FX

The phrase "special FX" has become synonymous with visual excitation that's out of the ordinary; something really awesome. Video games are becoming more and more like movies, and every game that comes out already has impressive graphics. However, there's always something that makes you go "*Wow!*" Let's work on making people go "*Wow!*"

Special effects can be anything from screen transitions and vivid explosions to weird, psychedelic graphics and what-have-you. For instance, I'm currently working on a particle system simulator that will "rip" monsters apart into a billion little atoms and throw them out along circular orbits. This should look pretty cool! I'm not sure where I'll use it—but when I do, it will turn some heads!

Most importantly, special effects is an area that you'll have to explore on your own, because it's one of the primary areas in which to exercise your creativity. Just remember one thing: in every game, have at least one really earth-shattering effect to catch the player's eye. Just to get you started, though, this section covers a few other possibilities.

Background Animation

This is an area that I just want to talk about for a moment. A video game must have more going on than the quest at hand. Adding little animations and effects that have nothing to do with the game can really add to the game's "fun factor."

For instance, imagine creating a Karate game. In this game, having some birds fly by every now and then or placing an erupting volcano right outside the door might be just the thing. In the game we make at the end of the book, I'm thinking of throwing in some fireflies that just twinkle around in the game world. They don't serve any purpose other than to make the universe seem a little more complex, a little more real.

These little effects and add-ons are definitely last-minute efforts you should put in after the game is done. However, always try to put a few out-of-the-ordinary animations and effects in to give your games some texture.

Screen Transitions

Video games are becoming more and more like movies. The credits on the boxes no longer list "programmers" or "engineers." These titles have been changed to "Directors" and "Producers." It then seems appropriate for us to think of the video display as a movie or television screen. In the movies or on TV we see *screen dissolves, blurs,* and other effects when the camera changes view or when we are taken to another place. Video games should also have these kinds of screen transitions. For instance, when you finish a level, maybe the screen fades away or melts—or whatever!

Having screen transitions can only add to the overall presentation of your game. Switching the screen to black and going to the next scene is boring. I'd much rather see the screen rip apart or do something exciting.

Programming screen transitions is relatively easy. Most transitions can be done in a few lines of code, with complex screen transitions only taking a few dozen lines. This is another area where you'll have to use your own creativity and talent to come up with some really wicked effects. However, I've written three different screen transitions and created a program (screenfx.c) to demo them. The program, shown in Listing 7.9, uses the PCX functions (created in Chapter 5, "The Mysteries of the VGA Card") and some library calls, so you'll have to link it to graph0.c.

The three effects that we are going to see are

- ■ Fade to black
- ■ Screen dissolve
- ■ Meltdown

Let's briefly go over the mechanics of each effect to get an idea of how they're done, and how to implement others.

Fade to Black

The fading-lights effect is an old favorite of many programmers. Its implementation is fairly simple and can be done in a few lines of code.

Basically, we slowly decrement the values of all color registers until they're zeroed out. As we learned in this chapter under "Illuminating Your Games," it's best to try and keep the color balance equal as you increase or decrease the intensity of any color. In the case of a light fade, we really don't care: the effect will only take a couple seconds, and the screen will get so dark so fast the colors will hardly be recognizable, anyway.

Therefore, the program in Listing 7.9 simply decreases each component of each color register by 5 until all components—red, green, and blue—are zero. When the fade is done, the function exits.

Screen Dissolve

This is a good effect to try to do in a single line of code. In fact, it's so easy to do I'll show you the single line of code in a minute.

A screen dissolve basically pixelates the screen image by putting black holes in it. All that must be done for a screen dissolve to occur is for thousands of randomly placed black dots to be plotted on the screen. Because the screen has the last video image (a room, scenery, or whatever), the plotting of these black dots makes that screen image look like it's "dissolving" into thin air.

Here are two of the coolest lines of code I can think of:

```
for (index=0; index<=300000; index++,
Plot_Pixel_Fast(rand()%320, rand()%200, 0));
```

This code simply plots 300,000 black pixels all over the screen. By plotting this many pixels, you're almost assured that most of the screen will be destroyed. (You could compute the exact number of iterations needed to completely erase the screen, but that would take a bit of math. The number 300,000 seems to work fine.)

This effect could be used to transition to another screen if the pixels of another video image were plotted rather than black pixels. Use x and y coordinates found randomly as the pixel coordinates of the source data in the new screen, as well as the destination pixel coordinates in the old screen.

Meltdown

This effect was inspired by DOOM and the way the DOOM screen seems to "melt" away. My version isn't as impressive. However, it only took 15 minutes to implement, and the results definitely look as though they were much harder to do.

The melt works by moving 160 little "worms" from the top to the bottom of the screen at random velocities, with gravity working on them. As these worms move down the screen, they eat up pixels. By the time most of them have hit bottom, the screen is just about gone and the meltdown complete. (I suspect the DOOM uses a similar technique. However, each vertical strip is scaled down instead of eaten up.)

Screen Transition Demo

Faded, dissolved, scaled, eaten, or disintegrated, it all looks good. Here's the main demo program to see them in effect (pun intended).

Listing 7.9. Screen transitions (screenfx.c).

```c
// I N C L U D E S //////////////////////////////////////////////

#include <io.h>
#include <conio.h>
#include <stdio.h>
#include <stdlib.h>
#include <dos.h>
#include <bios.h>
#include <fcntl.h>
#include <memory.h>
#include <malloc.h>
#include <math.h>
#include <string.h>
#include <graph.h>

#include "graph0.h" // Include our graphics library.

// D E F I N E S //////////////////////////////////////////////


// S T R U C T U R E S //////////////////////////////////////////

typedef struct worm_typ
        {
        int y;       // Current y position of the worm.
        int color;   // The color of the worm.
        int speed;   // The speed of the worm.
        int counter; // Counter.

        } worm, *worm_ptr;

// G L O B A L S //////////////////////////////////////////////

unsigned int far *clock = (unsigned int far *)0x0000046C;
        // Pointer to internal
        // 18.2 clicks/sec

pcx_picture screen_fx; // Our test screen.

worm worms[320]; // Used to make the screen melt.

//////////////////////////////////////////////////////////////

void Timer(int clicks)
{
// This function uses the internal timekeeper (the one that runs
// at 18.2 clicks/sec to time a delay). You can find the 32-bit
```

```
// value of this timer at 0000:046Ch.

unsigned int now;

// Get the current time.

now = *clock;

// Wait until the time has gone past the current time plus the
// amount we wanted to wait. Note that each tick is
// approximately 55 milliseconds.

while(abs(*clock - now) < clicks){}

} // end Timer

////////////////////////////////////////////////////////////////

void Fade_Lights(void)
{
// This function fades the lights by slowly decreasing the color
// values in all color registers.

int index,pal_reg;
RGB_color color,color_1,color_2,color_3;

for (index=0; index<30; index++)
    {

    for (pal_reg=1; pal_reg<255; pal_reg++)
        {
        // Get the color to fade.

        Get_Palette_Register(pal_reg,(RGB_color_ptr)&color);

        if (color.red   > 5) color.red-=3;
        else
           color.red = 0;

        if (color.green > 5) color.green-=3;
        else
           color.green = 0;
        if (color.blue  > 5) color.blue-=3;
        else
           color.blue = 0;

        // Set the color to a diminished intensity.

        Set_Palette_Register(pal_reg,(RGB_color_ptr)&color);

        } // end for pal_reg

    // Wait a bit...

    Timer(2);

    } // end fade for
```

continues

Listing 7.9. continued

```
} // end Fade_Lights

//////////////////////////////////////////////////////////////

void Dissolve(void)
{
// Dissolve the screen by plotting zillions of black pixels.

unsigned long index;

for (index=0; index<=300000; index++,
Plot_Pixel_Fast(rand()%320, rand()%200, 0));

} // end Dissolve

//////////////////////////////////////////////////////////////

void Melt(void)
{

// This function "melts" the screen by moving little worms at
// different speeds down the screen. These worms change to the
// color they're eating.

int index,ticks=0;

// Initialize the worms.

for (index=0; index<160; index++)
    {

    worms[index].color   = Get_Pixel(index,0);
    worms[index].speed   = 3 + rand()%9;
    worms[index].y       = 0;
    worms[index].counter = 0;

    // Draw the worm.

    Plot_Pixel_Fast((index<<1),0,(char)worms[index].color);
    Plot_Pixel_Fast((index<<1),1,(char)worms[index].color);
    Plot_Pixel_Fast((index<<1),2,(char)worms[index].color);


    Plot_Pixel_Fast((index<<1)+1,0,(char)worms[index].color);
    Plot_Pixel_Fast((index<<1)+1,1,(char)worms[index].color);
    Plot_Pixel_Fast((index<<1)+1,2,(char)worms[index].color);

    } // end index

// Do the screen melt.

while(++ticks<1800)
    {

    // Process each worm.
```

```
       for (index=0; index<320; index++)
           {
           // Is it time to move the worm?

           if (++worms[index].counter == worms[index].speed)
               {
               // Reset counter.

               worms[index].counter = 0;

               worms[index].color =
                 Get_Pixel(index,worms[index].y+4);

               // Has the worm hit bottom?

               if (worms[index].y < 193)
                   {

                   Plot_Pixel_Fast((index<<1),worms[index].y,0);

Plot_Pixel_Fast((index<<1),worms[index].y+1,
           (char)worms[index].color);

Plot_Pixel_Fast((index<<1),worms[index].y+2,
           (char)worms[index].color);

Plot_Pixel_Fast((index<<1),worms[index].y+3,
           (char)worms[index].color);

Plot_Pixel_Fast((index<<1)+1,worms[index].y,0);

Plot_Pixel_Fast((index<<1)+1,worms[index].y+1,
           (char)worms[index].color);

Plot_Pixel_Fast((index<<1)+1,worms[index].y+2,
           (char)worms[index].color);

Plot_Pixel_Fast((index<<1)+1,worms[index].y+3,
           (char)worms[index].color);

                   worms[index].y++;

                   } // End if the worm isn't at bottom yet.

               } // End if it's time to move the worm.

           } // end index

       // Accelerate the melt.

       if (!(ticks % 500))
           {

           for (index=0; index<160; index++)
               worms[index].speed—;

           } // End if it's time to accelerate the melt.
```

continues

Listing 7.9. continued

```
        } // end while

} // end Melt

// M A I N /////////////////////////////////////////////////////

void main(void)
{
int index,
    done=0,
    sel;

// Set the video mode to the 320x200, 256 color mode.

Set_Mode(VGA256);


PCX_Init((pcx_picture_ptr)&screen_fx);

PCX_Load("war.pcx", (pcx_picture_ptr)&screen_fx,1);

PCX_Show_Buffer((pcx_picture_ptr)&screen_fx);

PCX_Delete((pcx_picture_ptr)&screen_fx);

_settextposition(22,0);
printf("1 - Fade Lights.\n2 - Dissolve.\n3 - Meltdown.");

// Which special FX did the player want to see?

switch(getch())
      {
      case '1':  // Dim the lights.
            {

            Fade_Lights();

            } break;

      case '2': // Dissolve the screen.
            {
            Dissolve();

            } break;


      case '3': // Melt the screen.
            {

            Melt();

            } break;
```

```
    } // end switch

// Restore the video mode.

Set_Mode(TEXT_MODE);

} // end main
```

Textures, Anyone?

Because the main thrust of all these tortuous discussions is to learn how to make 3-D, texture-mapped, DOOM-style video games, we're going to need one little thing that I can't supply you: that's the darn textures. All those dark tunnels and rooms have to have some really cool textures to be mapped on them. The only problem is: if you're not an artist, where will you get them?

Well, you'd be surprised how easy they are to make if you stare at a lot of buildings and then spend some time with Deluxe Paint. Take a look at Figure 7.8. This figure shows some crude textures that I made in just a few minutes with Deluxe Paint.

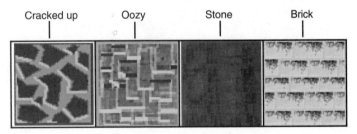

Figure 7.8. *Sample wall textures.*

These textures aren't that bad, and they give you an idea of what can be done by a non-artist. Therefore, even if you can't draw at all, making textures isn't too hard. However, if your drawing seems to look like the scratchings of an epileptic chicken, there are CD-ROMs you can purchase that have thousands of textures on them. You can import these textures and play with them as you wish.

(However you do it, please don't put any water faucets or bathrooms on the walls, like a certain game I won't mention...)

Bit-Mapped Image Scaling

People say "Leave the best for last." In our case, it's the hardest for last. I've tried to keep the math to a minimum because most video-game programmers cringe at the thought of trig functions, and aren't even too happy with multiplication. Unfortunately, however, 3-D games have to contain some fairly complex algorithms and mathematics to make things happen. Bit-mapped image scaling is one of these areas, and it's a topic that takes some time to get a good grip on.

We saw in Chapter 4, "The Mechanics of Two-Dimensional Graphics," how to scale a vector-based, polygon-type image. We simply multiply each vertex's components by the scaling factor and the result is a scaled point. When all the points were scaled this way and connected by the edges that make up the polygon, the image got bigger or smaller, and was therefore scaled as far as we were concerned.

Scaling bit-mapped images is a bit more of a challenge. The problem is that the image is really composed of hundreds of little pixels. To scale a bit-mapped image, we must somehow replicate the pixels proportionally to the scaling factor. For instance, if we wanted to scale the cowboy in Figure 7.9 by two, it would look as you see it in Figure 7.10.

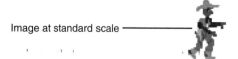

Image at standard scale ——————

Figure 7.9. *A standard bit-mapped image.*

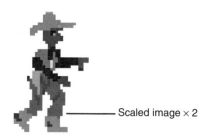

———— Scaled image × 2

Figure 7.10. *A scaled-by-two version of the image in Figure 7.9.*

If you look really close, you'll see that there are exactly twice as many pixels in Figure 7.10 as in Figure 7.9. In essence, we plotted each pixel in the source image of Figure 7.9 twice to come up with Figure 7.10.

Pixel doubling will work if we want to scale an image by a factor of two. However, if we want arbitrary scaling (as we will later to make our 3-D game), we must come up with a more general algorithm. It turns out that there's a really simple way to scale a bit-mapped image. In fact, it's so simple it should be illegal!

Let's start by considering an alternative approach to the problem, though. Instead of thinking of scaling an object .5 times or 6 times or whatever, think of *stretching* or *compressing* the bit map. In other words, we want to take a number of source pixels and stretch or compress them to fit into a number of destination pixels. Figure 7.11 shows a graphical representation of this.

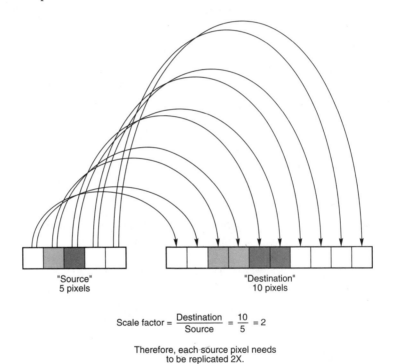

"Source"
5 pixels

"Destination"
10 pixels

$$\text{Scale factor} = \frac{\text{Destination}}{\text{Source}} = \frac{10}{5} = 2$$

Therefore, each source pixel needs
to be replicated 2X.

Figure 7.11. *Scaling pixels.*

For instance, if my source image is composed of strips 64 pixels long and I want to stretch the image into a new destination size of 100, I must replicate the source pixels each 100/64, or roughly 1.5, times.

Because we know the screen is an integer matrix, it may seem that stretching something a nonintegral number of times won't work. The reason it does work is that we sample the source image and continually place the sample on the destination image. Then we index into the next sample using the inverse of the scale factor.

For example (still using the previous example), I want to plot 100 pixels that somehow look like the original 64 scaled to fit in the space of 100. We computed that there would be a scale factor of 1.5; therefore, each pixel must be replicated 1.5 times. However, we can't really do that because we can't plot half a pixel. If we take our alternative approach, though, we could instead do something like the following:

- Have a destination index range from 0-99.

- Have a source index range from 0-63, but by a fraction of a unit, so that sometimes the same source pixel would be sent to the destination.

Viola! The image is scaled properly. The question is, what is the relationship between the fractional number and the scale factor? It's really hard! Here it is:

```
1/scale
```

That's all there is to it. Of course, the scaling must be done in both the x-axis and the y-axis. However, the same logic can be used on both. Furthermore, if the object has the same dimension in the x and y directions (that is, if it's MxM instead of MxN), the math can be done a little faster.

There is one teeny, weeny little detail: we have to use floating-point math, and that's a no-no because it's slower than integer-based math. In Chapter 18, "Optimization Techniques," we learn to use fixed-point math, and then we'll be able to rewrite the scaler function to be more efficient.

To show you the scaler in action, I've written a demo program, called scale.c, that lets you select one of four textures and scale it using the left-angle bracket (or "lesser-than") key and the right-angle bracket (or "greater-than") key. (These keys are the shifted versions of the comma and period keys, respectively.) Notice how the scaler really slows down when the object gets big. This performance just won't do, but it's a start. Again you will need to link the program to graph0.c. Listing 7.10 contains the code.

Listing 7.10. Scaling walls (scale.c).

```c
// I N C L U D E S /////////////////////////////////////////////

#include <io.h>
#include <conio.h>
#include <stdio.h>
#include <stdlib.h>
#include <dos.h>
#include <bios.h>
#include <fcntl.h>
#include <memory.h>
#include <malloc.h>
#include <math.h>
#include <string.h>
#include <graph.h>
```

```c
#include "graph0.h" // Include our graphics library.

// D E F I N E S ////////////////////////////////////////////////

// G L O B A L S ////////////////////////////////////////////////

sprite object;
pcx_picture text_cells;

// F U N C T I O N S ////////////////////////////////////////////

void Scale_Sprite(sprite_ptr sprite,float scale)
{

// This function scales a sprite by computing the number of
// source pixels needed to satisfy the number of destination
// pixels.

char far *work_sprite;
int work_offset=0,offset,x,y;
unsigned char data;
float y_scale_index,x_scale_step,y_scale_step,x_scale_index;

// Set the first source pixel.

y_scale_index = 0;

// Compute the floating-point step.

y_scale_step = sprite_height/scale;
x_scale_step = sprite_width/scale;

// Alias a pointer to the sprite for ease of access.

work_sprite = sprite->frames[sprite->curr_frame];

// Compute the offset of the sprite in the video buffer.

offset = (sprite->y << 8) + (sprite->y << 6) + sprite->x;

// Row by row, scale the object.

for (y=0; y<(int)(scale); y++)
    {
    // Copy the next row into the screen buffer, using memcpy
    // for speed.

    x_scale_index=0;

    for (x=0; x<(int)scale; x++)
        {
        // Test for a transparent pixel (that is, 0); if not
        // transparent, draw.

        if ((data=work_sprite[work_offset+(int)x_scale_index]))
            double_buffer[offset+x] = data;
```

continues

Listing 7.10. continued

```c
        x_scale_index+=(x_scale_step);

        } // end for x

    // Using the floating-scale_step, index to the next source
    // pixel.

    y_scale_index+=y_scale_step;

    // Move to the next line in the video buffer and in the
    // sprite bit-map buffer

    offset      += SCREEN_WIDTH;
    work_offset = sprite_width*(int)(y_scale_index);

    } // end for y

} // end Scale_Sprite

///////////////////////////////////////////////////////////////////

void Clear_Double_Buffer(void)
{
// This function clears the double buffer; kind of crude, but
// G.E. (good enough).

_fmemset(double_buffer, 0, SCREEN_WIDTH * SCREEN_HEIGHT + 1);

} // end Clear_Double_Buffer

// M A I N ///////////////////////////////////////////////////////

void main(void)
{
int index,
    done=0;

float scale=64;

// Set the video mode to the 320x200, 256 color mode.

Set_Mode(VGA256);

// Set the sprite system size so functions use the correct
// sprite size.

sprite_width = sprite_height = 64;

// Initialize the .PCX file that holds all the animation cells
// for net-tank.

PCX_Init((pcx_picture_ptr)&text_cells);

// Load the .PCX file that holds the cells.

PCX_Load("textures.pcx", (pcx_picture_ptr)&text_cells,1);
```

```
Sprite_Init((sprite_ptr)&object,0,0,0,0,0,0);

// Grab four interesting textures.

PCX_Grap_Bitmap((pcx_picture_ptr)&text_cells,
                (sprite_ptr)&object,0,0,0);
PCX_Grap_Bitmap((pcx_picture_ptr)&text_cells,
                (sprite_ptr)&object,1,1,0);
PCX_Grap_Bitmap((pcx_picture_ptr)&text_cells,
                (sprite_ptr)&object,2,2,0);
PCX_Grap_Bitmap((pcx_picture_ptr)&text_cells,
                (sprite_ptr)&object,3,3,0);

// Create some memory for the double buffer.

Init_Double_Buffer();


// Position the object in the center of the screen.

object.curr_frame = 0;
object.x          = 160-(sprite_width>>1);
object.y          = 100-(sprite_height>>1);

// Clear the double buffer.

Clear_Double_Buffer();

// Show the player the scaled texture.

Scale_Sprite((sprite_ptr)&object,scale);
Show_Double_Buffer(double_buffer);

_settextposition(24,0);
printf("Q - Quit, < > - Scale, Space - Toggle.");

// main loop

while(!done)
    {

    // Has the player hit a key?

    if (kbhit())
        {
        switch(getch())
            {
            case '.': // Scale the object larger.
                {
                if (scale<180)
                    {
                    scale+=4;
                    object.x-=2;
                    object.y-=2;
                    } // End if OK to scale larger.

                } break;
```

continues

Listing 7.10. continued

```
            case ',': // Scale the object smaller.
                {
                if (scale>4)
                    {
                    scale-=4;
                    object.x+=2;
                    object.y+=2;
                    } // End if OK to scale smaller.

                } break;

            case ' ': // Go to the next texture.
                {
                // Are we at the end?

                if (++object.curr_frame==4)
                    object.curr_frame=0;

                } break;

            case 'q': // Let's go!
                {
                done=1;
                } break;

            default:break;

            } // end switch


        // Create a clean slate.

         Clear_Double_Buffer();

        // Scale the sprite and render it into the double buffer.

         Scale_Sprite((sprite_ptr)&object,scale);

        // Show the double buffer.

         Show_Double_Buffer(double_buffer);

         _settextposition(24,0);
         printf("Q - Quit, < > - Scale, Space - Toggle.");

         }// end if

      } // end while

// Delete the .PCX file.

PCX_Delete((pcx_picture_ptr)&text_cells);

// Restore the video mode.
```

```
Set_Mode(TEXT_MODE);

} // end main
```

Bit-Mapped Image Rotation

Although we really won't be rotating many bit-mapped objects, let's cover the concept of rotation for completeness.

Rotating bit-mapped images is still an area of research. Computer scientists and graphics programmers are always looking for faster ways to do it. The problem is that a bit-mapped image is the conglomeration of hundreds, if not thousands, of pixels. To rotate such an image, each of the pixels must be rotated properly. This means that there's going to be a lot of math going on, and we know that that's something we try to avoid in a real-time application like a video game. Although there are fast algorithms available to do bit map rotation, they're just not fast enough.

So how did Chris Roberts make Wing Commander? Simple: he pre-rotated all the images using a modeling package, and made gigantic look-up tables of each ship in all of its possible rotations. Basically, he preprocessed all the rotations. The only time-consuming processing done during the game is the scaling, which can actually be done fairly quickly (again, with look-up tables). In any case, I'm going to follow this trend and take the position that you should pre-rotate your images using some other package, such as Electronic Arts' Deluxe Paint or, if you like spending money, AutoDesk's 3D Studio. Then, create a look-up table of rotated images, and have your software index this table using the angle as the index.

The drawback to using this technique is memory consumption. Having 32 or 64 bit maps for each object will eat memory alive. However, it's possible to have only partial look-up tables. For example, you could have a look-up table for a single quadrant, and then generate the other symmetrical quadrants during runtime. Because reflections about the x and y axes are simple to do, this is usually the tactic used.

To show you an example of bit map rotation using a look-up table, I've created a program that uses our scaler along with a .PCX file containing a few cells of a rotated asteroid. This program, called afield.c, moves the asteroid around in a 3-D starfield, scaling the asteroid as it gets closer to or farther away from the viewer. Listing 7.11 contains the code—and, by the way, the program needs the graphics library again.

Listing 7.11. Asteroids 3-D (afield.c).

```c
// I N C L U D E S ///////////////////////////////////////////

#include <io.h>
#include <conio.h>
#include <stdio.h>
#include <stdlib.h>
#include <dos.h>
#include <bios.h>
#include <fcntl.h>
#include <memory.h>
#include <malloc.h>
#include <math.h>
#include <string.h>
#include <graph.h>

#include "graph0.h" // Include our graphics library.

// D E F I N E S ///////////////////////////////////////////

#define NUM_STARS 30

// S T R U C T U R E S ///////////////////////////////////////

typedef struct star_typ
        {
        int x,y;    // The position of the star.
        int vel;    // The x component of star velocity.
        int color;  // The color of the star.

        } star, *star_ptr;

// G L O B A L S ///////////////////////////////////////////

star stars[NUM_STARS]; // The starfield
sprite object;
pcx_picture ast_cells;

////////////////////////////////////////////////////////////

// F U N C T I O N S ///////////////////////////////////////

////////////////////////////////////////////////////////////

void Star_Field(void)
{

static int star_first=1;

// This function creates a panning, 3-D starfield with 3-planes,
// like the one you'd see looking out of the Enterprise.

int index;

// Test whether we must initialize the starfield (that is,
// ascertain whether this is the first time function is being
// called.
```

```
if (star_first)
   {
   // Reset first time.
   star_first=0;

   // Initialize all the stars.

   for (index=0; index<NUM_STARS; index++)
      {
      // Initialize each star to a velocity, position,
      // and color.

      stars[index].x     = rand()%320;
      stars[index].y     = rand()%180;

      // Decide what star plane the star is in.

      switch(rand()%3)
         {
         case 0: // Plane 1 = the farthest star plane.
            {
            // Set the velocity and color.

            stars[index].vel = 2;
            stars[index].color = 8;

            } break;

         case 1: // Plane 2 = the mid-distance star plane.
            {

            stars[index].vel = 4;
            stars[index].color = 7;

            } break;

         case 2: // Plane 3 = The nearest star plane.
            {

            stars[index].vel = 6;
            stars[index].color = 15;

            } break;

         } // end switch

      } // end for index

   } // end if first time
else
   { // This must be the nth time in, so do the usual.

   // Erase, move, and draw.

   for (index=0; index<NUM_STARS; index++)
      {
```

continues

Listing 7.11. continued

```c
        if ( (stars[index].x+=stars[index].vel) >=320 )
           stars[index].x = 0;

        // Draw

        Plot_Pixel_Fast_D(stars[index].x,
                          stars[index].y,stars[index].color);

        } // end for index

   } // end else

} // end Star_Field

/////////////////////////////////////////////////////////////////

void Scale_Sprite(sprite_ptr sprite,float scale)
{

// This function scales a sprite by computing the number of
// source pixels needed to satisfy the number of destination
// pixels.

char far *work_sprite;
int work_offset=0,offset,x,y;
unsigned char data;
float y_scale_index,x_scale_step,y_scale_step,x_scale_index;

// Set the first source pixel.

y_scale_index = 0;

// Compute the floating-point step.

y_scale_step = sprite_height/scale;
x_scale_step = sprite_width/scale;

// Alias a pointer to the sprite for ease of access.

work_sprite = sprite->frames[sprite->curr_frame];

// Compute the offset of the sprite in the video buffer.

offset = (sprite->y << 8) + (sprite->y << 6) + sprite->x;

// Row by row, scale the object.

for (y=0; y<(int)(scale); y++)
    {
    // Copy the next row into the screen buffer, using memcpy
    // for speed.

    x_scale_index=0;

    for (x=0; x<(int)scale; x++)
        {
```

```
                    // Test for a transparent pixel (that is, 0); if not
                    // transparent, draw.

                    if ((data=work_sprite[work_offset+(int)x_scale_index]))
                        double_buffer[offset+x] = data;

                    x_scale_index+=(x_scale_step);

                    } // end for x

            // Using the floating-scale_step, index to the next source
            // pixel.

            y_scale_index+=y_scale_step;

            // Move to the next line in the video buffer and in the
            // sprite bit-map buffer.

            offset       += SCREEN_WIDTH;
            work_offset = sprite_width*(int)(y_scale_index);

            } // end for y

} // end Scale_Sprite

///////////////////////////////////////////////////////////////

Clear_Double_Buffer()
{
// This function clears the double buffer; kind of crude, but
// G.E. (good enough).

_fmemset(double_buffer, 0, SCREEN_WIDTH * SCREEN_HEIGHT + 1);

} // end Clear_Double_Buffer

// M A I N ///////////////////////////////////////////////////

void main(void)
{
int index,
    done=0,dx=5,dy=4,ds=4;

float scale=5;

// Set the video mode to the 320x200, 256 color mode.

Set_Mode(VGA256);

// Set the sprite system size so functions use the correct
// sprite size.

sprite_width = sprite_height = 47;

// Initialize the .PCX file that holds all the animation cells
// for net-tank.

PCX_Init((pcx_picture_ptr)&ast_cells);
```

continues

Listing 7.11. continued

```
// Load the .PCX file that holds the cells.

PCX_Load("asteroid.pcx", (pcx_picture_ptr)&ast_cells,1);

// Create some memory for the double buffer.

Init_Double_Buffer();

Sprite_Init((sprite_ptr)&object,0,0,0,0,0,0);

// Load in frames of rotating asteroid.

PCX_Grap_Bitmap((pcx_picture_ptr)&ast_cells,
                (sprite_ptr)&object,0,0,0);
PCX_Grap_Bitmap((pcx_picture_ptr)&ast_cells,
                (sprite_ptr)&object,1,1,0);
PCX_Grap_Bitmap((pcx_picture_ptr)&ast_cells,
                (sprite_ptr)&object,2,2,0);
PCX_Grap_Bitmap((pcx_picture_ptr)&ast_cells,
                (sprite_ptr)&object,3,3,0);
PCX_Grap_Bitmap((pcx_picture_ptr)&ast_cells,
                (sprite_ptr)&object,4,4,0);
PCX_Grap_Bitmap((pcx_picture_ptr)&ast_cells,
                (sprite_ptr)&object,5,5,0);
PCX_Grap_Bitmap((pcx_picture_ptr)&ast_cells,
                (sprite_ptr)&object,6,0,1);
PCX_Grap_Bitmap((pcx_picture_ptr)&ast_cells,
                (sprite_ptr)&object,7,1,1);

// Position the object in the center of the screen.

object.curr_frame = 0;
object.x          = 160-(sprite_width>>1);
object.y          = 100-(sprite_height>>1);

// Clear the double buffer.

Clear_Double_Buffer();

// Show the player the scaled texture.

Scale_Sprite((sprite_ptr)&object,scale);
Show_Double_Buffer(double_buffer);

// main loop

while(!kbhit())
     {
     // Scale the asteroid.

     scale+=ds;

     // Test whether the asteroid is too big or too small.
```

```
    if (scale>100 || scale < 5)
       {
       ds=-ds;
       scale+=ds;
       } // End if we need to scale in other direction.

    // Move the asteroid.

    object.x+=dx;
    object.y+=dy;

    // Test whether the object needs to bounce off the wall.

    if ((object.x + scale) > 310 || object.x < 10)
       {
       dx=-dx;
       object.x+=dx;
       } // End if hit a vertical boundary.

    if ((object.y + scale) > 190 || object.y < 10)
       {
       dy=-dy;
       object.y+=dy;
       } // End if hit a horizontal boundary.

    // Rotate the asteroid by 45 degrees.

    if (++object.curr_frame==8)
       object.curr_frame=0;

    // Create a clean slate.

    Clear_Double_Buffer();

    // Draw the stars.

    Star_Field();

    // Scale the sprite and render it into the double buffer.

    Scale_Sprite((sprite_ptr)&object,scale);

    // Show the double buffer.

    Show_Double_Buffer(double_buffer);

    } // end while

// Delete the .PCX file.

PCX_Delete((pcx_picture_ptr)&ast_cells);

// Restore the video mode.

Set_Mode(TEXT_MODE);

} // end main
```

Summary

This chapter covered many topics regarding advanced bit map graphic skills and special effects, but, mostly, it's the first time in the book we've really started talking about making the game *fun*. I think many programmers have forgotten about fun. They've replaced fun with megabyte after megabyte of digitized sound and graphics.

Just say no to such things!

High-Speed 3-D Sprites

In this chapter, we cover topics that aren't really new to us. They're just an application of the technology and concepts we've learned in the preceding chapters. Normally, I wouldn't even think to include applications of this type in a book. Applications are more of a creative topic rather than a technical one. In this case, however, I've changed my mind because it's such an important concept, and I want you to have firm grasp on it.

Just as DOOM rocked the world when it was released, another game did much the same thing a couple years ago. That game was Wing Commander, and the author was Chris Roberts. I remember seeing Wing Commander for the first time—and I was so impressed, it quickly became my favorite game. Wing Commander and games similar to it are done using the same techniques that we use for rendering sprites in a DOOM-type world.

by André LaMothe

The images in WC (Wing Commander) are simple models, computer-generated objects, or both that have been digitized into two-dimensional sprites. These sprites are moved around on the video screen using the proper mathematical transformations so that a sense of perspective is simulated. However, the images themselves are not 3-D in the sense that standard hidden-surface removal and 3-D computations are being done. The images are projections of 3-D objects onto flat, square polygons, which themselves are sprites.

Making a game like WC isn't too challenging as far as the complexity of the mathematics are concerned. However, a game like WC uses a lot of insights, tricks, and clever programming. Let's see if we can't get a grip on some of them by covering the following topics:

- The mechanics of 3-D sprites
- The perspective transform
- Computing the proper scale
- The viewing volume
- A new version of the scaler
- Clipping in 3-D space, "sprite style"
- Creating trajectories
- Angling in on the right sprite
- A perspective starfield
- Digitizing objects and modeling
- Creating a miniature production studio
- Digitizing and your color palette

The Mechanics of 3-D Sprites

Three-dimensional sprites are much like 2-D sprites. As a matter of fact, they're the same; we just *think* they're 3-D. This perception is based on the way they move on the screen and the size, or scale, at which we render them. Two-dimensional sprites can only move on the x and y axes of the view screen. However, 3-D sprites can move on all three axes: x, y, and z. The motion along the z-axis is only mathematical in nature, and the only way we perceive this motion is by somehow changing the x- and y-coordinates of the sprite, along with its scale, based on the z-coordinate of the sprite, to make the 2-D sprite look 3-D.

We're leaving a little detail out, though. How can a 2-D flat image look 3-D? The answer is that we draw the 2-D image so that if a 3-D object were viewed at a specific angle, invariant of distance, it would look like the 2-D image we just drew. As an example, for this chapter I took a toy of a little spaceship along with a video camera and digitizer card. I then placed the camera and objects at fixed positions from each other, as shown in Figure 8.1, and proceeded to scan the image.

Figure 8.1. *The video setup.*

Then I rotated the object a little by hand and took another snapshot. Soon I had 12 frames that were representative of what the 3-D object would look like from a viewpoint directly in line with the view angle at a specific distance. Those frames are shown in Figure 8.2.

If we were to render these frames on the screen, one after another, the resulting animation would look like a huge 3-D spaceship rotating a few hundred feet in front of us.

The three-dimensional aspects of 3-D sprites are really synthesized by two different factors:

■ First, we scan (or draw) the object in many different rotational positions. Ultimately, we'd like to scan the image in all possible rotations, although this wouldn't be feasible because of the memory requirements of each of the images.

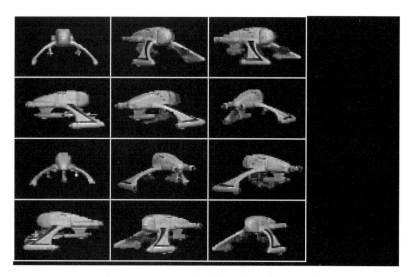

Figure 8.2. *The model.*

For instance, for this chapter I used objects that took 80x48 pixels to scan. This meant that each image took up 3840 bytes. That doesn't seem like much, but when you do some simple calculations based on the total number of frames (that is, the different view angles), you quickly realize that memory is eaten alive.

If we wanted to simply rotate the object parallel to the y-axis in 30-degree increments for four different pitches, we would have 12*4*3840 bytes, or roughly 184K. Imagine if we needed larger image sizes, more images, or both! The trick is to digitize only what you need and try to use algorithms to reflect the data during runtime. For instance, it might be possible to only digitize 180 degrees of rotation and generate the other 180 degrees from that first set of data.

■ The second way we synthesize the illusion of 3-D is by using perspective transformations when we position the sprites. This has the effect of making the sprites move toward and away from the projection point and horizons.

We can think of the sprites as points in a 3-D space and transform them based on this assumption. Then we can compute their scales and render them based on the distance from the viewer (that is, you). Finally, as the sprite moves around on the screen, we must select the proper frame to display.

This is how the illusion of 3-D is maintained. If the player gets "behind" a 3-D sprite that's traveling across the screen, we should see the back of the object—not the side of it, as we would when it was traveling from left to right in our perspective. This selection is done based on the trajectory vector of the object and the view vector of the player. We cover this little subtlety a bit later in this chapter, but for now I want you to have an overall idea of all the components involved in manipulating 3-D sprites.

The Perspective Transformation

We've seen this before (in Chapter 6, "The Third Dimension"). Perspective transformations and the math behind them are used to render objects on a computer screen in a way that results in a more realistic view than parallel (or orthogonal) projections. Perspective transformation computes the z-coordinate with the distance from the viewer to the view plane (in our case, the video screen) to alter the x- and y-coordinates of the object so they appear, well, in perspective.

To accomplish the aforementioned transformation for 3-D sprites, we simply use the center of the sprite as its position or *local origin*. This is important! If we use the upper-left corner of the sprite as its origin (as we have in the past), everything will look wrong. Always use the center of the object as its local origin. This is necessary because the object must scale evenly from its center, not its upper-left corner. (Get it? Got it. Good!)

Formula 8.1.

Sprite Perspective Projections.

The math to do the perspective transformation is simple: we need only the z-coordinate and view distance of the sprite. With those in hand, the new projected position of the sprite becomes:

```
x_Projected = view_distance * x_sprite/z_sprite
y_Projected = view_distance * y_sprite/z_sprite
```

This projection works properly: sprites move around along perspective lines in the view window. However, there's a detail we must discuss. That detail is what I have named *dimensional distortion*. Dimensional distortion occurs when you mix one virtual unit system with another. As an example, consider the situation in which you try to place 3-D sprites in a ray-cast world. The sprites will move and scale incorrectly relative to the ray-cast world. This is because the sprites and the walls are based on two different dimensional scales.

Alleviating this problem is a matter of a single multiplication, done during the projection. We must multiply sprite coordinates by the *inner dimensional scale* factors (the scale factors that map one mathematical space to another). In essence, we must scale the sprite universe to meet that of the ray-cast world (or whatever world we're trying to place them in). Of course, there's a mathematical way to compute this (and if you like punishment, just send me a letter and I'll show you how it's done). Personally, I just fiddle with the view distance until things look good.

I think we have a basic grasp on projecting the sprite on the screen. To reiterate:

- We use the center of the sprite as its position or origin.

- Then we divide the x- and y-coordinates of the sprite by the sprite's z-position.

- Then we multiply the results by a factor that takes into consideration the viewing distance and inner dimensional scale factor.

Sounds like we're building a time machine, right? Anyway, if we do the above operations and move the sprite around on the screen we will get a 2.5-D projection.

Now that we have the object properly positioned on the screen, we must scale it correctly so its size changes as it moves nearer or farther from the viewer's position.

Computing the Proper Scale

We're missing one thing; the scale of the sprite. We need to make the sprite get bigger and smaller based on its z-position relative to the viewer.

In other words, we need to come up with a formula that will give us a reasonable size or scale, in pixels, with which to draw the sprite. Well, scale is inversely proportional to the z-position of the sprite (that is, the total distance from sprite to viewer). Therefore, we can use the z-position along with a multiplication factor to compute the proper scale of the sprite—at least, a scale that looks good.

Again, inner dimensional distortion will occur if we mix virtual unit systems, so the factor by which we multiply is easiest come by through experimentation. Our scaling engine will generate the size, in pixels, that the bit-map texture must shrink or stretch to match. Formula 8.2 shows the math required to generate the proper scale based on the sprite's z-position.

Formula 8.2.

Computing the Scale.

```
scale = scale_distance/ sprite_z;
```

where *scale_distance* is chosen to give visually pleasing results.

We know that 3-D graphics *can't* be this easy. There has to be a catch! Yes, I admit it! There is one more teeny, weeny problem we must address: clipping. A lot of the rest of the chapter is about that.

The Viewing Volume

We learned in the chapters on polygon-based 3-D graphics (Chapter 6, "The Third Dimension," and Chapter 7, "Advanced Bit-Mapped Graphics and Special FX") that images must be clipped to a viewing volume (also called a viewing frustum). This is accomplished by taking the edges of each polygon and clipping them to the six sides of the viewing volume. Remember: in 3-D, the planes that have to be clipped to are the right, left, top, bottom, yon, and hither. The problem with clipping is that the viewing volume is a 3-D trapezoid constructed out of six intersecting planes, as shown in Figure 8.3.

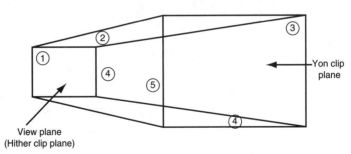

The viewing volume is the Interior space resulting
from the Intersection of six polygons (clip planes).

View plane
(Hither clip plane)

Yon clip
plane

Objects within the volume of
the clipping region are visible.

Figure 8.3. *The viewing volume.*

We surely don't want to compute the intersections of sprites with arbitrary planar equations. That would be a bummer! However, if we first project each sprite using perspective projection, and compute its scale appropriately, we can convert the viewing volume into a rectangular solid. Because we're doing an inverse operation, we can then clip the sprites in a much easier fashion than having to clip to arbitrary planes!

This works because the viewing volume is already a perspective object. If we clip the edges of the 3-D objects to the viewing volume before projecting them, we must use the trapezoidal form of the viewing volume. However, if we first project the objects in a perspective fashion and *then* clip them against the orthogonal version of the viewing volume, it's equivalent to clipping against the trapezoidal viewing volume and then projecting. Hither and yon clipping degenerates into a conditional statement that tests whether the sprite is too far or too close (that is, behind you) to see.

In the case of mode 13h, we can clip all sprites to the screen borders or the rectangle based on the corner points of (0,0) and (319,199). Hither and yon clipping is done using a simple pass/fail test: if the sprite is within the z-extents within which you wish it to be visible, render it; otherwise, disregard the sprite. The reason hither and yon clipping is so straightforward is that the sprite is really a square polygon perpendicular to the view direction, or parallel to the view plane. (We can think of it in either way; the two are synonymous.)

I suggest you experiment with the yon clip plane and set it so an object less than one pixel in either dimension (after scaling) is not drawn. Select the hither clip plane so that, as the object gets closer and closer, it doesn't get so close that it looks like an image seen through a microscope, with single pixels being scaled many times.

A New Version of the Scaler

Before we attempt to implement clipping, we should understand how the basic scaler operates. Because scaling and clipping go hand in hand, we must first write the scaler, then adapt it to do the clipping.

The scaler engine we saw in Chapter 7, "Advanced Bit-Mapped Graphics and Special FX" (Listing 7.9), used a slightly different approach to scaling wall textures. Each wall was not a 2-D sprite with a width and height. Instead, it was a 1-D vertical strip. Hence, the scaler would only be able to scale vertical strips or sprites having the width of a single pixel. (By the way, a single, textured pixel is called a *textel*.)

To do general 2-D sprite scaling, we use the same code we saw in Listing 7.9. However, the scaler is modified to use only integers, and the scaling indices are precomputed in look-up tables. The code for the new scaler is shown in Listing 8.1.

Listing 8.1. The new sprite scaler (without clipping).

```
/////////////////////////////////////////////////////////////////

void Scale_Sprite(sprite_ptr sprite,int scale)
{
// This function scales the sprite (without clipping). Scaling
// is done by looking into a precomputed table that determines
// how big each vertical strip should be. Another table is then
// used to compute how many of these vertical strips should be
// drawn based on the x scale of the object.

char far *work_sprite;  // The sprite texture.
int *row_y;             // Pointer to the y scale data
                        // (note: it's NEAR).
int far *row_x;         // Pointer to the x scale data
                        // (note: it's FAR).

unsigned char pixel;    // The current textel

int x,                  // Work variables
    y,
    column,
    work_offset,
    video_offset,
    video_start;


// If the object is too small, don't even bother rendering it.

if (scale<1) return;

// Compute needed scaling data.

row_y = scale_table_y[scale];
row_x = scale_table_x[scale];

// Access the proper frame of the sprite.

work_sprite = sprite->frames[sprite->curr_frame];

// Compute where the starting video offset will always be.

video_start = (sprite->y << 8) + (sprite->y << 6) + sprite->x;

// The image is drawn from left to right, top to bottom.

for (x=0; x<scale; x++)
    {

    // Recompute the next column address.

    video_offset = video_start + x;

    // Compute which column should be rendered based on
    // x scale index.

    column = row_x[x];
```

continues

Listing 8.1. continued

```
    // Now do the column, as we always have.

    for (y=0; y<scale; y++)
        {

        // Check for transparency.

        pixel = work_sprite[work_offset+column];

        if (pixel)
            double_buffer[video_offset] = pixel;


        // Index to the next screen row and data offset
        // in texture memory.

        video_offset += SCREEN_WIDTH;
        work_offset  =  row_y[y];

        } // end for y

    } // end for x

} // end Scale_Sprite

//////////////////////////////////////////////////////////////////
```

As you can see, the new scaler is very simple and short. It operates completely by using look-up tables. The scaler indexes into two tables: one for x scaling and one for y scaling. There are two tables because the width and height of the sprite may not necessarily be the same. If the sprites being scaled were always MxM, the scaler could be further simplified.

Note that the two look-up tables are in different memory regions: NEAR and FAR. The reasoning behind this is speed. The look-up table in the inner loop of the scaler (that is, the y scale) should be in the NEAR data segment for quicker access and dereferencing. The look-up table in the outer loop (the x scale) can be in a FAR segment as it's accessed, on average, only a few dozen times.

In general, it would be better to put both in the NEAR data segment. However, this would consume the NEAR memory quickly and we'd have a hard time allocating global variables. As a rule of thumb, if you're using look-up tables in C, try to make the tables accessed in the inner loops NEAR and other, less-accessed tables FAR. This rule of thumb goes away if you can manage to fit all of your tables and global variables into the 64K allotted to the NEAR data segment.

Now, let's see this new scaler in action. I've written a program that loads a set of predigitized images that are 80x48 pixels. The images were created by taking a model spaceship into my impoverished production studio (which you see later in this chapter) and taking snapshots of the ship at different angles. The program, called vyren.c, displays the ship at some z distance from the viewer (that's you) and allows you to translate it on the z-axis by pressing the ">" (left angle-bracket or "lesser-than") key and the "<" (right-angle bracket or "greater-than") key. (These keys are the shifted versions of the comma and period keys, respectively.) Anyway, you'll see how much faster the new scaler is with look-up tables as compared to the old one.

This program is shown in Listing 8.2. Take some time to study the main section and understand the sequence of steps the code goes through. As usual, the program must be linked with our evolving graphics library, graphics.c, and compiled using the medium memory model. The executable is vyren.exe. To exit the program, press the Q key.

Listing 8.2. Demo using the new scaler (vyren.c).

```
// I N C L U D E S ///////////////////////////////////////////

#include <io.h>
#include <conio.h>
#include <stdio.h>
#include <stdlib.h>
#include <dos.h>
#include <bios.h>
#include <fcntl.h>
#include <memory.h>
#include <malloc.h>
#include <math.h>
#include <string.h>

#include <graph.h>

#include "graphics.h" // Include our graphics library.

// P R O T O T Y P E S ///////////////////////////////////////

void Create_Scale_Data_X(int scale, int far *row);

void Create_Scale_Data_Y(int scale, int *row);

void Build_Scale_Table(void);

void Scale_Sprite(sprite_ptr sprite,int scale);

void Clear_Double_Buffer(void);

// D E F I N E S //////////////////////////////////////////////

#define MAX_SCALE      200      // Number of stars in star field.
#define SPRITE_X_SIZE  80       // Largest any bit map can be.
```

continues

Listing 8.2. continued

```c
#define SPRITE_Y_SIZE  48      // The size of a sprite texture.

// G L O B A L S ////////////////////////////////////////////////

sprite object;              // The generic sprite that will hold
                            // the frames of the ship.


pcx_picture text_cells;        // The .PCX file with the images

int *scale_table_y[MAX_SCALE+1];      // Table with precomputed
                                      // scale indices.

int far *scale_table_x[MAX_SCALE+1];  // Table with precomputed
                                      // scale indices.


////////////////////////////////////////////////////////////////

void Create_Scale_Data_X(int scale, int far *row)
{

// This function synthesizes the scaling of a texture sliver
// to all possible sizes, and creates a huge look-up table of
// the data.

int x;

float x_scale_index=0,
      x_scale_step;

// Compute scale step or number of source pixels to map to
// destination/cycle.

x_scale_step = (float)(sprite_width)/(float)scale;

x_scale_index+=x_scale_step;

for (x=0; x<scale; x++)
    {
    // Place data into proper array position for later use.

    row[x] = (int)(x_scale_index+.5);

    if  (row[x] > (SPRITE_X_SIZE-1)) row[x] = (SPRITE_X_SIZE-1);

    // Next index, please.

    x_scale_index+=x_scale_step;

    } // end for x

} // end Create_Scale_Data_X

////////////////////////////////////////////////////////////////

void Create_Scale_Data_Y(int scale, int *row)
{
```

```
// This function synthesizes the scaling of a texture sliver
// to all possible sizes, and creates a huge look-up table of
// the data.

int y;

float y_scale_index=0,
      y_scale_step;

// Compute the scale step or number of source pixels to map to
// destination/cycle.

y_scale_step = (float)(sprite_height)/(float)scale;

y_scale_index+=y_scale_step;

for (y=0; y<scale; y++)
    {
    // Place data into proper array position for later use.

    row[y] = ((int)(y_scale_index+.5)) * SPRITE_X_SIZE;

    if  (row[y] > (SPRITE_Y_SIZE-1)*SPRITE_X_SIZE)
         row[y] = (SPRITE_Y_SIZE-1)*SPRITE_X_SIZE;

    // Next index, please.

    y_scale_index+=y_scale_step;

    } // end for y

} // end Create_Scale_Data_Y

/////////////////////////////////////////////////////////////////

void Build_Scale_Table(void)
{

// This function builds the scaler tables by computing the scale
// indices for all possible scales from 1-200 pixels high.

int scale;


// Allocate all the memory.

for (scale=1; scale<=MAX_SCALE; scale++)
    {

    scale_table_y[scale] = (int *)malloc(scale*sizeof(int)+1);
    scale_table_x[scale] = (int far *)
                          _fmalloc(scale*sizeof(int)+1);

    } // end for scale

// Create the scale tables for both the x- and y-axes.

for (scale=1; scale<=MAX_SCALE; scale++)
```

continues

Listing 8.2. continued

```
    {
    // Create the indices for this scale.

    Create_Scale_Data_Y(scale, (int *)scale_table_y[scale]);
    Create_Scale_Data_X(scale, (int far *)scale_table_x[scale]);

    } // end for scale

} // end Build_Scale_Table

/////////////////////////////////////////////////////////////////

void Scale_Sprite(sprite_ptr sprite,int scale)
{
// This function scales the sprite (without clipping). Scaling
// is done by looking into a precomputed table that determines
// how big each vertical strip should be. Another table is then
// used to compute how many of these vertical strips should be
// drawn based on the x scale of the object.

char far *work_sprite;  // The sprite texture.
int *row_y;             // Pointer to the y scale data
                        // (note: it's NEAR).
int far *row_x;         // Pointer to x scale data
                        // (note: it's FAR).

unsigned char pixel;    // The current textel.

int x,                  // Work variables
    y,
    column,
    work_offset,
    video_offset,
    video_start;


// If the object is too small, don't even bother rendering it.

if (scale<1) return;

// Compute needed scaling data.

row_y = scale_table_y[scale];
row_x = scale_table_x[scale];

// Access the proper frame of the sprite.

work_sprite = sprite->frames[sprite->curr_frame];

// Compute where the starting video offset will always be.

video_start = (sprite->y << 8) + (sprite->y << 6) + sprite->x;

// The image is drawn from left to right, top to bottom.

for (x=0; x<scale; x++)
    {
```

```
            // Recompute the next column address.

            video_offset = video_start + x;

            // Compute which column should be rendered based on the
            // x scale index.

            column = row_x[x];

            // Now do the column, as we always have.

            for (y=0; y<scale; y++)
                {

                // Check for transparency.

                pixel = work_sprite[work_offset+column];

                if (pixel)
                    double_buffer[video_offset] = pixel;


                // Index to the next screen row and data offset in
                // texture memory.

                video_offset += SCREEN_WIDTH;
                work_offset  = row_y[y];

                } // end for y

        } // end for x

} // end Scale_Sprite

////////////////////////////////////////////////////////////////

void Clear_Double_Buffer(void)
{

// Take a guess...?

_fmemset(double_buffer, 0, SCREEN_WIDTH * SCREEN_HEIGHT + 1);

} // end Clear_Double_Buffer

// M A I N ////////////////////////////////////////////////////////

void main(void)
{

// This main loads in the 12 frames of a prescanned image and
// rotates them while allowing the player to change the z value
// of the object using the ',' and '.' keys.

int done=0,                      // Exit flag.
    count=0,                     // Used to count rtime until
                                 // frame change.
```

continues

Listing 8.2. continued

```
        scale=64;                    // Current sprite scale.

float scale_distance = 24000,        // Arbitrary constants to make
                                     // the flat texture scale
        view_distance = 256,         // properly in ray-cast world.

        x=0,                         // Position of texture or ship
                                     // in 3-D space.

        y=0,
        z=1024;


// Set the video mode to the 320x200, 256 color mode.

_setvideomode(_MRES256COLOR);

sprite_width  = 80;
sprite_height = 48;

// Create the look-up tables for the scaler engine.

Build_Scale_Table();

// Initialize the .PCX file that holds all the cells.

PCX_Init((pcx_picture_ptr)&text_cells);

// Load the .PCX file that holds the cells.

PCX_Load("vyrentxt.pcx", (pcx_picture_ptr)&text_cells,1);

// Create some memory for the double buffer.

Init_Double_Buffer();

Sprite_Init((sprite_ptr)&object,0,0,0,0,0,0);

// Load the 12 frames of the ship.

PCX_Grap_Bitmap((pcx_picture_ptr)&text_cells,
(sprite_ptr)&object,0,0,0);
PCX_Grap_Bitmap((pcx_picture_ptr)&text_cells,
(sprite_ptr)&object,1,1,0);
PCX_Grap_Bitmap((pcx_picture_ptr)&text_cells,
(sprite_ptr)&object,2,2,0);
PCX_Grap_Bitmap((pcx_picture_ptr)&text_cells,
(sprite_ptr)&object,3,0,1);
PCX_Grap_Bitmap((pcx_picture_ptr)&text_cells,
(sprite_ptr)&object,4,1,1);
PCX_Grap_Bitmap((pcx_picture_ptr)&text_cells,
(sprite_ptr)&object,5,2,1);
PCX_Grap_Bitmap((pcx_picture_ptr)&text_cells,
(sprite_ptr)&object,6,0,2);
PCX_Grap_Bitmap((pcx_picture_ptr)&text_cells,
(sprite_ptr)&object,7,1,2);
PCX_Grap_Bitmap((pcx_picture_ptr)&text_cells,
(sprite_ptr)&object,8,2,2);
```

```
PCX_Grap_Bitmap((pcx_picture_ptr)&text_cells,
(sprite_ptr)&object,9,0,3);
PCX_Grap_Bitmap((pcx_picture_ptr)&text_cells,
(sprite_ptr)&object,10,1,3);
PCX_Grap_Bitmap((pcx_picture_ptr)&text_cells,
(sprite_ptr)&object,11,2,3);

// Initialize the position of the ship.

object.curr_frame = 0;
object.x         = 0;
object.y         = 0;

Clear_Double_Buffer();


// Get player input and draw the ship.

while(!done)
    {

    // Has the player hit the keyboard?

    if (kbhit())
        {
        switch(getch())
            {
            case '.': // Move z farther.
                {
                z+=16;
                } break;

            case ',': // Move z closer.
                {
                z-=16;

                // Don't let object get too close!

                if (z<256)
                   z=256;

                } break;

            case 'q': // exit program
                {
                done=1;
                } break;

            default:break;

            } // end switch

        } // end if


    // Compute the size of the bit map.

    scale = (int)( scale_distance/z );
```

continues

Listing 8.2. continued

```
                    // Based on the size of the bit map, compute the
                    // perspective x and y.

                    object.x = (int)((float)x*view_distance /
                             (float)z) + 160 - (scale>>1);
                    object.y = 100 - (((int)((float)y*view_distance /
                             (float)z) + (scale>>1)) );


                    // Increment the frame counter to the next frame.

                    if (++count==2)
                        {
                        count=0;

                        if (++object.curr_frame==12)
                            object.curr_frame=0;

                        } // end if time to change frames


                    // Blank out the double buffer.

                    Clear_Double_Buffer();

                    // Scale the sprite to its proper size.

                    Scale_Sprite((sprite_ptr)&object,scale);

                    Show_Double_Buffer(double_buffer);


                    // Show the player some info.

                    _settextposition(24,0);
                    printf("Z Coordinate is %f",z);

                    } // end while
            // Delete the .PCX file.

            PCX_Delete((pcx_picture_ptr)&text_cells);

            // Put the computer back into text mode.

            _setvideomode(_DEFAULTMODE);

            } // end main

            ////////////////////////////////////////////////////////////
```

After executing the program in Listing 8.2, you should be somewhat excited at the possibilities of digitized models and this type of 3-D sprite animation. Who knows?

Maybe you'll go on to make a most excellent Wing Commander-type game in deference to a DOOM-type game. In any case, let's move on to the clipping algorithm.

Clipping in 3-D Space, "Sprite Style"

Clipping after a perspective transformation is easy. The algorithm basically tests the extents of the scaled sprite against the four edges of the screen, and also tests whether the sprite is within the z-extents within which it should remain visible. Therefore, the clipping problem boils down to testing a rectangle against the edges of the screen—which we've seen before (in Chapter 4, "The Mechanics of Two-Dimensional Graphics").

As you know, there are two ways to approach this: we can use either an image-space algorithm or an object-space algorithm. Image space is much easier. As we proceed to plot each pixel of the sprite, we test whether it's within the screen boundaries (view window) and, if so, plot the pixel. The problem with this approach is that it's inefficient (although in some cases image-space algorithms must be used due to the geometric complexity of the objects being rendered). In general, clipping at the image-space level is slower than at the object-space level.

Using an object-space technique, we must somehow decide before we draw the sprite what portions of it must be drawn and recompute new extents based on these computations. Basically, we must clip the rectangle generated by the scaled sprite against the screen boundaries to come up with a new rectangle. This turns out to be easy. We've seen code for this in the last chapter (Listing 7.3), but I'll show you again because, hey! That's the kind of guy I am.

Algorithm 8.1 does the clipping to the view window, given that:

- The screen is bounded by the points (0,0) and (`screen_x`,`screen_y`)

- The sprite has upper-left corner of (`sprite_x`,`sprite_y`)

- The sprite has the size `width` * `height`

Assume that the z-extent clip has already been done and visibility was found to be true, and that the object's scale and perspective x and y locations have been computed.

Algorithm 8.1. Sprite scaling.

```
// Test for complete invisibility.

if ( (sprite_x > SCREEN_X) or
     (sprite_y > SCREEN_Y ) or
```

continues

Algorithm 8.1. continued

```
      (sprite_x+Width < 0 ) or
      (sprite_y+height < 0) )
      {
      // Don't do anything.
      return;
      } // End if the sprite is invisible.
else
      {
      // The sprite is visible, so compute a new rectangle.

      // Save sprite extents so that they can be clipped.

      start_x  = sprite_x;
      start_y  = sprite_y;
      end_x  = sprite_x+Width-1;
      end_y  = sprite_y+Height-1;

      // Clip leftmost and topmost extents.

      if (sprite_x < 0) start_x = 0;
      if (sprite_y < 0) start_y = 0;

      // Clip rightmost and bottommost extents.

      if (sprite_x + Width > SCREEN_X) end_x = SCREEN_X;
      if (sprite_y + Height > SCREEN_Y) end_y = SCREEN_Y;

      // At this point the new sprite will have upper-left
      // corner (start_x,start_y) and lower-right corner
      // (end_x,end_y), these can be used by the renderer.

      return;

} // End, else sprite must be partially visible.
```

As with any algorithm, there are about a million little details that I've left out. However, I think you get the idea.

Here comes the hard part with sprite clipping: when we scale sprites, we must take a number of source pixels and "send" them to a destination (the screen) a number of times to obtain the correct scale. However, when we scale the sprite, its screen size may change. We must be extremely careful in the scaler to take this into consideration when drawing the scaled sprite. The sprite must still be scaled the same but, when it's drawn, we draw only the current portion of it. In other words, we still use the scale of the sprite to compute the scale factor (or the index into the look-up tables), but we bias the rendering so that only a subset of the scaled image is drawn because if the whole image was drawn, it would go off the screen and not be clipped—which is the whole point of this!

Creating Trajectories

Assuming that we have the sprites scaling and clipping properly, we then want to move them around in the environment. This means that we have to give them trajectories. We also need these trajectories in order to figure out the difference between the object's direction and the view direction, and select the proper frame to display. This action will uphold the illusion of 3-D when the sprite is moving around on the screen.

A trajectory is really a vector. To create a vector we need a terminal point and an initial point. Because a trajectory is really a velocity vector, it must have an initial point at the origin and terminal point somewhere else, as shown in Figure 8.4.

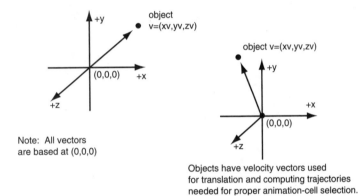

Figure 8.4. *Velocity vectors used for trajectories.*

The terminal point has two pieces of information:

- The first is the direction of the trajectory or velocity.

- The second is the magnitude of the velocity, or the speed.

Creating a velocity vector is simple. Let's say that we want the ship to have a direction of 50 degrees in the x-z plane, as shown in Figure 8.5.

Formula 8.3.

Computing a velocity vector.

We could use the following formula to compute this:

```
x_vel = cos(50) * speed
z_vel = sin(50) * speed
```

The final velocity vector can be expressed as

```
V = <x_vel, z_vel>
```

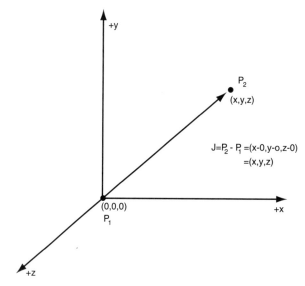

Figure 8.5. *Computing a velocity vector or trajectory.*

The V we have just computed is a valid vector quantity, and we can perform all the normal operations you would think, such as adding V to another vector.

> Note that V is in the x-z plane, or the *ground plane,* as you view the screen. In Wing Commander, you don't notice that the ships spend most of their time moving in this plane instead of in the whole x-y-z volume.

To use this vector to move the ship or some other object, we would just translate the object's coordinates using the velocity components as the translation factors. Obviously, we would only modify x and z, because our velocity vector only has these components. In general, however, we can create a three-component velocity vector and translate it in all dimensions.

If you like, the velocity vector could be generated randomly from a file or player input. Nonetheless, you need to know the direction of the object's travel (or its view direction) to compute the proper frame to display, because objects created using sprites are really 2-D!

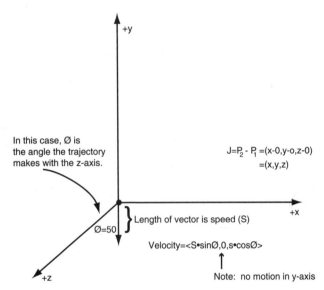

In this case, Ø is the angle the trajectory makes with the z-axis.

$J = P_2 - P_1 = (x-0, y-o, z-0)$
$= (x, y, z)$

Ø=50

Length of vector is speed (S)

Velocity=<S•sinØ,0,s•cosØ>

Note: no motion in y-axis

Figure 8.6. *Using trig functions to compute trajectories.*

Angling In on the Right Sprite

This topic is probably the most complex of any we've covered so far. Because a 3-D sprite moves around the view screen, it should look as though it's really 3-D to the viewer. The viewer in this case is the player, who is fixed at a specific position. This position is usually at (0,0,0), maybe slightly translated in the z-axis. In any case, as the sprite makes a turn (for instance), we want to display different views or frames of that sprite that coincide with the real, 3-D view that would be generated if the object we're rendering as a sprite was actually 3-D. (That was a mouthful!)

Solving this problem completely and in an elegant manner...is overkill as far as we're concerned. We're only interested in creating code, models, and algorithms that work and produce realistic results. Therefore, the algorithm we discuss in this section is hardly complete, and certainly something you can add to in the future. However, it's a good starting place, and I always would rather you have a good foundation to build on rather than a weak foundation that you can't reproduce.

As we would design any algorithm for any computer problem (or for any problem at all), we must first define the problem and then try to think of solutions to the problem. The problem we want to solve here is how to select an image to be rendered, based on the view angle of the player and the direction the object is facing.

> The object could be moving in a direction it's not facing. We won't consider this case, however, as it doesn't really add to the complexity of the problem. Instead, we'll assume in this book that the object is facing the direction it is moving.
>
> This assumption is reasonable because, for the code we write later in the book, we use a spaceship with rear thrusters. Moreover, this technique will work in Wolfenstein- and DOOM-type games that are inhabited by bipeds (creatures with two legs), which usually move in the direction in which they're pointed (or the opposite direction if they're backing up).

Let's begin analyzing the problem at hand. We have a view direction based on the player's view and an object's trajectory, or translation direction. As we said a moment ago, we can fix the player's view as always looking straight into the screen. Then we need only worry about the trajectory vector of the object we're displaying. Take a look at Figure 8.7 to see the relationship between the player's viewing vector and some possible object trajectories.

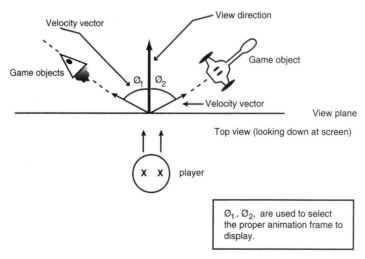

Figure 8.7. *The relationship between the player's viewing vector and the game object's trajectory.*

The next thing we should do is take a model of a toy car or something and move it around in front of you—in private, and try not to make motor noises during this exercise—while you continue looking forward. Doing this, you'll soon come to the conclusion that the image of the ship that should be displayed for a specific trajectory is roughly the same for all parallel paths, invariant of the position of the object. This is only partially correct, of course, but for our first attempt at an algorithm for computing the proper image it is a reasonable starting point.

What we must do is:

- Somehow compute the angle between the object's trajectory or direction of motion and the view angle (which is always straight into the screen).

- Divide the resulting angle up into quadrants and, based on the resulting index, select the image that most closely represents it from the ones that have previously been digitized or generated by means of computer models or artwork. (See the section in this chapter under "Digitizing Objects and Modeling" for more on creating images.)

- Display the proper frame using the perspective transformation to project the object on the screen, along with scaling of the object to present it at its proper size.

All these factors together create a realistic-looking object on the screen.

We're interested in finding the angle between the player's view and the object's trajectory. This can be accomplished using the dot product, or *inner product*. We know that if we have two vectors, we can find the angle between them by using the dot product, as shown in Figure 8.8.

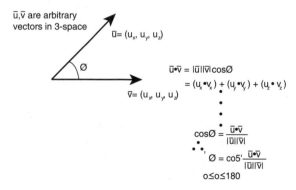

Figure 8.8. *The dot product revisited.*

Formula 8.4.

Computing the angle between viewer and object.

If we define the view vector as V and the object's velocity vector as O, the angle between then can be found by using following formula:

```
Given V=(vx,vy,vz) & O=(ox,oy,oz) then,
```

$$
\text{angle} = \cos^{-1} \frac{(vx*ox) + (vy*oy) + (vz*oz)}{\text{sqrt}(vx^2+vy^2+vz^2) \ * \ \text{sqrt}(ox^2+oy^2+oz^2)}
$$

If we wanted to verbalize this operation, we would say, "The angle between V and O is the inverse cosine of the dot divided by the product of the magnitudes."

This formula computes the angle between V and O, with one small catch: the angle is always the most interior angle; that is, between 0-180 degrees. That means that there are two different real angles that will give the same results when this formula is computed. This is because the dot product and the math behind it don't include which vector to use (that is, which way you wish to have the positive angles). Put another way, this formula gives the smallest delta between vectors, but not the largest. We can work around it with no trouble, but I want you to know about it because it could be a problem if you didn't know about it. (It's like the "off by one" problem that crops up all the time. If you didn't know about it, it could drive you crazy. The same goes here, so be forewarned!)

To see a graphic example of this problem, take a look at Figure 8.9. This figure shows the view vector along with two possible object trajectories and the resulting angle, computed using Formula 8.4.

Formula 8.4 is greatly simplified by the fact that we're only concerned with the ground plane (the x-z plane), because the view direction is always perpendicular to the view plane.

The final question you should be asking is: "How do I figure out the real angle?" Well, you could use the cross product to decide if the angle returned by Formula 8.4 is correct or if an extra 180 must be added. However, I hate math—that's why I have a degree in it—and I think we should use clever insights instead of brute force.

If we think of the object's trajectory vector as having the same origin as the view direction (which it does), and then test to see in which halfplane the x component of the trajectory vector lies relative to the view vector, we can figure out that the angle between each of the vectors should be less than or greater than 180 degrees, as shown in Figure 8.10.

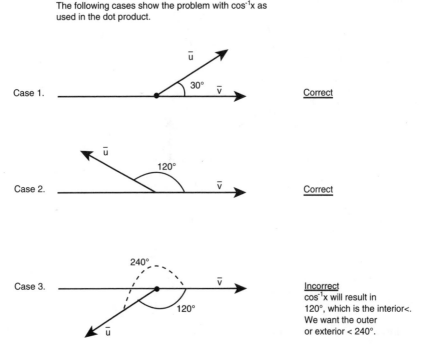

Figure 8.9. *The results of cos⁻¹ x.*

Using this technique of testing the x component, we can write a simple function that first computes the angle using the dot product, then tests the x component to see whether it's on the right side of the view vector (positive) or the left side (negative). If the x component is positive, we take the angle returned from Formula 8.4 and subtract that from 360. (This is the same as adding 180.) We would then take the final angle and divide it up into 12 quadrants. Alternatively, we could modulus it by 12. We then would use the resulting number as an index into the image cells. (Of course, the cells would have had to been in the proper order; that is, as the indices went from 0-11, the images were scanned as 30-degree rotations counterclockwise, with 0 degrees being the one looking into the screen.)

If the x component is negative, the process works the same—except that the other bank of image cells is used, and the absolute value of x would be taken before being placed in the equations.

The cells I created for the demo in this chapter are in the .PCX file named vryentxt.pcx. They're in order from left to right and from top to bottom. Each image is the previous image rotated 30 degrees counterclockwise, and I made 0 degrees pointing directly into the screen (or, from the viewer's point of view, the rear of the ship). We use these in the upcoming demo.

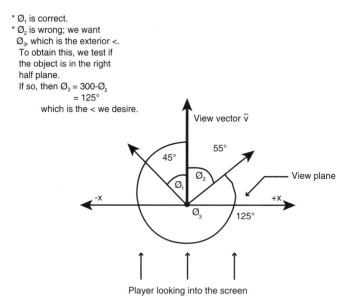

Figure 8.10. *Using the x halfplane to obtain the correct angle from the dot product.*

That full demo uses the angle to compute the correct view, but we just can't place a ship in the middle of nowhere. That would be boring! We need to add some action. I suggest a 3-D starfield. By 3-D, I mean that the stars are coming toward you instead of passing by from left to right, as we've seen before now. In the demo, we place the ship in the starfield and it looks very cool. So let's talk about how to create a perspective 3-D starfield.

A Perspective Starfield

The 3-D sprite techniques we have been discussing are used not only in games like Wing Commander, but also in DOOM and Wolfenstein. If you play DOOM, you'll notice that you can see different views of the sprites (the monsters) as they walk and chase you. In Chapter 6, "The Third Dimension," we talked about creating a ray-cast world and discussed how polygon-based worlds work. Now I'd like to take a bit of a detour and cover how we would create a simple, 3-D perspective starfield within which we could have a space battle.

In theory, creating a 3-D starfield is trivial. We would just create a few million random points in 3-D space, use a perspective transformation to view them, and always plot them as single pixels. This technique works fine and is actually used in high-end simulations. The only thing wrong with this technique is that it's slow, memory intensive, and boring. We are game designers, and we have to make the display look like it's a perspective starfield. No one ever said it really has to be! If you take a few moments and watch *Star Trek* or something similar, you'll see that the starfield is created by single pixels (stars) starting at some random location on the screen and slowly moving away from the center of the screen at higher and higher velocities as time progresses, until they're clipped from the view screen.

Realism

To make the stars look more realistic, we should increase their brightness as they come closer to the ship we're flying (our virtual viewpoint). It looks to me like we can do the following to create a 3-D starfield.

Here's a procedure for creating our 3-D starfield:

1. Create a star data structure that holds the position, color, and speed of a star.

2. Create an array of stars at different positions on the screen, with different speeds.

3. Set things up so the stars move away from the center of the screen.

4. Set things up so that, for each tick of the system timekeeper, the star is visibly sped up a little and made brighter.

5. Set things up so that, when a star reaches the end of the screen (an edge, in other words), it starts over again at another random position and speed.

6. Draw the stars.

7. Go back to Step 4.

This technique results in a totally real-looking starfield and yet is simple to implement. However, it does have a couple shortcomings:

■ First, you can't turn. You must always be moving forward.

■ Second, the stars will be moving at speeds that aren't realistically related to the motion of the objects within the starfield.

The first problem is a really big one; if you need to be able to change directions, you'd better try something else. The second problem is only artistic as far as I'm concerned. Who cares if you would have to be going millions of times the speed of light to pass stars that quickly? This is a video game, and we can make our universe do anything we like!

Creating a Starfield Using Integers

Let's talk about how we would go about implementing the starfield with integers only. We would technically like to use floating-point numbers to create a random velocity because it'd be more accurate. Floating-point numbers would allow us to create velocities such as, say, 2.5. However, we know that using floating-point numbers degrades system performance. Moreover, there are going to be 50-100 stars on the screen at any one time, and we want to make rendering the starfield as quick as possible so we can spend the rest of the PC's computational time on something more pressing (like the sprite blitting and game logic).

If we create the starfield using only integers as the velocity values, you'll hardly notice the quantization errors that occur due to using whole integral values instead of floating-point numbers.

We could come halfway and used fixed-point math, but it just isn't worth it. I've found that the stars will have such high velocities that the decimal portions of the speeds don't carry any weight, so they're really unneeded. Again, I'm probably beating this point into the ground, but I can't say this enough times: a video-game programmer must always find the simplest, fastest way to do things; otherwise, a display as seemingly simple as a starfield could take an insufferable amount of time to implement and execute. Remember, as long as the display looks good enough and it suspends the player in a world submerged in fantasy, it's good enough!

Listing 8.3 contains the completed version of the software that enables you to move your spaceship around in a 3-D starfield. (Note: the ship is locked in an x-z plane.) Use the numeric keypad to turn the ship, and the keys on the numeric keypad to move. The left- and right-arrow keys rotate the ship, and the up- and down-arrow keys speed it up and slow it down, respectively. To exit the program, press the Q key.

The name of the executable is finvyren.exe. When you create your own executable file you must link it with the graphics library named graphics.c.

Listing 8.3. The last shuttle (finvyren.c).

```c
// I N C L U D E S //////////////////////////////////////////////

#include <io.h>
#include <conio.h>
#include <stdio.h>
#include <stdlib.h>
#include <dos.h>
#include <bios.h>
#include <fcntl.h>
#include <memory.h>
#include <malloc.h>
#include <math.h>
#include <string.h>

#include <graph.h>

#include "graphics.h" // Include our graphics library
// P R O T O T Y P E S //////////////////////////////////////////

void Create_Scale_Data_X(int scale, int far *row);

void Create_Scale_Data_Y(int scale, int *row);

void Build_Scale_Table(void);

void Scale_Sprite(sprite_ptr sprite,int scale);

void Clear_Double_Buffer(void);

void Timer(int clicks);

void Init_Stars(void);

void Move_Stars(void);

void Draw_Stars(void);

// D E F I N E S //////////////////////////////////////////////

#define NUM_STARS      50        // Number of stars in starfield.
#define MAX_SCALE      200       // Largest any bit map can be.
#define SPRITE_X_SIZE  80        // The size of a sprite texture.
#define SPRITE_Y_SIZE  48

// S T R U C T U R E S //////////////////////////////////////////

// This is a star.

typedef struct star_typ
        {

        int x,y;       // Position of star.
        int xv,yv;     // Velocity of star.
        int xa,ya;     // Acceleration of star.
```

continues

Listing 8.3. continued

```
            int color;     // Color of star.
            int clock;     // Number of ticks star has been alive.
            int acc_time;  // This is the number of ticks to count
                           // before accelerating the acceleration
            int acc_count; // counter.

            } star, *star_ptr;

// G L O B A L S /////////////////////////////////////////////

unsigned int far *clock = (unsigned int far *)0x0000046CL;
        // pointer to internal timekeeper
        // 18.2 clicks/sec

sprite object;              // The generic sprite that will hold
                            // the frames of the ship.


pcx_picture text_cells;     // the .PCX file with the images.

int *scale_table_y[MAX_SCALE+1];     // Table with precomputed
                                     // scale indices.

int far *scale_table_x[MAX_SCALE+1]; // Table with precomputed
                                     // scale indices.

star star_field[NUM_STARS];          // The starfield.

/////////////////////////////////////////////////////////////

void Timer(int clicks)
{
// This function uses the internal timekeeper (the one that runs
// at 18.2 clicks/sec to time a delay). You can find the 32-bit
// value of this timer at 0000:046Ch.

unsigned int now;

// Get the current time.

now = *clock;

// Wait until time has gone past current time plus the amount we
// wanted to wait. Note: each click is approximately 55
// milliseconds.

while(abs(*clock - now) < clicks){}

} // end Timer

/////////////////////////////////////////////////////////////

void Init_Stars(void)
{

// This function initializes the starfield data structure when
// the system is started.
```

```
int index,divisor;

for (index=0; index<NUM_STARS; index++)
    {

    star_field[index].x      = 150 + rand() % 20;
    star_field[index].y      = 90  + rand() % 20;


    if (rand()%2==1)
       star_field[index].xv      = -4 + -2 * rand() % 3;
    else
       star_field[index].xv      = 4 + 2 * rand() % 3;

    if (rand()%2==1)
       star_field[index].yv      = -4 + -2 * rand() % 3;
    else
       star_field[index].yv      = 4 + 2 * rand() % 3;


    divisor = 1 + rand()%3;

    star_field[index].xa      = star_field[index].xv/divisor;
    star_field[index].ya      = star_field[index].yv/divisor;

    star_field[index].color      = 7;
    star_field[index].clock      = 0;

    star_field[index].acc_time  = 1 + rand() % 3;
    star_field[index].acc_count = 0;


    } // end index

} // end Init_Stars

/////////////////////////////////////////////////////////////////

void Move_Stars(void)
{
// This function moves the stars, and tests whether a star has
// gone off the screen. If so, the function starts the star
// again.

int index,divisor;

for (index=0; index<NUM_STARS; index++)
    {

    star_field[index].x += star_field[index].xv;
    star_field[index].y += star_field[index].yv;

    // Test whether the star is off-screen.

    if (star_field[index].x >= SCREEN_WIDTH  ||
        star_field[index].x < 0  ||
```

continues

Listing 8.3. continued

```
      star_field[index].y >= SCREEN_HEIGHT ||
      star_field[index].y < 0)
    {

    // Restart the star.

    star_field[index].x     = 150 + rand() % 20;
    star_field[index].y     = 90  + rand() % 20;

    if (rand()%2==1)
       star_field[index].xv    = -4 + -2 * rand() % 3;
    else
       star_field[index].xv    = 4 + 2 * rand() % 3;

    if (rand()%2==1)
       star_field[index].yv    = -4 + -2 * rand() % 3;
    else
       star_field[index].yv    = 4 + 2 * rand() % 3;


    divisor = 1 + rand()%3;

    star_field[index].xa    = star_field[index].xv/divisor;
    star_field[index].ya    = star_field[index].yv/divisor;

    star_field[index].color    = 7;
    star_field[index].clock    = 0;

    star_field[index].acc_time  = 1 + rand() % 3;
    star_field[index].acc_count = 0;

    } // end if

// Test whether it's time to accelerate.

if (++star_field[index].acc_count==star_field[index].acc_time)
   {
   // Reset the counter.

   star_field[index].acc_count=0;

   // Accelerate

   star_field[index].xv += star_field[index].xa;
   star_field[index].yv += star_field[index].ya;

   } // end if time to accelerate

// Test whether it's time to change color.

if (++star_field[index].clock > 5)
   {
   star_field[index].color = 8;

   } // end if > 10
else
```

```
    if (star_field[index].clock > 10)
        {
        star_field[index].color =255;

        } // end if > 20
    else
    if (star_field[index].clock > 25)
        {
        star_field[index].color = 255;

        } // end if > 25

    } // end for index

} // end Move_Stars

//////////////////////////////////////////////////////////////

void Draw_Stars(void)
{
// This function draws the stars into the double buffer.

int index;

for (index=0; index<NUM_STARS; index++)
    {

    Plot_Pixel_Fast_D(star_field[index].x,star_field[index].y,
                    (unsigned char)star_field[index].color);

    } // end for index

} // end Draw_Stars

//////////////////////////////////////////////////////////////

void Create_Scale_Data_X(int scale, int far *row)
{

// This function synthesizes the scaling of a texture sliver
// to all possible sizes, and creates a huge look-up table of
// the data.

int x;

float x_scale_index=0,
      x_scale_step;

// Compute scale step or number of source pixels to map to
// destination/cycle.

x_scale_step = (float)(sprite_width)/(float)scale;

x_scale_index+=x_scale_step;

for (x=0; x<scale; x++)
    {
    // Place the data into proper array position for later use.
```

continues

Listing 8.3. continued

```
    row[x] = (int)(x_scale_index+.5);

    if  (row[x] > (SPRITE_X_SIZE-1)) row[x] = (SPRITE_X_SIZE-1);

    // Next index, please.

    x_scale_index+=x_scale_step;

    } // end for x

} // end Create_Scale_Data_X

//////////////////////////////////////////////////////////////////

void Create_Scale_Data_Y(int scale, int *row)
{

// This function synthesizes the scaling of a texture sliver
// to all possible sizes, and creates a huge look-up table of
// the data.

int y;

float y_scale_index=0,
      y_scale_step;

// Compute the scale step or number of source pixels to map to
// destination/cycle.

y_scale_step = (float)(sprite_height)/(float)scale;

y_scale_index+=y_scale_step;

for (y=0; y<scale; y++)
    {
    // Place the data into proper array position for later use.

    row[y] = ((int)(y_scale_index+.5)) * SPRITE_X_SIZE;

    if  (row[y] > (SPRITE_Y_SIZE-1)*SPRITE_X_SIZE)
        row[y] = (SPRITE_Y_SIZE-1)*SPRITE_X_SIZE;

    // Next index, please.

    y_scale_index+=y_scale_step;

    } // end for y

} // end Create_Scale_Data_Y

//////////////////////////////////////////////////////////////////

void Build_Scale_Table(void)
{
```

```
// This function builds the scaler tables by computing the scale
// indices for all possible scales from 1-200 pixels high.

int scale;


// Allocate all the memory.

for (scale=1; scale<=MAX_SCALE; scale++)
    {

    scale_table_y[scale] = (int *)malloc(scale*sizeof(int)+1);
    scale_table_x[scale] = (int far *)
                           _fmalloc(scale*sizeof(int)+1);

    } // end for scale

// Create the scale tables for both the x- and y-axes.

for (scale=1; scale<=MAX_SCALE; scale++)
    {

    // Create the indices for this scale.

    Create_Scale_Data_Y(scale, (int *)scale_table_y[scale]);
    Create_Scale_Data_X(scale, (int far *)scale_table_x[scale]);

    } // end for scale

} // end Build_Scale_Table

/////////////////////////////////////////////////////////////////

void Scale_Sprite(sprite_ptr sprite,int scale)
{
// This function scales the sprite (without clipping). Scaling
// is done by looking into a precomputed table that determines
// how big each vertical strip should be. Another table is then
// used to compute how many of these vertical strips should be
// drawn based on the x scale of the object.

char far *work_sprite;  // The sprite texture.
int *row_y;             // Pointer to the y scale data
                        // (note: it's NEAR).
int far *row_x;         // Pointer to x scale data
                        // (note: it's FAR)

unsigned char pixel;    // The current textel

int x,                  // Work variables
    y,
    column,
    work_offset,
    video_offset,
    video_start;
```

continues

Listing 8.3. continued

```
// If the object is too small, don't even bother rendering it.

if (scale<1) return;

// Compute needed scaling data.

row_y = scale_table_y[scale];
row_x = scale_table_x[scale];

// Access the proper frame of the sprite.

work_sprite = sprite->frames[sprite->curr_frame];

// Compute where the starting video offset will always be.

video_start = (sprite->y << 8) + (sprite->y << 6) + sprite->x;

// The image is drawn from left to right, top to bottom.

for (x=0; x<scale; x++)
    {

    // Recompute next column address.

    video_offset = video_start + x;

    // Compute which column should be rendered based on the
    // x scale index.
    column = row_x[x];

    // Now do the column, as we always have.

    for (y=0; y<scale; y++)
        {

        // Ccheck for transparency.

        pixel = work_sprite[work_offset+column];

        if (pixel)
            double_buffer[video_offset] = pixel;


        // Index to next screen row and data offset in
        // texture memory.

        video_offset += SCREEN_WIDTH;
        work_offset  = row_y[y];

        } // end for y

    } // end for x

} // end Scale_Sprite
```

```
///////////////////////////////////////////////////////////

void Clear_Double_Buffer(void)
{

// Take a guess...?

_fmemset(double_buffer, 0, SCREEN_WIDTH * SCREEN_HEIGHT + 1);

} // end Clear_Double_Buffer

// M A I N ///////////////////////////////////////////////////

void main(void)
{

// This places the ship into a starfield and allows the player
// to fly around.

int done=0,                  // Exit flag.
    scale=64,
    direction=6;             // The direction of the ship
                             // (current frame).

float scale_distance = 24000, // Arbitrary constants to make the
                              // flat texture scale properly in
      view_distance = 256,    // a ray-cast world.

      x=0,                    // Position of texture or ship in
                              // 3-D space.
      y=0,
      z=1024,
      xv=0,zv=0,              // Velocity of ship in x-z plane.
      angle=180,              // Angle of ship.
      ship_speed=10;          // Magnitude of ship's speed.

// Set the video mode to the 320x200, 256 color mode.

_setvideomode(_MRES256COLOR);

// All sprites will have this size.

sprite_width  = 80;
sprite_height = 48;

// Create the look-up tables for the scaler engine.

Build_Scale_Table();

// Initialize the .PCX file that holds all the cells.

PCX_Init((pcx_picture_ptr)&text_cells);

// Load the .PCX file that holds the cells.

PCX_Load("vyrentxt.pcx", (pcx_picture_ptr)&text_cells,1);
```

continues

Listing 8.3. continued

```
// Create some memory for the double buffer.

Init_Double_Buffer();

// Initialize the starfield.

Init_Stars();

// Set up the ship's direction and velocity.

angle=direction*30+90;

xv = (float)(ship_speed*cos(3.14159*angle/180));
zv = (float)(ship_speed*sin(3.14159*angle/180));

Sprite_Init((sprite_ptr)&object,0,0,0,0,0,0);

// Load the 12 frames of the ship.

PCX_Grap_Bitmap((pcx_picture_ptr)&text_cells,
(sprite_ptr)&object,0,0,0);
PCX_Grap_Bitmap((pcx_picture_ptr)&text_cells,
(sprite_ptr)&object,1,1,0);
PCX_Grap_Bitmap((pcx_picture_ptr)&text_cells,
(sprite_ptr)&object,2,2,0);
PCX_Grap_Bitmap((pcx_picture_ptr)&text_cells,
(sprite_ptr)&object,3,0,1);
PCX_Grap_Bitmap((pcx_picture_ptr)&text_cells,
(sprite_ptr)&object,4,1,1);
PCX_Grap_Bitmap((pcx_picture_ptr)&text_cells,
(sprite_ptr)&object,5,2,1);
PCX_Grap_Bitmap((pcx_picture_ptr)&text_cells,
(sprite_ptr)&object,6,0,2);
PCX_Grap_Bitmap((pcx_picture_ptr)&text_cells,
(sprite_ptr)&object,7,1,2);
PCX_Grap_Bitmap((pcx_picture_ptr)&text_cells,
(sprite_ptr)&object,8,2,2);
PCX_Grap_Bitmap((pcx_picture_ptr)&text_cells,
(sprite_ptr)&object,9,0,3);
PCX_Grap_Bitmap((pcx_picture_ptr)&text_cells,
(sprite_ptr)&object,10,1,3);
PCX_Grap_Bitmap((pcx_picture_ptr)&text_cells,
(sprite_ptr)&object,11,2,3);

// Initialize the position of the ship.

object.curr_frame = 0;
object.x          = 0;
object.y          = 0;

Clear_Double_Buffer();


// Get player input and draw the ship.
```

```
while(!done)
    {

    // Has the player hit the keyboard?

    if (kbhit())
        {
      switch(getch())
            {
            case '4': // Turn the ship left.
                {

                if (++direction==12)
                    {

                    direction=0;

                    } // end if wrap around
                } break;

            case '6': // Turn the ship right.
                {

                if (--direction < 0)
                    {

                    direction=11;

                    } // end if wrap around

                } break;

            case '8': // Speed the ship up.
                {
                if (++ship_speed > 20)
                   ship_speed=20;

                } break;

            case '2': // Slow the ship down.
                {
                if (--ship_speed < 0)
                   ship_speed=0;

                } break;

            case 'q': // exit program
                {
                done=1;
                } break;

            default:break;

            } // end switch
```

continues

Listing 8.3. continued

```
// Reset velocity and direction vectors.

angle=direction*30+90;

xv = (float)(ship_speed*cos(3.14159*angle/180));
zv = (float)(ship_speed*sin(3.14159*angle/180));

} // end if

// Translate the ship each cycle.

x+=xv;
z+=zv;

// Clip to hither plane.

if (z<256)
    z=256;

// Compute the size of the bit map.

scale = (int)( scale_distance/z );

// Based on the size of the bit map, compute the
// perspective x and y.

object.x = (int)((float)x*view_distance /
        (float)z) + 160 - (scale>>1);
object.y = 100 - (((int)((float)y*view_distance /
        (float)z) + (scale>>1)) );

// Bound to screen edges.

if (object.x < 0 )
    object.x = 0;
else
if (object.x+scale >= SCREEN_WIDTH)
    object.x = SCREEN_WIDTH-scale;


if (object.y < 0 )
    object.y = 0;
else
if (object.y+scale >= SCREEN_HEIGHT)
    object.y = SCREEN_HEIGHT-scale;


// Set the current frame.

object.curr_frame = direction;

// Blank out the double buffer.

Clear_Double_Buffer();
```

```
        Move_Stars();

        Draw_Stars();

        // Scale the sprite to its proper size.

        Scale_Sprite((sprite_ptr)&object,scale);

        Show_Double_Buffer(double_buffer);

        // Show the player some info.

        _settextposition(23,0);
        printf("Position=(%4.2f,%4.2f,%4.2f)    ",x,y,z);

        // Slow things down a bit...

        Timer(1);

    } // end while

// Delete the .PCX file.

PCX_Delete((pcx_picture_ptr)&text_cells);

// Put the computer back into text mode.

_setvideomode(_DEFAULTMODE);

} // end main

/////////////////////////////////////////////////////////////////
```

As in the past, the main section is where most of the action takes place, so you don't have to do a lot of function tracing. This method is, in general, not the way you should program. You should try and make the code a little more modular, but not so much that each function call takes up more time than the function itself!

Now, that we have the mathematics and mechanics of displaying and transforming 3-D sprites on the screen, let's see how I created the images for this chapter.

Digitizing Objects and Modeling

This is the fun part: I felt like George Lucas when creating the models and digitizing them for this chapter. While it was fun, though, it wasn't the piece of cake many would think. (That means you, Mark!)

There are three approaches a game designer can use to create models or images for a game:

- Draw them.

- Model them with a 3-D program, such as 3D Studio.

- Digitize them with a video camera and frame-grabber card.

I'll admit that I am no artist. Although I can hold my own with 2-D art, I'm weak at drawing different-angled views of a 3-D object without a model sitting in front of me. Also, I hate using modeling programs because they're so complex. You need tons of polygons to make something look real, and the modeling software itself is extremely expensive. Alas, I decided to use real miniature models, a video camera, and a digitizer card to obtain the 3-D images of the objects for this chapter.

In theory, digitizing a miniature model is easy to do. Buy a digitizer card, borrow a video camera from someone, make a little stand and start taking snapshots of the object. *Wrong!* There are about 10 billion details that have to be considered first. Lighting, focal lengths, software, color palettes, repeatability, and resolution all must be considered.

In the end, I got everything to work—and to work almost to my satisfaction. (I'm never really satisfied.) I used Creative Labs Video Blaster SE (Special Edition) along with Microsoft's Video For Windows, Adobe Photostyler, and Electronic Art's Deluxe Animation. Also, I had a quite expensive video camera, which I borrowed from a good friend of mine whom I promised to mention. (Dione, I know you'll bring home the gold in the 1996 Olympics!) Anyway, once I had all that stuff, I had to practically build a small production studio with a blue screen, model stand, proper lighting, and a circular protractor to measure the angle the object was at so the model being filmed could be angled in a repeatable manner.

I forgot to mention that finding suitable toy models isn't as easy as it seems. Everything is trademarked, registered, or copyrighted. My advice to you, then, is to buy 20 different models of ships, boats, cars, spacecraft, and so on and build some weird object from all the models. Otherwise, you might get popped with a lawsuit!

I want to go through the order of operations to help ease the writhing pain you'll probably be introduced to when you digitize some objects of your own.

Creating a Miniature Production Studio

Here's what you need to do this:

- First, you need a well-lit, clean work area in which to place the video camera and backdrop. They should be at least four feet from each other. This will allow you to focus in and out.

- Next, I suggest that the room in which you do your filming be as monochromatic as possible. You don't want to film in a room with pink and blue walls. White walls with a black ceiling is the optimal situation.

- Make a little shooting area that allows you to change the backdrop, as shown in Figure 8.11. I took two pieces of Plexiglas and mounted them at 90 degrees to each other. Then I taped on colored construction paper to create a floor and backdrop for the object to be digitized in front of.

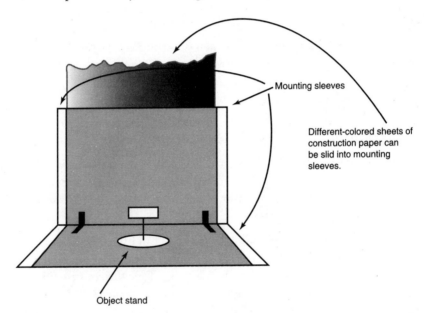

Figure 8.11. *A production studio that facilitates the use of different backdrop colors.*

The Backdrop

In the movies they use blue backdrops and then filter out the blue to obtain an image. Although this works great for them, I had problems with it. In the end, I used a black backdrop—the reason for using a blue backdrop is so that you can film a black object!—and played with the lighting so the object being digitized showed up against the backdrop with a high amount of contrast.

The Stand

Once you get your camera set up and have built a low-budget studio, you must build some kind of stand to hold the models. The stand can't be obtrusive to the image and must be something you can subtract out later with reasonable ease. At first I used a transparent Plexiglas stand, but I soon realized that the internal reflections within the stand created weird lighting effects. I then tried a paper clip, taping it to the bottom with one of the sides sticking up. I then drilled a small hole in the base of my model and mounted the model that way. This worked well. I could only rotate the model on one axis; I couldn't tilt or roll it. However, this was fine because I didn't really care about making such complex movements.

Lighting

Now comes the lighting problem. When digitizing video, you quickly realize how important lighting is, and how small changes can really affect the output of the digitizer. I finally settled on a halogen lamp along with a flashlight to create local specular effects (the flashlight is the Sun).

Studio Construction

Building a miniature studio is fairly hard when you have no resources to do it. If you're like me, and live in an apartment, you're really stuck because there's no convenient place to cut, drill, or paint. As I said, though, I used a couple of sheets of Plexiglas connected with angle brackets.

If you're allergic to tools and building stuff, you can probably get away with buying some black, white, and blue construction paper. I mention all three colors so that you can experiment and see what works best for you. Tape the construction paper to the wall and place your model on the ground in front of it, on a stand of some sort. This works fine, but is a little awkward because you'll be kneeling a lot and working on the floor.

I think the ultimate miniature studio would look like Figure 8.12. It would have a table that was some color with a parabolic-shaped backdrop. The drop could rotate and would be on a U-joint so that you could change the pitch and roll of the object along with rotating it on its pivot. Moreover, I'd have two cameras mounted at angles opposite the image so I could get two views at once.

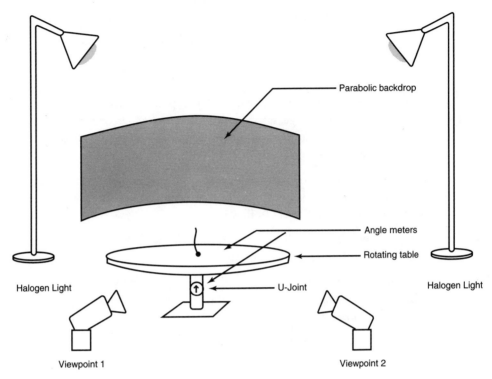

Figure 8.12. *The ultimate production studio.*

Video for Windows

Once all the physical problems have been solved and you have a clean video signal of your model, it's time to deal with the computer and the software (or, I should say, lack of software) with which to digitize the images. I didn't want to spend a lot of money on this, because I don't expect *you* to shell out hundreds or thousands of dollars on equipment and software. Therefore, we must use what comes with the digitizer card. This turns out to be Microsoft's Video for Windows, which is definitely designed for live video rather than taking the kind of snapshots we need.

Because just about all the digitizer cards you can buy come with Video for Windows, I want to describe how to use Video for Windows to obtain the images for your games.

- Use the single-frame option to capture each frame.

- Once you capture a frame, you save it as a .BMP file, and later convert this to a .PCX file with some other program.

To create frames of the object being rotated, I suggest mounting a circular protractor under the object so you can be sure the object is pointed in a certain direction. Then, when you capture the image, save it as *namexxx*.bmp, where *xxx* is the angle at which it's pointing. I found that using 30-degree rotations is more than enough to obtain a realistic-looking motion.

After obtaining all your frames, you must convert them to another format with either your paint program or some conversion program. (Most PC paint programs that support 320x200x256 like .PCX files.)

Once you have all the .PCX files, you must tediously subtract the border from each image, along with the stand if you can see it.

Then you take all the images and place them in cells so that they can be read as a single .PCX file with the same palette. I found that a resolution of no more than 128x128 was needed to obtain excellent realism.

The entire process just described is shown graphically in Figure 8.13.

The Color Palette

When digitizing live video, the software determines the optimal set of colors for each scanned frame. This won't work for our purposes, as we can only have one palette for each view of the object. If we really wanted to, we could have multiple palettes—but then we would have to change the palette every time an object changed views. This would be a problem.

I finally discovered that you could save a palette and force Video for Windows to use it all the time. To do this:

- Use the Capture Palette function to capture 20-30 frames of your object. Be sure not to allow your object to move.

- Using the 20-30 frames of imagery, the software averages the palettes for each frame, and arrive at an optimal palette. You can then use this palette for subsequent single-frame captures.

This is great, but the problem is that the whole palette is used. This means that any other computer-generated images have to be done using the palette that was generated by the frame grabber instead of a palette you like. How do we get around this?

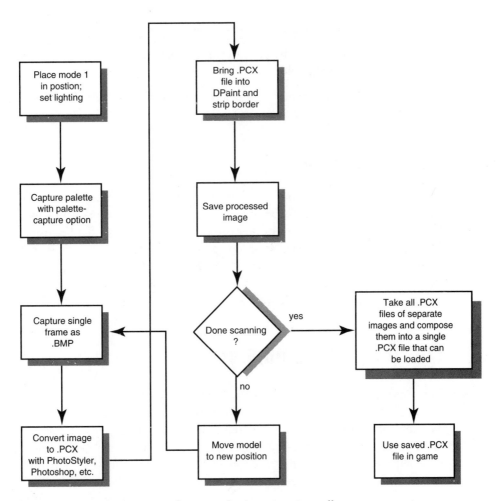

Figure 8.13. *The sequence of steps to obtain animation cells.*

Personally, I would want the frame grabber to have access to only 64 colors, and digitize the image using them. Then I could use the other 192 for other shades, color rotation, lighting, and game objects. I don't see a way to do this with the aforementioned setup. One other hope is to use image-processing software that you can give a palette, and force it to convert the images to this palette. I haven't seen anything like this, but I'm sure it's out there.

The last way to do it is by writing some software yourself. You could do a statistical scan of all the image data and find the most-used colors. Then you could:

- Create a palette of these with, say, 64 colors (or whatever).

- Remap the images pixel by pixel to the new palette and use colors that were nearest to the palette colors that were no longer available.

This way you could merge your game palette with the digitizer palette. This is actually the method I use, so I know it works.

The Wrap on Modeling

This is the basic procedure you should use to create your animation cells using models. There are no limits to what can be done with physical models. John Carmac used them for DOOM, and I'm sure many other games use them. I know that I'm using them. Models can be stored in a box, blown up, ignored for days, moved, and they still show up for work on time. Moreover, they work for nothing! You can't beat that, so I'd suggest that if you're planning to make a game by yourself and you're not an artist, modeling may be the best solution for getting realistic imagery in your games.

Cut! (I mean, Summary)

In this chapter we learned a few new tricks but, more importantly, we learned a little more about how to be creative and simulate something that would normally be very hard to do using simple techniques. We learned how to scale sprites and project them on the screen as if they were points using a perspective transform. We also learned how to do clipping (again). Finally, we covered the wonderful world of video production and real model usage in video games.

Sound FX and Music

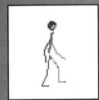

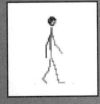

P laying video games without sound is like swimming without water. It shouldn't be done! It should be up there with the other video-game commandments like "Thou shalt not flicker!" Sound FX and music are two of the truly magical forces left on Earth. They can emote feelings of fear, excitement, and anticipation. I think excellent sound is more important than good graphics, because even if you have the most wicked 3-D, realtime, ray-traced video game, without sound it's just a moving picture.

In this chapter we study sound and its implementation on the PC. We talk solely about the Sound Blaster from Creative Labs, and compatibles. In this chapter we cover:

- The fundamentals of sound

- The Sound Blaster and its architecture

- Creating and playing digitized sound FX for video games

- The FM synthesizer

- Music and MIDI

- Advanced sound techniques

by André LaMothe

The Fundamentals of Sound

Sound is one of those things in life that isn't too complex to get a grasp on. Sound is basically a human interpretation of mechanical waves propagating within the medium of air, just as light is the propagation of electromagnetic waves through space. When a sound is created, the air around it expands and contracts. This expansion and contraction leads to a wavefront that eventually reaches your ears and creates pressure on your eardrums. Figure 9.1 shows a sound source and the propagation of mechanical waves from it.

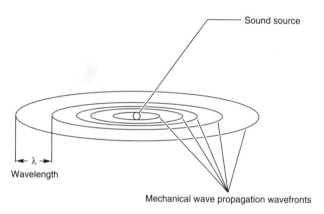

Figure 9.1. *A sound source and the propagation of mechanical waves.*

This wavefront then propagates through the air mechanically, meaning that air molecules transfer their kinetic energy from one to another. This allows the wave to move from one point to another. As the wave moves, it loses energy through friction (which we perceive as loudness), until finally it's completely absorbed by the air through which it travels.

Sound waves have some interesting properties. One of them is called the Doppler effect. We've all heard the sound of a train as it approaches, and the different sound it makes as it departs. This effect is caused by the propagation velocity of sound waves being modified by the speed of the train. You see, unlike light waves, sound is *slow*. It travels, on average, about 600 mph—so a train that's moving at 60 mph can change the way the sound propagates in an audible manner. If you recall, when a train approaches the sound gets louder and its *pitch*, or frequency, goes up. Then, as the train passes, the loudness and pitch go down. This occurs because the wavefronts are being emitted from a moving object, and compression is occurring. The train is moving and emitting the sound at the same time; this has the effect of making the frequency of the sound seem different when the train approaches and when it leaves.

Let's get a little technical and come up with some specific terms and conventions that we can use to describe and relate different sounds. People like to represent sounds on a two-dimensional graph like the one shown in Figure 9.2.

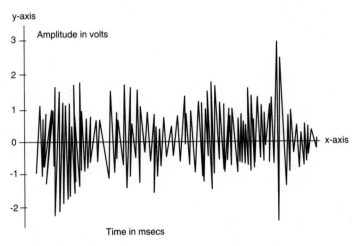

Figure 9.2. *The shape of sound.*

The x-axis is time, and the y-axis is the amplitude of the sound. A pure tone of middle C, which is 440Hz, would look like Figure 9.3.

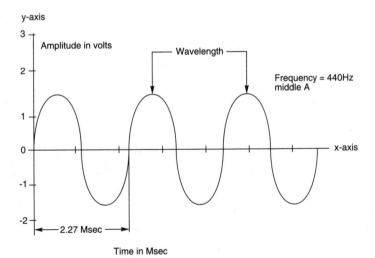

Figure 9.3. *A representation of a middle C note: 440Hz.*

As you can see, the wave replicates itself over and over as a function of time. This is one of the properties of a pure tone: it's a single sin wave of a specific frequency. It can be represented mathematically as:

```
F(t) = sin (2*π*F*t)
```

where F is the frequency we wish to generate.

As you can see from Figure 9.3, there are a few parameters we can extract from the wave form. One of them is the *amplitude* of the wave, or (more directly) its loudness. Amplitudes are usually measured in what are called *decibels*. Decibels are based on a logarithmic scale: a sound that's 5db is 10 times louder than a sound that is 4db. (Just like the scale by which we measure earthquakes. A 5 on the Richter scale is a little shake, but a 7 will definitely make you rock n' roll, as it's 100 times stronger than a 5!)

The next thing we can extract from Figure 9.3 is the wavelength of the sound. *Wavelength* is defined as the time, or distance, from one wavecrest to another. An easy way to picture this is the length of one complete cycle of the sound. Take a look at Figure 9.4. Here we have two different waveforms.

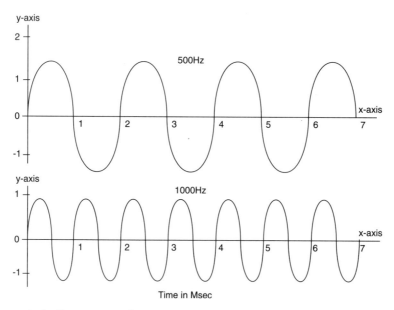

Figure 9.4. *Comparison of 500Hz to 1,000Hz waveforms.*

One of these waveforms represents a tone of 500Hz; the other represents a tone of 1000Hz. As you can see, the tone of 1000Hz has roughly twice as many complete cycles per unit of time as does the tone of 500Hz.

Now we should talk a little about *frequency response*. The average human has a frequency response something like that shown in Figure 9.5.

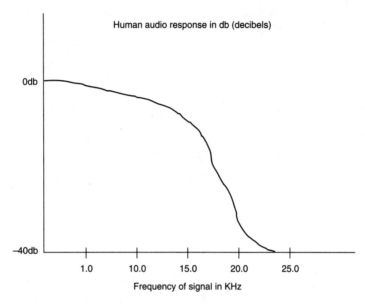

Figure 9.5. *The average human's frequency response.*

We hear well in the range of 20Hz-15KHz, and that response falls off until 20KHz (where most people become deaf). Therefore, we want to make sure that the sounds we make fall within these ranges.

Enough about what sound *is*. Let's start making some!

The Sound Blaster and Its Architecture

The Sound Blaster is a capable and complex card. Its operation is by no means simple, and we surely can't delve into all of its impressive capabilities in a single chapter. What we can do, however, is give a general description of the different models that are available, and their capabilities.

Currently, there are four different versions of the Sound Blaster. These are listed along with their functionality in Table 9.1.

Table 9.1. Sound Blaster versions and functionalities.

	Sound Blaster V2.0	Sound Blaster Pro V2.0	Sound Blaster 16	Sound Blaster 16 ASP
Function				
Sample Rates	4-15KHz	4-44.1KHz	4-44.1KHz	4-44.1KHz
Playback Rates	4-44.1KHz	4-44.1KHz	4-44.1KHz	4-44.1KHz
Stereo	No	Yes	Yes	Yes
DSP	8-Bit	8-Bit	8/16-Bit	8/16-Bit
FM Voices	11	20	20	20
Mic In	Yes *	Yes *	Yes *	Yes *
Mic Auto Gain	No	Yes	Yes	Yes
Line In	Yes	Yes	Yes	Yes
Speaker Out	Yes	Yes	Yes	Yes
Line Out	No	Yes **	Yes **	Yes **
CD Audio In	No	Yes	Yes	Yes
CD-ROM Connector	No	Yes	Yes	Yes
Mixer	No	Yes	Yes	Yes
Tone Control	No	No	Yes	Yes
Voice Recognition	No	No	No	Yes
Hardware Compression	No	No	No	Yes

* Mono

** Internal

The Sound Blaster can create two kinds of sounds:

- Synthesized sound
- Digitized sound

Synthesized sound is created electronically using analog or digital hardware. The Sound Blaster takes a state-of-the-art approach to synthesis, using what's called *FM synthesis*. FM synthesis is a sound creation based on frequency modulation, much the way music is transmitted by FM stations. We expand on this later in this chapter.

The Sound Blaster also has a *digital signal processor* (DSP). The DSP helps in synthesis and in the playback of *musical instrument digital interface* (MIDI) music. MIDI is basically a standard of describing songs and instruments in a manner that can be reproduced by computers or synthesizers, such as Yamaha's.

The second way the Sound Blaster creates sound is by digital playback. The Sound Blaster can digitize and play back samples of things such as speech and sound FX. This is useful for sounds that would be difficult, time consuming, or even impossible to synthesize with the FM synthesizer and DSP hardware alone. We'll rely on digitized sounds and MIDI music for our video-game sound FX.

The following sections describe how to use the Sound Blaster's digitizer.

Digitized Sound

All right, now we're getting somewhere! When I made my first digitized sound play on the Sound Blaster it was like I had sighted a new continent. Being able to play digitized sounds is *very* cool, and if used wisely can add orders of magnitude to the game play of a video game. First, let's talk about what digitized sound is. Take a look at Figure 9.6.

This is a snapshot of me saying "What's up?" As you can see, this looks different from the pure tones shown in previous figures. The question is, what's different? Answer: the human voice.

The human voice is *rich* and *textured*. This means that it has harmonics. When a person talks there are many overtones and undertones of the fundamental frequency that person is emitting at any instant. To digitize this information, or waveform, we must do two things:

- Convert the information into an electronic signal.
- Sample that signal at a continuous rate.

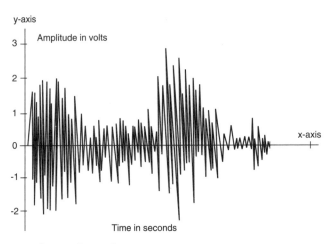

Figure 9.6. *A digitized sample.*

First, we must convert it into a form we can understand (that is, digital). This is done with an analog-to-digital (A/D) converter. The A/D converter converts the analog signal into a range of digital steps, usually represented by 8 or 16 bits each. That means that the signal we digitize gets converted into values that can be represented by 8 or 16 bits. If we use only 8 bits per sample, we have a range of only -127 to +128. However, if we use 16 bits, our range increases to -32767 to 32768, which is much higher quality.

Next, we must sample the signal at a continuous rate. For example, say we sampled a person speaking at 8KHz using one-byte samples for 10 seconds. This would take up *80K!!!* As you can see, digitizing costs memory; that's why the FM synthesizer is so important.

"So," you might say, "let's lower the sample rate." We can do that, but as we do something happens: we lose information due to what's called *quantization noise*. Say the signal we're sampling has a frequency of 10KHz, and we sample it at 6KHz. We aren't going to be able to reproduce the waveform accurately. As a rule of thumb— actually, it's not thumb's rule, but Shannon's Rule—you must sample a signal at twice its highest component's frequency if you are to reproduce it accurately. That means if you want to accurately reproduce music and speech, which ranges up to roughly 20KHz, you must digitize at two times that frequency, or 40KHz. CD players do just that: they digitize at 44.1KHz. At that rate you're not missing anything! The sound FX in DOOM were probably digitized somewhere around 11KHz, which is a good medium.

We definitely cannot be recording and playing samples at that rate. Digitizing at CD-quality rates consumes too much memory. While it's possible to play sounds off disk, for our purposes we'll try to sample at no greater than 6KHz at 8 bits.

Figure 9.7 illustrates sampling a signal.

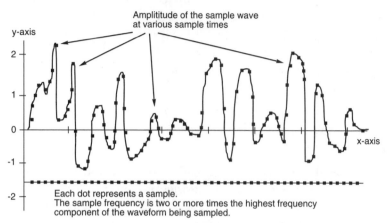

Figure 9.7. *Sampling a signal.*

Playing Digitized Sound

Let's start talking about how we play digitized sounds. I'm not going to show you how to digitize sounds; you can use one of dozens of software packages to digitize, play back, and manipulate sounds. Video games don't need to record sounds—they just need to know how to play them.

With that in mind, I'm suppling a piece of shareware called Blaster Master. This is a DOS application that lets you do everything with digitized sounds. It can convert sounds to different file formats and do special FX with the sounds (such as echoing, reverb, and pitch change).

> By the way, digitized sounds do have a format, just like everything else. The formats on the PC are called .WAV and .VOC. Both contain header information in addition to the actual sound data for the sample. As far as I can tell .WAV is a format that was invented for windows and .VOC is a format that's been around for a while.

Blaster Master converts between .WAV and .VOC, and more. The game we write in this book uses .VOC files only, so you must record or convert your sound files to .VOC format before using the software—or else the software will bail! We choose .VOC files for use in PC games because their format is much easier to understand. Moreover, .WAV files can only be recorded at 11KHz, 22KHz, and 44KHz, which is a restriction we must avoid because of memory limitations.

Where should we begin? Good question. Let's start with the driver. To play digitized sounds we must use a driver, called CT-VOICE.DRV, supplied by Creative Labs. This driver enables us to make calls, somewhat the way we make calls to BIOS, to tell the sound card to execute functions and commands.

However, the driver doesn't give us BIOS extensions the way the mouse driver or joystick driver does. This driver is an offspring of a fairly new technology called *loadable device drivers*. With this technology, the code of a driver is loaded into memory and chunks are then executed by jumping to a specific offset from the beginning of the driver with one or more specific register(s) loaded with the command(s) we want executed.

(Actually, I saw this technology about seven years ago. I've been programming for a long time, and there have been about a whole three times that I've had to manually load a driver into the computer and jump to offsets in the code segment.)

The CT-VOICE.DRV driver has a lot of commands, and I'm not going to explain all of them in detail. We talk only about the ones we need to load and play digitized sounds. Table 9.2 describes the driver functions we'll be using.

Table 9.2. A subset of CT-VOICE.DRV functions.

Function	Description
0	Get Driver Version
1	Set Base I/O Address
2	Set DMA Interrupt
3	Initialize Driver
4	Toggle Speaker
5	Set Status Word Address
6	Start Voice Output

Function	Description
8	Stop Voice Output
9	Terminate Driver
10	Pause Voice Output
11	Continue Voice Output
12	Break Voice Output Loop

Now let's look at each one of these in detail.

Function 0: Get Driver Version

This function queries the driver version number from the driver itself.

Entry   BX = 0

Exit   AH = Major Version Number

             AL = Minor Version Number

Function 1: Set Base I/O Address

This function sets the base I/O address used by the driver and the card, so the number you set it to should match the selected I/O port on the card itself. If you don't call this function, the driver defaults to 220h.

Entry   BX = 1

             AX = Base I/O address

Exit   None

Function 2: Set DMA Address

This function sets the direct memory access (DMA) interrupt number the driver uses to indicate that a DMA transfer has been completed by the Sound Blaster.

Entry   BX = 2

             AX = DMA interrupt number

Exit   None

Function 3: Initialize Driver

This function initializes and starts up the sound driver.

Entry   BX = 3

Exit   AX = 0 Driver successfully initialized

1 Incorrect driver version

2 I/O read/write failure

3 DMA interrupt failure

Function 4: Toggle Speaker (Sound Blaster base model only)

This function turns on or off the digitizer speaker output.

Entry   BX = 4

AL = 0 for Off

1 for On

Exit   None

Function 5: Set Status Word Address

This function tells the driver the address of a variable in which it will store various status information. You define a variable and then pass the segment and offset to this function so the driver can convey to you important information and status.

Entry   BX = 5

ES:DI = The segment and offset of the variable you want to use for status

Exit   None

Function 6: Start Voice Output

This function is the one that does the work. It plays a .VOC file using DMA to the speaker. However, we must point a pointer to the data.

Entry   BX = 6

ES:DI = The segment and offset of the beginning of the .VOC data you want played—note that we must be careful to pass the address of the actual data (that is, we must skip the `hteader` info; more on this later in this chapter)

Exit   AX = 0 if successful; nonzero otherwise

Function 8: Stop Voice I/O

This function stops any and all I/O operations and sets the `ct_voice_status` variable to 0.

Entry   BX = 8

Exit   None

Function 9: Terminate Driver

This function kills the drivers and stops all processing. However, it does not unload the driver from memory. You must do that yourself.

Entry   BX = 9

Exit   None

Function 10: Pause Voice Output

This function pauses the voice output. You can restart the sound by using the continuation command.

Entry   BX = 10

Exit   AX = 0 if successful, 1 if voice output is not active

Function 11: Continue Voice Output

This function continues a previously paused sound.

Entry   BX = 11

Exit   AX = 0 if successful, 1 if voice output is not paused

Function 12: Break Voice Output Loop

This function breaks a loop in the digitized data.

Entry   BX = 12

              AX = 0 Leave voice loop at end of current cycle

              1 Leave voice loop immediately

Exit   AX = 0 if successful

              1 if a voice loop is not active

Using the Driver Functions to Play .VOC Files

That about sums it up for the functions we'll be using. They're fairly self-explanatory and you should be able to write a driver and experiment with the Sound Blaster's digital channel by yourself... Gotcha! Did you think I'd leave you hanging in digital purgatory? No way! Let's make a driver and a demo program that play digitized sounds. You should be able to take this software and use it directly in your games.

The first thing we must do is load the CT-VOICE.DRV into a region of memory. We could just allocate some memory, open the file as pure binary, and load it in, byte by byte. However, there's a problem with this approach: the driver *must* be loaded on a paragraph boundary. That is, its segment can be anything, but its offset must be zero. What that means is that you can't use ALLOCATE or its derivatives to allocate the memory for the driver. You must use a function that allocates memory one paragraph at a time. The function that fills this requirement is called _dos_allocmem(). What we have to do, therefore, is:

- Open the file CT-VOICE.DRV.
- Figure out how big it is.
- Allocate the memory.
- Load it in.

The function in Listing 9.1 does just that.

Listing 9.1. Allocating memory for CT-VOICE.DRV.

```
//////////////////////////////////////////////////////////////

void Voc_Load_Driver(void)
{
// Load the ct-voice.drv.

int driver_handle;
```

```
    unsigned errno,segment,offset,num_para,bytes_read;

    // Open the driver file.

    _dos_open("CT-VOICE.DRV", _O_RDONLY, &driver_handle);

    // Allocate the memory.

    num_para = 1 + (filelength(driver_handle))/16;

    _dos_allocmem(num_para,&segment);

    // Point the driver pointer to the data area.

    _FP_SEG(driver_ptr) = segment;
    _FP_OFF(driver_ptr) = 0;

    // Load in the driver code.

    data_ptr = driver_ptr;

    do
     {
     _dos_read(driver_handle,data_ptr, 0x4000, &bytes_read);
     data_ptr += bytes_read;

     } while(bytes_read==0x4000);

    // Close the file.

    _dos_close(driver_handle);

    } // end Voc_Load_Driver

///////////////////////////////////////////////////////////////
```

You can break the function in Listing 9.1 into three parts:

■ First, we open up the CT-VOICE.DRV file using a pure binary mode. We do this so we get no character translations; that would be catastrophic, as we're reading in actual code and not an ASCII file.

■ The second part of the code computes how large the file is and then allocates the memory. Note that we allocate a number of blocks, where each block is a paragraph of 16 bytes.

■ Finally, the driver is loaded in 32k bytes at a time. This is one of the beauties of using the _dos_read() function in deference to the standard getch() functions: we can read large chunks at a time.

Now that we've loaded in the driver, we must keep a pointer to it so that we can vector to its start address. This pointer is kept in the global variable named driver_ptr. (I think the name is clear enough.)

Believe it or not, loading the driver was the hardest part. Let's see the code that loads a .VOC file. It looks much the same as the driver loader. Again, we must:

- Open the file in binary mode.
- Allocate memory.
- Load the entire .VOC file into the buffer.

Listing 9.2 contains the code to do this.

Listing 9.2. Loading a .VOC file.

```
///////////////////////////////////////////////////////////////

char far *Voc_Load_Sound(char *filename,
                         unsigned char *header_length)
{
// Load a sound off disk into memory and point a pointer to it.

char far *temp_ptr;
char far *data_ptr;

unsigned int sum;

int sound_handle,t;

unsigned errno,segment,offset,num_para,bytes_read;

// Open the sound file.

_dos_open(filename, _O_RDONLY, &sound_handle);

// Allocate the memory.
```

```
num_para = 1 + (filelength(sound_handle))/16;

_dos_allocmem(num_para,&segment);

// Point the data pointer to the allocated data area.

_FP_SEG(data_ptr) = segment;
_FP_OFF(data_ptr) = 0;

// Load in the sound data.

temp_ptr = data_ptr;

do
 {
 _dos_read(sound_handle,temp_ptr, 0x4000, &bytes_read);
 temp_ptr += bytes_read;

 sum+=bytes_read;

 } while(bytes_read==0x4000);

// Make sure it's a voc file; test for the word "Creative".

   if ((data_ptr[0] != 'C') || (data_ptr[1] != 'r'))
      {
      printf("\n%s is not a voc file!",filename);
      _dos_freemem(_FP_SEG(data_ptr));
      return(0);

      } // end if voc file

   *header_length = (unsigned char)data_ptr[20];


// Close the file.

_dos_close(sound_handle);

return(data_ptr);

} // end Voc_Load_Sound
```

//

The most exciting thing about the function in Listing 9.2 is that it returns the address of (or a pointer to) the region of memory into which the .VOC file was loaded. We use this pointer later, in the function that plays the sound.

The rest of the functions we implement are straightforward. We use in-line assembly to set up the registers and do an assembly language "call" to the driver by way of driver_ptr.

Let's take a look at a couple of the functions to get the hang of writing them. The driver must be initialized before we can use it. This is a reasonable request. To do this, we must implement Function 3 (Initialize Driver). Listing 9.3 contains the code to do this.

Listing 9.3. Initializing the driver.

```
////////////////////////////////////////////////////////////////

int Voc_Init_Driver(void)
{
// Initialize the driver and return the status.

int status;

_asm
    {
    mov bx,3            ; function 3 initialize the driver
    call driver_ptr     ; call the driver
    mov status,ax       ; store in version variable

    } // end in-line assembler

// Return status.

printf("\nDriver Initialized");

return(status);

} // end Voc_Init_Driver

////////////////////////////////////////////////////////////////
```

Another important function is the one that tells the driver the address of a variable to use to report back on its operational status. The code that sets this variable up, which I've called ct_voice_status, is contained in Listing 9.4.

Listing 9.4. Setting up the status variable to be accessed by the driver.

```
////////////////////////////////////////////////////////////////

Voc_Set_Status_Addr(char __far *status)
{

unsigned segm,offm;

segm = _FP_SEG(status);
offm = _FP_OFF(status);

_asm
    {
```

```
    mov bx,5          ; function 5 set status varible address
    mov es, segm       ; es gets the segment
    mov di, offm      ; di gets offset
    call driver_ptr   ; call the driver

    } // end in-line assembler

} // Voc_Set_Status_Addr
```

///

Finally, let's see the implementation of Function 6 (Start Voice Output), which is used to play a sound that's in memory. Listing 9.5 contains the code to do this.

Listing 9.5. Playing a .VOC file from memory.

///

```
int Voc_Play_Sound(unsigned char far *addr,
                   unsigned char header_length)
{
// Play a preloaded VOC file.

unsigned segm,offm;


segm = _FP_SEG(addr);
offm = _FP_OFF(addr) + header_length;

_asm
    {
    mov bx,6          ; Function 6: play a VOC file.
    mov ax, segm      ; Can only move a register into segment,
                      ; so we need this.
    mov es, ax        ; es gets the segment.
    mov di, offm      ; di gets offset.
    call driver_ptr   ; Call the driver.

    } // end in-line assembler

} // end Voc_Play_Sound
```

///

The Voc_Play_Sound function in Listing 9.5 works as follows:

■ The address of the .VOC file in memory we want played is passed to the function.

■ The function then uses two quite useful macros—_FP_SEG() and _FP_OFF()—to extract the segment and offset of the starting address of the .VOC sound buffer we want played.

■ The segment and offset are placed in ES:DI in accord with the driver requirements.

■ We vector to the driver.

And presto: the sound plays.

For the game we write in this book, and for your own first games, I suggest you stick
to simple digitized sounds. Playing music is not too much more difficult, but it does
take quite a bit of work and understanding. Anyway, Listing 9.6 contains the complete
sound software, along with a menu driven main() function that plays some familiar
sounds. When you execute the program, make sure that:

■ All the .VOC files are in the current directory.

■ The CT-VOICE.DRV file is also in the current directory.

One final note about digitized sound: after you start it, you don't have to do anymore
processing. You're free to continue your game loop. The sounds are processed and
driven completely by the Sound Blaster and its DMA hardware. The PC need not
waste time doing anything but starting the sound (and stopping it later), which takes
only a few microseconds.

Listing 9.6. The complete sound software.

```
// I N C L U D E S ////////////////////////////////////////////////

#include <io.h>
#include <stdio.h>
#include <stdlib.h>
#include <dos.h>
#include <bios.h>
#include <fcntl.h>

// G L O B A L S ////////////////////////////////////////////////

char __far *driver_ptr;
unsigned version;
char __huge *data_ptr;
unsigned ct_voice_status;

// F U N C T I O N S ////////////////////////////////////////////////

void Voc_Get_Version(void)
{
// Get the version of the driver and print it out.

_asm
   {
   mov bx,0        ; function 0 get version number
   call driver_ptr ; call the driver
   mov version,ax  ; store in version variable
```

```
    } // end in-line assembler

printf("\nVersion of Driver = %X.0%X",((version>>8) & 0x00ff), (version&0x00ff));

} // end Voc_Get_Version

//////////////////////////////////////////////////////////////////

int Voc_Init_Driver(void)
{
// Initialize the driver and return the status.

int status;

_asm
    {
    mov bx,3          ; function 3 initialize the driver
    call driver_ptr   ; call the driver
    mov status,ax     ; store in version variable

    } // end in-line assembler

// Return status.

printf("\nDriver Initialized");

return(status);

} // end Voc_Init_Driver

//////////////////////////////////////////////////////////////////

int Voc_Terminate_Driver(void)
{
// Terminate the driver.

_asm
    {
    mov bx,9          ; function 9 terminate the driver
    call driver_ptr   ; call the driver

    } // end in-line assembler

// Deallocate memory.

_dos_freemem(_FP_SEG(driver_ptr));

printf("\nDriver Terminated");

} // end Voc_Terminate_Driver

//////////////////////////////////////////////////////////////////

void Voc_Set_Port(unsigned port)
{

// Set the I/O port of the sound blaster.
```

continues

Listing 9.6. continued

```
_asm
   {
   mov bx,1          ; function 1 set port address
   mov ax,port       ; move the port number into ax
   call driver_ptr   ; call the driver

   } // end in-line assembler

} // Voc_Set_Port

///////////////////////////////////////////////////////////////////

void Voc_Set_Speaker(unsigned on)
{

// Turn the speaker on or off.

_asm
   {
   mov bx,4          ; function 4 turn speaker on or off
   mov ax,on         ; move the on/off flag into ax
   call driver_ptr   ; call the driver

   } // end in-line assembler

} // Voc_Set_Speaker

///////////////////////////////////////////////////////////////////

int Voc_Play_Sound(unsigned char far *addr,
                   unsigned char header_length)
{
// Play a preloaded VOC file.

unsigned segm,offm;


segm = _FP_SEG(addr);
offm = _FP_OFF(addr) + header_length;

_asm
   {
   mov bx,6          ; Function 6: play a VOC file.
   mov ax, segm      ; Can only move a register into segment,
                     ; so we need this.
   mov es, ax        ; es gets the segment.
   mov di, offm      ; di gets offset.
   call driver_ptr   ; Call the driver.

   } // end in-line assembler

} // end Voc_Play_Sound
```

```
/////////////////////////////////////////////////////////////////////

int Voc_Stop_Sound(void)
{
// Stop a sound that is playing.

_asm
    {
    mov bx,8            ; function 8 stop a sound
    call driver_ptr     ; call the driver

    } // end in-line assembler

} // end Voc_Stop_Sound

/////////////////////////////////////////////////////////////////////

int Voc_Pause_Sound(void)
{
// Pause a sound that is playing.

_asm
    {
    mov bx,10           ; function 10 pause a sound
    call driver_ptr     ; call the driver

    } // end in-line assembler

} // end Voc_Pause_Sound

/////////////////////////////////////////////////////////////////////

int Voc_Continue_Sound(void)
{
// Continue a paused sound that had previously been playing.

_asm
    {
    mov bx,11           ; function 11 continue play
    call driver_ptr     ; call the driver

    } // end in-line assembler

} // end Voc_Continue_Sound

/////////////////////////////////////////////////////////////////////

int Voc_Break_Sound(void)
{
// Break a sound loop.

_asm
    {
    mov bx,12           ; function 12 break loop
    call driver_ptr     ; call the driver
```

continues

Listing 9.6. continued

```
    } // end in-line assembler

} // end Voc_Break_Sound

//////////////////////////////////////////////////////////////////

void Voc_Set_DMA(unsigned dma)
{

_asm
    {
    mov bx,2          ; function 2 set DMA interupt number
    mov ax,dma        ; move the dma number into ax
    call driver_ptr   ; call the driver

    } // end in-line assembler

} // Voc_Set_DMA

//////////////////////////////////////////////////////////////////

Voc_Set_Status_Addr(char __far *status)
{

unsigned segm,offm;

segm = _FP_SEG(status);
offm = _FP_OFF(status);

_asm
    {
    mov bx,5          ; function 5 set status varible address
    mov es, segm      ; es gets the segment
    mov di, offm      ; di gets offset
    call driver_ptr   ; call the driver

    } // end in-line assembler

} // Voc_Set_Status_Addr

//////////////////////////////////////////////////////////////////

void Voc_Load_Driver(void)
{
// Load the ct-voice.drv.

int driver_handle;

unsigned errno,segment,offset,num_para,bytes_read;


// Open the driver file.

_dos_open("CT-VOICE.DRV", _O_RDONLY, &driver_handle);
```

```
// Allocate the memory.

num_para = 1 + (filelength(driver_handle))/16;

_dos_allocmem(num_para,&segment);

// Point the driver pointer to the data area.

_FP_SEG(driver_ptr) = segment;
_FP_OFF(driver_ptr) = 0;

// Load in the driver code.

data_ptr = driver_ptr;

do
 {
 _dos_read(driver_handle,data_ptr, 0x4000, &bytes_read);
 data_ptr += bytes_read;

 } while(bytes_read==0x4000);

// Close the file.

_dos_close(driver_handle);

} // end Voc_Load_Driver

//////////////////////////////////////////////////////////////

char far *Voc_Load_Sound(char *filename,
                         unsigned char *header_length)
{
// Load a sound off disk into memory and point a pointer to it.

char far *temp_ptr;
char far *data_ptr;

unsigned int sum;

int sound_handle,t;

unsigned errno,segment,offset,num_para,bytes_read;

// Open the sound file.

_dos_open(filename, _O_RDONLY, &sound_handle);

// Allocate the memory.

num_para = 1 + (filelength(sound_handle))/16;

_dos_allocmem(num_para,&segment);

// Point the data pointer to the allocated data area.

_FP_SEG(data_ptr) = segment;
_FP_OFF(data_ptr) = 0;
```

continues

Listing 9.6. continued

```c
// Load in the sound data.

temp_ptr = data_ptr;

do
 {
 _dos_read(sound_handle,temp_ptr, 0x4000, &bytes_read);
 temp_ptr += bytes_read;

 sum+=bytes_read;

 } while(bytes_read==0x4000);

// Make sure it's a voc file.

    if ((data_ptr[0] != 'C') ¦¦ (data_ptr[1] != 'r'))
       {
       printf("\n%s is not a voc file!",filename);
       _dos_freemem(_FP_SEG(data_ptr));
       return(0);

       } // end if voc file

    *header_length = (unsigned char)data_ptr[20];


// Close the file.

_dos_close(sound_handle);

return(data_ptr);

} // end Voc_Load_Sound

/////////////////////////////////////////////////////////////////

void Voc_Unload_Sound(char far *sound_ptr)
{

// Delete the sound from memory.

_dos_freemem(_FP_SEG(sound_ptr));

} // end Voc_Unload_Sound


/////////////////////////////////////////////////////////////////

void main(void)
{

char far *sounds[4];
unsigned char lengths[4];
int done=0,sel;
```

```
Voc_Load_Driver();

Voc_Init_Driver();

Voc_Set_Port(0x220);

Voc_Set_DMA(5);

Voc_Get_Version();

Voc_Set_Status_Addr((char __far *)&ct_voice_status);

// Load in sounds.

sounds[0] = Voc_Load_Sound("beav.voc"  , &lengths[0]);
sounds[1] = Voc_Load_Sound("ed209.voc" ,&lengths[1]);
sounds[2] = Voc_Load_Sound("term.voc"  , &lengths[2]);
sounds[3] = Voc_Load_Sound("driver.voc",&lengths[3]);

Voc_Set_Speaker(1);

// Main event loop: let the player select a sound to play. Note
// that you can interupt a sound that is currently playing.

while(!done)
    {
    printf("\n\nSound Demo Menu");
    printf("\n1 - Beavis");
    printf("\n2 - ED 209");
    printf("\n3 - Terminator");
    printf("\n4 - Exit");
    printf("\n\nSelect One ? ");
    scanf("%d",&sel);

    switch (sel)
        {
        case 1:
            {
            Voc_Stop_Sound();
            Voc_Play_Sound(sounds[0] , lengths[0]);
            } break;

        case 2:
            {
            Voc_Stop_Sound();
            Voc_Play_Sound(sounds[1] , lengths[1]); ;
            } break;

        case 3:
            {
            Voc_Stop_Sound();
            Voc_Play_Sound(sounds[2] , lengths[2]); ;
            } break;

        case 4:
            {
            done = 1;
            } break;
```

continues

Listing 9.6. continued

```
                default:
                        {
                printf("\nFunction %d is not a selection.",sel);
                        } break;

                } // end switch

        } // end while

// Terminate.

Voc_Play_Sound(sounds[3] , lengths[3]); ;

// Wait for end sequence to stop. The status variable will be -1
// when a sound is playing, and 0 otherwise.

while(ct_voice_status!=0) {}

Voc_Set_Speaker(0);

// Unload sounds.

Voc_Unload_Sound(sounds[0]);
Voc_Unload_Sound(sounds[1]);
Voc_Unload_Sound(sounds[2]);
Voc_Unload_Sound(sounds[3]);

Voc_Terminate_Driver();

} // end main
```

The FM Synthesizer

The FM synthesizer is the heart of the Sound Blaster's music- and voice-synthesis capabilities. As I said earlier in this chapter, the FM synthesizer synthesizes a waveform by modulating a carrier wave. This allows for the creation of harmonics. Moreover, the waveforms of musical instruments and human vocal cords can be approximated with this technique.

The FM synthesizer has 18 operator cells. Each cell consists of two sections:

■ A modulator cell

■ A carrier cell

Figure 9.8 shows a typical FM synthesizer operator cell, where A is the overall amplitude, Wc is the carrier-wave frequency in radians/sec, and Wm is the modulator frequency in rads/sec.

The output of the modulator cell is added to the carrier cell. This has the effect of creating a wave that "rides" on top of another wave. The math that describes this operation is the composition of two sin waves. Here's the output wave function:

```
F(t) = A sin (Wc*t + sin Wm*t)
```

Unfortunately, we don't have the time to go into the FM synthesizer; we have a game to write! (Even though music for our game would be really cool.)

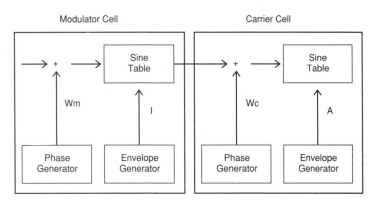

f(t) = A Sin (Wct + I Sin Wmt)
A = Output amplitude
I = Modulation amplitude (modulation index)
Wc = Carrier frequency
Wm =Modulator frequency
t = time in seconds

Figure 9.8. *A typical FM synthesizer operator cell.*

Music and MIDI

As with the FM synthesizer we don't have the time to go into playing music using the Sound Blaster. There's quite a bit to it, and you should obtain a complete reference. However, I want to at least tell you what to look forward to. The Sound Blaster does come with a driver, similar to the CT-VOICE.DRV driver discussed earlier, to play MIDI music. (If you've forgotten, MIDI stands for *musical instrument digital interface*.) Anyway, the music driver that plays MIDI files is called SBFDRV.DRV, and is loaded by the program SBFMDRV.EXE. The driver's functions are described in Table 9.3.

Table 9.3. SBFMDRV.DRV functions.

Function	Description
0	Get FM Drive Version
1	Set Music Status Byte Address
2	Set Instrument Table
3	Set System Clock Rate
4	Set Driver Clock Rate
5	Transpose Music
6	Play Music
7	Stop Music
8	Reset FM Driver
9	Pause Music
10	Resume Music
11	Set User-Defined Trap for System Exclusive

That's all I'm going to say about the music driver. I'll bet you that a game-programming guru could figure it out with just the above information and what he or she knew about the CT-VOICE.DRV. Hmmmm?

Using Sound in Video Games

I cannot overemphasize the proper use and timing of sound in a video game. I have watched people come to near-life experiences when the proper sound was played at the right time.

Because the computer has a limited amount of memory, you must pick your sounds wisely and use them to really enhance the world that you've created. Also, sounds should all be exaggerated: you should make them bigger than life. No one wants to hear a gun shot that sounds like "Bang." They want to hear a photon torpedo! So what if it's unrealistic? We are little demigods, and these are our universes; therefore we can do anything we want!

Let's talk about the architecture of the sound interface for a video game. We will want to play different sounds as a function of time. Let's take as an example the game we are going to construct, which I've named Warlock. During the game play it's possible that we may want to play multiple digitized sounds at one time. Unfortunately, we only have one digital channel. Alas, we can play only one data stream at a time. Being the brilliant software sorcerers that we are, however, there are ways around this little problem, which we discuss briefly next.

Let's talk about some philosophies that we must adhere to in any case. In Warlock I anticipate growls, wind, and maybe some weapons. All of these sounds could happen simultaneously. What we must do is create a method of prioritizing the sounds and allowing the preemption of lower-priority sounds for a higher-priority sound. One algorithm we could use is shown in Algorithm 9.1.

Algorithm 9.1. Psuedocode of a sound scheduler.

```
while(true)
// Age queued sounds. If they've been waiting too long, dequeue
// them. If there is no sound playing, play the requested sound.

else
// If the sound being requested is of a higher priority (you
// fired your gun or something), preempt the current sound and
// play the higher-priority sound.

else
// If the requested sound is of lower priority, queue it to be
//  played later.

end
```

Algorithm 9.1 is a good first draft of a sound scheduler. It allows for sounds to be queued and even preempted.

Now, if the video game could only play one digitized sound at a time, that would be pretty boring. So how can we play multiple sounds simultaneously? We can do the following "trick."

Say we have the sound of a laser and the sound of a growl that must be played at the same time, and that they were started at the same time. Assume, also, that they have the same priority. With Algorithm 9.1, we would have to toss a coin and play one or the other. But why not just add the sounds together and play the result?

We can do exactly that. We use the *theorem of superposition*, which states that any two waves in space or time can superimpose on each other, and the result is a wave. In our case, we must add the .VOC data.

There's a problem with this approach: space and time have no limits, but 8-bits do! During the addition of the two waveforms, we might overflow the range of 8 or 16 bits. There are two ways to deal with this:

- We can just clip the sound at the range.

- We can take only a percentage of each wave, guaranteeing that the sum never overflows.

Algorithm 9.2 implements a superimposer.

Algorithm 9.2. Pseudocode for the superimposer.

```
length one  =length(sound one)
length two = length(sound two)

if  length one > length two
        // Process the first part of the sound.
    for index=0 to length two
    new sound[index] =
    .5 * sound one[index] + .5 * sound two[index]

    // Process the second part of the sound: just copy the
    // rest of sound one but attenuate it.
    for index=length two+1 to length one
    new sound[index] = .5 * sound one[index]
else
    // Process the first part of the sound.
    for index=0 to length one
    new sound[index] =
    .5 * sound one[index] + .5 * sound two[index]

    // Process the second part of the sound: just copy the
    // rest of sound one but attenuate it.
    for index=length one+1 to length two
    new sound[index] = .5 * sound two[index]
end
```

In essence, Algorithm 9.2 is what you need to add sounds together. It adds only two sounds, of course, but it could be generalized. There's only one problem with adding sounds in this way: it takes up time and memory. If there are two .VOC files in memory and they're both 60K, you must do 60 thousand additions, which can be done in a few milliseconds. That's reasonable, as a human won't be able to perceive the delay. But the result of the addition must go into a new buffer that consumes another 60K. So, beware!

Summary

Within this chapter we talked about the art of noise in PC games:

- We covered The Sound Blaster card and how to play digitized sounds using the CT-VOIDE.DRV driver supplied by Creative Labs.

- We also learned some of the theory behind sounds and what the Sound Blaster is capable of.

- We took a stab at some advanced topics relating to sound scheduling and superposition algorithms.

Also, you got to hear me imitate a few celebrities.

That about raps it up...get it, rap music? Meet you in the next chapter. Later!

Implementing Computer Game Music

by John W. Ratcliff

B y now you know about optimization techniques and other graphics tricks and twiddles. You have learned how to do dazzling graphics, create brilliant artificial intelligence, and maybe even how to read the joystick port. In this chapter, you learn about the most powerful technique available to create a lasting impact on the user. Sound and music enable you to directly control a user's emotions interactively and within the context of your game. Well-designed sound effects can create a more vivid "virtual reality" than the most advanced 3D graphics. Emotionally compelling music can communicate a greater sense of dread, excitement, victory, sadness, or even horror, than the most exacting computer art.

Music and sound effects are the most powerful tools available to impact the user emotionally. If you don't understand that intuitively, watch *Jurassic Park* again. But this time when the Tyrannosaurus Rex shows up to eat the Land Rover, turn off the sound and see how much of

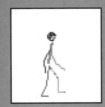

the terror generated in that scene is fueled directly by the power of the music and sound. While graphics enable the user see the reality of your world, music and sound effects let the user know how to feel about it.

While many of you know this intuitively, you should test this for yourself in a literal fashion. Rent *Terminator II*, *Conan the Barbarian*, *Star Wars*, *Aliens*, or *Jurassic Park*. Every single time you hear your heart racing during the film, close your eyes and think very hard about what you are hearing at that time. Listen to how the primary melody of the film's music score is interwoven and allowed to build and evolve during different portions of the film. Occasionally during a really loud action sequence, turn off the volume. You will feel the tension of the situation vanish as if you had closed the spigot to a faucet of rushing water.

Nothing is created with sound and music in film that you cannot—or wouldn't want to—emulate with multimedia. With one caveat. In our multimedia titles, we want the sound effects, dialogue, foley, and music to be both interactive and contextual to the environment. By adding interactive elements to the soundtrack, the emotional content becomes magnified.

A soundtrack contains four major components: dialogue, sound effects, foley, and music. The following sections take a brief look at each, and how you should apply them to your product.

> **Dialogue.** Most dialogue you hear in movies has been redone in a studio after the scene was shot. This procedure allows the actor to focus on how he or she sounds, and it gives the sound designer the capability to control the exact balance of the audio in the finished soundtrack. All of your dialogue should be done professionally and in a recording studio. Unless you have been given a gloriously huge budget, however, you probably can't afford Hollywood actors and an expensive studio. The alternative is to look to the number of multimedia sound engineers who are offering full audio services to the industry. These professionals cannot only provide you with composing services, but they can also provide voice actors, custom digital sound effects, and mixing. They can even deliver the audio in computer data format at the resolution you need, customized for the hardware platforms you are targeting.

> **Sound Effects.** Although more and more sound effects libraries are available, many products call for custom effects. Common sense suggests that you use clip-sound libraries where you can, but go to a professional sound engineer to get effects that exactly match the content of your product.

> **Foley.** Foley effects are those ambient supporting sound effects that you don't notice when you watch a film, but that you would notice if they were absent. Foley effects include footsteps, cars, wind, birds, or any other environmental sounds that support the content of the film. In Hollywood, every footstep and

rustle of fabric is added to the soundtrack and synchronized frame by frame to the film as a post-production process.

Foley effects create a greater sense of "virtual reality" than the most exacting computer graphics. Foley effects are greatly enhanced if used with special processing like Qsound, reverb, and other digital signal processing effects. *Reverb* is a technique where sounds are fed through a signal processing phase to approximate the echo and reflections found in a real environment. For example, on the Creative Labs AWE32 sound card you can program the exact characteristics of the shape of a room you might be in at any given time. This programming is accomplished through MIDI events; instantly all foley effects sound as though there were occurring in a room of the specified shape and size.

Foley and digital sound effects are the most highly interactive tools you can apply to your soundtrack. With foley, you let the user hear footsteps, gunshots, growls of a monster around a corner, the wind blowing, birds chirping, and street noise. Provided that these sounds are in real time, contextual to where they are in your "virtual reality," they will draw the user deeply into your created world. This magnification of the virtual reality experience through the use of interactive digital sound effects overpowers goggles, gloves, head-tracking devices, or any of the other virtual reality gadgetry out there. From a technology standpoint, without the soundtrack, you have plunged the user back into the days of silent movies.

Music. There has been a lot of discussion about how to adapt music to the interactive nature of multimedia products. In film, the music score unfolds in a linear fashion. The composer knows exactly the amount of time required to build up to that great suspense scene. But in an interactive title, the point at which the suspense scene occurs is unknown; it depends on when the user is ignorant enough to open the door marked "Pit From Hell." While some games simply score a different song for each level—providing almost no interactively—others have tried experiments with branching in and out of MIDI sequences to create a seamless transition. Some have even attempted algorithmic music—music is actually created in real time by the computer.

Probably the best middle-ground approach is to come up with all possible variations of emotion you want to communicate in the product, and then have your composer score as if it were for film. Your composer should provide branching points into and out of these sequences to communicate the emotional context in pseudo-realtime. These branches will not be instantaneous, but they will model the underlying context of the game state very closely, such that when you enter a danger state, or a suspense state, the music will branch to reflect that emotion.

Another approach is to simply use the music to communicate the base ambiance for the current level, and make heavy use of interactive foley, dialogue, and digital sound effects to communicate the action. Obviously gunshots, explosions, and screams of terror are going to do a very good job of conveying that information to the user.

We, as game developers, are very fortunate as to have this powerful tool made available to us. For years, PC game developers have had to settle with audio devices which could do little more than beep, warble, and fart. The only emotional reaction we could elicit from the user was a deep desire to find the "turn off music" button. The first generation of sound cards weren't that big of an improvement. While new sound cards, such as the Adlib Personal Music System, did allow us to add important interactive audio cues to a game, they had a very limited emotional range. The fundamental weakness inherent in a cheesy FM synthesis device enabled our orchestrations to carry about as much emotional content as grade schooler's FlutoFone.

Fortunately for us, things have improved dramatically with the proliferation of CD-ROM, digital sound cards, and wave-table synthesis MIDI devices. Now we can use sound and music in ways that contain more emotional content than a Steven Spielberg movie. That's right, more! More because watching a Spielberg movie, as compelling as it is, is a passive experience. We watch the dinosaur attack the Land Rover, but we have no control over the situation. In an interactive product, we are afforded the opportunity to try to get away from the dinosaur. As we attempt to escape the vicious beast, the music and sound effects communicate that emotional distress in direct correlation to our own actions. This results in a heightened sense of awareness that only an interactive environment can bring.

One of the best examples of interactive digital sound in a gaming environment is Id Software's Doom. How many of you have jumped back in your chair when you heard the eerie growls and snorts of a monster somewhere around a corner? Note that although you didn't see the monster, simply hearing it precipitated an emotional response. This emotional response is so strong that when the beast lurches out and you cut it down in a hail of bullets, you feel a much greater sense of accomplishment. It is these types of subtle audio cues that enable you to orchestrate the emotional response in the user. Done properly, this effect will bring the game player deeper into the environment you are trying to create.

At this time, I should sound a note of warning. While good use of sound and music can greatly enhance your product, poor quality sound and music can have just the opposite effect. Sound and music that are of poor quality or don't support the emotional direction of your product are a waste of time, money, and disk space. Bad or unprofessional production values, while they may not destroy a product, will leave the user with an overall poor impression, regardless of how well done the rest of elements might be.

To avoid these mistakes, following are some steps you can take to make the sound and music in your product as good and effective as possible:

- Use professional sound effects. Either hire a sound effects specialist or be extraordinarily choosy about utilizing clip sounds. Do not steal your sound effects from movies, records, or television. It is a copyright violation to do so. Your product will not be accepted by a publisher and you may even be sued. Just because you download a great *Star Trek* sound effect from a bulletin board system doesn't mean that you have rights to use it. If you can't get sound effects that fit your exact needs from clip sound libraries, you may want to have custom sounds produced by a professional sound effects specialist.

- Use professional music, either by hiring an interactive media composer or using high quality music clips that fit your project. Interactive media composers and sound effects specialists are listed later in this chapter. Remember, just as you wouldn't hire a bass player to play the saxophone, you should be aware that the talent to compose for MIDI and interactive environments is unique. Just because someone is a great musician doesn't mean that they can provide you with the quality MIDI composition you want for your game. Production values need to be high, and squeezing quality out of limited music devices is a talent your composer will need.

- Ensure that all the music supports at any given time the emotional content, theme, and direction of the game. Think about the interactive nature of your music and how you want it to shift in context to game play. The more attention you give this, the greater the effect.

- Look at films of a similar genre as your game. Every time you watch a movie, try to be consciously aware of how your emotions are being manipulated by the music and sound effects. If you don't have a good ear for music, or you are unclear about how to use sound and music effectively, you should be willing to turn over that part of the project to someone who does.

- Listen to your composer. Look for a composer with an established track record composing for the target hardware and who is familiar with interactive media. Communicate very strongly to your composer exactly what you want. Give your composer specific music, either from CD or film, that matches the emotional content you want to communicate. You will get much better music and have a more fruitful relationship if you communicate very clearly to the composer what you want to accomplish. A lot of wasted money and hard feelings can occur if you don't let your composer know exactly what it is you are looking for.

Effective use of sound and music in interactive media make the difference between the user feeling as if he or she "played a game" versus feeling that he or she "experienced a game." I think you will find adding compelling interactive sound effects and music the most rewarding user interface design you will ever create.

Types of Audio

You can implement audio on the PC architecture in the following ways.

Digital Sound. Ever since the release of the Creative Labs's SoundBlaster, the PC architecture has had a solid platform for implementing digital sound. Other entries such as the Covox Speech Thing, the Walt Disney Sound Source, and the MediaVision ProAudio Spectrum card, all provided this capability. With digital sound your program can play back anything that can be recorded with a microphone, including sound effects, human speech, and music. Digital sound requires enormous amounts of memory and disk storage, but has been used very effectively as a method for delivering sound effects and voice recorded responses.

Digital sound is what you hear when you play a compact disc recording. Sound is simply a waveform. Sound from a speaker is a voltage level being applied to a coil, causing the speaker cone to move in and out in direct correlation to the strength of the signal. The motion of the speaker cone creates a sound wave to be generated in the air. Conversely, a sound wave can be converted to digital form by converting the voltage levels into numeric values. This process is called *analog-to-digital conversion*, or *ADC*. A wave form is approximated by taking many repeated samples. Thus, an analog-to-digital converted waveform has two components: the bit resolution of the sampled data, and the frequency with which the waveform has been sampled. On your standard audio compact disc, the data is stored at 16 bits of resolution with a 44kHz frequency response in stereo. This means that a single stereo sample consumes 32 bits, with 44 thousand of those a second. Thus, one second of sound on a compact disk takes up 176,000 bytes of storage. One minute of sound is over 10 megabytes!

Typically, computer games use much lower resolution data. To pump digital audio data out at CD quality would consume all of the machine's resources. Games generally deal with audio at 8-bit resolution sampled at 11kHz. Even at this low data rate it only takes a little bit of sound to use all the memory in a computer. So, while digital sound is a powerful way to deliver environmental effects, like thunder and explosions, it is generally considered too expensive a resource to perform music in an interactive environment.

Another problem of digital sound is that although it will allow you to play back exact recordings, it is almost impossible to use it to create real-time interactive music. With a MIDI device, this problem is not an issue because the application uses a musical notation interface under software control. In short, you actually send the computer equivalent of sheet music in real time.

FM Synthesis. The earliest popular PC sound card was the Adlib Personal Music System. This card contained a Yamaha YM3812 (OPL2) FM synthesis chip. This is a device that creates waveforms by using oscillators that enable you to apply frequency modulation and attack, sustain, decay, and release operators to a semi-programmable waveform, including a white-noise generator. If this sounds complicated, it is! This device is phenomenally difficult to program; even your best programming efforts sound pretty lame. Fortunately, the importance of FM synthesis is declining in the wake of the new generation of General MIDI wave table synthesis devices. There are a number of systems that allow the YM3812 to emulate a MIDI device, thus alleviating the need to deal with the arcane nature of this device.

MIDI. The Musical Instrument Digital Interface (or MIDI) specification is an internationally supported *de facto* standard that defines a serial interface for connections among music synthesizers, musical instruments, and computers. MIDI, which is maintained by the MIDI Manufacturers Association (Los Angeles, California), is based on hardware (such as I/O channels, and cables) and software (encoded messages defining device, pitch, volume, and so forth). According to the specification, the receiving device in a MIDI system interprets the musical data even though the sending device has no way of knowing what the receiver can do. This can be a problem, however, if the receiving device doesn't have the capability to interpret the data correctly. General MIDI addresses this problem by identifying hardware capabilities in advance.

All general MIDI devices have 128 sound effects as well as musical instrument and percussion sounds. General MIDI systems support simultaneous use of 16 MIDI channels with a minimum of 24 notes each, and they have a specified set of music controllers. This means that with general MIDI, the sender knows what to expect of the receiver. Consequently, a file created with one general-MIDI device is recognizable when played on any other—without losing notes or changing instrumental balance. This, however, is only valid in theory. In practice, a general MIDI file tends to have significantly different characteristics from one device to another. This is due to the fact that while the instruments are standardized for general MIDI, the balance of those instruments, timbre, and quality, has not been. Thus, each general MIDI instrument has different performance characteristics. Composing a piece of general MIDI that sounds good on all MIDI devices requires the composer to remove subtleties in the composition that tend to be synthesizer specific. Because MIDI files typically are quite small, to take advantage of the strengths of each, I tend to have my music tweaked for individual and more popular MIDI synths. A number of vendors are offering General MIDI synthesizers. These include the Roland Sound Canvas, the Roland RAP-10, the Creative Labs AWE32, the Logitech SoundWave, the Ensoniq SoundScape, the Gravis Ultrasound, the Turtle Beach Maui card, the Sierra Semiconductor Aria card, and many more in development. Additionally, general MIDI emulation is available for FM synthesis devices such as the SoundBlaster through third-party developer toolkits such as MIDPAK. The future of interactive music appears to be the general MIDI platform. This allows you to hire a composer to create fully orchestrated scores that will play back at high quality on a large, installed base of sound cards. MIDI data streams are small, have a relatively low interrupt rate, and require low CPU bandwidth. Most current-day MIDI synthesizers use what is called *Wave Table synthesis*. Wave Table synthesis uses large ROMs that store actual digital recordings of various instruments. If your MIDI data stream specifies a piano, for example, then an actual digitized sound recording of a real piano is used. Wave Table devices give the MIDI music an extremely realistic feel. Typically, the larger the set of ROMs and the inclusion of features such as chorus and reverb effects will imbue your music with a very high aesthetic value.

MODs. MOD files became popular on the Commodore Amiga computer. The Amiga was an extremely exciting game machine that provided phenomenal multimedia capabilities for its time. It supported four channels of digital audio sound in hardware. Because many of the game authors working with the Amiga wanted the capability to play music, they devised a scheme whereby they could play fully orchestrated music called MOD files. MOD files basically are a software-based method of performing wavetable synthesis. Recall from the MIDI section that with wavetable synthesis, actual digital sound recordings of instruments are stored on the device in ROM. When the MIDI stream says to play a piano note, it pulls out an actual digital recording of a piano note from the ROM and modulates its frequency. MOD files do the same thing, only in software. This requires RAM to store the digital sound effects, and software to perform frequency modulation in real time. This is a very memory-intensive and CPU-intensive task. Additionally, composing music for MOD files is much more difficult than composing for MIDI.

So, while MOD files provide the richest, most realistic method of producing music on low-end devices such as the SoundBlaster, they don't compare to a true general MIDI synthesizer. Additionally, your digital channel now is tied up with music, and it becomes more difficult to use it for environmental support sounds. Because the marketplace is moving to general MIDI synthesizers, the safest bet is to compose your music score as MIDI and support the game's environmental sounds with digital sound. The DIGPAK and MIDPAK development kit enclosed enables you to do this.

CD RedBook Audio. One benefit of CD-ROM drives, which are becoming more popular, is that they can play standard CD audio tracks. You cannot, however, have your game run from the CD and play music simultaneously. Accessing the data portion of a CD and the audio portion of the CD are mutually exclusive. You also cannot switch CD audio tracks instantaneously to achieve any semblance of interactively or smooth transition. Many developers, however, find benefits in placing portions of their music score on the CD as an audio track, and you may find some uses for it in your game design.

Software Digital Mixing. With the exception of the Gravis Ultrasound and the Creative Labs AWE32, almost every sound card on the market supports a single channel of digital audio only. In the context of an interactive environment, you are going to want to play many sound effects at once, which you can do by implementing a software-based digital mixer. Because sound is additive, this process is fairly simple; just take all the sounds that are playing at any given time, add them together into a buffer, clip for overflow, and pass that buffer to the sound card. Several development packages support software-based digital mixing in their API specification.

Customized Downloadable Patches. On the Gravis Ultrasound and the Creative Labs AWE32, an application can download musical instruments or digital sound effects into memory on the sound card. After these sounds are on the card, you can trigger them simply by issuing a MIDI event. This concept is very powerful because not only do you get multichannel support, customized instruments, a lower burden on both system RAM and CPU, but you also get the capability to manipulate those sound effects in real time using pitch shifting, pan-pot controls, and even chorus and reverb effects.

The DIGPAK & MIDPAK Developers Kit

As we find ourselves approaching the new millennium, developers should not have to worry about the mechanics of programming individual sound devices at the hardware level. Under Windows 3.1, a driver mechanism already exists for playing digital sound and MIDI music for application software. There are a number of systems that relieve you of this burden and allow you to focus on the sound and music you want to deliver under DOS real mode or DOS protected mode. Some commercial systems include the Audio Interface Library from Miles Design and the Sound Operating System from Human Machine Interfaces.

One of the most popular systems developed has been DIGPAK and MIDPAK from The Audio Solution. DIGPAK provides a device-independent API layer to play digital audio on virtually any sound card under DOS. MIDPAK enables you to play fully orchestrated general MIDI music on virtually any sound card, including even non-MIDI devices, such as the SoundBlaster, by using exceptional MIDI emulation. As of January 1, 1994, the DIGPAK and MIDPAK developers kit was released into the public domain for non-commercial use. A nominal license fee is required for commercial distribution of the drivers. This license fee functionally serves as a maintenance fee to keep the drivers up to date and to run the SoundBytes OnLine bulletin board system.

DIGPAK and MIDPAK were created to provide a mechanism for DOS-based game developers to deal with the overwhelming number of sound cards flooding the market. These drivers have been revised, updated, and enhanced for over five years by myself, John Miles of Miles Design, and many engineers at sound board companies. The complete DIGPAK and MIDPAK programmers kit is being provided to you on the enclosed CD and the API is documented later in this chapter. Be sure to examine the on-line documentation files on the CD for more detailed information, and make use of the extensive set of demo programs.

I would like to extend thanks and give credit to the engineers who have helped create these drivers:

- John Miles, Miles Design
- Scott Sindorf, Creative Labs
- Doug Codey, Mediavision
- Mike Leibow, Forte
- Mike Dabbs, Simutronics
- Kerchen Heller, Sierra Semiconductor
- Milo Street, Street Electronics
- Brad Craig, Advanced Gravis
- Richard Mazzerese, Turtle Beach

Following are some of the companies that use DIGPAK and MIDPAK in their products:

Electronic Arts	Epyx
Activision	Fun Univ Netwk
Spectrum Holobyte	Home Brew Software
The Software Toolworks	Humongous Entertainment

SSI, Strategic Simulations Inc.	ICOM Simulations
Milliken Publishing Company	Interplay
Commodore Computer	IntraCorp
Virgin Games	Kram
Compu-Teach	Legacy Software
Knowledge Adventure	Macmillan/McGraw Hill
Gametek	Magnetic Images
Access Software	MECC
Alive Software	Merit Software
Azeroth Publishing	Microleage Sports Assc.
Bethesda Softworks	Ninga
C.R.A.P.O., Inc.	Norsehelm Productions
Concepteva	Objects, Inc.
Cooper, R.J. & Assc.	Optimum Resource
DC True	Presage Software Co., Inc.
Dennis Cunningham	Quantum Quality Productions
Three-Sixty Pacific	Redwood Games
Destiny Software	Saddleback Graphics
Edmark Corporation	Safari Software
Simutronics	White Wolf Productions, Inc.
Stragem	XOR Corporation
T&t Research	Trilobyte
Waterford Institute	Masque Publishing
Wesson International	Iterated Systems

Following are just some of the products that use DIGPAK and/or MIDPAK. (AIL stands for the Audio Interface Library from Miles Design, a superset of MIDPAK.)

Name	Manufacturer	Type
Guardians of Eden	Access Software	MidPak
Return to Zork	Activision	DigPak
Mechwarrior II	Activision	DigPak
Animal Quest	Alive Software	DigPak+MidPak
Magic Crayon	Alive Software	DigPak+MidPak
VGA Jigsaw	Alive Software	DigPak+MidPak
Inspector Gadget	Azeroth Publishing	DigPak+MidPak
Terminator 2029	Bethesda Softworks	DigPak

continues

Name	Manufacturer	Type
Le Ponctueur	C.R.A.P.O., Inc.	DigPak
Bilou	Concepteva	DigPak
Switch Progressions	Cooper, R.J. & Assc.	DigPak+MidPak
Switch Quik	Cooper, R.J. & Assc.	DigPak+MidPak
Stepping Stones Bonus	Compu-Teach, Inc.	DigPak+MidPak
Shadow President	DC True	DigPak
T-Zero	Dennis Cunningham	DigPak+MidPak
Battle Cruiser 3000AD	Three-Sixty Pacific	DigPak
Creepers	Destiny Software	DigPak+MidPak
Millie's Math House	Edmark Corporation	DigPak
KidDesk	Edmark Corporation	DigPak
Fun Univ Ntwk Intfc	Fun Univ Netwk	DigPak+MidPak
Wheel of Fortune	Gametek	DigPak+MidPak
Gateworld Trilogy	Home Brew Software	MidPak
PuttPutt's FunPack	Humongous Entertainment	DigPak+MidPak
PuttPutt Joins Parade	Humongous Entertainment	DigPak+MidPak
Fatty Bear	Humongous Entertainment	DigPak+MidPak
Fatty Bear's FunPack	Humongous Entertainment	DigPak+MidPak
PuttPutt Goes to the Moon	Humongous Entertainment	DigPak+MidPak
Beyond Shadowgate	ICOM Simulations	DigPak+MidPak
Battle Chess 4000	Interplay	DigPak
Grandmaster Chess	IntraCorp	DigPak+MidPak
Space Adventure	Knowledge Adventure	DigPak
Dinosaur Adventure	Knowledge Adventure	DigPak
Realms of Avarton	Kram	DigPak
Mutanoid Math Challenge	Legacy Software	DigPak+MidPak
Mutanoid Word Challenge	Legacy Software	DigPak+MidPak

Sights & Sounds	Macmillan/McGraw Hill	DigPak
Places to Play	Magnetic Images	DigPak
Oregon Trail Deluxe	MECC	DigPak+MidPak
Tom Landry Football	Merit Software	DigPak+MidPak
MicroLeague Baseball IV	Microleague Sports Assc.	DigPak+MidPak
MicroLeague Football II	Microleauge Sports Assc.	DigPak+MidPak
Microleage Cards	Microleage Sports Assc.	DigPak
Math Zone	Milliken Publishing	DigPak
Marvin The Moose	Milliken Publishing	DigPak
Milliken Storyteller	Milliken Publishing	DigPak
Math Sequences	Milliken Publishing	DigPak
Cribbage Master	Ninga	DigPak
Ragarok (Valhalla)	Norsehelm Productions	DigPak
Layout for DOS	Objects, Inc	DigPak+MidPak
Stickybear Townbuilder	Optimum Resource	DigPak
Contraption ZAck	Presage Software Co., Inc.	DigPak+MidPak
Spaceward Ho PC	Presage Software Co., Inc.	DigPak+MidPak
Solitaire's Journey	Quantum Quality Productions	DigPak+MidPak
Pickle Wars	Redwood Games	DigPak+MidPak
Guzzle Puzzles	Redwood Games	DigPak
My Paint	Saddleback Graphics	DigPak
Space Chase 1,2,3	Safari Software	MidPak
GemStone III	Simutronics	DigPak+MidPak
Cyberstrike	Simutronics	DigPak+MidPak
WorldAtlas	The Software Toolworks	DigPak+MidPak
Chessmaster 3000	The Software Toolworks	DigPak
BodyLink	Stragem	DigPak

continues

Name	Manufacturer	Type
Pools of Darkness	Strategic Simulations Inc.	DigPak
Gateway to the Savage	Strategic Simulations Inc.	DigPak
DNA Parrot	T&t Research	DigPak
Monopoly Deluxe	Virgin Games	DigPak
Waterford Mental Math	Waterford Institute	DigPak+MidPak
ATC/Tracon	Wesson International	DigPak
Empire Deluxe	White Wolf Productions, Inc.	DigPak+MidPak
NFL Challenge	XOR Corporation	DigPak
Chess Maniac 5,000,001	Spectrum Holobyte	DigPak+AIL
The 7th Guest	Virgin/Trilobyte	DigPak+AIL
SSN-21 Seawolf	Electronic Arts	DigPak+MidPak
KaleidoSonics	Masque Publishing	DigPak+MidPak
Gambit	Electronic Arts	DigPak+MidPak
Warlords II	SSG	DigPak+MidPak

What is "eXtended MIDI"?

MIDPAK, because it uses the AIL drivers from Miles Design, does not play MIDI files directly. Your MIDI file must be converted into *eXtended MIDI format*. This is a pre-parsed MIDI file format created by Miles Design. The eXtended MIDI file format supports multiple MIDI sequences in a single file that MIDPAK enables you to switch to almost instantly using the PlaySequence command. You add multiple MIDI files to a single eXtended MIDI file (XMI) as follows. Suppose that you have three song files called SONGA.MID, SONGB.MID, and SONGC.MID, and you want to put them all in one XMI file. You would do the following from the DOS command line:

```
MIDIFORM SONG.XMI SONGA.MID SONGB.MID SONGC.MID
```

This places the three MIDI sequences into the single eXtended MIDI file, SONG.XMI. You can access them in MIDPAK as `PlaySequence(0)` `PlaySequence(1)` and `PlaySequence(2)`.

Tricks *of the*
Game-Programming
Gurus

Color Gallery

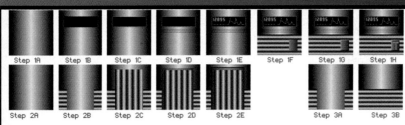

BUILDING A SET OF TILES FOR A CONTROL PANEL

TILE 1   Step A – A 64x64 box with a horizontal gradient is drawn in shades of gray, to look like
                    stainless steel or aluminum.
          Step B – A black box is drawn in for the display area
          Step C – A copper-colored border is added around the display area
          Step D – Black lines, at 25% strength, are added for a little definition on the control panel
          Step E – The display graphics are added to the black box
          Step F – To add interest to the bottom area, vertical gradients are added to give the
                    illusion of some three-dimensional shapes in the panel.
          Step G – Highlights and shadows are added to the recessed area in the bottom of the
                    3D panel area
          Step H – The control panel switch is added.

TILE 2   Step A – start with the same box as tile 1, step A.
          Step B – Clip some of the 3D effect from step 1F, and add to each side of the tile
          Step C – Add some horizontal gradients in the center section
          Step D – Surround the center section with a copper-colored border on sides and top
          Step E – Outline the outer section of the copper border with a black line for definition

TILE 3   Step A – Start with tile 2, step B
          Step B – Completely fill the bottom with the vertical gradients

The three tiles placed together in random sequences

Hedge   Cave   Placed side by side,   Left half of   The joint is
                             you see an obvious   hedge is   edited and
                             seam.   joined to   smoothed for
                                                         right half of   a nicer
                                                         cave.   transition

Hedge   Transition   Cave

The three tiles placed side by side

CREATING TRANSITION TILES

This is a transition from the hedge to the cave graphic. Don't forget
that you might want to also create a cave-to-hedge transition also,
using the left half of the cave tile and the right half of the hedge file
in a similar manner!

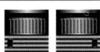

Control panel tiles created   First tile   Second tile modified into
earlier   modified into   doors, one for each
                                   a jamb   sliding direction

DOOR AND JAMB TILES

ANIMATED TILES

The display area in each tile is slightly different. When animated, the green numbers will change, the
LED's will appear to flash, and the blue line will rise and fall. The last three tiles will be used for when
the switch is pulled.

Have you ever looked out the window of a moving car and noticed that nearby objects appear to move by at a faster rate than objects farther away? This common experience has the somewhat-intimidating name of parallax. Parallax scrolling is a graphics technique where two or more layers of graphics move at different rates. This relative motion between layers provides some of the visual cues necessary for realistic simulation of depth and motion. This is a sample background of a sky that will move slower in the background than the foreground.

The foreground layer, which will move faster, gives the impression of moving fast.

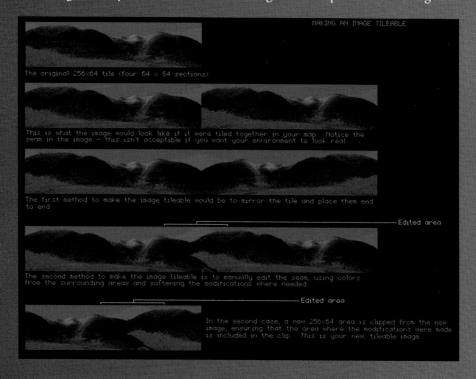

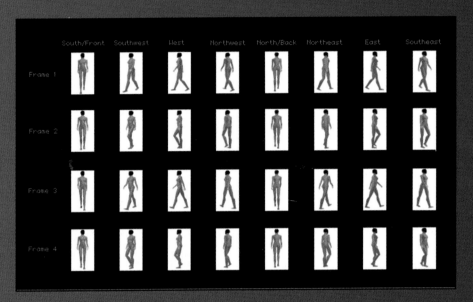

The above frames were created as guides to help you create characters walking in eight different views. Four frames of each view are provided. When these four frames are played as an animation, smooth movement from one step to the next gives the illusion that the character is walking.

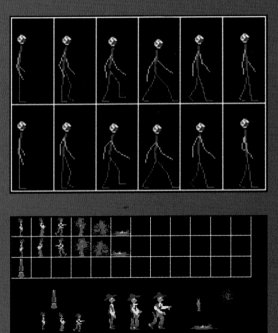

The simplest form of animating character motion is the stickman. Note the placement of the arms and legs to create a smooth motion.

To further illustrate the concept, the stickman example is tranformed into a realistic game character. The cowboy is a simple character that walks forward frame by frame. The other character is a spinning asteroid. Motion of other characters like asteroids is done with the same concept.

Our cowboy would be out of place without a realistic setting like a western town. Note the scale of the cowboy's size in relation to the size of the buildings in the town.

We can place our cowboy character in his western town and now the animation and realism can take place.

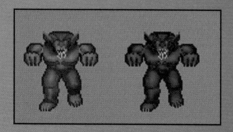

A front view of a venomous, man-eating creature running toward its prey. You get the feeling of motion from the nature of its position and stature.

Rotating a tank around a 360-degree turn is done in the same way as creating creatures that walk and run. Frame-by-frame rotation of the tank continues until it has completed the circle.

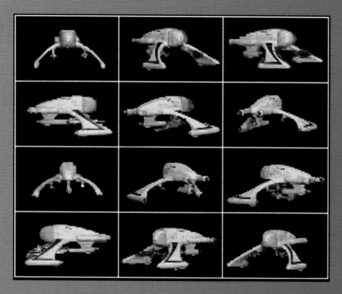

Rotating 3-D objects is demonstrated here by turning the spaceship 360 degrees around the x axis. Keep in mind that rotating 3-D objects entails partially hiding parts of the other side of the object. You must maintain the proper perspective and scale of the 3-D object as it rotates.

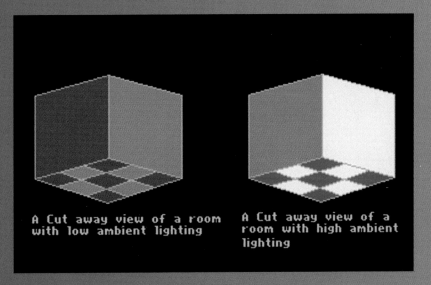

Ambient light is the average light in a room coming from all directions. For instance, if you have an adjustable ceiling lamp, you can increase or decrease the level of ambient light in a room. These are two rooms with different levels of ambient light.

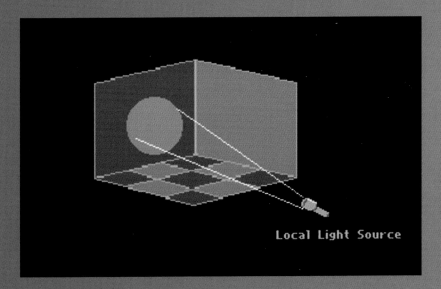

Local lighting is a concentration of light intensity in a specific location to highlight something. For example, if you were in your bedroom and had the lights on, you would have an average, or ambient, light level in your room. Now imagine shining a flashlight on the wall. You'd see an increase of reflected light from the wall area at which the flashlight was pointed.

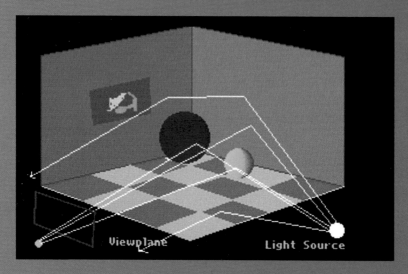

Ray tracing creates an image by simply building it according to the physical model by which we see real objects. This, of course, consists of rays of light hitting objects and being absorbed, refracted, reflected, and so on until they finally find their way to our eyes. The above illustration demonstrates the way light is reflected from various objects.

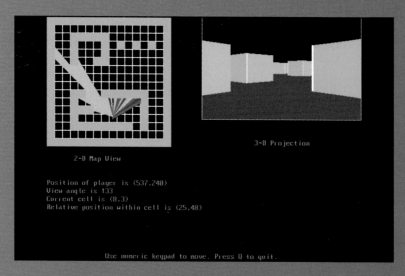

Ray casting is a technique used in video games to create a realistic 3-D view. The display on the left side of the screen is a 2-D overview, or map view, of the world being rendered. The world is a matrix composed of cells or blocks, each being 64x64x64 virtual units. From this 2-D database, a full 3-D model is created through the use of ray casting. This 3-D view is seen through a viewport on the right side of the screen.

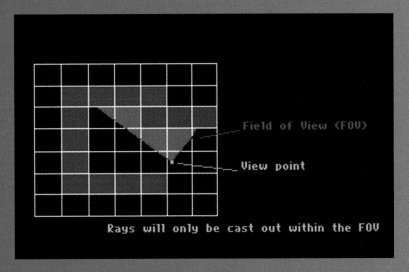

If we could see 45 degrees in each direction relative to the view direction, we would have an Field of View of 90 degrees. Most humans have a large Field of View: 90 degrees or more. However, for our discussions, I have picked 60 degrees.

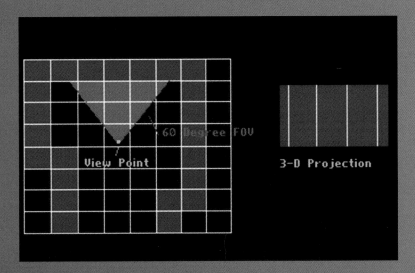

At this point we know that we need to cast out a collection of rays that spans a certain FoV. We then must calculate the intersections of these rays with the walls, and use the information about each intersection to generate a 3-D view. The player is in an 8x8 world. We've set the player's viewpoint looking straight up; that is, 90 degrees. If we wanted to have a 60-degree field of view, we would start casting out rays from the view direction less 30 degrees to the view direction plus 30 degrees, or from 30 to 120 degrees. As you can see, I've shown the casting of a few rays and the final result of the cast.

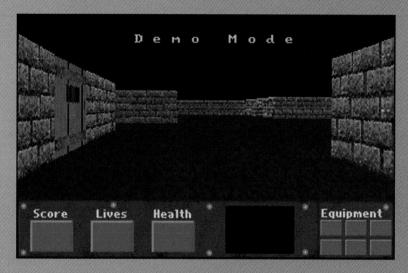

Look at this 3-D world. Notice the wall with textures that obscures our point of view. The distant walls appear smaller than the near walls. This creates a distance effect that adds even more realism to the game.

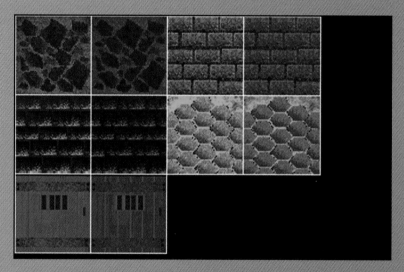

Textures are important in creating a game like WARLOCK. They give dimension and visual appeal to the game. Textures can be walls, floors, and ceilings.

Clipping means drawing only the portions of a video image that are within some predefined boundary. Consider, for example, the case in which you see an object in a game move off the screen. This asteroid is moving out of the Field of View, thus part of it needs to be clipped as it passes from our sight.

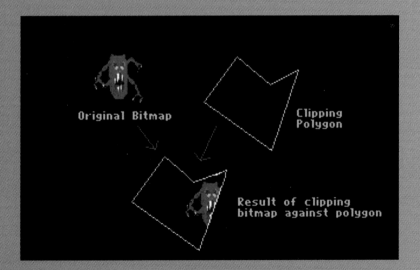

Bit clipping means clipping a bit map to the edges of the screen or some other arbitrary shape. The only clipping that's done with a sprite or bit-mapped image is against some polygon, such as the edges of the screen or some other, smaller rectangle within the boundaries of the screen. This figure shows a bit-mapped image clipped against a polygon.

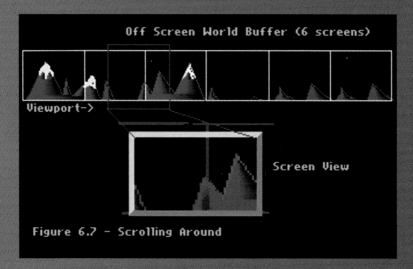

Figure 6.7 - Scrolling Around

Many video games have really huge game worlds. In fact, these worlds are so large that displaying the entire world at once is impossible. Therefore, a technique called scrolling (or panning) is used to display a window into the game universe. This window may be the same size as the video display, or smaller. Here is an example game world that has six screens' worth of image data. The view port has some position within the game world, and everything within the view port is mapped to the screen. The scrolling effect occurs when the view port is continually moved in some direction, and the data within it is continually mapped to the view screen.

Here gradient colors are used to give objects a 3-D look. The upper example of the circle, box, and cylinder is drawn with a singular medium value of red. This does not give the shapes a three-dimensional look. When you add several values of red (32 in this case) in a gradient range, a 3-D look can be achieved using a 2-D paint program.

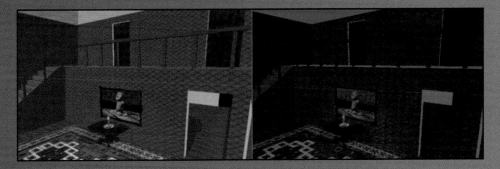

(Left) A scene of the interior of a house shown in daylight. (Right) The same scene shown as it would appear at night. Blue overtones were added to the scene, giving the illusion that moonlight is shining through a window of the house.

This image is identical to the last image except that the palette has been altered into gradients. Doing this allows you to add hand-drawn art with a 3-D look very easily.

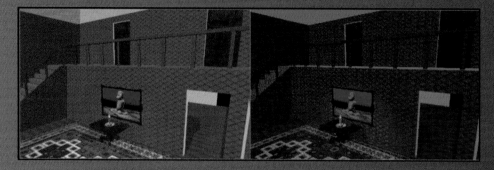

Again, the same image, but the palette has been reduced to 128 colors, leaving 128 additional colors in your palette for other items. Notice that the image quality is still somewhat acceptable in this case.

Now, with the colors reduced down to 64 in this palette, the image begins to suffer some degradation. When you reduce the colors in an image, some manual editing may be necessary to make the image retain good quality.

If you use a full palette and combination of texture and perspective, you can create a great hallway for any game.

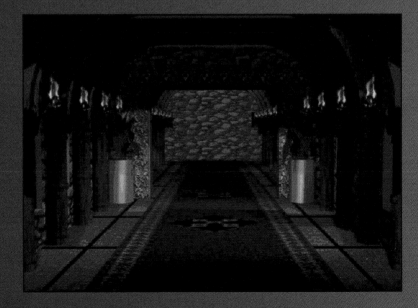

The same hallway reduced to 64 colors. With only 64 colors, this image suffers a lot of deterioration, and may not be acceptable for use in the game without a great deal of editing.

With a little imagination, you can make a good scene into a great scene. When you add railing, create different textures, and change color and lighting, you can add realism to the game environment.

What Format Should the MIDI Data Be In?

On a true MIDI device such as an MPU401 MT-32 or SoundCanvas, exactly what is found in the MIDI stream is passed to the device (excluding SysEx messages).

On an Adlib or SoundBlaster, however, MIDPAK emulates a MIDI device, and that emulation has the following certain restrictions:

> Channels 2-9 are the melodic tracks.
> Channel 10 is percussion.
> The patch set is in the general MIDI format.

Professional Interactive Media Composers

I must admit that, personally, I know very little about MIDI, and rely heavily on professional MIDI composers to provide my music. To get your MIDI music into MIDPAK compatible format so that is sounds great, you can contact the following composers:

> Wallace Music & Sound
> Rob Wallace, Executive Producer
> 6210 West Pershing Avenue
> Glendale, Arizona 85304-1141
> 1-602-979-6201

(KaleidoSonics, Miracle Piano Teaching System, Mario's Missing Deluxe, Snoopy's Game Club, MIG 29, Monster Bash & Hocus Pocus, Odell Down Under, Blackjack, Video Poker, ChessNet, World Series of Poker Adventure, Casino Lite Series, Tom Landry Strategy Football, Wayne's World, Empire Deluxe)

> Computer Music Consulting
> Donald S. Griffin
> 239 Richland Avenue
> San Francisco, CA 94110
> 415-285-3852

(Aladdin, Sega, Rules of Engagement, Mario's Time Machine, PC, Monopoly Deluxe, Aegis, Jungle Book, Carrier Strike, Wild Learning Safari)

> The Fat Man
> 7611 Shoal Creek Blvd.
> Austin, TX 78757
> 1-512-454-5775

(The 7th Guest, SSN-21 Seawolf, Seal Team, Wing Commander, Putt Putt Goes to the Moon)

All these extremely talented composers have done numerous projects composing with both AIL and MIDPAK. They know how to make an Adlib, SoundBlaster, and SoundCanvas sound great. They also are professionals. Please, *do not call* any of these professional composers unless you are prepared to accept a bid for a project. Original music composition for an interactive product easily can run into thousands of dollars.

Questions and Answers

The following sections answers questions that are commonly asked about adding sound to games.

When I Play My MIDI Music with MIDPAK, Some of the Music Seems to Be Missing

Check your channel assignments. MIDI emulation on SoundBlaster *et al*, occurs on channels 2-9 for melodic tracks, and channel 10 for percussion. A lot of sequencing software saves MIDI out starting with channel 1. Channel 1 is ignored under MIDPAK's MIDI emulation. MIDPAK channel assignments were designed to emulate those of a Roland MT-32. Even though we have provided a set of General MIDI patch assignments, the channel assignments are still limited to 2-9 and 10 as indicated here.

The Music on MIDPAK Sounds Different than Inside My Sequencer. Why?

Your sequencer is using a different set of patches than MIDPAK uses. Contact any of the previously mentioned composers to get your MIDI tweaked to sound good with the MIDPAK patches. You should be prepared to pay a reasonable fee for this service, however.

When I Specify a Volume Change with MIDPAK, Nothing Happens. Why?

MIDPAK's volume changes are relative to the base volume for that channel. If you didn't specify a base volume for each channel in your MIDI file, then MIDPAK can't change the volume. You specify the base volume for a MIDI channel with a controller 7.

Can I Use the Same MIDI File for All Sound Cards?

No, but you can come close. Start by scoring for general MIDI. It's best, however, to tweak for SoundCanvas, General MIDI, OPL2/OPL3, and re-patch for MT-32. Base volumes on each device are quite a bit different, and different patches sound better or worse across these devices. The source code to the SETM (MIDPAK configuration program) is provided within (SETUP.ZIP) and depending on which sound driver the user selects, you can copy different versions of your music.

DIGPAK API Documentation

The DIGPAK kit includes one set of sources that works in all memory models, as well as both DOS real mode and DOS protected mode interfaces. DIGPAK drivers are fully compatible with MIDPAK drivers. Even though all DIGPAK drivers execute in real mode, they work in flat mode throughout the DIGPLAY linkable interface layer. Protected mode support requires version 3.4 DIGPAK drivers.

Not all DIGPAK sound drivers are at the 3.4 level yet. Drivers not yet converted are the Gravis Ultrasound and the Turtle Beach Multisound. Additionally, none of the 8253 timer-based drivers will work in protected mode due to the performance penalties incurred and potential conflicts with high interrupt rate timer code.

The set of digitized sound drivers hook into user interrupt vector 66h to provide a clean programmers interface. This document describes the two ways you can access the digitized sound package. The first is the interrupt level interface. The second is a link library interface that provides a set of C or assembly language callable functions to access not only the digitized sound drivers but also to provide useful support routines. These glue code functions are located in the DIGPLAY.ASM source file.

```
**************************************************************************
*************** INT 66h Interface Specification ***********************
**************************************************************************
```

When invoking digplay functions to play sound, you pass the address of a sound structure (SNDSTRUC) that contains the basic information describing the sound effect you want to play. The following code shows you how.

```
*** REAL MODE:

typedef struct
{
    unsigned char far *sound;       // Far address of audio data.
    unsigned short sndlen;      // Length of audio sample.
    short far *IsPlaying;               // Address of play status flag.
    short  frequency;               // Playback frequency.
} SNDSTRUC;

*** PROTECTED MODE:

typedef struct
{
    unsigned char *sound;       // MUST BE OFFSET:SEGMENT IN 1MB ADRESS SPACE!
    unsigned short sndlen;// Length of audio sample. < 64k
    short *IsPlaying;       // Address of play status flag. REAL PTR OFFSET:SEGMENT!!
    short      frequency;       // Playback frequency.
} SNDSTRUC;

********* DIGPAK functions ***********************************
```

> Any function numbers not listed are obsolete.

Function #1: DigPlay

DigPlay plays an 8-bit digitized sound. It is the basic DIGPAK function to play a sound effect. The application sets up a sound structure to describe where in memory the sound effect is located, and the length of that sound effect. By using the DigPlay function, the contents of the audio buffer might get modified. If you know you need to play the sound effect more than once from memory, use the MassageAudio, DigPlay2 combination. You use this same function for playing back audio in any resolution or even to record audio because the DigPak API has evolved over the years and originally only had this one single API function. To allow for downward compatibility, these functions were enhanced by setting various play and record modes.

The C function prototype for this function is in DIGPLAY.H. It is found in DIGPLAY.OBJ, which is the object file produced from DIGPLAY.ASM. You may use this link layer interface, or call the INT 66h function directly.

INPUT:	AX = 688h	Command Number
	DS:SI	*REAL* Point to a sound structure that describes the sound effect to be played.
	ESI	*FLAT* If using 32-bit interface passing, ESI points to flat-model address in the first 1M of address space to the sound structure. Will be converted into a valid segment offset by DIGPAK driver.
OUTPUT:	None	

Function #2: SoundStatus

This function checks current status of sound driver, and reports version number of the driver, 3.1 and later. It is used to query the current status of a sound effect. If a sound effect is playing, a return code of 1 will be found in the AX register. This function is also used to report the version number of the DigPak sound driver, which is located in the BX register starting with v3.1 of the drivers. You use the C function ReportVersionNumber to get this amount returned.

INPUT:	AX = 689h	
OUTPUT:	AX = 0	No sound is playing.
	= 1	Sound effect currently playing.
	BX =	Version starting with version 3.1, the BX register of the SoundStatus call will return the version number. The version number is in decimal, and multiplied times 100, meaning that a return of 310 is equal to version 3.10. Versions before 3.1 did not set the BX register to anything, so you should zero out the BX register before you check the version number. If the BX register still is zero, then the DigPak driver loaded is less than 3.1.

Function #3: MassageAudio

This function preformats audio data into output hardware format. It will massage into any hardware-specific format required by the audio data pointed to by the sound structure. On some devices, the audio does not play back in straight unsigned 8-bit data. After the contents of this memory have been reformatted, you may then issue the DigPlay2 call as many times as you want without reloading the sound data.

INPUT: AX = 68Ah

           DS:SI   *REAL* Point to a sound structure that describes the sound effect to be played.

           ESI   *FLAT* If using 32-bit interface passing, ESI points to flat-model address in the first 1M of address space to the sound structure. Will be converted into a valid segment offset by DIGPAK driver.

Function #4: DigPlay2

This function plays preformatted audio data. In conjunction with the MassageAudio call, it plays back preformatted audio data without changing the contents of the audio buffer.

INPUT: AX = 68Bh

           DS:SI   *REAL* Point to a sound structure that describes the sound effect to be played.

           ESI   *FLAT* If using 32-bit interface passing, ESI points to flat-model address in the first 1M of address space to the sound structure. Will be converted into a valid segment offset by DIGPAK driver.

OUTPUT: None

Function #5: AudioCapabilities

This function reports capabilities of hardware device. It reports all the restrictions and support information for any resident DIGPAK driver in a series of bitcodes that you can easily test.

INPUT: AX = 68Ch

OUTPUT: AX = Bit 0 ->   On, supports background playback.

                                  Off, driver only plays as a foreground process.

             Bit 1 ->   On, source data is reformatted for output device.

                                  Off, device handles raw 8-bit unsigned audio.

             Bit 2 ->   On, device plays back at a fixed frequency, but the audio driver will downsample input data to fit.

                                  Off, device plays back at user specified frequency.

                                  (NOTE: You still can play back an audio sample at the frequency you want. The driver simply downsamples the data to fit the output hardware. It currently does not support upsampling, however.)

             Bit 3 ->   On, this device uses the timer interrupt vector during sound playback.

             Bit 4 ->   Driver supports timer sharing (not available in flat model).

             Bit 5 ->   Supports audio pending.

             Bit 6 ->   Supports stereo panning.

             Bit 7 ->   Supports 8-bit PCM stereo playback.

             Bit 8 ->   Supports audio recording.

             Bit 9 ->   Supports DMA backfilling.

                                  DX = If this device plays back at a fixed frequency, then the DX register will contain that fixed frequency playback rate.

Function #8: StopSound

This function immediately halts the currently playing sound effect.

INPUT: AX = 68Fh

OUTPUT: None   Will cause any currently playing sound
                          effect to be terminated.

Function #12: SetTimerDivsorRate

This function is not valid in protected mode. It allows the application to inform a timer-based DigPak sound driver of the reprogrammed 8253 interrupt rate. This function is only applicable in real mode because none of the timer-based DigPak drivers function in protected mode. If your computer game has reprogrammed the 8253 to a new rate, you must inform DigPak of that reprogrammed rate. When you play a digital sound effect through a timer-based driver, DigPak must reprogram the 8253 to a very high interrupt rate to service play that sound. Normally DigPak defaults to the standard 18.2 time per second interrupt rate and puts the timer back to that value when the sound effect has completed. This function, however, allows you to inform DigPak of the new programmed rate, and while the sound effect is playing, it services the original hardware interrupt at this rate, and puts it back when finished.

INPUT: AX = 693h

         DX =   Countdown timer divisor rate so that
                         timer-based drivers can service application
                         timer interrupts at their previous rate.
                         Service rate will be an approximation that
                         is fairly close. To reset timer divisor to
                         default of 18.2, pass a 0 in the DX register.
                         WARNING!!! If you make use of timer
                         sharing, be sure to reset it back to the
                         normal 18.2 time per second rate when you
                         exit.

OUTPUT: None

Function #14: PostAudioPending

This function allows you to queue up a second sound effect for DigPak. Starting with DigPak v3.0, an application can specify a second sound effect to be played—as soon as the current sound effect is completed. This technique, called *double-buffering*, allows your application to do very sophisticated sound processing. By using double-buffering, you can do software-based digital mixing, and/or spool continuous digital audio from disk or EMS memory. Look at the example program PEND.C to see how a large sound effect is played back in small pieces. By modifying this demo program, you can stream audio from disk, or do software-based digital mixing, by adding multiple sound effects into a continually streaming dual buffer system.

INPUT:	AX = 695h	
	DS:SI	*REAL* Pointer to a sound structure that describes the sound effect to be played.
	ESI	*FLAT* If using 32-bit interface passing, ESI points to flat-model address in the first 1M of address space to the sound structure. Will be converted into a valid segment offset by DIGPAK driver.
OUTPUT:	AX = 0	Sound was started playing.
	AX = 1	Sound was posted as pending to play.
	AX = 2	Already a sound effect pending, this one not posted.

Function #15: AudioPendingStatus

This function allows you to query the current status of the PostAudioPending double-buffered state. In a double-buffered system, you can be in one of three states. In state 0, no sound is playing. In state 1, a sound effect is playing, but no second sound effect is queued (meaning it's time to post another one before the sound channel goes dead.) In the third state, a sound is playing and a second sound effect is queued up to play, which will be an idle state for your application.

INPUT:	AX = 696h	
OUTPUT:	AX = 0	No sound is playing.
	AX = 1	Sound playing, sound pending.
	AX = 2	Sound playing, no sound pending.

Function #16: SetStereoPan

Currently, this function is supported on just a few devices, such as the SoundBlaster Pro. You can check the AudioCapabilities call to learn whether or not the current driver supports stereo panning. On some stereo sound cards like the SoundBlaster Pro, you can pan shift a mono digital sound effect. With this function call, you tell the sound card what percentage to play the sound effect from the left speaker versus the right speaker. You can call this function as rapidly as you want—even while a sound effect is playing—to make a sound effect quickly pan from speaker to speaker. This effect can add a cool, cheesy element to your game.

INPUT:	AX = 697h	
	DX =	Stereo pan value. 0 full volume right. 64 full volume both. 127 full volume left.
OUTPUT:	AX = 0	Command ignored, driver doesn't support stereo panning.
	AX = 1	Pan set.

Function #17: SetPlayMode

This function allows you to set the playback/record mode for the resident DigPak driver. Because DigPak began in 1987 to provide a single API function (play sound effect) only, a separate PlayMode API call was the easiest way to expand the functionality while maintaining downward compatibility with preexisting software. With this function, you can specify the resolution at which a sound effect should be played or recorded.

INPUT:	AX = 698h	
	DX = Play Mode function.	
	DX = 0 ->	8-bit PCM
	= 1 ->	8-bit Stereo PCM (left/right)
	= 2 ->	16-bit PCM
	= 3 ->	16-bit PCM stereo
		Once the play mode has been changed, all DigPak functions work exactly the same as

before but expect data passed as specified by this play mode. 8-bit PCM Stereo has left/right unsigned channel pairs. Supported by Stereo FX card and Sound Blaster Pro. All 16-bit data is signed, left/right paired for stereo.

OUTPUT: AX = 1 ->   Mode set.

              AX = 0 ->   Mode not supported by this driver.

Function #18: Report pending status flag address and Semaphore address

This API call provides the application with an address in memory pointing to DigPak's internal PendingFlag. This technique is called a *semaphore*, and it allows your application to monitor the status of the flag without performing a function call. Whenever your application sees this semaphore change value, you know that you can post the next sound effect in the pending queue.

```
int far *ReportPendingAddress(void);
```

Reports the far address of the pending flag. If this memory location pointed to by this address is 1, then a pending sound effect is still pending. When this becomes zero, your application software can post the next piece of audio to play. It is preferable to use this semaphore to know when to post the next buffer rather than to use the `AudioPendingStatus` call.

```
int far *ReportSemaphoreAddress(void);
```

Report the address of the DigPak semaphore. This returns a far address to a word location inside DigPak. When this is true, DigPak is currently active, and you shouldn't invoke any DigPak function from a hardware interrupt at this time.

INPUT: AX=699h

OUTPUT: AX:DX ->   Form far Address of Pending status flag.

              BX:DX ->   Form far address of digpak semaphore. (When using DIGPLAY.ASM in flat-model, this address returned will be converted into a valid flat-model address.)

Function #19: Set audio recording mode

This function allows you to set DigPak to play or record sound. Although you still invoke the DigPlay call, if audio record mode is set, this function causes DigPak to record audio into the buffer rather than to play it. This function is only supported on SoundBlaster cards.

INPUT:	AX = 69Ah	
	DX = 0	Turn ON audio recording.
	= 1	Turn OFF audio recording.
OUTPUT:	AX = 0	Sound driver doesn't support audio recording.
	AX = 1	Audio recording mode is set.

Function #21: Set DMA backfill mode

This function allows you to turn DMA backfilling on. Ideally, everyone would use the PostAudioPending double-buffered calls and be happy. Most sound cards, however, do not allow you to play two sound effects, one right after the other, without causing an audio glitch. Now, although Creative Labs has sold over two million SoundBlaster cards without this problem, most new sound cards have it. The only way to work around this glitch is a technique called *DMA backfilling*. Ideally, the PostAudioPending calls would automatically use DMA backfilling, but that would take a long time to implement for all drivers. The method by which DigPak supports DMA backfilling is somewhat crude, but it will work until I can reengineer the drivers to more cleanly support DMA backfilling.

If you look at the demo program PEND.C, you see an example of where the DMA backfill functions are used instead of the PostAudioPending calls—if the sound card supports it. Simply use this shell program to implement double-buffered audio in your applications.

Normally when you play a sound effect on a sound card, a DMA transfer is set up, the sound effect is played, and the DMA transfer is stopped when the end of the sound effect is reached. This method is a normal one-shot sound effect mode, which is how all sound effects are played using the normal DigPlay calls. With auto-init DMA, when the end of the sound effect is reached, the DMA controller immediately goes back to the beginning of the buffer; it never finishes playing the sound effect. Consequently, if you had a sound effect that said, "hello," and you started an auto-init DMA transfer, you would hear "hello" repeatedly until you shut off the effect. Because only a single transfer is occurring, there are no audio glitches between one "hello" and the next.

How do you use auto-init DMA to do double-buffered audio? First you must set up a transfer buffer of a fixed size—perhaps 2K. If your buffer size is 2K, you would set up two buffers for a total of 4K. You start that 4K buffer playing, and you query DigPak to learn which half of the buffer is currently playing. Every time the DMA transfer crosses a 2K boundary, you copy the next snippet of audio *behind* the buffer! Thus the term *DMA backfilling*—you are filling the audio behind the current DMA transfer. To make things a little more difficult, you cannot use just any 4K buffer. The DMA transfer address you use cannot cross a page boundary. A page boundary is every 64K in the low 1M of address space of the machine. Thus, DigPak has an API function to allow you to determine whether the buffer you have chosen crosses one of these boundaries. If it does, just use the next 4K buffer beyond it; it will then not cross a boundary.

If all of this sounds complicated... it is. That's why I have provided a simple demonstration program called PEND.C that you can model your code after. With auto-init DMA transfers and double-buffering, you can stream audio continuously from disk, do real-time software-based digital mixing, and stream continuous audio interleaved in movies or FLIC files.

INPUT:	AX = 69Ch	
	DX = backfill	Mode 0 means turn it off, and a 1 means to turn it off.
OUTPUT:	AX = 1 ->	Back fill mode set.
	0 ->	Driver doesn't support DMA backfill.

Function #22: Report current DMAC count

This function reports the current DMA transfer counter for an auto-init DMA transfer. In other words, if you start a 4K transfer, this function will count down from 4097 to 0 as it plays back. By monitoring this counter, you will know when to fill the next half of the buffer. Look at the example program PEND.C to see how this is done.

INPUT:	AX = 69Dh	
OUTPUT:	AX = Current DMAC	Count (counts down, not up)

Function #23: Verify DMA block

This function allows you to verify that the buffer you want to use for an auto-init DMA transfer does not cross a 64K page boundary. See PEND.C for an example.

INPUT:	AX = 69Eh	
	ES:BX ->	*REAL* address of sound.
	EBX ->	*FLAT* 32-bit flat model address in the first 1M of address space. DIGPAK converts it into a valid offset:segment.
	CX ->	Length of sound effect.
OUTPUT:	AX = 1	Block is OK; doesn't cross 64k boundary.
	AX = 0	Block failed; does cross 64k boundary.

Function #24: Set PCM volume

This function is only implemented on a few sound cards. It allows you to set the overall relative digital sound volume for the sound card.

INPUT:	AX = 69Fh	
	BX =	Left channel volume (or both if mono) 0-100.
	CX =	Right channel volume (or both if mono) 0-100.
OUTPUT:	AX = 1	Volume set.
	AX = 0	Device doesn't support volume setting.

Function #25: SetDPMIMode

This function informs the DigPak driver to respond to 32-bit register addressing. Because originally the DigPak drivers were only meant to be used in real mode, I did not think about any other addressing considerations. (Since the first DigPak drivers were developed in 1987, I would have had to be pretty psychic to think otherwise.) Because many of the DigPak functions use the combination of a segment and offset register to form an address, this consideration causes problems in protected mode. In protected mode, segment registers are now selectors, so it is difficult to form a real-mode address out of them. After this API call is issued, DigPak knows it is being invoked by a protected mode application and will respond to the full 32-bit addresses found in ESI rather than the normal DS:SI combination. This processing of address translation is handled automatically by the link layer interface DIGPLAY.ASM found in the flat subdirectory.

INPUT: AX = 6A0h

            DX = Mode on/off 1/0

OUTPUT: None

```
/*********************************************************************
*** DigPlay, linkable interface to the Digitized Sound Package.  ***
*********************************************************************/

/*********************************************************************
** REAL MODE DIGPLAY.H linkable interface layer, all procedures are
**                    prototyped and use segment names such that
**                    they will link in any memory model.
*********************************************************************/

#ifndef LOADABLE_DRIVERS
#define LOADABLE_DRIVERS 1 // Conditional compilation, set to true if
#endif

/* Bit flags to denote audio driver capabilities. */
/* returned by the AudioCapabilities call.        */
#define PLAYBACK     1     // Bit 0,  true if can play audio
                           //         in the background.
#define MASSAGE      2     // Bit 1,  is true if data is massaged.
#define FIXEDFREQ    4     // Bit 2.  is true if driver plays
                           //         at fixed frequency.
#define USESTIMER    8     // Bit 3,  is true, if driver uses timer.
#define SHARESTIMER 16     // Bit 4,  timer can be shared (BETA!!!!!)
#define LOOPEND     32     // Bit 5,  support looped samples, and
                           //         pending sounds (BETA!!!)
#define STEREOPAN   64     // Bit 6,  supports stereo panning.
#define STEREOPLAY 128     // Bit 7,  supports 8 bit PCM stereo playback.
#define AUDIORECORD 256    // Bit 8,  supports audio recording!
#define DMABACKFILL 512    // Bit 9,  support DMA backfilling.
#define PCM16       1024   // Bit 10, supports 16 bit digital audio.
#define PCM16STEREO 2048

typedef struct
{
  char far *sound;        // address of audio data.
  unsigned short sndlen;  // Length of audio sample.
  short far *IsPlaying;    // Address of play status flag.
  short      frequency;   // Playback frequency.
} SNDSTRUC;

extern short far cdecl DigPlay(SNDSTRUC far *sndplay);
                    // 688h -> Play 8 bit digitized sound.
```

```
extern short far cdecl SoundStatus(void);
                        // 689h -> Report sound driver status.
extern void  far cdecl MassageAudio(SNDSTRUC far *sndplay);
                        // 68Ah -> Preformat 8 bit digitized sound.
extern void  far cdecl DigPlay2(SNDSTRUC far *sndplay);
                        // 68Bh -> Play preformatted data.
extern short far cdecl AudioCapabilities(void);
                        // 68Ch -> Report audio driver capabilities.
extern short far cdecl DigPakIdentityString(char far *str);
                        // 68Ch -> reports ID string of
                        // sound driver. returns string length.
extern void  far cdecl StopSound(void);
                        // 68Fh -> Stop current sound from playing.
extern short far cdecl PostAudioPending(SNDSTRUC far *sndplay);

#define NOTPLAYING        0 // No sound is playing.
#define PLAYINGNOTPENDING 1 // Playing a sound, but no sound is pending.
#define PENDINGSOUND      2 // Playing, and a sound is pending.

extern short  far cdecl AudioPendingStatus(void);

#define FULLRIGHT         0
#define FULLLEFT          127
#define FRONTANDCENTER    64

extern short far cdecl SetStereoPan(short panvalue);
                        // 0-127, 0 full right.

#define PCM_8_MONO        0
#define PCM_8_STEREO      1
#define PCM_16_MONO       2
#define PCM_16_STEREO     3

extern short far cdecl SetPlayMode(short playmode);
                        // Return 0 if mode not available, 1 if mode set.

extern short far cdecl SetRecordMode(short mode);
                        // Set audio recording mode.

extern short far * far cdecl PendingAddress(void);

// Reports the far address of the pending
// flag. If this memory location pointed to by this address is 1 that means
// a pending sound effect is still pending.  When this becomes zero, then your
// application software can post the next piece of audio to play. It is
// preferable to use this semaphore to know when to post the next buffer
// rather than to use the AudioPendingStatus call.

extern short far * cdecl ReportSemaphoreAddress(void);

// Reports the far address of the DigPak
// semaphore. If this semaphore is true, then DigPak is currently active
// and you shouldn't post any DigPak calls. This is EXTREMELY important if
// you are trying to invoke DigPak functions via a hardware interrupt, where
// you could potentially have interrupted DigPak itself.

extern void far cdecl SetTimerDivisorRate(short rate);

// Set the 8253 timer divisor rate.
```

```
// If your program, has reprogrammed the 8253 timer to another rate, then
// you must be sure to tell DigPak what that reprogrammed rate it. Be
// sure to set this BACK to zero when your program exits!!!

extern short far cdecl ReportVersionNumber(void);
// Report the DigPak version number.
// Return code is times 100, meaning that version 3.1 would be returned
// as the decimal number 310. This function wasn't supported prior to
// version 3.1 release, so it will be returned as 0, for versions prior
// to 3.1.

extern short far cdecl SetBackFillMode(short mode);

// Turn DMA backfill mode on/off, return code
// of 1 means mode was set. Return code of 0 means driver doesn't support
// DMA backfill.

extern unsigned short far cdecl ReportDMAC(void);
                         // Report current DMA counter.

extern short far cdecl VerifyDMA(char far *data,short length);

// Verify this buffer block
// doesn't cross a 64k boundary. Return code of 1 means the block is OK.
// return code of 0 means the block can't be used, try another.

extern void far cdecl NullSound(char far *sound,short sndlen,short null);

/* Support routines */

extern void  far cdecl WaitSound(void);
                         // Wait until sound playback completed.
extern short far cdecl CheckIn(void);
                         // Is sound driver available? 0 no, 1 yes.


/***********************************************************************
*** Warning, it you enable LOADABLE_DRIVERS you must provide      ***
*** memory allocation functions, and access to DOSCALLS.OBJ.      ***
***********************************************************************/

extern short far cdecl InitDP(short segment);
                         // initialize digpak driver.
extern void  far cdecl DeInitDP(short segment);
                         // uninitialize digpak driver.
```

MIDPAK API Documentation

The MIDI driver, MIDPAK, hooks into user interrupt vector 66h to provide a clean, clear programmers interface. This document describes the two ways you can access the MIDI sound package. The first is the interrupt level interface. The second is a link library interface that provides a set of C or assembly language callable functions to access the MIDI sound drivers and it also provides useful support routines. These glue code functions are located in the source file MIDPAK.ASM.

MIDPAK uses the same interrupt vector as DIGPAK. DIGPAK describes the complete set of Digitized sound drivers provided by The Audio Solution. MIDPAK is fully compatible with DIGPAK. If your application needs to play back both MIDI music and digitized sound, you first load the digitized sound driver you need, and then load the MIDPAK MIDI driver on top of it. The MIDPAK driver detects the presence of the DIGPAK sound driver and re-routes all calls through it. If the digitized sound hardware does not support independent playback of digitized sound (DMA support: SoundBlaster, and ProAudio Spectrum), then MIDI music playback will shut down while the digitized sound effect is playing. MIDI music playback will continue once the digitized sound effect has completed. This is completely transparent to the running application.

MIDPAK uses the set of MIDI sound drivers developed by Miles Design Incorporated. These drivers vary in size and can be noted by the extension of .ADV. MIDPAK will always load the sound driver MUSIC.ADV when started. The application should copy the appropriate sound driver over as MUSIC.ADV before loading MIDPAK.

MIDPAK does not play MIDI files directly. You must convert the MIDI file (with the extension of .MID) into an eXtended MIDI file (.XMI) by using the program MIDIFORM or the MENU utility. The Miles eXtended MIDI drivers support MIDI channels 2-9 melodic and channel 10 for percussion.

Any function numbers not listed are obsolete or unused.

Function #1: UnloadMidPak

This function removes the MIDPAK TSR from memory, not to be used by application software! Used internally by MIDPAK, simply included here for documentation purposes.

INPUT: AX = 700h   Command number

OUTPUT: None

Function #2: DigPakAvailable

This function determines whether a digpak sound driver is available, underneath the MIDPAK driver.

INPUT:	AX = 701h	Command number.
OUTPUT:	AX = 0	Digpak is not available.
	AX = 1	Digpak is available.

Function #3: PlaySequence

This function plays a sequence from the currently registered XMIDI file.

INPUT:	AX = 702h	Command number.
	BX = SEQ	Sequence number, numbered starting from zero.
OUTPUT:	AX = 1	Sequence is being played.
	AX = 0	Sequence not available.

Function #4: SegueSequence

This function registers a new sequence to be segued in at the next trigger event, with the activation code specified. If the activation code passed is a -1, then this sequence will be changed to at the next trigger. A trigger is placed into the MIDI stream by using a Controller 119, with a specified event code. Controller 119s may be placed at any point into the MIDI data stream to communicate positional information to your application.

INPUT:	AX = 703h	Command number.
	BX = SEQ	Sequence number to segue to.
	CX = ACT	Activation event code, -1 means next trigger.

Function #5: RegisterXmidi

This function registers an XMIDI file by address for playback.

| INPUT: | AX = 704h | Command number. |
| | BX = Offset | Offset portion of far address of XMIDI data. |

	CX = Segment	Segment portion of far address of XMIDI data.
	SI = Low len	Low word of length of XMIDI data.
	DI = High len	High word of length of XMIDI data.
OUTPUT:	AX = 0	Unable to register XMIDI data.
	AX = 1	XMIDI file registered resident. This means that the XMIDI file was able to be held entirely in MIDPAK's internal buffer area. The application can throw away the memory associated with this XMIDI file because MIDPAK has made a copy of it for itself. This is very useful in virtual memory environments where the application program does not always have fixed addresses in memory. It also allows MIDPAK to play back MIDI files in the background from DOS.
	AX = 2	XMIDI file was registered to the application. The caller is responsible for making sure that this fixed memory address always contains the data as passed.

Function #6: MidiStop

This function stops playing current MIDI sequence.

INPUT	AX = 705h	Command number
OUTPUT:	None	

Function #8: ReportTriggerCount

This function returns trigger event counter, and last event code.

INPUT:	AX = 707h	Command number.
OUTPUT:	AX = COUNT	Count of # of callbacks since last reset.
	DX = ID	Event ID of last callback. See callback trigger in XMIDI spec.

Function #9: ResetTriggerCount

This function resets the trigger event counter to zero.

INPUT: AX = 708h   Command number.

OUTPUT: None

Function #12: ResumePlaying

This function resumes playing stopped sequence.

INPUT: AX = 70Bh   Command number.

Function #13: SequenceStatus

This function reports sequence status.

INPUT: AX = 70Ch   Command number.

OUTPUT: AX = Status

               SEQ_STOPPED 0   // Equates for SequenceStatus().

               SEQ_PLAYING 1   // Sequence is currently playing.

               SEQ_DONE 2   // A sequence is DONE playing.

Function #14: RegisterXmidiFile

This function registers by filename.

INPUT: AX = 70Dh   Command number.

           BX = Offset   Offset portion of filename address.

           CX = Segment   Segment portion of filename address.

Function #15: RelativeVolume

This function reports relative volume for music, as a percentage.

INPUT:	AX = 70Eh	Command number.
OUTPUT:	AX = VOL	Report current relative volume, as a percentage 0-100.

Function #16: SetRelativeVolume

This function sets relative volume for music, as a percentage.

INPUT:	AX = 70Fh	Command number.

Function #17: BootstrapMidPak

This function is the application install of MIDPAK driver.

INPUT:	AX = 710h	Command number.
	BX:CX ->	segment:offset of ADV driver.
	DX:SI ->	segment:offset of AD file.

Function #18: PollMidPak

INPUT:	AX = 711h

This function is used in conjunction with PMIDPAK.COM. PMIDPAK is the polled version of MIDPAK. Normal MIDPAK steals either the timer interrupt or the real-time clock interrupt and services it as a rate of 120h. However, some more advanced applications may want to service the hardware interrupts themselves, may want to play back the music at a different quantization rate, or may want to sync the service rate to graphics routines to avoid any potential of their graphics routines being interrupted by the music.

After MIDPAK is installed, it restores the timer interrupt vector and is acquiescent until the application program invokes int 66h with the command 0711h. You should invoke this interrupt at 120h or to the quantization rate you used when running MIDIFORM. When running MIDIFORM, you can specify a quantization rate for your music other than the default of 120h. As you lower the quantization rate, you will hear some degradation in the quality of the music since ASDR will not be responding as quickly. Reducing it to 60h, for example, won't make much of a noticeable difference; however, reducing it to 15h to 30h will cause noticeable degradation. Obviously, running many channels of MIDI music out of an FM synthesis device such as an Adlib is going to take some CPU. By requantizing your music and servicing MIDPAK at the rate you are comfortable with, you can balance machine resources nicely.

Function #19: MidpakClock

This function reports the current heartbeat count for MIDPAK.

INPUT:	AX = 712h	
OUTPUT:	AX:DX	Current heartbeat count since MidPak startup. 120h heart beat, application can use this for timing.
	BX:CX ->	Forms the far address pointing to this heartbeat counter.
	BX->	Is the offset portion.
	CX->	Is the segment portion.

This function reports the heartbeat counter for MidPak. Starting at zero since MidPak startup, this value is the long word result of the heartbeat counter for MidPak. MIDPAK uses a 120h timer your application software can use for timing by simply polling this function.

Function #20: TriggerCountAddress

This function reports the address in memory of the trigger count.

INPUT:	AX = 713h	
OUTPUT:	AX:DX	Form for address to point to the integer TriggerCount. This is the counter that gets incremented each time a Controller 119 is encountered in the MIDI file.

Function #21: EventIDAddress

This function reports the address in memory of the EventID.

INPUT: AX = 714h

OUTPUT: AX:DX   Forms an address to point to the integer EventID, which is the EventID of the last controller 119 trigger event encountered.

Function #23: ReportSequenceNumber

This function reports current sequence being played.

INPUT: AX = 716h

OUTPUT: Reports currently playing sequence number.

```
extern short cdecl CheckMidiIn(void);
                // Returns 1 if MIDPAK is installed, 0 if not.
extern short cdecl DigPakAvailable(void);
                // Returns 1 if DIGPAK is installed, 0 if not.


/*************************************************************************
*** These flags are returned by the XMIDI registration call.       ***
*************************************************************************/

#define FAILURE_TO_REGISTER     0  // Xmidi file registration failed.
#define REGISTERED_RESIDENT     1  // Resident driver holds midi file now
                                   // The application can throw away the
                                   // memory if it wants to.
#define REGISTERED_APPLICATION 2   // Driver didn't have a big enough buffer
                                   // area reserved to hold the audio data
                                   // so the application is responsible for
                                   // keeping the memory for this sequence
                                   // while it is registered.

extern short cdecl PlaySequence(short seqnum);
                // Play a particular sequence number from
                // the currently registered xmidi file.

#define NEXT_CALLBACK -1  // Activation on next callback.

extern short cdecl SegueSequence(short seqnum,short activate);
                // Switch sequence to this sequence when next
                // callback trigger event is hit with the
                // event number equal to activate. If activate
                // is set to -1 then the next event causes the
                // segue to occur.

extern short cdecl RegisterXmidi(char *xmidi,long int size);
                // Registers an extended midi file for playback.
                // This call will register all sequences.
```

```
extern short cdecl MidiStop(void);
                     // Stop playing current sequence.

extern long int cdecl ReportCallbackTrigger(void);
                          // Low word is trigger count.
                          // High word is last event ID.

extern void cdecl ResetCallbackCounter(void);
                     // Reset callback counter to zero.

extern void cdecl ResumePlaying(void);
                     // Resume playing last sequence.

#define SEQ_STOPPED 0   // equates for SequenceStatus()
#define SEQ_PLAYING 1
#define SEQ_DONE    2

extern short cdecl SequenceStatus(void);
                     // Report current sequence play status.

extern short cdecl RelativeVolume(short vol);
                     // Report current volume.

extern void  cdecl SetRelativeVolume(short vol,short time);
                     // Set volume, over time period.

#define NOBUFFER         1 // No resident buffer available.
#define FILENOTFOUND     2 // The file was not found.
#define FILETOBIG        3 // The file exceeds the reserved buffer size.
#define REGISTRATIONERROR 4 // Error registering the XMI file.

extern short cdecl RegisterXmidiFile(char *fname);
                     // Register by filename.
extern void  cdecl PollMidPak(void);
                     // Poll MidPak for music processing.
extern long int cdecl MidPakClock(void);
                          // Return MIDPAK heartbeat count (120hz)
extern long int * cdecl MidPakClockAddress(void);
                          // Return address of midpak clock.
extern short * cdecl TriggerCountAddress(void);
                          // Report address of trigger count.
extern short * cdecl EventIDAddress(void);
                          // Report address of event id.
extern short cdecl ReportSequenceNumber(void);
extern short cdecl InitMP(char *midpak,char *adv,char *ad);
                     // Init MIDI driver.
extern void cdecl DeInitMP(char *midpak);
                     // Unload a previously loaded sound driver.
```

Lunch with The Fat Man—Music in Software

I asked my friend George Alistair Sanger, who goes by the pseudonym "The Fat Man," to talk about how, when, and why music should be used in software. The Fat Man is a popular interactive media composer who provides wide ranging services to the multimedia industry.

The Fat Man works on audio production and composition from his home in Austin, Texas. Clients from Los Angeles to New York to Hong Kong include Warner/Elektra/Atlantic, Cannon Films, and Southwest Airlines. Credits include musical contributions to dozens of software products, including producing music for Wing Commander from Origin Systems, The 7th Guest from Virgin/Trilobyte, and SSN-21 Seawolf from Electronic Arts.

Why?

Why should music and sound be used in a computer program? For the same reasons we've all surrendered to using icons—because it's the next logical step in computer software development. Icons and graphics save the viewers from having to figure out what they are supposed to be seeing; music helps them know what they are supposed to be feeling.

I don't intend to demean the intelligence of the average user, but there's a little bit of analytical work (Which side of the brain does that again? Brains ought to be color-coded to match the big companies; one side blue and the other rainbow) that goes into reading—reading is slow, somewhat detached from our more natural experiences, and the user doesn't really like to do it. That's what makes icons work. It already has been established that icons speed up productivity by giving us images from the "real world" (whatever that is) and enables us to relate our feelings about a file cabinet or a wizard, for example, to the items represented on-screen. Music and sound take this to the next logical step.

The user associates with graphics the feelings that are appropriate to the real world object that is represented. Music and sound are even more direct. They expose him or her directly to those feelings—the user now can experience an angry wizard or an efficient filing cabinet. And feelings can be very useful tools. In a feature article about multimedia in *PC Magazine*, a veteran of interactive video suggests that emotions associated with data may be the answer to information overload—in fact, they may prove more important than the data itself.

Sound and music can do the following:

- Increase throughput
- Enhance the pleasantness of a computer experience
- Increase entertainment value of a program

When?

Music and sound should be used in more than just games.

Although computers and film are very different media, the relative maturity of the latter sometimes makes it useful for developers to look at film as a model for the future of some aspects of computer software. Especially with the importance of multimedia, we can look for examples not only in feature films, but all types of video applications, such as educational and industrial films, training, advertising and news programs—anything that's been on a film or videotape. When do they use music and sound?

Other than dialogue, a general rule of thumb is that films use music and sound when and only when there is a need to enhance the emotions felt by the viewer. In the case of computer programming, it follows that it is appropriate to use music and sound for the following:

■ To enhance emotion where it already exists. Some folks like happy faces or other graphics when their computers start up—a happy tune can triple the happy effect. A business logo can be enhanced by an audio swirl. Action games can be scored like action pictures, but remember that strategy games can be scored like mysteries or documentaries.

■ To inject emotion where it is desired but doesn't already exist. If the attention of the user really is required, consider how much more effective a klaxon is than the word "Warning!" in a dialog box. Clicking keystrokes gives a sense of security to some typists. Any place an interesting graphic is used to change boredom to interest, an interesting piece of sound can enhance that change.

■ To manipulate or change an emotion that might already exist. A child safety multimedia presentation might show a picture of a cute baby near a swimming pool. Something like the *Jaws* theme might keep the user from focusing on the cuteness of the baby. A short, simple title tune might make a database program seem less complex and frightening. In the case of the "bad news" dialog box, consider how much more palatable a warning a pleasant "ping" is than an explosive sound (or a picture of a bomb, for that matter.) With audio, the developer, like a film director, can control the degree of emotion the user feels.

Moreover, it's a mistake to use music or sound in the following situations:

■ When emotional response is inappropriate. When music is just thrown in as filler, or is so poorly composed that it doesn't adequately support the purpose of the program, it annoys the user and cheapens the software.

■ When it gives music itself a bad name—Muzak.

Which leads us to the next question....

How?

Like graphics, music and sound must be done right. Simply filling up space with spectacular graphics done by an "artist friend" (everybody's got one) is simply not the way to create an effective program, and the same applies to music. There is as much an art to using music and sound in software as there is in film, and it's too big a subject to address here.

By way of a cheap conclusion, here's a good rule of thumb. To judge the quality of your sound, regardless of the technical limitations of your platform, ask yourself the following three questions:

1. Does every bit of the audio support the emotional direction of the program?

2. Does the audio maximize musical interest?

3. Can you dance to it?

Say, this was great. Let's have lunch more often.

User Interface Design with Voice-Recognition Systems

I would like to take a moment to discuss a new form of user interface design relating to sound. It is becoming more prevalent that we have the ability to utilize voice-recognition systems as part of our user interface design. I would like to give some common-sense guidelines on how to incorporate voice recognition into your application software.

A voice-activated system should be the most intuitive method of interacting with a computer. So why was it usually done wrong in the past? Most current systems are passive; they sit in the background making hackneyed guesses at what they think you might have said. Then they go off and erase a file or do something else equally stupid.

Most people would say the problem is with the voice-recognition software. It's not. The problem is with the user interface design. A voice-recognition user interface should be active. It should query the user for confirmation when in doubt, and it should acknowledge the user when given a request. It should also be personified through a combination of conversational techniques and audio cues.

Try carrying on a conversation with a friend who never responds. Feel like you're being ignored? At the minimum, you need that occasional "yeah" and "uh-huh" to know the person is listening. Take the following case. A parent asks a child to do something, and the child doesn't respond "OK, Dad." Typically Dad will get annoyed and shout, "Hey, did you hear me?!" (At least that's what happens at my house.) In conversational English, we require a response to know we are being understood. A voice-activated computer interface needs those same audio cues: "Sure." "OK, Boss." "Pardon?"

A few audio cues like this make the interface more natural and allow us to navigate complex systems with only a few simple verbal commands. There is no real problem with voice-recognition systems today. They can generally recognize discrete vocabularies with a high level of accuracy. We have commercial software that enables us to do complex operations simply by using a few pull-down menus and icons. A well-designed voice-activated menu system can be equally powerful, and eminently more appealing to interact with.

One final note about interacting with a computer verbally. Talking machines got a bad name in the early 80s because of the Japanese jabbering car: "The door is ajar, the door is ajar." Everybody hated them. People bragged about how they had "rewired" their new cars to cut down on the nagging. For the record, the problem isn't that talking machines aren't cool; the problem is that until this point, they have had the wrong user interface.

Many of us may have heard as children that we were not to speak unless spoken to. The same corollary applies to talking machines. If a machine babbles at you, interrupting your current train of thought and what you are doing at the time, it is very annoying. If, however, you ask the machine for some information and it can verbally respond, it is a very, very cool machine. Eminently, exceedingly, cool. If the machine has something really important to tell you, it shouldn't burst into your personal space unannounced, interrupting your own train of thought, or private conversation. No, it should simply issue a gentle, "Ahem" or "Excuse me"; or it should simply clear its computer throat. When you have a moment to respond and say, "OK, Simon," the computer can then continue to deliver pressing information. If voice-activated systems don't feel completely natural, they are practically useless. We should continue to use mice and keyboards where appropriate, but voice-activated systems should be conversational, interactive, and, above all, natural.

Personifying the machine by using conversational English, variety, accents, and humor are all equally appealing. Some fear adding this conversational tone to the software because they feel it might somehow undermine the seriousness of the product. But who wants to hear another perfectly intoned pseudo-British "voice mail" computer voice? How boring. Instead, your computer might respond with, "Yeah Boss, anything you say," "Sure dude, no problem," or "Initiating file save sequence; that cool with you?" Obviously, these examples are irreverent, and not meant to be taken literally so much as to demonstrate the amount of fun we can inject into working with the computer. And isn't making the computer more natural, easy to use, and less threatening the ultimate goal of good user interface design?

In conclusion I would like to say that the examples given here were only presented to spark your creativity. When designing voice-activated user interface, just ask yourself one question: "How would it work if I were talking to a real person?" Then, given your technology limitations, do your best to approximate. Keep in mind that while your recognition system may have a limited vocabulary, the machine is capable of "saying" anything. Keep your command sets simple, and do not allow them to be susceptible to frequent misinterpretation. Within context, attempt to adapt to the users' preferences, including inferences to common responses. Allow the voice responses to have variety and character, and, most of all, to be natural.

TEST.C

The following is a simple demonstration C program that shows how to load a DIGPAK and MIDPAK driver, and to play both music to and sound effects. It uses the link layer interfaces DIGPLAY.ASM and MIDPAK.ASM to hook into the API function calls.

```
/**************************************************************************/
/* TEST.C DIGPAK & MIDPAK test application. Dynamically loads DIGPAK and  */
/* MIDPAK drivers, SOUNDRV.COM and MIDPAK.COM/MIDPAK.ADV/MIDPAK.AD         */
/* then plays the MIDI file TEST.XMI and allows you to play sound          */
/* effects TEST1.SND and TEST2.SND                                         */
/**************************************************************************/
/*          Written by John W. Ratcliff  1994                             */
/*          Compuserve: 70253,3237                                        */
/*          Genie: J.RATCLIFF3                                            */
/*          INTERNET:70253.3230@compuserve.com                            */
/*          BBS: 1-314-939-0200 14.4kb                                    */
/*          Address:                                                      */
/*          747 Napa Lane                                                 */
/*          St. Charles, MO 63304                                         */
/**************************************************************************/

#include <stdio.h>
#include <stdlib.h>
#include <malloc.h>

#include "keys.h"        // Include #define's for keyboard commands
#include "loader.h"      // Include header for midpak/digpak dynamic loader
```

```c
#include "midpak.h"       // Include header for link layer to MIDPAK functions.
#include "digplay.h"      // Include header for link layer to DIGPAK functions.
#include "doscalls.h"     // Include header to assembly DOS support functions.

#define NOBJ 4            // #define for number of sound effects to load

static char *Names[NOBJ] = // Filenames for demo sound effects.
{
        "TEST1.SND",
        "TEST2.SND",
        "PEND.SND",
        "TEST.SND"
};

static SNDSTRUC snd;            // DigPak sound structure
static char *soundbuffer=0;     // Address of sound buffer
static long int ssize[NOBJ];    // Contains length of loaded sound effects.
char *Sounds[NOBJ];             // addresses of the test sound effects.

void UnloadSounds(void);        // Unload test sound effects from memory
int  LoadSounds(void);          // Load test sound effects into memory.
void PlaySound(int sound);      // Play one of the loaded sound effects.
void TestDigPak(void);          // Test DigPak play routines.

// Application provided memory allocation and de-allocation routines.  Used by the
// loader and by doscalls.
// You may replace these function to any other far memory allocation system you
// might use.

unsigned char far * far memalloc(long int siz)
{
  unsigned char far *mem;

  mem = farmalloc(siz); // C's far memory allocation functions.
  return(mem);
}

void far memfree(char far *memory)
{
  farfree(memory);         // Call C's far memory free routine.
}


void main(void)
{
  long int siz;
  char *fname;

// Invoke loader to boostrap the default DIGPAK sound driver.
  if ( !LoadDigPak("SOUNDRV.COM") )
  {
    printf("Failed to load DIGPAK sound driver 'SOUNDRV.COM'.\n");
    exit(1);
  }

  if ( !InitDigPak() ) // Initialize DigPak sound driver.
  {
    // Unload driver from memory if it failed to initialize, and exit.
    UnLoadDigPak();
```

```
    printf("Failed to initialize DIGPAK sound driver 'SOUNDRV.COM'.\n");
    exit(1);
  }

  if ( LoadMidPak("MIDPAK.COM", "MIDPAK.ADV", "MIDPAK.AD") )
  // load MIDPAK components
  {
    printf("Loaded MIDPAK.COM MIDPAK.ADV and MIDPAK.AD into Low Mem\n");
    if ( InitMidPak() )
    {
      printf("MIDPAK driver initialized.\n");
      fname = fload("TEST.XMI",&siz); // Load demonstration song.
      if ( fname )
        {
          printf("Loaded TEST.XMI %d bytes long.\n",siz);
          RegisterXmidi(fname,siz); // Register XMIDI sequence with MIDPAK
          printf("Sequence registered, now playing.\n");
          PlaySequence(0); // Tell MIDPAK to play the first sequence.
          SegueSequence(1,-1); // Tell MIDPAK to segue to the second sequence
          // in the test MIDI file when the first controller 119 event is hit.
        }
    }
    else
      printf("Failed to initialize MIDPAK driver.\n");
  }

  TestDigPak(); // Test/demonstrate the DigPak functions.

  UnLoadMidPak(); // Unload MIDPAK from memory, unhook the hardware.
  UnLoadDigPak(); // Unload DIGPAK from memory, unhook the hardware.
}

void TestDigPak(void)
{
  int i,key,sound;

  printf("Loading digital sound effects.\n");
  if ( LoadSounds() )  // Load the sound effects into memory.
  {
        // Display menu of sound effects.
    printf("Select an sound effect to play. [ESC] when finished playing around.\n");
    for (i=0; i<NOBJ; i++)
    {
      printf("%c %s\n",i+'A',Names[i]);
    }
    do
    {
      if ( keystat() ) // If a key was pressed.
        {
          key = getkey(); // Get the key pressed.
          if ( key >= 'a' && key <= 'z') key-=32; // convert lower-case to upper
case.
          if ( key >= 'A' && key <= 'Z')
          {
            sound = key-'A';
            if ( sound < NOBJ ) PlaySound(sound);
          }
        }
```

```
    } while ( key != 27 );
    UnloadSounds();
  }
}

// Load all of the sound files into memory.
int LoadSounds(void)
{
  int fph;
  long int siz,end;
  int i,handle,j;
  int select;

  for (i=0; i<NOBJ; i++)
  {
    Sounds[i] = fload(Names[i], &siz);
    if ( !Sounds[i] )
    {
      printf("File '%s' not found.\n",Names[i]);
      return(0);
    }
    ssize[i] = siz;
    snd.frequency = 11000;
    snd.sound = Sounds[i];
    snd.sndlen = ssize[i]; // Specify length of sound effect in bytes.
    MassageAudio(&snd);
    printf("Sound Loaded '%s'.\n",Names[i]);
   }
  return(1);
}

void UnloadSounds(void)
{
  int i;

  for (i=0; i<NOBJ; i++) memfree(Sounds[i]);
}


void PlaySound(int sound)
{
  StopSound(); // Wait for previous sound to complete.
  snd.frequency = 11000;
  snd.sound = Sounds[sound];
  snd.sndlen = ssize[sound]; // Specify length of sound effect in bytes.
  DigPlay2(&snd); // play preformated sound effect.
}
```

Video Game Algorithms, Data Structures, and Methodologies

This chapter contains the "glue" that you'll use to put together all the pieces that make up a video game on the PC. A video game is a *synergistic program*, meaning it's more than the sum of its parts. I say this because, once a game is written and played, it's possible to temporarily suspend the player in another dimension. This new dimension exists solely within the computer and the player's mind. To accomplish this task, we must consider many factors about the look and feel of the game from the player's point of view, and from our own points of view as software architects.

In this chapter we cover many topics: some related, some not. Nevertheless, all this information is necessary if a successful video game is to emerge from the primal ooze of your brain.

by André LaMothe

This chapter is mostly insights and reflections, so pay close attention! Here's the potpourri of topics within:

- Data structures used to represent game universes
- What happens when objects collide
- Representing game objects
- Using data structures in video games
- Cloning game objects
- States of being
- User interfaces
- Demo modes
- Saving the game
- Modeling the real world

Data Structures Used to Represent Game Universes

Representing an entire universe seems as if it would be quite an undertaking—and if we had to take into consideration every possible detail, this chapter would be about 10,000,000,000,000,000,000 pages long. However, in PC video games we are dealing with approximations of reality. We need not have complete models of our game worlds. We need just enough to get by.

Because we're concerned with games similar to Wolfenstein and DOOM, let's bias our discussions toward how game worlds such as these are represented. Using this concept as a foundation, you should be able to think up appropriate constructions for any universe. However, before we do that, let's briefly discuss the "standard" way a 3-D polygon-based world is represented.

Let's use a hypothetical 3-D racing game as an example. In our game we want to have buildings, trees, a single track, some stands, and a control tower. In a standard, polygon-based world this information would be represented at the object level, meaning there would be models of the 3-D objects. These models would be represented by lists of polygons, and further defined by the vertices that make up each polygon. Then, each object would have a position, orientation, and scale. If we wanted 10 different buildings, therefore, we would have 10 different object definitions: one for each building.

We might then take each of these objects and create a linked list. When the list was traversed, we would build (that is, *render*) each object in the list. We would have similar lists of data structures for trees, stands, and so on.

Finally, the track itself would be a list of polygons that built up a continuous road, without cracks or discontinuities. Therefore, in essence, the game universe would be made of lists of objects that made up the universe. Figure 11.1 shows an *object-space representation* (that is, a representation of the geometrical properties) of a game universe.

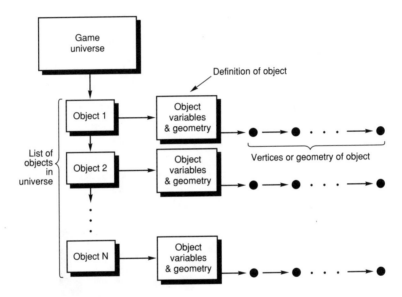

Figure 11.1. *A standard object-space representation of a game universe.*

This representation is fine and can work perfectly well. However, having such representations makes things such as collision detection, multiple levels, and data storage more complex. In a video game, we want to be able to create new levels quickly based on simple primitives. Therefore, we want to think in terms of what data structures and methods of representing our worlds make creating new worlds easy. We may lose some flexibility using this approach, but it's worth it in the long run.

As an example, let's leave the racetrack and begin again with a 2-D game world representation, which we then can extend into 3-D. In Chapter 14, "Linking Up," we see how to make a complete video game that takes place in a cell-based world. Let's cover how we make cell-based worlds.

In most video games there are a lot of objects and images that are repeated over and over, but in different patterns. If you take a look at PacMan, you'll see that there are many mazes—however, each maze is based on the same objects. There also are power pills, little dots, right turns, left turns, straightaways, and so on. If you took your time and analyzed each screen of Pac Man, you would realize that the screens' graphics are made out of a set of "cells." These cells are placed in certain ways to make turns, straightaways, and all the rest. This is the technique we're interested in using. It will enable us to represent large worlds with very little data; moreover, it permits simplification of collision detection within the game universe.

To implement a cell-based universe, we do the following:

■ First, we decide how many cells our universe will have. As an example, let's say the universe is 10x10.

■ Then we decide how big each cell will be. In a bit-mapped 2-D game, we may choose 16x16 pixels. Hence, we would have a game grid such as that shown in Figure 11.2.

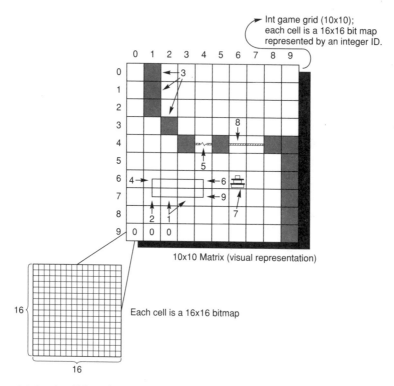

Figure 11.2. *A cell-based representation of a game grid.*

- We then go about drawing the cells we want in the game. We might have a cell with a little tree in it, a cell with a solid block in it, a cell with a food pellet in it, and so on.

- We then assign an integer to each cell type.

- We then create a data structure (usually, a 2-D matrix) and fill the matrix with the IDs that represent each cell.

Take a look at Figure 11.3, which shows a data representation of the game grid for our cell-based universe.

0	3	0	0	0	0	0	0	0	0
0	3	0	0	0	0	0	0	0	0
0	3	0	0	0	0	0	0	0	0
0	0	3	0	0	0	0	0	0	0
0	0	0	3	5	3	8	8	3	3
0	0	0	0	0	0	0	0	0	3
0	4	1	1	6	0	7	0	0	3
0	2	1	1	9	0	0	0	0	3
0	0	0	0	0	0	0	0	0	3
0	0	0	0	0	0	0	0	0	3

10x10 - Data representation

Figure 11.3. *Data representation of the game grid in Figure 11.2.*

At this point we have an entire universe stored in an indirect manner. Instead of storing each universe as a complete bit map, we broke one universe down into a collection of bit maps. Then we created a game matrix that uses integers, or IDs, to differentiate which bit maps or cells should be drawn at each cell location.

Now when we want to render the screen, it's easy: we have the game grid, which is our representation of the graphics we wish displayed. We also have the actual bit maps of each cell stored somewhere. To draw the screen, we go cell by cell and look at the integer, or ID, in the cell. With this information we draw the bit map represented by that particular ID number.

Figure 11.4 shows a sample game grid, along with each cell's bit map and the cell IDs.

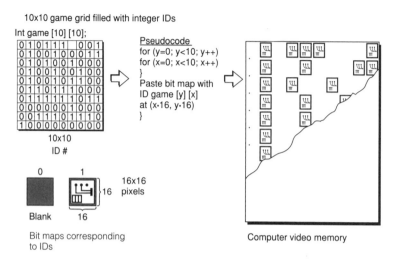

Figure 11.4. *Building up the screen display with a cell-based world representation.*

As you can see in Figure 11.4:

■ We fill the game grid data structure (usually, a 2-D matrix) with integers, where each integer is the ID of a specific bit map we want in that location.

■ Then we do a double FOR loop through the game grid data structure.

■ For each ID, we grab and render the proper bit map. These bit maps are cells that, when combined in groups or patterns, can represent things such as buildings, roads, game objects, and so forth.

The only thing we have to concern ourselves with is the proper positioning of each bit map. As each bit map in this example is 16x16 pixels, we must move one full cell size—16 pixels—every time we move to another cell. Therefore, if we drew our 10x10 game grid on the screen, it would fill a total of 160x160 pixels.

Using cell-based worlds is the only way to fly, and it makes creating a new game grid a simple task. It also enables us to create tools to easily draw new levels. You can write a program that draws a grid on the screen and then uses icons or colors to represent the actual bit maps you wish to place in the game world. You place the icons or colors into each cell location on the grid. This is then translated into the IDs that represent the bit maps, and saved for later use. With this technique, you can quickly make dozens of levels—and they each only take a tiny amount of memory space.

The only setback to cell-based worlds is that we can't place objects exactly where we want them. They always must be within a cell boundary. However, usually this isn't a problem.

We can use the same process to create a cell-based world similar to Wolfenstein or DOOM. However, instead of the cells representing bit maps, they represent 3-D cubes with one or more specific texture(s) on them. We would therefore build up our game grid with a set of IDs that represents which texture to place on each cell in the game.

If you've played Wolfenstein, you'll have noticed that the Wolfenstein world is built with a collection of cubes that have textures mapped onto each of the four vertical sides. Each of these cubes is really a cell in a 2-D grid. The IDs in each cell are the textures to be placed on the four sides, respectively. The program then reads the game grid and builds a 3-D universe from it.

The reason a 3-D universe can be built from a 2-D grid is that the game grid is regular, and the height of each cube is always the same. In essence, the game world is an extrusion of a 2-D cell world.

In a real game, you'll be able to get by with a cell-based world. However, sometimes you may need to add a few of the techniques mentioned during our previous discussions of object-based worlds or worlds built of polygons (or any arbitrary geometry other than cells). The cell-based world is used for creating the overall environment. However, certain types of objects sometimes just don't fall into this mold, and you may have to use another data structure. For instance, if there are smaller objects that the player must be able to place anywhere in the game, additional data structures are necessary.

DOOM has a 3-D universe, and also has 2-D bit maps that are placed in the universe as stationary objects: things such as food, weapons, and so on. I suspect that these objects are in another data structure, maybe one that's attached to each room. This extra data structure gives the specific position and type of object that should be placed within the room.

In any case, use whatever works. Make sure, however, that creating new levels and changing things is as easy as possible. You don't want to have to re-create the wheel for each new level. You want to use tools and low-level primitives to build things up.

Now that we have a universe to play with, let's find out how to bump into it.

When Objects Collide

In general, a collision occurs when the bounding regions of any two objects occupy the same space; see Figure 11.5.

However, in a PC video game, calculating intersections with actual perimeters is too time consuming. Most game programmers use the *bounding box*: a rectangle that bounds the object.

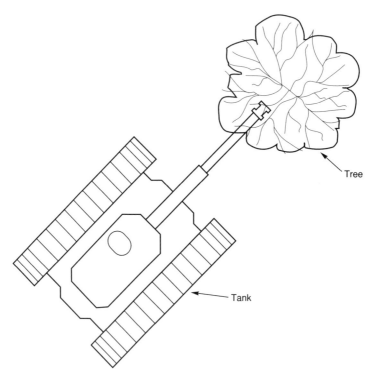

Figure 11.5. *Collision between two game objects.*

Testing for collisions between rectangles is much easier. Given rectangle R1 and R2, Algorithm 11.1 tests for collision.

Algorithm 11.1. Bounding-box collision detection.

```
For (each vertex of P1) do

if (vertex lies within P2 that is, is it within the x- and y-extents of P2)
    {
    there has been a collision
    exit
    }
} // end for
```

There are faster ways to do this test, but you get the idea. Using bounding boxes is great. However, as we're using a bounding box around the object, and not the exact geometry of the object itself, we can sometimes get collisions when there aren't any. Figure 11.6 shows an example.

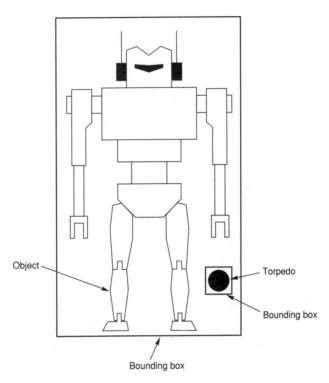

Figure 11.6. *Collision due to bounding boxes.*

To remedy this, we can either find the bounding box of an object and shrink it by some percentage, or we can do collision detection in two phases:

■ First, we use the bounding-box test in Algorithm 11.1 to see if we have a possible collision.

■ If the situation passes the test, we do a more exhaustive test to verify our hypothesis of a collision using the exact geometry of the object.

My advice to you is: use a bounding-box test with a bounding box that is 10-percent smaller, and let the player just wonder if the hit occurred or not!

We've covered general collision detection (in Chapter 4, "The Mechanics of Two-Dimensional Graphics"), so let's talk about collision with walls and the game universe, which is usually taken care of as a separate task.

Using our cell-based world to represent the game universe makes collision detection a snap. All we do is compute what cell our player is in and see if that cell is solid. For example, in our earlier discussion on game grids we had one that was 10x10, where each cell was 16x16 pixels. Therefore, the image on the screen would be 160x160. If our player was at location 50,92, he or she would be within a specific cell boundary. If this cell has something in it, the player shouldn't be there!

To compute the player's cell location, we divide the coordinates by 16. In our case, the result of dividing 50,92 by 16 would result in cell 3,5 (throw away the fractional part). We then would look into the 2-D game-grid matrix and, if anything else was there, we would back the player up, or execute logic that would let a player know he or she was encroaching on a solid object.

You can extend this technique into three dimensions. In a Wolfenstein-type game, the player is always on the same level—so we need only track the player's x and y. The player's height, or z, is irrelevant, because it's always the same. This would be a little more complex in a game such as DOOM because the player can move in z (that is, up and down by way of stairs and elevators).

Game Objects

So you have this great idea for a video game and you're ready to write 50,000 or so lines of C! You have one problem: this is your first game, and you don't know the best way to represent objects in the game. Should you use arrays, structures, linked list, binary trees, or what? My motto is: "Keep it simple; clever comes later."

We'll be using arrays, structures, and linked lists from time to time. Binary search trees and other, more advanced structures probably won't be of too much use until you're writing advanced algorithms, or maybe A.I. systems. A little bit of philosophy: use what works. If you can do something more elegantly (for example, using a linked list instead of an array), do so if it makes things easier. Otherwise, don't.

Try to use the most basic structures possible that are efficient and get the job done. For instance, if you want to have a collection of objects, and know that you'll have 10 at most, you could use a linked list and add to the list as the objects were created. This saves on memory, but it makes things *so* much more obtuse. For 10 objects, who cares? Just make an array and be done with it!

A video game is so intricate that if you sit down and go through a complex decision-making process for each aspect of the game, you'd be there forever (and I do mean forever). Get a rough draft going, then go back and clean it up if you wish. I'm friends with one of the most famous video-game designers of all time. He did much of the work in the 70s and 80s, and he's always told me: "Write the game, then rewrite it, then write it once more for good measure." So it's all right to start off rough and polish the game when you're done.

Using Data Structures in Video Games

I want to discuss a subset of data structures used in video games. These are the structures used to represent the game objects. Game objects can include the creatures, the weapons, the trinkets you can pick up, and on and on. When you create a static object or a character to partake in your universe, you must think up a few attributes that object or character has, and then create an appropriate structure to encapsulate these.

As an example, let's take a look at what we would need for a static object. By *static*, I mean an object you can pick up (as opposed to a *dynamic* object, which can move). The object does nothing otherwise; it just sits there. When you pick it up, it gives you health, food, or more energy. Listing 11.1 contains a reasonable structure for such objects.

Listing 11.1. A static object data structure.

```
typedef struct static_typ
    {
    int x,y;        // The position of the object.
    int type;       // The type of object: food, energy, or
                    // health.
    char *data;     // A pointer to the bit map that represents
                    // the object.
    int state;      // The state of the object: exists, amount
                    // of energy left, and so on.
    int amount;     // An extra field to further qualify the
                    // "type."
    } static, *static_ptr;
```

The `static` declaration in Listing 11.1 suffices as a good start, and we can add to it later. We could build up a linked list of these so that we have several in a game. However, if there are only a few of these in a game, we could make an array using the following line:

```
static stuff[10];
```

We would then go about initializing the `stuff` array, and that would be it. We could then refer to this array for static objects.

As another example, let's see what we'd need for a player in a game. In the game we make later in the book—Warlock—the player is a type of sorcerer who can pick things up and has different spells, health, lives, and some bit-map hands that are visible in front of the screen. Listing 11.2 might be a first attempt at the necessary variables.

Listing 11.2. A structure for the player in Warlock.

```
typedef struct player_typ
        {
        int x,y;                    // The position of the player.
        int lifes;                  // How many lives the player has
                                    // remaining.
        int health;                 // The player's health points.
        int weapons[3];             // An array that holds the types of
                                    // weapons the player has.
        int spells[10];             // An array that holds the types of
                                    // spells the player has.
        char *hands_stationary;     // The player's hands when
                                    // they aren't doing anything.
        char *hand_motion[4];       // four bit maps of the player's
                                    // game hands casting a spell.
        int state;                  // the player's state: alive,
                                    // dead, or dying.

        } player, *player_ptr;
```

(We get into the game state briefly in the section of this chapter called "States of Being," and more completely in Chapter 13, "Synthetic Intelligence.")

As you can see, we've got most of the important variables covered now. More are added later, and some deleted, but it's a good start. This is just how you go about creating the objects in your games: come up with a set of information that you feel will be needed, create a structure, and go from there.

Once you have your game objects, both static and dynamic, you must write software to make the objects be drawn, move, collide, and be erased. However, you don't want to write a separate function for each instance of a tree! Let's see how to clone game objects.

Cloning Game Objects

By *cloning* game objects, I mean reusing the same code to create multiple instantiations of the same object type, where each object type has its own copy of the data that represents the object in question. Figure 11.7 is a graphical representation of this.

To implement cloning, each algorithm (whether it be for drawing, motion, or collision detection) is written to operate on an instance of data. Therefore, each function is written to loop through all the instances of the object type.

For example, say we have code that implements a fly that just flies around in the game world and doesn't do much else. We might have a set of functions that look like those in Listing 11.3.

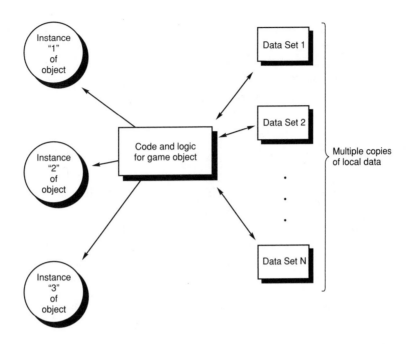

Figure 11.7. *Cloning game objects with multiple data sets.*

Listing 11.3. Sample fly functions.

```
void Erase_Flies(void)
{
for (each fly in the fly data structure ) do
     {
     erase the fly
     } // end for

} // end Erase_Flies

void Move_Flies(void)
{

for (each fly in the fly data structure) do
     {
     current_fly.x += current_fly.xv;    // Move in the x
                                          // direction.
     current_fly.y += current_fly.yv;    // Move in the y
                                          // direction.

     } // end for

} // end Move_Flies
```

We would make similar functions to draw the flies (no pun intended) and check for collisions. However, I think you get the point. We make one routine for each action that is to be performed on the object, and then create multiple data objects. These data objects are then fed into the functions and operated on. If we had an array of 1,000 flies, each of the functions would operate on 1,000 structures.

States of Being

At this point, I want to discuss a philosophical topic. I call it philosophical because it is one game-programming guru's method of doing things, and many other gurus may do it differently. In my experience, I've found it convenient to represent my game objects with a set of variables that includes a "state." This state helps qualify the object in some manner that could change as a function of temporal space or environment.

For instance, I always like to have a variable in each structure that indicates whether the game object is alive, dead, or dying. Having this variable helps in writing the functions that do the death animation, or the final extraction of the object when the object is dead and gone.

The reason for having state fields in the object's data structure is that doing so makes use of the same functions that draw the object when the object is healthy as when it's dying. This extra information is retrieved by way of the state or state variables. We cover states and finite state machines (FSMs) at length in Chapter 13, "Synthetic Intelligence." However, for now, know that (as in real life) a system or object in a video game can sequence through a series of states. To keep track of this we use state variables within the structure of each game object.

As an example of using a state to qualify some aspect of a game object, let's take a look at a small program that creates a little ant. The ant will walk in the same direction until it hits a wall or a rock, then choose another direction (NORTH, SOUTH, EAST, or WEST). Because the directions north, south, east, and west are such a simple item to track, we might forgo the use of a state to record this; however, north, south, east, and west could have as easily been "emotions" such as hungry, tired, happy, and angry.

To make things more exciting, let's make a whole colony of ants using our technique of cloning. Listing 11.4 contains the program ants.c.

Listing 11.4. An ant farm (ants.c).

```
// I N C L U D E S /////////////////////////////////////////////////

#include <dos.h>
#include <bios.h>
```

```c
#include <stdio.h>
#include <math.h>
#include <conio.h>
#include <graph.h>

// D E F I N E S ///////////////////////////////////////////////

#define ANT_NORTH 0
#define ANT_EAST  1
#define ANT_SOUTH 2
#define ANT_WEST  3
#define NUM_ANTS  50

// S T R U C T U R E S /////////////////////////////////////////

// Ant structure:

typedef struct ant_typ
        {
        int x,y;              // The position of the ant.
        int state;            // The state of the ant.
        unsigned char color;  // The color of the ant: red
                              // or green.
        unsigned back_color;  // The background under the ant.

        } ant, *ant_ptr;

// G L O B A L S ///////////////////////////////////////////////

unsigned char far *video_buffer = (char far *)0xA0000000L;
// vram byte pointer

unsigned int far *clock = (unsigned int far *)0x0000046C;
// Pointer to internal

// Our little ants:

ant ants[NUM_ANTS];


// F U N C T I O N S ///////////////////////////////////////////

void Timer(int clicks)
{
// This function uses the internal timekeeper (the one that runs
// at 18.2 clicks/sec to time a delay). You can find the 32-bit
// value of this timer at 0000:046Ch.
unsigned int now;

// Get current time:

now = *clock;

// Wait until the time has gone past the current time plus the
// amount we wanted to wait. Note that each click is
// approximately 55 milliseconds.

while(abs(*clock - now) < clicks){}
```

continues

Listing 11.4. continued

```
} // end Timer

///////////////////////////////////////////////////////////////

void Plot_Pixel_Fast(int x,int y,unsigned char color)
{

// Plot the pixel in the desired color a little quicker using
// binary shifting to accomplish the multiplications.

// Use the fact that 320*y = 256*y + 64*y = y<<8 + y<<6.

video_buffer[((y<<8) + (y<<6)) + x] = color;

} // end Plot_Pixel_Fast

///////////////////////////////////////////////////////////////

unsigned char Read_Pixel_Fast(int x,int y)
{

// Read a pixel from the video buffer.

// Use the fact that 320*y = 256*y + 64*y = y<<8 + y<<6.

return(video_buffer[((y<<8) + (y<<6)) + x]);

} // end Read_Pixel_Fast

///////////////////////////////////////////////////////////////

void Draw_Ground(void)
{
int index;

// Draw a bunch of gray rocks:

for (index=0; index<200; index++)
    {
    Plot_Pixel_Fast(rand()%320,rand()%200, 7 + rand()%2);

    } // end for index

} // end Draw_Ground

///////////////////////////////////////////////////////////////

void Initialize_Ants(void)
{
int index;

for (index=0; index<NUM_ANTS; index++)
    {
    // Select a random position, color, and state for each ant.
    // Also: scan their background.

    ants[index].x     = rand()%320;
    ants[index].y     = rand()%200;
```

```
        ants[index].state = rand()%4;

        if (rand()%2==1)
           ants[index].color = 10;
        else
           ants[index].color = 12;

        // Scan the background:

        ants[index].back_color = Read_Pixel_Fast(ants[index].x, ants[index].y);

        } // end for index

} // end Initialize_Ants

////////////////////////////////////////////////////////////////

void Erase_Ants(void)
{
int index;

// Loop through the ant array and erase all ants by replacing
//   what was under them.

for (index=0; index<NUM_ANTS; index++)
    {
    Plot_Pixel_Fast(ants[index].x, ants[index].y, ants[index].back_color);
    } // end for index

} // end Erase_Ants

////////////////////////////////////////////////////////////////

void Move_Ants(void)
{

int index,rock;

// Loop through the ant array and move each ant, depending on
// its state.

for (index=0; index<NUM_ANTS; index++)
    {

    // What state is the ant in?

    switch(ants[index].state)
        {

        case ANT_NORTH:
            {
            ants[index].y--;

            } break;

        case ANT_SOUTH:
            {
            ants[index].y++;
```

continues

Listing 11.4. continued

```
                    } break;

            case ANT_WEST:
                {
                ants[index].x--;

                } break;

            case ANT_EAST:
                {
                ants[index].x++;

                } break;

            } // end switch

        // Test whether the ant hit a screen boundary or a rock.

        if (ants[index].x > 319)
            ants[index].x = 0;
        else
        if (ants[index].x <0)
            ants[index].x = 319;

        if (ants[index].y > 200)
            ants[index].y = 200;
        else
        if (ants[index].y <0)
            ants[index].y = 199;

        // Now test whether we hit a rock.

        rock = Read_Pixel_Fast(ants[index].x, ants[index].y);

        if (rock)
            {
            // Change states.

            ants[index].state = rand()%4;  // Select a new state.

            } // end if

        } // end for index

} // end Move_Ants

/////////////////////////////////////////////////////////////

void Behind_Ants(void)
{
int index;
// Loop through the ant array and scan what's under the ants.

for (index=0; index<NUM_ANTS; index++)
    {
    // Read the pixel value and save it for later.
```

```
      ants[index].back_color =
      Read_Pixel_Fast(ants[index].x, ants[index].y);
      } // end for index

} // end Behind_Ants

//////////////////////////////////////////////////////////////

void Draw_Ants(void)
{
int index;
// Loop through the ant array and draw all the ants green or red,
// depending on their type.

for (index=0; index<NUM_ANTS; index++)
    {
    Plot_Pixel_Fast(ants[index].x,
                    ants[index].y, ants[index].color);
    } // end for index
} // end Draw_Ants

// M A I N //////////////////////////////////////////////////

void main(void)
{

// Set the 320x200x256 color mode.

_setvideomode(_MRES256COLOR);

_settextposition(2,0);
printf("Hit any key to exit.");

// Draw the world:

Draw_Ground();

// Set up all the ants:

Initialize_Ants();

while(!kbhit())
    {
    // Erase all the ants:

    Erase_Ants();

    // Move all the ants:

    Move_Ants();

    // Scan what's under the ant:

    Behind_Ants();

    // Now draw the ant:

    Draw_Ants();
```

continues

Listing 11.4. continued

```
    // Wait a little...
    Timer(2);

    } // end while

// Restore the old video mode:
_setvideomode(_DEFAULTMODE);

} // end main
```

If you execute the program in Listing 11.4, you'll see a bunch of little dots on the computer screen. The red and green dots represent ants, and the gray dots are rocks. When the ants bump into a rock, they change direction. This program illustrates the use of state variables. Later, we learn to use state variables to implement more complex computational structures, called *state machines*.

Now let's change gears and take a look at the game from the player's point of view.

User Interfaces

When players play your game, they'll experience it mostly through the graphics and sound. However, there's one more area of interactivity players will be involved in: the user interface.

A user interface (or UI) is necessary for a video game to allow the player to change the state of the game, select options, change number of players, and so on. When making a UI, make it as simple as possible. There's nothing more frustrating than an overwhelming UI. (Sports games are notorious for this. They have about a billion options, and by the time you've got everything set up you don't want to play any more.)

In a video game there are two major areas for which we need a UI:

- The first UI is active during run time. This UI displays vital information about the state of the game, your score, and so on.

- The second UI is the one that's activated to change game options and playing features.

Both of these must be easy to understand and update. The UI the player sees during play should focus on the most important aspects of the character's state. Moreover, it should use text when possible. Icons are cool and look great, but I've seen many icons that look similar to Vulcan symbols, and no one knows what they mean!

As far as the game-options UI goes:

- It should be accessible from any point in the game, if possible.

- It should use large letters and have few options per screen.

- It should allow the player to change game options; however, it should have a great deal of error protection and data checking.

- It should assume the player does not know what he or she is doing.

UIs are the icing on the cake, and you must think of the best possible way to implement yours. Remember: keep it simple, make no assumptions, and stay away from symbols (unless they are *extremely* clear).

Demo Modes

Once you've created the ultimate video game, you'll surely want to give it a *demo mode* that will show it off. Implementing a demo mode is rather easy, if you approach the task from a certain perspective: one of redirecting the input source to a file rather than the player.

When a player plays a game, that player changes the state of an input device. (See Chapter 3, "Input Device Basics," for more information on this.) This device is then used by the player to control the game. Within the game, the control logic obtains its input from a specific function, such as Get_Input(). This function retrieves the state of an input device.

What if we were to replace the inner logic of the input function to get the input from a pre-recorded file instead of from the physical input device? The game wouldn't know the difference. Figure 11.8 shows how this is done.

"But," you ask, "how do I create the file?" What's needed is a special mode of the game that only we can play. What this mode does is digitize the input-device state at some constant time interval; say, .1 second. We create a file of this digitized information, and that file is used as the source for the input function during demo mode.

This is how demo or playback modes usually are implemented. There are other ways to do this, of course, but they all rely on having either prerecorded data or some kind of artificial intelligence system to control the player's input.

You may think that digitizing all this information will consume a lot of memory. Let's see. If we sample 10 times a second, we would need to store 600 bytes/minute, or roughly 6K for a 10-minute demo. That's definitely not a problem, so I suggest you use this technique. However, have it in mind *before* you write the game so you don't have to hack your input functions. They should have a "source" switch that can select from among the mouse, keyboard, joystick, or playback file. Having the ability to play back a file will also make "instant replays" a snap.

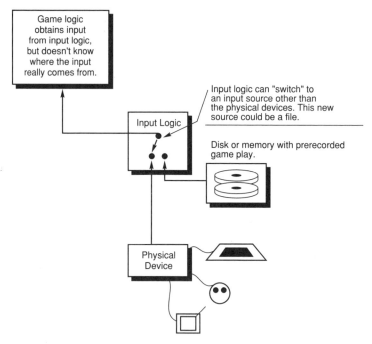

Figure 11.8. *Using a file as an input source to implement a demo mode.*

Saving the Game

Many physicists believe that if you knew the position and state of every particle in the universe, you could predict the next click in time. We aren't going to argue that point. However, we do need to save the state of our game universe somehow.

Let's state the problem this way: "How do we save a game and restore it back to the same position, so that game play can be continued at another time?" The answer is simple: we make a list of all the game objects and factors that can change during the game. Then we create some kind of file format to store all this information in. Then, when the player wants to save a game, we simply save each and every piece of information needed to restore the game on disk.

As an example, let's see how we would do a "save game" in Wolfenstein or DOOM:

- Each game has a collection of objects that are, for the most part, always in the same position, so we need not save their position. However, we do need to save the fact that they are still in existence at the time of the save game.

- Then we have to consider all of the game creatures. For every living creature in the game, we should save a copy of their structure. Within the structure would be their position, state, and so on.

- Finally, we would save the state of the player, along with any objects and or extra information relating to position, health, and so on that will be necessary to restore the state of the game. That's all there is to it. In essence, we're digitizing our universe by taking a snapshot in time. (By the way, while this works in video games, it doesn't work in real life because of Chaos, Non-Deterministic Dynamics, and other large words...)

Modeling the Real World

This topic is kinda off the wall; nevertheless, it's one that we must address at least briefly. Within a video game, there will undoubtedly be effects that you want to have within your game world. These effects could be such things as friction, the trajectory of a missile, and conservation of momentum. Examples of where we would use these concepts could be in a racing game, firing a missile in a combat game, and two balls hitting each other in a pool simulation. In any case, I want to give you a little refresher course on basic mechanics, which is the study of motion.

Everyone has a good feel for velocity. Velocity is just a gauge of change of distance per unit of time. For instance, if I want to move an object at two pixels per second, I might express it this way:

```
Object_Position += 2;
```

If we looked at the position of the object as a function of time we would obtain a graph such as the one shown in Figure 11.9.

What about acceleration? Acceleration is the change of velocity per unit time—in other words, how much the velocity is changing. When you press the accelerator in your car, you begin an acceleration curve that keeps moving your car at a faster and faster velocity. To implement acceleration we would do this:

```
Object_Position += velocity;
velocity+=acceleration_factor;
```

Every time through this code fragment, the velocity would increase—which, in turn, would cause the object to translate more. This would be perceived as an acceleration. One of the most familiar accelerations we experience is the acceleration of gravity. If an object is dropped from a position above the ground, it will experience an acceleration of 9.8 ft/sec*sec, or 32 M/sec*sec. To put it another way, if the object is dropped, in one second it will be moving at 9.8 ft/sec and in two seconds it will be moving at 19.6 ft/sec.

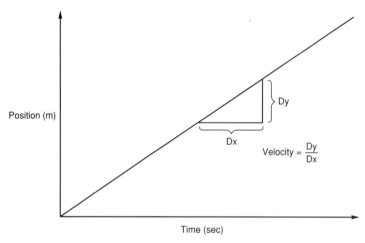

Figure 11.9. *A graph of position versus time for a constant velocity.*

To see acceleration at work, take a look at the ball.c program shown in Listing 11.5. It drops a virtual ball, which then accelerates due to gravity. You can see the effects of changing the gravitational constant by pressing the + or - keys.

Listing 11.5. Dropping a virtual ball (ball.c).

```
// I N C L U D E S ///////////////////////////////////////////////

#include <stdio.h>
#include <math.h>
#include <graph.h>

// D E F I N E S ///////////////////////////////////////////////

#define EARTH_GRAVITY 9.8

// G L O B A L S ///////////////////////////////////////////////

unsigned int far *clock = (unsigned int far *)0x0000046C;
// Pointer to internal.
```

```
// F U N C T I O N S //////////////////////////////////////////////

Timer(int clicks)
{
// This function uses the internal timekeeper (the one that runs
// at 18.2 clicks/sec to time a delay). You can find the 32-bit
// value of this timer at 0000:046Ch.

unsigned int now;

// Get current time:
now = *clock;

// Wait until time has gone past the current time plus the
// amount we wanted to wait. Note that each click is
// approximately 55 milliseconds.

while(abs(*clock - now) < clicks){}

} // end Timer

// M A I N ////////////////////////////////////////////////////////

void main(void)
{

float ball_x   = 160,
      ball_y   = 50,
      ball_yv  = 0,
      ball_acc = EARTH_GRAVITY;

int done=0,key;

// Use all MS graphics routines for a change:

_setvideomode(_MRES256COLOR);

_settextposition(0,0);
printf("Q to quit, use +,- to change gravity.");

while(!done)
    {
    // Has there been a keyboard press?
    if (kbhit())
       {

       // Test what key:

       switch(getch())
            {
            case '-':
                   {
                   ball_acc-=.1;

                   } break;

            case '=':
```

continues

Listing 11.5. continued

```
                        {
                        ball_acc+=.1;

                        } break;

                case 'q':
                        {
                        done=1;

                        } break;

                } // end switch

        // Let the player know what the gravity is:
        _settextposition(24,2);
        printf("Gravitational Constant = %f",ball_acc);

        } // end if keyboard hit

    // Erase the ball:

    _setcolor(0);

    _ellipse(_GBORDER, ball_x,ball_y,ball_x+10,ball_y+10);

    // Move the ball:
    ball_y+=ball_yv;

    // Add acceleration to velocity:
    ball_yv+=(ball_acc*.1);
// The .1 is to scale it for viewing.

    // Test whether the ball has hit bottom.
    if (ball_y>190)
        {
        ball_y=50;
        ball_yv=0;

        } // end if
    // Draw the ball:
    _setcolor(1);
    _ellipse(_GBORDER, ball_x,ball_y,ball_x+10,ball_y+10);

    // Wait a bit...
    Timer(2);

    } // end while

// Restore the old video mode:
_setvideomode(_DEFAULTMODE);

} // end main
```

Creating physics models in a video game is necessary if things are to look real. Even if they aren't to look real, we still need models of how they will interact with other objects.

As a final example, let's implement a perfectly elastic collision. The program in Listing 11.6 creates a group of virtual atoms that are trapped in a container. When the atoms hit the edge of the container, they bounce off and conserve momentum. We *could* use a bunch of physics equations; however, we only need a reasonable model that looks good. If you've ever bounced a pool ball off the edge of a table, you'll have noticed that it always reflects at the same angle at which it was incident. Figure 11.10 shows this.

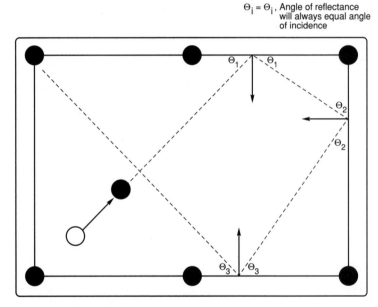

Figure 11.10. *A tricky shot.*

To implement this, we need only reflect the sign of the velocity of the atom, and it will bounce off the edge in a way that looks PC (that is, "physically correct"). Listing 11.6 shows the code.

Listing 11.6. A perfect gas (gas.c).

```
// I N C L U D E S //////////////////////////////////////////////

#include <dos.h>
#include <bios.h>
#include <stdio.h>
#include <math.h>
```

continues

Listing 11.6. continued

```
#include <conio.h>
#include <graph.h>

// D E F I N E S ///////////////////////////////////////////

#define NUM_ATOMS 200

// S T R U C T U R E S ///////////////////////////////////////

// Atom structure:

typedef struct ant_typ
        {
        int x,y;          // The position of the atom.
        int xv,yv;        // The velocity of the atom.

        } atom, *atom_ptr;

// G L O B A L S ///////////////////////////////////////////

unsigned char far *video_buffer = (char far *)0xA0000000L;
// vram byte pointer.

unsigned int far *clock = (unsigned int far *)0x0000046C;
// Pointer to internal.

// Our atoms:

atom atoms[NUM_ATOMS];


// F U N C T I O N S ///////////////////////////////////////

void Timer(int clicks)
{
// This function uses the internal timekeeper (the one that runs
// at 18.2 clicks/sec to time a delay). You can find the 32-bit
// value of this timer at 0000:046Ch.

unsigned int now;

// Get the current time:
now = *clock;

// Wait until time has gone past the current time plus the
// amount we wanted to wait.  Note that each click is
// approximately 55 milliseconds.

while(abs(*clock - now) < clicks){}

} // end Timer

//////////////////////////////////////////////////////////////

void Plot_Pixel_Fast(int x,int y,unsigned char color)
{
// Plot the pixel in the desired color a little quicker using
```

```
// binary shifting to accomplish the multiplications.

// Use the fact that 320*y = 256*y + 64*y = y<<8 + y<<6.

video_buffer[((y<<8) + (y<<6)) + x] = color;

} // end Plot_Pixel_Fast

//////////////////////////////////////////////////////////////

void Initialize_Atoms(void)
{
int index;

for (index=0; index<NUM_ATOMS; index++)
    {
    // Select a random position and trajectory for each atom

    atoms[index].x    = 5 + rand()%300;
    atoms[index].y    = 20 + rand()%160;
    atoms[index].xv   = -5 + rand()%10;
    atoms[index].yv   = -5 + rand()%10;

    } // end for index

} // end Initialize_Atoms

//////////////////////////////////////////////////////////////

void Erase_Atoms(void)
{
int index;

// Loop through the atoms and erase them.

for (index=0; index<NUM_ATOMS; index++)
    {
    Plot_Pixel_Fast(atoms[index].x, atoms[index].y, 0);
    } // end for index

} // end Erase_Atoms

//////////////////////////////////////////////////////////////

void Move_Atoms(void)
{
int index;;

// Loop through the atom array and move each atom. Also: check
// for collisions with the walls of the container.

for (index=0; index<NUM_ATOMS; index++)
    {
    // Move the atoms:

    atoms[index].x+=atoms[index].xv;
    atoms[index].y+=atoms[index].yv;
```

continues

Listing 11.6. continued

```c
      // Did the atom hit a wall? If so, reflect the
      // velocity vector.

      if (atoms[index].x > 310 || atoms[index].x <10)
        {
         atoms[index].xv=-atoms[index].xv;
         atoms[index].x+=atoms[index].xv;
         } // end if hit a vertical wall

      if (atoms[index].y > 190 || atoms[index].y <30)
        {
         atoms[index].yv=-atoms[index].yv;
         atoms[index].y+=atoms[index].yv;
         } // end if hit a horizontal wall

      } // end for index

} // end Move_Atoms

////////////////////////////////////////////////////////////////

void Draw_Atoms(void)
{
int index;
// Loop through the atoms and draw them.

for (index=0; index<NUM_ATOMS; index++)
    {
    Plot_Pixel_Fast(atoms[index].x, atoms[index].y, 10);
    } // end for index

} // end Draw_Atoms

// M A I N ////////////////////////////////////////////////////

void main(void)
{
// Set the 320x200x256 color mode:
_setvideomode(_MRES256COLOR);

_settextposition(2,0);
printf("Hit any key to exit.");

// Draw the container:
_setcolor(9);
_rectangle(_GBORDER,0,16,319,199);

// Set up all the ants.

Initialize_Atoms();

while(!kbhit())
    {
    // Erase all the atoms.

    Erase_Atoms();
```

```
    // Move all the atoms.
    Move_Atoms();

    // Now draw the atoms.
    Draw_Atoms();

    // Wait a little...
    Timer(1);

    } // end while

// Restore the old video mode.
_setvideomode(_DEFAULTMODE);

} // end main
```

That's enough physics for me! I think you get the idea: when you want to model something, sit down and come up with a few rules or equations that will create a model that responds the way you want it to. Then figure out a clean, simple way to implement it in the game.

Summary

This chapter was a crash course in ideas and techniques used to represent game worlds and the actions that take place in them. Among other things, we covered:

- Object-based and cell-based representations of worlds
- Demo modes
- Physics modeling

The main idea you should take away with you is: there is no right way to do any of this stuff. There are just *ways*. If you have a better way, use it. However, the framework we laid here should give you some directions to go with your own creativity.

12

Surreal Time, Interrupts, and Multitasking

I f you've ever played a video game...well, that's a dumb way to start a chapter in a book like this! You've probably noticed how everything in a video game looks like it's happening at the same time. I can assure you that 99.9 percent of the time, it's not! The computer is just doing things so fast, over and over, that it seems like it's multitasking. In this chapter we explore the crude multitasking capabilities of the PC. We also explore how to create "game loops" that seem to do many things at once, and discuss some architectural topics relating to video-game design and writing "self-contained" functions. Here's what we cover:

- The way a player perceives the game

- Multitasking

- Implementing multitasking with interrupts

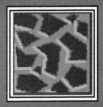

by André LaMothe

- Creating interrupts handlers with C
- Game loops
- Autonomous functions
- Responder functions
- Reprogramming the internal clock
- Putting it all together
- ISR Case Study I—It's Full of Stars...
- ISR Case Study II—Keying Up!

A Player's Perception

When a person plays a video game, he or she expects it to be interactive. By *interactive* I mean that the graphics should be crisp and fast, the music should play at the right tempo, and player input should be responded to instantly (from the player's point of view). To the player, the graphics and sound of the game seem to be happening simultaneously. Now let's cross the tracks to the programmer's points of view.

In fact, the different elements of the game are hardly happening simultaneously. The PC is not a multitasking computer (at least not in DOS games). Moreover, the PC has only one processor. Therefore, the illusion of reality or "real time" is simulated in some other manner. This other manner is pure speed. The PC can operate so fast relative to a human's perception that it can do things in a sequential manner and make it look like it's all happening at once.

This is how the illusion of video games is possible. We get the input, execute the game logic, draw the objects, and make the sounds; then we do that sequence over again. Of course, this happens dozens of times, if not hundreds of times, a second, fooling the player into believing in our virtual world.

What is Multitasking?

Multitasking is simply the execution of two or more processes at once on a single computer. For instance, Microsoft Windows is a multitasking operating system (although some would tend to argue that it needs a few additions to be truly multitasking. However, it will do for the purposes of our discussion.) Windows enables the user to execute a program, and then execute another if the user wishes. The computer slices up each second into a group of *time slices*. Each process or program gets one slice of the processor's time. The processor then goes to the next process or program and gives it a slice of time. This continues until each program has been serviced, when it starts all over again. The PC is so fast, though, it seems as though all the programs are running simultaneously. Take a look at Figure 12.1 to see multitasking in action.

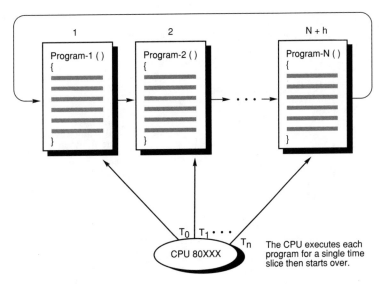

Figure 12.1. *Example of multitasking.*

In video-game design we aren't interested in multitasking, for example, a word processor with our game. We're interested in multitasking different portions of the game. What that means is we want to execute each portion of the game for a short amount of time, making sure to give each piece of the game its chance. (By *piece of the game* I mean the graphics, sound, and logic portions of the game.) Then, when each section of the game has executed, the game loops back to the beginning and completes the cycle again.

We could argue that a single C program that has one main section calling several functions is like a little virtual computer, where each one of the functions is a task and each task is executed in such a way that a form of multitasking occurs. However we want to look at it, the fact of the matter is that the main section controls the execution of these functions, and a game can be written so these functions and the main execution stream are never interrupted by another process.

Actually, this is fine: complete video games can and are being written with a single main section and no interrupts. However, interrupts allow a crude form of true multitasking to occur:

■ When the main section is executing, it can be stopped in its tracks at some unknown point. The state of the machine is saved so that the main section can be resumed later.

■ Control of the PC then is given to the interrupt handler, which is a complete program.

■ When the interrupt handler or *interrupt-service routine* (ISR) is finished, it exits and execution continues where it left off in the main section.

Figure 12.2 shows how an interrupt is serviced.

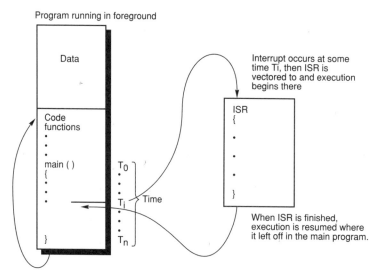

Figure 12.2. *An interrupt server routine being serviced.*

You might say, "Why on Earth would you want to do that?" There are many reasons to use interrupts. For instance, say you have a program that needs keyboard input. Say the player presses a key, but at that point the program is drawing graphics. The key press will be lost. If, however, when a key was pressed an ISR was called, the processor would stop what it was doing, process the interrupt, and then resume, and the key press is never lost.

In the case of PC video games, we aren't so much interested in the keyboard as we are with timing. Timing is everything in a game. The graphics have to be drawn at specific times. The sounds must be played at a constant tempo. Sometimes we want things to occur at specific time intervals, such as 1/30th of a second or 1/60th of a second. This can become a problem if you don't have interrupts: the PC would have to keep track of time, and this might tax the processor.

Another problem that can occur is that you may be able to make a time delay on a specific PC exactly one second long, but on another, faster PC the same code may take only .25 seconds. In that case, your time base becomes machine-dependent.

Yet another problem solved with interrupts and multitasking is that the main section doesn't have to poll everything. It would be a real pain if the main section, on top of running an entire game, had to keep asking whether the serial port was ready, if the joystick moved, if the keyboard was pressed, if the sound system was done, and so on.

We want to try to separate tasks that could run independently of the game and the main section and place them into interrupts. Now, don't get me wrong. The PC doesn't have a zillion interrupts we can latch onto. In actuality there are only a couple we ever use, and we use them for specific reasons.

If I've confused you beyond recognition...isn't that what friends are for? Let's try to clarify this confusion with an explanation of how multitasking is accomplished in DOS.

Implementing Multitasking with Interrupts

Under DOS, the only way we're going to get any multitasking at all is through the use of interrupts. Some of the interrupts happen based on external events, and some are based on internal events. As an example, let's talk first about the most famous interrupt of all: the keyboard interrupt.

Whenever a key is pressed, your program stops—no matter what it's doing—and execution begins in the keyboard ISR. (I'll bet you didn't realize that every time you press a key your program stops. But it does!) The keyboard ISR does its thing and then relinquishes control back to your program. Your program, data, and everything else is left unscathed by the whole process. This is Rule Number One of writing ISRs: don't irritate anything unless you mean to. For example, if during an ISR you fry all the registers, you'd better have saved them beforehand so that you can restore them on exit.

Before we get into the nuts and bolts of writing and installing an interrupt handler, let's take a look at what kinds of interrupts are available on the PC. Take a look at Table 12.1.

Table 12.1. The interrupts on a PC.

Number	Address	Function
0H	000-003H	Divide by zero
1H	004-007H	Single step
2H	008-00BH	Nonmaskable interrupt
3H	00C-00FH	Breakpoint
4H	010-013H	Overflow
5H	014-017H	Print screen
6H	018-01BH	Reserved
7H	01C-01FH	Reserved
8H	020-023H	Timer 18.2
9H	024-027H	Keyboard
AH	028-02BH	Reserved
BH	02C-02FH	RS-232 Port 1
CH	030-033H	RS-232 Port 0
DH	034-037H	Hard disk
EH	038-03BH	Diskette
FH	03C-03FH	Reserved
10H	040-043H	Video I/O call
11H	044-047H	Equipment check call
12H	048-04BH	Memory check call
13H	04C-04FH	Diskette I/O call
14H	050-053H	Serial I/O call
15H	054-057H	Cassette I/O call
16H	058-05BH	Keyboard I/O call
17H	05C-05FH	Printer I/O call
18H	060-063H	ROM BIOS entry code
19H	064-067H	Bootstrap loader

Number	Address	Function
1AH	068-06BH	Time of day call
1BH	06C-06FH	Get control on break
1CH	070-073H	Get control on timer
1DH	074-077H	Video initialization table
1EH	078-07BH	Diskette parameter table
1FH	07C-07FH	Graphics character table
20H	080-083H	DOS program terminate
21H	084-087H	DOS universal function
22H	088-08BH	DOS terminate address
23H	08C-08FH	DOS Ctrl break
24H	090-093H	DOS fatal error vector
25H	094-097H	DOS absolute disk read
26H	098-09BH	DOS absolute disk write
27H	09C-09FH	DOS terminate and stay resident
28-3FH	0A0-0FFH	Reserved for DOS
40-7FH	100-1FFH	Not used
80-F0H	200-3C3H	Reserved by Basic
F1-FFH	3C4-3FFH	Not used

Table 12.1 is the interrupt-handler table. It represents the first 1,024 bytes of memory on every PC. There are a total of 256 entries, each being four bytes, which represents the FAR address to the ISR. As you can see, all 256 interrupts aren't used by the PC yet. However, the number is growing.

The PC supports both hardware and software interrupts. Software interrupts are created by an extension in the 80xxx instruction set, designed to allow the current process being executed to be interrupted momentarily by something other than a physical hardware interrupt. Most interrupts on the PC are of the software type. However, a few are created purely by hardware (such as the nommaskable interrupt and keyboard interrupt). As game programmers, this delineation doesn't affect us: both types work the same way from a programmer's point of view.

> When experimenting with interrupts, I suggest that you be very careful: you're playing with fire. If you make a mistake you can crash the computer and cause it to lose data. So watch it!

So, our game plan is to pick an interrupt that we want to replace or chain into. This selection isn't clear yet, but we get to that in this chapter. Then we simply install our ISR. That's it.

The only thing we are missing is the ISR, so let's learn how to make one using C.

Creating Interrupts Handlers with C

Be glad you're programming when you are. Otherwise, you'd probably shudder at the thought of writing an ISR in pure assembly language. Luckily for us, the new C compilers have extensions that allow interrupts to be written in C code with the proper keywords. Moreover, C takes care of a great deal of the housekeeping on entry and exit from the ISR. All you have to do is write the ISR, which is standard C code. To make a function an ISR you use the keyword interrupt.

For example, say we wanted to create an interrupt that we plan to link into the timekeeper interrupt 0x1C. We might begin like this:

```
void _interrupt _far Timer(void)
{


} // end timer
```

The _far keyword is needed because all interrupts are 32-bit calls (an offset and segment).

Within the function you can do anything you want as long as whatever you do is reentrant. That means you should be extremely careful when calling DOS functions or complex C functions such as printf. I suggest you not use any extensions to the C language. As far as saving registers goes, you needn't worry: the C compiler saves all registers on entry and restores them on exit, except the stack segment SS. Also, for ease of access, the DS register points to the global data segment of your C program on entry to the ISR, so the ISR can access global variables. It's almost too good to be true, but that's how it works.

Now that we have an ISR, let's learn how to install it.

Installing an ISR

Once we have the ISR routine written we "install" it into the computer by placing its start address into the interrupt table at the proper interrupt entry. Now, there are two ways of doing this:

■ We could just change the interrupt address to point to our own interrupt and leave it at that. However, the old handler then would never be called.

Besides, what happens if an interrupt occurs when we're halfway done changing an address? Crunch, crunch, crunch—that's what happens! Therefore, it's better to let DOS do this for you with the function _dos_setvect(). We also use the function _dos_getvect() to save the old vector. Both functions are guaranteed to change the vectors without disturbing the operating sytem or causing a problem.

■ Many times, we want to add functionality to the system without replacing it entirely, so we chain interrupts. By *chain*, I mean we save the old ISR address and replace it with our own, then make our ISR jump to the old ISR when ours is done. This way we don't throw out anybody's ISRs or terminate-and-stay-resident programs (TSRs)—unless we wanted to!

Take a look at Figure 12.3 to see the two approaches to installing ISRs.

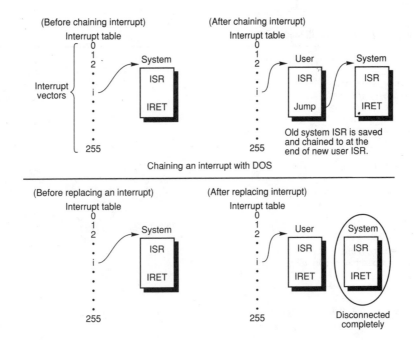

Figure 12.3. *Installing ISRs.*

Listing 12.1 shows how to install our example timer() ISR (which still does nothing).

Listing 12.1. Installing an ISR.

```
void (_interrupt _far old_isr)(); // Function pointer to save
                                  // old ISR.

// Save old timekeeper ISR.

old_isr = _dos_getvect(0x1C);

// Install our new ISR.

_dos_setvect(0x1C,Timer);
```

That was hard...*not!* To replace the old ISR we would do this:

```
_dos_setvect(0x1C, old_isr);
```

That's all there is to it. As an example, let's make our timer ISR actually do something now, like update a global variable. Listing 12.2 contains the program spy.c, which has a main section that sits in a loop and prints out the variable. The only way the variable can change, therefore, is if some other program—for example, an ISR—were to change it.

Listing 12.2. Spying on the clock (spy.c).

```
// I N C L U D E S ////////////////////////////////////////////////

#include <dos.h>
#include <bios.h>
#include <stdio.h>
#include <math.h>
#include <conio.h>
#include <graph.h>

// D E F I N E S ////////////////////////////////////////////////

#define TIME_KEEPER_INT 0x1C

// G L O B A L S ////////////////////////////////////////////////

void (_interrupt _far *Old_Isr)();
     // Holds old com port interrupt handler.

long time=0;

// F U N C T I O N S ////////////////////////////////////////////////
```

```
void _interrupt _far Timer(void)
{

// Increment global time variable. Note: we can do this because,
// on entry, DS points to global data segment.

time++;

} // end Timer



// M A I N //////////////////////////////////////////////////

void main(void)
{

// Install our ISR.

Old_Isr = _dos_getvect(TIME_KEEPER_INT);

_dos_setvect(TIME_KEEPER_INT, Timer);

// Wait for the player to hit a key.

while(!kbhit())
    {
    // Print the time variable. Note: the main
    // does NOT touch it...

    _settextposition(0,0);
    printf("\nThe timer reads:%ld   ",time);

    } // end while

// Replace old ISR.

_dos_setvect(TIME_KEEPER_INT, Old_Isr);


} // end main
```

When you run the program in Listing 12.2, you'll notice the counter incrementing quickly. Actually, it's incrementing 18.2 times a second. This is the current setting of the internal timekeeper counter. (Don't worry, we'll terrorize that in a while, also.) The most important thing to note is that the main section does not increment the time variable. Instead, the ISR does.

We've now created an ISR, installed it, and seen that it works—and we did this in just a few lines of code. Amazing, huh? We're going to write more complex ISRs later, but for now lets switch gears and talk about game loops.

The Game Loop

At this point in your game-programming guru training you've learned quite a bit about all the elements that are combined to make a video game. However, you probably have a few questions about the architecture of a video game. In this section, I lay down the framework for a typical game.

A video game isn't all that complex if you look at it from a sufficiently lofty view. You must:

- Initialize all the systems.

- Begin a game loop.

- Get input from the player.

- Do the game logic and transformations to the game objects.

- Render the graphics.

- Loop back to the top.

In essence, that's all there is to it. As you know, however, the details of all these tasks are quite complex. You see, in a video game we may need some events to occur asynchronously from the game itself. For instance, you may need some variable updated precisely every 1/30th of a second, or you may need the game to wait for some kind of synchronization (like the vertical retrace) before continuing with its next cycle. These factors tend to obscure the cleanliness of the game loop.

When designing a video game, we first must decide what kind of game it will be, the kinds of creatures that will be in the game, the types of graphics and sounds the game will have, and so on. Then we must make a rough flowchart of how the game will operate, or how the overall software is going to look. We need not consider low-level details (such as blitting and sound drivers) at this point. We're more interested now in the Big Picture.

As a video-game designer, it's up to you to decide how you implement your games. There is no correct way to do it. If the end result works, *how* it works is irrelevant. However, some designs are better than others, and "better" must be qualified by these factors:

- The time it takes to implement the game

- The speed of execution

- The ease of modification

- The ease of debugging

There are more factors we could add to the list, but these are the most important.

In Chapter 14, "Linking Up," we go into a game I wrote called Net-Tank. It's a serially linked tank simulation with sound effects, cool graphics, weapons, and fully interactive play. Let's take a look at its game loop, shown in Figure 12.4.

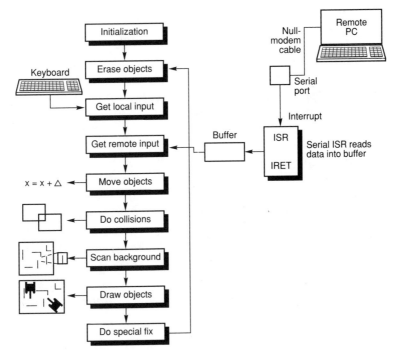

Figure 12.4. *A sample game loop.*

As you can see, the game loop has all the parts that we've discussed:

- Initializing the game objects
- Erasing the objects
- Getting input from the local player
- Getting input from the remote player
- Doing the transformations
- Computing collisions
- Calling a routine that moves the missiles
- Rendering the graphics in an off-screen buffer, which (when the time is right) is blasted to the video screen

This is a good example of a game loop. It has all of the elements of a more complex game. However, the game itself is simple in nature, and I could get away with not using interrupts and timing functions. (Actually, that's not true: the serial communications had to be done with an interrupt handler. You'll learn more about this in Chapter 14, "Linking Up.") Anyway, I didn't have any asynchronous events going on, I didn't have a complex sound engine, and I didn't do any time-critical processing that would have needed close timing control using an interrupt.

Now lets talk about some software techniques that will help solve game-related problems that might occur. The thing to remember is, a video game could be made without them; however, they make it easier.

Autonomous Functions

In a video game, there are hundreds (if not thousands) of things going on every second, and the main section must keep track of a lot of different variables and states. Many actions that are done in a game don't need such tight control, and it'd be nice if some of the functions were "self contained" and took some of the burden of initialization, timing, and operation off the caller. I call these functions *autonomous.* I've given them this name to describe their inherent ability to operate without needing much attention. The main section can call a function of this type once during the game loop and the function does its job.

Say, for example, that we wanted to make a function that slowly changes a certain color register's value. This color register could be used to draw little gadgets on the video display. When the function executes, it changes the color of the register, thereby changing the color on the display. This effect would be for appearance only. A function like this is ideal to make run autonomously. Listing 12.3 takes a look at how we would implement the function.

Listing 12.3. An autonomous light strobe.

```
void Strobe_Lights(void)
{
static clock=0,        // The function's own clock "memory" so
        first_time=1;  // the function can initialize on its
                       // first call.

// Test whether this is the first time.

if (first_time)
    {
    first_time=0;  // Reset first-time flag.
    // Do initializations.
    } // end if first time
```

```
else // not first time i.e. nth time
    {
    // Test whether it's time to do action.
    if (++clock==100)
        {
        change color register
        // Reset the clock.
        clock=0;

        } // end if time to do action

    } // end else

} // end Strobe_Lights
```

The interesting thing about `Strobe_Lights()` is that it's self-contained. The caller need not call it with specific parameters to tell it to initialize or run normally. Moreover, it has local `static` variables that stay in existence even after the function ends. This is the key to autonomous functions. The main section can call the function once every cycle of the game loop and know that the lights will be strobed. The main section doesn't have the burden of tracking variables, initializing the function, and so on.

This is good. However, it lacks one more facet: machine-independence. You see, the function counts up to 100 and then does its thing—but this counting is machine-dependent. The faster the machine, the faster the counting, and the result is that some machines will have faster strobe lights than others. To remedy this problem, we must have some kind of time reference.

Time references are important, and we need them for many things other than just doing events as specific times. For example, we may want a little bird to fly out every five seconds, or the screen to be rendered 30 times a second. The only way to do this kind of thing is to have some kind of time reference and be able to access it.

Let's talk about responder functions, which can be used for this and more.

Responder Functions

A *responder function* does what its name would indicate: it responds to some kind of event, whether it be a temporal event, a variable change, or something else. In our case, we use responders to react to some state or event, and to take an action based on this.

For instance, we could have a responder function watch the internal clock and play a sound every five seconds. In this case the responder function "responds" to a five-second interval by reacting with a sound. On the other hand, we could have a responder function "watch" some variable that was changed by the main section, or by an interrupt, and react to that.

Take a look at Figure 12.5 to see the relationship between responder functions and the rest of the system.

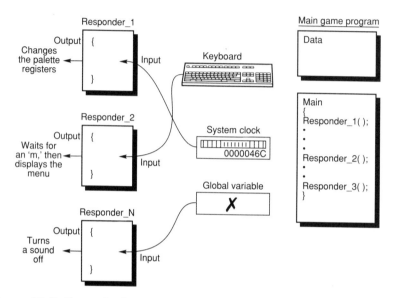

Figure 12.5. *Responder functions.*

All the concepts we're talking about are "real-time" programming techniques that aren't normally taught in schools or books. (That's why they may seem a bit strange.)

Let's go ahead and implement a responder function that tracks the timer variable from Listing 12.2 and waits for it to tick five times. When it does, the function resets the time variable and plots a random pixel on the screen. See Listing 12.4.

Listing 12.4. Responder (pres.c).

```
// I N C L U D E S /////////////////////////////////////////////

#include <dos.h>
#include <bios.h>
#include <stdio.h>
#include <math.h>
#include <conio.h>
#include <graph.h>

// D E F I N E S ///////////////////////////////////////////////

#define TIME_KEEPER_INT 0x1C


// G L O B A L S ///////////////////////////////////////////////
```

```
void (_interrupt _far *Old_Isr)();
    // Holds old com port interrupt handler.

long time=0;

// F U N C T I O N S //////////////////////////////////////////

void _interrupt _far Timer(void)
{

// Increment global time variable. Note: we can do this because,
// on entry, DS points to global data segment.

time++;

} // end Timer

//////////////////////////////////////////////////////////////

void Plot_Responder(void)
{

static int first_time=1;
static long old_time;

// Test whether this is the first time.

if (first_time)
   {
   // Reset first time.

   first_time=0;

   old_time = time;

   } // end if first time
else
   { // not first time

   // Have five clicks passed?

   if ( (time-old_time)>=5)
      {
      old_time = time; // Save new old time.

      // Plot the pixel.

      _setcolor(rand()%16);
      _setpixel(rand()%320,rand()%200);

      } // end if

   } // end else

} // end Plot_Responder

// M A I N //////////////////////////////////////////////////
```

continues

Listing 12.4. continued

```
void main(void)
{

_setvideomode(_MRES256COLOR);

printf("Hit any key to exit...");

// Install our ISR.

Old_Isr = _dos_getvect(TIME_KEEPER_INT);

_dos_setvect(TIME_KEEPER_INT, Timer);

// Wait for the player to hit a key.

while(!kbhit())
    {
    // ... game code.

    // Call all responders.

    Plot_Responder();

    // ... more game code.

    } // end while

_setvideomode(_DEFAULTMODE);

// replace old ISR

_dos_setvect(TIME_KEEPER_INT, Old_Isr);

} // end main
```

Listing 12.4 uses a responder function to track the time and plot a pixel every five clicks, or 5*55.4 ms. The 55.4 milliseconds comes from the fact that the timekeeper is set to generate an interrupt 18.2 times/second, or every 55.4 ms. Note that the responder is an autonomous function, too, meaning it's self sustaining and self initializing.

Autonomous and responder functions can be used for many things, helping to separate your software into "task groups" that allow operations that aren't tightly coupled to the game itself to occur without much work from the main section. The game logic is complicated enough to keep you busy, and you shouldn't have to worry about blinking lights and so on.

On the PC the only way we can keep time and dispatch events based on time is to use the internal timers. Unfortunately, most of them are in use for other things. One of them, however, is used for the computer's timekeeper. It "beats" 18.2 times/second.

This is an unusual time base and, I have to admit, I don't know why the designers chose this. In any case, we can reprogram it to obtain a more reasonable time base, such as 20, 30 or 60 times/second. These are times bases that are more appropriate for video games. Let's learn how to reprogram the internal timer.

Programming the Internal Clock

The internal clock on the PC, which keeps time, isn't really a clock at all. It's a timer/counter chip that counts at a certain rate based on its settings. The chip on the PC that contains these functions is called the 8253 timer chip. The 8253 timer chip contains three 16-bit counters. These counters can be programmed in many ways, and as a result the chip is quite versatile. Table 12.2 shows the counters currently in use, and their functions.

Table 12.2. The 8253 timer chips counter allocation.

I/O Port	Counter #	Usage
40h	Counter 0	Timer/Disk
41h	Counter 1	Memory refresh
42h	Counter 3	Tape Drive/Speaker
43h	Control Register	Controlling timer functions

The timer chip can be accessed through ports 40h-43h. As you can see, counter 0 and 3 are our only hope—we definitely don't want to mess with counter 1! We see that counter 0 is already used by DOS as the timekeeper; therefore, why not keep it that way, but speed it up to the time base that we desire?

This works fine; the computer won't crash. The only drawback is that the computer's time will be wrong. The way around this is to save the time when you change the counter (that is, the timer speed), and keep track of time, taking into consideration the newly installed time base. Then, when the program exits, reset the timer and update the time. You can use C functions to save and restore the time.

Changing the Timer's Value

Let's talk about how we can go about changing the timer's value. The timer uses a value loaded into it to count down with. When it's done counting, it sends out an interrupt. The counter is then reset and counts down again. In the case of counter 0, the interrupt is sent out 18.2 times/second, or every 55.4 ms. That time is calculated as follows: the timer chip is fed with a 1.19318MHz clock rate. This is divided by the value in the counter. In the case of the timekeeper interrupt, the value in the counter is 65536. If you take 1.19318MHz and divide by 65536, you get 18.206 cycles/second, or 54.925 ms. As you can see, the builders of the PC used the largest divisor possible that would fit into 16 bits: 65535. (The timer actually goes one extra pulse; that's where I got 65536.)

Anyway, all we need to do is compute the 16-bit number that, when divided into 1.19318MHz, gives us the desired frequencies. I've done this for you for some popular rates; take a look at table 12.3.

Table 12.3. 16-bit counter values for different clock rates.

Hex Value	Decimal Value	Time Base
4DAE	19886	60Hz
965C	39772	30Hz
E90B	59659	20Hz

What we want to do, then, is reprogram counter 0 so it generates an interrupt at a more reasonable pace that our game can use to track time at a higher resolution than 18.2 times/second.

Let's talk about how we go about placing these values into the counter registers. I/O ports 40-43h are the ports of interest, and in our case all we care about are ports 40h and 43h: counter 0 and the control register, respectively. The control register has the bit designations shown in Table 12.4.

Table 12.4. 8253 Control Register Bit Designations.

Bit 0 - 0 = Count in binary, 1 = Count in BCD.
Bits 1-3 are used to select the counter mode.

Bit 3	Bit 2	Bit 1	Mode
0	0	0	0 - Interrupt on terminal count
0	0	1	1 - Hardware retriggerable one-shot
X	1	0	2 - Rate generator
X	1	1	3 - Square wave
1	0	0	4 - Software retriggerable strobe
1	0	1	5 - Hardware retriggerable strobe

Bits 4 and 5 control the reading and writing.

Bit 5	Bit 4	Function
0	0	Counter latch operation
0	1	Read/Write least significant byte of counter
1	0	Read/Write most significant byte of counter
1	1	Read/Write least, then most, significant byte

Bits 6 and 7 select the counter that will be accessed for the operation.

Bit 7	Bit 6	Counter #
0	0	0
0	1	1
1	0	2
1	1	Illegal

After viewing Table 12.4, we see that there are quite a few options that can be set. However, I'm going to take care of that problem right now: we're only going to alter counter 0. With that in mind, the settings of the other bits are as follows:

- The mode of operation is mode 2: rate generator.

- The method of counting is binary.

- We'll access the counter registers using "Read/Write least, then most, significant byte."

Therefore, what we must do is first write the control word to port 43h and then make two writes to port 40h. The first write will be the low byte of our new counter value. The next byte will be the high byte. The hardware sorts the bytes out, so don't worry. Listing 12.5 contains outatime.c, a function that reprograms the timer.

Listing 12.5. Reprogramming the internal clock (outatime.c).

```
// I N C L U D E S /////////////////////////////////////////////

#include <stdio.h>
#include <conio.h>

// D E F I N E S /////////////////////////////////////////////

#define CONTROL_8253   0x43  // The 8253's control register.
#define CONTROL_WORD   0x3C  // The control word to set mode 2,
                             // with binary counting and
                             // least/most significant.
#define COUNTER_0      0x40  // counter 0

#define TIMER_60HZ     0x4DAE // 60Hz
#define TIMER_30HZ     0x965C // 30Hz
#define TIMER_20HZ     0xE90B // 20Hz
#define TIMER_18HZ     0xFFFF // 18.2Hz (the standard count).

// M A C R O S /////////////////////////////////////////////

#define LOW_BYTE(n) (n & 0x00ff)
#define HI_BYTE(n) ((n>>8) & 0x00ff)

// F U N C T I O N S /////////////////////////////////////////////

void Change_Time(unsigned int new_count)
{

// Send the control word, mode 2, binary, least/most.

_outp(CONTROL_8253, CONTROL_WORD);

// Now write the least significant byte to the counter register.

_outp(COUNTER_0,LOW_BYTE(new_count));
```

```
// And now the high byte.

_outp(COUNTER_0,HI_BYTE(new_count));

} // end Change_Time

// M A I N ///////////////////////////////////////////////////////

void main(void)
{
// Reprogram the timer to 60 hz instead of 18.2 hz.

Change_Time(TIMER_60HZ);

} // end main
```

After running the program, the system timer will, of course, be running too fast. You can do either of the following to remedy this:

■ Reset the computer.

■ Run the program again with the constant in `Change_Time()` changed to TIMER 18HZ.

Putting It All Together

We've covered the basics behind interrupts, multitasking, and some software techniques to make video-game architecture a little easier. The software techniques are by no means the best or even an extensive collection. We covered them to simply get you thinking in different ways about the structure of a video game. You undoubtedly will come up with techniques and tricks of your own to implement your video game. However, this chapter serves as a starting point to get you in the correct frame of mind. Now I'd like to summarize what we have learned and again produce some examples of what to use the techniques for. After discussing those topics, were going to take a look at two more code examples to try to solidify some of these concepts.

First, we learned about multitasking on the PC and how we can implement it using interrupts. An interrupt is just a momentary change in the execution of one program, usually the main section, to another interrupt-service routine (ISR) that performs a job related to what initiated the interrupt. Interrupts are useful because they allow a form of "coarse-grained" multitasking to be achieved on the PC. Moreover, they can be used to handle time- or event-related tasks that would be too hard for the main section to keep track of due to the nature of the event or task. ISRs are typically used for tasks such as keyboard processing and serial communications. However, we can use them for other functions (such as the sound system, the I/O system, doing housekeeping chores, and so on).

We can achieve this by hooking our ISRs into interrupts that we know occur at certain times or are based on specific events. For instance, the timekeeper interrupt 0x1C is quite useful. We can place an ISR in the interrupt table that will be executed at every system tick (that is, 18.2 times/second). This way we're guaranteed that no matter how bogged down the system becomes, our ISR is always called promptly. We also learned that we can change the system clock to count at different rates, such as 20Hz, 30Hz and 60Hz, and so on. We may want to do this to have a more reasonable interrupt interval if we're using the timekeeper interrupt to do something that must be done more frequently than 18.2 times/second.

Finally, we learned that we can use interrupts to toggle global flags that are, in essence, messages that can be responded to by other functions in the game program. This may be needed for the game to do time-critical operations, synchronization, or both.

The next topics we discussed were related to designing the game loop. The game loop is simply a method of setting up the software and functions in a video game so that everything gets done in a timely and logical manner. We learned that a game should have an initialization section followed by a main event loop, which erases imagery, obtains input, does transformations, renders the graphics, and then displays them. Of course, this order may change and the elements themselves may change. However, we always must create an event loop that does all the operations needed for a single cycle in an efficient and logical manner.

After talking about game loops we then discussed some seemingly esoteric topics in software design. We covered a couple types of new functions, called autonomous and responder functions. These techniques were shown to detail how many activities and processes in a video game need to be self sustaining and have local memory. Video games are so complex that we'd like to write functions that do their own thing without being supervised by the main section. Autonomous functions help solve these kinds of problems. Then we talked about responder functions which are used in video games to "respond" to events and take actions.

All of these discussions are to help you in understanding the way "real-time" programming is done—in other words, how to make many things seem like they're happening simultaneously. In video games this is absolutely necessary.

The last thing we covered was reprogramming the internal clock, which is located on the 8253 timer chip. We learned that counter 0 holds a 16-bit value used to divide down an incoming signal of 1.19318MHz. The resulting signal is used to create a *tick*, a kind of heartbeat that initiates the timekeeper interrupt and can be hooked into by way of interrupt vector 0x1C. In 100 percent of video games, this timer is reprogrammed to a more suitable speed, such as 30Hz or 60Hz, and the computer is synchronized to this new time base. Furthermore, the game's sound system and I/O system usually are placed in a background task that executes in an ISR initiated by timekeeper interrupt 0x1C. This makes the music and I/O run at a steady pace even if the game slows due to computations and visual complexity.

This chapter was one of the hardest to write because there are so many things that you need to know. In reality, however, only experience will teach you the millions of subtleties that a video-game programmer considers. Nevertheless, your eyes are open to a new way of thinking, and that's a good start.

As I promised, we're going to write a couple more ISR routines to do some cool things.

ISR Case Study I—It's Full of Stars...

To show just how useful interrupts and multitasking can be, I've written a 3-D starfield that is an interrupt handler. Every time the internal time counter increments, it sends out an interrupt that can be "hooked" into at interrupt 0x1C. I've linked my starfield into this interrupt; therefore, 18.2 times a second my starfield code is called and the starfield is updated. We'd use something like this in a game that was played on a single screen (maybe one of the shoot-em'-up type games). No matter what's happening in the foreground, our starfield keeps on running flawlessly.

Note how the starfield ISR is self-contained, meaning that it initializes itself the first time it's called (when it creates the starfield database), then renders the starfield on subsequent calls.

One final little fact: when you exit the program, you can leave it resident by pressing the E key. Then you'd see a starfield running across the DOS prompt, which is rather bizarre! The reason this works is that when you exit by pressing the E key, the old ISR isn't reinstalled. The PC continues to call the starfield. You wouldn't think this would work! However, when the program exits, it leaves much of the code intact in the main memory, so the ISR survives the exit of the main section. Nevertheless, if you try to run anything the computer will probably crash, as this is not the method you should use to make a terminate-and-stay-resident program (TSR). (There's a DOS function called dos keep to do this, but we aren't interested in TSRs. We just happened to create one accidentally.) If the system does crash, you'll have to reboot.

Listing 12.6 contains our 3-D starfield.

Listing 12.6. A 3-D starfield (stars.c).

```c
// I N C L U D E S ///////////////////////////////////////////////

#include <dos.h>
#include <bios.h>
#include <stdio.h>
#include <math.h>
#include <conio.h>
#include <graph.h>


// D E F I N E S ///////////////////////////////////////////////

#define TIME_KEEPER_INT 0x1C
#define NUM_STARS 50

// S T R U C T U R E S ///////////////////////////////////////////////

typedef struct star_typ
        {
        int x,y;     // Position of the star.
        int vel;     // X component of star velocity.
        int color;   // Color of the star.

        } star, *star_ptr;


// G L O B A L S ///////////////////////////////////////////////

void (_interrupt _far *Old_Isr)(void);
        // Holds old com port interrupt handler.

unsigned char far *video_buffer = (char far *)0xA0000000L;
        // vram byte ptr.

int star_first=1;  // Flags first time into starfield.

star stars[NUM_STARS]; // The starfield.


// F U N C T I O N S ///////////////////////////////////////////////

void Plot_Pixel_Fast(int x,int y,unsigned char color)
{

// Plots the pixel in the desired color a little quicker using
// binary shifting to accomplish the multiplications.

// Use the fact that 320*y = 256*y + 64*y = y<<8 + y<<6.

video_buffer[((y<<8) + (y<<6)) + x] = color;

} // end Plot_Pixel_Fast

///////////////////////////////////////////////////////////////

void _interrupt _far Star_Int(void)
```

```
{

// This function creates a panning, 3-D starfield with 3-planes,
// like looking out of the Enterprise.

// Note: this function had better execute faster than 55.4ms;
// otherwise, it will be called again reentrantly—and kaboom!

int index;

// Test whether we must initialize starfield (that is, if the
// first time function is being called.

if (star_first)
    {
    // Reset first time
    star_first=0;

    // Initialize all the stars.

    for (index=0; index<NUM_STARS; index++)
        {
      // Initialize each star to a velocity, position, and color.

        stars[index].x      = rand()%320;
        stars[index].y      = rand()%180;

        // Decide what star plane the star is in.

        switch(rand()%3)
              {
            case 0: // Plane 1 = the farthest star plane.
                  {
                  // Set velocity and color.

                  stars[index].vel = 2;
                  stars[index].color = 8;

                  } break;

            case 1: // Plane 2 = the mid-distance star plane.
                  {

                  stars[index].vel = 4;
                  stars[index].color = 7;

                  } break;

            case 2: // Plane 3 = the nearest star plane.
                  {

                  stars[index].vel = 6;
                  stars[index].color = 15;

                  } break;

            } // end switch
```

continues

Listing 12.6. continued

```c
          } // end for index

      } // end if first time
else
      { // must be nth time in, so do the usual

      // Erase, move, draw.

      for (index=0; index<NUM_STARS; index++)
          {
          // erase

          Plot_Pixel_Fast(stars[index].x,stars[index].y,0);

          // move

          if ( (stars[index].x+=stars[index].vel) >=320 )
             stars[index].x = 0;

          // draw

          Plot_Pixel_Fast(stars[index].x,stars[index].y,
                          stars[index].color);

          } // end for index

      } // end else

} // end Star_Int

// M A I N ///////////////////////////////////////////////////
void main(void)
{
int num1, num2,c;

_setvideomode(_MRES256COLOR);

// Install our ISR.

Old_Isr = _dos_getvect(TIME_KEEPER_INT);

_dos_setvect(TIME_KEEPER_INT, Star_Int);

// Wait for the player to hit a key.

_settextposition(23,0);

printf("Hit Q - to quit.");
printf("\nHit E - to see something wonderful...");

// Get the character.

c = getch();

// Does the player feel adventurous?
```

```
if (c=='e')
   {
   printf("\nLook stars in DOS, how can this be ?");

   exit(0);  // Exit without fixing up the old ISR.
   } // end if

// Replace old ISR.

_dos_setvect(TIME_KEEPER_INT, Old_Isr);

_setvideomode(_DEFAULTMODE);

} // end main
```

ISR Case Study II—Keying Up!

As we learned in Chapter 3, "Input Device Basics," we can use BIOS to read any key that's pressed by checking a *scan code*. This works great and will suffice in most cases, but what about the case when you want to press two keys simultaneously? (One example of this might be pressing an up- or down-arrow key and the right-arrow key to obtain a diagonal.) The only way to accomplish this is to dig deeper into the operation of the keyboard. BIOS only gives us one layer more of control than the standard C functions. We need to go deep, deep, *deep* down into the keyboard hardware itself if we want to have the kind of functionality that's needed in a professional video game.

The PC's keyboard actually has an entire microcomputer in it, called the 8048. When a key is pressed or released, the keyboard creates a serial stream and sends it to the PC for processing. BIOS tells us about key presses; however, it neglects the releases. That's the very information we need to implement multiple simultaneous key presses. You see, if we know when a key is pressed and when it's released, we can write an algorithm that tracks the state of a collection of keys. When a key is pressed, we flag it as pressed; when it's released, we clear this flag. With this technique we can register multiple key presses, but until a corresponding release is performed we keep the key in the down position in our data structure.

The proper terminology for the key press and key release is *make* and *break*, respectively. Moreover, when a key is pressed, the *make code* is sent, and when the key is released the appropriate *break code* is sent. These make codes and break codes are similar to scan codes. The difference is that when a key is pressed and the make code is sent, whatever that value is will have a 128 added to it when the key is released and the break code is sent.

To gain control of the keyboard, we're going to boot DOS out and install our own driver that will receive a key code, whether it's a make or break, and then stuff it into a global variable that a C program can access. Then a C function can use the current make or break code to figure out what keys are pressed and released, and detail that in a table. The keyboard interrupt is INT 0x09, so all we have to do is write and install an ISR to accomplish the task we've described.

Before we dive in, however, let's take a look at a couple of I/O ports and their function. The keyboard I/O port is at 60h and the keyboard control register is at 61h. These ports are on the *peripheral interface adapter* (PIA) chip. In any case, we must make sure our ISR does a bit of housekeeping when it's called and before it exits. The flow of operations is as follows:

1. Enter into the ISR. This occurs whenever a key is pressed.

2. Read the key code from I/O port 60h and place it into a global variable for later processing by the main section, or update the data table.

3. Read the control register from I/O port 61h and perform a logical OR operation on it with 82h.

4. Write the result back to the control register port 61h.

5. Perform a logical AND operation on the control register with 7fh. This resets the keyboard flip-flop, indicating to the hardware that a key has been processed and another can be read.

6. Reset the 8259 interrupt controller. (This may or may not be necessary, but it's better to be safe than sorry.) To accomplish this we write a 20h to port 20h; what a coincidence, huh?

7. Exit the ISR.

Listing 12.7 contains our keyboard ISR, and then has some code to track the arrow keys. While it runs you can use the arrows to move a little dot around the screen in any direction or combination of directions.

Listing 12.7. Cyber Dot (cyber.c).

```
// I N C L U D E S /////////////////////////////////////////////

#include <dos.h>
#include <bios.h>
#include <stdio.h>
#include <math.h>
#include <conio.h>
#include <graph.h>
```

```
// D E F I N E S /////////////////////////////////////////////

#define KEYBOARD_INT    0x09
#define KEY_BUFFER      0x60
#define KEY_CONTROL     0x61
#define INT_CONTROL     0x20

// Make and break codes for the arrow keys.

#define MAKE_RIGHT      77
#define MAKE_LEFT       75
#define MAKE_UP         72
#define MAKE_DOWN       80

#define BREAK_RIGHT     205
#define BREAK_LEFT      203
#define BREAK_UP        200
#define BREAK_DOWN      208

// Indices into arrow key state table.

#define INDEX_UP        0
#define INDEX_DOWN      1
#define INDEX_RIGHT     2
#define INDEX_LEFT      3

// G L O B A L S ///////////////////////////////////////////////

void (_interrupt _far *Old_Isr)(void);
     // Holds the old com port interrupt handler.

unsigned char far *video_buffer = (char far *)0xA0000000L;
     // vram byte ptr

int raw_key;  // The global raw keyboard data.

int key_table[4] = {0,0,0,0}; // The arrow key state table.

// F U N C T I O N S ///////////////////////////////////////////

void Plot_Pixel_Fast(int x,int y,unsigned char color)
{

// Plot the pixel in the desired color a little quicker using
// binary shifting to accomplish the multiplications.

// Use the fact that 320*y = 256*y + 64*y = y<<8 + y<<6.

video_buffer[((y<<8) + (y<<6)) + x] = color;

} // end Plot_Pixel_Fast

///////////////////////////////////////////////////////////////

void Fun_Back(void)
{
int index;
```

continues

Listing 12.7. continued

```c
// Draw a background that should jog your memory.

_setcolor(1);
_rectangle(_GFILLINTERIOR, 0,0,320,200);

_setcolor(15);

for (index=0; index<10; index++)
    {
    _moveto(16+index*32,0);
    _lineto(16+index*32,199);

    } // end for index

for (index=0; index<10; index++)
    {
    _moveto(0,10+index*20);
    _lineto(319,10+index*20);

    } // end for index

} // end Fun_Back

/////////////////////////////////////////////////////////////

void _interrupt _far New_Key_Int(void)
{

// I'm in the mood for some in-line!

_asm
    {
    sti                     ; Reenable interrupts.
    in al, KEY_BUFFER       ; Get the key that was pressed.
    xor ah,ah               ; Zero out upper 8 bits of AX.
    mov raw_key, ax         ; Store the key in global.
    in al, KEY_CONTROL      ; Set the control register.
    or al, 82h              ; Set the proper bits to reset
                            ; the FF.
    out KEY_CONTROL,al      ; Send the new data back to the
                            ; control register.
    and al,7fh
    out KEY_CONTROL,al      ; Complete the reset.
    mov al,20h
    out INT_CONTROL,al      ; Reenable interrupts.
                            ; When this baby hits 88 mph, your
                            ; gonna see some serious @#@#$%.

    } // end inline assembly

// Now for some C to update the arrow state table.

// Process the key and update the table.

switch(raw_key)
    {
    case MAKE_UP:     // Pressing up
```

```
                {
                key_table[INDEX_UP]    = 1;
                } break;

        case MAKE_DOWN:  // Pressing down
                {
                key_table[INDEX_DOWN]  = 1;
                } break;

        case MAKE_RIGHT: // Pressing right
                {
                key_table[INDEX_RIGHT] = 1;
                } break;

        case MAKE_LEFT:  // Pressing left
                {
                key_table[INDEX_LEFT]  = 1;
                } break;

        case BREAK_UP:    // Releasing up
                {
                key_table[INDEX_UP]    = 0;
                } break;

        case BREAK_DOWN:  // Releasing down
                {
                key_table[INDEX_DOWN]  = 0;
                } break;

        case BREAK_RIGHT: // Releasing right
                {
                key_table[INDEX_RIGHT] = 0;
                } break;

        case BREAK_LEFT:  // Releasing left
                {
                key_table[INDEX_LEFT]  = 0;
                } break;

        default: break;


        } // end switch

} // end New_Key_Int

// M A I N ///////////////////////////////////////////////////

void main(void)
{
int done=0,x=160,y=100; // Exit flag and dot position.

// Set the video mode to the 320x200, 256 color mode.

_setvideomode(_MRES256COLOR);

Fun_Back(); // Light cycles, anyone?
```

continues

Listing 12.7. continued

```c
printf("\nPress ESC to Exit.");

// Install our ISR.

Old_Isr = _dos_getvect(KEYBOARD_INT);

_dos_setvect(KEYBOARD_INT, New_Key_Int);

// Main event loop.

while(!done)
    {
_settextposition(24,2);

printf("raw key=%d    ",raw_key);

    // Look in the table and move the little dot.

    if (key_table[INDEX_RIGHT])
       x++;

    if (key_table[INDEX_LEFT])
       x--;

    if (key_table[INDEX_UP])
       y--;

    if (key_table[INDEX_DOWN])
       y++;

    // Draw the cyber dot.

    Plot_Pixel_Fast(x,y,10);

    // This is our exit key. The make code for "esc" is 1.

    if (raw_key==1)
       done=1;

    } // end while

// Replace old ISR.

_dos_setvect(KEYBOARD_INT, Old_Isr);

_setvideomode(_DEFAULTMODE);

} // end main
```

Th— th— th— that's all, folks!

Summary

Within this chapter we learned some of the most advanced topics that can be mastered on the PC. We covered the timer, interrupts (including keyboard interupts), and more.

We learned to write interrupts in C and how to link them into the interrupt table. Moreover, we learned about some of the timing and synchronization structures used in PC games, such as responders and automonous functions.

Finally, we took what we learned and wrote some programs that took control of the PC—and, in one case, didn't give it back!

Synthetic Intelligence

The human mind is an abyss filled with the past, the present, and the future. It is aware of its own existence, and is the only known device that is self-organizing and questions its own understanding. Computer science is at the doorstep to understanding the mechanisms of thought, memory, and consciousness. However, as PC game programmers we really don't need to be too sophisticated to make reasonably intelligent games. The creatures in our games only have to *seem* like they have intelligence.

In this chapter we trek across waters that are still uncharted by even the most advanced video games. We discuss topics that range from the practical to the theoretical to the completely esoteric. Nevertheless, complex "thinking" models can be derived with just a little knowledge. These models will definitely be able to handle simple tasks such as combat, search, and evasion. The following "gray matter" will be covered:

■ An overview of how video games think

■ Chase and evasion algorithms

by André LaMothe

- Patterned thoughts
- Random walks
- Finite-state machines
- Probability machines
- Memory and learning
- Search algorithms
- Game theory

How Video Games Think: An Overview

A day will come when the computer is as formidable an opponent as the most brilliant human mind. However, today's computers (at least, PCs) are not of the complexity needed to initiate thoughts and creativity. The good news is: we don't care! We're making video games, not androids.

In a game we have creatures and game objects. All we need to accomplish is having them do reasonable things in their universe. The player can then, for a short time, be suspended in a realm where he or she thinks the aliens attacking the ship are real! To accomplish these goals we must analyze what intelligence we must impart to our game objects. This "intelligence" depends on what kind of games and creatures we're creating. For instance, the creatures in Pac Man spend most of their time either chasing you or running away from you. If we were the people who wrote Pac Man we'd be …well, we'd be in Hawaii, maybe, but we'd also be implementing an algorithm to accomplish this chasing and retreating. On the other hand, if we were writing a game like Space Invaders, the intelligence for the creatures wouldn't require much more than a couple of dozen lines of computer code. The pseudocode would read something like:

1. Continue moving in the direction you are moving (right or left).

2. When you hit the edge of the screen, change directions and move down a cell height.

3. Go to 1.

Not too terribly complex an intelligence function for a game that raked in 50 to 100 million in revenues over its entire lifetime!

The 3-D video games we're interested in are really no different than this: the intelligence functions are the same as they would be in a 2-D game. A 3-D view merely gives an extra dimension to the life and reality of a game and, when playing a 3-D game, players seem more able to believe that the game is real. However, the same algorithms are used in 3-D games as are used in 2-D games. For instance, Terminator Rampage has a really simple intelligence system—something on the same order of complexity as that of Pac Man. However, when 3-D graphics are added, along with the sound and combat, the creatures seem to have complex personalities. I assure you they have the reasoning capacity of sponges.

Here's the common denominator for most video games: the intelligence is rather primitive and is made up for by the graphics and sound. Video-game programmers have gotten away with this for so long because the games they make are mostly combat and shoot-em'-up types. Our mission in this chapter is to understand the methods used to implement intelligence, and the major categories into which "thinking" algorithms fall.

Remember: games don't think. They just look like they do. The reason for this, as I said earlier, is most of the time we will be implementing primal intelligence, such as combat and destruction. (The thought process for combat is fairly simple: find your enemy and destroy him/her/it—or, in terms of computer code: move toward the enemy, point barrels in enemy's direction, then fire all weapons.) When you're done reading this chapter you'll have the game brains to do anything!

Chase and Evasion Algorithms

Let's begin at the beginning. One of the simplest game algorithms to implement is the so called *chase algorithm* and its opposite, the *evade algorithm*. Basically, they make the game object either—wait for it—chase the player or evade the player. Of course, the game universe must be taken into consideration, and the player shouldn't try to phase through walls and such. Let's go through the process of how to make a creature chase the player.

The Chase

First, we need to know the locations of both objects. We have that because we have the coordinates of the player and the game object that's the enemy.

Next, we need to implement an algorithm that will make the enemy chase the player. Algorithm 13.1 does this.

Algorithm 13.1. The chase algorithm.

```
// Let px,py be the player's position and ex,ey be the
// enemy's position:

while(game is running)
        {
    ....game code

    // First the x component:
    if ex > px then ex=ex+1
    if ex<px then   ex=ex-1
    // Now the y component:
    if ey>py then ey=ey+1
    if ey<py then ey=ey-1

    ...game code
    }
```

Algorithm 13.1 does exactly what we want it to:

■ If the player is to the right of the enemy—that is, if the player's x-coordinate is greater—the enemy increments its own x position by one and moves in the direction of the player.

■ The same logic is applied to the y-coordinate.

When this algorithm runs, the enemy chases down the player much the same way a T1000 would: *relentlessly*. It doesn't stop until it catches the player. We could ease it up a little by adding some extra logic to relax its tracking a bit. However, before we do that let's take a look at a program that implements the chasing. The program in Listing 13.1 creates two dots: one blue (you) and one red (the computer). The red dot chases you down no matter what you do. To move (or, I should say, run!) press the U key for up, the N key for down, the H key for left, and the J key for right. To exit the program, press the Q key.

Listing 13.1. The Terminator (term.c).

```
// I N C L U D E S/////////////////////////////////////////////

#include <stdio.h>
#include <graph.h>


// G L O B A L S ///////////////////////////////////////////////

unsigned int far *clock = (unsigned int far *)0x0000046C;
    // pointer to internal timekeeper
    // 18.2 clicks/sec
```

```
/////////////////////////////////////////////////////////////////

void Timer(int clicks)
{
// This function uses the internal timekeeper (the one that runs
// at 18.2 clicks/sec to time a delay). You can find the 32-bit
// value of this timer at 0000:046Ch.

unsigned int now;

// Get current time.

now = *clock;

// Wait until time has gone past current time plus the amount we
// wanted to wait. Note: each click is approximately 55
// milliseconds.

while(abs(*clock - now) < clicks){}

} // end Timer

// M A I N /////////////////////////////////////////////////////

void main(void)
{
int px=160,py=100, // Starting position of player.
    ex=0,ey=0;      // Starting position of enemy.

int done=0; // exit flag

_setvideomode(_MRES256COLOR);
printf("      The Terminator - Q to Quit");

// Main game loop

while(!done)
    {
    // Erase dots

    _setcolor(0);

    _setpixel(px,py);
    _setpixel(ex,ey);

    // Move player

    if (kbhit())
        {
        // Which way is player moving?

        switch(getch())
            {

                case 'u': // Up
                    {
                    py-=2;
```

continues

Listing 13.1. continued

```
                        } break;

            case 'n': // Down
                    {
                py+=2;
                    } break;

            case 'j': // Right
                    {
                px+=2;
                    } break;

            case 'h': // Left
                    {
                px-=2;
                    } break;

            case 'q':
                    {
                    done=1;
                    } break;
            } // end switch
        } // end if player hit a key
    // move enemy

    // Begin brain

    if (px>ex) ex++;
    if (px<ex) ex - ;
    if (py>ey) ey++;
    if (py<ey) ey - ;

    // End brain

    // Draw dots:
    _setcolor(9);
    _setpixel(px,py);
    _setcolor(12);
    _setpixel(ex,ey);

    // Wait a bit...
    Timer(2);

    } // end while

_setvideomode(_DEFAULTMODE);

} // end main
```

Listing 13.1 shows how simple it is to implement a seemingly complex intelligence response. This proves that a few lines of code can go a long way when it comes to implementing intelligence.

Evasion

While we're at it, we might as well complete the discussion with the converse of chasing: evasion. To make the creature evade the player, we would do the exact opposite of what we did to chase the player. Algorithm 13.2 outlines this.

Algorithm 13.2. The evasion algorithm.

```
// Let px,py be the player's position and ex,ey be the
// enemy's position.

while(game is running)
        {
    ....game code

    // First the x component:
    if ex > px then ex=ex-1
    if ex<px then   ex=ex+1
    // Now the y component:
    if ey>py then ey=ey-1
    if ey<py then ey=ey+1

    ...game code
    }
```

At this point it should start to sink in that games don't think; they simply act and react to the player and to the environment. (Some scientists say that humans are nothing more then a complex set of actions and reactions...)

On to the next topic: patterns.

Patterned Thoughts

In the early days of video games, programmers were in too much trouble trying to plot dots on the screen to be worried about simulating good combat tactics and writing complex algorithms to control the creatures in the universe. Alas, they thought they could simulate intelligent behavior with *patterns*, that is, by digitizing the motions of the creatures and having the creatures "play back" these motions. For example, in the game Galaxian the little bugs do a few circles, fire at you a few times, and then take their place in the flock of other Galaxians. Take a look at Figure 13.1.

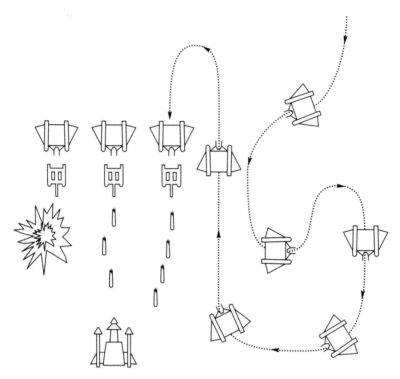

Figure 13.1. *A Galaxian following a pattern.*

When they execute these motions, they're simply following the commands of prerecorded patterns.

Implementing patterns is quite easy, and they find use in many scenarios. As an example, let's use patterns and a random number to implement a brain that could be used to control a little spaceship. The spaceship tries to evade you while trying to get a clear shot at you at the same time. What we could do is implement Algorithm 13.3.

Algorithm 13.3. Patterns with a random selector.

```
// Let pattern be an array that holds the translational
// information for ten different patterns:

while(game is running)
      {
    ...game code

        // Is the creature done with current pattern?
```

```
if (creature is done with pattern)
        {
    // Select a new pattern.
    current_pattern  = pattern[rand()%10]
    }

creature's position = old position + next element in current pattern

increment pattern index
...game code
  }
```

Algorithm 13.3 seems more complex than the previous chase-and-evade algorithms, but actually it's not. In essence:

- We select a pattern at random.

- We then move the creature every game cycle in the direction the pattern indicates.

- We then move to the next element in the pattern. Each pattern may consist of a different number of elements. Some patterns may have 10 elements, some may have 1,000. However, when the creature is done with the pattern, it would select another.

- Finally, we could have the random number generated with some coupling logic to another algorithm, such as Algorithm 13.1.

Now, as you can see in that last step, there's a facet of Algorithm 13.3 that makes it more complex: it has a two-stage thought process. A random number is input into the pattern selector, which then gives the creature a new pattern to "play." We can think of the random number as a synapse and the pattern a result of the synapse. Take a look at Figure 13.2 to see the input/output relationship of which I speak.

The brain could work by testing the distance to the player: if the creature is outside a certain radius, it chases the player. However, when the creature gets close enough, it starts performing patterns using a randomly selected pattern. This is handled by Algorithm 13.4.

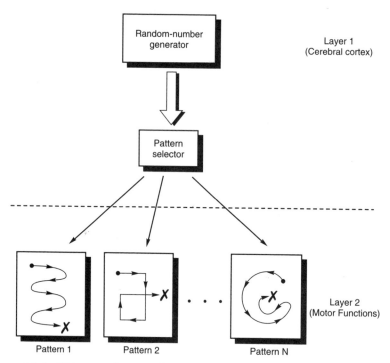

Figure 13.2. *Using random numbers to select patterns.*

Algorithm 13.4. Chasing and dancing.

```
while(game is running)
     {
    ...game code

    if (player is within 50 pixels) then chase player
    else
    select a random pattern and execute it

    ...game code
     }
```

To show you an example of patterns in action, I've rewritten the original chase program shown in Listing 13.1 to do exactly what Algorithm 13.4 says. The new program is shown in Listing 13.2. When the enemy dot gets close to the player (you), the enemy dot selects one of three patterns and executes it until the pattern is complete. Then the dot either chases the player or selects another pattern, depending in its distance.

Listing 13.2. The Fly (fly.c).

```c
// I N C L U D E S //////////////////////////////////////////////

#include <stdio.h>
#include <graph.h>
#include <math.h>

// G L O B A L S /////////////////////////////////////////////////

unsigned int far *clock = (unsigned int far *)0x0000046C;
    // pointer to internal timekeeper
    // 18.2 clicks/sec


// The x and y components of the patterns that will be played.
// (I just made them up.)

int patterns_x[3][20]= { 1,1,1,1,1,2,2,-1,-2,-3,-1,
                   0,0,1,2,2,-2,-2,-1,0,
                   0,0,1,2,3,4,5,4,3,2,1,3,3,3,3,3,
                   2,1,-2,-2,-1,
                   0,-1,-2,-3,-3,-2,-2,
                   0,0,0,0,0,0,1,0,0,0,1,0,1 };

int patterns_y[3][20] = { 0,0,0,0,-1,-1,-1,-1,-1,
                   0,0,0,0,0,2,2,2,2,2,2,
                   1,1,1,1,1,1,2,2,2,2,2,2,
                   3,3,3,3,3,0,0,0,0,
                   1,1,1,2,2,-1,-1,-1,-2,-2,
                   -1,-1,0,0,0,1,1,1,1,1 };


//////////////////////////////////////////////////////////////////

void Timer(int clicks)
{
// This function uses the internal timekeeper (the one that runs
// at 18.2 clicks/sec to time a delay). You can find the 32-bit
// value of this timer at 0000:046Ch.

unsigned int now;

// Get current time

now = *clock;

// Wait until time has gone past current time plus the amount we
// wanted to wait. Note: each click is approximately 55
// milliseconds.

while(abs(*clock - now) < clicks){}

} // end Timer

// M A I N //////////////////////////////////////////////////////
```

continues

Listing 13.2. continued

```c
void main(void)
{

int px=160,py=100, // Starting position of player.
    ex=0,ey=0;      // Starting position of enemy.

int done=0,            // Exit flag.
    doing_pattern=0,   // Flags if a pattern is being executed.
    current_pattern,   // Current pattern 0-2 that's being done
                       // by brain.
    pattern_element;   // Current element of pattern being
                       // executed.

_setvideomode(_MRES256COLOR);

printf("        The Fly - Q to Quit");

// Main game loop

while(!done)
    {
    // Erase dots

    _setcolor(0);

    _setpixel(px,py);
    _setpixel(ex,ey);

    // Move player

    if (kbhit())
        {

        // Which way is player moving?

        switch(getch())
            {

            case 'u': // Up
                    {
                    py-=2;
                    } break;

            case 'n': // Down
                    {
                    py+=2;
                    } break;

            case 'j': // Right
                    {
                    px+=2;
                    } break;


            case 'h': // Left
                    {
```

```
                    px-=2;
                        } break;

            case 'q':
                    {
                    done=1;
                    } break;

        } // end switch

    } // end if player hit a key

// Move enemy

// Begin brain

if (!doing_pattern)
    {

    if (px>ex) ex++;
    if (px<ex) ex—;
    if (py>ey) ey++;
    if (py<ey) ey—;

    // Check whether it's time to do a pattern (that is, is
    // enemy within 50 pixels of player?)

    if (sqrt(.1 + (px-ex)*(px-ex) + (py-ey)*(py-ey)) < 15)
        {
        // Never ever use a SQRT in a real game!

        // Get a new random pattern.

        current_pattern = rand()%3;

        // Set brain into pattern state.

        doing_pattern = 1;

        pattern_element = 0;

        } // end if within a radius of 50

    } // end if doing a pattern
else
    {
    // Move the enemy using the next pattern element of the
    // current pattern.

    ex+=patterns_x[current_pattern][pattern_element];
    ey+=patterns_y[current_pattern][pattern_element];

    // Are we done doing pattern?

    if (++pattern_element==20)
        {
```

continues

Listing 13.2. continued

```
            pattern_element = 0;
            doing_pattern = 0;
            } // end if done doing pattern

     } // end else do pattern

   // end brain

   // draw dots

   _setcolor(9);
   _setpixel(px,py);

   _setcolor(12);
   _setpixel(ex,ey);

   // Wait a bit...

   Timer(1);

   } // end while

_setvideomode(_DEFAULTMODE);

} // end main
```

When you run the program in Listing 13.2, you see why I named it "The Fly." The dot seems to come alive with the personality of a fly. It comes toward you and then flies around you rapidly. This intelligence and response was created by a few lines of code with some very basic concepts. (Hmmm; do you think, maybe, that people *are* just a bunch of actions and reactions?)

Let's continue our discussion by taking a random walk.

Random Walks

What I mean by *random walks* is doing something randomly just as we did in Listing 13.2. However, we can extend this concept not only to selecting responses, but to being a response itself. There's no reason we can't add one more type of behavior to our fly brain, that being random motion.

Random motion is used in the brains of many video games as one of the responses a virtual enemy can take. This topic has recently been celebrated in the mainstream under the heading "fuzzy logic." *Fuzzy logic* refers to selecting a solution without all the information, or without any of the information at all.

In a video game we can use random variables and fuzzy logic to select the trajectories or actions of our creatures. For instance, when you're faced with a decision such as walking around an obstacle that's in the middle of your path, do you avoid it by walking around to the right or to the left? All else being equal, the decision is rather random and is, therefore, a "fuzzy decision." If someone later asked you why you chose the solution you did, you wouldn't really have a good answer. In any case, we can use a random variable to select a direction for our little fly to move in. Algorithm 13.5 makes the little dot, which has now been deemed a fly, move in random directions:

Algorithm 13.5. Random walking.

```
while(game is running)
     {
    ..game code

     if (dot is done with current trajectory) then
        {
        select a new trajectory; that is, select a new
                translation factor for X and Y
        }
     move the dot a few times with the new trajectory

     .. game code
     }
```

Algorithm 13.5 implements a crude brain that selects a random direction and then moves the fly in that direction. Let's write a program that creates a lone dot (a fly) in a world by itself with this brain. Check out Listing 13.3.

Listing 13.3. A Dumb Fly. (dfly.c).

```
//I N C L U D E S/////////////////////////////////////////////

#include <stdio.h>
#include <graph.h>
#include <math.h>

// G L O B A L S ///////////////////////////////////////////////

unsigned int far *clock = (unsigned int far *)0x0000046C;
    // pointer to internal timekeeper
    // 18.2 clicks/sec.


////////////////////////////////////////////////////////////////

void Timer(int clicks)
```

continues

Listing 13.3. continued

```
{
// This function uses the internal timekeeper (the one that runs
// at 18.2 clicks/sec to time a delay). You can find the 32-bit
// value of this timer at 0000:046Ch.

unsigned int now;

// Get current time.

now = *clock;

// Wait until time has gone past current time plus the amount we
// wanted to wait. Note: each click is approximately 55
// milliseconds.

while(abs(*clock - now) < clicks){}

} // end Timer

// M A I N ///////////////////////////////////////////////////

void main(void)
{

int ex=160,ey=100; // Starting position of fly.

int curr_xv=1,curr_yv=0, // Current translation factors.
    clicks=0;               // Times when the fly is done moving in
                            // the random direction.

_setvideomode(_MRES256COLOR);

printf(" The Dumb Fly - Any Key to Quit");

// Main game loop

while(!kbhit())
    {
    // Erase dots

    _setcolor(0);

    _setpixel(ex,ey);

    // Move the fly

    // Begin brain

    // Are we done with this direction?

    if (++clicks==20)
        {
        curr_xv = -5 + rand()%10; // -5 to +5
        curr_yv = -5 + rand()%10; // -5 to +5
        clicks=0;
```

```
        } // end if time for a new direction

    // Move the fly

    ex+=curr_xv;
    ey+=curr_yv;

    // Make sure the fly stays on paper.

    if (ex>319) ex=0;
    if (ex<0)   ex=319;
    if (ey>199) ey=0;
    if (ey<0)   ey=199;

    // end brain

    // Draw fly

    _setcolor(12);
    _setpixel(ex,ey);

    // Wait a bit...

    Timer(1);

    } // end while
_setvideomode(_DEFAULTMODE);

} // end main
```

After watching Listing 13.3 execute, I think you'll agree that we've definitely got all we need to make a fly brain...That doesn't sound too impressive, but it really is quite amazing when you think about it. With a few simple rules, some patterns, and a couple random numbers we've created a reasonable simulation of an insect. I'm impressed!

OK, so you want more ? How's about a bit of finite-state machines?

Finite-State Machines

Finite-state machines (FSMs) are truly incredible machines. They exist totally in the virtual space of the computer. They're used in hardware design, software design, and even in genetic engineering. As far as we're concerned, an FSM is a machine, simulated in software, that moves from "state" to "state" based on some input. Moreover, the FSM remembers the state it's in at all times. Take a look at Figure 13.3 to see a diagram of a particular FSM. (What this one does doesn't matter for the moment.)

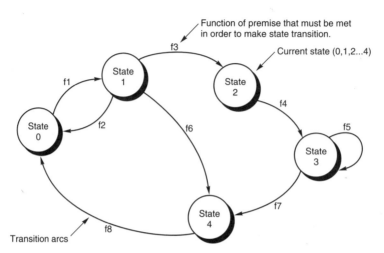

Figure 13.3. *A general finite-state machine.*

As you see, the FSM has a collection of states, represented by circles, and a set of arcs from state to state. These arcs show rules that denote what must occur to trigger a "transition" from one state to another using the arc in question.

FSMs can be used in video games as the "high-level" control logic that dictates the commands to the "low-level" logic. Just as each of our brains has a cerebral cortex that transmits our abstract will to the lower-level motor portions of our brain, an FSM can be used to initiate, control, and monitor the low-level actions being performed by the simulated brain.

As an example, we could take what we've already learned about chasing, evading, patterns, and random walks and implement an FSM that would move from state to state, where each state performs one of these functions. Now, we have a couple of decisions to make:

■ What will cause the state machine to change state?

■ How will the state machine select the next state?

These are good questions—and the stuff that video games are really made of. Before we address them, I want you to take a look at Figure 13.4 to see the abstract representation of our proposed FSM without the logic for state transitions in yet.

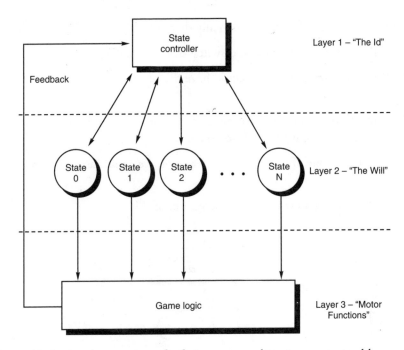

Figure 13.4. *An abstract view of a finite-state machine in a game world.*

An Environment-Driven FSM

Now, here comes the fun part! We can make the FSM make state transitions based on a set of variables that have to do with the game world. In other words, we control the FSM with the very environment it's in, just as our own brains act and react to our environments.

Let me put this another way. In a moment we look at an implementation of an FSM that uses random selection to select the next state from one of the following:

- Chase
- Evade
- Random
- Pattern

However, in a complete video game, we could instead use the "state" of the video game as input the FSM state control.

Here's an example of a environmentally driven FSM:

- If the player is near, we could switch over to the Pattern state.

- If the player isn't near, we could have the computer hunt him or her down using the Chase state.

- If the player was firing a barrage of bullets at our poor little computer creature, we could switch it to the Evade state.

- Finally, if none of those premises was met, we could just switch over to the Random state.

Figure 13.5 shows a graphical representation of this.

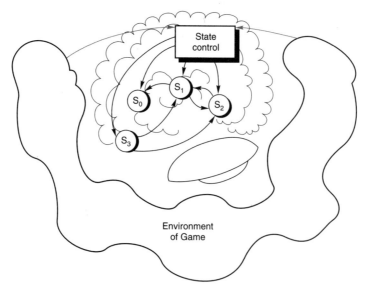

Figure 13.5. *A finite-state machine being driven by its own environmental aspects.*

As I said, I want to show you an FSM that changes state based on factors in its environment. In our case, we don't have much of a game world to work with: just a blank screen and a couple dots. However, it will get the point across. The program in Listing 13.4 uses an FSM and implements a really annoying fly that bugs the player. Note how the current state is displayed at the bottom of the screen.

Listing 13.4. A Brainy Fly (bfly.c).

```c
// I N C L U D E S///////////////////////////////////////////

#include <stdio.h>
#include <graph.h>
#include <math.h>

// D E F I N E S ///////////////////////////////////////////

#define STATE_CHASE    1
#define STATE_RANDOM   2
#define STATE_EVADE    3
#define STATE_PATTERN  4

// G L O B A L S ///////////////////////////////////////////

unsigned int far *clock = (unsigned int far *)0x0000046C;
    // pointer to internal timekeeper
    // 18.2 clicks/sec


// The x and y components of the patterns that will be played.
// (I just made them up.)

int patterns_x[3][20]= { 1,1,1,1,1,2,2,-1,-2,-3,-1,0,0,1,2,2,-2,-2,-1,0,
                         0,0,1,2,3,4,5,4,3,2,1,3,3,3,3,2,1,-2,-2,-1,
                         0,-1,-2,-3,-3,-2,-2,0,0,0,0,0,0,1,0,0,0,1,0,1 };


int patterns_y[3][20] = { 0,0,0,0,-1,-1,-1,-1,-1,
                          0,0,0,0,0,2,2,2,2,2,2,
                          1,1,1,1,1,1,2,2,2,2,2,
                          3,3,3,3,3,0,0,0,0,
                          1,1,1,2,2,-1,-1,-1,-2,-2,
                          -1,-1,0,0,0,1,1,1,1,1 };

//////////////////////////////////////////////////////////////

void Timer(int clicks)
{
// This function uses the internal timekeeper (the one that runs
// at 18.2 clicks/sec to time a delay). You can find the 32-bit
// value of this timer at 0000:046Ch.

unsigned int now;

// Get current time

now = *clock;

// Wait until time has gone past current time plus the amount we
// wanted to wait. Note: each click is approximately 55
// milliseconds.

while(abs(*clock - now) < clicks){}
```

continues

Listing 13.4. continued

```c
} // end Timer

// M A I N /////////////////////////////////////////////////////

void main(void)
{

int px=160,py=100,    // Starting position of player.
    ex=0,ey=0,        // Starting position of enemy.
    curr_xv,curr_yv;  // Velocity of fly during random walk.


int done=0,           // Exit flag.
    doing_pattern=0,  // Flags if a pattern is being executed.
    current_pattern,  // Current pattern 0-2 that is being done
                      // by brain.
    pattern_element,  // Current element of pattern being
                      // executed.
    select_state=0,   // Flags whether a state transition must
                      // take place.
    clicks=20,        // Used to time the number of cycles a
                      // state stays active.
    fly_state = STATE_CHASE;  // Start fly off in chase state.

float distance;       // Used to hold distance between fly and
                      // player.

_setvideomode(_MRES256COLOR);

printf("     Brainy Fly - Q to Quit");

// Main game loop

while(!done)
    {
    // Erase dots

    _setcolor(0);

    _setpixel(px,py);
    _setpixel(ex,ey);

    // Move player

    if (kbhit())
       {

       // Which way is player moving?

       switch(getch())
           {
               case 'u': // Up
                     {
                   py-=2;
```

```
                        } break;

            case 'n': // Down
                    {
                py+=2;
                    } break;

            case 'j': // Right
                    {
                px+=2;
                    } break;


            case 'h': // Left
                    {
                px-=2;
                    } break;

            case 'q':
                    {
                    done=1;
                    } break;

            } // end switch

    } // end if player hit a key


// Move enemy

// Begin brain

// What state is brain in? Let FSM sort it out.


switch(fly_state)
        {

        case STATE_CHASE:
                {
                _settextposition(24,2);
                printf("current state:chase   ");

                // Make the fly chase the player.

                if (px>ex) ex++;
                if (px<ex) ex—;
                if (py>ey) ey++;
                if (py<ey) ey—;

                // Time to go to another state.

                if (—clicks==0)
                   select_state=1;

                } break;
```

continues

Listing 13.4. continued

```
case STATE_RANDOM:
    {
    _settextposition(24,2);
    printf("current state:random  ");

    // Move fly in random direction.

    ex+=curr_xv;
    ey+=curr_yv;

    // Time to go to another state.

    if (—clicks==0)
        select_state=1;

    } break;


case STATE_EVADE:
    {
    _settextposition(24,2);
    printf("current state:evade  ");


    // Make fly run from player.

    if (px>ex) ex—;
    if (px<ex) ex++;
    if (py>ey) ey—;
    if (py<ey) ey++;

    // Time to go to another state.

    if (—clicks==0)
        select_state=1;

    } break;

case STATE_PATTERN:
    {
    _settextposition(24,2);
    printf("current state:pattern  ");

    // Move the enemy using the next pattern element
    // of the current pattern.

    ex+=patterns_x[current_pattern][pattern_element];
    ey+=patterns_y[current_pattern][pattern_element];

    // Are we done doing pattern?

    if (++pattern_element==20)
        {
        pattern_element = 0;
        select_state=1;
        } // end if done doing pattern
```

```
        } break;


default:break;

} // end switch fly state

// Does brain want another state?

if (select_state==1)
   {

   // Select a state based on the environment and on
   // fuzzy logic.
   // Uses distance from player to selct a new state.

   distance =
 sqrt(.5+fabs((px-ex)*(px-ex)+(py-ey)*(py-ey)));

   if (distance > 5 && distance <15 && rand()%2==1)
      {
      // Get a new random pattern.

      current_pattern = rand()%3;

      // Set brain into pattern state.

      fly_state = STATE_PATTERN;

      pattern_element = 0;

      } // end if close to player
   else
   if (distance < 10) // too close let's run!
      {
      clicks=20;
      fly_state = STATE_EVADE;

      } // else if too close
   else
   if (distance > 25 && distance <100 && rand()%3==1)
      // Let's chase the player.
      {
      clicks=15;
      fly_state = STATE_CHASE;

      }  // end if chase player
   else
   if (distance > 30 && rand()%2==1)
      {
      clicks=10;
      fly_state = STATE_RANDOM;

      curr_xv = -5 + rand()%10; // -5 to +5
      curr_yv = -5 + rand()%10; // -5 to +5

      } // end if random
```

continues

Listing 13.4. continued

```
                else
                    {
                    clicks=5;
                    fly_state = STATE_RANDOM;

                    curr_xv = -5 + rand()%10; // -5 to +5
                    curr_yv = -5 + rand()%10; // -5 to +5

                    } // end else

                // Reset need another state flag.

                select_state=0;

                } // End if we need to change to another state.

        // Make sure fly stays on paper.

        if (ex>319) ex=0;
        if (ex<0)   ex=319;
        if (ey>199) ey=0;
        if (ey<0)   ey=199;

        // end brain

        // Draw dots

        _setcolor(9);
        _setpixel(px,py);

        _setcolor(12);
        _setpixel(ex,ey);

        // Wait a bit...

        Timer(1);

        } // end while

_setvideomode(_DEFAULTMODE);

} // end main
```

Play with Listing 13.4 and ponder its apparent complexity, keeping in mind the simple model it's derived from. Maybe you'll see, as I do, that the human mind is not beyond our grasp; we've just been approaching it in the wrong way.

Preemptive State Control

There's one more dimension we can add to FSMs: *preemptive state control.* This means changing states before a state is complete, based on some variable or function. In the fly simulation, each state executes until completion. We could add the condition that, if enough factors were met during the execution of a state, the FSM would "jump" out of the state.

This concludes our discussion of FSMs. They can be used in your video games to make the creatures in your universe seem highly intelligent and lifelike.

Now that we have a high-level control system, let's keep adding to the low-level functionality.

Probability Machines

We've already seen how probability and random numbers can be used to select directions, states, and whatever else we think up for them. We have been using random numbers in a crude manner to implement personalities. By *personalities* I mean that the fly in our previous example would select different states, based on its environment and a random number. If we were to change the random-number part of the selection (that is, if we were to make it either harder or easier to select a certain state), we would, in essence, be changing the personality of the fly.

For instance, say we wanted to have two flies in a game. If we used the same code for the brain of each fly, they would act in the same way. In many cases, this would be fine. However, it'd be much more interesting to have many flies, each with a slightly different personality. Implementing this would change the size of the random number in each one of the lines of code that selects a random number—but this is crude, and a hacker's approach. What we want to do is create a general method of implementing personalities using probability.

In our context, *personality* means the chances of a creature performing a certain action under certain conditions. As an example, I have friends who are pretty aggressive and would punch your lights out if you rubbed them the wrong way. On the other hand, I have friends who are more passive and would probably try to talk instead of fight. What we see here is "personality." How it works is unimportant; the end result—the final result—is all that matters.

In video games, we might have enemies that like to chase you a lot, while others may like to sit still and fire. Still others may prefer to run rather than fight. Analyzing the situation, we see that only a few states exist, but the probability of entering a state is different for each creature. To implement this, we would refer to a *probability table* during the portion of the code that selects a new state. This probability table would contain the various probabilities pertaining to the actions of the creature in question.

These probabilities would be used along with the environment to select a new state. For example, take a look at Table 13.1 to see a group of probabilities for three different enemies in a game.

Table 13.1. Probability distributions for three enemies in a game.

State	Creature 1: Annihilator
Attack	50%
Evade	5%
Random	10%
Flock	20%
Pattern	15%

State	Creature 2: Brainiac
Attack	20%
Evade	30%
Random	20%
Flock	20%
Pattern	10%

State	Creature 3: Wimpoid
Attack	5%
Evade	60%
Random	20%
Flock	10%
Pattern	5%

As you can see from the probability distributions, Annihilator does a lot of attacking and Wimpoid does a lot of running away. Brainiac is a cross between these.

Before moving on to how to implement these probabilities, I want to talk about another state that you should have noticed: Flock. Flock causes the creatures in the game to flock together and try to group up; for example, the way real soldiers or insects sometimes want to group together and stay close. This is really nothing more than everyone (that is, all game objects) selecting a common meeting point and heading toward it. We can use this as another state, so that sometimes the creatures seem to group together.

Implementing this new state is simple:

- Select the creatures you want to flock together.

- Take the average of all their positions. This point in space is the *centroid*, and can be used to compute the trajectories for all the objects to follow.

- Compute trajectories so that each creature heads toward the centroid.

This will keep the group together. You could go into the Flock state when too many of the computer-generated bad guys were getting flamed. You could, possibly, make them close ranks and turn the tables against the player. Take a look a Figure 13.6 to see a geometrical representation of flocking.

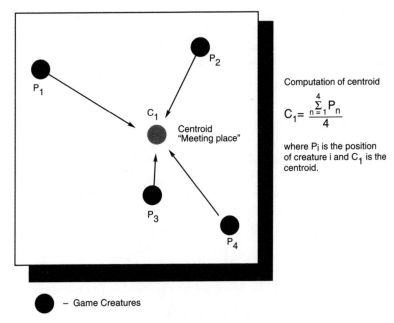

Computation of centroid

$$C_1 = \frac{\sum\limits_{n=1}^{4} P_n}{4}$$

where P_i is the position of creature i and C_1 is the centroid.

Figure 13.6. *A geometrical view of flocking.*

Now on to how we would implement probability look-up tables. Let's take another look at our game brain at this point, shown in Figure 13.7.

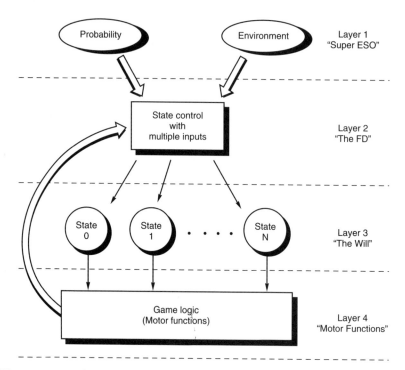

Figure 13.7. *The evolution of our game brain.*

We have the high-level state control starting up new states based on the environment and a probability. This new state is "acted out" by the low-level state control, which is (in essence) analogous to the motor portion of your brain. Now we're going to add another level to the brain. This new level overlaps slightly with, but is at a higher level than, state control. This new level takes into consideration both the environment and a probability distribution. A separate probability distribution can exist for each creature so that, with the same overall brain architecture, we can extract many different personalities.

There are about a billion ways to implement probability look-up tables. This just happens to be the way I like doing it when coupled to finite-state machines:

■ First, you must enumerate all the states you'll have in you game. For example, let's use the ones we already have. They are:

1	Chase
2	Evade
3	Random
4	Pattern

| 5 | Flock |
| 6 | Motionless |

(I've added the state Motionless, which does exactly what you would think. This may seem like a boring state, but it makes the enemy look like it's thinking or waiting for the player to make a move—that is, it creates tension and suspense.)

■ At this point, we would come up with the environmental variables that drive our decisions. Let's pick two variables to help select the different states:

Distance from player
State of the player's weapon: firing or not

■ We then need to build up the probability tables. To do this we fill arrays with the numbers 1-6, which represent the different states. We'll make the tables 20 elements long.

To select a state, we index into the table with a random number, from 0-19. Of course, when we select a random number as shown here:

```
sel = rand()%20
```

the numbers from 0-19 are equally likely. How do we make the states come up more often or less often? Well, what you do is fill the table with the distribution you wish. For instance, if you wanted 50 percent chasing, you would place ten 1s in the table. If you wanted a 20 percent chance of flocking, you would place four 5s in the table. Your table would start to look like this:

```
int table_1[20] = {1,1,1,1,1,1,1,1,1,1,5,5,5,5,...the rest of the states};
```

To put this mathematically: we're using a random variable that has equal distribution from 0-19 to index into a table that represents a skewed-probability density function, where the element indexed is the next state.

I hope you get that—but if you don't, at least it sounds cool!

Now that you see the form of the look-up tables, we can talk about state selection. As we saw in the Brainy Fly program (Listing 13.4), the distance from the player was used along with a random number to select the next state. We're going to do pretty much the same thing here. We'll use the distance along with the state of the player's weapon to select one of two probability densities: one is used when enemies are far away, and the other is used when they're closer.

For this example only one personality is used by all the enemies, but adding more personalities is as easy as making more tables. The algorithm for the new brain is shown in Algorithm 13.6.

Algorithm 13.6. Using probability densities in state selection.

```
table_1 = {1,1,1,2,2,3,3,4,4,4,4,4,5,5,5,5,6,6,6,6}
table_2 = {1,1,2,2,2,2,3,3,3,3,3,3,4,4,5,5,5,5,5,6}

While(game is running)
      {
    ...game code
    if (executing a state then continue with state}
          {
          ..do state
      }
    else  // Select a new state.
      {
    if (distance between player and enemy is > 100)
            {
            new state = table_1[rand()%20];
            }
        else
            {
        if (distance between player and enemy is < 100
            and player is shooting at enemy)
              {
              new state = table_2[rand()%20];
              }
          else  // Just pick a random state.
              {
              new state = rand()%7;
              }
          } // end else
      } // end else select new state
    } // end main while
```

Algorithm 13.6 will probably do very weird things, but I guarantee it will do something interesting. If you tweak the probabilities and tune it up, you'll be able to get quite a good response. You can then add more IF statements, more environmental cues and, finally, more probability tables to increase the number of personalities of your game creatures.

Anyway, let's keep moving. The next few topics we talk about are part of what I call the "esoteric collection." They're interesting, but are not being used much in the games of today. Hopefully, the games of tomorrow will take full advantage of these advanced concepts.

Memory and Learning

If I were to define memory and learning, I'd probably say they're the ability to use past experience to solve new problems, along with the ability to consume and interpret new information. It's possible to make the creatures in our games "learn" and "memorize" in a crude manner. All we need to do is keep track of certain variables and use these in our state selection and motor functions.

For instance, we could allow each creature in the game to have an internal map of the game grid. If the creature had been in the room before and found that there were a lot of his dead friends there, we might turn up his aggressiveness the next time he went into the room. As another example, if during the creature's combat with the player the player kept moving to the left and then firing, the game creatures could learn this by counting how many times the player moved in each direction. The direction the player moved in most could be used against him or her, as the creature used this information to improve its own tactics.

These are only a couple examples of what memory and learning can be used for. However, anything *you* can remember in a game, you can probably make the game remember about you and use it against the player. Does that seem a little self destructive? Hmmmm—that's all I'm going to say, I forgot the rest...

Search Algorithms...Tracking Down the Player

The brains we've been building are getting fairly advanced, and we could probably give an insect or maybe even a slug a run for the money. However, now I want to cover a simple topic: how searches should be done.

Do you remember the story about Theseus and the Minotaur? Well, there was a Minotaur (a man with a bull's head) who was chasing Theseus. Theseus stole the Minotaur's CD player or something. Anyway, Theseus was trapped in a maze (actually the contractor who built it, named Daedalus, called it a labyrinth) with the Minotaur and had to get out before the Minotaur got him. The question is, how should someone go about finding his or her way out of a maze, or even finding the way to a point in the maze without getting trapped forever? Take a look at Figure 13.8 to see a sample maze.

There's a simple algorithm, shown here as Algorithm 13.7, that will help you find your way out of any maze.

Pay close attention; you may need it someday!

Start

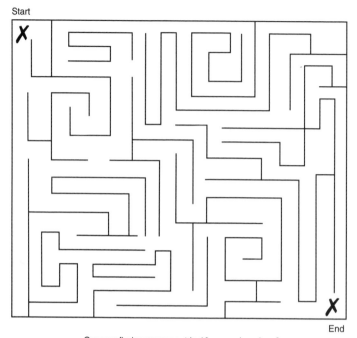

End

Can you find your way out in 10 seconds or less?

Figure 13.8. *A sample maze.*

Algorithm 13.7. The Way Out.

```
Do
    {
    move forward keeping the wall on your right
    if you come to a junction turn right
    if you come to a dead end turn completely around
    } until out of maze;
```

This algorithm works perfectly: try it in your house! Start at any point in the house and follow the algorithm. You'll eventually find your way to every door in the house.

As far as we're concerned in video games, we can use this algorithm (or a modification of it) to help the creatures in the game track down the player while avoiding the walls and such. (Or, of course, we could just cheat and let the creatures "phase" right through all the walls!) The algorithm could have a problem if there are circular-shaped objects in the room that can be traveled down. However, we could avoid this case, or add logic to take care of it.

Game Theory

The next topic isn't too closely related to action video games, but is more related to strategy games like chess. However, I want to at least cover it in some manner to give you some ideas.

Game Theory is a branch of mathematics that is, to put it lightly, *very* hard and *very* theoretical. It has to do with coming up with a set of rules, "the game," and computing the optimal solution or algorithm to winning the game. This is usually done with a ton of matrices, probability, and linear programming. However, we can extract from Game Theory a couple tidbits for our use.

In general, game theorists try to solve a problem by weighing their current position or state in the game, meaning they gauge how they're doing at a point in time and then try to improve their position. To do this in a computer:

- We first create some kind of objective function that would score or rate our current position.

- We then try a new tactic or position to see if making this new move would improve our position.

- If it does, we execute that move.

- If it doesn't, we try another.

This is exactly how a chess program works. The computer computes its own and its opponent's "scores," depending on the current position of the pieces, and then tries to select a move that will maximize its own score while minimizing its opponent's score. This "thought" process can actually go to many levels. The computer will test each possibility: "If I were to do this, then my opponent could do that; then if I did the other..." This can go and on—although human players can be beat if the computer only goes to "two ply," executing two iterations of action and reaction.

In video games this tactic can be used as a "very high-level" control of the lower-level brain functions. For instance, every minute or so the computer could count things up and decide how it's doing. If it's doing well, it would keep doing what it's doing. However, if things are amiss, maybe it's time for a change.

Summary

We covered a plethora of interesting topics in this chapter, and even implemented a small prototype brain that has many of the properties of a household fly. Using combinations of the techniques in this chapter, along with your own creativity, you should be able to create virtual brains that will give any player a run for the money. I do have a couple of suggestions, though:

■ Try to keep it simple.

■ Don't try to create a HAL 2000 your first time out. Shoot for something more like Robbie the Robot!

We've discussed some of the most state-of-the-art methods used in video games today. If you have an understanding of them, you'll be able to make games that will be as good as, or better than, anything out there. The industry has been moving toward dazzling graphics and sounds, and has been forgetting about the little detail of "game play." Hopefully, you'll be able to bring some brains and strategy into the next generation of games.

Linking Up

J ust as a single brain cell wouldn't make much headway in a chess game, a single player on a computer isn't very exciting. With recent advances in telecommunications, however, multiplayer video games are becoming more common. Today, many video games support two players over modems. In this chapter we begin to unravel the complexities of the PC's communications system and learn techniques to create serially linked, multiplayer video games. The following topics are communicated:

- Video game communications

- The PC's serial interface

- ROM BIOS routines

- Linking up with a null modem

- Building a communications library

- Video-game communication strategies

- State-vector synchronization

- I/O state synchronization

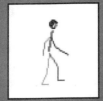

by André LaMothe

■ Temporal synchronization

■ The modem

■ Net-Tank: a two-player tank simulation on a circuit board

In this chapter we'd like to concentrate on the aspects of video-game design that have to be taken into consideration for multiplayer games, with as little emphasis on the communications medium itself as possible. Unfortunately, we don't have time to learn how to do full modem communications. However, we do learn how to communicate with a serial port over a null modem to another machine in the same room. With this knowledge and some late nights, you'll be able to communicate over a modem. You'll have all the elements you need and, with a little work, you should be able to get things working.

We want to learn how to write games that can be played on two or more computers simultaneously without getting out of sync and having problems. Therefore, the essence of this chapter is on communication tactics in video-game architecture and not on the physical communication link itself.

Video Game Communications

At this point in the book, you're ready to write a video game. You've learned just about everything you need to know, from beginning to end. However, there's one major area still missing: multiplayer video games.

This is a relatively new field that hasn't yet been explored to its fullest. There are video games that support modem communications, but most people either don't take advantage of this feature or feel it's too complex to get working. In any case, the canvas is still pretty open in this area, and there's lots of work to be done by video game programmers.

Because we're primarily concerned with writing video games for the consumer, we'll concentrate on using the serial port as our communications medium (and not network communications such as IPX/SPX and other obscure acronyms). I pick the serial port in deference to using Ethernet for two reasons:

■ First, everyone has a serial port.

■ Second, lots of people own modems, which is the primary way two-player games are played today.

When writing a video game for two or more players, we must design this aspect into the game from the very beginning. You cannot write an entire game and *then* at the end decide to make it a multiplayer game. Making two separate games run on two different computers and remain in synchronization takes a fair amount of work and planning.

As usual we can't count on anyone else writing the software we need to do the low-level dirty work, so we'll make it ourselves. (Get used to this; it's the way of the game-programming guru.) With that in mind, let's talk about the communication channel we'll be using for our discussions.

The PC's Serial Interface

The serial port(s) on the PC are implemented by a system comprised of many different components. As programmers, we need not be too concerned about its exact hardware implementation. We do, however, need to have some clue about how it works. Otherwise, we just won't be able to use it.

Before we get into a description of the PC's serial communications system, let's lay out the foundation of its capabilities we're interested in using in our video games.

PCs can support up to seven serial ports, although most PCs only have one or two. We can configure these serial ports to communicate at various baud rates, up to 115,200 baud. We can also select the type of parity, number of stop bits, number of data bits, and types of interrupts that we want serviced. (If you don't know what I'm talking about, just hold on for a minute more.)

Once we configure the port(s), we can have a conversation with another computer or device by writing to or reading from the serial port. The PC's hardware takes care of many of the details of transmitting and receiving data. All we have to do is supply the serial port with a character to send, or process a character that is waiting.

For video games, we'll primarily be sending packets of information that describe the state of the game to the other machine, and vice versa. These packets are based on standard characters, eight bits long. All we're really interested in, then, is how to open up a serial port, write characters to it, and read characters from it. Let's get down to business and see what the PC has to offer (incidentally clarifying some terms used a moment ago).

The UART

The PC is equipped with a *universal asynchronous receiver/transmitter* (UART), a chip that sends and receives serial data. There are two popular UARTS on PCs out there:

- The 8250
- The 16650

These are completely compatible from our standpoint, and we really don't care which one we're using. The only important difference between them is that the 16650 has an internal first-in, first out (FIFO) buffer that buffers incoming data so that, if the data isn't processed in a timely fashion, it isn't lost.

Now, let's look at each of the registers in the UART and how to access them. After that we undertake writing a complete serial library from scratch, one that can open a serial port, read from it, and write to it. Once we have this, we can concentrate on game topics.

UART Settings and Status

The UART settings and status are controlled through the use of a collection of internal registers. These registers are accessed as I/O ports that begin at a specific base address. The base address is based on the serial port with which you wish to communicate. Take a look at Table 14.1 to see these base addresses.

Table 14.1. UART control-register base addresses.

Serial Port	Base Port Address
COM1	3F8h
COM2	2F8h
COM3	3E8h
COM4	2E8h

As you can see, if we want to play with serial port number 1's registers we'd use 3F8h as the base of the I/O address. Each port has nine registers that can be written to or read from, depending on their type. Therefore, to access register 1 of COM1, you'd use the I/O address 3F8h plus 1, or 3F9h.

Now that we know where the registers can be found, what do each of the registers do?

Register 0: The Transmitter-Holding Register (THR)

Bit 7 6 5 4 3 2 1 0

| X | X | X | X | X | X | X | X |

The transmitter-holding register is where the next character to be transmitted is placed. If it's a single byte and you're using a transmission scheme that uses less than 8 bits, they will be ignored.

Register 0: The Receive-Buffer Register (RBR)

Bit 7 6 5 4 3 2 1 0

| X | X | X | X | X | X | X | X |

Register 0 also doubles as the receive-register buffer. Depending on whether you write to or read from this register, it's the transmit buffer or the receive buffer, respectively. In any case, if you read this register it contains the last character that was received.

Register 1: The Interrupt Enable Register (IER)

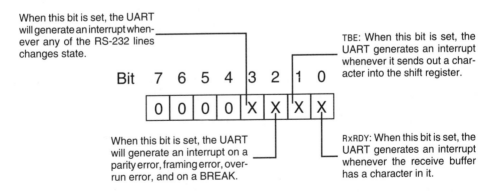

When this bit is set, the UART will generate an interrupt whenever any of the RS-232 lines changes state.

TBE: When this bit is set, the UART generates an interrupt whenever it sends out a character into the shift register.

Bit 7 6 5 4 3 2 1 0

| 0 | 0 | 0 | 0 | X | X | X | X |

When this bit is set, the UART will generate an interrupt on a parity error, framing error, overrun error, and on a BREAK.

RxRDY: When this bit is set, the UART generates an interrupt whenever the receive buffer has a character in it.

The receive buffer register is used to enable the type of interrupts that the UART can generate. It can either be read from or written to. When we set up the serial port, we don't want to poll the serial port all the time, so the common way of receiving input is to write an interrupt-service routine (ISR) that's called when a character has been received. This register allows us to tell the UART what events will generate an interrupt. In our case, we're only interested in the RxRDY interrupt, which is generated when a character has been received by the UART.

Register 2: The Interrupt-Identification Register (IIR)

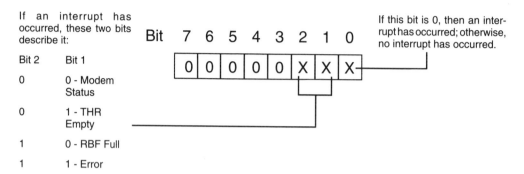

If an interrupt has occurred, these two bits describe it:

Bit 2	Bit 1	
0	0	- Modem Status
0	1	- THR Empty
1	0	- RBF Full
1	1	- Error

If this bit is 0, then an interrupt has occurred; otherwise, no interrupt has occurred.

The interrupt-identification register is used to determine what caused the UART to be interrupted. This may seem redundant. However, if you had previously set the UART to send an interrupt on two or more different actions, when an interrupt occurred you wouldn't have any way to tell which action actually caused the interrupt. This register qualifies what type of interrupt has occurred.

Register 3: The Line-Control Register (LCR)

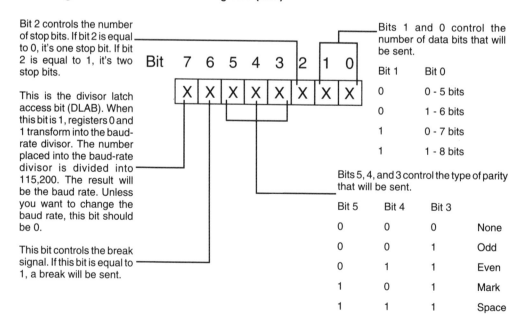

Bit 2 controls the number of stop bits. If bit 2 is equal to 0, it's one stop bit. If bit 2 is equal to 1, it's two stop bits.

This is the divisor latch access bit (DLAB). When this bit is 1, registers 0 and 1 transform into the baud-rate divisor. The number placed into the baud-rate divisor is divided into 115,200. The result will be the baud rate. Unless you want to change the baud rate, this bit should be 0.

This bit controls the break signal. If this bit is equal to 1, a break will be sent.

Bits 1 and 0 control the number of data bits that will be sent.

Bit 1	Bit 0	
0	0	- 5 bits
0	1	- 6 bits
1	0	- 7 bits
1	1	- 8 bits

Bits 5, 4, and 3 control the type of parity that will be sent.

Bit 5	Bit 4	Bit 3	
0	0	0	None
0	0	1	Odd
0	1	1	Even
1	0	1	Mark
1	1	1	Space

The line-control register is used to control some of the settings for the serial port, such as the number of data bits and the type of parity. This register also doubles as the baud-rate divisor latch, which is responsible for controlling both the low-and high-order bytes that comprise the final baud-rate divisor WORD. This register can be read from and written to.

Register 4: The Modem-Control Register (MCR)

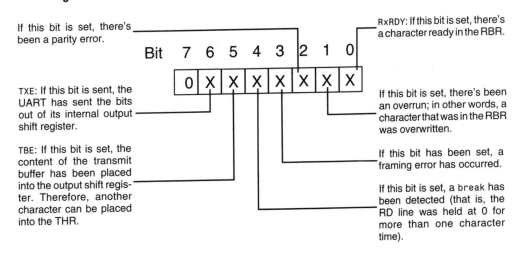

This bit enables local loopback. If this bit is set, the output of the UART is electronically connected back to the input.

This bit controls general-purpose output number 2 (GP02). It must be one for the UART to be able to send interrupts.

This bit controls the modem's data terminal ready (DTR) line. The DTR line will reflect this bits setting.

This bit controls the modem's request to send (RTS) line. The RTS line will reflect this bits setting.

This bit controls general-purpose output number 1 (GP01). It is used to reset various vendor defined functions on a modem.

The modem-control register controls some of the outputs on the modem control lines. However it's most important use as far as we're concerned is the GP02 bit. When set, this bit allows interrupts to occur.

Register 5: The Line-Status Register (LSR)

If this bit is set, there's been a parity error.

RxRDY: If this bit is set, there's a character ready in the RBR.

TXE: If this bit is sent, the UART has sent the bits out of its internal output shift register.

TBE: If this bit is set, the content of the transmit buffer has been placed into the output shift register. Therefore, another character can be placed into the THR.

If this bit is set, there's been an overrun; in other words, a character that was in the RBR was overwritten.

If this bit has been set, a framing error has occurred.

If this bit is set, a break has been detected (that is, the RD line was held at 0 for more than one character time).

The line-status register is used to figure out the status of the communications port. In our case, we're concerned with bit 5 (TBE) this status is used to determine whether we can place another character into the transmitter holding register.

Register 6: The Modem-Status Register (MSR)

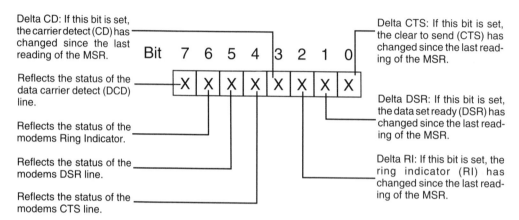

The modem-status register is used to figure out the status of the modem-control lines. In our case, we won't be using them. However, you might be able to find use for the ring indicator. You could write software that monitors it and, when your house is called, it detects that fact and does something (...like turning on a hidden camera?).

Register 7: The Scratch-Pad Register

The scratch-pad register is not used.

Register 8: The Baud-Rate Divisor Latch Least-Significant Byte (DLL)

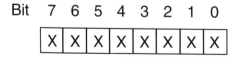

The baud-rate divisor latch least-significant byte register is used to hold the low byte of the divisor used to compute the actual baud rate of the serial port. The final baud rate is computed by taking the low byte and high byte and using them as a divisor to divide the number 115,200. The result is the baud rate. This register is accessed by having register 0 with bit 7 (DLAB) of the line-control register (LCR) set.

Register 9: The Baud-Rate Divisor Latch Most-Significant Byte (DLM)

```
Bit   7  6  5  4  3  2  1  0
    ┌──┬──┬──┬──┬──┬──┬──┬──┐
    │X │X │X │X │X │X │X │X │
    └──┴──┴──┴──┴──┴──┴──┴──┘
```

The baud-rate divisor most-significant byte register is used to hold the high byte of the divisor used to compute the actual baud rate of the serial port. The final baud rate is computed by taking the low byte and high byte and using them as a divisor to divide the number 115,200. The result is the baud rate. This register is accessed by having register 1 with bit 7 (DLAB) of the line-control register (LCR) set.

UART Hardware

Now that you've seen the software behind the UART, let's take a look at the hardware. The only thing we need to know is where to plug the cable in and how to make the physical connection.

PCs can have two types of serial ports:

- A nine-pin (DB 9 connector)
- A 25-pin (DB 25 connector)

Table 14.2 shows the pin out of both.

Table 14.2. The pin out for PC serial ports.

Pin	Function	Symbol
9-Pin Connector		
1	Carrier Detect	CD
2	Receive Data	RXD
3	Transmit Data	TXD
4	Data Terminal Ready	DTR
5	Signal Ground	GND
6	Data Set Ready	DSR

continues

Table 14.2. continued

Pin	Function	Symbol
7	Request To Send	RTS
8	Clear To Send	CTS
9	Ring Indicator RI	

25-Pin Connector

Pin	Function	Symbol
2	Transmit Data	TXD
3	Receive Data	RXD
4	Request To Send	RTS
5	Clear To Send	CTS
6	Data Set Ready	DSR
7	Signal Ground	GND
8	Carrier Detect	CD
20	Data Terminal Ready	DTR
22	Ring Indicator	RI

The ROM BIOS Routines

Before we move on to writing our own serial communications system, let's stop and see if ROM BIOS could be of service. The BIOS does support serial communication, although in a limited way. The functions are accessed through interrupt 14h. There are functions to open a serial port, configure it, read a character, and write a character. There's just one little problem: they don't work! (I can't believe it, but they really don't work.) Well, they work under specific conditions, but for what we need they'll hardly suffice. For one thing, there isn't any support for interrupt-driven I/O, which in our case is an absolute necessity.

We can't be sitting around polling everything. We must have interrupt-driven event systems in video games. Because of that factor, and the small detail that the BIOS routines barely even work, we can summarily dismiss them as a feasible solution to blasting bits across the wire.

Now that I've said that, let's move on to linking up two PCs and creating a small, networked game.

Linking Up with a Null Modem

As I said in the beginning, we won't have enough time to go into all the details of using the modem to link our game up. There are just too many subjects we'd have to touch upon, all of them having little to do with video-game design. What I've decided to do instead is create a communication system that uses a null-modem connection; that is, no modem at all. A *null modem* is simply a connection made from one serial port of one computer to the serial port of another computer. Figure 14.1 shows a null-modem connection.

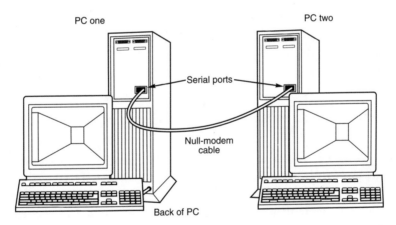

Figure 14.1. *Linking up two PCs.*

To make this connection, we must make a null-modem cable with the proper gender connectors. This can be a bit tricky but, if you're careful, it'll work on the first try. We'll be using only three pins of the connector:

■ The transmit data line

■ The receive data line

■ The ground

Take a look at Figure 14.2 to see how to make a null-modem cable for your particular type of connectors.

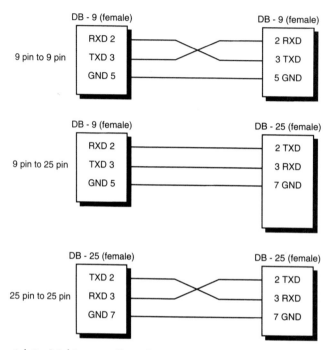

Figure 14.2. *Making a null-modem cable for various serial connectors.*

If you don't want to make a null-modem cable, you can purchase one from almost any computer store. (Please don't pay more than $15.00, though. I hate seeing people get ripped off for $1.50 of wire and plastic!) Now, an official null-modem cable and connection uses more than the three pins I described. It uses all of them, thereby simulating a modem being connected. However, we aren't interested in simulating connected modems. As long as we have the TXD, RXD, and ground lines, we're in business. (The extra lines are used for hardware handshaking, and we aren't going to be using them.)

All right, we have a null-modem cable and we know what registers do what in the UART. I think it's time to start writing the communications software.

Building a Communications Library

We are not going to need many functions in our library. In fact, we only need six. Roughly, we only need functions that:

- Initialize the serial port.
- Install an interrupt service routine (ISR).
- Read a character from the serial port.
- Write a character to the serial port.
- Get the status of the port.
- Close the serial port.

They all look reasonable, so let's discuss them one by one.

Initializing a Serial Port

The steps we must take are as follows:

- First, we set the number of bits, the number of stop bits, and the parity. This is done with the line control register (LCR) number 3.
- Next, we set the baud rate with the baud rate least-significant and most-significant divisor latches.
- Next, we set the UART up to handle interrupts.
- We then must tell the PC's programmable interrupt controller (PIC) chip that it should allow the serial-port interrupts.
- Finally, we activate the proper serial interrupt at bit 3 or 4, (being careful not to mess up the interrupt mask register).

Now let's discuss these steps in detail.

To initialize the port we must first set the number of bits, the number of stop bits, and the parity. This is done with the line control register (LCR) number 3.

Next, we set the baud rate with the baud rate least-significant and most-significant divisor latches. This one is a bit complicated. You see, registers 0 and 1 double as the low and high bytes of a word used to divide into the magic number 115,200, which results in the final baud rate used by the UART. However, as we know, registers 0 and 1 are the transmitter-holding register (THR) and the interrupt-enable register (IER).

When bit 7 of the line-control register is set to 1, they become registers 8 and 9—but they're still addressed as 0 and 1. Get it?

As an example, let's set the baud to 9600. We would compute a number that when divided into 115,200 was equal to 9600. That number is 12. Then we would break this number into a low byte and a high byte. In this case, the low byte would be 12 and the high byte would be 0. We would then set bit 7 (DLAB) of the line control register to 1 and write the low byte into register 0 and the high byte into register 1, which are really 8 and 9 but are addressed as 0 and 1. Then we would reset bit 7 (DLAB) in the line-control register.

That wasn't too bad, was it? Next, we set the UART up to handle interrupts. Let's talk about this for a minute.

When the UART receives a character, the character will sit in the receive buffer only until another character arrives. Then it's obliterated by the new character. We can't have this happening because we'd lose information. There are two solutions to this problem:

- First, we could poll the receive buffer register fast enough that we never lose any data, but this would be a waste of time.

- Second (and a better solution), we could use an interrupt-service routine or ISR.

As we learned in Chapter 12, "Surreal Time, Interrupts, and Multitasking," the C language has a really easy way of creating ISRs using the _interrupt keyword. Therefore, we'll use an ISR that's activated whenever an interrupt occurs. How do we tell the UART to signal this interrupt? Well, if you stare long enough at all the registers you'll figure out that you need to set a bit here and a bit there, and the UART will do its job.

To enable interrupts, we must set the following bits in the UART:

- Bit 0 (RxRDY) of the interrupt enable register (IER) must be set to 1.

- Bit 3 (GP02) of the modem control register (MCR) must be set to 1.

Then we should be ready to receive interrupts, right? Wrong! We have to do one more thing. We must tell the PC's programmable interrupt controller (PIC) chip that it should allow the serial-port interrupts. To accomplish this we must change the settings in the PIC's interrupt mask register (IMR), which is accessed at port 21h. Table 14.3 shows the bit designations of the IMR.

Table 14.3. The PIC's Interrupt Mask Register (IMR).

Bit 0: IRQ 0—Used for time keeper

Bit 1: IRQ 1—Used for Keyboard

Bit 2: IRQ 2—Reserved

Bit 3: IRQ 3—COM 2 or COM 4

Bit 4: IRQ 4—COM 1 or COM 3

Bit 5: IRQ 5—Fixed Disk

Bit 6: IRQ 6—Floppy Disk

Bit 7: IRQ 7—Printer

Therefore, the last thing we need to do to get the interrupts up and running is activate the proper serial interrupt at bit 3 or 4. But watch out! The register is inverted, so a 0 means on and a 1 means off.

Be careful when you play with the interrupt mask register. You can really mess up the computer with it. It's a hacker's dream! I suggest reading the data first and masking it with a pattern that you want to impose on it, then writing the new data back.

Installing an ISR

Once we have gone through all these stunts to achieve a simple little interrupt, we can finally install our ISR into the proper vector depending on the COM port. The vectors we're interested in changing are listed in Table 14.4. Note that ports 3 and 4 use the same interrupts as ports 1 and 2, respectively.

Table 14.4. Serial-port interrupt vectors.

Vector	Number	Address	Function
0x0B	0x002C - 0x002F		RS-232 port 1
0x0C	0x0030 - 0x0033		RS-232 port 2

To install our ISR, all we need to do is use the C functions _dos_getvect() to get the old ISR, and _dos_setvect() to install our new one in its place. Then, when an interrupt occurs (when a character is received) our ISR will be called. That all sounds great, but what is our ISR going to do?

Well, our ISR has one mission in life: to get the character out of the receive-buffer register (RBR) and place it into a software buffer. We're going to buffer the input so the main program can take its time reading the input. We implement this buffer as an n-byte recirculating buffer.

For our use I've set the size of the buffer to 128 bytes, although it could be anything. The buffering algorithm operates by getting the next character from the RBR and placing it in the next position in the buffer. Then the current buffer position is incremented. When the buffer index hits the end, it wraps around back to the beginning and starts overwriting the data that's there. Hopefully, before it can do that the main program has read the buffer and consumed the buffered data. Figure 14.3 shows a picture of the recirculating buffer.

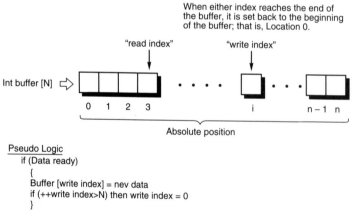

Figure 14.3. *A recirculating buffer.*

We must cover one more subtlety before we conclude the ISR discussion. Before the ISR leaves, it must reissue an enable interrupts command to the PIC. This is done through the I/O port 20h, called the interrupt control register (ICR). To reenable interrupts, a 20h must be written to the ICR. In general, you don't really need to do this when using the C-based interrupt function. If you were using pure asembly, however, it would be necessary, so we cover it here for completeness. Listing 14.1 contains the listing for the ISR routine.

Listing 14.1. The ISR routine.

```
////////////////////////////////////////////////////////////////

void _interrupt _far Serial_Isr(void)
{

// This is the interrupt-service routine (ISR) for the com port.
// It's quite simple. When it gets called, it gets the next
// character out of the receive buffer register 0 and places it
// into the software buffer. Note: C takes care of all the
// register saving and housework. Cool, huh!?

// Lock out any other functions so the buffer doesn't become
// corrupted.

serial_lock = 1;

// Place the character into the next position in the buffer.

ser_ch = _inp(open_port + SER_RBF);

// Wrap buffer index around.

if (++ser_end > SERIAL_BUFF_SIZE-1)
    ser_end = 0;

// Move the character into the buffer.

ser_buffer[ser_end] = ser_ch;

++char_ready;

// Restore the PIC.

_outp(PIC_ICR,0x20);

// Undo the lock.

serial_lock = 0;

} // end Serial_Isr

////////////////////////////////////////////////////////////////
```

The code in Listing 14.1 does exactly what we said it would. However, there is one added feature: a variable called serial_lock. All this variable does is keep the main program from messing with the buffer while the ISR is updating it. This technique is called a *lock* or *semaphore*. In the case of DOS, this problem never occurs. The problem arises in a fully preemptive operating system. However, locking is just a good habit to get into even if it's not necessary at this point.

We are almost done!

Reading a Character from the Buffer

Next, we need to be able to read a character out of the buffer. This is easy. All we do is keep another index, which points to the current position from which the data buffer is accessed for reading. We use this pointer to consume a character and increment it. If both the read and write indices are the same, the consumer (the main program) has consumed all the input from the producer (the ISR), and no more data is ready. In that case, the read character function returns a zero. Listing 14.2 contains the pertinent code.

Listing 14.2. The `Serial_Read` **function.**

```
//////////////////////////////////////////////////////////////////

int Serial_Read(void)
{

// This function reads a character from the circulating buffer
// and returns it to the caller.

int ch;

// Wait for ISR to end.

while(serial_lock){}

// Test whether there's a character(s) ready in buffer.

if (ser_end != ser_start)
    {

    // Wrap buffer index if needed.

    if (++ser_start > SERIAL_BUFF_SIZE-1)
        ser_start = 0;

    // Get the character out of buffer.

    ch = ser_buffer[ser_start];

    // There's one less character in the buffer now.

    if (char_ready > 0)
        —char_ready;

    // Send data back to caller.

    return(ch);

    } // end if a character is in buffer
else
```

```
    // Buffer was empty; return a NULL (that is, 0)
    return(0);

} // end Serial_read
```

//

The `Serial_Read()` function gets the next available character out of the data buffer and returns it. If there isn't a character available, it returns a 0.

Writing to the Serial Port

The last important function we need is something to write to the serial port. To accomplish this, we need only to write to the transmitter-holding register. However, we must make sure that two criteria are met:

- First, the ISR can't be active.

- Second, the transmitter-holding register must be empty.

The first premise takes care of itself. However, the second one must be determined by way of the line-status register bit 5. When this bit is set, the transmitter is empty and another character can be sent. Listing 14.3 contains the code to send a character.

Listing 14.3. The `Serial_Write` function.

//

```
void Serial_Write(char ch)
{

// This function writes a character to the transmit buffer, but
// first it waits for the transmit buffer to be empty. Note: the
// function is not interrupt-driven, and it turns off interrupts
// while it's working.

// Wait for transmit buffer to be empty.

while(!(_inp(open_port + SER_LSR) & 0x20)){}

// Turn off interrupts for a bit.

_asm cli

// Send the character.

_outp(open_port + SER_THR, ch);
```

continues

Listing 14.3. continued

```
// Turn interrupts back on.

_asm sti

} // end Serial_Write

/////////////////////////////////////////////////////////////
```

The only tricky thing Serial_Write() does is turn off interrupts.

A Terminal Program: NLINK

That completes our crash course in serial communications on the PC. To show you how to put it all together, I've written a little terminal program called NLINK. It connects two PCs by way of COM1 or COM2, and lets two players type to each other over a null-modem cable. To exit the program, press the Esc key. Listing 14.4 contains the complete communications library and the main section to NLINK.

Listing 14.4. NLINK (nlink.c).

```
// I N C L U D E S /////////////////////////////////////////

#include <dos.h>
#include <bios.h>
#include <stdio.h>
#include <math.h>
#include <conio.h>
#include <graph.h>

// D E F I N E S ///////////////////////////////////////////

// Registers in UART

#define SER_RBF      0    // The read buffer.
#define SER_THR      0    // The write buffer.
#define SER_IER      1    // The int. enable register.
#define SER_IIR      2    // The int. identification register.
#define SER_LCR      3    // Control-data config. and divisor
                          // latch.
#define SER_MCR      4    // Modem-control register.
#define SER_LSR      5    // Line-status register.
#define SER_MSR      6    // Modem-status of cts, ring, etc.
#define SER_DLL      0    // The low byte of baud rate divisor.
#define SER_DLH      1    // The high byte of divisor latch.

// Bit patterns for control registers.
```

```
#define SER_BAUD_1200   96    // Baud-rate divisors for
                              // 1200-19200 baud.
#define SER_BAUD_2400   48
#define SER_BAUD_9600   12
#define SER_BAUD_19200   6

#define SER_GP02         8    // Enable interrupt.


#define COM_1           0x3F8 // Base port address of port 0.
#define COM_2           0x2F8 // Base port address of port 1.

#define SER_STOP_1       0    // 1 stop bit per character.
#define SER_STOP_2       4    // 2 stop bits per character.

#define SER_BITS_5       0    // Send five-bit characters.
#define SER_BITS_6       1    // Send six-bit characters.
#define SER_BITS_7       2    // Send seven-bit characters.
#define SER_BITS_8       3    // Send eight-bit characters.

#define SER_PARITY_NONE  0    // No parity
#define SER_PARITY_ODD   8    // Odd parity
#define SER_PARITY_EVEN 24    // Even parity

#define SER_DIV_LATCH_ON 128  // Used to turn reg 0,1 into
                              // divisor latch.

#define PIC_IMR         0x21  // PIC's interrupt mask register.
#define PIC_ICR         0x20  // PIC's interupt control register.


#define INT_SER_PORT_0   0x0C // Port 0 interrupt COM1 and COM3.
#define INT_SER_PORT_1   0x0B // Port 0 interrupt COM2 and COM4.

#define SERIAL_BUFF_SIZE 128  // Current size of circulating
                              // receive buffer.


// G L O B A L S ///////////////////////////////////////////

void (_interrupt _far *Old_Isr)();  // Holds old com-port
                                    // interrupt handler.


char ser_buffer[SERIAL_BUFF_SIZE];  // The receive buffer.

int ser_end = -1,ser_start=-1;      // Indexes into the receive
                                    // buffer.
int ser_ch, char_ready=0;           // Current character and
                                    // ready flag.
int old_int_mask;                   // The old interrupt mask
                                    // on the PIC.
int open_port;                      // The currently open port.
int serial_lock = 0;                // Serial ISR semaphore so
                                    // the buffer isn't altered
                                    // while it is being written
                                    // to by the ISR.
```

continues

Listing 14.4. continued

```c
////////////////////////////////////////////////////////////////

void _interrupt _far Serial_Isr(void)
{

// This is the interrupt-service routine (ISR) for the com port.
// It's quite simple. When it gets called, it gets the next
// character out of the receive buffer register 0 and places it
// into the software buffer. Note: C takes care of all the
// register saving and housework. Cool, huh!?

// Lock out any other functions so the buffer doesn't become
// corrupted.

serial_lock = 1;

// Place character into next position in buffer.

ser_ch = _inp(open_port + SER_RBF);

// Wrap buffer index around.

if (++ser_end > SERIAL_BUFF_SIZE-1)
    ser_end = 0;

// Move character into buffer.

ser_buffer[ser_end] = ser_ch;

++char_ready;

// Restore PIC.

_outp(PIC_ICR,0x20);

// Undo lock

serial_lock = 0;

} // end Serial_Isr

////////////////////////////////////////////////////////////////

int Ready_Serial(void)
{

// This functions returns true if there are any characters
// waiting, and 0 if the buffer is empty.

return(char_ready);

} // end Ready_Serial

////////////////////////////////////////////////////////////////
```

```c
int Serial_Read(void)
{

// This function reads a character from the circulating buffer
// and returns it to the caller.

int ch;

// Wait for ISR to end

while(serial_lock){}

// Test whether there's a character(s) ready in buffer.

if (ser_end != ser_start)
   {

   // Wrap buffer index if needed.

   if (++ser_start > SERIAL_BUFF_SIZE-1)
       ser_start = 0;

   // Get the character out of the buffer.

   ch = ser_buffer[ser_start];

   // There's one less character in the buffer now.

   if (char_ready > 0)
       —char_ready;

   // Send data back to caller.

   return(ch);

   } // end if a character is in buffer
else
   // Buffer was empty; return a NULL (that is, 0)
   return(0);

} // end Serial_read


/////////////////////////////////////////////////////////////////

void Serial_Write(char ch)
{

// This function writes a character to the transmit buffer, but
// first it waits for the transmit buffer to be empty. Note: the
// function is not interrupt-driven, and it turns off interrupts
// while it's working.

// Wait for transmit buffer to be empty.

while(!(_inp(open_port + SER_LSR) & 0x20)){}

// Turn off interrupts for a bit.
```

continues

Listing 14.4. continued

```
_asm cli

// Send the character.

_outp(open_port + SER_THR, ch);

// Turn interrupts back on.

_asm sti

} // end Serial_Write

////////////////////////////////////////////////////////////////

void Open_Serial(int port_base, int baud, int configuration)
{

// This function opens up the serial port, sets its
// configuration, turns on all the little flags and bits to make
// interrupts happen, and loads the ISR.

// Save the port for other functions.

open_port = port_base;

// First set the baud rate.

// Turn on divisor latch registers.

_outp(port_base + SER_LCR, SER_DIV_LATCH_ON);

// Send low and high bytes to divisor latches.

_outp(port_base + SER_DLL, baud);
_outp(port_base + SER_DLH, 0);

// Set the configuration for the port.

_outp(port_base + SER_LCR, configuration);

// Enable the interrupts.

_outp(port_base + SER_MCR, SER_GP02);

_outp(port_base + SER_IER, 1);

// Hold off enabling PIC until we have the ISR installed.

if (port_base == COM_1)
    {
    Old_Isr = _dos_getvect(INT_SER_PORT_0);
    _dos_setvect(INT_SER_PORT_0, Serial_Isr);
    printf("\nOpening Communications Channel Com Port #1...\n");

    }
else
    {
```

```c
   Old_Isr = _dos_getvect(INT_SER_PORT_1);
   _dos_setvect(INT_SER_PORT_1, Serial_Isr);
   printf("\nOpening Communications Channel Com Port #2...\n");
   }


// Enable interrupt on PIC.

old_int_mask = _inp(PIC_IMR);

_outp(PIC_IMR, (port_base==COM_1) ? (old_int_mask & 0xEF) : (old_int_mask & 0xF7 ));


} // Open_Serial

/////////////////////////////////////////////////////////////////


void Close_Serial(int port_base)
{

// This function closes the port, which entails turning off
// interrupts and restoring the old interrupt vector.

// Disable the interrupts.

_outp(port_base + SER_MCR, 0);

_outp(port_base + SER_IER, 0);

_outp(PIC_IMR, old_int_mask );

// Reset old ISR handler.

if (port_base == COM_1)
   {
   _dos_setvect(INT_SER_PORT_0, Old_Isr);
   printf("\nClosing Communications Channel Com Port #1.\n");
   }
else
   {
   _dos_setvect(INT_SER_PORT_1, Old_Isr);
   printf("\nClosing Communications Channel Com Port #2.\n");
   }

} // end Close_Serial

/////////////////////////////////////////////////////////////////


void main(void)
{

char ch;
int done=0;

printf("\nNull Modem Terminal Communications Program.\n\n");
```

continues

Listing 14.4. continued

```
// Open COM1

Open_Serial(COM_1,SER_BAUD_9600,SER_PARITY_NONE | SER_BITS_8 | SER_STOP_1);

// main loop

while(!done)
     {

     // Try to get a character from local machine.

     if (kbhit())
        {
        // Get the character from keyboard.

        ch = getch();
        printf("%c",ch);

        // Send the character to other machine.

        Serial_Write(ch);

        // Has the player pressed Esc? If so, bail!

        if (ch==27) done=1;

        // Test for CR; if so, add an line feed.

        if (ch==13)
           {
           printf("\n");
           Serial_Write(10);
           }

        } // end if kbhit
     // Try to get a character from remote.

     if (ch = Serial_Read())
        printf("%c", ch);

     if (ch == 27)
        {
        printf("\nRemote Machine Closing Connection.");
        done=1;
        } // end if remote close


     }  // end while

// Close the connection and blaze.

Close_Serial(COM_1);

} // end main
```

Learning about serial communications is like going to the dentist. No one likes to do it, but it has to be done. I'm sorry that I had to submit you to that torture, but it's something we needed to cover. (And a little torture is kinda fun once in a while!)

Now, onto the more interesting topic of video-game communications.

Video Game Communication Strategies

Linking two PCs and having them run the same game world is a rather complex problem, and one without any best or right answers. Your particular solution—the way you architect your game(s) for linked play—can and probably will change for each game you write. However, there are some issues that we always have to consider, and that's what we're going to talk about now.

In a two-player game running on a single computer, each player has the chance to control his or her character and change its state once during the main game loop. Figure 14.4 shows two different representations of this kind of setup.

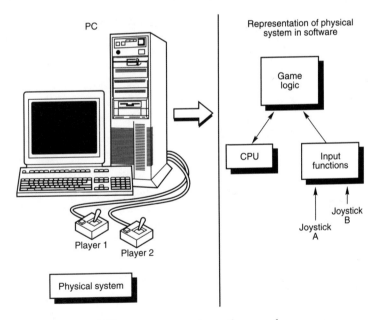

Figure 14.4. *Two different representations of a two-player game.*

In a two-player game that runs on two different computers, however, the situation becomes more complex, as shown in Figure 14.5.

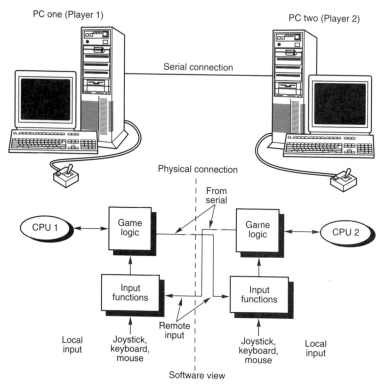

Figure 14.5. *A two-player game with two PCs.*

Problems can arise with this configuration, primarily because there isn't really another player. Somehow we have to give the local computer information about the remote computer's state. Moreover, it must be enough information to permit the local computer to figure out what the other computer's player is doing, and reflect that locally.

There are a couple of ways to accomplish this functionality:

■ One way is to send over information about the input device of the other player. In that case, the communications port is like a virtual input device being driven by another computer. When a remote player moves a character, this movement is sent to the remote system by sending the status of the input device. The other system then can update its remote virtual player's position based on this.

■ The second method is called *state-vector synchronization*. In this system, instead of sending the I/O devices, we send the "state" of the remote machine so the local machine can synchronize to the remote machine, as shown in Figure 14.6. This system works quite well. However, it can take up a lot of bandwidth sending all this state information over the wire.

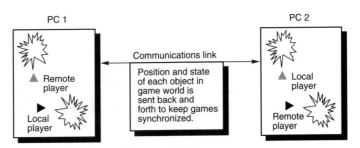

Figure 14.6. *State-vector synchronization.*

We delve deeper into each method in a moment, but for now let's think about what can go wrong when linking up two PCs.

■ The biggest problem occurs when the two machines get out of synchronization. Say that one PC is a 586 and the other is a 386. It's possible for one machine to be able to get ahead of the other machine, and for the two games to get out of synchronization. This factor must be considered, and methods to keep the machines synchronized have to be addressed in the overall design.

■ The next potential problem can be called *nondeterministic aliasing*. (By the way, I just made that up. It does describe the problem, though.) Both games must be totally deterministic. By this I mean that little mines can't be placed at different positions on both machines. If mines are placed on one machine at some location, they'd better be at the same location on the other machine. Also, random-number generators can't be used to drive logic unless the same numbers are generated at the same time on both machines.

The only way around this nondeterministic aliasing is to send enough state information so that even if there is something that happens randomly on one machine, the other machine is apprised of it.

These are really the most important issues with which you need to concern yourself.

We've briefly discussed a couple methods of synchronization, now let's expand on them.

State-Vector Synchronization

State-vector synchronization is simple in concept: continually send the state of the remote machine and update the local machine with this information.

As an example, let's use a hypothetical game that has two players linked up and dueling in an asteroid field. To send the state of one machine to the other, we have to know everything about the game. We must send the position and attributes (such as speed and size) of each asteroid. We also must send the position of the player. If either player fired a weapon, we'd have to send a message saying that a weapon was fired, and describing the weapon's attributes. Also, if a new object were to come into existence in either machine, we'd have to send a message to tell the remote machine to create a similar object.

In essence, we create a snapshot of the game universe and send it to the remote machine every cycle. We also must do this at a reasonable rate, so that when one player blows up an asteroid that's about to hit the other player's character, the asteroid explodes before the little character is obliterated. Figure 14.7 shows an exaggeration of what can happen if the systems start getting out of synchronization.

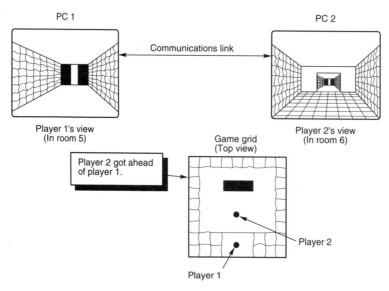

Figure 14.7. *When two PCs get out of state.*

State-vector synchronization works fine, and is quite reliable because everything happening on one machine is sent to the other. However, as I mentioned, it's not so easy to implement: all possible states have to be taken into consideration and the amount of information sent over the communications channel gets to be fairly big.

A system that's easier to understand is called I/O state synchronization, which we will talk about next.

I/O State Synchronization

I/O state synchronization is a method in which the state of the input device is sent to the remote computer in real time. Whatever the player does locally, the remote system gets as input and uses to make that player's character do on the remote system what the character has been told to do by way of the communications channel. Take a look at Figure 14.8 to see this pictorially.

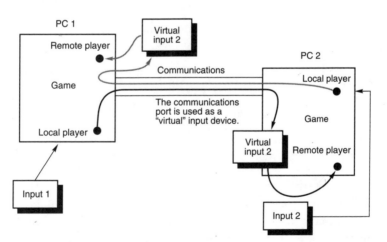

Figure 14.8. *Sending the input devices to another machine.*

This system works flawlessly as long as both systems stay in sync and nothing random happens. Otherwise, the remote machine will have no idea that the state of the other machine has changed, because nothing changed with the input device.

If you needed to have some random thing happen, you'd send a message that would tell the remote system about it. However, then you've mixed state-vector and I/O state synchronization together—which is fine (and, as you'll see, almost inevitable).

To implement I/O state synchronization:

- We would first collect the input device's current states. These would include joystick and keyboard.

- Then we would package them together in a packet and send it over the communications channel.

The term *packet* denotes a conglomeration of information. To send packets, we must come up with a set of conventions so the serial communications systems know what these packets mean. For example, say we decided to send the state of the joystick over the communications channel, along with the state of the buttons. We might come up with a packet that looks like Table 14.5.

Table 14.5. A sample I/O space information packet.

Packet byte#	Value	Meaning
0	J	A joystick status is being sent.
1	data_x	A byte that represents the x position of the joystick.
2	data_y	A byte that represents the y position of the joystick.
3	buttons	A byte that represents the button status.
4	. (period)	End of transmission.

This is an extremely simple packet; it consists of a J followed by three bytes and, finally, a period to denote the end of the packet. The local machine would create this packet and send it to the remote machine a number of times per second so that the remote machine could keep in synchronization. At the same time, the remote machine would be sending its joystick packets back.

Here's a little tidbit to confuse you: the game that runs on each computer is the same piece of software. When it runs on one machine it thinks of the other computer as the remote player, while the other machine thinks of the other player as remote also. (Sort of like time travel—and can it give you a headache!)

That's about all there is to I/O state synchronization. We've talked about keeping the games in sync, but we need to lock down a gray area we can call temporal synchronization.

Temporal Synchronization

Temporal synchronization means keeping both machines locked to some common clock. This clock can be internal or external. As I said before, we want both games to run at the same speed, and we want the same action to be happening on each machine. To accomplish this we must have an allowance to keep both machines on the same cycle.

There are many ways to do this, but here are just a couple:

- One way is to have both computers sending their "state" based on a time interval that's the same for both machines. For instance, the machine sends its state every 1/30th of a second. Using this technique, each machine will get a maximum 1/30th of a second out of sync.

- Another technique is to pass an imaginary token back and forth, as shown in Figure 14.9.

PC 1 sends a token to PC 2. When PC 2 sends it back, PC 1 continues and knows that both games are synchronized.

Figure 14.9. *Sending a token to keep things in synchronization.*

Computer 1 sends its state to computer 2. Only when computer 2 acknowledges this and sends its state can computer 1 continue. And remember: from computer 2's point of view, this is reversed. Therefore, when the communication begins, one computer will get to the punch first and the messages will go back and forth.

This method has an interesting side effect: the computers will synchronize to the slower computer's speed and stay there. Again, there will be a maximum time lag, based not on the speed of the computers, but on how long it takes for each message to be sent back and forth from each machine.

OK, now you're a communications expert. That was easy, wasn't it? Even if you're not an expert you at least have a good idea of what to expect and some techniques to handle possible problems. Before we get to the game Net-Tank, I want to talk about the modem itself.

The Modem

Communicating over the modem takes a lot of overhead and setup that would add a zillion pages we don't have time for. The modem is controlled by the same serial port it connects to. The only difference is that the modem listens to the serial port and, if it hears a special sequence of characters, it thinks you're talking to it and it will interpret the command and execute it. These commands are called the *AT command set*. They support all the functionality you need to dial, answer, and make the telephone connection.

Once the connection is made, it's transparent to you. You can forget you're connected by a modem.

Well, I'm about ready to hang up. Let's get to the game!

Net-Tank: A Two-Player Tank Simulation

Net-Tank is a one- or two-player game that I've written to enable you to get an understanding of how to implement multiplayer games, along with some of the problems that can occur. The game is rudimentary (it took me three days to write), and is played on a single screen. Moreover, the game is 2-D with the view being that of the player looking down on the game grid. We make a full, 3-D, Wolfenstein-type game in Chapter 19, when we write Warlock, but for now I want to keep the game simple enough that we can analyze the communication part of it without a lot of complex game logic and graphics blurring your vision.

Before we start taking the game apart, I suggest that you play it with someone, or at least play it in solo mode so that you'll have an idea of what I'm talking about during the explanation. As I mentioned before, a game-programming guru has to be able to write code specifically for each game, and try not to "make" already existing code work. That said, I had to modify some of our old software and create new modules. I used the approach of creating libraries so as not to have to include a ton of source code that didn't have to do directly with game play. I created the following libraries:

SNDLIB.C	The sound library
GRAPH1.C-	The low-level 2-D sprite and graphics library
KEYLIB.C-	The keyboard input library
SERLIB.C -	The communication library

These library files all have headers with the same names:

```
SNDLIB.H
GRAPH1.H
KEYLIB.H
SERLIB.H
```

All these modules are put into one big library using Microsoft's library manager, LIB. To create the library:

1. Compile each C module with the following batch file, name CO.BAT:

   ```
   cl -AM -Zi -c -Fc -Gs -G2 %1.c
   ```

   This tells the compiler to compile using the MEDIUM memory model, codeview information, no stack probes, and 286-instruction compatibility.

2. After compiling each module, make one big library called MYLIB.LIB. To do so, call the library manager by entering the following:

   ```
   lib mylib.lib
   ```

3. The system informs you the library doesn't exist and queries whether you want the library created. Answer Yes.

4. On the operations line, add all the modules into the library, as follows:

   ```
   operations: +SNDLIB  +GRAPH1  +KEYLIB  +SERLIB
   ```

5. The system then prompts you with a list file and output file. Press Enter in both cases.

You now have a library called MYLIB.LIB, which you can link in as you would any other library.

To create the game you must make two executables:

■ One executable is for the local player on computer 1.

■ The second executable is for the remote player.

To do so:

1. Compile both NET1.C and NET2.C (the two versions of the game) with the following small batch file, named CC.BAT:

```
cl -AM -Zi -c  -Fc -Gs -G2 %1.c
if errorlevel 1 goto c_fail
link /ST:16384 /CO %1,,,graphics.lib+mylib.lib,,
:c_fail
```

This batch file compiles the game and links it with library to create an executable. Do this to create the executables NET1.EXE and NET2.EXE.
(Just in case you don't feel like doing all this, I've created both executables for you already.)

2. Place NET1.EXE on one machine and NET2.EXE on the other. Make sure a null-modem cable is connecting to both machines on COM1.

3. You're ready to go. Just type NET1.EXE on one machine and NET2.EXE on the other. The machines will link up and play.

The controls are as follows:

Right Arrow	Turn Right
Left Arrow	Turn Left
Up Arrow	Move Forward
Down Arrow	Move Backward
Esc Key	Exit Game
Spacebar	Fire Missile
T Key	Irritate Other Player

Play the game for a while and try to notice things like:

■ Time lag in the movement

■ Whether the games get out of synchronization

■ If they do, when they do

Also, notice all the sound effects. I made them with samples of my voice and the shareware program BLASTER MASTER.

Finally, both games use whatever keyboard repeat rate is installed. If you have problems with the keyboard beeping, try slowing the keyboard down. To do this use the program TURBOKEY.COM, supplied on the companion CD.

Analysis of Net-Tank

Net-Tank is what would be considered a pre-Neanderthal video game. I'd have to agree. However, it does contain some interesting techniques that you can use (and that are used later, during Warlock). All the game logic is contained in the main() function of the C program. I did this so that you could trace out the entire game in a single bound without a lot of function jumping. Any functions called are low-level, and usually do what their names say they do (such as Draw_Sprite()). The main section is only a couple hundred lines long, and if you can get a handle on it you're in good shape. Let's cover the game section by section.

Section I: Initialization

In this section of the code we load up all the sound files and load in the graphics for the game. The animation cells for the tanks are scanned from the loaded files, and the memory is allocated for the double buffer. Net-Tank uses the double buffer technique to eliminate flickering. The graphics are drawn in an off-screen buffer. Then, at the end of all the rendering, the double buffer is blasted into the video buffer. Another thing that happens during initialization is that the players' and missiles' data structures are all zeroed or set up in the proper position (or both).

This brings us to the first point of a networked game. The software is almost identical, but there must be one difference: the local player's position on one machine must be identical to the remote player's position on the other machine at start up. This means we must have the positions of the players hardcoded, loaded in by way of a file, or selected at run time. The manner in which it's done doesn't matter. However, when the game starts, the remote player on one machine is the local on the other and the state had better be the same! Otherwise, there will be a bit of a synchronization problem.

Section II: The Game Loop

The next section of the game begins the main game loop. This is the loop that's executed over and over again.

Notice the game loop has another inner loop. The outer game loop is used to initialize a couple of things. Then the inner game loop begins. This is where all the action is!

Notice that the game pays attention to whether it's linked or solo.

Section III: Erasing the Objects

As we know from all the previous graphics chapters, we must erase the gamefield before we can draw it. The next section of the code does just that: it erases the players and their missiles. The erasing is done by replacing what was under them on the last cycle. This is done so as not to destroy the background (the circuit board).

Section IV: Getting Input and Sending Status to the Remote System

Here's the fun part. This section of the code is broken into two segments:

- Part one gets the input from the local player.
- Part two gets the input from the remote player.

What's interesting is that both sections are relatively the same. The only difference is that the remote section looks for input from the serial port rather than the keyboard, as does the local player section.

Let's stop and talk for a moment on how the communication is done. As I said a few pages back, there are two main methods by which to implement communications:

- You can send the state of the entire game every cycle.
- You can make the communications link an extension of the input devices, and treat it as another joystick or keyboard.

The second method is the one I chose for Net-Tank. For every cycle, the local player sends whatever he or she is doing with the keyboard to the remote. Moreover, during the remote phase of the input scan, the serial line is read and interpreted as if it were another keyboard.

Summing up: in the input section, both players' input is queried by way of the local keyboard and the serial line. Then actions are taken on these inputs. Hopefully, the remote does the same thing. If it does not, the games will become unsynchronized.

Remember that for this technique to work, the two games must be completely deterministic. There can be no randomness in either game unless the randomness is in sync. In Net-Tank, I've followed this rule everywhere except in one portion of the game, which is the explosion. Usually, I can get away with it—but sometimes, after a player is killed, the games get out of synchronization.

Section V: Moving the Objects

The next portion of the code moves the objects. We simply use the information from the local and remote input to translate or rotate the tanks.

The way the tanks are moved is kind of interesting. The tanks are drawn in 16 different directions, each 22.5 degrees apart. Normally, if we wanted to move the tank forward we'd have to know its direction and then find the angle and compute the sine and cosine to figure out the translation factors. This would enable us to move the tank in the direction it was pointed. In Net-Tank, however, what I did was to precompute the sines and cosines of the translations of the tank. Therefore, the way the tank is pointing (which is just the current frame) is used as an index into a table that has these translation values precomputed.

If that seems a little contrived, believe me: it's better than using floating-point math along with transcendental functions! You learn more about these tricks in Chapter 18, "Optimization Techniques."

Anyway, after the tanks have been moved, the missiles are all moved at once.

Section VI: Collision Detection

Once all the objects have found their new home, it's time to see if anyone is stepping on anyone; that is, whether they're breaking Pauli's Exclusion Principle, which states that "no two particles can be at the same two positions at the same time." In our case, we want to ask the question, "Have the missiles hit anyone?" To do this, the missiles are all tested against the bounding box of each tank. If there's a hit, it's flagged so that an explosion can occur at the end of the game cycle. Currently, the tanks can "phase" right through each other. (I'll leave fixing that to you.)

Finally, I want to talk about how I make the tanks bump off the walls. If you recall from Chapter 6, "The Third Dimension," a game grid is represented by a matrix of cells that each have a certain dimension. In the case of Net-Tank, the game grid is 20x11, where each cell is 16x16 pixels. Therefore, to see if a tank has bumped into a wall (that is, gone into an occupied cell), we simply:

- Divide the tank's x and y positions by 16.
- Truncate the decimal portion.
- Index into the game grid to see if a block is there. If a block is there, we back the player up equal to the distance that player just moved forward.

Section VII: Drawing the Objects

Now we're ready to draw all the objects. To do this we must first scan the backgrounds under the locations in which we're planning to place the objects. After that, we can place the objects. At this point, the entire screen has been built up in the double buffer, so it's time to see what we have created.

Section VIII: Displaying the Double Buffer

Net-Tank uses the double-buffering technique to eliminate flicker. In this portion of the game, an extremely tight assembly-language loop does a copy of the double buffer to the screen buffer. However, we only move the first 176 lines of the double buffer to the screen. This is because the lower part of the screen is the gauges, and they don't need to be redrawn.

Section IX: Odds and Ends

The game has gone another cycle. We have displayed the new frame and are ready to go to the next cycle. Before we do, however, we should take care of a few odds and ends. During this phase of the game, the gauges are redrawn, the lights on the circuitry are blinked, and any variables that need resetting are reset.

Section X: Here We Go Again and Again and Again and ...

GOTO Section I.

Summary

Not only have we learned the mysteries of the serial communication port, we've created an entire library that can be used in the future with little modification.

We also learned how to network two players together, and the factors that must be taken into consideration to do this.

Finally, we have a complete (well, almost complete) game to experiment with.

15

The Toolchest

Writing a video game is like building a house: you need the right tool for the right job! In this chapter we "hammer" information on bit-map editors, "wrench" animation packages into place, "wire up" sound editors and, finally, "lay the foundation" of our own map-editor system for Warlock. Here are the topics we'll "tool" around with:

- Defining "tools"
- Which tools do we really need?
- Bit-map editors
- Animation packages
- Making movies
- Sound editors
- The map editor—WAREDIT
- Using WAREDIT
- A functional description of WAREDIT
- Improving WAREDIT

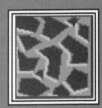

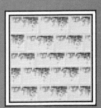

by André LaMothe

What Are Tools?

Tools are anything that make life easier on us! When creating a complex piece of software such as a video game, we must be able to solve a problem once, and then have the solution to similar problems automated. For instance, if we wanted to change the pitch of a sampled sound, we could write a piece of software that did the necessary mathematical operation to accomplish this. However, when we want to change the pitch of another sound, we surely don't want to do all that programming again! We'd like to reuse the software already created. There are many tasks relating to computers and computing that are so redundant, time consuming, or both, that people have created tools and utilities to make these tasks more simplified.

In the case of a video-game programmer, we must think about what we need to create a game. Then we must consider how hard it would be to improve our game: to change it or add levels. After going through that mental experiment we could generate a list of the tools that we'll need to accomplish our goals in a timely fashion. Our list might look like this:

- A bit-map graphics editor
- Some animation software to animate our bit maps
- A sound digitizer with many operations and features
- A program to draw the game levels and place the game objects

The first three are all common needs of any video-game programmer, and I suggest you use someone else's software. If you try to write your own, you'll probably take up at least a few months—if not a couple years!

The fourth one is where we come in. Many games today have dozens, if not hundreds, of levels. The game writers don't actually write a dozen or hundreds of games and put them all on your disk! Instead, the game programmer has a game engine that uses some kind of database representing a specific level. This database is loaded, and the game executes the level. When the level is complete, the next level is loaded. If you've taken a close look at Net-Tank (the game we made in Chapter 14, "Linking Up"), you'll have noticed that the game grid (or battle ground) is a 2-D matrix of characters that are translated into the actual bit maps that comprise the game.

The Net-Tank game grid is so simple that a text editor sufficed as the tool to draw levels. However, it would have been nice to have a more complex tool that had icons, bit-map previews, and so on with which to draw the battle ground. In the case of Net-Tank, creating a level took about 10 minutes. To create a tool to create levels would have taken a couple days, so it wasn't worth it. However, in a game like Wolfenstein, DOOM, or even our own game, Warlock, a map-editor tool is a must.

As video-game programmers, we're primarily interested in creating specific tools for the games we make. These tools are usually going to be map editors, or programs that have something specific to do with the game we're working on. Having tools to create new levels and new worlds allows unsophisticated users to create new levels without knowledge of how the game works. Also, being able to churn out level after level is financially rewarding if the public is dying for more levels and new environments.

Now that we've talked about what tools are, and some specific tools that are usually required to get the job done, let's explore the capabilities of the tools that we should acquire.

Bit-Map Editors

The graphics and imagery of today's video games must be dauntingly impressive, to say the least. They must look professional, realistic, and have some dimension to them. Of course, no tool in the world is going to make up for lack of artistic ability—and without a real artist at the helm, your graphics may look like Crayola drawings! Use whatever program you wish, but here's a minimum list of features:

- The program should be able to operate in any graphics mode, especially mode 13h (that is, 320x200x256.)

- The program should have multiple file formats for both reading and writing.

- The interface should be graphical and enable you to draw the images in a high-precision manner if need be. This means a zoom utility must be available.

- Color is important. The program should have a full repertoire of color-palette controls and operations.

- The images must be able to be printed out on a printer, and the program should support color laser printers if possible.

- After drawing a bit map, the program must allow certain geometrical operations such as rotation, scaling, shearing, and stretching.

- The program should support anti-aliasing (smoothing of the edges) and as many cool color effects as possible.

- Finally, the program should have multiple "pages" so that an artist can cut and paste from different areas and other screen pages. Then these "brushes" can be put together to create a final image.

Today the trend is slowly moving away from "paint" programs to "illustration" programs. Illustration programs are based more on vectors and objects. Either way you go, it may take some time to find a good art program. I suggest Electronic Arts' Deluxe Paint or Deluxe Animation, or maybe PC Paintbrush.

Animation Packages

This area isn't as important as is the graphics bit-map editor; however, it's a necessity if the artwork is going to be done in parallel with game design. Ultimately, the game will do all the animation and timing using the cells of animation drawn by the artist— but it's nice for the artist to get an idea of what these cells look like prior to their being placed into the game (which might not exist yet).

You may not even want to purchase an animation package. You may decide to write a simple one yourself. All you really need is to select a sequence of cells from all your bit maps and then cycle through them with some timing parameters. A decent program to do this would take a few days to complete. If you don't feel like writing one, there are packages available. However, they're high-priced. (Maybe we're in the wrong business!) Anyway, they are invariably overkill for our purposes.

There's still one company, Electronic Arts, that creates a high-quality product for a low price: Deluxe Animation. The product is designed solely for mode 13h—maybe that's why it's so inexpensive! It's simple and has been the tool of choice for hundreds of published games. It's also an incredible paint system for mode 13h, and is what I use for the most part.

Movie Making

A new trend in video games is using real actors and digitized scenery. My feelings on using actors is, "Just Say No!" It's a video game—it's supposed to look like one!

Anyway, digitizing scenery isn't so bad if the computer makes it look "computerish" so it doesn't clash with the game objects. An interesting technique that can make the worst of artists seem artistic is using models of the creatures in a game along with a camera and a frame grabber. Figure 15.1 shows how you might use real models and video hardware for this purpose.

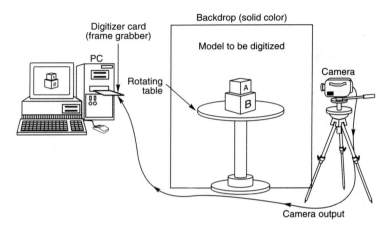

Figure 15.1. *Using real models and video hardware to create artwork and imagery.*

In Chapter 8, "High-Speed 3-D Sprites," we go into the detail of building a small studio and using video for this kind of work. In brief, though:

■ A model of some creature is placed on a platform with a blue, black or white background that can be subtracted out later.

■ You then digitize the image using the PC, a video camera, and frame grabber.

This is for the most part how the images for DOOM were created. A modeler made models of the creatures, placed them on a platform and digitized them. Then he fixed up their colors and gave them to the programmers to use in the game.

Using this technique, a video-game programmer can get realistic images from models of mechs, creatures, or whatever. Moreover, obtaining different 3-D views of the object is as easy as rotating or moving the model. If you have a little money, therefore, and your graphic arts talents aren't at their peak, this may be the way to go.

Sound Editors

There are two kinds of sounds in a video game:

■ Digitized effects

■ Music

As far as digitized sound goes, many tools are available to the public that enable you to sample and do interesting things to the raw sounds. The raw sounds themselves can be obtained from anywhere or anything you can imagine. There are even CDs with hundreds of digitized sound effects: explosions, cars, rockets, and so on. However, if you don't have access to a CD or to a digitized sound library, you'd be surprised what sounds you can make yourself. The entire set of digitized effects for Net-Tank was made with my vocal cords!

Music is a whole other ball game. It's an area that many video-game programmers leave to the experts: music is to be made by musicians, not by programmers! If you happen to be both, all the more power to you. There are many "sequencers" and musical composition products you might be able to take advantage of. However, I suggest you take already-made songs and short ballads and use them as your foundation.

Another approach you may want to explore is having a musician record the music using a synthesizer with a MIDI output digitized by the PC.

Whatever you decide to do, the music for a game must have the proper tempo, and the "mood" of the music must be right for each level and set of conditions. For these reasons, many video-game programmers contract out the musical parts of the game to professional musicians so the job gets done right. Moreover, you may need a fairly advanced sound driver, which you'll have to obtain or create yourself. If, however, you feel that the sound effects you need are simple, a digitizer, some samples, and a little creativity will go a long way.

The Map Editor—WAREDIT

We have talked about some of the commercially available tools that a video-game programmer needs, and how they're used. Now I want to cover tools that are specific to the game we're creating. In our case, we're making a 3-D textured game called Warlock. The game will be very simple; as of the moment I write this, I'm still not sure it'll even have any monsters in it. However, I want to make a tool that will allow us to easily create levels for the game. Warlock consists of a 3-D world comprised of a set of cubes. Each cube has textures on all four sides of it. The world is approximately 200x200 cubes, as shown in Figure 15.2.

We could have represented the world as a text file and typed in 40,000 little characters. However, I didn't think that would be any fun! Instead, I decided to create a simple map editor that allows the user to "draw" the world from a top-down view. The map editor enables us to easily create new levels and new environments in which our game objects can exist.

You can use a mouse to draw on a surface that will represent the entire game universe. The color you draw with represents different textures and objects that can be in the world. There are a few controls on the map editor. We get to their operation shortly.

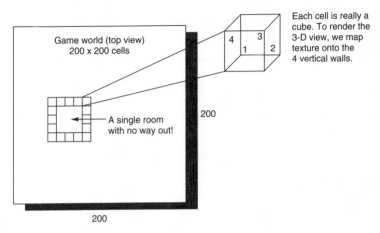

Game world (top view)
200 x 200 cells

A single room
with no way out!

200

200

Each cell is really a
cube. To render the
3-D view, we map
texture onto the
4 vertical walls.

4 3
1 2

Figure 15.2. *The game world for Warlock.*

I decided to represent the game world using a cell-based technique. Therefore, all I need do is generate some kind of 2-D matrix that represents the game world, and fill it with integers that represent the types of objects that go in those positions. The objects can be walls, foods, potions, monsters, scrolls, or doors.

Now, if a wall or door is placed in a cell, it fills a square up exactly. However, other objects, such as food and scrolls, are much smaller than the size of a wall (which is really a six-sided cube; the top and bottom are always invisible). Therefore, when a scroll is placed down on the map, we can only place it within a square. We cannot be any more accurate than that. When the game engine recognizes a scroll in the data structure, it places a scroll randomly within the square. A better solution would have been to make the editor have a more advanced data structure so that objects smaller than a single square could be placed more accurately. However, what the editor does now is good enough for our purposes.

You generate a level by drawing walls, doors, and so on with different colors, selecting the object by clicking on a color. I used colors to represent objects because it's the easiest method to implement, although it would have been much better to use scaled down icons. The problem with that approach would have been that the screen, or map area, would have had to be many times larger to represent a 200x200 matrix of icons: it would have to be scrolled with scroll bars. I didn't want to implement all kinds of gadgets, so we're stuck with colors to represent the walls, door, potions, and so on. The good news is that when you select a color, the object that color represents is placed into the preview box so you can see what you're drawing with.

The software is absolutely crude and took about three days to write. A proper map editor, with full control and the works, would take months to implement. (The map editor ID used for DOOM took six months to complete!) Therefore, although making a good tool and spending time on it is crucial, WAREDIT will suffice for our needs. WAREDIT will enable us to draw a level, place objects in the world, and then save the level.

As a final feature, WAREDIT has a zoom window that continually zooms around the cursor as it moves in the map area. This helps with the placement of doors and creating of fine detail.

Using WAREDIT

To run WAREDIT, enter:

```
wedit
```

at the DOS prompt. The program begins by loading in the textures and all the imagery for the preview window. As it's doing this you see images flash on the screen. When the loading of all the textures is complete, you see the interface.

The controls on WAREDIT are simple. To start drawing a map or level:

1. Click on the object you wish to use.

   The objects are listed down the right side of the screen; there are walls, doors, scrolls, potions, food, and monsters.

   To see a preview of the texture or object represented by any color, click that color. I tried to choose colors so there was some correlation between the color of the icon and the texture it represents (for example, gray colors for the stone textures). However, the shades are really irrelevant. A darker shade doesn't mean a darker texture; it means a different texture.

2. Once you've selected a color and, ultimately, a texture or object, move the mouse into the large rectangle on the left side of the screen. This is the area where you draw your level.

   I suggest first drawing all the walls and doors. When the level is complete, place your game objects: scrolls, potions, monsters, and so on. If you make a mistake, use the right mouse button as an eraser.

When you're satisfied with the level:

1. Click the START color in the lower-right portion of the interface.

2. Place a single pixel somewhere in the game area. This is where the player will start. The player will always be looking upward.

To load or save a map, use the controls in the upper-right portion of the interface. File names can be up to eight characters long, with no extensions. To start all over (that is, to clear the screen), click the CLEAR button. The screen is cleared.

That is about all there is to using the editor.

> You may have a more up-to-date version of WAREDIT. However, the database that this version creates will be almost fully compatible with any further updates. I can guarantee the artwork and textures will be different, and the colors may also change. However, if you placed potion number 1 somewhere, no matter what potion number 1 looks like or what color represents it, the new WAREDIT will be able to load it in and use your levels. I could give you the final version now; however, this is more realistic. You can see what changes will be made and why we made them in the next chapter. If I do make such a change, I'll let you know with a readme file.

Now that we've talked about WAREDIT from a user's point of view, let's talk about the general program structure and database format.

A Functional Description of WAREDIT

The WAREDIT program is fairly understandable. In general, most tools aren't too complex to write; they're just time consuming. The factor that just kills you is all the graphical user-interface code! Because we're using DOS and not MS Windows, we must write everything ourselves. If we want buttons, we have to write button code. If we want dialog boxes, we have to write routines to make dialog boxes. And on it goes.

This is an important factor to consider. If you're going to start making tools with GUIs, you'd better first make a library that you can rely on to do the graphics. Otherwise, you'll be writing thousands of lines of interface code!

Let's go through the design process a little and see what was needed to implement WAREDIT. Then we cover some of the more interesting functions.

WAREDIT was designed to do one thing: draw the map of the Warlock world based on all the textures and objects that could be in the world. We had to be able to load and save levels and see a preview of these textures as they were being used. Also, I realized that a 200x200 map matrix with a single pixel to represent a block is too small for most people to see; moreover, the color of a single pixel is hard to discern from the color of another that's close by. With that in mind, I decided to create a zoom window that would continually zoom the area around the mouse pointer whenever the mouse was in the map region. As far as software goes, I needed the following functionality:

- A way to load .PCX files
- A way to draw sprites and scale objects
- A mouse library
- Dialog boxes
- A routine that could figure out where the mouse was clicked
- A function that could zoom an image
- Some I/O functions to load and save the data
- A predrawn, loadable user interface

We've already written the first three items. I had to implement the rest of the functions using new code, or additions to existing code.

Let's begin with that last one. I knew that if I had to algorithmically draw the GUI, it was going to take me days. Instead, I decided to draw the GUI using Deluxe Paint and load it in as a .PCX file. After I drew the GUI, I recorded (with pencil and paper) the position of all the icons and windows so I could create constants in the editor program that would point to these areas of interest.

Selecting all the colors was the hardest part. I knew that I'd have about four different wall types, each having up to six different textures. I also knew that the walls would be based on four different colors: gray, red, green, and blue. Therefore, I used shades of each of those colors to represent the different textures.

I knew that the user would have a hard time seeing each shade on the screen, so I decided to create the zoom utility. The zoom window works by tracking the mouse cursor and grabbing the pixels around it within a six-pixel radius. These pixels are then made larger by replicating each single pixel in the map area into a large, 3x3 pixel. The image is then rendered in the zoom window.

Back to all the icons. When you click on an icon, which is really a color that represents a texture or object, you see a preview of the object in the preview window. This is accomplished by taking the bit map for the texture or object and scaling it to fit within the preview window. Now, you use that icon color to draw with. However, the color itself is not what goes into the database when you draw on the map area. A look-up table translates the color to a value that will be used by the game software as the actual data that represents a texture or object. Listing 15.1 contains the defines section delineating the different data types:

Listing 15.1. The defines section of WAREDIT.

```
#define WALLS_START       64
#define NUM_WALLS         24

#define DOORS_START       128
#define NUM_DOORS         4

#define SCROLLS_START     144
#define NUM_SCROLLS       4

#define POTIONS_START     160
#define NUM_POTIONS       4

#define FOODS_START       176
#define NUM_FOODS         2

#define MONSTERS_START    192
#define NUM_MONSTERS      2

#define WALL_STONE_1      (WALLS_START+0)    // for now only 6
#define WALL_STONE_2      (WALLS_START+1)
#define WALL_STONE_3      (WALLS_START+2)
#define WALL_STONE_4      (WALLS_START+3)
#define WALL_STONE_5      (WALLS_START+4)
#define WALL_STONE_6      (WALLS_START+5)
#define NUM_STONE_WALLS   6

#define WALL_MELT_1       (WALLS_START+6)    // for now only 6
#define WALL_MELT_2       (WALLS_START+7)
#define WALL_MELT_3       (WALLS_START+8)
#define WALL_MELT_4       (WALLS_START+9)
#define WALL_MELT_5       (WALLS_START+10)
#define WALL_MELT_6       (WALLS_START+11)
#define NUM_MELT_WALLS    6

#define WALL_OOZ_1        (WALLS_START+12)   // for now only 6
#define WALL_OOZ_2        (WALLS_START+13)
#define WALL_OOZ_3        (WALLS_START+14)
#define WALL_OOZ_4        (WALLS_START+15)
#define WALL_OOZ_5        (WALLS_START+16)
#define WALL_OOZ_6        (WALLS_START+17)
#define NUM_OOZ_WALLS     6

#define WALL_ICE_1        (WALLS_START+18)   // for now only 6
#define WALL_ICE_2        (WALLS_START+19)
#define WALL_ICE_3        (WALLS_START+20)
#define WALL_ICE_4        (WALLS_START+21)
```

continues

Listing 15.1. continued

```
#define WALL_ICE_5        (WALLS_START+22)
#define WALL_ICE_6        (WALLS_START+23)
#define NUM_ICE_WALLS     6

#define DOORS_1            (DOORS_START+0)   // for now only 4
#define DOORS_2            (DOORS_START+1)
#define DOORS_3            (DOORS_START+2)
#define DOORS_4            (DOORS_START+3)

#define SCROLLS_1         (SCROLLS_START+0) // for now only 4
#define SCROLLS_2         (SCROLLS_START+1)
#define SCROLLS_3         (SCROLLS_START+2)
#define SCROLLS_4         (SCROLLS_START+3)

#define POTIONS_1         (POTIONS_START+0) // for now only 4
#define POTIONS_2         (POTIONS_START+1)
#define POTIONS_3         (POTIONS_START+2)
#define POTIONS_4         (POTIONS_START+3)

#define FOODS_1            (FOODS_START+0)    // for now only 2
#define FOODS_2            (FOODS_START+1)

#define MONSTERS_1        (MONSTERS_START+0) // for now only 2
#define MONSTERS_2        (MONSTERS_START+1)

#define GAME_START 255 // Put the player here. The player will
                       // always start wherever this value is.
```

As you can see in Listing 15.1, there's a define for each texture or object that can be in the world. For instance, all the walls in the world will always have values from 64-127. All scrolls start at value 144 and end at value 159. Currently, there are only 24 walls and four scrolls, but I left room in the coding for up to 16 scrolls and 64 walls. The same approach was used on all game objects, so that the data structure could be improved without a lot of changes.

Therefore, when you're drawing in the map area you're really filling up the database, which is a long array that's accessed like a 2-D matrix.

When the array is built up and the level is complete, we must save the data somehow. This is where the LOAD and SAVE buttons come into play. When these are clicked, a dialog box makes sure you know what's happening. If you accept the action, a file is opened using standard fopen(), and the data is saved to or loaded from the file. You enter the file name using a custom line editor, which I made and which understands only the alphanumeric keys (along with Enter and Backspace).

NOTE

> I had to make my own line editor because the only other way to receive input in C is with scanf(), and that would permit too many potential errors in typing and editing (for example, you'd be able to type right over the boundaries of the input box). See how much trouble obtaining a single line of text can be!

Let's talk about the dialog box I just mentioned. It's really a bit map I drew, with two buttons on it. The buttons are just pictures. However, I know where they are relative to the upper-left corner of the dialog-box bit map. All I have to do is figure out whether the mouse is on the button, and if you clicked the mouse button.

To do this test, I created a general function that would take a few parameters, such as:

- The size of each button
- How many buttons there were per row and per column
- The location of the first button
- The distance between buttons

The function would then figure out which button had been pressed. (Remember: there's no magical way to do these things! We have to do them ourselves. We don't have a nice window manager and button engine sending us messages—although you could write one. However, I didn't want to write an entire windowing system for this editor!)

Listing 15.2 contains the function that detects what button is pressed.

Listing 15.2. Detecting a button press.

```
////////////////////////////////////////////////////////////////

int Icon_Hit(int xo, int yo, int dx, int dy,
             int width, int height,
             int num_columns, int num_rows,
             int mx, int my)
{
// Given the geometry of the set of buttons or icons, this
// function computes which one the mouse has clicked.

int row, column, xs,ys,xe,ye;

for (row=0; row<num_rows; row++)
    {
```

continues

Listing 15.2. continued

```
// Compute starting and ending y of current row.

ys = row*dy + yo;
ye = ys+height;

for (column=0; column<num_columns; column++)
    {
    xs = column*dx + xo;
    xe = xs+width;

    // Test whether the mouse pointer is within bounding box
    // of the current icon.

    if (mx>xs && mx<xe && my>ys && my<ye)
        {
        return(column + row*num_columns);

        } // end if a hit

    } // end for column scan

} // end for row scan

return(-1); // no hit

} // end Icon_Hit

////////////////////////////////////////////////////////////////
```

That's really all there is to the map editor: some collision detection, a little scaling, a couple of look-up tables, and a nicely drawn GUI. I suggest you play with the editor and get a feel for it before we have the next discussion about improvements that could be made to it.

Finally, to create an executable version of WAREDIT, you should use the two objects I have created called GRAPH0.OBJ and MOUSELIB.OBJ. I suggest putting them into a library and then linking to wedit.c. (However, you can do whatever you want.) Of course, GRAPH0.OBJ was created with graph0.c and graph0.h, and MOUSELIB.OBJ was created with mouselib.c, which we've seen before.

Improving WAREDIT

WAREDIT will work for our needs, but it's hardly a complete product. It lacks many features that we don't require for our present purposes, but that will be needed to make detailed levels. Here are some things you might think about for future implementation:

- Using colored dots to represent game objects is too cryptic. The optimal solution would be to have a scrolling window in which the game world could be viewed. Each block of the game would be represented by an icon instead of a single pixel.

- Another limitation: all objects have to be placed on block or cell boundaries. What if we want to put two "foods" in the same cell? The way to do this would be to have a cell zoom. This would allow you to place objects smaller than a cell in multiple positions within the same cell.

- Also, what about special effects such as lighting? We should be able to change the light levels in an area.

- What about setting the characteristics of the monsters? We should be able to do more than place them in a cell: we should be able to point them in a direction, give them an aggressiveness, and so on.

- We should also have some kind of ability to teleport the player. However, then we'd need to create a source and a destination for the teleportations.

- An important technique not used by WAREDIT is *polymorphism*: a technique that allows the abstraction of data types so that multiple forms can be referred to using the same reference. All the data structures and defines are hardcoded in the program, and they'll have to be imported into the game in an include file. It would have been better to have some kind of parser read an .INI file that would have all the game objects and their values.

We could go on and on adding to the editor, and that's what most people do until they have the ultimate editor. In fact, we could take a few days and improve the editor and bring it up to the level where we could create maps with the detail of Wolfenstein 3-D. (Giving it the detail of DOOM would take months!) In any case, I think you have some food for thought, and if your first editor is even twice as good as WAREDIT, it will probably be good enough to create a good game.

Summary

We've traveled a long way—and, if you're still with me, you must be one of the chosen few destined to create other worlds in the realm of the PC. I bet you had no idea of all the details that needed to be taken into consideration, all the knowledge from so many areas that had to be mastered. Video games are truly massive in nature and anybody who can create one has accomplished a great goal. Pat yourself on the back; you deserve it!

I've been promising you as we went through our journey that we would make a 3-D game at the end. Well, we're almost at the end. In a few more chapters—in Chapter 19, to be exact—we see the Warlock game engine.

For now, back to work!

16

Creating Art for Your Game

There are many different graphics programs available in the shareware and retail markets. Each available program has its strengths and weaknesses. Sometimes it may take more than one program to provide all the functions and features you might desire for your game's graphic development.

Popular paint programs available as shareware are MVP Paint, NeoPaint, and Desktop Paint 256. One advantage shareware programs have over retail packages is that you can "try them before you buy them." It's important to point out here that shareware is widely available, but it is not *free*. Some shareware games, programs, and utilities are included on the CD furnished with this book to help you learn the concepts discussed by the authors. Please read the registration information for the software programs that interest you. Typically, you do not have license to use these programs beyond the evaluation period of the software (typically, 10 to 30 days) unless the software is purchased and

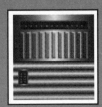

by Denise Tyler

registered. By registering the software with the developer, you help promote the availability of higher quality software through this method. You also have the peace of mind of using a fully licensed version of the software, and gaining technical support when needed.

Commercially, there are a wide variety of graphics programs. Their prices range from under one hundred dollars to thousands of dollars. One software package that's reasonably priced and quite popular within the game community is Electronic Arts' Deluxe Paint II Enhanced. A version that creates animations, Deluxe Paint Animator, is also available. Programs that combine raster-based and vector-based graphics are also popular: CorelDRAW! and Micrografx Designer are two such programs. Another inventive and powerful graphics program is Fractal Design Painter, which simulates traditional art media in a remarkable way. On the higher end, animation software such as Autodesk Animator Pro and 3D Studio offer unlimited possibilities in image development and animation.

Handy Features and Tools

What are some of the handy features you should look for in a graphics program? Well, there are quite a few I look for and use frequently, and I'm happy to share some pointers with you on this:

- Look for the ability to import and export a variety of file formats. Images can come in a variety of bit-map formats that may have to be converted into the format you finally use. For example, you may want your final output to be a .PCX file, but you've found some photos that have been saved in GIF, BMP, or TIF format. It's nice to be able to convert these other formats into your project, edit them as necessary, and then save them into your final format. These four file formats are the most commonly used for 256-color PC paint programs.

- Look for complete control over the colors in and arrangement of the palette. You may have gathered images from several different sources in addition to creating your own. Your goal is to make a palette that will produce the best results with all these different types of images. You'll find that combining these images results in a palette that is haphazardly arranged. Having the ability to rearrange these colors into logical gradient ranges is a handy feature that I get into in more detail later in this chapter.

- Another good feature is the ability to reduce the number of colors in an image to a user-specified amount. You'll find quickly that 256 colors don't go a long way when working with a variety of photos or canned textures. You may need some way of reducing the colors of each individual image (say, from 256 colors down to 64 colors, or perhaps even 32 colors).

■ An especially good feature is the ability to combine palettes from two or more images and intelligently select the best colors for the combined image. Using the preceding example, after the palettes of individual images have been reduced, you can combine several smaller palettes into one. If you cannot find a program that does this, consider a 24-bit (true-color) paint program. This type of program enables you to cut and paste different images into one file and then convert the combined image to the best 256 colors for your palette.

■ You'll also want features that can employ gradients. *Gradient routines* blend a color from one to another, and are available in many different forms. Some gradient routines work with two colors and vary the ratio of one color to the next, blending (or *dithering*) the two colors. Other gradient routines enable you to select a range of colors in the palette and blend between them, using the entire range. The latter method is the one I prefer, because the results are softer and quite handy for dimensional drawing. Electronic Arts' Deluxe Paint series has nice gradient features.

■ Lastly, you'll be happier if you can perform softening and anti-aliasing. (*Anti-aliasing* is a technique that smooths the jagged appearance of diagonal or round areas by blending intermediate colors into the jagged areas.) Used carefully, they can help smooth transitions from very dark colors to very light colors and give the image a more pleasing and nonjagged appearance.

There are some important tools your money can't buy, however. These other tools—essential to developing good graphics—are desire, patience, and a good eye for detail. Whether it be programming, cooking, or drawing, perfecting any task takes practice. Don't be discouraged if your initial artwork doesn't come out the way you saw it in your mind's eye. Consider that you learned something by making it, and continue onward!

Now, let's look at the basics of creating game graphics, shall we?

Plan First: Take an Inventory

You've just been handed a game engine and a description of the plot of the game. In the description is a list of wall graphics, characters, and objects that have to be developed. What's the next step?

Well, before you start drawing the pictures you have to create a palette that contains all the colors you'll use in the game. Sometimes this is pretty straightforward, especially in the case where all the tiles and characters will be drawn by hand. However, if you intend to use graphics obtained from other sources, such as photos or rendered graphics, palette development will take a little planning.

Before you begin to develop your palette, you should consider a few things about the game you're creating the graphics for. Some of the factors you should keep in mind are discussed here.

Game Resolution and the Number of Colors

Some games are developed in 16 colors, and others in 256 colors. In this book we've been concentrating on developing 256-color games. Screen resolutions can be 320x200, 320x240, or 640x480 and higher. Larger resolutions present some performance problems on anything but a really fast computer, but the principles of the graphic development remain the same.

Art for Your Target Audience

Is your game intended for children, for adolescents, for teenagers, or for adults? Children's games are generally done in bright, cheery colors. Think of the types of things children are attracted to: cartoons, circuses, and parades! All these things have bright colors associated with them. Teenagers generally like games with a lot of action and monsters—the more, the better! Games targeted for older audiences are probably influenced more by the subject matter of the game, discussed next.

Subject Matter and General Mood

Does your game require graphics that reflect high-tech, such as a space adventure? This might require a combination of bright and dark colors, the bright colors for the high-tech metallic looks and the darker colors for the starry skies of the universe. Medieval scenes might require a rich-looking palette with earthy, antiqued colors to reflect days of old. Horror games would probably require dark, gloomy colors. If your game will require scenes in both day and night lighting, take that into consideration as well.

What and What Not to Detail

Certain situations will arise that dictate how your palette is created and the colors that appear in it. If you have some photographs or 3-D renderings that you'll be using for your game, you'll want them displayed as accurately as possible. Later we discuss how to optimize the palette to incorporate as many of the required colors as possible so that your images look their best.

A Bit About Color

From the "artistic" point of view, most colors can be created from three primary colors—red, *yellow*, and blue. When painting or coloring, if you mix equal portions of these three colors you arrive at a color that's very close to black. White is one color that you cannot obtain by mixing these colors.

In the computer world, where color is made from light, all the colors on your CRT are made of varying levels of red, *green*, and blue light. Many programs describe the colors on your screen with three numbers, separated by commas. For example, the color black on the computer would be represented as R0, G0, B0 (meaning all three color light guns are "off"). In the computer world, white is achieved by pushing all three values to their fullest (R63, G63, and B63 for 8-bit registers, or R255, G255, and B255 for 24-bit registers).

Color can be divided into "warm" colors and "cool" colors. Some examples are shown in Table 16.1.

Table 16.1. Color temperatures.

Warm colors	Cool colors
Red	Green
Yellow	Blue
Orange	Purple
All earth tones	All gray shades, including white and black

Now, here's the tricky part. Warm colors can be "cooled down" by being tinted or mixed with a cool color. Likewise, a cool color can be "warmed up" by tinting it with a warm color. It's generally a good idea to create a scene that contains all warm or all cool colors. This creates an image that is more pleasing to the eye. For cool scenes, tinting your warm colors just a tad with a cool color, such as green or blue, is a good choice. For warm scenes, tinting your cool colors slightly with a value close to brown generally works quite well.

Another thing worth mentioning is that colors look quite different depending on the background color or colors they're placed against. To show you a simple example of this, take a look at the file EXAMP16.PCX (on the CD). This file shows two monsters, a gray one and a red one, which are placed on both a medium gray and a white background. The monsters are the same colors in both instances, but those viewed against the white background appear darker.

You should also experiment to see what a warm color would look like on a cool background color, or vice versa. The colors will fight with each other and hurt your eyes. This is the main reason for keeping the same color theme in the entire image.

Development of a 256-Color Game Palette

There are a few different approaches to take in developing palettes for 256-color games. One method, commonly used in adventure-type games, is to designate a portion of the palette to remain the same in each image. These colors are used for items that appear in more than one screen of the game (for example, user-interface elements, characters, and objects). Usually, 64 colors are sufficient to reserve for this. The remaining 192 colors in the palette will change from screen to screen, depending on the background images created for the game.

Another approach is to create a single palette to be used for all screens, objects, and characters in your game. This is the method we discuss here.

The Best Colors to Use

If you're developing all of your game images from scratch, you have a wide choice of colors to use within your game palette. As a rule, however, you'll probably want to include the following color ranges:

- Gray shades (from pure white to pure black)
- Ranges of each of the primary colors (red, yellow, and blue)
- Ranges of each of the secondary colors (orange, green, and purple)
- Flesh tones for your characters
- Earth tones for hair, earth, wood, and so on

Graduated Ramps of Colors

What do I mean by a "range of colors" or a "graduated ramp of color"? Let's refer to the .PCX file named EXAMP01.PCX on the companion CD. You want to create a red ball and make it look as though it's round and three dimensional. The ball appears on a black background, and light is shining onto the ball from its right front side.

In the two-dimensional world, this ball would be represented by a circle filled with a singular color—a medium shade of red, as shown in the upper portion of Figure 16.1.

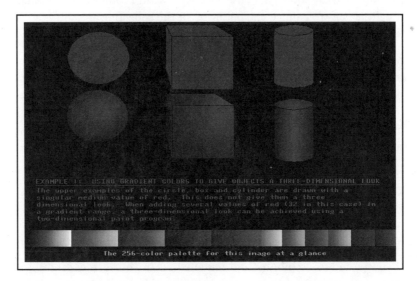

Figure 16.1. *Using gradient colors to achieve a 3-D look with a 2-D paint program (EXAMP01.PCX on the companion CD).*

This hardly looks convincing, does it? To make the ball appear as though it's round, the shades of red must vary from light to dark values, as shown on the lower portion of the figure. This gives the object shape, highlight, and sheen. The same technique applies to square or cylindrical shapes, as shown in the example picture.

These light-to-dark shades of red are what I mean as a *range of colors* or a *graduated ramp of color*. Notice when looking at the palette for this sample PCX file that several color ranges have been developed. Feel free to experiment with this palette and modify it to suit your color preferences.

Saving a Color for Transparency

One important factor to mention during development of your palette is that you must reserve a color for use as transparency in your sprites and characters. If any image contains this color, you'll see holes in that image! Keep this in mind when working with your images, and check to be sure that any usage of your transparent color is changed to another color that works well in that image.

Obtaining Palettes from Other Images

There are commercial libraries of clip art and photographs available on the market that offer royalty-free usage of the images contained in the collection. It's important to note, however, that you should read the licensing agreements of such collections carefully to be sure you have the right to use the images within your product. If there's any doubt, it's always safe to contact the publisher of the collection.

Using clip art or images from bulletin boards and communication services is not recommended. Many graphic files on these types of boards have been copied from magazines, copyrighted photographs, and movies without prior permission from the publisher or creator. Unless permission is given in the accompanying documentation to do so, you'd be wise not to use these images in your game. The safest thing to do, of course, is to take your own photos and develop your own rendered graphics, or hire someone to develop them for you if you aren't able.

In the previous section we discussed what colors would be best to place in a palette to give you a wide range of colors to use. If you try to fit a photograph into this palette, you quickly see that the appearance of the photograph has been severely altered. It might be great "pop art," but hardly sufficient for your game. To get around this, you must create your palette around the colors that exist in the images you've collected.

If you intend to use photos and rendered art in your game, careful selection of the images can make a difference in how far the 256 colors in your palette will go. Keep some of these pointers in mind:

- ■ **DO** select images with a common color theme throughout the collection, and colors that come close to those you want to see in your final game. Maintaining this consistency allows your final versions of these tiles to be displayed more accurately.

- ■ **DO** select images with good contrast and fairly good color consistency. Having a photo or image with light areas on one side and dark areas on the other will be difficult to make tileable, which is a necessity in 3-D games. We will discuss making images tileable later on.

- ■ **DON'T** select images with a lot of "little things" in them. For example, let's say you have a high-resolution photograph of a crowd of people sitting on bleachers. When reduced to a 64x64 tile, this image would not look as you think. You might see faces represented by only one pixel, or not at all! Folks will say, "What is that?"

It's probably a good idea to rescale your photos or renderings, if necessary, to the approximate size your finished tiles will be. The best time to rescale would be before you optimize your palette. There are two reasons I can think of for doing this:

■ First, you'll only optimize the colors you actually need, rather than any other extraneous colors that might appear in the larger image.

■ Second, when it comes time to gather all your images into one file to create the palette, you can fit many of them in one image file.

Approaches to creating the final 256-color palette differ depending on whether you're using a 256-color paint program or a 24-bit, true color paint program.

Using a 256-color paint program, how can you combine several images into one palette without affecting the quality of the image? One approach is to squeeze the colors of each image down to the fewest number of colors it can use without degrading its quality.

Let me show you an example of this. First, let's take a look at Figure 16.2 (or EXAMP02.PCX on the companion CD), which shows two images of a room in a house. The left side of the image is what the room would look like during the day, and the right side of the image shows the same view at night. Figure 16.3 (EXAMP03.PCX) is the same image, but the palette has been rearranged into gradients. This will make the creation of hand-drawn 3-D art easier while keeping the same colors that the image already contains.

Figure 16.2. *A palette with its colors in the "default" arrangement, as provided with a graphic file.*

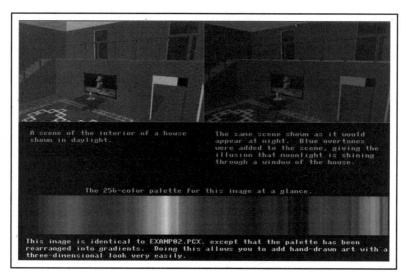

Figure 16.3. *The same image as EXAMP02.PCX, but with its palette rearranged into gradients (EXAMP03.PCX).*

Now let's take a look at Figure 16.4 (EXAMP04.PCX). In this file, the colors contained in the image have been reduced to 128 colors. There is some degradation of the image quality, but enough detail remains to portray the image effectively. By reducing the colors in the image, you now have 128 spaces for colors that can be used for other images.

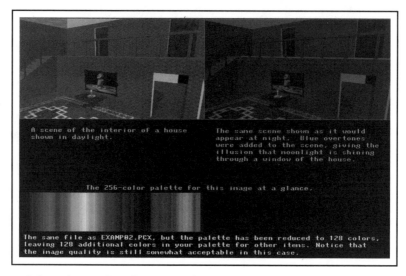

Figure 16.4. *Reducing the colors to 128 frees up 128 colors for additional images and characters (EXAMP04.PCX).*

Let's see what happens if we reduce the number of colors in half again, to 64 colors. Load in EXAMP05.PCX for this example, shown in Figure 16.5. Again, there's even more degradation in the image, and some retouching may have to be done. Only you can decide whether the quality is still good enough for your game.

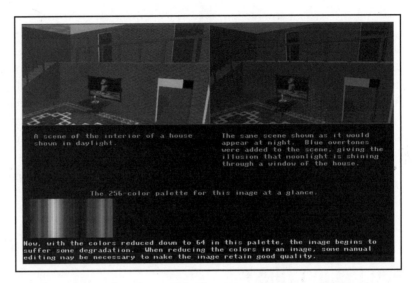

Figure 16.5. *Reducing the colors to 64 colors increases color availability, but can also affect the quality of the image. Use caution when reducing colors in the image, or touch up areas that do not appear correctly (EXAMP05.PCX).*

Each image you want to incorporate into your game should be similarly handled. However, take care that the total number of colors in all images combined does not exceed 256 individual colors.

The next step would be to combine all the images you've reduced into one graphic file. Some programs also enable you to merge palettes from multiple images into one palette. You can then use this palette to develop the remainder of your hand-drawn art.

In a 24-bit paint program, create a new image large enough to contain all or most of your gathered, rescaled images. Generally, fifty to sixty 64x64 tiles will fit into a 640x480 image, leaving space between them so that the clipping areas are easily identifiable. With a 24-bit program, you wouldn't have to worry about squeezing the palettes of each image down to fewer colors. The approach here would be to put all of your images into one 24-bit graphic file, and then convert that larger image to 256 colors. The 24-bit paint program would make the selection of colors for you, probably incorporating the 256 colors most used in the image into your palette.

Special Considerations for Digitized Video

Digitized video sequences are sometimes used for characters, rather than using hand-drawn or rendered art. Since the advent of Microsoft Video for Windows, incorporating digitized video segments into game and multimedia software is quite easy.

If your game is to incorporate digitized video sequences, make sure the same palette is pasted into each frame of the video. There should be tools to accomplish this task with your video digitizing software. Reducing colors in a digitized video sequence is difficult, especially if a lot of movement has been filmed. In general, stationary "talking head" sequences translate fairly well because the colors remain fairly consistent. Another approach would be to film a character in front of a blue screen with good lighting that casts no shadows on the background. The character then can be brought in and superimposed over other backgrounds using a technique called Chroma keying. This technique is commonly used in broadcast television to superimpose your local meteorologists over the weather maps during their reports. (For more information on this procedure, see Chapter 8, "High-Speed 3-D Sprites.")

Give Me My Space! (Developing Wall, Floor, and Ceiling Tiles)

Guess what? We're ready to start developing images now! This is the part you have been curious about, and I hope I can tell you enough of the basics to get you started.

For the purpose of these examples, let's concentrate on development of images for a 3-D arcade adventure. These games are extremely popular at this time. The same basic principles would apply to any type of game, however.

Detail, Detail, and Detail

One of the most challenging aspects of game-graphics development is to try to cram as much image detail into as small a space as you can. This is a skill that comes with practice, but it's worth getting the technique down. Paying attention to the little things helps also. It's nice to have a blank stone wall, but adding cracks, moss and other little extras enhance the tile's quality. Such added touches can make a big difference in the final result of your product. Remember: each of these tiles is a window into your imaginary world, and you have to make your players believe they're really in that world!

While developing wall, floor, and ceiling tiles, it's helpful to use a program that enables you to zoom in on the small tile and give you a better picture of it. This is helpful for two reasons:

- First, when adding the details to the tile, it helps your hand-to-eye coordination to work with a larger area and pick the exact pixels you need to change.

- Second, it gives you an idea of what the tile looks like close up, and you can make modifications as necessary to make it look better.

Let's take a look at what is involved in creating a wall tile, step by step. The steps are shown in color in EXAMP06.PCX.

1. For the first tile, the one in the top row, I began with a 64x64 box filled with a horizontal gradient ranging from very dark gray to almost white and back again. This gives the illusion that the control panel is made of stainless steel or aluminum, and also creates a more "high-tech" appearance, as shown in Figure 16.6.

Figure 16.6. *A 64x64 box filled with a gray-to-white gradient (INSERT01.PCX).*

2. Next, I added a black box where the control-panel display would be located, as shown in Figure 16.7.

Figure 16.7. *A black rectangle added where the control-panel display is located (INSERT02.PCX).*

3. Following that, I surrounded the black box by a gradient range of copper colors (dark brown to brownish-orange), as shown in Figure 16.8.

Figure 16.8. *A copper-colored border, one pixel wide, added around the black box. (INSERT03.PCX).*

4. I also added some lines in a 25-percent strength of black, just below the control-panel display, shown in Figure 16.9. This tinted the gray shades already there to a slightly darker value, adding some interest to the top section.

Figure 16.9. *Three black lines, at 25-percent strength, added to the top section for enhancement (INSERT04.PCX).*

5. In the fifth step, I added the details of the control panel shown in Figure 16.10. I drew red and yellow singular pixels for LEDs, bright green hand-drawn numbers, and bright blue oscilloscope-type lines.

Figure 16.10. *LEDs, numbers, and other details added to the display area of the control panel (INSERT05.PCX).*

6. Now that the top is done, the bottom looks rather bare, so we have to fill it with something to make it more interesting. To add a 3-D effect to the panel, I selected the same gray shades and applied them in vertical gradients. I left a boxed-in area untouched for placement of the control-panel switch. These changes are reflected in Figure 16.11.

Figure 16.11. *More gray gradients on the lower half of the tile, leaving an area for the switch (INSERT06.PCX).*

7. I then shaded the area for the switch in light and dark values along each side to give indication of a recessed area, as shown in Figure 16.12.

Figure 16.12. *The switch area, shaded with light and dark values of gray to make it appear recessed into the control panel (INSERT07.PCX).*

8. Finally, I added the switch itself, in the copper shades.

There, we have a control-panel face! The final result is shown in Figure 16.13.

Figure 16.13. *The finishing touch: a copper-colored switch added to the control panel (INSERT08.PCX).*

For the surrounding walls I made modifications to the tile already developed. Using cutting and pasting techniques, I built new tiles from the existing tile to make sure adjacent areas match up against each other. This gives consistency to the area that will appear in the game, and also helps give a seamless, non-tiled appearance to the rooms. The steps taken here are outlined in EXAMP06.PCX.

Giving Wall Tiles Depth in the 3-D World

Your little tiles might look absolutely *perfect* on your monitor—but when you get them into the three-dimensional world of your game, something looks wrong. What is it?

As a rule, when the tiles are observed at an angle in the 3-D world, anything that's a dark value appears recessed inward, and anything that's a lighter value appears in the foreground. Bear this in mind when creating your images, and use it to your advantage. To give your tiles depth and shape, consider the examples discussed and displayed in Figure 16.1. Vary the shades of colors gradually from light to dark, with light values toward the front and dark values toward the back. Sometimes, to give the appearance that certain parts of your wall tile are sticking outward, the light-to-dark shading has to be abrupt.

Rescaling Images

There are a couple of things that should be mentioned about rescaling images that you will be using as tiles.

Let's say you've created a background scene in a landscape rendering program, such as Vista Pro. You want to rescale this so the mountains can be used as background tiles in your game. The original image you created is 640x480. The upper portion of the image contains a lot of sky, and the lower portion contains a lot of grass. The center section, that with the mountains and hills, is the part you're interested in using. For an example of this, see Figure 16.14.

It wouldn't make sense to use this image as one 64x64 tile, because the mountains will squeeze together horizontally during the rescaling. It would make more sense to create multiple tiles out of this background image and place them together in your map.

If you want your final image to be placed in two 64x64 tiles, you must crop your original image to 640x320 (the height being half of the width). For three tiles, you would have to crop until you have a 640x213 area from your original image (the height being one-third the width). For four tiles, the image would have to be reduced to 640x160 (the height being one-fourth the width). Let's say, in this case, that we want to make four tiles out of this image, because the section you want to keep will fit within the 640x160 dimension.

You have to "eyeball" things a little bit here. When cropping your image, don't start off with *exactly* a 160-pixel height. You may find out that you want to keep a little more area for the sky, or have a little more grass showing. Leave a bit of extra to play with during your initial crop, because the image will look a lot different once the extraneous sky and grass are taken away from it. Figure 16.15 highlights the area that was removed in our example, and Figure 16.16 shows the resulting 640x160 image that was kept.

Figure 16.14. *A scene rendered in Vista Pro (EXAMP13.PCX).*

Figure 16.15. *The highlighted areas in this photo are to be removed from the image. The final image size will be 640x160 pixels (EXAMP12.PCX).*

Figure 16.16. *The final 640x160 image after all cropping is complete (EXAMP11.PCX).*

The next step would be to rescale the image from 640x160 down to 256x64 (or the size of four of your tiles placed end to end). Many graphic programs allow rescaling of images. Some of them enable you to enter the new width and height of the destination image, and others work on a percentage entry. To determine the percentage, divide the destination width (in this case, 256) by the source width (in this case, 640). For this example, the destination image would be 40 percent of the original size.

Creating Seamless Tileable Images

Seamless images are those that can be placed end to end without noticing where one image starts and the other ends. In some games, the images only have to be seamless horizontally (because they'll only be used end-to-end in the game). However, some games require that images be seamless both horizontally *and* vertically. This would be the case in a flight simulation game when the planes are flying over texture-mapped landscapes. These landscapes use seamless tiles that join together both horizontally and vertically.

Figure 16.17 shows you how to make a tile that's seamless in the horizontal direction only.

Figure 16.17. *When the mountain scene is placed alongside a copy of itself, an obvious seam appears (INSERT10.PCX).*

Here, our mountain range is shown rescaled to 256x64 (the size of four tiles) and placed next to a copy of itself. Notice that the seam where the two images join is obvious, and the two tiles do not flow smoothly, one right into the next. This seam should be edited so the joined images appear as one contiguous picture.

There are two basic approaches to make a seamless tile. The first way, which would work in this example, is to make a mirrored copy of the original tile. These two images would then be placed side-by-side in your game map, as shown in Figure 16.18.

Figure 16.18. *One method of creating a seamless tile: make a mirrored copy and place it alongside the original tile (INSERT11.PCX).*

This technique might not work for some images, however. In those cases, you'll have to place two copies of the original tile end to end and make modifications to the seam. Picking colors from the area surrounding the seam, edit the image so the transitions blend smoothly from one image to the other. The image in Figure 16.19 shows what the center would look like after the modifications.

Figure 16.19. *Another method of creating a seamless tile: edit the seam using surrounding colors and softening the edited areas (INSERT12.PCX).*

A new section, equal to the size of your original tile (in this case, 256x64 pixels) then is cut out of the image, making sure that the area that was edited is contained within this new section. The cutout is your seamless tile, shown in Figure 16.20.

Figure 16.20. *An area equal to the size of the original tile (and including the edited area), cropped out and used for the final, seamless tile (INSERT13.PCX).*

The above tiling examples can be seen in color in EXAMP10.PCX.

Special Situations

There are other considerations to take into account when creating wall tiles. Sometimes, the engine requires that certain effects, such as doors that open and close, be developed in a certain way. Additionally, there may be areas where the player enters into a new and different realm during the adventure, which might require the creation of a transition tile. Some of the wall tiles might be animated to add interest to the journey. This section discusses these kinds of situations.

Transitions: One Tile Type to Another

Sometimes in your map, you'll have scenes that change from one type of tile to another. Let's say you have a section in your map that's composed of shrubbery, and then suddenly you're in an area made of stone, such as a cave. You must make a *transition tile* if you want the change between the two tiles to be less abrupt.

Let's take the case of a hedge tile and a tile of a cave lined with boulders. Refer to the tiles shown in Figure 16.21 for the two areas for which we want to create a transition tile. As shown in Figure 16.21, these two tiles are seamless—that is, they work well when lined up against themselves in your game map. It's only when placed next to each other directly, as in Figure 16.22, that an obvious seam is seen. Our purpose here is to make a tile that would make the transition of the two tiles appear smoother.

Figure 16.21. *This shrub tile and boulder tile, when placed alongside copies of themselves, are seamless (INSERT14.PCX).*

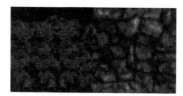

Figure 16.22. *When the shrub tile and the boulder tile are placed side by side, you can see an obvious seam (INSERT15.PCX).*

It's a good idea when creating transition tiles such as this to make a tile that transitions from tile 1 to tile 2, and another that transitions from tile 2 to tile 1. Let's say, for the first example, that you want to create a tile that transitions from tile 1 (the hedge) to tile 2 (the cave).

Use these steps:

1. Take the left half of the shrub tile and join it to the right half of the cave/boulder tile in one 64x64 image. The left half of the shrub tile was selected so that it would fit properly with the right side of the full shrub tile (as shown in Figure 16.23).

Figure 16.23. *The left half of the shrub tile, placed against the right half of the boulder tile (INSERT16.PCX).*

Likewise, the right half of the boulder tile was selected so that it would properly fit with the full boulder tile.

2. Edit the joint of the two images to give a softer appearance in how the two areas fit together. In this case, the illusion of space between the shrubs and the boulders was given by drawing in a random shape between the two areas. This area was then softened so that it blended into the black background (as shown in Figure 16.24).

Figure 16.24. *The area where the seam of the two halves join, edited to soften the transition between the two types of tiles (INSERT17.PCX).*

For the tile that transitions from the boulders to the shrubbery, you would take the left half of the boulder tile and join it to the right half of the shrub tile and edit it similarly.

Now you can have a smooth transition from one area to the next, no matter which direction it's coming from! Figure 16.25 shows what the transition tile we just created looks like when placed in the proper location in your game map.

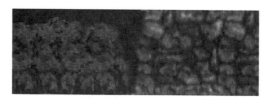

Figure 16.25. *The shrub tile, the edited transition tile, and the boulder tile, placed side by side (INSERT18.PCX).*

Doors and Elevators

Sliding doors and elevator doors are composed of two tiles: a door tile and a jamb tile. For the purpose of this next example, I've selected two of the tiles that were created when making the control-panel area. These two images work extremely well for an elevator door. The tile on the right will be perfect for a jamb, and the tile on the left will be perfect for the elevator door (as shown in Figure 16.26).

Figure 16.26. *Two of the tiles developed while creating our control-panel tile, selected to create an elevator (INSERT19.PCX).*

For the jamb tile, think of what the opening in the side of a sliding kitchen door looks like. The object of the jamb tile is to give the appearance that the sliding door is recessing into the wall. To make a jamb and door from these tiles:

1. Draw a dark box in the center of the tile.

2. Soften the edges a little so that the lines aren't as abrupt.

3. Add a little detail to the tile, such as LEDs or buttons.

The results are shown in Figure 16.27.

Figure 16.27. *The right tile shown in Figure 16.26, modified to create a door jamb (INSERT20.PCX).*

You need two tiles for an elevator door:

■ The first tile is for a door that slides from left to right. The pushbuttons in this tile are located on the left edge: the side of the door that will be visible the longest while the door recesses into the wall (as shown in Figure 16.28).

Figure 16.28. *Two door tiles—one for sliding left and one for sliding right—created from the left tile shown in Figure 16.26 (INSERT21.PCX).*

■ The second door tile has its pushbuttons on the right side of the door. When opened, this door will slide from right to left.

In many cases, you can just mirror the first tile and make modifications to it to create the second tile.

Special Effects and Animated Walls

Walls can be animated in a series of different frames to add interest to your scene. For instance, you can add torches with flickering lights on your walls, or a fireplace, or an animated control panel.

Because we already have our first control-panel tile done, we can now look at the steps involved in animating it. Take a look at the following six tiles, three in Figure 16.29 and three in Figure 16.30. You'll see that each tile is slightly different. Some of the LEDs are blacked out in different spots. The number display changes, and the blue oscilloscope line varies in height in places. The last three tiles show the control-panel switch going from its upper position to its lower position, which can be used when the control panel is activated or deactivated.

Figure 16.29. *The control-panel display is slightly different in each of these three tiles (INSERT22.PCX).*

Figure 16.30. *In addition to changes in the control-panel display, the switch moves from top to bottom in these three tiles (INSERT23.PCX).*

When animated, these tiles will look as though the control panel is operating. The LEDs will flash, and the numeric display will rapidly change as if the control panel is making calculations.

To make these tiles, you need only to make as many copies as desired in your sequence and modify them slightly in each successive tile.

Avoiding "the Jaggies"

When you look at your tiles in perspective in your 3-D world, you'll notice that some areas are heavily jagged when displayed on your screen at an angle. The way to avoid this is to draw any horizontal lines in a 2-pixel width, use softening or anti-aliasing (or both) around the line to soften it.

It's sometimes impossible to avoid "the jaggies," especially on small objects and sprites. Intelligent use of color sometimes helps the situation somewhat. Sometimes what can help is to develop your characters or other sprites on a background color similar in hue and tone to a color that's predominant in the sprite. You can then anti-alias the sprite to this background color. After that, the remaining background color can be replaced with your "transparent" color, and the image edited as necessary to work out any pixels that affect the appearance of the sprite. It's a tricky process, but one that gets easier with practice and experience.

Avoiding Color Problems with the Engine

If your engine makes farther objects appear darker than closer objects, you may need to avoid using the deepest one or two colors in each of your color ranges. Do not remove them from your palette, though, because the game engine will use them. Some engines replace the colors that have been used in your tiles with a value that is a shade or two darker to accomplish this effect. If a deeper shade does not exist, the engine will take a guess at a color that comes close in RGB value, and at times the color replacement can be objectionable.

(Chapter 6, "The Third Dimension," has more on the inner workings of distance shading and the color look-up table.)

If Only I Had Weapons and Food! (Object Development)

No game is complete without items that can be picked up and used during the course of your adventure. It'd be a difficult task to fight off those attacking monsters and enemies without weapons or food to replenish your strength. The walls you developed would also look pretty sparse without having some objects in the room to fill up the spaces a bit.

Object development is similar to wall-tile development, with one major difference: invisible, or "see-through," areas. Wall tiles are used in the game in a boxed area, where all of the pixels in the box are usually displayed on the screen. Some games also allow transparent areas in wall tiles as well, making the creation of tiles such as gates, crumbling walls, and opening/closing doors possible.

Objects and characters are also clipped into a box, but the parts of the box you wish not to be displayed on the screen are filled with your transparent color. Any use of your selected transparent color in the objects or characters will show the background environment through it.

Maintaining Object Size in Relation to Walls

When developing objects, create them at a size that will look fairly proportional to the walls surrounding it. I try to keep in mind when doing this that the average wall height in a house is eight feet. If we divide the 64-pixel height of the wall tiles by eight feet, we come up with a figure of eight pixels representing one foot. This rule of thumb works well for larger objects, such as furniture and trunks.

For smaller objects, however, this thumb rule just doesn't work. It would be difficult to draw a pistol, which would be something along the line of eight inches in height in reality; you'd have to fit the picture of this pistol into a box only five or six pixels high. In the case of smaller articles and objects, some artistic license has to be used. Draw the objects in the smallest amount of space you can while making the object as detailed and recognizable as possible.

Remember Perspective

Notice that when walking down the corridors of your 3-D world that the viewpoint toward the horizon is angled a bit. Adding a similar angle to objects adds interest to the way it looks. If the eyes of the character you're portraying in your journey would be above the level of the top of the object, you can depict that by adding a slight bit of an angle to the view. Take care not to give the object too great a perspective, however, because it won't fit in with the rest of the surroundings. All you need is a touch of perspective drawing.

Bring On the Enemies! (Character Development)

Now that all the spaces and objects are created for the game, you must give life to some inventive characters with which to interact. Character development is probably the most tedious part of the game. You often have to create at least four frames and up to as many as eight frames for each view of their movement. Each one of these frames has to be in synchronization—that is, in the same relative position—with each of the others so the character's movement doesn't appear jerky.

Is There an Easy Way?

One way to create characters is to create and render them in a 3-D animation program, such as 3D Studio, and render the actions in each of eight views (front, back, right, left, and each angle in between). The modeling, animation, and subsequent editing of the characters can sometimes take as long as hand drawing, but the perspectives and shading of the characters will be more realistic.

If all you have access to is a two-dimensional paint program, you have no alternative but to draw each of these frames by hand. There are some techniques that will make this a little easier, and these are discussed in a moment.

Proportions

Proportions of a human body are different depending on age. For an adult, the body is divided into eight sections:

- The head takes up one-eighth of the total height of the body. The upper eighth portion would be for the head, stopping at the bottom of the chin.

- Sections two and three would be for the neck and torso, with the bottom of the third section being at waist level.

- Section four would be the area from waist to hip level.

- Sections 5 and 6 would contain the upper leg region, with the knees being placed slightly above the bottom of the sixth level.

- Sections 7 and 8 would contain the lower leg region.

- In regard to the arms, the elbow would be placed slightly above waist level, and the forearm would end about where the third and fourth sections meet. The hand would extend from the forearm through about four-fifths of the fifth section.

Books on anatomy can give you some good insight as to skeletal and muscular proportion and structure. Sometimes these proportions are somewhat exaggerated in games and cartoon art; for example, longer arms and legs, overdeveloped muscles and facial features, and other characteristics that would make a character look more fierce or more heroic.

Guidelines for a Person Walking in Eight Views

EXAMP15.PCX is a graphic file provided to assist you in developing a human character walking in eight viewpoints. These frames were rendered in 3D Studio, and accurately reflect what this character would look like at each angle when taking the same step. Four frames of each view are provided. When animated and played back at the appropriate speed, the motion is quite fluid and believable.

EXAMP15.PCX, illustrated in Figure 16.31, shows four frames each of a character walking in eight views. You can use this as a guide when creating your own humanoid characters.

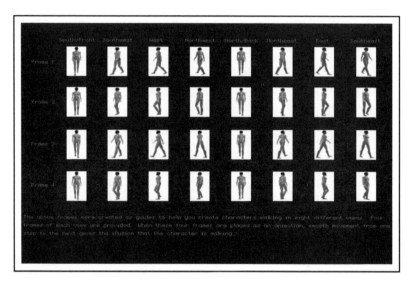

Figure 16.31. *Four frames each of a character walking in eight views (EXAMP15.PCX).*

Animation Techniques

If you study each of the frames in EXAMP15.PCX, you see that certain portions of each frame remain relatively stationary. The head and the torso of the character remain in the same basic position in each frame. To make your animation a little easier:

1. Draw these types of areas first.

2. Then make a copy of the stationary portions of each frame of the desired character.

3. Finally, add the parts of the character that move from one frame to the next.

This approach also provides an added benefit: it gives you a guide as to how to set each image one on top of the other. By basing your character animation around portions that remain stationary, you can superimpose the final frames and have the motion appear smooth. Even a one-pixel shift can create a situation where your character's movement will appear jerky.

Monsters and Other Gory Characters

I think it goes without saying that there is no "proportion" rule to making monsters—some of them have heads that could be half the size of their body! The ruling principle here is a good imagination: you can make your monster look any way you want. That's the fun of it—you don't have to worry about realism, because no one really knows what a monster is supposed to look like!

There are a wealth of sources around you to inspire ideas. Your local library has books about cartooning, or some that contain fantasy art drawn by some of the world's leading artists. Comic books can also be a good source for ideas. The depiction of monsters and demons in art goes back a long way, so you have many centuries of artwork to draw from. Remember, though: keep your monsters as original as possible to avoid copyright infringement!

The graphic file EXAMP16.PCX shows one frame of a monster. Here, you can see that the monster will look quite different just by changing its color. (That's one of the fun parts of doing character development—once you have one character made, it can be modified just a little for a totally different character!) Eventually, you'll build up quite a library of those nasty creatures that everyone loves to assault!

EXAMP16.PCX, illustrated in Figure 16.32, shows how the appearance of a character can change just by revising the colors. Changes of this type add variety to your characters in the game while cutting down on development time.

Figure 16.32. *Our two monsters again: changing color makes them look completely different (EXAMP16.PCX).*

The Finishing Touches

You might think that your graphic development is done—but there are still a *few* more screens that have to be created. These are the screens with which the user will interact— the screens that open and close the game, the border screen that surrounds the play area, and the screens that let the player know his or her progress throughout the game.

It's a good idea to maintain consistency in appearance with all of these screens. Doing so will make your game appear more professional. The key rule here, in both color and mood, is *continuity*.

Opening and Closing Screens

The opening and closing screens are probably two of the most important in your game. Of the two, the opening screen is the one that will bear the most weight. Here, you want to create a "first impression" of the game in your player's mind. If the opening screen is successful at drawing the player's attention, he or she will continue on into the game and begin playing it.

It's a good idea to develop your opening screen in the same resolution as the game. If the opening screen is drawn at a higher resolution, or with more colors, the player will expect that the rest of the game is depicted that way—and will be disappointed to find out that it is not.

Here are some ideas for your opening screen:

■ Try a scene from the game, or a depiction of the area in which it is to take place. You can, if desired, take a screen shot from the game and introduce your player to the game in that manner, but you might want to give the scene more detail in your opening screen.

■ You might have a detailed drawing of the "hero" of the game in an action pose.

■ Depict the arch enemy of the game in all his (or her) glory, taunting you in the opening screen as if to say "Come and get me!"

■ Try one or more monsters from the game, drawn in attack poses.

■ Another good choice is using the same artwork that your game will use for the package art, scaled down to your final game resolution.

For the closing screen, similar art can be used. The purpose of this screen would be to leave your player with the desire to come back for more!

User-Interface Art

The user-interface screen is the one that shows while the border and status display as you are playing the game. Here are some items this screen can include:

■ An area for score and level of play

■ An area that shows what weapon the player is currently using

■ An area that displays the condition of the player's health

■ Areas for the ammunition and food or health regeneration items the player has left

■ A display of the map that shows the location of the player in relation to where he is and where important items can be located

Screens for Status, Game Configuration, Credits...

Here are some other screens that can be displayed throughout the game:

■ The current status of the level the player is engaged in, showing level score, how many more monsters are left, what items are still necessary to obtain before the level is finished, and so on

■ The overall status of the game, including the current score and the percentage of the game completed

■ A game-configuration screen

■ A help screen

■ An instruction screen

■ A screen to select difficulty of play

Animations

Animations are also very effective for starting and ending the game. You can use animations to draw attention to your company logo, to display a background story of the game, or to end the game with previews of what's to come.

The most common format for animation is Autodesk's FLI or FLC format. FLI animations are restricted to 320x200 in size, which would be suitable for many shareware games. The FLC format was developed later, and animations of this type can be developed in any desired resolution.

If you do not have access to an animation program, a series of still frames can be created and then converted to FLI/FLC animation with Dave Mason's shareware program "Dave's Targa Animator." This is a popular shareware program that packs a lot of power and does a lot of *neat* things. The file can be found on Compuserve, in the Graphic Developers' Forum under Library 12 (Animations). If you don't have access to Compuserve, your local bulletin board may have this file in its collection; it's quite popular.

Promotional Shots

Once all your walls, characters, objects, and interface screens are created and incorporated into your game, you might want to capture a few screen shots to place on bulletin boards and on-line services to help promote interest in your game.

There are several shareware and commercial screen-capture programs available, but you should make sure that they support capturing "non-standard" video modes, such as those found in games. It's also nice to find a screen-capture program that automatically captures a screen and saves it to your hard drive. This enables you to play through the game naturally without having to pause and enter the key sequence for the capture, allowing real "action shots" to be taken.

The other option, of course, is to create code in your engine to capture screen shots at the press of a button.

Summary

Entertainment and game software is experiencing an exciting growth phase right now. As computers become faster and more powerful, it opens the door for production of games with higher resolution and more sophisticated animation. I, as well as many of you, can hope to see high-resolution true-color graphics in computer games someday, leaving the concerns about palette limitations a thing of the past.

As your graphic and animation skills improve, you can prepare yourself for development of future high-resolution games. By perfecting your skills and finding software that produces the results you desire, you pave the way for your future. Learn as much as you can about working with images, video, and animation, because the knowledge will go a long way toward creating high-quality games. By doing so, you will experience great joy as you hear that people throughout the world are enjoying your work. In my book, that's the definition of success!

Parallax Scrolling Techniques

H ave you ever looked out the window of a moving car and noticed that nearby objects appear to move by at a faster rate than objects farther away? This common experience has the somewhat-intimidating name of *parallax*. You experience parallax so often in everyday life that you probably take it for granted.

Parallax is just one of many visual cues or hints that our brains use to help interpret what our eyes "see." Another familiar visual cue is *perspective*. Perspective and parallax are combined with non-visual cues, such as balance and hearing, to form a complete picture of your immediate environment.

What, then, is *parallax scrolling*, and what does it have to do with game programming? Parallax scrolling is a graphics technique where two or more layers of graphics move at different rates. This relative motion between layers provides some of the visual cues necessary for realistic simulation of depth and motion.

by Mark Seminatore

More on Mode 13h

Before developing any scrolling code, let's first review the video mode of choice. As discussed in Chapter 5, "The Mysteries of the VGA Card," the most popular video mode for games is the standard VGA/MCGA mode 13h. Reason Number One for the popularity of mode 13h is its compatibility across different VGA chipsets. The race to be Reason Number Two is probably tied between programming ease and color depth.

The following is a brief review of mode 13h programming basics. For a more in-depth review, see Chapter 5; on the other hand, if you're experienced at programming the VGA you may want to skip to the next section. Otherwise, pay close attention: programming mode 13h is nice and simple.

Mode 13h supports a resolution of 320x200 pixels and 256 simultaneous colors, where each pixel is represented by a single byte. An entire screen therefore includes 320 times 200, or 64,000 bytes. This 64K "window" is mapped into the PC's memory space starting at A000:0000 through A000:FFFF.

All that is required to draw pixels in mode 13h is a pointer to VGA memory. You can easily create such a pointer using the following code:

```
char far *VideoMem=MK_FP(0xa000,0);
```

To draw an individual pixel at location (200,100) with a color value of 2, you need only calculate the pixel offset into video memory. The pixel offset is calculated either by multiplying the y-coordinate by 320—there are 320 pixels per row—and adding in the x-coordinate:

```
PixelOffset = y * 320 + x;
```

or using the screen coordinates:

```
PixelOffset = 100 * 320 + 200 = 32,200
```

You can then access the video display memory as if it were a one-dimensional array of characters:

```
VideoMem[PixelOffset]=2;
```

You can draw an entire rows of pixels at one time using the standard C library function `memcpy()`. This function is one of the fastest (non-optimized) ways to copy data from one memory location to another. Some compilers can even generate this function in-line for additional speed.

As an example, the following code copies 320 bytes from the array `Src` to `VideoMem`:

```
memcpy(VideoMem,Src,320);
```

Assuming that `VideoMem` points to the start of video memory, this function draws one full row of pixels on the display.

All graphics are drawn to a buffer allocated in system memory. Once an entire frame is generated, it's block-copied to the display using another call to `memcpy()`.

That's all you need to know about mode 13h at this point so let's move on.

Notes on the Demo Code

I've put together several small demos to illustrate some of the techniques described in this chapter. The code uses video mode 13h, for reasons explained above and in Chapter 5, to implement some simple parallax scrolling demos. The code is not highly optimized; the emphasis is on readability, not performance.

All code in this chapter was written for Borland C++ 3.1 and Turbo Assembler 3.1. The C code was carefully written to avoid Borland-specific language extensions, so it should compile with minimal changes under different C/C++ compilers. The assembler routines were written using Borland's IDEAL mode. Note that an assembler is not required to use the demos in this chapter. The assembly language routines are supplied as optional drop-in replacements for particular C functions.

The First Step

Before we can scroll multiple layers of graphics, we first need a method for scrolling a single layer of graphics. There are certainly many different ways to implement scrolling graphics. The first method we discuss is fairly straightforward and works well for simple, repeated scrolling.

In *repeated scrolling* the image moves horizontally and, eventually, wraps around from one edge of the screen to the other. In other words, all the image data that scrolls off the right edge of the screen gets drawn back on the left edge of the screen. Similarly, data that scrolls off the left edge gets drawn on the right edge of the screen.

Although it may not seem like this would be a terribly useful technique, it's one of the simplest to implement and may be used in a number of places. For example, the background layers of an action game don't attract too much attention, so users aren't likely to notice that the cloudy blue sky periodically repeats.

So how do you draw a bit map and force it to wrap around when we reach the edge of the screen? One simple way is to draw the bit map on the screen in two halves. Start by logically dividing our bit map into two pieces—a left and a right half. Keep track of where the logical division is using a simple integer counter. This counter stores the width of the logical left half of the bit map. For now, let's call this counter LeftHalf and set the left half width equal to one pixel.

The width of the logical right half is then the total width of the bit map minus the width of the left half. Now—and this part is *most* important—you draw the logical right half of the bit map on the left half of the screen. Likewise, you draw the left half of the bit map on the right side of the screen. Take a look at Figure 17.1 to see this process.

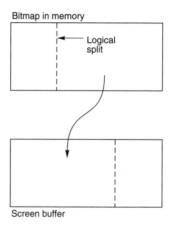

Figure 17.1. *A continuously scrolling bit map.*

So how does this strange arrangement lead to a scrolling image? To understand what's going on, let's look at what happens when you decrement LeftHalf. Decrementing LeftHalf decreases the left-half width. As a result, the last pixel of the left half becomes the first pixel of the right half. This logical shifting of image data from one half to the other is what simulates scrolling.

Next, draw the two bit map halves on the screen. Starting at the left edge of the screen, draw the logical right half of the bit map:

■ First, draw a row of bit map pixels starting at the column defined by LeftHalf. The number of pixels to draw is the total bit map width minus LeftHalf.

■ Continue by drawing pixels from the start of the bit map to column LeftHalf.

As the location of the logical split is updated and the two halves are redrawn, the image appears to move across the screen.

Take a look at the following example code, which demonstrates drawing a bit-map scanline in two halves. (Recall that a *scanline* is an entire horizontal row of pixels):

```
// Draw the bit map left half
   memcpy(Screen+320-LeftHalf,Bitmap,LeftHalf);
// Draw the bit map right half
   memcpy(Screen,Bitmap+LeftHalf,320-LeftHalf);
```

where `Screen` is a pointer to video memory, `LeftHalf` is the width of the logical left half of the bit map, and `Bitmap` is a pointer to the scrolling image. This process is repeated for every scanline of the bit map.

Each time you increment or decrement `LeftHalf`, you must make sure that it stays within the bounds of the bit map:

■ If `LeftHalf` is greater than the bit map width, set it equal to one.

■ If `LeftHalf` is less than one, set it equal to the total bit map width minus one.

Remember that because you have to draw both a left and a right half, the width of each logical half must be less than the total bit map width.

I should point out that there's no reason to limit the size of the bit map to a single screen width. It may be desirable, for example, to double the width of the bit map. The bit map would then wrap around half as often. The size of the bit map is limited by the amount of available memory.

Listing 17.1 contains the header file, Paral.h, used by the demo program in Listing 17.2, Paral.c. Paral.h contains the various manifest constants, data structures, and function prototypes used by Paral.c.

Listing 17.1. Repeat-scrolling demo header file (Paral.h).

```
//
//  Paral.h: This header defines the constants and data
//           structures used in the parallax demos.
//
    #define KEYBOARD 0x09
//
// Keyboard press/release codes for the INT 9h handler.
//
    #define RIGHT_ARROW_PRESSED    77
    #define RIGHT_ARROW_REL       205
    #define LEFT_ARROW_PRESSED     75
    #define LEFT_ARROW_REL        203
    #define ESC_PRESSED           129
    #define UP_ARROW_PRESSED       72
```

continues

Listing 17.1. continued

```c
#define UP_ARROW_REL         200
#define DOWN_ARROW_PRESSED    80
#define DOWN_ARROW_REL       208

#define VIEW_WIDTH   320
#define VIEW_HEIGHT  150
#define MEMBLK       VIEW_WIDTH*VIEW_HEIGHT
#define TRANSPARENT  0  // Color of see-thru pixels.
#define TOTAL_SCROLL 320

enum {NORMAL,RLE};
enum {FALSE,TRUE};

typedef struct
{
  char manufacturer;     /* Always set to 0 */
  char version;          /* 5 for 256-color files */
  char encoding;         /* Always set to 1 */
  char bits_per_pixel;   /* 8 for 256-color files */
  int  xmin,ymin;        /* Coords for top left corner */
  int  xmax,ymax;        /* Width and height of image */
  int  hres;             /* Horiz resolution of image */
  int  vres;             /* Vert resolution of image */
  char palette16[48];    /* EGA palette */
  char reserved;         /* Reserved for future use */
  char color_planes;     /* Color planes */
  int  bytes_per_line;   /* bytes in 1 line of pixels */
  int  palette_type;     /* 2 for color palette */
  char filler[58];       /* Nothing but junk */
} PcxHeader;

typedef struct
{
  PcxHeader hdr;
  char *bitmap;
  char pal[768];
  unsigned imagebytes,width,height;
} PcxFile;

#define PCX_MAX_SIZE 64000L
enum {PCX_OK,PCX_NOMEM,PCX_TOOBIG,PCX_NOFILE};

#ifdef __cplusplus
extern "C" {
#endif

    int ReadPcxFile(char *filename,PcxFile *pcx);
    void _interrupt NewInt9(void);
    void RestoreKeyboard(void);
    void InitKeyboard(void);
    void SetAllRgbPalette(char *pal);
    void InitVideo(void);
    void RestoreVideo(void);
    int InitBitmaps(void);
    void FreeMem(void);
    void DrawLayers(void);
```

```
    void AnimLoop(void);
    void Initialize(void);
    void CleanUp(void);
    void OpaqueBlt(char *,int,int,int);
    void TransparentBlt(char *,int,int,int);

#ifdef __cplusplus
   }
#endif
```

The program in Listing 17.2, Paral.c, demonstrates a repeated scrolling image. The moving image is that of a cloudy sky at sunset. While it may look like a continuously varying image, it's actually a single image with wrap-around at the edges of the screen.

The most important function in the code is OpaqueBlt(). This routine draws the left and right halves of the bit map, as defined by LeftHalf, in a system memory buffer. When finished, the contents of the memory buffer are copied to the screen.

When you run Paral.c, use the left- and right-arrow keys to change the direction of movement. To exit the demo, hit the escape key. When you exit the program, it calculates and displays the animation frame rate. The performance on a 386SX/25 was nearly 35 frames per second with a viewport size of 320x100 pixels.

Listing 17.2. Repeated scrolling demo (Paral.c).

```c
    #include <stdio.h>
    #include <stdlib.h>
    #include <string.h>
    #include <time.h>
    #include <dos.h>
    #include "paral.h"

    char *MemBuf,          // Pointer to memory buffer

           *BackGroundBmp, // Pointer to background bit map

           *VideoRam;      // Pointer to VGA memory

    PcxFile pcx;           // Structure for .PCX files

    int volatile KeyScan;  // Modified by keyboard handler

    int frames=0,          // Total frames drawn

         PrevMode;         // Original video mode

    int background;        // Left-half position in background

// Pointer to BIOS keyboard handler
    void _interrupt (*OldInt9)(void);
```

continues

Listing 17.2. continued

```c
//
// This routine loads a 256-color PCX file.
//
    int ReadPcxFile(char *filename,PcxFile *pcx)
    {
      long counter;
      int mode=NORMAL,nbytes;
      char abyte,*pchar;
      FILE *fileptr;

      fileptr=fopen(filename,"rb");
      if(fileptr==NULL)
        return PCX_NOFILE;
      fread(&pcx->hdr,sizeof(PcxHeader),1,fileptr);

      pcx->width=1+pcx->hdr.xmax-pcx->hdr.xmin;
      pcx->height=1+pcx->hdr.ymax-pcx->hdr.ymin;
      pcx->imagebytes=(unsignedint)(pcx->width*pcx->height);

      if(pcx->imagebytes > PCX_MAX_SIZE)
        return PCX_TOOBIG;

      pcx->bitmap=(char*)malloc(pcx->imagebytes);
      if(pcx->bitmap == NULL)
        return PCX_NOMEM;

      pchar=pcx->bitmap;
      for(counter=0;counter<pcx->imagebytes;counter++)
      {
        if(mode == NORMAL)
        {
          abyte=fgetc(fileptr);
          if((unsigned char)abyte > 0xbf)
          {
            nbytes=abyte & 0x3f;
            abyte=fgetc(fileptr);
            if(-nbytes > 0)
              mode=RLE;
          }
        }
        else if(-nbytes == 0)
          mode=NORMAL;
        *pchar++=abyte;
      }

// Get the color palette from the .PCX file
    fseek(fileptr,-768L,SEEK_END);
    fread(pcx->pal,768,1,fileptr);
    pchar=pcx->pal;
// Perform 8-bit to 6-bit shift on the palette for the VGA
    for(counter=0;counter<768;counter++)
      *pchar++=*pchar >>2;
    fclose(fileptr);
    return PCX_OK;              // Return success

    }
```

```
//
//  This is the new int 9h handler. This allows for smooth
//  interactive scrolling. If the BIOS keyboard handler was
//  not disabled, holding down one of the arrow keys would
//  overflow the keyboard buffer and cause a very annoying
//  beep.
//
    void _interrupt NewInt9(void)
    {
      register char keybyte;

      KeyScan=inp(0x60);    // Read key code from keyb
      keybyte=inp(0x61);    // Tell keyb key processed
      outp(0x61,(keybyte|0x80));
      outp(0x61,keybyte);

      outp(0x20,0x20);      // Send End-Of-Interrupt to 8259 PIC.
   // Check for key releases
      if(KeyScan == RIGHT_ARROW_REL ||
         KeyScan == LEFT_ARROW_REL)
         KeyScan=0;    // Clear the key flag.
    }

//
//  This routine restores the original BIOS keyboard
//  interrupt handler.
//
    void RestoreKeyboard(void)
    {

// Restore BIOS keyboard interrupt
      _dos_setvect(KEYBOARD,OldInt9);
    }

//
//  This routine saves the original BIOS keyboard interrupt
//  handler and then installs a custom handler for this
//  program.
//
    void InitKeyboard(void)
    {

// Save BIOS keyboard interrupt handler
      OldInt9=_dos_getvect(KEYBOARD);

// Install custom keyboard handler
      _dos_setvect(KEYBOARD,NewInt9);
    }

//
//  This routine calls the video BIOS to set all the DAC
//  registers of the VGA based on the contents of pal[].
//
    void SetAllRgbPalette(char *pal)
    {
      struct SREGS sregs;
      union REGS regs;
```

continues

Listing 17.2. continued

```
// Get segment values
    segread(&s);

// Point ES to pal
    sregs.es=FP_SEG((void far*)pal);

// Get offset to pal
    regs.x.dx=FP_OFF((void far*)pal);

// BIOS 10h sub 12h
    regs.x.ax=0x1012;

// Starting DAC register
    regs.x.bx=0;

// Ending DAC register
    regs.x.cx=256;

// Call video BIOS
    int86x(0x10,&regs,&regs,&sregs);
    }

//
//   This routine sets up the video mode to BIOS mode 13h.
//   This mode is the MCGA-compatible 320x200x256 mode.
//
    void InitVideo()
    {
      union REGS regs;

// BIOS func 0fh
    regs.h.ah=0x0f;

// Call video BIOS
    int86(0x10,&regs,&regs);

// Save current video mode
    PrevMode=regs.h.al;

// Set video mode 13h
    r.x.ax=0x13;

// Call video BIOS
    int86(0x10,&r,&r);

// Create a pointer to video memory
    VideoRam=MK_FP(0xa000,0);
    }

//
//   This routine restores the video mode to its original
//   state.
//
    void RestoreVideo()
    {
      union REGS regs;
```

```
   // Restore previous mode
      regs.x.ax=PrevMode;

  // Call video BIOS
      int86(0x10,&regs,&regs);
    }

//
// This routine loads the bit map layers.
//
    int InitBitmaps()
    {
      int results;

  // Initial left-half split location
      background=1;

// Read in the background bit map
      result=ReadPcxFile("backgrnd.pcx",&pcx);
      if(result != PCX_OK)                     // Check for errors
        return FALSE;
      BackGroundBmp=pcx.bitmap;        // Save bit map pointer
      SetAllRgbPalette(pcx.pal);       // Set up VGA palette

      MemBuf=malloc(MEMBLK);  // Create system memory buffer
      if(MemBuf == NULL)        // Check for errors
        return FALSE;

      memset(MemBuf,0,MEMBLK);          // Clear buffer
      return TRUE;                      // Success!
    }

//
//  This routine frees all memory allocated by the program.
//
    void FreeMem()
    {
      free(MemBuf);
      free(BackGroundBmp);
    }

//
//  This routine draws a scrolling bit map layer where all
//  pixels are opaque. It uses the C function memcpy() for
//  speed. The argument ScrollSplit defines the column
//  that splits the bit map into two halves.
//
    void OpaqueBlt(char *bmp,int StartY,int Height,
      int ScrollSplit)
    {
      char *dest;
      int counter;

      dest=MemBuf+StartY*320;   //Calc start in mem buffer.
      for(counter=0;counter<Height;counter++)
      {
// Draw the left bit map half in the right half of the memory
// buffer.
```

continues

Listing 17.2. continued

```
        memcpy(dest+ScrollSplit,bmp,VIEW_WIDTH-ScrollSplit);

// Draw the right bit map half in the left half of the memory
// buffer.
        memcpy(dest,bmp+VIEW_WIDTH-ScrollSplit,ScrollSplit);

        bmp+=VIEW_WIDTH;        //Update pointer to bit map
        dest+=VIEW_WIDTH;       //Update pointer to mem buffer
    }
  }

//
// This routine draws the parallax layers. The order of
// the functions determines the z-ordering of the layers.
//
    void DrawLayers()
    {
      OpaqueBlt(BackGroundBmp,0,100,background);
    }

//
// This routine handles the animation. Note that this is
// the most time-critical section of code. To optimize
// parallax drawing, this routine and its children
// (functions called by this routine) could be rewritten
// in assembly language. A 30% increase in drawing speed
// would be typical.
//
    void AnimLoop()
    {
      while(KeyScan != ESC_PRESSED)   // Loop until Esc key
      {
        switch(KeyScan)               // Process key that was hit
        {
        case RIGHT_ARROW_PRESSED:     // Right arrow is down
          background-=1;              // Scroll background left
                                      // two pixels
          if(background < 1)          // Did we reach the end?
            background+=VIEW_WIDTH;   // ... yes, wrap around.

          break;
        case LEFT_ARROW_PRESSED:          // Left arrow is down
          background+=1;              // Scroll background right
          if(background > VIEW_WIDTH-1)    // Reach the end?
            background-=VIEW_WIDTH;   // ... yes, wrap around.

          break;
        default:                      // Handle all other keys
          break;
        }
        DrawLayers();    // Draw parallax layer(s) in MemBuf
// Block copy MemBuf to VGA memory
        memcpy(VideoRam,MemBuf,MEMBLK);
        frames++;                // Count total frames drawn
      }
    }
```

```
//
// This routine performs all the initialization.
//
    void Initialize()
    {
      InitVideo();          // Set up mode 13h
      InitKeyboard();       // Install keyboard handler
      if(!InitBitmaps())    // Read in the bit maps
      {
        CleanUp();          // Free up memory
        printf("\nError loading bitmaps\n");
        exit(1);     // Quit to DOS.
      }
    }

//
// This routine performs all the necessary cleanup.
//
    void CleanUp()
    {
      RestoreVideo();       // Put VGA in original state
      RestoreKeyboard();    // Restore BIOS keyboard
      FreeMem();            // Release all memory
    }

//
// This is the main program start. This function calls the
// initialization routines. It then gets the current clock
// ticks, calls the animation loop and, finally, gets the
// ending clock ticks. The clock ticks are used to
// calculate the animation frame rate.
//
    int main()
    {
      clock_t begin,fini;

      Initialize();     // Set video mode, load bit maps, etc

      begin=clock();    // Clock ticks at animation start
      AnimLoop();       // Do the animation.
      fini=clock();     // Get clock ticks at animation end

      CleanUp();             // Free mem, etc
      printf("Frames: %d\nfps:%f\n",frames,
        (float)CLK_TCK*frames/(fini-begin));
      return 0;
    }
```

Multiple Scrolling Layers

You now know how to scroll a bit map left and right and make it wrap around at the edges of the screen. The next step is to add some additional scrolling layers and move them at different rates. The varying scroll rates, or relative motion, between different layers are what provide the illusion of 3-D depth.

You might be wondering how you determine what rates of motion to use for different layers. To make things simple, let's make the assumption that the rates at which layers appear to move decrease linearly with increasing distance. This assumption satisfies the requirement that nearby layers move faster than distant layers. Also, in the limiting case in which a layer is very far away, there would be almost no apparent motion. This is perfect for stars, clouds, or distant mountain ranges. Note that the linear assumption is not entirely correct, but it is a reasonable compromise.

It's not important to attempt to calculate accurate scroll rates. (If you did, you'd most likely end up with a floating-point number, and for performance reasons the scroll rate should be an integer value.) Actually, the parallax demo in Listing 17.3 uses just a single rule for scroll rates. Each layer moves half as fast as the layer in front. Just remember that what's important is that the relative motion between different layers produces pleasing results.

Each layer of graphics is drawn from back to front. This allows nearby layers to overlap and hide portions of more distant layers. (This method, the Painter's Algorithm, is discussed in more detail in Chapter 6, "The Third Dimension.") This hiding of distant layers by nearby layers provides a feeling of perspective. The amount of overlap to use is dependent on the images. Also, remember that there's no value added in double-drawing too many pixels, so keep overlap to a minimum. The OpaqueBlt() function can be used to draw overlapping layers. By changing the bit map drawn, you can then simulate depth and motion.

Unfortunately, though, OpaqueBlt() only draws opaque, rectangular regions. This isn't very practical for most types of scenery. What we would really like is a way to overlay two layers, yet allow parts of the background layer to show through.

Transparent Pixels

One way that transparent pixels can be implemented is by checking the color value of each pixel just before it's drawn. If the pixel color equals the transparent color, we skip to the next pixel. This additional logic carries with it a significant burden in terms of performance. That's because we can no longer use memcpy() to draw entire rows of pixels with a single function. Instead we must use a for() loop to draw each pixel individually.

Listing 17.3 contains a new function called TransparentBlt(). This function is a direct replacement for OpaqueBlt(). The only difference is that TransparentBlt() does not draw transparent pixels. (It also happens to be quite a bit slower.)

How does `TransparentBlt()` know which pixels are transparent? In this case I decided that any pixel with a color value of 0 (usually black) will be transparent. The function skips any pixel that has a color value equal to the manifest constant TRANSPARENT.

The program in Listing 17.3, Paral.c, is a demonstration of dual-parallax scrolling using two repeated layers. The farthest layer is opaque, while the closest layer is transparent. These layers use the `OpaqueBlt()` and `TransparentBlt()` functions, respectively. There are only two moving layers, but the effect is still pretty realistic.

As in the Paral.c program in Listing 17.2, the left- and right-arrow keys move the image left and right, respectively, and pressing Esc exits the demo. Notice that the frame rate decreased significantly. That's due entirely to the added transparent pixel logic. On a 386SX/25 I managed to get about 10 frames per second—not too bad for a program written entirely in C.

Listing 17.3. Simple dual-parallax (Paral.c).

```
#include <stdio.h>
#include <stdlib.h>
#include <string.h>
#include <time.h>
#include <dos.h>
#include "paral.h"

char *MemBuf,             // Pointer to memory buffer
     *BackGroundBmp,      // Pointer to background bit map
                          // data
     *ForeGroundBmp,      // Pointer to foreground bit map
                          // data
     *VideoRam;           // Pointer to VGA memory

PcxFile pcx;              // Data structure for reading .PCX
                         // files

int volatile KeyScan;     // Modified by keyboard interrupt
                          // handler

int frames=0,            // Number of frames drawn
    PrevMode;            // Holds original video mode

int background,  // Tracks scroll position in background
                 // bit map
    foreground,  // Tracks scroll position in foreground
                 // bit map
    position;    // Tracks total scroll distance

// Pointer to BIOS keyboard handler
    void _interrupt (*OldInt9)(void);


//
//  This routine loads a 256-color PCX file.
```

continues

Listing 17.3. continued

```
//
    int ReadPcxFile(char *filename,PcxFile *pcx)
    {
      long counter;
      int mode=NORMAL,nbytes;
      char abyte,*pchar;
      FILE *fileptr;

      fileptr=fopen(filename,"rb");
      if(fileptr==NULL)
        return PCX_NOFILE;
      fread(&pcx->hdr,sizeof(PcxHeader),1,fileptr);

      pcx->width=1+pcx->hdr.xmax-pcx->hdr.xmin;
      pcx->height=1+pcx->hdr.ymax-pcx->hdr.ymin;
      pcx->imagebytes=(unsigned int)(pcx->width*pcx->height);

      if(pcx->imagebytes > PCX_MAX_SIZE)
        return PCX_TOOBIG;
      pcx->bitmap=(char*)malloc(pcx->imagebytes);
      if(pcx->bitmap == NULL)
        return PCX_NOMEM;

      pchar=pcx->bitmap;
      for(counter=0;counter<pcx->imagebytes;counter++)
      {
        if(mode == NORMAL)
        {
          abyte=fgetc(fileptr);
          if((unsigned char)abyte > 0xbf)
          {
            nbytes=abyte & 0x3f;
            abyte=fgetc(fileptr);
            if(-nbytes > 0)
              mode=RLE;
          }
        }
        else if(-nbytes == 0)
          mode=NORMAL;
        *pchar++=abyte;
      }
// Get color palette from the .PCX file
      fseek(fileptr,-768L,SEEK_END);
      fread(pcx->pal,768,1,fileptr);
      pchar=pcx->pal;
// Perform 8-bit to 6-bit shift on the palette for the VGA.
      for(counter=0;counter<768;counter++)
        *pchar++=*pchar >>2;
      fclose(fileptr);
      return PCX_OK;                    // Return success
    }

//
// This is the new int 9h handler. This allows for smooth
// interactive scrolling. If the BIOS keyboard handler was not
// disabled, holding down one of the arrow keys would overflow
```

```
//   the keyboard buffer and cause a very annoying beep.
//
    void _interrupt NewInt9(void)
    {
      register char keybyte;

      KeyScan=inp(0x60);        // Read key code from keyboard
      keybyte=inp(0x61);        // Tell keyboard that a key was
                                // processed.
      outp(0x61,(keybyte¦0x80));
      outp(0x61,x);
      outp(0x20,0x20);   // Send End-Of-Interrupt to the 8259 PIC
// Check for key releases.
      if(KeyScan == RIGHT_ARROW_REL ¦¦
         KeyScan == LEFT_ARROW_REL)
         KeyScan=0;      //Clear the key flag
    }


//
// This routine restores the original BIOS keyboard interrupt
// handler.
//
    void RestoreKeyboard(void)
    {
  // Restore BIOS keyboard interrupt handler
      _dos_setvect(KEYBOARD,OldInt9);
    }


//
//  This routine saves the original BIOS keyboard interrupt
//  handler and then installs a custom handler for this
//  program.
//
    void InitKeyboard(void)
    {
  // Save BIOS keyboard interrupt handler
      OldInt9=_dos_getvect(KEYBOARD);
  // Install custom keyboard interrupt handler
      _dos_setvect(KEYBOARD,NewInt9);
    }


//
//  This routine calls the video BIOS to set all the DAC
//  registers of the VGA based on the contents of pal[].
//
    void SetAllRgbPalette(char *pal)
    {
      struct SREGS sregs;
      union REGS regs;

      segread(&sregs);        // Get current segment reg values
      sregs.es=FP_SEG((void far*)pal);  // Point ES to pal
      regs.x.dx=FP_OFF((void far*)pal); // Get offset to pal
      regs.x.ax=0x1012;                 // BIOS func 10h sub 12h
      regsx.bx=0;                       // Starting DAC register
      regs.x.cx=256;                    // Ending DAC register
      int86x(0x10,&regs,&regs,&sregs);  // Call video BIOS
```

continues

Listing 17.3. continued

```
    }

//
//   This routine sets up the video mode to BIOS mode 13h. This
//   mode is the MCGA compatible 320x200x256 mode.
//
    void InitVideo()
    {
       union REGS regs;

  // BIOS func 0fh, Set Video Mode
       regs.h.ah=0x0f;

  // Call the video BIOS.
       int86(0x10,&regs,&regs);

  // Save the original video mode
       PrevMode=regs.h.al;

  // Set the video mode to 13h: 320x200x256
       regs.x.ax=0x13;

  // Call the video BIOS
       int86(0x10,&regs,&regs);

  // Create a pointer to video memory
       VideoRam=MK_FP(0xa000,0);
    }

//
//   This routine restores the video mode to its original state.
//
    void RestoreVideo()
    {
       union REGS regs;

  // Restore the original video mode.
       regs.x.ax=PrevMode;
  // Call the video BIOS
       int86(0x10,&regs,&regs);
    }

//
//   This routine loads the bit-map layers.
//
    int InitBitmaps()
    {
       int results;

  // Initial left-half split location
       background=foreground=1;

  // Read in the background bit map
       result=ReadPcxFile("backgrnd.pcx",&pcx);
  // Check for errors
       if(results != PCX_OK)
          return FALSE;
```

```
  // Save bit map pointer
     BackGroundBmp=pcx.bitmap;
  // Set up the VGA palette
     SetAllRgbPalette(pcx.pal);

  // Read in the foreground bit map
     result=ReadPcxFile("foregrnd.pcx",&pcx);
  // Check for errors
     if(result != PCX_OK)
       return FALSE;
  // Save bit map pointer
     ForeGroundBmp=pcx.bitmap;

  // Create a system-memory buffer.
     MemBuf=malloc(MEMBLK);
  // Check for errors
     if(MemBuf == NULL)
       return FALSE;

     memset(MemBuf,0,MEMBLK);                   // Clear buffer
     return TRUE;                               // Success!
   }

//
//  This routine frees all memory allocated by the program.
//
   void FreeMem()
   {
     free(MemBuf);
     free(BackGroundBmp);
     free(ForeGroundBmp);
   }

//
//  This routine draws the parallax layers. The order of the
//  functions determines the z-ordering of the layers.
//
   void DrawLayers()
   {
     OpaqueBlt(BackGroundBmp,0,100,background);
     TransparentBlt(ForeGroundBmp,50,100,foreground);
   }

//
//  This routine handles the animation. Note that this is the
//  most time-critical section of code. To optimize the
//  parallax drawing this routine and its children (functions
//  called by this routine) could be rewritten in assembly
//  language. A 30% increase in drawing speed would be typical.
//
   void AnimLoop()
   {
     while(KeyScan != ESC_PRESSED)             // Loop until Esc key
                                               // is hit
     {
       switch(KeyScan)                         // Process the key that
                                               // was hit.
```

continues

Listing 17.3. continued

```
        {
      case RIGHT_ARROW_PRESSED:          // Right arrow is down
        position--;                      // Update scroll total
        if(position < 0)           // Stop scrolling if end is
                                   // reached
        {
          position=0;
          break;
        }
        background-=1;              // Scroll background left.
        if(background < 1)         // Did we reach the end?
          background+=VIEW_WIDTH;  // ...then wrap around.

        foreground-=2;             // Scroll foreground left.
        if(foreground < 1)         // Did we reach the end?
          foreground+=VIEW_WIDTH;  // ...then wrap around.

        break;
      case LEFT_ARROW_PRESSED:           // Left arrow is down
        position++;                      // Update scroll total
        if(position > TOTAL_SCROLL)      // Stop if end is
                                   // reached
        {
          position=TOTAL_SCROLL;
          break;
        }
        background+=1;                   // Scroll background right.
        if(background > VIEW_WIDTH-1) // Did we reach the end?
          background-=VIEW_WIDTH;        // ...then wrap around.

        foreground+=2;                   // Scroll foreground right.
        if(foreground > VIEW_WIDTH-1)    // Did we reach the
                                   // end?
          foreground-=VIEW_WIDTH;        // ...then wrap around.

        break;
      default:                           // Handle all other keys.
        break;
      }
      DrawLayers();          // Draw parallax layer(s) in MemBuf.
// Block Copy MemBuf to VGA memory.
      memcpy(VideoRam,MemBuf,MEMBLK);
      frames++;                    // Count total frames drawn.
    }
  }

//
//  This routine performs all the initialization.
//
  void Initialize()
  {
    position=0;
    InitVideo();             // Set up mode 13h
    InitKeyboard();          // Install our keyboard handler
    if(!InitBitmaps())       // Read in the bit maps
```

```
    {
      CleanUp();              // Free up memory
      printf("\nError loading bitmaps\n");
      exit(1);            // Quit to DOS.
    }
  }

//
//  This routine performs all the necessary cleanup.
//
  void CleanUp()
  {
    RestoreVideo();      // Put VGA back in original state
    RestoreKeyboard();   // Restore BIOS keyboard handling
    FreeMem();           // Release all memory
  }

//
//  This is the main program start. This function calls the
//  initialization routines. Then it gets the current clock
//  ticks, calls the animation loop and, finally, gets the
//  ending clock ticks. The clock ticks are used to calculate
//  the animation frame rate.
//
  int main()
  {
    clock_t begin,fini;

    Initialize();        // Set video mode, load bit maps, etc.

    begin=clock();       // Get clock ticks at animation start
    AnimLoop();          // Do the animation.
    fini=clock();        // Get clock ticks at animation end

    CleanUp();           // Free mem, etc
    printf("Frames: %d\nfps: %f\n",frames,
           (float)CLK_TCK*frames/(fini-begin));
    return 0;
  }
```

Optimized Versions of OpaqueBlt() and TransparentBlt()

Listing 17.4 contains optimized assembly language versions of the OpaqueBlt() and TransparentBlt() routines, which are also on disk. These routines replace the C versions and are about 30 percent faster. The demo program Paral uses these assembly language versions.

These routines were written to be compatible with 286 machines. Because the routines draw to a system memory buffer, they could be optimized further by using 32-bit memory move instructions.

Listing 17.4. Optimized blit routines (Blit.asm).

```
        ideal
        model compact,c
        p286
        dataseg

        VIEW_WIDTH  equ 320
        VIEW_HEIGHT equ 100
        TRANSPARENT equ 0
        global MemBuf:dword

        codeseg

        public OpaqueBlt
        public TransparentBlt

;
; This routine copies a bit map to MemBuf.  It also scrolls
; the bit map left and right depending on the status of
; ScrollSplit.
;
        proc OpaqueBlt
        ARG Bitmap:dword,StartY:word,Height:word,ScrollSplit:word
        USES si,di

        les     di,[MemBuf]       ; get pointer to memory buffer
        mov     ax,[StartY]       ; get starting y-coordinate
        mov     bx,ax                 ; make a copy
        sal     ax,6                  ; mult by 64
        sal     bx,8                  ; mult by 256
        add     ax,bx             ; result is same as mult by 320
        add     di,ax             ; calc offset into MemBuf

        mov     bx,[Height]           ; get height of bit map
        mov     dx,[ScrollSplit]      ; get bit map right half
        push    ds                    ; save data segment
        lds     si,[Bitmap]           ; get pointer to bit map

        mov     ax,VIEW_WIDTH     ; get screen width
        sub     ax,dx             ; calc left half length
        cld                       ; set direction to forward
@@loop01:
        add     di,dx             ; calc screen starting pos
        mov     cx,ax             ; get left half length
        shr     cx,1              ; turn into words
        rep     movsw             ; draw left half of bit map
        jnc     short @@skip01    ; skip if done
        movsb                     ; move last pixel
@@skip01:

        sub     di,VIEW_WIDTH     ; adjust screen pointer offset
        mov     cx,dx             ; get right half length
        shr     cx,1              ; turn cx into words
        rep     movsw             ; draw right half of bit map
        jnc     short @@skip02    ; skip if done
        movsb                     ; move last pixel
```

```
@@skip02:

        add   di,ax              ; add right width to get next row
        dec   bx                 ; decrement row counter
        jnz   short @@loop01     ; do it again

        pop   ds                 ; restore data segment
        ret                      ; back to the caller
    endp OpaqueBlt

;
; This routine copies a bit map to MemBuf.  It also scrolls
; the bit map left and right depending on the status of
; ScrollSplit.  This routine does not draw pixels if the
; color index is equal to TRANSPARENT.
;
    proc TransparentBlt
    ARG Bitmap:dword,StartY:word,Height:word,ScrollSplit:word
    USES si,di

        les   di,[MemBuf]        ; get pointer to memory buffer
        mov   ax,[StartY]        ; get starting y-coordinate
        mov   cx,ax              ; make a copy
        sal   ax,6               ; mult by 64
        sal   cx,8               ; mult by 256
        add   ax,cx              ; result is same as mult by 320
        add   di,ax              ; add offset to MemBuf

        mov   dx,[ScrollSplit]   ; get bit map left half
        mov   bx,VIEW_WIDTH      ; get view width
        sub   bx,dx              ; calc right half length

        push  ds                 ; save data segment
        lds   si,[Bitmap]        ; get pointer to bit map
@@loop01:
        add   di,dx              ; calc screen starting pos
        mov   cx,bx              ; get right half length

;
;  Draw the right half
;
@@loop02:
        mov   al,[si]            ; get bit map pixel
        inc   si                 ; point to next pixel
        cmp   al,TRANSPARENT     ; is pixel transparent?
        je    short @@skip01     ; ...yes skip next instr
        mov   [es:di],al         ; otherwise draw it
@@skip01:
        inc   di                 ; point to next byte of MemBuf
        dec   cx                 ; decrement counter
        jnz   short @@loop02

        sub   di,VIEW_WIDTH      ; adjust screen pointer offset
        mov   cx,dx              ; get left half length

;
;  Draw the left half
;
```

continues

Listing 17.4. continued

```
@@loop03:
        mov   al,[si]           ; get bit map pixel
        inc   si                ; point to next pixel
        cmp   al,TRANSPARENT    ; is pixel transparent?
        je    short @@skip02    ; ...yes skip next instr
        mov   [es:di],al        ; otherwise draw it
@@skip02:
        inc   di                ; point to next byte of MemBuf
        dec   cx                ; decrement counter
        jnz   short @@loop03    ; loop till done

        add   di,bx             ; add right width
        dec   [Height]          ; decrement row counter
        jnz   short @@loop01    ; do it again

        pop   ds                ; restore data segment
        ret                     ; back to the caller
        endp TransparentBlt

        end
```

Scrolling Tiled Bit Maps

One of the problems with the repeated scrolling code previously presented is the amount of memory occupied by the image. The practical limit on the size of a single image under DOS is 64K. This works out to maximum image sizes of 320x200 or 640x100. Remember that in mode 13h one pixel equals one byte, and 640x100 equals 64,000 bytes. Even if you could have a single image larger than 64K, you'd soon run out of memory: at best, there's only 640K available.

Don't worry: we don't go into a discussion of 16-bit code, extended memory, or segmentation here. Let's just say that these restrictions are due to basic limitations of good old, real-mode DOS. Some day this may change, but for now we must accept it and continue.

One clever approach to the memory problem is to use *tiled bit maps*. Instead of using a single bit map, you create a large virtual bit map composed of many smaller bit maps, or *tiles*. These tiles may be viewed as fundamental building blocks that are combined to form a much larger image.

The key to this technique is the tile look-up table. This look-up table, usually implemented as an array, maps the small tiles into the virtual image. The look-up table doesn't require much memory (approximately one or two bytes per tile) and may be as large as your imagination. Imagine a scrolling virtual image that's up to 5400 tiles wide by 12 tall, with each tile drawn as 16x16 bit maps. That means the size of the virtual bit map would be 86,000x192 pixels, which is far larger than any single image could possibly be.

One restriction of this method is that the amount of detail is entirely dependent upon the detail in the individual tiles. Each tile should be small and general enough to be used in several places. However the tiles must be interesting enough to form an attractive image.

For practical reasons the tiles must have a width that's a power of two and an even integer fraction of the screen width. For example, the tiles could be 2, 4, 16, or up to 320 pixels wide in mode 13h. The importance of these restrictions is explained later in this chapter.

Like repeated bit maps, the tiles come in two main flavors: opaque and transparent. The former are extremely fast, and excellent for distant layers or nearby layers that have no transparent regions. Well, actually, the last statement isn't quite true. There can be transparent regions in an opaque tiled image if you make provisions for a null or empty tile. When the tile map has a null tile, that tile isn't drawn. This leaves a square hole in the tile, which allows background images to show through.

Transparent tiled layers are slower, again because of the additional overhead required by checks for transparent pixels. I don't present code for transparent tiled layers in this chapter, but you can implement them using the transparent pixel logic from the repeated bit maps. In your own programs you're free to use any combination of repeated and tiled layers with either opaque or transparent pixels, keeping in mind the various performance trade-offs involved.

To create a tiled image we make use of the fact that there are never more than two partial tiles on the screen at any point in time. The rest of the tiles are always fully visible. If you're not yet convinced of this property, take a look at Figure 17.2 (or work it out with a piece of graph paper).

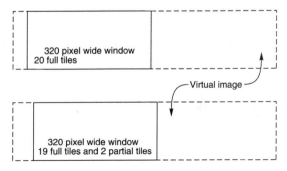

Figure 17.2. *Tiled bit map properties.*

This useful result is one of the benefits of the tile width constraint just spoken of. What this means is that drawing the tiled image involves three steps:

1. Draw the first (possibly partial) tile.

2. Next, draw several full tiles.

3. Last, draw the last (possibly partial) tile.

Also, we need to keep an integer counter, which tracks the location of the visible screen within the virtual image.

The program in Listing 17.6, Tile.c, demonstrates an implementation of tiled layers. The closest layer is composed of several tiles. The definition of the virtual image is kept in an ASCII file called TILEMAP.DAT, which is processed during initialization. The numbers in the file represent the names of the .PCX tile files. (For example, tile 1 becomes TILE1.PCX, and so on.) Note that tile 0 is reserved for the null (or empty) tile. Figure 17.3 shows a small sample tile map.

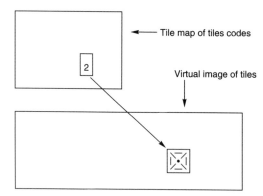

Figure 17.3. *Sample tile map.*

The important difference between this code and the dual-parallax demo in Listing 17.3 is the addition of the function DrawTile(). This routine draws a tile at a given screen location. The two arguments offset and width define the starting column and width, respectively, for drawing the partial tiles. For partial tiles:

■ offset is the first column of the tile to draw

■ width is some value less than the tile width

For full tiles:

■ offset is zero

■ and width is set to the tile width

The program in Listing 17.6, again, uses the arrow keys to control movement and the escape key to exit. The demo shows the wall of a house in the foreground made up of bit map tiles, and the now-familiar mountain range and skyline in the background. The performance is slightly slower due to the addition of the tiling code, but only by a couple of frames per second.

Listing 17.5 contains the header file for the tiled bit map demo shown in Listing 17.6. The header defines the constants and function prototypes for the demo.

Listing 17.5. Tiled-scrolling header (Tile.h).

```
//
// Tiles.h
// This header includes definitions for scrolling
// tiled images.
//

    #define NUM_TILES      17       // Number of tile files
    #define TILE_WIDTH     16       // Width in pixels of a tile
    #define TILE_HEIGHT    16       // Height in pixels of a tile
    #define TILE_COLS      40       // Width of tile map
    #define TILE_ROWS       6       // Height of tile map
    #define TILES_TOTAL    (TILE_COLS*TILE_ROWS)
    #define TILES_PER_ROW  (VIEW_WIDTH/TILE_WIDTH)

    #define SHIFT 4

#ifdef __cplusplus
extern "C" {
#endif

    void ReadTiles(void);
    void FreeTiles(void);
    void ReadTileMap(char *);
    void DrawTile(char *,int,int,int,int);
    void DrawTiles(int,int);

#ifdef __cplusplus
   }
#endif
```

Listing 17.6. Tiled layer-scrolling demo (Tiles.c).

```
    #include <stdio.h>
    #include <stdlib.h>
    #include <string.h>
    #include <time.h>
    #include <dos.h>
    #include "paral.h"
    #include "tiles.h"
```

continues

Listing 17.6. continued

```c
    char *MemBuf,           // Pointer to memory buffer
        *BackGroundBmp,     // Pointer to background bit map
                            // data
        *ForeGroundBmp,     // Pointer to foreground bit map
                            // data
        *VideoRam;          // Pointer to VGA memory

    PcxFile pcx;            // Data structure for reading
                            // .PCX files

    int volatile KeyScan;   // Modified by keyboard interrupt
                            // handler

    int frames=0,           // Number of frames drawn
        PrevMode;           // Holds original video mode

    int background,  // Tracks scroll position in background
                     // bit map
        foreground,  // Tracks scroll position in foreground
                     // bit map
        position;    // Tracks tile scroll position

    char *tiles[NUM_TILES+1];
    int tilemap[TILES_TOTAL];

// Pointer to BIOS keyboard interrupt handler.
    void _interrupt (*OldInt9)(void);

//
//  This routine loads a 256-color PCX file.
//
    int ReadPcxFile(char *filename,PcxFile *pcx)
    {
      long counter;
      int mode=NORMAL,nbytes;
      char abyte,*pchar;
      FILE *fileptr;

      fileptr=fopen(filename,"rb");
      if(fileptr==NULL)
        return PCX_NOFILE;
      fread(&pcx->hdr,sizeof(PcxHeader),1,fileptr);

      pcx->width=1+pcx->hdr.xmax-pcx->hdr.xmin;
      pcx->height=1+pcx->hdr.ymax-pcx->hdr.ymin;
      pcx->imagebytes=(unsigned int)(pcx->width*pcx->height);

      if(pcx->imagebytes > PCX_MAX_SIZE)
        return PCX_TOOBIG;

      pcx->bitmap=(char*)malloc(pcx->imagebytes);
      if(pcx->bitmap == NULL)
        return PCX_NOMEM;

      phar=pcx->bitmap;
      for(counter=0;counter<pcx->imagebytes;counter++)
```

```c
    {
      if(mode == NORMAL)
      {
        abyte=fgetc(fileptr);
        if((unsigned char)abyte > 0xbf)
        {
          nbytes=abyte & 0x3f;
          abyte=fgetc(fileptr);
          if(--nbytes > 0)
            mode=RLE;
        }
      }
      else if(--nbytes == 0)
        mode=NORMAL;
      *pchar++=abyte;
    }
// Get color palette from the .PCX file.
    fseek(f,-768L,SEEK_END);
    fread(pcx->pal,768,1,fileptr);
    pchar=pcx->pal;
// Perform 8-bit to 6-bit shift on the palette for the VGA.
    for(counter=0;counter<768;counter++)
      *pchar++=*pchar >>2;
    fclose(fileptr);
    return PCX_OK;                  // Return success
    }


//
//   This is the new int 9h handler. This allows for smooth
//   interactive scrolling. If the BIOS keyboard handler was not
//   disabled, holding down one of the arrow keys would overflow
//   the keyboard buffer and cause a very annoying beep.
//
    void _interrupt NewInt9(void)
    {
      register char keybyte;

      KeyScan=inp(0x60);      // Read key code from keyboard
      keybyte=inp(0x61);      // Tell keyboard key was processed
      outp(0x61,(keybyte|0x80));
      outp(0x61,keybyte);
      outp(0x20,0x20);        // Send End-Of-Interrupt to 8259 PIC
// Check for key releases.
      if(KeyScan == RIGHT_ARROW_REL ||
         KeyScan == LEFT_ARROW_REL)
         KeyScan=0;          // Clear key flag.
    }


//
//   This routine restores the original BIOS keyboard
//   interrupt handler.
//
    void RestoreKeyboard(void)
    {
// Restore the BIOS keyboard interrupt handler/
      _dos_setvect(KEYBOARD,OldInt9);
    }
```

continues

Listing 17.6. continued

```
//
//  This routine saves the original BIOS keyboard interrupt
//  handler and then installs a custom handler for this
//  program.
//
    void InitKeyboard(void)
    {
// Save the BIOS keyboard interrupt handler.
        OldInt9=_dos_getvect(KEYBOARD);
// Install the custom keyboard interrupt handler.
        _dos_setvect(KEYBOARD,NewInt9);
    }


//
//  This routine calls the video BIOS to set all the DAC
//  registers of the VGA based on the contents of pal[].
//
    void SetAllRgbPalette(char *pal)
    {
      struct SREGS sregs;
      union REGS regs;

      segread(&sregs);                // Get current segment values
      sregs.es=FP_SEG((void far*)pal);  // Point ES to pal
      regs.x.dx=FP_OFF((void far*)pal); // Get offset to pal
      regs.x.ax=0x1012;               // BIOS func 10h sub 12h
      regs.x.bx=0;                    // Starting DAC register
      regs.x.cx=256;                  // Ending DAC register
      int86x(0x10,&regs,&regs,&sregs); // Call the video BIOS
    }


//
//  This routine sets up the video mode to BIOS mode 13h. This
//  mode is the MCGA compatible 320x200x256 mode.
//
    void InitVideo()
    {
      union REGS regs;

      regs.h.ah=0x0f;            // BIOS func 0fh
      int86(0x10,&regs,&regs);   // Call video BIOS
      PrevMode=regs.h.al;        // Save current video mode
      regs.x.ax=0x13;            // Set video mode 13h
                                 //   13h: 320x200x256
      int86(0x10,&regs,&regs);   // Call the video BIOS
// Create a pointer to video memory.
      VideoRam=MK_FP(0xa000,0);
    }


//
//  This routine restores the video mode to its original state.
//
    void RestoreVideo()
    {
      union REGS regs;

      regs.x.ax=PrevMode;     // Restore original video mode.
```

```
    int86(0x10,&regs,&regs);    // Call the video BIOS.
    }

//
//  This routine loads the bit-map layers.
//
    int InitBitmaps()
    {
      int result;

 // Initial left-half split location
      background=foreground=1;

// Read in the background bit map.
      r=ReadPcxFile("backgrnd.pcx",&pcx);
// Check for errors
      if(result != PCX_OK)
        return FALSE;
      BackGroundBmp=pcx.bitmap;       // Save bit-map pointer
      SetAllRgbPalette(pcx.pal);      // Set up VGA palette
// Read in the foregound bit map.
      result=ReadPcxFile("foregrnd.pcx",&pcx);
// Check for errors
      if(result != PCX_OK)
        return FALSE;
      ForeGroundBmp=pcx.bitmap;   // Save bit-map pointer.

//Create a system-memory buffer.
      MemBuf=malloc(MEMBLK);
// Check for errors.
      if(MemBuf == NULL)
        return FALSE;

      memset(MemBuf,0,MEMBLK);              // Clear buffer
      return TRUE;                          // Success!
    }

//
//  This routine frees all memory allocated by the program.
//
    void FreeMem()
    {
      free(MemBuf);
      free(BackGroundBmp);
      free(ForeGroundBmp);
      FreeTiles();
    }

//
//  This routine draws the parallax layers. The order of the
//  functions determines the z-ordering of the layers.
//
    void DrawLayers()
    {
      OpaqueBlt(BackGroundBmp,0,100,background);
      TransparentBlt(ForeGroundBmp,50,100,foreground);
      DrawTiles(position,54);
    }
```

continues

Listing 17.6. continued

```
//
// This routine handles the animation. Note that this is the
// most time-critical section of code. To optimize the parallax
// drawing, this routine and its children (functions called by
// this routine) could be rewritten in assembly language. A
// 30% increase in drawing speed would be typical.
//
    void AnimLoop()
    {
      while(KeyScan != ESC_PRESSED) // Loop until Esc is hit.

      {
        switch(KeyScan)  // Process the key that was hit.
        {
        case RIGHT_ARROW_PRESSED:  // Right arrow is down.
          position+=4;          // Update tile scroll total.
          if(position > TOTAL_SCROLL) // Stop if end reached.

          {
            position=TOTAL_SCROLL;
            break;
          }

          background-=1;              // Scroll background left.
          if(background < 1)          // Did we reach the end?
            background+=VIEW_WIDTH;  // ...then wrap around.

          foreground-=2;              // Scroll foreground left.
          if(foreground < 1)          // Did we reach the end?
            foreground+=VIEW_WIDTH; // ...then wrap around.

          break;
        case LEFT_ARROW_PRESSED:     // Left arrow is down.
          position-=4;               // Update tile scroll total.
          if(position < 0)           // Stop if end is reached.
          {
            position=0;
            break;
          }

          background+=1;              // Scroll background right
          if(background > VIEW_WIDTH-1) // Did we reach the end?
            background-=VIEW_WIDTH;  // ...then wrap around.

          foreground+=2;              // Scroll foreground right.
          if(foreground > VIEW_WIDTH-1) // Did we reach the end?
            foreground-=VIEW_WIDTH;  // ...then wrap around.

          break;
        default:                      // Handle all other keys.
          break;
        }
        DrawLayers();        // Draw parallax layer(s) in MemBuf.
// Block copy MemBuf to VGA memory.
        memcpy(VideoRam,MemBuf,MEMBLK);
        frames++;            // Count total frames drawn.
                                    // drawn
```

```
      }
    }

//
//  This routine performs all the initialization.
//
    void Initialize()
    {
      position=0;
      InitVideo();     // Set up the video mode.
      InitKeyboard();  // Install the cusom keyboard handler.

      if(!InitBitmaps())  // Read in the bit maps.

      {
        CleanUp();  // Free up memory.
        printf("\nError loading bitmaps\n");
        exit(1);      // Quit to DOS.
      }
      ReadTileMap("tilemap.dat");   // Read in the tile map.
      ReadTiles();                  // Read in the tile bit maps.
    }

//
//  This routine performs all the necessary cleanup.
//
    void CleanUp()
    {
      RestoreVideo();     // Restore the original video mode.
      RestoreKeyboard();  // Restore the BIOS keyboard handler.
      FreeMem();          // Release all memory.
    }

//
// This routine loads the individual title bit maps. The file
// names have the form T##.PCX.
//
    void ReadTiles(void)
    {
      PcxFile pcx;
      char buf[80];
      int counter,result;

      tiles[0]=NULL;          // setup empty tile
      for(counter=1;counter<=NUM_TILES;counter++)
      {
        sprintf(buf,"t%d.pcx",counter); // Build the filename.
        result=ReadPcxFile(buf,&pcx);   // Load tile bit map.
        if(result != PCX_OK)
        {
          printf("\nerror reading file: %s\n",buf);
          exit(1);                      // Quit to DOS.
        }
        tiles[counter]=pcx.bitmap;    // Save bit-map pointers.
      }
    }

//
```

continues

Listing 17.6. continued

```
// This routine frees all the memory allocated for the various
// tile bit maps.
//
    void FreeTiles()
    {
      int counter;

      for(counter=0;counter<NUM_TILES;counter++)
        free(tiles[counter]);
    }
//
// This routine loads the tilemap from the given filename.
//    void ReadTileMap(char *filename)
    {
      int counter;
      FILE *fileptr;

      fileptr=fopen(filename,"rt");
      for(counter=0;counter<TILES_TOTAL;counter++)
      {
        fscanf(fileptr,"%d",&(tilemap[counter]));
      }
      fclose(fileptr);
    }

//
//  This routine draws a bit map tile in a memory buffer. The
//  routine can draw portions of the tile smaller. The argument
//  'offset' defines the starting column within the tile. The
//  argument 'width' defines the length of the tile to draw.
//
    void DrawTile(char *bmp,int x,int y,int offset,int width)
    {
      char *dest;
      int counter;

      if(bmp == NULL) return;  // Don't draw empty tiles.
      dest=MemBuf+y*VIEW_WIDTH+x;  // Calc offset in memory buf.
      bmp+=offset;              // Get bit map to draw.

  // Draw each scanline of the bit map.
      for(counter=0;counter<TILE_HEIGHT;counter++)
      {
        memcpy(dest,bmp,width);  // Copy from bit map to MemBuf.
        dest+=VIEW_WIDTH;        // Get next row of MemBuf.
        bmp+=TILE_WIDTH;         // Get next row of bit map.
      }
    }

//
//  This routine draws a screen full of tiles. The argument
//  vloc is the left corner x location within the virtual
//  screen.
//
    void DrawTiles(int VirtualX,int Starty)
    {
      int counter,xcoord,index,offset,row,limit;
```

```
// Get index of first visible tile
    index=VirtualX>>SHIFT;
    offset=VirtualX-(index<<SHIFT);
    limit=TILES_PER_ROW;
    if(offset==0)
      limit—;
    for(row=Starty;row<Starty+TILE_HEIGHT*TILE_ROWS;
                    row+=TILE_HEIGHT)
    {
      xcoord=TILE_WIDTH-offset;

// Draw the leftmost tile of the current row.
// May be a partial tile.
      DrawTile(tiles[tilemap[index]],0,row,
              offset,TILE_WIDTH-offset);
      for(counter=index+1;counter<index+limit;counter++)
      {
// Draw the next tile on the current row; always a full tile.
        DrawTile(tiles[tilemap[counter]],xcoord,
              row,0,TILE_WIDTH);
        xcoord+=TILE_WIDTH;
      }
// Draw right-most tile of the current row.
// (May be a partial tile.)
      DrawTile(tiles[tilemap[counter]],xcoord,row,0,offset);
      index+=TILE_COLS;
    }
  }


//
//  This is the main program start. This function calls the
//  initialization routines. It then gets the current clock
//  ticks, calls the animation loop and, finally, gets the
//  ending clock ticks. The clock ticks are used to calculate
//  the animation frame rate.
//
    int main()
    {
      clock_t begin,fini;

  // Set video mode, load bit maps, etc
      Initialize();

  // Get clock ticks at animation start
      begin=clock();
  // Do the animation.
      AnimLoop();
  // Get clock ticks at animation end
      fini=clock();

      CleanUp();                // Free mem, etc
      printf("Frames: %d\nfps:%f\n", frames,
        (float)CLK_TCK*frames/(fini-begin));
      return 0;
    }
```

Avoiding Shear

On slower machines or machines with slower video cards, it's possible to see some shearing of the image as it is copied to the screen. *Shearing* makes the image look like it is being torn or shredded.

This interesting but undesirable effect occurs because the monitor "refreshes" the display approximately 60 times per second. If your code is in the middle of drawing a new frame while the monitor is refreshing the display, you get to see some shearing effects.

The VGA does provide a means for checking the status of the screen refresh. There is a register on the VGA card that can be polled to see if the screen is currently being refreshed. All that is required is that we wait until the screen refresh is completed and then start our drawing.

The code fragment in Listing 17.7 contains loops until the monitor completes one screen refresh. This provides you with about 1/60th of a second to draw the next frame of graphics. This code could be placed before the code that moves the frame from system memory to the video display. Perform this check before copying the memory buffer to video display and keep the viewport size small. It's the best we can do to avoid shear in mode 13h.

Listing 17.7. Vertical retrace check.

```
    asm mov dx,0x3da
NoRetrace:
    asm in  al,dx
    asm and al,8
    asm jz NoRetrace      // Wait till current retrace ends
Retrace:
    asm in  al,dx
    asm and al,8
    asm jnz Retrace       // Wait till next retrace starts
```

The code in this chapter does not perform vertical retrace checking. This was done to keep the use of assembly language to a minimum. However, I do provide the code in Listing 17.7 for reference and personal use.

Only on very fast machines or machines with small viewport sizes will 1/60th of a second be long enough to draw several layers of graphics and copy them to the screen. This is the main disadvantage of mode 13h. The only other alternative is to use a tweaked video mode that provides multiple pages and page flipping.

PCX Graphics

For convenience, all the bit maps used in this chapter are stored on disk as 256-color .PCX files. The PCX format was chosen mainly because it's easy to read and does a reasonable job of compressing image data. Just as important is that .PCX files are supported by most paint programs. (For lots more information on .PCX files, see Chapter 5, "The Mysteries of the VGA Card.")

Notes on Performance

It should be clear that the performance of our scrolling code suffers somewhat because the code is often drawing the same pixel more than once. Actually, a run with a profiler will show that a great deal of time is spent performing the copy from system memory to the video display.

For the most part, the cost of copying from system memory to the display will dwarf the cost of redrawing some pixels. This is because system memory is accessed much faster than VGA memory. Note that this is not true in all cases. Some adapters, such as local bus video cards, are quite fast.

There are a number of ways we could speed things up a bit. Wherever possible and practical, you should avoid function calls and use macros instead. The instructions that call and return from a function are pure overhead.

Another performance hit occurs when you pass arguments to a function. These arguments get pushed and popped off the stack each and every time the function gets called, and this wastes time. A few well-chosen global variables can significantly speed up some critical loops.

Use the block memory move functions wherever possible. These functions are optimized for moving memory around quickly, and are perfect for drawing runs of pixels. If you absolutely must use a FOR loop, try unrolling the loop if possible. Some optimizing compilers will attempt to unroll loops, but many times it is just as simple to do it manually. (See Chapter 18, "Optimization Techniques," for more on unrolling loops.)

Lastly, if performance is critical (and it usually is in games), there's no substitute for a little assembly language. Typically, only a couple of critical routines need be handcoded in assembly language. A solid strategy:

1. Write everything in C as you develop new algorithms.

2. Refine your algorithms until you're certain they are correct and appropriate for the tasks at hand.

3. Go find the performance bottlenecks and rewrite those routines in assembler.

 Did you like the graphics used with the demos in this chapter? *I* sure did. It cannot be overstated how important quality graphics are to the impact of a game. All the graphics used in this chapter were kindly contributed by Denise Tyler, the author of Chapter 16 of this book and a very talented artist. Thanks, Denise!

Summary

There are many different ways parallax scrolling can be implemented. The methods presented in this chapter aren't necessarily the fastest or the most elegant. They do, however, have the virtue of being relatively easy techniques to implement and understand.

By combining the techniques outlined in this chapter with others—perhaps even some you develop yourself—you'll be well on your way toward developing your own games. Don't be afraid to experiment! This is really fun stuff.

Optimization
Techniques

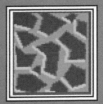

L ast year I asked Santa Claus for a Cray
XMP supercomputer—and, as usual,
he didn't bring me one. And unless
you'll be using a supercomputer with femto-
second execution cycles and terrabytes of RAM,
we're both stuck with the PC. Therefore, we
must make our PC video-game programs as fast
and efficient as possible. To do this we must
extract every possible ounce of power from the
PC. In this chapter we cover the following
optimization techniques and tactics:

- Parameter passing

- Global variables

- Pointer and value aliasing

- Using registers

- Compiler optimizations

- Expanding loops

- Binary multiplication

- Look-up tables

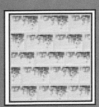

by André LaMothe

- Fixed-point mathematics
- The in-line assembler
- Case Study I: Optimizing Pixel Plotting
- Case Study II: Optimizing Line Drawing

Introduction

Before we dive into all the interesting optimizations that can be done to make our PC video games run faster, I want to talk about a couple of issues relating to optimizations and coding in general.

- When you optimize your software, don't try to optimize the entire program at once. Look for areas that are time-critical and using up the most machine cycles. Take these functions and "work" them, one at a time, until you're satisfied with their performance.

  Optimizing an entire game at once will probably transform it into a mess and you'll never be able to debug it and or add to it. Optimizations should be weighed against other factors. If optimizing a function will make it 5 percent faster and 50 percent more cryptic, try to find another area to optimize. Trying to debug optimized code is rather arduous.

- Don't try to use all kinds of clever C code for everything. If you have 10 lines of code that execute once every time through the main loop, don't try to mash them into one line. I hate to see stuff like this:

  ```
  *(x+(y++)> = *( &(x++) >> 2) + (char far *)y;
  ```

  Get the picture? Not only would this confuse the inventors of C themselves, but Codeview can't help you on lines like this, and your debugging time will increase.

- Because we're making video games, I can guarantee that 90 percent of the execution of the game will be spent not in the game logic, but in rendering the graphics. Therefore, make all the drawing functions as fast as possible, and make the game logic clean and understandable. A function that plots a pixel can be thought of as a "black box," but your game logic can't. Keep it clean.

We're about to study a veritable plethora of optimizations that can be done. Any function you can think of can usually be optimized from two to 10 times using some or all of the optimizations we study herein—not to mention that you'll really impress your friends!

Parameter Passing

After reading Chapter 2, "Assembly Language Basics" (and from your own experience), you should know that passing parameters to functions is not "free." They must be pushed onto the stack, accessed using the base pointer and, finally, popped off the stack. If you have a function that adds 10 numbers that are passed as parameters, you might have something like this:

```
int Add_Em_All(int n1,int n2,int n3,int n4,int n5,int n6,int n7,int n8,int n9, int n10)
{
return(n1+n2+n3+n4+n5+n6+n7+n8+n9+n10);
} // end Add_Em_All
```

(Admittedly, this isn't a terribly realistic function. We're using it to exaggerate the point.) After we compiled the function, the body of the function would look something like this:

```
clc
mov ax,00h
adc ax,n1
adc ax,n2
adc ax,n3
adc ax,n4
adc ax,n5
adc ax,n5
adc ax,n6
adc ax,n7
adc ax,n8
adc ax,n9
adc ax,n10
```

Of course, the stack frame must be created and deleted at the end. However, the real time consumer is the 10 pushes and pops that are done when the variables are passed. If you look at the execution times of the adc instruction and compare the times of the push and pop instructions, you find that they can take up to three times the number of cycles the adc does. Wow! Passing the parameters alone costs more than the body of the function. However, as the function itself got much larger, the effects of parameter passing would be diminished and overcome by the function body. This shows us that we must try to pass only the variables that are necessary for the function to operate. When you write a function, then, don't add all kinds of bells and whistles; just send the bare minimum of parameters to make the function operate in a reasonable manner.

Never ever send structures as values. If you define a structure and send like this:

```
typdef struct point_typ
    {
    int x[10],y[10],z[10]
    } point, point_ptr;
```

and make a call with the structure like this:

```
Display(point point_1);
```

the entire structure will be passed on the stack! To avoid this, always use pointers when passing structures. Use "pass by value" only when passing integers and standard C data types.

You may be asking, "Why not use global variables instead of parameters?" Let's take a look at that idea.

Global Variables

We're writing video games, and sometimes rules *have* to be broken. Everyone has learned somewhere that global variables are a no-no and should be avoided. Here's a game-programming guru's point of view: go ahead and use global variables if they help with speed in a noticeable manner. Moreover, design your functions so that, if they use a common variable all the time (such as color), they use a global `color` variable to which they all have access.

For instance, let's say we have a set of drawing functions that plot pixels, draw lines, and draw circles. These functions all have different types of coordinates sent to them; the plot function needs a pair of coordinates, the line function needs four parameters, and so on. However, all of them probably use a single color. Why not make each function draw in the current, global pen color? You could have a variable called `draw_color`, which all functions would use internally. If you change this color and make 100 calls to the pixel plotter, you only have to change the color once—and you just saved 200 pushes and pops!

Keep in mind that using global variables can be a bit like a drug: the more you use them, the more you need them. A good programmer can balance their use and squeeze a good 5 to 10 percent more performance out of the code if they're used properly.

Pointer and Value Aliasing

This subject is a tactic that few programmers use, or have even thought about using. Let's say you have a fragment of code like the one here:

```
for (t = y->stars[index].left; t<starts[index].left+100; t++)
    {
    position = point->x + point->y + point->z;
```

```
pitch      = point->x *  point->y * point->z;
roll       = point->ang + sin(t) * point->ang;
}
```

This fragment looks harmless enough—but lurking within it are some possible aliasing optimizations. You see, it takes a few instructions to dereference a pointer. The tactic we can use to rectify this is to alias values that are used two or more times into simple variables, and use them in the code. This means the above function could be rewritten as:

```
t1 = y->stars[index].left;
x = point->x;
y = point->y;
z = point->z;
ang = point->ang;

for (t =t1; t<t1+100; t++)
    {
    position = x+ y + z;
    pitch     = x * y * z;
    roll      = ang + sin(t) * ang;
    }
```

Although the new version is longer, it executes faster because there are only five pointer dereferences instead of 800. Of course the variables x, y, z, and ang take some time to be accessed, but it's an order of magnitude less than dereferencing structures and pointers. You can bank on that.

To conclude: whenever a variable is used more than two times and is accessed by way of complex dereferencing, alias the variable to a simple, local variable and use it in the calculations.

Now, on to registers.

Using Registers

Ultimately, all the C code we write will be converted to assembly language and appropriately executed. During this conversion, some of the general-purpose registers are used to accomplish the tasks the code was written to accomplish. However, we can't be sure that registers will be used instead of slower stack memory. To ensure that a function uses a register for an index variable (or whatever), we can force the compiler—at least, *try* to force it—to use a register if possible. Using a register is many times faster than using memory, because registers are internal to the CPU and memory is not.

We can use the register keyword to instruct the compiler to use a register. As an example, let's write a function that does a swap without registers:

```
void Swap(int num_1, num_2)
{
int  temp;

// swap num_1, num_2

temp = num_1;
num_1 = num_2;
num_2 = temp;

} // end Swap
```

Now, let's rewrite the function using a register as the temporary variable:

```
Swap(int num_1, num_2)
{
register int  temp;

// swap num_1, num_2

temp = num_1;
num_1 = num_2;
num_2 = temp;

} // end Swap
```

That's all there is to it. If the compiler can, it will use a register for the temp variable—and the code will speed up a good 10 to 15 percent. Well worth the effort.

There are a couple of caveats when using the register keyword:

- The compiler doesn't create registers; it uses the standard CPU registers.

- Sometimes, forcing the compiler to use a register actually makes the code slower. Be careful. However, you can usually get away with using one or two registers in a small function.

Next, let's talk about general compiler optimizations.

Compiler Optimizations

The Microsoft compiler is said to be optimizing and, marginally, this is a true statement. Although the optimizer can make your code slower sometimes, or even introduce bugs, it does do classic optimizations (as defined by computer scientists and others). However, as video-game programmers, we can't trust it. Therefore, we never use any of these optimizations (well, maybe some little ones). That way we're always safe. When your video game is fully functioning and bug-free and you want to play with the compiler options to speed things up, go ahead. Just don't count on it during development.

About the only optimization I suggest and feel good about is turning off the stack probes. *Stack probes* are little prolog code fragments that the compiler introduces to make sure there's enough stack space to allocate the function frame. Just make the stack a few kilobytes and you'll never have a problem. Then you can turn stack probes off, which speeds up the function call quite a bit. (Use the -Gs compiler directive to turn off stack probes.)

I'm probably going to get a lot of flack for saying not to use the optimizer. However, I think it can potentially cause more problems that it solves—and I'd rather write efficient code than rely on the optimizer to fix things for me! The optimizer can actually introduce bugs into your code in some cases, and that's another reason not to use it. (I've already documented dozens of bugs in the new Microsoft Visual C++ 1.5 compiler, so this statement has a lot of foundation. I actually still use C/C++ 7.0, finding it to be much more reliable.)

Expanding Loops

This is an old one. Back in the late 70s and early 80s, in the heyday of Apple, the 6502 processor was king. People were always finding clever ways to make it do the impossible. One trick that has found its way from the past into the present is called *loop unrolling*. This is a technique where the programmer actually undoes a loop structure manually, therefore defeating the entire purpose of the loop. The loop structure itself has a bit of overhead, and we can use this to our advantage.

For example, say we wanted to initialize the fields of 10,000 structures. We could do the following:

```
for (index=0; index<10000 index++)
    {
    player[index].men = 3;
    } // end for index
```

This would work fine. However, the variable index is incremented and compared 10,000 times, and the loop itself runs 10,000 times, meaning there are 10,000 NEAR jumps. We can unroll the loop a little and get a bit of a performance increase. Here's what we would do:

```
for (index=0; index<1000 index+=10)
    {
    player[index+0].men = 3;
    player[index+1].men = 3;
    player[index+2].men = 3;
    player[index+3].men = 3;
    player[index+4].men = 3;
    player[index+5].men = 3;
```

```
    player[index+6].men = 3;
    player[index+7].men = 3;
    player[index+8].men = 3;
    player[index+9].men = 3;
    } // end for index
```

Now the loop executes only 1,000 times; therefore, index has only 1,000 increments and compares, and there are only 1,000 NEAR jumps.

I've also written this example to show you that unrolling the loop may not be worth it. Look closely at the new code. We had to add offsets to each index in the array indexing, and the time it takes to do the additions will probably undo the gains we made by unrolling the loop. However, we can add a trick to fix it. We'll use the loop to count the number of times the operation is done, but we'll use a secondary index variable to index into the structure. This will put us over the top, and this time we *do* get a speed improvement. Take a look:

```
new_index=0;  // add this line

for (index=0; index<1000 index+=10)
    {
    player[new_index++].men = 3;
    player[new_index++].men = 3;
    player[new_index++].men = 3;
    player[new_index++].men = 3;
    player[new_index++].men = 3;
    player[new_index++].men = 3;
    player[new_index++].men = 3;
    player[new_index++].men = 3;
    player[new_index++].men = 3;
    player[new_index++].men = 3;
    } // end for index
```

Now the new code works faster than the old code! Cool, huh?

Loop unrolling used to be so important that people would unroll loops 10,000 to 20,000 times! Today, this can really backfire because of the internal instruction caches in advanced CPUs. Unrolling the loop too many times can cause a multitude of cache-thrashing problems. However, if you use it sparingly (that is, unroll only four to eight times) you should get good results.

Let's move on to another old trick: using shifting to multiply numbers.

Binary Multiplication

This trick is a subtle one and most people don't know about it. However, it's a breeze. We first perused it in Chapter 5, "The Mysteries of the VGA Card."

On the PC (and almost every computer on this planet), the binary number system is used to represent numbers in the computer (although I hear that Martians use ternary computers). Because binary numbers are base 2, and each number is held in a WORD as a collection of digits, shifting a WORD to the right or left shifts each digit into the next place in the binary WORD. This operation automatically multiplies the number by 2 or divides the number by 2 respectively. Take a look at Figure 18.1 to see this pictorially.

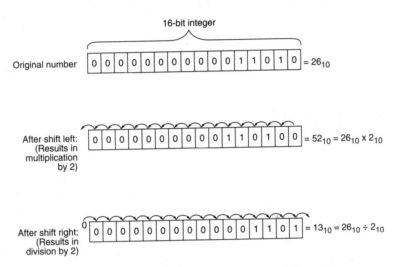

Figure 18.1. *Shifting bits to perform multiplication and division.*

That's great, but how is it going to help us multiply a number by 26? Well, if you shift a number to the left each time, you're multiplying by 2. Do this four times and you multiply by 16, five times and you multiply by 32, and so on. In this way we can multiply a number by any power of 2—but what about numbers that aren't a power of 2, like 26? To accomplish this, we break the multiplication into a group of multiplications by, again, powers of 2. For instance, 26 can also be thought of as 16 + 8 + 2. Therefore, if we were to multiply a number by 2, add that to the same number multiplied by 8, and finally add *that* to the same number multiplied by 16, then take the result, the answer would be the original number times 26! Take a look:

```
Y = X * 26 = X * 16 + X * 8 + X * 2 = X << 4 + X << 3 + X << 1
```

It doesn't take a rocket scientist to know that shifting is much faster than multiplication, and we can save a lot of time using this technique. A shift is a simple binary operation—in contrast to multiplication, which is at least an order of magnitude more complex.

There are two other issues we should touch upon here:

■ First, division can be accomplished by shifting the number to the right, although division is done less frequently because, generally, division by shifting is more complex to implement than multiplication.

■ Second, this technique only works on integers and nonfloating-point numbers. FLOATs and DOUBLEs are in IEEE format, and shifting them will thrash them—so don't do it. (Unless, of course you intend to thrash them; then go right ahead.)

Now, let's "shift" gears and move on to look-up tables.

Look-Up Tables

Look-up tables, as their name implies, are tables in which we look things up. What we look up can be anything. In the realm of video-game design, however, we usually want to look up something that's somehow going to improve our performance. This means that instead of actually performing a calculation during runtime, we precompute all possible calculations that could occur and store them in a giant table. Then, during runtime, we look in the table using the parameter of the calculation rather than performing the actual, complex calculation.

The most classic use for look-up tables is the precomputation of transcendental functions, such as sin, cos, tan, and so on. These functions take quite a bit of time to perform, even with a math co-processor. Using look-up tables, we could do the following.

We know that we're going to need the sin and cos of an angle computed, where the angle can be anything from 0-360 degrees and is an integer (that is, there are never angles with decimal components, such as 3.3 degrees). The following code would create a sin and cos look-up table:

```
float sin_table[360], cos_table[360];

for (index=0; index<360; index++)
    {
    sin_table[index] = sin(index*3.14159/180);
    cos_table[index] = cos(index*3.14159/180);
    } // end for index
```

This code fragment would create two tables, each containing 360 values, which would be the precomputed values for sin and cos.

Now, let's see how to use the look-up tables. As an example, take a look at this expression:

```
x = cos(ang*3.14159/180)*radius;
y = sin(ang*3.14159/180)*radius;
```

Using our new look-up tables, and assuming ang is an integer that represents an angle in degrees, we would have:

```
x = cos_table[ang]*radius;
y = sin_table[ang]*radius;
```

Using look-up tables can greatly increase the speed of your PC games. The only drawback is that they take up a lot of space. For instance, the game Wing Commander from Sierra On-Line uses look-up tables that hold the precomputed views of the ships at any rotation. DOOM uses look-up tables to help figure out what could possibly be visible at every location in the game universe. In other words, the computer moves the player's character to every position in the universe and rotates the player's view around at each position. A look-up table is built that stores what could be seen in each view. This data is computed before the game is played, or is loaded in from disk. Then, during game play, the look-up table is referred to and, if some part of the universe can't possibly be seen, the hidden-surface removal system ignores those invisiblle parts. This means that fewer calculations are done, speeding up the rendering.

I'm a firm believer in the idea that an entire video game can be made with look-up tables alone, and with little or no logic. As in electrical engineering, video games use finite-state machines (which we first encountered in Chapter 13, "Synthetic Intelligence"). However, instead of using logic to move from state to state (as we did in Chapter 13), it's possible to move from state to state with look-up tables. This is the technique digital engineers use most frequently to implement FSMs, and we can also do this in software. All that's needed is a table that contains the current state and the next state—but, as I said, we see more of this later. (I'm getting a bit theoretical, but it's definitely food for thought.)

The wrap: look-up tables are great. Use them all you want if you can spare the memory. Furthermore, when making look-up tables, try to use symmetry wherever possible to decrease the size of the look-up table. For instance, sin and cos are the same function, out of phase by 90 degrees. Take a look at Figure 18.2.

We see that sin and cos have the same shape. In fact, they're related by the following formulas:

```
sin(angle) = cos(angle-90)
cos(angle) = sin(angle+90)
```

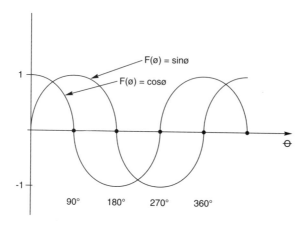

Figure 18.2. *The phase difference between sin and cos.*

If we felt like it, therefore, we could make a single look-up table for cos and then, when we wanted the sin of an angle, we could add 90 degrees to the angle and use the new result as the look-up index. Of course, you'd have to take care of the fact that the new angle could be greater than 360. You'd have to make it "wrap around" with something like:

```
if (angle>360)
   angle=angle-360;
```

To prove to you that look-up tables can increase the speed of execution of a program, I've created a program that uses the ordinary sin and cos functions provided by C, along with a look-up table of sin and cos to draw 1,000 circles on the screen. The program, shown in Listing 18.1, starts by computing the tables. It then draws 1,000 circles with the internal functions, and stops and waits for a keyboard press. It then draws 1,000 circles using the look-up tables. Type the program in and see the difference for yourself. Notice, also, that this code is quite compact. It really takes very little to do graphics.

Listing 18.1. Comparing the performance of look-up tables and runtime functions (Looknup.c).

```
#include <math.h>
#include <stdio.h>
#include <graph.h>


float sin_table[360], cos_table[360];

void main(void)
{

int index,x,y,xo,yo,radius,color,ang;
```

```c
char far *screen = (char far *)0xA0000000;

// Use Microsoft's library to go into 320x200x256 mode.
_setvideomode(_MRES256COLOR);

// Create look-up tables.

for (index=0; index<360; index++)
    {
    sin_table[index]= sin(index*3.14159/180);
    cos_table[index] = cos(index*3.14159/180);

    } // end for index

// Draw 1,000 circles using built-in sin and cos.

for (index=0; index<1000; index++)
    {
    // Get a random circle.
    radius = rand()%50;
    xo = rand()%320;
    yo = rand()%200;
    color = rand()%256;

    for (ang=0; ang<360; ang++)
        {
        x = xo + cos(ang*3.14159/180) * radius;
        y = yo + sin(ang*3.14159/180)*radius;
        // Plot the point of the circle.
        screen[(y<<6) + (y<<8) + x] = color;
        } // end for ang
    } // end for index

// Done. Halt the system and wait for the player to hit a key.
printf("\nHit a key to see circles drawn twith look-up tables.");

getch();
_setvideomode(_MRES256COLOR);

// Draw 1,000 circles using look-up tables.

for (index=0; index<1000; index++)
    {
    // Get a random circle.
    radius = rand()%50;
    xo = rand()%320;
    yo = rand()%200;
    color = rand()%256;

    for (ang=0; ang<360; ang++)
        {
        x = xo + cos_table[ang] * radius;
        y = yo + sin_table[ang] *radius;
        // Plot the point of the circle.
        screen[(y<<6) + (y<<8) + x] = color;
        } // end for ang
    } // end for index
```

continues

Listing 18.1. continued

```
// Let the player hit a key to exit.

printf("\nHit any key to exit.");
getch();

_setvideomode(_DEFAULTMODE);

} // end main
```

After running looknup.c, you should agree that look-up tables are extremely useful and can radically change the performance of a program.

The next stop in our evolution of optimization techniques is fixed-point mathematics.

Fixed-Point Mathematics

Fixed-point mathematics? No, it's not a new revision of broken-point mathematics. It's a different way of looking at computer math.

There are two distinct forms of math done on a computer:

■ Integer math

■ Floating-point math

Integer math uses CHARs, INTs, LONGs, and so on. Floating-point math uses FLOATs, DOUBLEs, and so on. The difference in the two kinds of math is in the way the numbers are internally represented, and what the numbers can represent numerically. Integers are represented in the computer in straightforward binary without any encoding. As you know, integers can represent both positive and negative whole numbers (without decimal places). On the other hand, floating-point numbers are used to represent numbers that *do* have decimal places (that is, are nonintegral).

Why all the concern about numbers? Well, the PC can do math reasonably fast. However, reasonably is not reasonable enough for video games! Even with a math co-processor, the PC still leaves much to be desired in the real-time, 3-D graphics department. Calculations done with integers are much faster than those done with floating-point numbers.

You may ask, then: "Why do we have to use floating-point numbers in the first place?" The answer is that, by the nature of the type of programming we do (3-D computer graphics), we're going to inevitably need accuracy in our calculations, meaning we need to use floating-point numbers and calculations. And floating-point calculations are so time-consuming because of the way the floating-point numbers are represented. They're not in straight binary. Instead, they're in a special IEEE format that holds the number and mantissa (the exponent) in a weird, biased form that has to be decoded and encoded for calculations.

A number is just an abstract concept: a tool with which to count objects. If we wanted to, we could make our own number systems and conventions as programmers—as long as they do the job. This is where fixed-point math comes in to play. It's possible to represent a number that has a whole part and a decimal part all within a single integer. How we do this is: we pretend there's a decimal somewhere within the integer, and that the binary digits to the left are the whole part of the number and the binary digits to the right are the decimal part. Figure 18.3 should help you picture this.

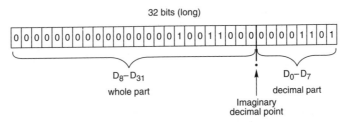

Figure 18.3. *The representation of 152.05 in fixed-point with 24 bits of whole part and 8 bits of decimal part.*

Where you put the decimal is up to you. The more you put it to the left, the more decimal places you'll have—at the expense of the whole places. Conversely, the more you move the imaginary decimal to the right, the more whole places you'll have—at the expense of decimal accuracy.

We must come up with a decimal position and a base data type that will fill our needs. I suggest that we use a LONG data type, which has a full 32 bits of accuracy. We then place the decimal somewhere in the middle of it, breaking it into two halves. In general, you should place the decimal where it needs to be for your particular application. For this discussion, we can place the decimal after the eighth digit. By placing the decimal eight digits from the right, we have eight digits to hold the decimal part and 24 digits to hold the whole part. This is more than ample for our needs, because the video games we'll be writing won't be using extremely large numbers, and we won't need more than a couple decimal places of accuracy.

To use fixed-point math we need only to figure out how to do a few operations on it. These are:

- Assignment
- Addition
- Subtraction
- Multiplication
- Division
- Comparison

Before we can figure out ways to implement these operations, though, we must first figure out how to declare a fixed-point number! Take a look below—it's really difficult:

```
long fix_1, fix_2, fix_3;
```

Fooled you for a second, huh? Isn't that simple? As I said before, we use the LONG data type for our fixed-point numbers and just *imagine* a decimal place. Therefore, a plain old declaration is all we need to create a fixed-point number.

Assignment

Now, let's talk about assignment. If we want to assign the whole part of the fixed number, we do the following:

```
int a=300;
long fix_1=0;  // 00000000000000000000000.00000000
fix_1 = ((long)a << 8);
```

That's how you place an integer into a fixed-point number: you first cast the integer to a LONG data type, then shift it into the proper position (that is, eight bits to the left).

Assigning a floating-point number is relatively the same, but we can't use shifting. Instead, we must use a floating-point multiplication combined with a cast to LONG. (Remember: it doesn't make sense to shift a floating-point number.) Here's how to do the assignment:

```
long fix_1 = (long)(23.45 * 256);
```

We multiply by 256 because this is equivalent to shifting eight times to the left.

Addition and Subtraction

We can use the standard C operators to add or subtract fixed-point numbers; for example, to add two fixed-point numbers and place the result in a third we would have the following:

```
fix_3 = fix_1 + fix_2;
```

Subtraction works in the same manner. Moreover, negative values also work because the internal representation of LONG data types takes care of negative values without disturbing our fixed-point numbers.

Multiplication

The hardest of all the operations is multiplication. We must be careful here: there are a lot of little subtleties that can create bugs. For one thing, when multiplying two fixed-point numbers, the worst-case result can take up twice the number of bit places as the multiplier and multiplicand had. In other words, if the multiplier and the multiplicand are both 32-bit, it's possible for the product to be a 64-bit result. We'll be using the CPU's standard multiplication, and must pay close attention to the magnitude of the fixed-point numbers we're multiplying. Otherwise, they'll overflow.

To multiply two fixed-point numbers, we use the multiply operator as usual. However, when the multiplication is done we must shift the result eight places back to the right. This is because, when we created each of the fixed-point numbers, we artificially multiplied them by 256 (that is, shifted them left eight times). When we perform a multiplication on them now, the imaginary decimal place moves to the left (just as it would if you did a decimal multiplication). To remedy this, we must shift the final result back eight times to the right—or a constant of 256 will be multiplied by the result. (That would make 2*5 equal 2*5*256 instead of the proper answer of 10!) Here's how to do a multiplication.

```
fix_1 = (fix_2 * fix_3) >> 8;
```

If you want to do a sum of products, shifting does not have to be done after each multiplication. It can be done at the end. Here's an example:

```
fix_1 = (fix_2 * fix_3 + fix_4 * fix_5) >> 8;
```

This property of fixed-point numbers could come in handy if you're trying to optimize further and get rid of all the shifts.

Division

To perform division, I suggest not using the division (/) bar but, instead, multiplying by the reciprocal. In general, you can always multiply by the reciprocal of a number instead of dividing by the number. Remember that division, whether it's integer, floating-point, or fixed-point, is always slower than multiplication.

Here's an example of how a division would be accomplished:

```
// Create fix_1, which is the reciprocal of 34.
fix_1 = (long)(256 * 1/34);

// Equivalent to the operation (fix_3 / fix_1)
fix_2 = (fix_3 * fix_1) >> 8;
```

Before we move onto the next topic, I'd like to take up a couple of short discussions on some details that most authors don't like to discuss. These are accuracy and maximum numerical representations.

Accuracy

With our conventions and fixed-point representation we'll use eight bits to represent the decimal portion. This means the smallest number we can resolve is 1/256 (or, roughly, .004). Therefore, our maximum error will occur during the multiplication of two numbers. With our system, the largest number we can have as a product is 32761. (I explain that shortly.) Therefore, the greatest error can be .004*32761, or 131.004. Wow—that's pretty big! In reality, you never have errors this big. You should only be doing two to five multiplications on any fixed-point number, and the numbers you should be multiplying shouldn't be as large as 32761. You'll find your errors to be in the ballpark of .01 to .5 most of the time, which is reasonable because 90 percent of the time the results are used as pixel locations on the screen, itself an integer matrix.

Enough about accuracy. Let's move on to figuring out the maximum number that can be represented in our fixed-point system.

Maximum Numerical Representation

We have 24 bits to hold the whole part of the number and eight to hold the decimal part. You'd think, therefore, that we'd have 2^{24}, or 16,777,216. Almost, but not quite. Because fixed-point numbers can be both positive and negative, we have a range of half that, or -8,388,608 to +8,388,608. Now, there's a really big "gotcha" lingering in the midst of fixed-point math. We can add and subtract numbers that will fit into the range, but when we multiply we must be exceedingly careful not to overflow the LONG.

When I studied fixed-point math for the first time and tried to implement it, I made a big mistake. I used a scheme similar to ours (that is, 24 bits for the whole part and eight for the decimal part). I thought that the largest numbers I could multiply together would be any two numbers that, when multiplied, would fit into 24 bits. *Wrong!* That would have meant that I could multiply 4096 * 4096 and still be OK. This is completely incorrect. I was forgetting about the other eight bits sitting there causing the 4096 to be scaled by 256! Therefore, I was really multiplying (4096*256) * (4096*256), which equals about 1.09×10^{12}. Because a LONG is 2^{32}, it can hold signed numbers from -2,147,483,648 to +2,147,483,648 (which is 1,000 times smaller than the result I was getting). The moral of the story is that fixed-point numbers are still LONGs and, if they contain numbers interpreted as LONGs that will overflow if multiplied, you've got a problem.

In our case, the largest result of a multiplication that can fit in our fixed-point system is roughly 32761, or 181^2. The 181 was computed as follows: find a number that, when multiplied by 256 and squared, will be less than or equal to the largest number that a LONG can represent (or +2,147,483,648). We use 256 because we have eight decimal digits, and 2^8 is 256.

Does it seems strange that the largest number that can be a result of a multiplication can only be roughly 3276, but the result of and addition can be roughly 8,000,000? Well...you win some, you lose some.

To help you experiment with fixed-point numbers and see some of their interesting properties, I've created a little library and a main() program to demo their use (Listing 18.2). I suggest you take your time and really get a firm grasp on them, because they're an important topic unto themselves and there's little published about them. Also, remember: the decimal point is imaginary!

Listing 18.2. The fixpoint library functions (Fix.c).

```
/// I N C L U D E S ///////////////////////////////////////////////

#include <math.h>
#include <stdio.h>

// Define our new magical fixed-point data type.

typedef long fixed;

// F U N C T I O N S ///////////////////////////////////////////////

fixed Assign_Integer(long integer)
{

return((fixed)integer << 8);
```

continues

Listing 18.2. continued

```
} // end Assign_Integer

/////////////////////////////////////////////////////////////////

fixed Assign_Float(float number)
{

return((fixed)(number * 256));

} // end Assign_Float

/////////////////////////////////////////////////////////////////

fixed Mul_Fixed(fixed f1,fixed f2)
{

return((f1*f2) >> 8);

} // end Mul_Fixed

/////////////////////////////////////////////////////////////////

fixed Add_Fixed(fixed f1,fixed f2)
{

return(f1+f2);

} // end Add_Fixed

/////////////////////////////////////////////////////////////////

void Print_Fixed(fixed f1)
{

printf("%ld.%ld",f1 >> 8, 100*(unsigned long)(f1 & 0x00ff)/256);

} // end Print_Fixed

//M A I N /////////////////////////////////////////////////////////

void main(void)
{

fixed f1,f2,f3;

f1 = Assign_Float(15);
f2 = Assign_Float(233.45);

f3 = Mul_Fixed(f1,f2);

printf("\nf1:");
```

```
Print_Fixed(f1);

printf("\nf2:");
Print_Fixed(f2);

printf("\nf3:");
Print_Fixed(f3);

} // end main
```

Of course, in your programs you wouldn't actually use function calls for addition and multiplication. I just put them there to separate things for you to experiment with the properties of fixed-point numbers.

On to the in-line assembler.

The In-Line Assembler

To assemble or not to assemble: that is the question. It was (more or less) the question in Shakespeare's time and it's true today. As I've said before, you should only use assembly language and the in-line assembler if you really need to. Otherwise, the operation you're doing is machine-dependent in nature. You shouldn't need assembly for anything other than doing graphics and sound. You definitely should not be using assembly for game logic and algorithms. Moreover, if you do need assembly language for speed, try to use the in-line assembler in deference to MASM because the in-line assembler is easier to implement and takes less development time.

We have looked at a collection of methods that, if implemented in your video games, will increase their performance many times. Now let's take a look at some of the functions we've written in the previous chapters and optimize them with our new techniques.

Case Study I: Optimizing Pixel Plotting

In the game we make in Chapter 19, and in the ones you'll be making, plotting pixels is a function that must be as fast as possible. Let's take the Plot_Pixel() function from Listing 5.5 (in Chapter 5, "The Mysteries of the VGA Card"), and see if we can optimize it further. Listing 18.3 contains the new function.

Listing 18.3. A function to plot pixels faster.

```
/////////////////////////////////////////////////////////////

void Plot_Pixel_Fast(int x,int y,unsigned char color)
{

// Plot the pixel in the desired color a little quicker using
// binary shifting to accomplish the multiplications.

// Use the fact that 320*y = 256*y + 64*y = y<<8 + y<<6.

video_buffer[((y<<8) + (y<<6)) + x] = color;

} // end Plot_Pixel_Fast

/////////////////////////////////////////////////////////////
```

Unfortunately for us, this function is almost as optimized as it's going to get. Here are the only suggestions I'd make:

- Convert it to in-line assembly.

- Don't pass any parameters.

- Possibly, create a humongous look-up table with 64,000 entries, each holding the address of a pixel given an x and y coordinate.

Now that I think of it, a look-up table might be slower because the operation of indexing the table may turn out to take more time than the two shifts and addition that are done to compute the address. However, let's implement the first two, starting with using globals instead of passed parameters.

We could create the following globals:

```
int plot_x, plot_y, plot_color;
```

We also could rewrite the function as shown in Listing 18.4.

Listing 18.4. Another version of the pixel-plotting function.

```
/////////////////////////////////////////////////////////////

void Plot_Pixel_Global(void)
{

// Plot the pixel in the desired color a little quicker using
// binary shifting and globals.

// Use the fact that 320*y = 256*y + 64*y = y<<8 + y<<6.
```

```
video_buffer[((plot_y<<8) + (plot_y<<6)) + plot_x] = plot_color;

} // end Plot_Pixel_Global
```

//

This will be much faster, but we still have to assign the variables plot_x, plot_y, and plot_color before the call. The question is, therefore: "Does the assignment to the globals take less time than the passing of the parameters, along with the creating and deletion of the function frame, along with the dereferencing of the parameters?" (That was a mouthful!) Maybe, maybe not; it depends on the situation, but it's worth a try. Now, let's convert the procedure to assembly language. The result is shown in Listing 18.5.

Listing 18.5. An assembly language version of the pixel plotter (plasm.c).

//

```
Plot_Pixel_Asm(int x,int y,int color)
{

// Plot the pixel in the desired color a little quicker using
// binary shifting and assembly.
// Do it in assembly.

  _asm
    {
    les di,video_buffer    // Create a pointer to the screen
                           // buffer.
    mov di,y               // Get the row.
    shl di,6               // Multiply by 64.
    mov bx,di              // Save the result.
    shl di,2               // Two more times equals 256.
    add di,bx              // Combine the results.
    add di,x               // Add the x component.
    mov al,BYTE PTR color  // Move color into a register.
    mov es:[di], al        // Plot the pixel.
    }  // end assembly

} // end Plot_Pixel_Asm
```

//

Surprisingly enough, the assembly language version using the in-line assembler is only about 2 percent faster than the C version. There are two reasons for this:

■ First, the C version is "pure," and the compiler does a good job of converting it to assembly—almost as well as we can do manually.

■ Second, when you use the in-line assembler it saves all the registers and restores them. This operation uses the fractional saving we made with our hand assembly, and evens the score. The only way to get rid of registers being saved and restored is to write an external assembly function using MASM, which I would say is permissible in this case because we're trying to optimize such an important operation (pixel plotting).

As a final example, I want to show you an optimization that is VGA-dependent and can make your rendering engine up to twice as fast.

Case Study II: Optimizing Line Drawing

Games like Wolfenstein 3-D and DOOM don't use a lot of generally accepted 3-D graphics techniques, as do flight simulators and polygon-based graphics engines. They use quite clever methods to generate their 3-D views. These methods are based on drawing a great many lines in a single direction. These lines usually are vertical or horizontal, but only in remote cases diagonal. Therefore, we should understand ways to draw horizontal or vertical lines really fast. In this analysis, we study the horizontal line.

As we learned in Chapter 5, "The Mysteries of the VGA Card," to draw a horizontal line we simply do a memcpy from the starting address in the video buffer to the ending address (Listing 5.6). These addresses are computed based on the starting x and ending x of the line. The only drawback to this method is that it uses a BYTE write to accomplish the data transfer. A game-programming guru knows that the VGA card works best with WORDs, not BYTEs. (By "best" I mean fastest.) Therefore, when possible, we want to blast the video buffer a WORD at a time instead of a BYTE at a time. What I have done is rewrite the horizontal line-drawing function to draw lines a WORD at a time.

This is not as easy as it seems, because the endpoints have to be taken care of separately. You see, when you write a WORD to the video buffer, in essence you plot two pixels. You must be careful to take this into consideration when drawing a line. Say we wanted to draw a line from the point (51,100) to the point (100,100). We'd have a line that looked something like Figure 18.4.

Close analysis of this line shows that each endpoint really only has one byte turned on, not two. Therefore, we must write software that can handle when the endpoints are on BYTE or WORD boundaries. The program in Listing 18.5 does this.

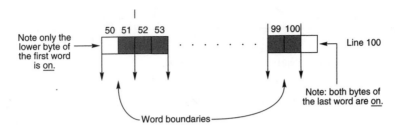

Figure 18.4. *A horizontal line.*

Listing 18.6. A horizontal-line drawing program based on WORD writes (hlinef.c).

```
////////////////////////////////////////////////////////////////////

void H_Line_Fast(int x1,int x2,int y,unsigned int color)
{
// A fast horizontal-line renderer uses WORD writes instead of
// BYTE writes. The only problem is the endpoints of the h line
// must be taken into account. Test whether the endpoints of the
// horizontal line are on WORD boundaries (that is, whether
// they're evenly divisible by 2). Basically, we must consider
// the two endpoints of the line separately if we want to write
// WORDs at a time (that is, two pixels at a time). Note:
// x2 > x1.

unsigned int first_word,
            middle_word,
             last_word,
           line_offset,
                 index;


// Test the 1's bit of the starting x.

if ( (x1 & 0x0001) )
   {

   first_word = (color<<8);

   } // end if starting point is on a word boundary
else
   {
   // Replicate color into both bytes.
   first_word = ((color<<8) | color);

   } // end else

// Test the 1's bit of the ending x.

if ( (x2 & 0x0001) )
   {
```

continues

Listing 18.6. continued

```
    last_word = ((color<<8) ¦ color);

    } // end if ending point is on a WORD boundary
else
    {
    // Place color in high byte of WORD only.

    last_word = color;

    } // end else

// Now we can draw the horizontal line, two pixels at a time.

line_offset = ((y<<7) + (y<<5));
// y*160, because there are 160 WORDs/line.

// Compute middle color.

middle_word = ((color<<8) ¦ color);

// Left endpoint

video_buffer_w[line_offset + (x1>>1)] = first_word;

// The middle of the line

for (index=(x1>>1)+1; index<(x2>>1); index++)
    video_buffer_w[line_offset+index] = middle_word;

// Right endpoint

video_buffer_w[line_offset + (x2>>1)] = last_word;

} // end H_Line_Fast

/////////////////////////////////////////////////////////////////
```

The function operates by first testing whether the line's endpoints are on BYTE boundaries. Based on that, the function creates two WORDs: one that will be the beginning of the line and one that will be the end of the line. These two WORDs have the byte that represents the color replicated in them once or twice. The function then draws the line by:

- Writing the first WORD that represents the left endpoint

- Doing a FOR loop to write the WORDs in the middle of the line

- Writing the WORD that represents the endpoint of the line

Even though the function is many times longer than the original H_Line function, it's nearly twice as fast. (There's a bit of overhead for the endpoint calculations.) To make it even faster I would convert the part that draws the middle into in-line, but this I leave up to you.

Summary

We've covered a great many topics in this chapter, and even if you never write a video game you definitely will be a more efficient programmer with the knowledge you've obtained. You have some formidable ammo within your reach! Don't think that these are the best or the only optimizations that can be done in a video game, though. You'll undoubtedly discover more, and improve on what I've showed you.

Our long journey is coming to a close and I want to go out with a thermonuclear, time-distorting bang. I'll be waiting for you in Chapter 19, where at last we get into the core of Warlock. Strap your overalls on and let's wrench!

Warlock

I f you made it this far, you have definitely got the right stuff! You have traversed many perils and uncovered many secrets. Within the pages of the previous chapters we learned about so many different areas of computing, it's almost unfathomable that anyone could keep it all straight! You must be one of the special people who have the ability.

Anyway, I promised I'd supply you with a full, 3-D game. Well...I fibbed. A little. If I gave you a complete game, there would be nothing for you to do! You wouldn't learn anything by it. Therefore, what I've done is create the skeleton of a game; a game core. I've created a 3-D ray-casting engine that operates in real time. Furthermore, throughout the book we've been writing functions that can be used to complete the game.

Take a look at Figure 19.1 to see some screen shots of Warlock.

by André LaMothe

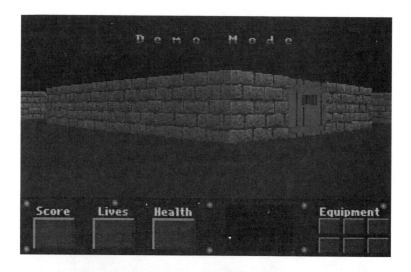

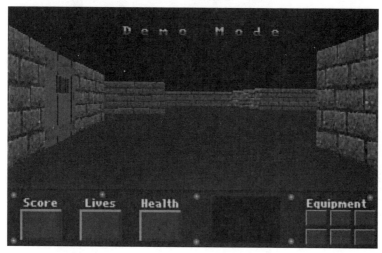

Figure 19.1. *Screen shots of Warlock.*

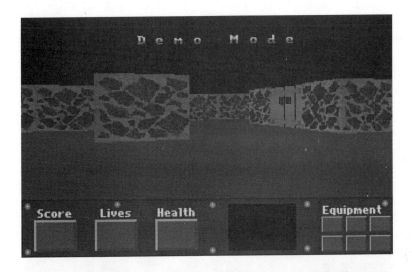

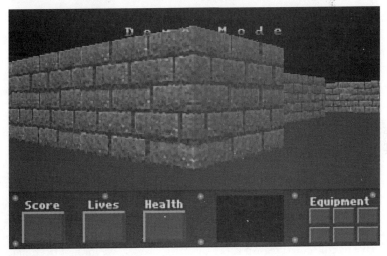

Figure 19.1. *continued.*

I want you to take what I've given you and create something with it. Maybe you'll make a simple game of Capture the Flag. Maybe you'll make some kind of D&D game. Whatever you decide, I'd like to see what you do with the engine and what you come up with. Therefore, at the end of the chapter I give you an address where you can send any submissions, questions, answers, or comments. (I might even publish your game in an upcoming book or magazine!)

This final chapter covers the logic and some of the architecture of the game core that I've created for you to use and enhance. We briefly talk about the following areas:

- The story behind Warlock
- The components of the game
- The new ray caster
- Texture mapping
- Shading
- The use of assembly language
- The game loop
- The game grid
- Demo mode
- Placing objects in the world
- Picking up some speed
- A few last words

The Story Behind Warlock

The first thing I do when I design a game is think up the game itself. Warlock is supposed to be a sword-and-sorcery version of DOOM. My basic vision was to have the player be a sorcerer who can use magical weapons, along with verbal spells, to accomplish tasks. He (the character as currently written is male) would begin at Level One and traverse three different subdomains, each containing a specific object that he'd have to collect to create a superpowerful magical weapon. This magical weapon, when complete, would be the only way to destroy the evil necromancer found on the final level. Within the game you'd be able to pick up food, potions, and scrolls. The potions would do the usual things: make you healthier, stronger, and so on. The scrolls would be spells that you could verbalize (using a digitized voice). These scrolls could be used in serious situations where you just don't have the firepower.

In this vision, the game also would have a couple of floating-type monsters—maybe two or three—rather than friction-based bipeds.

That's about all I wanted to see: a few levels with some really cool textures; a couple of monsters; and some neat, digitized sounds. Along with the 3-D view, that should bring our game up to par with something like Wolfenstein 3-D. Of course, you can do anything you wish with the game core; the story line for Warlock is just a suggestion.

The Components of the Game

Before we start confusing ourselves, let's take a look at the game to get an idea of what it has and what it doesn't.

A Note on Sound

The game uses the Sound Blaster for digitized effects, and you must have your Sound Blaster set to the following to hear anything:

- DMA #1
- IRQ #5
- I/O port 220h

These are the settings with which I compiled the executable file. If your settings differ, you can always recompile the executable and make appropriate changes to the Voc functions in the beginning of the main.

Whether you have a sound card or not, just run the program to see it in action.

Loading Warlock

The executable is called warlock.exe. Just enter

```
warlock
```

at the DOS prompt. The executable automatically loads everything for you and executes.

Compiling Warlock

The game uses three main modules and a few assembly language modules for some of the rendering. The names and function of the modules are as follows:

warlock.c	This is the source code to the game core.
sndlib.c	This is the source code to the sound system. (We've seen the functions before, but I've created a cleaner interface for Warlock and placed it in this file.)
sndlib.h	This is the header file for sndlib.c.

graphics.c	This is the final graphics library (almost identical to graph0.c).
graphics.h	This is the header file for graphics.c.
drawg.asm	This function draws the black sky and the gray ground using 32-bit instructions.
render32.asm	This function moves the double buffer to the video buffer. It also uses 32-bit instructions.
sliver.asm	This function draws a single sliver of texture into the double buffer. This is how the 3-D view (a collection of vertical strips) is generated. I had to use assembly for speed. Again, I used 32-bit instructions for speed and so you have access to the extra segment registers.

The C files are compiled, the assembly files assembled, and the whole thing linked together using warlock.c as the main module. What I did was create a library that included the sound library, the graphics library, and the extra assembly language functions. I then compiled and linked it to the main program, warlock.c.

Remember to compile everything using the MEDIUM memory model, and use the /G2 option on the compiler to allow 286 specific, in-line instructions.

Here was my standard batch file, which I used to compile everything using Microsoft's C/C++ 7.0:

```
cl -AM -Zi -c  -Fc -Gs -G2 %1.c
```

This line translates as "Compile only using MEDIUM memory model, 286 instructions, no stack probes, and generate code listings."

To get an overall view of how the software goes together, take a look at Figure 19.2. It shows graphically how the pieces fit together.

Demo Mode

The game starts out in demo mode, and you notice an indication of this at the top of the screen. You see a first-person point of view as the demo engine plays back a segment of a minute or so of me running around in the universe.

When you've had enough, hit the Esc key. This takes the game out of demo mode and into walkthrough mode.

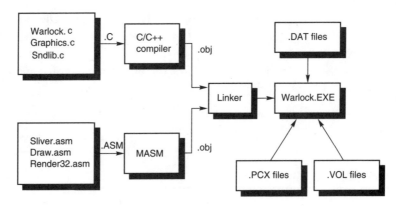

Figure 19.2. *The modules of Warlock.*

Walkthrough Mode

In walkthrough mode, use the arrow keys to move around in the universe. To open a door, press the Spacebar.

As you can see, Warlock's environment looks like a dungeon. You should notice that there are no objects in the universe. There also are no ceilings, floors, or shading. We discuss all these topics later in this chapter.

When you're done experimenting, press the Esc key again and the game exits.

Go ahead and check it out. I'll wait here.

Ready? Now let's talk a little about each aspect of the game core that has something interesting about it.

The New Ray Caster

The ray caster that you saw in Chapter 6, "The Third Dimension," was (to put it bluntly) about as fast as a dot-matrix printer printing a gray scale, high-resolution picture! It was, in a word, slow. This is because it was quite annotated, used straightforward techniques, was all in C, used floating-point math, and didn't use all the look-up tables and clever insights it could have. The ray caster we use in Warlock is a little different. It's highly optimized; I would say that the code itself could only be about twice as fast as it is now. To get that, however, the ray caster would become so totally weird that you probably couldn't follow it anymore. (As it is, I can barely figure it out myself, and I wrote it!)

Ultimately, the ray caster's speed is not the bottleneck. The bottleneck is the movement of the double buffer to the video buffer. It would have been much better to interleave the ray caster's texturing with the video scan. The ray caster's computation time then would literally be absorbed within the video rendering, and it would be as if the ray casting was taking zero time.

We talk a bit more about this interleaving and some other ideas later in the chapter. Listing 19.1 contains the new ray caster.

Listing 19.1. The new ray-casting engine.

```
///////////////////////////////////////////////////////////////

void Ray_Caster(long x,long y,long view_angle)
{

  // This is the heart of the system. It casts out 320 rays and
  // builds the 3-D image from their intersections with the
  // walls. It was derived from the previous version used in
  // ray.c. However, it has been extremely optimized for speed
  // by the use of many more look-up tables and fixed-point
  // math.

  int cell_x,      // The current cell the ray is in.
      cell_y,
      ray,         // The current ray being cast, 0-320.
      casting=2,   // Tracks the progress of the x and y
                   // component of the ray.
      x_hit_type,  // Records the block that was intersected;
                   // used to figure out which texture to use.
      y_hit_type,  //
      x_bound,     // The next vertical and horizontal
                   // intersection point.
      y_bound,
      next_y_cell, // Used to figure out the ray's quadrant.
      next_x_cell,
      xray=0,      // Tracks the progress of a ray looking for
                   // y intersections
      yray=0,      // Tracks the progress of a ray looking for
                   // x intersections.
      x_delta,     // The amount needed to move to get to the
                   // next cell position.
      y_delta,
      xb_save,
      yb_save,
      xi_save,     // Used to save exact x and y intersection
                   // points.
      yi_save,
      scale;


  long cast=0,
       dist_x,     // The distance of the x and y ray intersections
                   // from the viewpoint.
       dist_y;
```

```
float xi,       // Used to track the x and y intersections.
      yi;

// S E C T I O N  1 //////////////////////////////////////////

  // Initialization

  // Compute starting angle from the player. Field of view is 60
  // degrees, so subtract half of that current view angle.

  if ((view_angle-=ANGLE_30) < 0)
  {
    view_angle=ANGLE_360 + view_angle;
  } // end if

  // Loop through all 320 rays.

  for (ray=319; ray>=0; ray—)
  {

// S E C T I O N  2 //////////////////////////////////////////

    // Compute the first x intersection.

    // We need to know which halfplane we're casting from
    // relative to the y-axis.

    if (view_angle >= ANGLE_0 && view_angle < ANGLE_180)
    {
      // Compute the first horizontal line that could be
      // intersected with the ray. Note: it will be above the
      // player.

      y_bound = (CELL_Y_SIZE + (y & 0xffc0));

      // Compute delta to get to next horizontal line.

      y_delta = CELL_Y_SIZE;

      // Based on the first possible horizontal intersection
      // line, compute the x-intercept so casting can begin.

      xi = inv_tan_table[view_angle] * (y_bound - y) + x;

      // Set cell delta

      next_y_cell = 0;

    } // end if upper half plane
    else
    {
      // Compute the first horizontal line that could be
      // intersected with the ray. Note: it will be below the
      // player.

      y_bound = (int)(y & 0xffc0);
```

continues

Listing 19.1. continued

```
// Compute the delta to get to next horizontal line.

y_delta = -CELL_Y_SIZE;

// Based on the first possible horizontal intersection
// line, compute the x-intercept so casting can begin.

xi = inv_tan_table[view_angle] * (y_bound - y) + x;

// Set cell delta

next_y_cell = -1;

} // end else lower half plane

// S E C T I O N  3 ///////////////////////////////////////////////

// Compute the first y intersection.

// We need to know which halfplane we're casting from
// relative to the x-axis.

if (view_angle < ANGLE_90 || view_angle >= ANGLE_270)
{

// Compute the first vertical line that could be
// intersected with the ray. Note: it will be to the right
// of the player.

x_bound = (int)(CELL_X_SIZE + (x & 0xffc0));

// Compute delta to get to next vertical line.

x_delta = CELL_X_SIZE;

// Based on the first possible vertical intersection line,
// compute the y intercept so casting can begin.

yi = tan_table[view_angle] * (x_bound - x) + y;

// Set cell delta

next_x_cell = 0;

} // end if right half plane
else
{

// Compute the first vertical line that could be
// intersected with the ray. Note: it will be to the left
// of the player.

x_bound = (int)(x & 0xffc0);

// Compute delta to get to next vertical line.

x_delta = -CELL_X_SIZE;
```

```
          // Based on the first possible vertical intersection line,
          // compute the y intercept so casting can begin.

          yi = tan_table[view_angle] * (x_bound - x) + y;

          // Set cell delta

          next_x_cell = -1;

     } // end else right half plane


     // begin cast

     casting      = 2;        // Two rays to cast simultaneously.
     xray=yray    = 0;        // Reset intersection flags.


// S E C T I O N  4 /////////////////////////////////////////////

     while(casting)
     {

        // Continue casting each ray in parallel.

        if (xray!=INTERSECTION_FOUND)
        {

          // Compute the current map position to inspect.

          cell_x = ( (x_bound+next_x_cell) >> CELL_X_SIZE_FP);

          cell_y = (int)yi;
          cell_y>>=CELL_Y_SIZE_FP;

          // Test whether there's a block where the current x ray
          // is intersecting.

          if ((x_hit_type = world[cell_y][cell_x])!=0)
          {
            // Compute the distance.

            dist_x  = (long)((yi - y) * inv_sin_table[view_angle]);
            yi_save = (int)yi;
            xb_save = x_bound;

            // Terminate x casting.

            xray = INTERSECTION_FOUND;
            casting—;

          } // end if a hit
          else
          {

            // Compute the next y intercept.

            yi += y_step[view_angle];
```

continues

Listing 19.1. continued

```
                // Find the next possible x intercept point.

                x_bound += x_delta;

            } // end else

        } // end if x ray has intersected

// S E C T I O N  5 ////////////////////////////////////////////////

        if (yray!=INTERSECTION_FOUND)
        {

            // Compute the current map position to inspect.

            cell_x = xi;
            cell_x>>=CELL_X_SIZE_FP;

            cell_y = ( (y_bound + next_y_cell) >> CELL_Y_SIZE_FP);

            // Test whether there is a block where the current y ray
            // is intersecting.

            if ((y_hit_type = world[cell_y][cell_x])!=0)
            {

                // Compute the distance.

                dist_y  = (long)((xi - x) * inv_cos_table[view_angle]);
                xi_save = (int)xi;
                yb_save = y_bound;

                yray = INTERSECTION_FOUND;
                casting—;

            } // end if a hit
            else
            {

                // Terminate y casting.

                xi += x_step[view_angle];

                // Compute the next possible y intercept.

                y_bound += y_delta;

            } // end else

        } // end if y ray has intersected

    } // end while not done

// S E C T I O N  6 ////////////////////////////////////////////////

    // At this point we know that the ray has successfully hit
    // both a vertical wall and a horizontal wall. We must see
```

```
// which one was closer, and then render it.

if (dist_x < dist_y)
{

  // There was a vertical wall closer than the horizontal.

  // Compute the actual scale and multiply it by the view
  // filter so that spherical distortion is cancelled.

  scale = (int)(cos_table[ray]/dist_x);

  // Clip wall sliver against viewport.

  if (scale>(MAX_SCALE-1)) scale=(MAX_SCALE-1);

    scale_row      = scale_table[scale-1];

    if (scale>(WINDOW_HEIGHT-1))
    {
      sliver_clip = (scale-(WINDOW_HEIGHT-1)) >> 1;
      scale=(WINDOW_HEIGHT-1);
    }
    else
      sliver_clip = 0;

    sliver_scale   = scale-1;

    // Set up parameters for assembly language.

    sliver_texture = object.frames[x_hit_type];
    sliver_column  = (yi_save & 0x003f);
    sliver_top     = WINDOW_MIDDLE - (scale >> 1);
    sliver_ray     = ray;

    // Render the sliver in assembly.

    Render_Sliver_32();

} // end if

else // The ray must have hit a horizontal wall first.
{

  // There was a vertical wall closer than the horizontal.

  // Compute the actual scale and multiply by view filter
  // so that spherical distortion is cancelled.

  scale = (int)(cos_table[ray]/dist_y);

  // Do clipping again.

  if (scale>(MAX_SCALE-1)) scale=(MAX_SCALE-1);

    scale_row      = scale_table[scale-1];

    if (scale>(WINDOW_HEIGHT-1))
```

continues

Listing 19.1. continued

```
    {
      sliver_clip = (scale-(WINDOW_HEIGHT-1)) >> 1;
      scale=(WINDOW_HEIGHT-1);
    }
    else
      sliver_clip = 0;

    sliver_scale   = scale-1;

    // Set up parameters for assembly language.

    sliver_texture = object.frames[y_hit_type+1];
    sliver_column  = (xi_save & 0x003f);
    sliver_top     = WINDOW_MIDDLE - (scale >> 1);
    sliver_ray     = ray;

    // Render the sliver.

    Render_Sliver_32();

  } // end else

// S E C T I O N  7 ////////////////////////////////////////////////

  // Cast the next ray.

  // Test whether the view angle needs to wrap around.

  if (++view_angle>=ANGLE_360)
  {

    view_angle=0;

  } // end if

 } // end for ray

} // end Ray_Caster

//////////////////////////////////////////////////////////////////////
```

The new ray caster has relatively the same architecture as the first one we saw (in ray.c in Chapter 6). The optimizations have been made at a microscopic rather than macroscopic level, meaning I optimized the code line by line instead of changing the basic techniques being used. This worked fine, and I got an increase of about an order of magnitude in speed. I used a lot of fixed-point math, integers, logical operations, and a few more look-up tables to increase the performance to a reasonable level. Finally, I had to resort to assembly to get that *last few percent*. All in all, though, the pure C version fared well on a 486 machine, although it was pretty slow on a 386. (At least that's what my friend Ashvin said about it when he ran it. But I think we can trust him.)

Each section of the code does the same thing as it does in the previous version; the difference is in the optimizations. The overall new theme to the code is the use of integers and fixed-point math rather than floating-point. This is where most of the speed increase was squeezed from.

Let's briefly cover the changes made in each section to get an idea of the overall effect. Here's a section-by-section overview of the optimization changes.

Section 1

Here we didn't change anything.

Section 2

Notice how y_bound is computed now: it uses all integers and logical operations. The major premise here is that any integral number modulo N is equivalent to the same number logically combined with (N-1) using the AND function. In other words:

```
X % 64 == X AND 63
```

This is the trick I used here to really cut the code size down and increase the execution speed enormously for this section.

Section 3

Section 3 uses the same tactics as Section 2. However, the data being operated on was the x intersections rather than the y intersections.

Section 4

This is where testing for further intersections begins. I paid closer attention to this section and the following section for possible optimizations because this code is in the inner loop of the ray caster. In general, you want to optimize the innermost loop of any program before worrying about the outer loops.

In any case, I took a long, hard look at the computation of cell_x and cell_y and optimized them using shifting for division, realizing that there was a multiplication that was canceling out a division (so why do it?).

Finally, all the calculations were done in fixed-point except for the calculation of distance, which I left in floating-point. I benchmarked the difference between fixed-point and floating-point and found it wasn't worth it for the added complexity, so I elected to stick with floating-point math for the calculation of distance.

Section 5

This section has the same optimizations as section 4; the difference is merely that another axis is taken into consideration.

Section 6

This section has changed quit a bit:

- First, the computation of scale has changed dramatically. I have pre-multiplied the viewing distortion with the viewing scale together to get a single array that has the result. This decreased the computation of scale by one multiplication.

- Next, I rearranged the terms and reduced it to what you see.

- Next, there's a bunch of code to do clipping. This code works by clipping each vertical strip by the screen viewport, and then sending the new information along with the original scale to the texture engine.

   The texture engine is in assembly language and receives its data through a global variable area instead of the stack. This was done for speed. The texturing is very simple. When an intersection is found, the point along the 64x64 block is computed and sent to the texturer. This location, 0-63, is used as an index into the texture memory to extract a single column of the texture.

Section 7

Nothing too exciting here.

All in all, I'm quite happy with the ray caster. It works great for such a simple program and for the short time in which it was developed: three days! It shows what's possible with the PC and a little foresight and planning.

Texture Mapping

We discussed this topic at length in Chapter 7, "Advanced Bit-Mapped Graphics and Special FX," so I'm not going to delve into the technicalities again. I do want to explain, however, the way texturing is done in Warlock.

The texturing amounts to drawing vertical strips extracted from a larger bit map. These bit maps are predrawn and located somewhere in memory. Take a look at Figure 19.3 to see the textures I drew for Warlock.

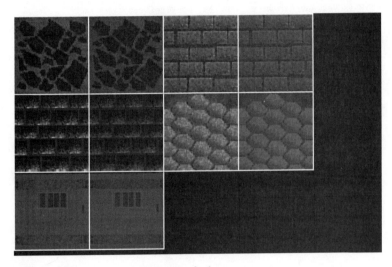

Figure 19.3. *The textures used in Warlock.*

These textures are 64x64 and were drawn using DPaint. As we learned before, the texture mapping in a ray-cast game is really the conglomeration of a lot of vertical strips scaled and drawn with a specific texture. This texture is scaled by mapping a number of source texture pixels to a destination size. The trick is to do this operation quickly.

To accomplish this, I decided to make the "sliver engine" in assembly language. The sliver engine is just the function that draws these scaled, textured, vertical strips. The sliver engine works on the same algorithm we saw before; the only difference is that I precomputed the scaling indices. In essence, I scaled all possible wall sizes, from 1 to 220, and computed what the result of each iteration would be if the scaling algorithm did the computations. Then I made a massive table (approximately 40K) that held all these precomputed scaling indices as the elements of each row. Therefore, if you want a scale of 100, you go to row 100 in the look-up table and draw 100 pixels. Each pixel is extracted from the source bit map using the array data at the 100th row and the nth column, where n is the current pixel being drawn.

I'm probably making this seem hard. Sorry; maybe the code is easier to understand! Listing 19.2 contains the C version of the sliver engine, and Listing 19.3 contains the assembly version. The C version lacks the clipping stuff, but don't pay that any mind. Just look at the inner loop of the C version and compare it to the loop of the assembly version.

Listing 19.2. The C version of the "sliver" engine.

```
void Render_Sliver(sprite_ptr sprite,int scale, int column)
{
  // This is yet another version of the sliver scaler; however,
  // this one uses look-up tables with precomputed scale indices.
  // In the end I converted this to assembly for speed.

  char far *work_sprite;
  int far  *row;

  int work_offset=0,offset,y,scale_off;

  unsigned char data;

  // Alias proper data row.

  row = scale_table[scale];

  if (scale>(WINDOW_HEIGHT-1))
  {
    scale_off = (scale-(WINDOW_HEIGHT-1)) >> 1;
    scale=(WINDOW_HEIGHT-1);
    sprite->y = 0;
  }

  // Alias a pointer to the sprite for ease of access.

  work_sprite = sprite->frames[sprite->curr_frame];

  // Compute the offset of the sprite in the video buffer.

  offset = (sprite->y << 8) + (sprite->y << 6) + sprite->x;

  for (y=0; y<scale; y++)
  {

    double_buffer[offset] = work_sprite[work_offset+column];

    offset      += SCREEN_WIDTH;
    work_offset =  row[y+scale_off];

  } // end for y

} // end Draw_Sliver
```

Listing 19.3. The assembly version of the "sliver" engine.

```
.MODEL MEDIUM,C          ; Use the MEDIUM memory model and C
                         ; function names.

.CODE                    ; Begin code segment.

EXTRN double_buffer:DWORD    ; The external double buffer.
EXTRN sliver_texture:DWORD   ; A pointer to the texture memory.
EXTRN sliver_column:WORD     ; The current texture column.
EXTRN sliver_top:WORD        ; The starting y of the sliver.
EXTRN sliver_scale:WORD      ; The overall height of the sliver.
EXTRN sliver_ray:WORD        ; The current video column.
EXTRN sliver_clip:WORD       ; How much of the texture is being
                             ; clipped?
EXTRN scale_row:WORD         ; The pointer to the proper row of
                             ; precomputed scale indices.


PUBLIC Render_Sliver_32      ; Export the function to the linker.

Render_Sliver_32 PROC FAR C  ; This is a C function and is FAR.

.386                         ; Use 80386 instructions; we
                             ; need them for the extra
                             ; segments fs,gs.

        push si              ; Save registers we will
                             ; obliterate.
        push di

        les di, double_buffer    ; Point es:di to double buffer.

        mov dx,sliver_column     ; Hold the column in dx.

        lfs si, sliver_texture   ; fs:si points to texture memory.

        ; offset = (sprite->y << 8) + (sprite->y << 6) + sprite->x

        mov bx,sliver_top        ; Multiply y by 320 to get
                                 ; the proper offset.
        shl bx,8
        mov ax,bx
        shr bx,2
        add bx,ax
        add bx,sliver_ray        ; Add x.
        add di,bx

        mov bx,sliver_clip       ; Move important constants
                                 ; into registers.
        mov ax,sliver_scale
        add ax,bx

Sliver_Loop:                     ; Main loop
```

continues

Listing 19.3. continued

```
                        ; double_buffer[offset] = work_sprite[work_offset+column]

        xchg dx,bx              ; Exchange dx and bx as only bx
                                ; can be used as an index.
        mov cl, BYTE PTR fs:[si+bx] ; Get the texture pixel.

        mov es:[di], cl         ; Move it to the screen.

        xchg dx,bx              ; Restore dx and bx.

        mov cx,bx              ; Get ready to access the
                                ; proper scale index.

        ; row = scale_table[scale]

        mov dx, scale_row

        shl bx,1

        add bx,dx

        mov dx, WORD PTR [bx]    ; Get the scale index out
                                ; of the array.

        add dx,sliver_column

        mov bx,cx

        ; offset      += SCREEN_WIDTH;

        add di,320              ; Move down to the next
                                ; video line.

        inc bx                  ; Increment counter.
        cmp bx, ax
        jne Sliver_Loop         ; Are we done?

        pop di                  ; Restore registers.
        pop si

        ret                     ; Blaze

Render_Sliver_32 ENDP

END
```

In general, the assembly version does the same thing as the C version. The assembly version just uses globals, does a little clipping, and does it all faster. I was forced to use 386 instructions and the extra segment registers to make it as fast as possible. Without the extra segment registers, I would have had to put things on the stack (which would have decreased performance a bit).

Now, I'd like to apologize for something I told you a long time ago. I said earlier that we have to use the 386 and 486 as fast 8086s. That wasn't really true. We can use the 32-bit registers and so on, but the only way to do so is with assembly language (unless, of course, you use a DOS extender along with a 32-bit compiler). Back then, though, it was better to keep things simple.

Shading

When you've played the game core, you'll have noticed the lack of shading. Actually, the walls may *look* shaded, but they aren't. I just have two versions of each wall:

■ On vertical walls, I use one version of the texture.

■ On horizontal walls I use a brighter version of the wall texture.

I had shading in the engine, but it decreased the performance of the engine by about 5 percent. That didn't bother me too much. It was the palette problems that came with the shading technique I used. I had to break the palette up into zones of the same hue with different shades. I thought that would just be too constrictive for you.

If you want shading, you can make your own palette and use the techniques described in Chapter 6, "The Third Dimension," to select the proper shade for such things as angle and distance.

The Use of Assembly Language

Using assembly language is sometimes the only resort a programmer has to speed up a specific portion of code to an acceptable rate. In Warlock I used about 100 lines of assembly to optimize only the most time-critical portions of the game. These, of course, were the rendering of the graphics. This is the rough norm among PC video game programmers: we'll write an entire game in C and then convert only a few functions to pure assembly to push the PC's performance envelope. These functions are almost solely the graphics functions that do the rendering. (If you find yourself using assembly for the artificial intelligence or the game logic, something is definitely wrong with your overall design and you need to rethink it.)

I can almost guarantee that the world's best programmer could make your (or my) C programs just as fast without the use of assembly. Keep that in mind and, when you catch yourself using assembly for more than graphics-related functions and low-level programming, recognize that it's time to take a step back (and a step forward...and now we're Cha-Cha-ing!) and start over again.

Anyway, the only other two functions that I converted to assembly language are the functions that move the double buffer to the video buffer (Listing 19.4) and draw the sky and ground (Listing 19.5). The assembly for them is about five to ten lines, if that.

Listing 19.4. The function that moves the double buffer to the video buffer (renderb.asm).

```
;//////////////////////////////////////////////////////////////
;
; This function draws the ground and sky. It does this using the
; 32-bit registers and the "store double word" instruction. Note:
; there are two separate parts to the fill. One fills the sky;
; the other fills the ground.
;
;//////////////////////////////////////////////////////////////

.MODEL MEDIUM,C             ; Use the MEDIUM memory model
                           ; and C names.

.CODE                      ; Begin code segment.

EXTRN double_buffer:DWORD   ; The double buffer is elsewhere.

PUBLIC Draw_Ground_32       ; Export function name to linker.

Draw_Ground_32 PROC FAR C   ; This function is C callable
                           ; and FAR.

.386                       ; Use 80386 instruction (that
                           ; is, 32-bit stuff).

push di                    ; Save di

cld                        ; Set direction to foward.

les di, double_buffer       ; Point es:di to double buffer.

xor eax,eax                ; Put a zero into eax.
mov cx,320*76/4            ; We must fill 76 lines of the
                           ; screen.
rep stosd                  ; Do that.


mov eax,01E1E1E1Eh         ; Now put a gray into eax.
mov cx,320*76/4            ; Fill the remaining 76 lines
                           ; (the ground).
rep stosd                  ; Do that.

pop di                     ; Restore di.

ret                        ; Blaze!

Draw_Ground_32 ENDP

END
```

Listing 19.5. The sky- and ground-rendering function (drawg.asm).

```asm
;///////////////////////////////////////////////////////////////
;
; This function simply copies the double buffer into the video
; buffer. Note: it uses the 32-bit instructions and registers
; for a little bit more speed, even though the video RAM access
; will ultimately be the bottleneck.
;
;///////////////////////////////////////////////////////////////

.MODEL MEDIUM,C             ; Use the MEDIUM memory model C
                            ; function names.

.CODE                       ; Begin the code segment.

EXTRN double_buffer:DWORD   ; The double buffer is elsewhere.
EXTRN video_buffer:DWORD    ; The video buffer is elsewhere.

PUBLIC Render_Buffer_32     ; Export the function name to
                            ; the linker.


Render_Buffer_32 PROC FAR C ; This function is C callable
                            ; and FAR.

.386                        ; Use 80386 stuff.

push ds                     ; Save the data segment register.

cld                         ; Set direction to foward.
lds si, double_buffer       ; Make the double buffer the
                            ; source for the move.
les di, video_buffer        ; Make the destination the
                            ; video buffer.
mov cx,320*152/4            ; Move the whole 3-D portion of
                            ; the screen.

rep movsd                   ; Do that.

pop ds                      ; Restore the registers.

ret                         ; Blaze!!

Render_Buffer_32 ENDP

END
```

The Game Loop

As I've said, Warlock is hardly a complete game—in fact, it's basically a walkthrough. I've provided the 3-D engine; I want you to provide a game. Nevertheless, the skeleton does have some structure to it and there is a crude event loop. That's what we are now going to discuss.

The source module warlock.c is where all the action takes places, and where all of the game code is. I decided to keep all the source in one module, and keep the main section in one piece instead of breaking it up. This enables you to comprehend it more easily and add to it as you wish.

The game is based on an event-driven structure. By *event-driven*, I mean that the game loop is looking for player input to act upon. This player input comes in the form of keyboard input only. The player presses a key and then the position of the character, view angle, or both is changed. This information is reflected in the next frame. The game has the following event structure:

1. Initialization: imagery is loaded, sounds are loaded, and look-up tables are created. Also, the new keyboard ISR is installed so we can obtain simultaneous key presses.

2. The keyboard is queried. If there have been any key presses or releases, they're reflected in the keyboard motion look-up table. This information is used for movement.

3. If the player's character was moved or rotated in Step 2, the character is moved and his new coordinates are computed. If they're valid, all is well. Otherwise, the character is sent back to his previous position.

4. Tests are made to see whether the player has pressed the Spacebar. He or she would do this in an effort to open a door. If there's a door in front of the character, the door-opening responder function is started. The responder then processes the door animation sequence and removes the door from the world.

5. Warlock has random sounds of moaning, wind, and growling. If a random variable is a certain value, a random sound is selected and played.

6. The system waits for the vertical sync (described in Chapter 7, "Advanced Bit-Mapped Graphics and Special FX"). This keeps the game running at a specific rate and helps minimize the visibility of the screen being updated.

7. The screen is rendered by using the call to the ray caster.

8. The game loops back to Step 2.

The game is void of game logic or creatures. These are the things that you'll have to put in. I admit that the 3-D engine is lacking the code to place sprites in the world, but if I'd put them in, the code would have had to be more optimized, and I would have had to use more assembly. I wanted to keep it simple and let you take it from here. You already have everything you need to put sprites in the world, but I'll give you some hints in a bit (in the section called "Placing Objects in the World") to point you in the right direction.

Now let's talk about the representation of the game world.

The Game Grid

The game world, or game grid, is represented by a 2-D matrix, 64x64 cells in size. This matrix holds integers that represent whether a cell is solid, and the texture that should be mapped onto the walls of the cell. The name of the file Warlock loads to obtain this data is raymap.dat.

The editor program WAREDIT (which we made in Chapter 15, "The Toolchest") works on Warlock—with some modification that, again, I want you to make. WAREDIT uses a 200x200 cell game world. Warlock uses a 64x64 cell game world. This and the integer codes are all that need be changed, and you're in business.

Take a look at Figure 19.4 to see the game world you've been running around in.

```
5555555555555555555555555555555555555555555555555555555555555555555555
5              5              55                              55
5              5              55                              55
5   55555   5555555555555555   555555555                      55
5   5        5        55555   5        5   55555555555555555555555
5   5        5         5555   5        5  5                    55
5   5        5           5    5        5  5                    55
5   5        5           5    5      5555    555555555555   55555
5   55555   5555555555755555   5                  5        55
5                              7                  5        55
5                              5        5         5        55
5              55              5        5         5        55
5      5555    55              555555555555555555555555    55
5      5   5                                      5        55
5                              5555555555555   333333   5555555   55
5   333333333333333333333   5                  3      5        55
5   3                       3   5              3      5        55
5   3                       3   5   3333333333   3      5        55
5   3                       3   5   3      3 3   3        55
333333                      333333333          3   3333333        55
3      3                                       3      3        55
3      3   3333333333                   3   3   3        3333   55
3      3   3      3   333333333333   3   3333            333311
3      3   3      3   3   33333      3                  3   11
3      3   3      3   3   3333            3333733333        11
3   3   3      3   3   7      3   33333      3   3        11
3   3   3   33333   3   333333   3   3   3   3   3        11
3   3   3      3   3   3      3   3   3   7   3   3        11
3   3   3      3          3   3   33333   3   33333        11
3   3   3      3          3   3          3   3        11
3   33333333   333333333333333333   3              333        11
3                                                  111111111
3                                          111      1      11
3                                          111      1      11
3   333333333   3333333      333   111              11111   11111
3   3              3   333   111              1   7   11
333333              3                              1   11111
3      3              3                              11
3   3333333333333333333              111111111111111      11
3                       3              1              1      11
3                       7              1              1      11
3                       3              117111111111111111111      11
3   3333333333333333333   111   1   1                      11
3   3                    111   1   1                      11
3   3                    111   1   1   111111111111111   11
3   3                          1   1   1              1   11
3   3   1111111111   11          1   1   1              1   11
333333   1              1   111   1   1   1              11
1              1              1   111   1   1   1        11
1              1   11111111   111   1   1   1              1   11
1   1   1      1              1   1   1              1   11
111111   1      1                      1   1   111111111111   11
1      1      1                      1   1              11
1   1111111111111111111111111111111      11111              11
1   1   1711   11111      1              1   1   1              11
1   1      1   1              1         1   7              11
1   1      7   7              1   1      111111111111111111111111111
1   1      1   1   1              1   1              1   11
1   1   1711   1   1         1      1   1              1   11
1   1111111111   111111111      111111   1   1   1        11
1              11                      1              11
1              11                      1              11
111111111111111111111111111111111111111111111111111111111111111111111111
```

Figure 19.4. *The game grid.*

As you can see, it looks like a bunch of numbers. The numbers have the following meanings:

1	Use texture number 1 for these blocks.
3	Use texture number 2 for these blocks.
5	Use texture number 3 for these blocks.
7	This is a door; use texture number 4 for these blocks.

The texture numbers are really the texture indices as they're loaded into memory. The integers ascend by two because there are really two shades of each texture; that is, there are texture pairs: (1,2), (3,4), (5,6), and so on. The textures can be found in the .PCX file named walltext.pcx. They're loaded from left to right and from top to bottom.

That about sums it up for the representation of the world. There's not really much to it. In WAREDIT, if you remember, we used all kinds of defines to delineate the different cell types and their meanings. In Warlock, we see that most of this stuff isn't currently needed. It will be, however, once you start making a game with the core.

One of the interesting things about Warlock is the demo mode. Let's discuss the mechanics of it.

The Demo Mode

I have to admit it: the demo mode gave me a real headache! I was trying to make it marvelously easy to implement, but none of the techniques I used took into consideration the temporal aspects of the game and its lack of synchronous timing. In other words, I was messing the timing up! Basically, I wanted to digitize the keyboard input and play it back from a file as if it were the real keyboard. The software wouldn't know the difference. The problem with this was that there's an ISR getting input for me instead of using standard getch(). This was messing me up, as I kind of forgot about using the ISR.

Anyway, when I digitized the keyboard and played it back, the playback didn't do the same thing as it did when I recorded it because the input wasn't interrupt-driven anymore. The lack of interrupts changed the timing of the game and made the game run into walls and do other weird things.

To solve this problem, I took the approach of digitizing the actions of the game rather than the inputs that caused them: I'd digitize when the character moved, not when he was told to move. This required packing the character's motion into a packet that does a logical OR operation on whether the character translated and rotated simultaneously (which is a possibility). In the end, this worked perfectly. The demo runs for about a minute.

To get out of demo mode, you simply press the Esc key. If you want to make your own demo you can uncomment the MAKING_DEMO define and change the state of the variable demo_mode to 0. This creates a demo called demo.dat. Then you can reset the changes, recompile the game, and run the game: the demo will be yours. However, be careful! There's no checking for overuse of memory and so on, and the program will crash hard if you exceed the demo length (which is set at about 1,000 samples).

Placing Objects in the World

I feel as though I've left you out to dry by not putting sprites into the world. I'm sorry, but I really want you to do this yourself. It will build your character. I will give you some hints, though.

The sprites are placed in the world separately from the ray casting. They're just ordinary sprites, placed somewhere in the universe. To render them we first must see if they're within the field of view of the player. This is accomplished by finding their position relative to the player and computing their angles. If they're within the field of view, they are rotated and translated relative to the player. Once this is done they can be rendered—but what about the hidden surface problem?

During the ray cast, you keep an array that holds the distance from the player to each sliver. It's like a really small z-buffer. This z-buffer is used to compare the distance of each vertical strip of the sprite that's drawn. The sprite's distance is computed from the player's position and, as each sliver of the sprite is drawn, its distance from the player is compared to the precomputed z-buffer values accumulated from the ray casting. If the sprite's sliver is closer, it's drawn. If not, it must be occluded by a wall: don't draw it.

Summing up, sprites are really standard 3-D objects, except that they're always on planes perpendicular to the viewer (which makes them easy to render and texture). However, all the 3-D stuff you learned about polygon-based systems in Chapter 6, "The Third Dimension," applies to sprites. You could think of them as being placed into the world after it has been drawn, as the world and they are really done in completely different ways.

Faster, Faster, Faster!

There are some things you can do to make the ray caster faster.

- First, the first part of the ray caster (Sections 2 and 3) could be done a little better. They probably could be done in 1/100th of the time by doing a little preprocessing.

- Second, the last floating-point math operation could be extracted.

- Third, we could separate the x and y ray cast into two separate sections. This would get rid of a few hundred IFs.

- Fourth, we could interleave the ray casting with the rendering so that, while the CPU is waiting for the video buffer to be available, the ray casting is going on or the texturing is being done.

- Finally, rather than use mode 13h, we could use mode X, which is 320x240 and is the fastest mode available for this kind of work.

But that's another story for another book....

Last Words

I really don't have much more to say about PC games. You have the technical information you need. The rest of it is pure imagination, and you're the only one who can supply that. Hopefully, you can make an incredible game that makes another person smile. That's the reason I do it. Whatever motivates you, I hope to see a new explorer charting worlds within the virtual universe of the computer. And if we ever meet in the Andromeda Galaxy, you better have your shields up!

May your journeys be magical...

You can send any questions, submissions, and so forth to:

Andromeda Industries
P.O. Box 641744
San Jose, CA 95164-1744

Index

Symbols

Add to Your Sams Library Today with the Best Books for Programming, Operating Systems, and New Technologies

The easiest way to order is to pick up the phone and call

1-800-428-5331

between 9:00 a.m. and 5:00 p.m. EST.
For faster service please have your credit card available.

ISBN	Quantity	Description of Item	Unit Cost	Total Cost
0-672-30448-1		Teach Yourself C in 21 Days	$24.95	
0-672-30471-6		Teach Yourself Advanced C in 21 Days (book/disk)	$34.95	
0-672-30309-4		Programming Sound for DOS and Windows (book/disk)	$39.95	
0-672-30468-6		C Programmer's Guide to Serial Communication, 2nd Edition	$39.95	
0-672-48470-6		Assembly Language: For Real Programmers ONLY!	$44.95	
0-672-30361-2		Virtual Reality and the Exploration of Cyberspace (book/disk)	$26.95	
0-672-30365-5		C for Fun and Profit (book/disk)	$29.95	
0-672-27395-0		Microsoft C/C++ 7 Developer's Guide (book/disk)	$49.95	
0-672-30308-6		Tricks of the Graphics Gurus (book/disk)	$49.95	
0-672-30319-1		The Waite Group's New C Primer Plus, 2nd Ed.	$29.95	
0-672-30292-6		Programming Windows Games with Borland C++ (book/disk)	$34.95	
0-672-30313-2		Programming Games for Beginners for Windows (book/disk)	$26.95	
0-672-30311-6		Borland C++ 4 Object Orientated Programming	$39.95	
❏ 3 ½" Disk		Shipping and Handling: See information below.		
❏ 5 ¼" Disk		TOTAL		

Shipping and Handling: $4.00 for the first book, and $1.75 for each additional book. Floppy disk: add $1.75 for shipping and handling. If you need to have it NOW, we can ship product to you in 24 hours for an additional charge of approximately $18.00, and you will receive your item overnight or in two days. Overseas shipping and handling adds $2.00 per book and $8.00 for up to three disks. Prices subject to change. Call for availability and pricing information on latest editions.

201 W. 103rd Street, Indianapolis, Indiana 46290

1-800-428-5331 — Orders   1-800-835-3202 — FAX   1-800-858-7674 — Customer Service

ISBN 0-672-30507-0

What's on the CD-ROM

The *Tricks of the Game-Programming Gurus* CD-ROM contains

- Warlock, a hot 3-D adventure framework created specifically for this book. Working from the foundation laid by Warlock, you can make your own awesome, shoot-'em-up 3-D hit!

- All the source code, libraries, utilities, and support files discussed and developed in the book. Using these tools, you can develop powerful and professional games!

- Hot games that showcase the techniques taught in this book. The games include DOOM 1.2, Wolfenstein 3-D, Blake Stone, Traffic Department 2192, and Pinball Super Android.

- DigiPak and MidiPak Developer's Kit, created by John Ratcliff. DIGPAK allows playback of digital sound and MIDPAK allows the playback of General MIDI music on all sound cards.

Installing the CD-ROM

To install the files your hard drive, complete the following steps:

1. At the DOS prompt, change to the CD-ROM drive containing the installation disc. For example, if the disc is in drive E:, type E: and press Enter.

2. Type INSTALL and press Enter.

> To install the files on the disc, you'll need at least 40M of free space on your hard drive.

You will then see a menu from which you can choose to install all the programs on the disc, or any one of the programs individually. The installation program will copy the selected files to a directory named \GURU, which will be created automatically. The files are arranged by application in subdirectories, with the book's source files in a directory called \SOURCE, arranged by chapter.